A note about the cover

Is everything *really* an argument? Seeing the images on the cover of this book might make you wonder. The "Black Lives Matter" protest, for example, instantly calls to mind the very public unrest across the United States and around the world following a series of controversial police actions. But what does an image of a red pepper with a bar code say about the origin and value of food? Does a student using a tablet argue for or against the ways that technology is shaping how we communicate with one another? The honeybee might remind you of organic farming—or of the fact that bees have been dying off in droves while scientists speculate about the causes. And as for the gorgeous view on the smartphone, what's your best call? A comment on the power of mobile devices? Criticism of how beauty is now commonly treated as something to post online rather than simply to enjoy? What's your take?

everything's an argument/with readings

Top left: © Lynn Johnson/Aurora/Getty Images; top right: © Steven Barrymore; bottom left: © Bill Coster/age fotostock; bottom right: Frederick M. Brown/Getty Images; center row, left to right: Red DaxLuma Gallery/Shutterstock; Pacific Press/Getty Images; AP Photo; A. S. Alexander Collection of Ernest Hemingway. Department of Rare Books and Special Collections, Princeton University Library; © Mel Longhurst/Photoshot; © imageBROKER/age fotostock

Seventh Edition

EVERYTHING'S AN argument with readings

Andrea A. Lunsford
STANFORD UNIVERSITY

John J. Ruszkiewicz
UNIVERSITY OF TEXAS AT AUSTIN

Keith Walters
PORTLAND STATE UNIVERSITY

BEDFORD/ST. MARTIN'S
A Macmillan Education Imprint
Boston • New York

For Bedford/St. Martin's

Vice President, Editorial, Macmillan Higher Education Humanities: Edwin Hill
Editorial Director, English and Music: Karen S. Henry
Publisher for Composition, Business and Technical Writing, and Developmental Writing: Leasa Burton
Executive Editor: John E. Sullivan III
Developmental Editors: Rachel Goldberg and Sherry Mooney
Editorial Assistant: Jennifer Prince
Senior Production Editor: Rosemary R. Jaffe
Senior Production Supervisor: Jennifer Wetzel
Marketing Manager: Joy Fisher Williams
Copy Editor: Steven Patterson
Indexer: Leoni Z. McVey
Photo Researcher: Sheri Blaney
Director of Rights and Permissions: Hilary Newman
Senior Art Director: Anna Palchik
Text Design: Anna Palchik and Graphic World, Inc.
Cover Design: John Callahan
Cover Images (top to bottom): © Hero/age fotostock; c. byatt-norman/Shutterstock; © Robert Walls/age fotostock; Lee Thomas/Alamy; © Christin Gilbert/age fotostock
Composition: Graphic World, Inc.
Printing and Binding: RR Donnelley and Sons

Manufactured in the United States of America.

2 3 4 5 6 20 19 18 17 16

For information, write: Bedford/St. Martin's, 75 Arlington Street, Boston, MA 02116 (617-399-4000)

ISBN 978-1-319-08574-2 (paperback)
ISBN 978-1-319-01632-6 (hardcover)

Acknowledgments

Text acknowledgments and copyrights appear at the back of the book on pages 800–803, which constitute an extension of the copyright page. Art acknowledgments and copyrights appear on the same page as the art selections they cover. It is a violation of the law to reproduce these selections by any means whatsoever without the written permission of the copyright holder.

PREFACE

We've long described *Everything's an Argument with Readings* as a labor of love, in part because working on the book keeps us connected to the neighborhoods our students inhabit. In teaching them how to persuade powerfully and ethically, we broaden our own horizons and learn more with each edition. But the core principles of this book endure.

We believe that language—taken broadly—provides the most powerful means of understanding and shaping the world. We know that arguments seldom if ever have only two sides; rather, they present a dizzying array of perspectives. We assume that arguments always come in response to other claims, part of an ongoing conversation that builds throughout our lives. Understanding arguments, then, calls for exercising judgment across a full range of rhetorical situations, perspectives, and media.

For good reason, we give enhanced attention to media this time around. *Everything's an Argument with Readings* first appeared just as new technologies were reshaping the ways ideas could be framed and shared; our earliest edition included chapters on "Visual Argument" and "Arguments in Electronic Environments"—which then meant email, newsgroups, and Web sites. Each subsequent edition advanced our game. But with social media now stretching the boundaries of rhetoric, particularly in the arenas of culture and politics, keeping up requires more than just acknowledging change; it means adapting our understanding of persuasion to these compelling contexts.

To that end, we offer in this seventh edition of *Everything's an Argument with Readings* a thoroughly reworked Part 3, "Style and Presentation in Arguments": its *four* chapters now outline the rhetorical opportunities students encounter across a wider range of media, both in and out of school. Whether in an updated and augmented section on style or in a chapter about "Multimedia Arguments" composed almost from scratch, our readers will find much to challenge their views of audiences, arguments, texts, and images. But the advice always remains practical, focused on providing tools writers need, whether they're polishing an academic essay or evaluating claims trending across social media.

The opening part of *Everything's an Argument with Readings*—which introduces core rhetorical principles, including ethos, pathos, and logos—has been more subtly reworked and tightened to make its six chapters even clearer and more readable. Users of this book routinely praise its timely examples of public discourse, and we've pushed ourselves to make this opening section especially memorable, illustrating just how pervasive—and occasionally entertaining—arguments can be. Topics covered in the seventh edition include hashtag politics, pickup trucks, the appeal of fatty foods, and the real reason college alumni donate money to their schools. More often than in past editions, we've linked our examples, occasionally even extending connections across chapter boundaries. In other words, we've allowed ourselves to have some serious fun.

Part 2 of our text opens with a chapter on "Structuring Arguments" (which now includes more on invitational arguments, in addition to classical, Toulmin, and Rogerian arguments), followed by chapters devoted to the genres that students are often assigned in their college courses. In this section, we have provided many new, timely examples along with new Readings we hope students will find especially engaging. And in recognition of the importance of design when composing in a digital world, each genre chapter's "Guide to Writing" now has a section devoted to "Considering Format and Media."

In Part 4, we have increased our coverage of academic arguments (including a new annotated student essay on the effects of depriving young people of direct contact with nature). In addition, we've paid careful attention to giving advice on how to find useful evidence in online sources (including social media) and how to evaluate sources, using what technology critic Howard Rheingold calls an effective "crap detector." And in our chapter on "Plagiarism and Academic Integrity," we have expanded our discussions of fair use as well as of sampling and mashups across time (including today). Finally, the chapter on MLA style and APA style has been updated to reflect the most current advice from those organizations and to provide even more examples that can guide students as they document their sources.

While much new material has been added (or updated), much remains familiar in *Everything's an Argument with Readings*, a best seller in its field since its debut. We're pleased that it seems to strike a chord with students and instructors who expect a book on argument to be candid, balanced, and attuned to everyday events. Users have also come to expect a stylish and visually striking presentation of issues and concepts, rendered in language that is personable and even occasionally personal. We have worked hard, too, to maintain the precision and economy of our most recent edition, knowing that students appreciate books that get to the point.

As in previous editions, we have tried to balance attention to the critical reading of arguments (*analysis*) with attention to the writing of arguments (*production*), demonstrating both activities with lively—and realistic—examples, on the principle that the best way to appreciate an argument is to see it in action. Texts of every kind beckon for reactions, including a close look at a politician's *kairotic* address on the floor of the U.S. Senate, selections from a commencement address by Ruth Simmons at Smith College and by then First Lady Michelle Obama, the photo lead-in to an essay by LeBron James, a selfie that includes Pope Francis, an oral presentation outline sketched by a student, and cartoons, infographics, and other visual arguments. The new edition features seven new full-length essays—chosen for their topicality and usefulness as models of argument—on topics ranging from professional gaming to arrests of NFL players to what friendship really means in the era of social media. We have kept the best and most popular materials from previous editions but have also searched for new items—including visual and multimedia ones—that we believe embody the spirit of the times. As always, we want students to page through the book to find the next intriguing argument or to discover one of their own.

After all, our purpose in *Everything's an Argument with Readings* is to present persuasion as an essential and instinctual activity—something we do almost from the moment we are born (in fact, an infant's first cry is as poignant a claim as we can imagine). But we also want writers to think of argumentation as a craft both powerful and professional. So we have designed *Everything's an Argument with Readings* to be itself a case for civil persuasion, with a voice that aims to appeal to readers cordially but that doesn't hesitate to make demands on them when appropriate.

In selecting themes and arguments for the anthology, we've tried to choose topics of interest and concern to the students we teach as well as issues and texts worth arguing about. We've sought readings that will challenge students to consider new perspectives on topics they may feel they already understand and, in particular, to contextualize themselves in a world characterized by increasing globalization and divisive rhetoric on many topics. We have retained several of the chapter topics that have worked especially well in earlier editions—stereotypes in popular culture, sustainability and food, and the possible meanings of diversity on college campuses. In refocusing and revising these chapters, we have sought to find a balance between including texts that students and teachers found provocative, instructive, and useful and adding new ones that treat contemporary issues while leading us to think about argumentation in novel, timely ways. For example, how can research analyzing the characters in video games help us understand how stereotyping works in our society? How might the meaning of "sustainable food" change, depending on whether we're focusing on the United States or on developing countries? What challenges do Muslim women on college campuses face, and what does their situation teach us about campus dynamics?

In addition to updating these chapters from the sixth edition, we have added chapters on two new topics: how globalization is affecting language and how technological advances are influencing our understanding of privacy. In the chapter on the first topic, we encourage students to begin thinking of themselves as global citizens and to examine the privileges and perhaps the responsibilities that come with speaking English as a first or additional language. The chapter also helps students begin to examine the consequences of the spread of English for some less widely used languages. In many ways, the topics raised in this chapter relate to the same questions of sustainability raised in the discussions of food. The chapter on the changing meaning of privacy considers two major issues: Big Data and how data are used by industry and government, on the one hand, and privacy and cell phones in light of the 2014 *Riley v. California* Supreme Court ruling, on the other.

In choosing new selections for the anthology, we have first looked for new genres (including multimodal genres) that bring home to students the message conveyed by the book's title. Furthermore, we have tried to build upon the emphasis on academic argument in the earlier part of the book. We have searched for examples of research writing that use a range of methodologies, including case studies, quantitative research, and professional reports, with the goal of giving students practice for analyzing the sorts of arguments they will be assigned in their various courses. The readings in this edition include excerpts from ten books treating a range of topics and written for a variety of audiences. We have also included part of a Supreme Court ruling to help students see stasis theory in action and to help them appreciate the role that such rulings play in all our daily lives. Finally, we have sought arguments, whether written or visual, that will help students see themselves "among others," to use Clifford Geertz's memorable turn of phrase.

Here is a summary of the key features that continue to characterize *Everything's an Argument with Readings* and of the major new features in this edition.

Key Features

Two books in one, neatly linked. The beginning of the book provides a brief guide to argument; later chapters offer a thematically organized anthology of readings in a wide range of genres. The two parts of the book are linked by cross-references in the margins, leading students from the argument chapters to specific examples in the readings and from the readings to appropriate rhetorical instruction.

An imaginative and winning approach, going beyond traditional pro/con assumptions to show that argument is everywhere—in essays, tweets, news articles, scholarly writing, speeches, advertisements, cartoons, posters, bumper stickers, debates, Web sites, blogs, text messages, and other electronic environments.

Student-friendly explanations in simple, everyday language, with many brief examples and a minimum of technical terminology.

Fresh and important chapter themes that encourage students to take up complex positions. Readings on topics such as "How Does Popular Culture Stereotype *You*?," "What Should 'Diversity on Campus' Mean and Why?," and "Why Is Sustainability Important When It Comes to Food?" demand that students explore the many sides of an issue, not just pro/con.

A real-world, full-color design, with readings presented in the style of the original publication. Different formats for newspaper articles, magazine articles, essays, writing from the Web, radio transcripts, and other media help students recognize and think about the effect that design and visuals have on written and multimodal arguments, and the full-color design helps bring the many images in the text to life.

New to This Edition

Two new chapters—on how globalization is changing language and what privacy means in the digital age—treat issues relevant to students as citizens and scholars. Although students may not give the topic much conscious thought, globalization is influencing language and languages, including English, in complex ways. And if you mention *Riley v. California* in class, many students will recognize it as the recent Supreme Court ruling mandating that their cell phones can be searched only by law enforcement officials who have first obtained a warrant to do so. Although students may give a great deal of thought to privacy and technology, they—and all of us—have much to learn on the topic.

Forty-six new selections in the guide and readings chapters draw from a variety of sources and genres, including student newspaper articles, infographics, and media reviews:

- Seven new full-length arguments in the guide—on topics ranging from arrests of NFL players to Google Glass—provide engaging, topical models for specific kinds of arguments.
- The transcript from an NPR radio program examines the standard practice of colleges and universities of overrepresenting students of color in their promotional materials.
- A chapter from Georgetown University law professor Sheryll Cashin's most recent book, *Place, Not Race: A New Vision of Opportunity in America*, questions the fairness of affirmative action in ways that challenge partisans on both the right and the left ends of the political spectrum.
- An excerpt from Barbara Kingsolver's *Animal, Vegetable, Miracle* argues passionately against genetically modified foods, while other selections argue just as passionately for them.

A heavily revised four-chapter section on "Style and Presentation in Arguments" provides up-to-date advice and commentary on the ways arguments are now routinely adapted to different audiences and media. Additions to these chapters include the following:

- A revised chapter on style that shows in more detail precisely how writers shape their words and sentences (even their punctuation) to influence readers. The entries describing particular rhetorical tropes and schemes are now arranged alphabetically for easier reference.
- A chapter on "Presenting Arguments" that has been redesigned to provide a clearer path to effective presentations. It features the actual notes that a student prepared for an oral report.
- A chapter on "Visual Rhetoric" that has been reworked to focus specifically on the rhetorical appeals (pathos, ethos, logos) that photographs, graphic design, typefaces, and even colors can generate.
- A thoughtful yet practical new chapter on "Multimedia Arguments" that examines what happens to arguments and audiences as they move between and among media as old as books and as new as Twitter.

Examples now occasionally work across chapters to reinforce their points more memorably.

A new "Considering Format and Media" section appears in the "Guide to Writing" in each genre chapter.

Get the Most Out of Your Course with *Everything's an Argument with Readings*

Bedford/St. Martin's offers resources and format choices that help you and your students get even more out of your book and course. To learn more about or to order any of the following products, contact your Bedford/St. Martin's sales representative, email sales support (**sales_support@bfwpub.com**), or visit the Web site at **macmillanhighered.com/everythingsanargumentwithreadings/catalog**.

LaunchPad for *Everything's an Argument with Readings*: Where Students Learn

LaunchPad provides engaging content and new ways to get the most out of your course. Get an **interactive e-book** in a fully customizable course space; then assign and mix our resources with yours.

- **LearningCurve adaptive quizzing** offers four new modules on argument.
- **Pre-built units**—including readings, videos, quizzes, discussion groups, and more—are **easy to adapt and assign** by adding your own materials and mixing them with our high-quality multimedia content and ready-made assessment options.
- LaunchPad also provides access to a **gradebook** that gives a clear window on the performance of your whole class, individual students, and even individual assignments.
- A **streamlined interface** helps students focus on what's due, and social commenting tools let them **engage**, make connections, and learn from one another. Use LaunchPad on its own or integrate it with your school's learning management system so that your class is always on the same page.

To get the most out of your course, order LaunchPad for *Everything's an Argument with Readings* packaged with the print book. (LaunchPad for *Everything's an Argument with Readings* can also be purchased on its own.) An activation code is required. To order LaunchPad for *Everything's an Argument with Readings* with the print book, use **ISBN 978-1-319-03950-9**.

Choose from Alternative Formats of *Everything's an Argument with Readings*

Bedford/St. Martin's offers a range of affordable formats, allowing students to choose the one that works best for them. For details, visit **macmillanhighered.com/everythingsanargumentwithreadings/catalog**.

- *Paperback brief or hardcover high school edition* To order the paperback edition of *Everything's an Argument*, use **ISBN 978-1-319-08575-9**. To order the hardcover high school edition of *Everything's an Argument with Readings*, use **ISBN 978-1-319-01632-6**.
- *Popular e-book formats* For details, visit **macmillanhighered.com/ebooks**.

Select Value Packages

Add value to your text by packaging one of the following resources with *Everything's an Argument with Readings*. To learn more about package options for any of the following products, contact your Bedford/St. Martin's sales representative or visit **macmillanhighered.com/everythingsanargumentwithreadings/catalog**.

Writer's Help 2.0 for Lunsford Handbooks offers Andrea Lunsford's smart advice with *Writer's Help* smart search. *Writer's Help* is a powerful online handbook with "the simplicity and usability of Google," according to one student user, but with the *instruction* that free online resources lack. Its trusted content from Andrea Lunsford helps students whether they are searching for writing advice on their own or working on an assignment. Its tools, built around a smart search that recognizes nonexpert terminology, are as simple as they are innovative. *Writer's Help* saves teachers time by helping them assign pages and track progress, providing a window into student use and achievement. User-friendly help for college writers also means useful data for instructors and administrators. To order *Writer's Help 2.0 for Lunsford Handbooks* packaged with the print book, contact your sales representative for a package ISBN.

i-series This popular series presents multimedia tutorials in a flexible format—because there are things you can't do in a book.

- *ix visualizing composition 2.0* helps students put into practice key rhetorical and visual concepts. To order *ix visualizing composition* packaged with the print book, contact your sales representative for a package ISBN.
- *i-claim: visualizing argument* offers a new way to see argument—with six multimedia tutorials, an illustrated glossary, and a wide array of multimedia arguments. To order *i-claim: visualizing argument* packaged with the print book, contact your sales representative for a package ISBN.

Make Learning Fun with *Re:Writing 3*

bedfordstmartins.com/rewriting

New open online resources with videos and interactive elements engage students in new ways of writing. You'll find tutorials about using common digital writing tools, an interactive peer review game, Extreme Paragraph Makeover, and more—all for free and for fun. Visit **bedfordstmartins.com/rewriting**.

Instructor Resources

macmillanhighered.com/everythingsanargumentwithreadings/catalog

You have a lot to do in your course. Bedford/St. Martin's wants to make it easy for you to find the support you need—and to get it quickly.

***Instructor's Notes for* Everything's an Argument with Readings** is available as a PDF that can be downloaded from the Bedford/St. Martin's online catalog at the URL above. In addition to chapter overviews and teaching tips, the instructor's manual includes sample syllabi and possible discussion points for the Respond questions in the book.

Teaching Central offers the entire list of Bedford/St. Martin's print and online professional resources in one place. You'll find landmark reference works, sourcebooks on pedagogical issues, award-winning collections, and practical advice for the classroom—all free for instructors. Visit **macmillanhighered.com/teachingcentral**.

Bits collects creative ideas for teaching a range of composition topics in an easily searchable blog format. In her *Teacher to Teacher* blog, Andrea Lunsford shares ideas inspired by her teaching, reading, and traveling. Her "Multimodal Mondays" posts offer ideas for introducing low-stakes multimodal assignments to the composition classroom. A community of teachers—leading scholars, authors, and editors—discuss revision, research, grammar and style, technology, peer review, and much more. Take, use, adapt, and pass the ideas around. Then come back to the site to comment or share your own suggestions. Visit **community.macmillan.com** and follow *Bedford Bits* to see for yourself.

Acknowledgments

We owe a debt of gratitude to many people for making *Everything's an Argument with Readings* possible. Our first thanks must go to the thousands of people we have taught in our writing courses over nearly four decades, particularly students at the Ohio State University, Stanford

University, the University of Texas at Austin, and Portland State University. Almost every chapter in this book has been informed by a classroom encounter with a student whose shrewd observation or perceptive question sent an ambitious lesson plan spiraling to the ground. (Anyone who has tried to teach claims and warrants on the fly to skeptical first-year writers will surely appreciate why we have qualified our claims in the Toulmin chapter so carefully.) But students have also provided the motive for writing this book. More than ever, they need to know how to read and write arguments effectively if they are to secure a place in a world growing ever smaller and more rhetorically challenging.

We are grateful to our editors at Bedford/St. Martin's who have contributed their many talents to our book. With this edition we welcome new editors, Rachel Goldberg and Sherry Mooney, to *Everything's an Argument with Readings*. Not only did they bring new ideas to the project and a superb editorial sense (particularly in suggesting what works best where), but they have also been extraordinarily helpful in sorting through the increasingly complicated issue of acquiring first-rate examples and images for the book.

We are similarly grateful to others at Bedford/St. Martin's who contributed their talents to our book: Rosemary Jaffe, senior production editor; Diana Blume, art director; Sheri Blaney, art researcher; Margaret Gorenstein, permissions researcher; Steven Patterson, copy editor; Arthur Johnson and Linda McLatchie, proofreaders; and Jennifer Prince, editorial assistant.

We'd also like to thank the astute instructors who reviewed the sixth edition: Nolan Belk, Wilkes Community College; Hailie Bryant, Appalachian State University; James Bryant-Trerise, Clackamas Community College; Don Carroll, College of DuPage; Matthew Davis, University of Wisconsin–Stevens Point; Josh Herron, Anderson University; Susan Hubbard, University of Central Florida; Calvin Jones, South Piedmont Community College; Jeff Kosse, Iowa Western Community College; Edwin Kroll, Kalamazoo Valley Community College; Charles Poff, Central Virginia Community College; David Rude, Heald College; Timothy Shonk, Eastern Illinois University; Mary Ann Simmons, James Sprunt Community College; James Stokes, University of Wisconsin–Stevens Point; Bobby Vasquez, University of Nebraska; Lorena Williams, Duquesne University; and Stephanie Zerkel-Humbert, Maple Woods Community College.

Thanks, too, to John Kinkade, who once again has prepared the instructor's notes for this seventh edition, and to Margo Russell for her invaluable help finding (and in some cases helping transcribe) new reading selections. Finally, we are grateful to the students whose fine argumentative essays or materials appear in our chapters: George Chidiac, Manasi Deshpande, Charlotte Geaghan-Breiner, Sean Kamperman, Rachel Kolb, Taylor Pearson, and Natasha Rodriguez. We hope that *Everything's an Argument with Readings* responds to what students and instructors have said they want and need.

Andrea A. Lunsford
John J. Ruszkiewicz
Keith Walters

BRIEF CONTENTS

Part 3: Style and Presentation in Arguments 305

Part 4: Research and Arguments 377

Part 5: Arguments 505

CONTENTS

Part 1 photo: AP Photo/L'Osservatore Romano, Riccardo Aguiari; top to bottom: Pacific Press/Getty Images; © Bob Englehart/Cagle Cartoons, Inc.; Michael N. Todaro/FilmMagic/Getty Images

Top to bottom: Used with permission of Gary Varvel and Creators Syndicate. All rights reserved; Kevin C. Cox/Getty Images; AP Photo/L'Osservatore Romano, Riccardo Aguiari; © NBC/Photofest, Inc.

Top: © Bish/Cagle Cartoons, Inc.; second from top: Tim Boyle/Getty Images; bottom: Kittipojn Pravalpatkul/Shutterstock

Part 2 photo: Cal Sport Media via AP Images; top to bottom: © Gary A. Vasquez/USA Today Sports Images; © World History Archive/Alamy; PhotoLink/Getty Images; National Archives

Top to bottom: Alfred Eisenstaedt/Getty Images; USAID; AP Photo/The Philadelphia Inquirer, Tom Gralish, Pool; Frederick M. Brown/Getty Images

Top to bottom: Bill Wight/Getty Images; Red DaxLuma Gallery/Shutterstock; PHOTOEDIT/PhotoEdit, Inc.; Mario Tama/Getty Images

Top to bottom: Cal Sport Media via AP Images; © Ildi Papp/age fotostock; Robyn Beck/AFP/Getty Images; © Bill Coster/age fotostock

Top to bottom: © Florian Kopp/agefotostock.com; Ron Sanford/Science Source®/Photo Researchers; © Lucy Nicholson/Reuters/LANDOV; AP Wide World Photos

Part 3: Style and Presentation in Arguments 305

Part 4 photo: Mike Nelson/AFP/Getty Images; top to bottom: knape/Getty Images; AP/Invision/Charles Sykes: Mike Nelson/AFP/Getty Images; © Andy Singer/Cagle Cartoons, Inc.

Top to bottom: © Zoonar M Kang/age fotostock; © Bartomeu Amengual/age fotostock; © imageBROKER/age fotostock; © imagineasia/age fotostock

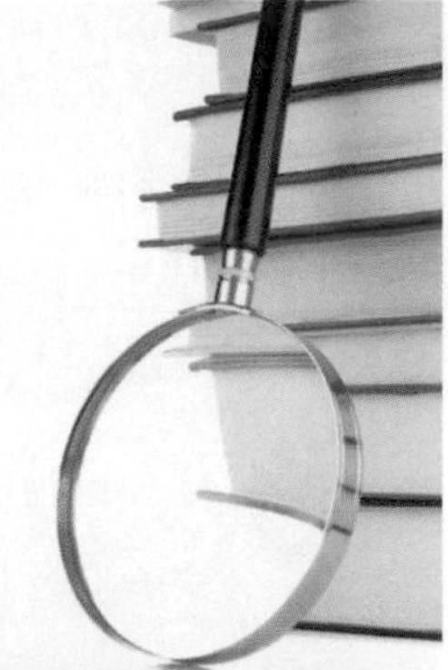

Part 5 photo: Christian Charisius/picture-alliance/dpa/AP Images; top to bottom: Seregram/Shutterstock; B. Deutsch, leftycartoons.com; Everett Collection; Jeff Siner/Charlotte Observer/MCT/Getty Images

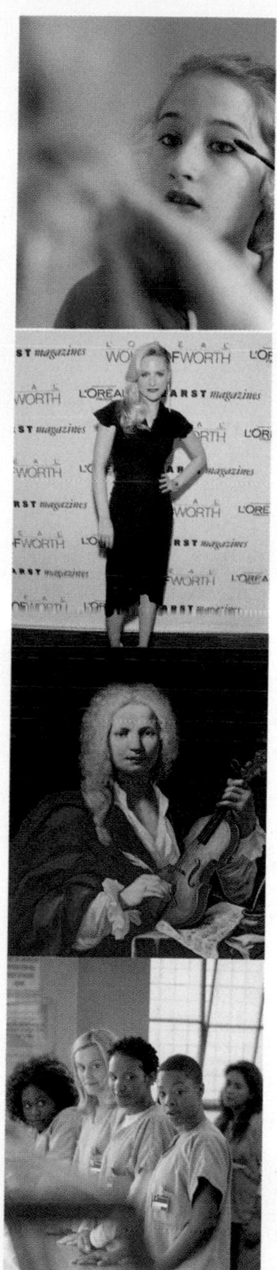

Top to bottom: Melanie Stetson Freeman/© 2011 The Christian Science Monitor (www.CSMonitor.com). Reprinted with permission; Eugene Gologursky/Wire Image/Getty Images; Civico Museo Bibliografico Musicale, Bologna, Italy/Alinari/Bridgeman Images; The Kobal Collection at Art Resource, NY

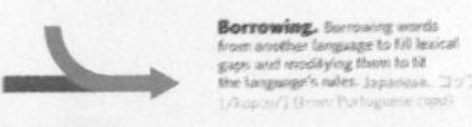

Top to bottom: Makeshift Magazine (mkshft.org); © Frank Fell/age fotostock; AP Photo/John McConnico; AP Photo/Journal Inquirer, Jared Ramsdell

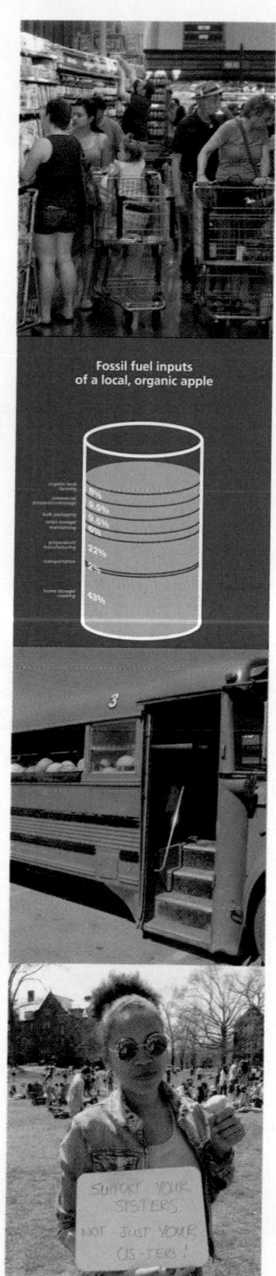

Top to bottom: AP Photo/The Philadelphia Inquirer, Clem Murray; © Claire Ironside, all rights reserved; AP Photo/The Herald-Palladium, John Madill; Megan Haaga, for Open Gates, by permission

Top to bottom: © Jake Nicolella for Penn State University; © Jim West/Photoshot; A. S. Alexander Collection of Ernest Hemingway. Department of Rare Books and Special Collections, Princeton University Library; AP Photo/The Miami Herald/Marsha Halper

Top to bottom: AP Photo, 1943; AP Photo; AP Photo/Kin Cheung; AP Photo/Pablo Martinez Monsivais

everything's an argument/with readings

PART 1

READING AND UNDERSTANDING arguments

1
Everything Is an Argument

Left: Pacific Press/Getty Images; right: © Akintunde Akinleye/Corbis

On May 7, 2014, First Lady of the United States Michelle Obama turned to new media to express her concern over the kidnapping of more than 200 young Nigerian girls by the terrorist group Boko Haram. Her tweet, along with an accompanying photo highlighting the trending hashtag #BringBackOurGirls, ramped up an argument over what the international community could do to stop an organization responsible for thousands of deaths in northeastern Nigeria. In bringing her appeal to Twitter, the First Lady acknowledged the persuasive power of social media like Facebook, YouTube, Instagram, and innumerable political and social blogs. The hashtag itself, it would appear, had become a potent tool for rallying audiences around the globe to support specific ideas or causes. But to what ends?

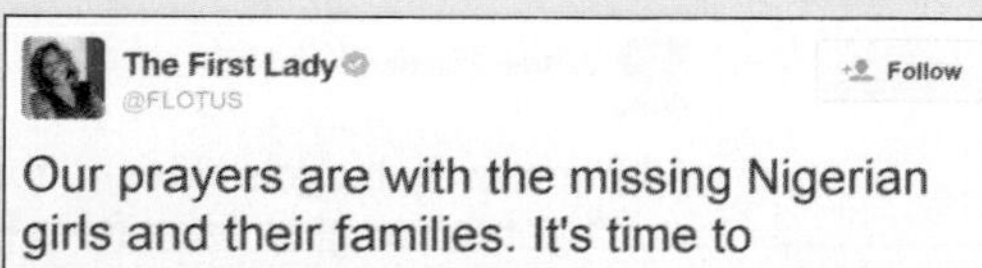
The First Lady
@FLOTUS
Follow

Our prayers are with the missing Nigerian girls and their families. It's time to #BringBackOurGirls. -mo

Just weeks before Obama's notable appeal, a U.S. State Department spokesperson Jen Psaki drew attention with a tweet of her own aimed at countering attempts by Russian social media to co-opt the U.S. State Department's #UnitedforUkraine hashtag:

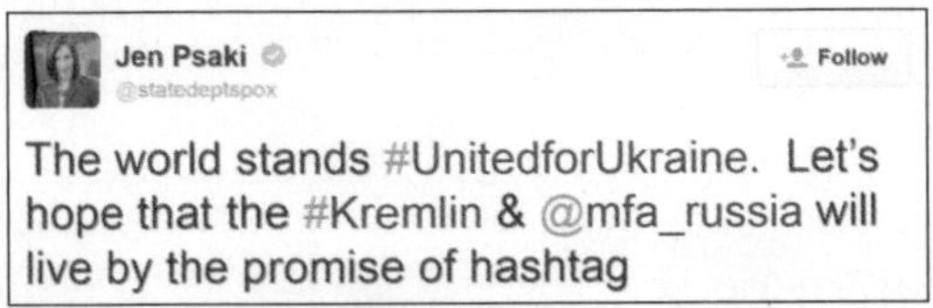

The Russian government, it seems, having just annexed the Crimea region and threatening all of Ukraine, was showing more skill than Western nations at using Twitter and other social media to win propaganda points in the diplomatic crisis. Yet Psaki's response via Twitter earned her disapproval from those who interpreted her social media riposte as further evidence of U.S. weakness. For instance, Texas senator Ted Cruz tweeted in reply to Psaki:

Even Michelle Obama took heat for her earnest appeal on behalf of kidnapped girls the same age as her own daughters. While celebrities such as Amy Poehler and Mary J. Blige posted supportive items, Obama's tweet got quick international pushback from those who argued (in 140 characters) that the anti-terrorist use of drones by the U.S. military was no less reprehensible than the tactics of Boko Haram. And domestic critics saw Obama's message as a substitute for real action, with columnist Jeffrey Goldberg chiding well-intentioned activists with a dose of reality:

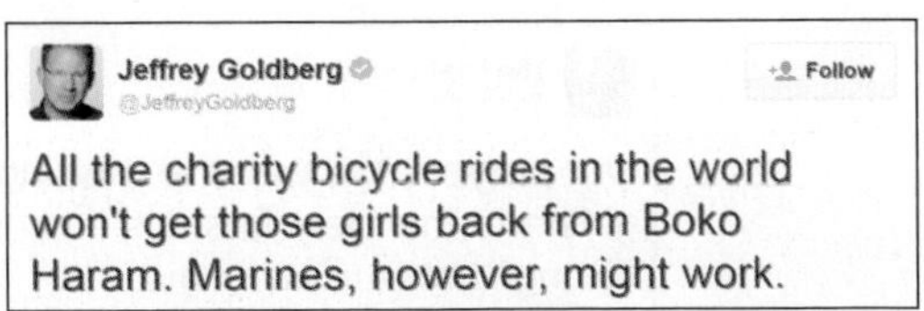

Clearly, social media play out on crowded, two-way channels, with claims and counterclaims whizzing by, fast and furious. Such tools reach audiences and they also create them, offering an innovative way to make and share arguments. Just as important, anyone, anywhere, with access to a phone, tablet, or other electronic device, can launch arguments that circle the globe in seconds. Social networking and digital tools are increasingly available to all.

We've opened this chapter with dramatic, perhaps troubling, examples of Twitter controversies to introduce our claim that arguments are all around us, in every medium, in every genre, in everything we do. There may be an argument on the T-shirt you put on in the morning, in the sports column you read on the bus, in the prayers you utter before an exam, in the off-the-cuff political remarks of a teacher lecturing, in the assurances of a health center nurse that "This won't hurt one bit."

The clothes you wear, the foods you eat, and the groups you join make nuanced, sometimes unspoken assertions about who you are and what you value. So an argument can be any text—written, spoken, aural, or visual—that expresses a point of view. In fact, some theorists claim that language is inherently persuasive. When you say, "Hi, how's it going?" in one sense you're arguing that your hello deserves a response. Even humor makes an argument when it causes readers to recognize—through bursts of laughter or just a faint smile—how things are and how they might be different.

More obvious as arguments are those that make direct claims based on or drawn from evidence. Such writing often moves readers to recognize problems and to consider solutions. Persuasion of this kind is usually easy to recognize:

> **The National Minimum Drinking Age Act, passed by Congress 30 years ago this July, is a gross violation of civil liberties and must be repealed. It is absurd and unjust that young Americans can vote, marry, enter contracts, and serve in the military at 18 but cannot buy an alcoholic drink in a bar or restaurant.**
>
> —Camille Paglia, "The Drinking Age Is Past Its Prime"

> **We will become a society of a million pictures without much memory, a society that looks forward every second to an immediate replication of what it has just done, but one that does not sustain the difficult labor of transmitting culture from one generation to the next.**
>
> —Christine Rosen, "The Image Culture"

RESPOND•

Can an argument really be any text that expresses a point of view? What kinds of arguments—if any—might be made by the following items?

a Boston Red Sox cap

a Livestrong bracelet

the "explicit lyrics" label on a best-selling rap CD

the health warnings on a package of cigarettes

a Tesla Model S electric car

a pair of Ray-Ban sunglasses

Why We Make Arguments

In the politically divided and entertainment-driven culture of the United States today, the word *argument* may well call up negative images: the hostile scowl or shaking fist of a politician or news "opinionator" who wants to drown out other voices and prevail at all costs. This winner-take-all view turns many citizens off to the whole process of using reasoned conversation to identify, explore, and solve problems. Hoping to avoid personal conflict, many people now sidestep opportunities to speak their mind on issues shaping their lives and work. We want to counter this attitude throughout this book.

Some arguments, of course, *are* aimed at winning, especially those related to politics, business, and law. Two candidates for office, for example, vie for a majority of votes; the makers of one smartphone try to outsell their competitors by offering more features at a lower price; and two lawyers try to outwit each other in pleading to a judge and jury. In your college writing, you may also be called on to make arguments that appeal to a "judge" and "jury" (perhaps your instructor and classmates). You might, for instance, argue that students in every field should be required to engage in service learning projects. In doing so, you will need to offer better arguments or more convincing evidence than potential opponents—such as those who might regard service learning as a politicized or coercive form of education. You can do so reasonably and responsibly, no name-calling required.

There are many reasons to argue and principled ways to do so. We explore some of them in this section.

Arguments to Convince and Inform

We're stepping into an argument ourselves in drawing what we hope is a useful distinction between *convincing* and—in the next section—*persuading*. (Feel free to disagree with us.) Arguments to convince lead audiences to accept a claim as true or reasonable—based on information or evidence that seems factual and reliable; arguments to persuade then seek to move people beyond conviction to *action*. Academic arguments often combine both elements.

In the excerpt from his book *Disability and the Media: Prescriptions for Change*, Charles A. Riley II intends to convince other journalists to adopt a less stereotypical language for discussing diversity.

LINK TO P. 527

Many news reports and analyses, white papers, and academic articles aim to convince audiences by broadening what they know about a subject. Such fact-based arguments might have no motives beyond laying out what the facts are. Here's an opening paragraph from a 2014 news story by Anahad O'Connor in the *New York Times* that itself launched a thousand arguments (and lots of huzzahs) simply by reporting the results of a recent scientific study:

> **Many of us have long been told that saturated fat, the type found in meat, butter and cheese, causes heart disease. But a large and exhaustive new analysis by a team of international scientists found no evidence that eating saturated fat increased heart attacks and other cardiac events.**
>
> **—Anahad O'Connor, "Study Questions Fat and Heart Disease Link"**

Wow. You can imagine how carefully the reporter walked through the scientific data, knowing how this new information might be understood and repurposed by his readers.

Similarly, in a college paper on viability of nuclear power as an alternative source of energy, you might compare the health and safety record of a nuclear plant to that of other forms of energy. Depending upon your findings and your interpretation of the data, the result of your fact-based presentation might be to raise or alleviate concerns readers have about nuclear energy. Of course, your decision to write the argument might be driven by your conviction that nuclear power is much safer than most people believe.

Even an image can offer an argument designed both to inform and to convince. On the following page, for example, editorial cartoonist Bob Englehart finds a way to frame an issue on the minds of many students today, the burden of crushing debt. As Englehart presents it, the problem is impossible to ignore.

© Bob Englehart/Cagle Cartoons, Inc.

Arguments to Persuade

Today, climate change may be the public issue that best illustrates the chasm that sometimes separates conviction from persuasion. The weight of scientific research may convince people that the earth is warming, but persuading them to act on that knowledge doesn't follow easily. How then does change occur? Some theorists suggest that persuasion—understood as moving people to do more than nod in agreement—is best achieved via appeals to emotions such as fear, anger, envy, pride, sympathy, or hope. We think that's an oversimplification. The fact is that persuasive arguments, whether in advertisements, political blogs, YouTube videos, or newspaper editorials, draw upon *all* the appeals of rhetoric (see p. 21) to motivate people to act—whether it be to buy a product, pull a lever for a candidate, or volunteer for a civic organization. Here, once again, is Camille Paglia driving home her argument that the 1984 federal law raising the drinking age in the United States to 21 was a catastrophic decision in need of reversal:

> What this cruel 1984 law did is deprive young people of safe spaces where they could happily drink cheap beer, socialize, chat, and flirt in a free but controlled public environment. Hence in the 1980s we immediately got the scourge of crude binge drinking at campus fraternity keg parties, cut off from the adult world. Women in

that boorish free-for-all were suddenly fighting off date rape. Club drugs — Ecstasy, methamphetamine, ketamine (a veterinary tranquilizer) — surged at raves for teenagers and on the gay male circuit scene.

Paglia chooses to dramatize her argument by sharply contrasting a safer, more supportive past with a vastly more dangerous present when drinking was forced underground and young people turned to highly risky behaviors. She doesn't hesitate to name them either: binge drinking, club drugs, raves, and, most seriously, date rape. This highly rhetorical, one might say *emotional*, argument pushes readers hard to endorse a call for serious action — the repeal of the current drinking age law.

Admit it, Duchess of Cornwall. You *knew* abandoned dogs need homes, but it was heartrending photos on the Battersea Dogs & Cats Home Web site that *persuaded* you to visit the shelter. WPA Pool/Getty Images

RESPOND.

Apply the distinction made here between convincing and persuading to the way people respond to two or three current political or social issues. Is there a useful distinction between being convinced and being persuaded? Explain your position.

Arguments to Make Decisions

Closely allied to arguments to convince and persuade are arguments to examine the options in important matters, both civil and personal—from managing out-of-control deficits to choosing careers. Arguments to make decisions occur all the time in the public arena, where they are often slow to evolve, caught up in electoral or legal squabbles, and yet driven by a genuine desire to find consensus. In recent years, for instance, Americans have argued hard to make decisions about health care, the civil rights of same-sex couples, and the status of more than 11 million immigrants in the country. Subjects so complex aren't debated in straight lines. They get haggled over in every imaginable medium by thousands of writers, politicians, and ordinary citizens working alone or via political organizations to have their ideas considered.

For college students, choosing a major can be an especially momentous personal decision, and one way to go about making that decision is to argue your way through several alternatives. By the time you've explored the pros and cons of each alternative, you should be a little closer to a reasonable and defensible decision.

Sometimes decisions, however, are not so easy to make.

www.CartoonStock.com

Arguments to Understand and Explore

Arguments to make decisions often begin as choices between opposing positions already set in stone. But is it possible to examine important issues in more open-ended ways? Many situations, again in civil or personal arenas, seem to call for arguments that genuinely explore possibilities without constraints or prejudices. If there's an "opponent" in such situations at all (often there is not), it's likely to be the status quo or a current trend which, for one reason or another, puzzles just about everyone. For example, in trying to sort through the extraordinary complexities of the 2011 budget debate, philosophy professor Gary Gutting was able to show how two distinguished economists—John Taylor and Paul Krugman—draw completely different conclusions from the exact same sets of facts. Exploring how such a thing could occur led Gutting to conclude that the two economists were arguing from the same facts, all right, but that they did not have *all* the facts possible. Those missing or unknown facts allowed them to fill in the blanks as they could, thus leading them to different conclusions. By discovering the source of a paradox, Gutting potentially opened new avenues for understanding.

The infographic "Speak My Language" by Santos Henarejos explores how technology has affected the way we communicate around the world.

LINK TO P. 585

Exploratory arguments can also be personal, such as Zora Neale Hurston's ironic exploration of racism and of her own identity in the essay "How It Feels to Be Colored Me." If you keep a journal or blog, you have no doubt found yourself making arguments to explore issues near and dear to you. Perhaps the essential argument in any such piece is the writer's realization that a problem exists—and that the writer or reader needs to understand it and respond constructively to it if possible.

Explorations of ideas that begin by trying to understand another's perspective have been described as **invitational arguments** by researchers Sonja Foss, Cindy Griffin, and Josina Makau. Such arguments are interested in inviting others to join in mutual explorations of ideas based on discovery and respect. Another kind of argument, called **Rogerian argument** (after psychotherapist Carl Rogers), approaches audiences in similarly nonthreatening ways, finding common ground and establishing trust among those who disagree about issues. Writers who take a Rogerian approach try to see where the other person is coming from, looking for "both/and" or "win/win" solutions whenever possible. (For more on Rogerian strategies, see Chapter 7.)

"You say it's a win-win, but what if you're wrong-wrong and it all goes bad-bad?"

The risks of Rogerian argument © David Sipress/The New Yorker Collection/The Cartoon Bank

RESPOND.

What are your reasons for making arguments? Keep notes for two days about every single argument you make, using our broad definition to guide you. Then identify your reasons: How many times did you aim to convince? To inform? To persuade? To explore? To understand?

Occasions for Argument

In a fifth-century BCE textbook of **rhetoric** (the art of persuasion), the philosopher Aristotle provides an ingenious strategy for classifying arguments based on their perspective on time—past, future, and present. His ideas still help us to appreciate the role arguments play in society in the twenty-first century. As you consider Aristotle's occasions for argument, remember that all such classifications overlap (to a certain extent) and that we live in a world much different than his.

Arguments about the Past

Debates about what has happened in the past, what Aristotle called **forensic arguments**, are the red meat of government, courts, businesses, and academia. People want to know who did what in the past, for what reasons, and with what liability. When you argue a speeding ticket in court, you are making a forensic argument, claiming perhaps that you weren't over the limit or that the officer's radar was faulty. A judge will have to decide what exactly happened in the past in the unlikely case you push the issue that far.

More consequentially, in 2014 the federal government and General Motors found themselves deeply involved in arguments about the past as investigators sought to determine just exactly how the massive auto company had allowed a serious defect in the ignition switches of its cars to go undisclosed and uncorrected for a decade. Drivers and passengers died or were injured as engines shut down and airbags failed to go off in subsequent collisions. Who at General Motors was responsible for not diagnosing the fault? Were any engineers or executives liable for covering up the problem? And how should victims of this product defect or their families be compensated? These were all forensic questions to be thoroughly investigated, argued, and answered by regulatory panels and courts.

From an academic perspective, consider the lingering forensic arguments over Christopher Columbus's "discovery" of America. Are his expeditions cause for celebration or notably unhappy chapters in human history? Or some of both? Such arguments about past actions—heated enough to spill over into the public realm—are common in disciplines such as history, philosophy, and ethics.

Mary Barra, the chief executive officer of General Motors, testifies before a congressional panel looking into problems with ignition switches in the company's cars. AP Photo/Ron Sachs/picture-alliance/dpa/AP Images

Amy Davidson's article "Four Ways the *Riley* Ruling Matters for the NSA" predicts some probable outcomes of an important Supreme Court decision.

LINK TO P. 786

Arguments about the Future

Debates about what will or should happen in the future—**deliberative arguments**—often influence policies or legislation for the future. *Should local or state governments allow or even encourage the use of self-driving cars on public roads? Should colleges and universities lend support to more dual-credit programs so that students can earn college credits while still in high school? Should coal-fired power plants be phased out of our energy grid?* These are the sorts of deliberative questions that legislatures, committees, or school boards routinely address when making laws or establishing policies.

But arguments about the future can also be speculative, advancing by means of projections and reasoned guesses, as shown in the following passage from an essay by media maven Marc Prensky. He is arguing that it is time for some college or university to be the first to ban physical, that is to say *paper*, books on its campus, a controversial proposal to say the least:

> Colleges and professors exist, in great measure, to help "liberate" and connect the knowledge and ideas in books. We should certainly pass on to our students the ability to do this. But in the future those liberated ideas—the ones in the books (the author's words), and the ones about the books (the reader's own notes, all readers' thoughts and commentaries)—should be available with a few keystrokes. So, as counterintuitive as it may sound, eliminating physical books from college campuses would be a positive step for our 21st-century students, and, I believe, for 21st-century scholarship as well. Academics, researchers, and particularly teachers need to move to the tools of the future. Artifacts belong in museums, not in our institutions of higher learning.
>
> —Marc Prensky, "In the 21st-Century University, Let's Ban Books"

Arguments about the Present

Arguments about the present—what Aristotle terms **epideictic** or **ceremonial arguments**—explore the current values of a society, affirming or challenging its widely shared beliefs and core assumptions. Epideictic arguments are often made at public and formal events such as inaugural addresses, sermons, eulogies, memorials, and graduation speeches.

Members of the audience listen carefully as credible speakers share their wisdom. For example, as the selection of college commencement speakers has grown increasingly contentious, Ruth J. Simmons, the first African American woman to head an Ivy League college, used the opportunity of such an address (herself standing in for a rejected speaker) to offer a timely and ringing endorsement of free speech. Her words perfectly illustrate epideictic rhetoric:

> Universities have a special obligation to protect free speech, open discourse and the value of protest. The collision of views and ideologies is in the DNA of the academic enterprise. No collision avoidance technology is needed here. The noise from this discord may cause others to criticize the legitimacy of the academic enterprise, but how can knowledge advance without the questions that overturn misconceptions, push further into previously impenetrable areas of inquiry and assure us stunning breakthroughs in human knowledge? If there is anything that colleges must encourage and protect it is the persistent questioning of the status quo. Our health as a nation, our health as women, our health as an industry requires it.
>
> —Ruth J. Simmons, Smith College, 2014

Perhaps more common than Smith's impassioned address are values arguments that examine contemporary culture, praising what's admirable and blaming what's not. In the following argument, student Latisha Chisholm looks at the state of rap music after Tupac Shakur:

> With the death of Tupac, not only did one of the most intriguing rap rivalries of all time die, but the motivation for rapping seems to have changed. Where money had always been a plus, now it is obviously more important than wanting to express the hardships of Black communities. With current rappers, the positive power that came from the desire to represent Black people is lost. One of the biggest rappers now got his big break while talking about sneakers. Others announce retirement without really having done much for the soul or for Black people's morale. I equate new rappers to NFL players that don't love the game anymore. They're only in it for the money. . . . It looks like the voice of a people has lost its heart.
>
> —Latisha Chisholm, "Has Rap Lost Its Soul?"

As in many ceremonial arguments, Chisholm here reinforces common values such as representing one's community honorably and fairly.

Are rappers since Tupac—like Jay Z—only in it for the money? Many epideictic arguments either praise or blame contemporary culture in this way. Michael N. Todaro/FilmMagic/Getty Images

RESPOND.

In a recent magazine, newspaper, or blog, find three editorials—one that makes a forensic argument, one a deliberative argument, and one a ceremonial argument. Analyze the arguments by asking these questions: Who is arguing? What purposes are the writers trying to achieve? To whom are they directing their arguments? Then decide whether the arguments' purposes have been achieved and how you know.

Occasions for Argument

	Past	*Future*	*Present*
What is it called?	Forensic	Deliberative	Epideictic
What are its concerns?	What happened in the past?	What should be done in the future?	Who or what deserves praise or blame?
What does it look like?	Court decisions, legal briefs, legislative hearings, investigative reports, academic studies	White papers, proposals, bills, regulations, mandates	Eulogies, graduation speeches, inaugural addresses, roasts

Kinds of Argument

Yet another way of categorizing arguments is to consider their status or stasis—that is, the specific *kinds of issues they address*. This approach, called **stasis theory**, was used in ancient Greek and Roman civilizations to provide questions designed to help citizens and lawyers work their way through legal cases. The status questions were posed in sequence because each depended on answers from the preceding ones. Together, the queries helped determine the point of contention in an argument—where the parties disagreed or what exactly had to be proven. A modern version of those questions might look like the following:

- Did something happen?
- What is its nature?
- What is its quality or cause?
- What actions should be taken?

Each stasis question explores a different aspect of a problem and uses different evidence or techniques to reach conclusions. You can use these questions to explore the aspects of any topic you're considering. You'll discover that we use the stasis issues to define key types of argument in Part 2.

Did Something Happen? Arguments of Fact

There's no point in arguing a case until its basic facts are established. So an **argument of fact** usually involves a statement that can be proved or disproved with specific evidence or testimony. For example, the question of pollution of the oceans—is it really occurring?—might seem relatively easy to settle. Either scientific data prove that the oceans are being dirtied as a result of human activity, or they don't. But to settle the matter, writers and readers need to ask a number of other questions about the "facts":

- Where did the facts come from?
- Are they reliable?
- Is there a problem with the facts?
- Where did the problem begin and what caused it?

For more on arguments based on facts, see Chapters 4 and 8.

What Is the Nature of the Thing? Arguments of Definition

Some of the most hotly debated issues in American life today involve questions of definition: we argue over the nature of the human fetus, the meaning of "amnesty" for immigrants, the boundaries of sexual assault. As you might guess, issues of definition have mighty consequences, and decades of debate may nonetheless leave the matter unresolved. Here, for example, is how one type of sexual assault is defined in an important 2007 report submitted to the U.S. Department of Justice by the National Institute of Justice:

> **We consider as incapacitated sexual assault any unwanted sexual contact occurring when a victim is unable to provide consent or stop what is happening because she is passed out, drugged, drunk, incapacitated, or asleep, regardless of whether the perpetrator was responsible for her substance use or whether substances were administered without her knowledge. We break down incapacitated sexual assault into four subtypes. . . .**
>
> **—"The Campus Sexual Assault (CSA) Study: Final Report"**

The specifications of the definition go on for another two hundred words, each of consequence in determining how sexual assault on college campuses might be understood, measured, and addressed.

Of course many **arguments of definition** are less weighty than this, though still hotly contested: Is playing video games a sport? Can Batman be a tragic figure? Is Hillary Clinton a moderate or a progressive? (For more about arguments of definition, see Chapter 9.)

What Is the Quality or Cause of the Thing? Arguments of Evaluation

Arguments of evaluation present criteria and then measure individual people, ideas, or things against those standards. For instance, a *Washington Post* story examining long-term trend lines in SAT reading scores opened with this qualitative assessment of the results:

> Reading scores on the SAT for the high school class of 2012 reached a four-decade low, putting a punctuation mark on a gradual decline in the ability of college-bound teens to read passages and answer questions about sentence structure, vocabulary and meaning on the college entrance exam. . . . Scores among every racial group except for those of Asian descent declined from 2006 levels. A majority of test takers—57 percent—did not score high enough to indicate likely success in college, according to the College Board, the organization that administers the test.
>
> —Lyndsey Layton and Emma Brown, "SAT Reading Scores Hit a Four-Decade Low"

The final sentence is particularly telling, putting the test results in context. More than half the high school test-takers may not be ready for college-level readings.

In examining a circumstance or situation like this, we are often led to wonder what accounts for it: *Why are the test scores declining? Why are some groups underperforming?* And, in fact, the authors of the brief *Post* story do follow up on some questions of cause and effect:

> The 2012 SAT scores come after a decade of efforts to raise test scores under the No Child Left Behind law, the federal education initiative crafted by President George W. Bush. Critics say the law failed to address the barriers faced by many test takers.
>
> "Some kids are coming to school hungry, some without the health care they need, without the vocabulary that middle-class kids come to school with, even in kindergarten," said Helen F. Ladd, a professor of public policy and economics at Duke University.

Although evaluations differ from causal analyses, in practice the boundaries between stasis questions are often porous: particular arguments have a way of defining their own issues.

For much more about arguments of evaluation, see Chapter 10; for causal arguments, see Chapter 11.

What Actions Should Be Taken? Proposal Arguments

After facts in a controversy have been confirmed, definitions agreed on, evaluations made, and causes traced, it may be time for a **proposal argument** answering the question *Now, what do we do about all this?* For example, in developing an argument about out-of-control student fees at your college, you might use all the prior stasis questions to study the issue and determine exactly how much and for what reasons these costs

STASIS QUESTIONS AT WORK

Suppose you have an opportunity to speak at a student conference on the impact of climate change. You are tentatively in favor of strengthening industrial pollution standards aimed at reducing global warming trends. But to learn more about the issue, you use the stasis questions to get started.

- **Did something happen?** Does global warming exist? *Maybe not*, say many in the oil and gas industry; at best, evidence for global warming is inconclusive. *Yes*, say most scientists and governments; climate change is real and even seems to be accelerating. To come to your conclusion, you'll weigh the facts carefully and identify problems with opposing arguments.
- **What is the nature of the thing?** Skeptics define climate change as a naturally occurring event; most scientists base their definitions on change due to human causes. You look at each definition carefully: *How do the definitions foster the goals of each group? What's at stake for each group in defining it that way?*
- **What is the quality or cause of the thing?** Exploring the differing assessments of damage done by climate change leads you to ask who will gain from such analysis: *Do oil executives want to protect their investments? Do scientists want government money for grants? Where does evidence for the dangers of global warming come from? Who benefits if the dangers are accepted as real and present, and who loses?*
- **What actions should be taken?** If climate change is occurring naturally or causing little harm, then arguably *nothing* needs to be or can be done. But if it is caused mainly by human activity and dangers, action is definitely called for (although not everyone may agree on what such action should be). As you investigate the proposals being made and the reasons behind them, you come closer to developing your own argument.

The No Child Left Behind Act was signed in 2002 with great hopes and bipartisan support.
AFP/Getty Images

are escalating. Only then will you be prepared to offer knowledgeable suggestions for action. In examining a nationwide move to eliminate remedial education in four-year colleges, John Cloud offers a notably moderate proposal to address the problem:

> **Students age twenty-two and over account for 43 percent of those in remedial classrooms, according to the National Center for Developmental Education. . . . [But] 55 percent of those needing remediation must take just one course. Is it too much to ask them to pay extra for that class or take it at a community college?**
>
> **—John Cloud, "Who's Ready for College?"**

For more about proposal arguments, see Chapter 12.

Appealing to Audiences

Exploring all the occasions and kinds of arguments available will lead you to think about the audience(s) you are addressing and the specific ways you can appeal to them. Audiences for arguments today are amazingly diverse, from the flesh-and-blood person sitting across a desk when you negotiate a student loan to your "friends" on social media, to the "ideal" reader you imagine for whatever you are writing. The figure on the next page suggests just how many dimensions an audience can have as writers and readers negotiate their relationships with a text, whether it be oral, written, or digital.

As you see there, texts usually have **intended readers**, the people writers hope and expect to address—let's say, routine browsers of a

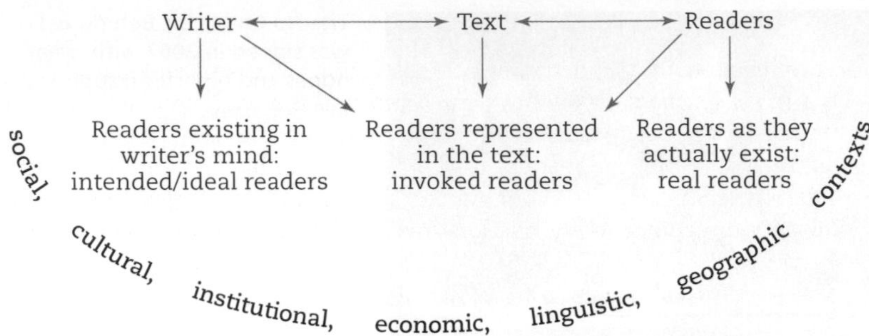

Readers and writers in context

newspaper's op-ed page. But writers also shape the responses of these actual readers in ways they imagine as appropriate or desirable—for example, maneuvering readers of editorials into making focused and knowledgeable judgments about politics and culture. Such audiences, as imagined and fashioned by writers within their texts, are called **invoked readers**.

Making matters even more complicated, readers can respond to writers' maneuvers by choosing to join the invoked audiences, to resist them, or maybe even to ignore them. Arguments may also attract "real" readers from groups not among those that writers originally imagined or expected to reach. You may post something on the Web, for instance, and discover that people you did not intend to address are commenting on it. (For them, the experience may be like reading private email intended for someone else: they find themselves drawn to and fascinated by your ideas!) As authors of this book, we think about students like you whenever we write: you are our intended readers. But notice how in dozens of ways, from the images we choose to the tone of our language, we also invoke an audience of people who take writing arguments seriously. We want you to become that kind of reader.

So audiences are *very* complicated and subtle and challenging, and yet you somehow have to attract and even persuade them. As always, Aristotle offers an answer. He identified three time-tested appeals that speakers and writers can use to reach almost any audience, labeling them *pathos*, *ethos*, and *logos*—strategies as effective today as they were in ancient times, though we usually think of them in slightly different terms. Used in the right way and deployed at the right moment, emotional, ethical, and logical appeals have enormous power, as we'll see in subsequent chapters.

RESPOND.

You can probably provide concise descriptions of the intended audience for most textbooks you have encountered. But can you detect their invoked audiences—that is, the way their authors are imagining (and perhaps shaping) the readers they would like to have? Carefully review this entire first chapter, looking for signals and strategies that might identify the audience and readers invoked by the authors of *Everything's an Argument*.

Emotional Appeals: Pathos

Emotional appeals, or **pathos**, generate emotions (fear, pity, love, anger, jealousy) that the writer hopes will lead the audience to accept a claim. Here is an alarming sentence from a book by Barry B. LePatner arguing that Americans need to make hard decisions about repairing the country's failing infrastructure:

> When the I-35W Bridge in Minneapolis shuddered, buckled, and collapsed during the evening rush hour on Wednesday, August 1, 2007, plunging 111 vehicles into the Mississippi River and sending thirteen people to their deaths, the sudden, apparently inexplicable nature of the event at first gave the appearance of an act of God.
>
> —*Too Big to Fall: America's Failing Infrastructure and the Way Forward*

If you ever drive across a bridge, LePatner has probably gotten your attention. His sober and yet descriptive language helps readers imagine the dire consequence of neglected road maintenance and bad design decisions. Making an emotional appeal like this can dramatize an issue and sometimes even create a bond between writer and readers. (For more about emotional appeals, see Chapter 2.)

Ethical Appeals: Ethos

When writers or speakers come across as trustworthy, audiences are likely to listen to and accept their arguments. That trustworthiness (along with fairness and respect) is a mark of **ethos**, or credibility. Showing that you know what you are talking about exerts an ethical appeal, as does emphasizing that you share values with and respect your audience. Once again, here's Barry LePatner from *Too Big to Fall*, shoring up his authority for writing about problems with America's roads and bridges by invoking the ethos of people even more credible:

> For those who would seek to dismiss the facts that support the thesis of this book, I ask them to consult the many professional engineers in state transportation departments who face these problems on a daily basis. These professionals understand the physics of bridge and road design, and the real problems of ignoring what happens to steel and concrete when they are exposed to the elements without a strict regimen of ongoing maintenance.

It's a sound rhetorical move to enhance credibility this way. For more about ethical appeals, see Chapter 3.

Logical Appeals: Logos

Appeals to logic, or **logos**, are often given prominence and authority in U.S. culture: "Just the facts, ma'am," a famous early TV detective on *Dragnet* used to say. Indeed, audiences respond well to the use of reasons and evidence—to the presentation of facts, statistics, credible testimony, cogent examples, or even a narrative or story that embodies a sound reason in support of an argument. Following almost two hundred pages of facts, statistics, case studies, and arguments about the sad state of American bridges, LePatner can offer this sober, logical, and inevitable conclusion:

> We can no longer afford to ignore the fact that we are in the midst of a transportation funding crisis, which has been exacerbated by an even larger and longer-term problem: how we choose to invest in our infrastructure. It is not difficult to imagine the serious consequences that will unfold if we fail to address the deplorable conditions of our bridges and roads, including the increasingly higher costs we will pay for goods and services that rely on that transportation network, and a concomitant reduction in our standard of living.

For more about logical appeals, see Chapter 4.

Bringing It Home: *Kairos* and the Rhetorical Situation

In Greek mythology, Kairos—the youngest son of Zeus—was the god of opportunity. In images, he is most often depicted as running, and his most unusual characteristic is a shock of hair on his forehead. As Kairos

dashes by, you have a chance to seize that lock of hair, thereby seizing the opportune moment; once he passes you by, however, you have missed that chance.

Kairos is also a term used to describe the most suitable time and place for making an argument and the most opportune ways of expressing it. It is easy to point to shimmering rhetorical moments, when speakers find exactly the right words to stir an audience: Franklin Roosevelt's "We have nothing to fear but fear itself," Ronald Reagan's "Mr. Gorbachev, tear down this wall," and of course Martin Luther King Jr.'s "I have a dream . . ." But *kairos* matters just as much in less dramatic situations, whenever speakers or writers must size up the core elements of a rhetorical situation to decide how best to make their expertise and ethos work for a particular message aimed at a specific audience. The diagram below hints at the dynamic complexity of the rhetorical situation.

But rhetorical situations are embedded in contexts of enormous social complexity. The moment you find a subject, you inherit all the knowledge, history, culture, and technological significations that surround it. To lesser and greater degrees (depending on the subject), you also bring personal circumstances into the field—perhaps your gender, your race, your religion, your economic class, your habits of language. And all those issues weigh also upon the people you write to and for.

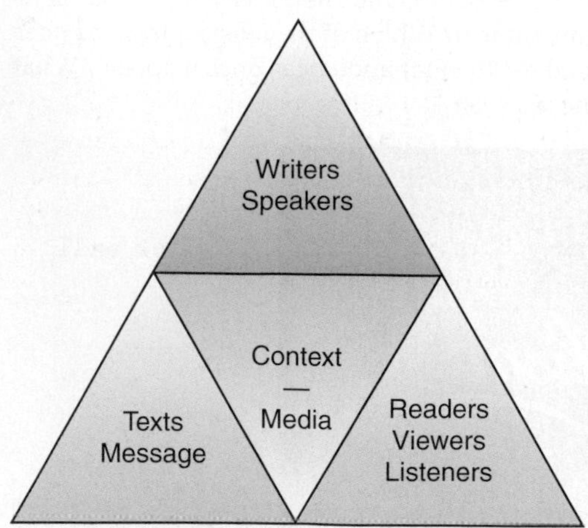

The rhetorical situation

Ronald Reagan at the Berlin Wall, June 12, 1987: "Mr. Gorbachev, tear down this wall!" © Dennis Brack/PhotoShot

So considering your rhetorical situation calls on you to think hard about the notion of *kairos*. Being aware of your rhetorical moment means being able to understand and take advantage of dynamic, shifting circumstances and to choose the best (most timely) proofs and evidence for a particular place, situation, and audience. It means seizing moments and enjoying opportunities, not being overwhelmed by them. Doing so might even lead you to challenge the title of this text: is everything an argument?

That's what makes writing arguments exciting.

RESPOND

Take a look at the bumper sticker below, and then analyze it. What is its purpose? What kind of argument is it? Which of the stasis questions does it most appropriately respond to? To what audiences does it appeal? What appeals does it make and how?

© Kevin Lamarque/Reuters/Corbis

CULTURAL CONTEXTS FOR ARGUMENT

Considering What's "Normal"

If you want to communicate effectively with people across cultures, then learn about the traditions in those cultures and examine the norms guiding your own behavior:

- Explore your assumptions! Most of us regard our ways of thinking as "normal" or "right." Such assumptions guide our judgments about what works in persuasive situations. But just because it may seem natural to speak bluntly in arguments, consider that others may find such aggression startling or even alarming.
- Remember: ways of arguing differ widely across cultures. Pay attention to how people from groups or cultures other than your own argue, and be sensitive to different paths of thinking you'll encounter as well as to differences in language.
- Don't assume that all people share your cultural values, ethical principles, or political assumptions. People across the world have different ways of defining *family*, *work*, or *happiness*. As you present arguments to them, consider that they may be content with their different ways of organizing their lives and societies.
- Respect the differences among individuals *within* a given group. Don't expect that every member of a community behaves—or argues—in the same way or shares the same beliefs. Avoid thinking, for instance, that there is a single Asian, African, or Hispanic culture or that Europeans are any less diverse or more predictable than Americans or Canadians in their thinking. In other words, be skeptical of stereotypes.

2
Arguments Based on Emotion: Pathos

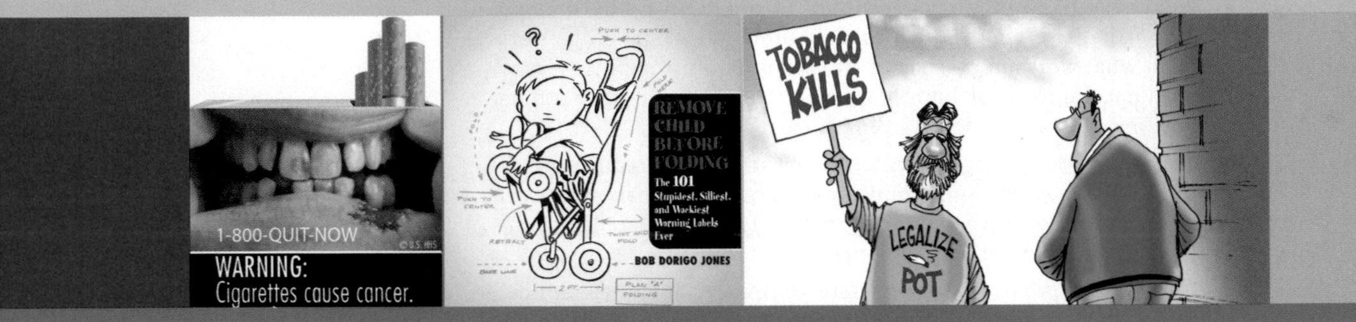

Center: PRNews Photo/Wide World/AP Photo; right: Used with permission of Gary Varvel and Creators Syndicate.

Emotional appeals (*appeals to pathos*) are powerful tools for influencing what people think and believe. We all make decisions—even including the most important ones—based on our feelings. That's what the Food and Drug Administration hoped to capitalize on when it introduced nine tough warning labels for cigarettes, one of which you see above. One look at the stained, rotting teeth and the lip sore may arouse emotions of fear strong enough to convince people not to smoke.

In the second panel, Bob Dorigo Jones, an opponent of lawsuit abuse, takes concerns about product liability in a different direction, publishing a book entitled *Remove Child before Folding: The 101 Stupidest, Silliest, and Wackiest Warning Labels Ever* to make us laugh and thereby, perhaps, to wonder why common sense seems in such short supply. In the third panel, editorial cartoonist for the *Indianapolis Star* Gary Varvel uses the anti-smoking meme to point out a potent irony in burgeoning campaigns to legalize marijuana.

The arguments packed into these three images all appeal to emotion, and research has shown us that we often make decisions based on just such appeals. So when you hear that formal or academic arguments should rely solely on facts to convince us, remember that facts alone often won't carry the day, even for a worthy cause. The largely successful case made this decade for same-sex marriage provides a notable example of a movement that persuaded people equally by virtue of the reasonableness and the passion of its claims. Like many political and social debates, though, the issue provoked powerful emotions on every side—feelings that sometimes led to extreme words and tactics.

Of course, we don't have to look hard for arguments fueled with emotions such as hatred, envy, and greed, or for campaigns intended to drive wedges between economic or social groups, making them fearful or resentful. For that reason alone, writers should not use emotional appeals rashly or casually. (For more about emotional fallacies, see p. 72.)

Reading Critically for Pathos

On February 24, 2014, Senator Tom Harkin of Iowa, fresh from two "fact-finding" trips to Cuba, described his experiences on the Senate floor in a rambling, forty-minute speech, praising that island nation's accomplishments in health care and education and urging a normalization of Cuban–American relationships. Later that day, Florida senator Marco Rubio, expecting to speak about growing repression in Venezuela, found it impossible to ignore Harkin's rosy view of the "fascinating" socialist experiment ninety miles from the coast of the United States. Seizing a kairotic moment, the first-term senator delivered a passionate fifteen-minute rejoinder to Harkin without a script or teleprompter—though Rubio did use posters prepared originally for the Venezuelan talk. After a sarcastic taunt ("Sounded like he had a wonderful trip visiting what he described as a real paradise"), Rubio quickly turned serious, even angry, as he offered his take on the country Harkin had toured:

> **I heard him also talk about these great doctors that they have in Cuba. I have no doubt they're very talented. I've met a bunch of them. You know where I met them? In the United States because they defected. Because in Cuba, doctors would rather drive a taxi cab or work in a hotel than be a doctor. I wonder if they spoke to him about the outbreak of cholera that they've been unable to control, or about the**

> three-tiered system of health care that exists where foreigners and government officials get health care much better than that that's available to the general population.

The speech thereafter settles into a rhythm of patterned inquiries designed to raise doubts about what Senator Harkin had seen, Rubio's informal language rippling with contempt for his colleague's naïveté:

> I heard about their [the Cubans'] wonderful literacy rate, how everyone in Cuba knows how to read. That's fantastic. Here's the problem: they can only read censored stuff. They're not allowed access to the Internet. The only newspapers they're allowed to read are *Granma* or the ones produced by the government. . . .
>
> He talked about these great baseball players that are coming from Cuba—and they are. But I wonder if they informed him [that] every single one of those guys playing in the Major Leagues defected. They left Cuba to play here. . . .
>
> So it's great to have literacy, but if you don't have access to the information, what's the point of it? So I wish somebody would have asked about that on that trip. . . .
>
> I wonder if anybody asked about terrorism, because Cuba is a state sponsor of terrorism. . . .

Language this heated and pointed has risks, especially when a young legislator is taking on a genial and far more experienced colleague. But Rubio, the son of Cuban immigrants, isn't shy about allowing his feelings to show. Segueing to his original topic—growing political repression in socialist Venezuela—he uses the kind of verbal repetition common in oratory to drive home his major concern about Cuba, its influence on other nations:

> Let me tell you what the Cubans are really good at, because they don't know how to run their economy, they don't know how to build, they don't know how to govern a people. What they are really good at is repression. What they are really good at is shutting off information to the Internet and to radio and television and social media. That's what they're really good at. And they're not just good at it domestically, they're good exporters of these things.

Rubio's actual audience in the U.S. Senate was very small, but today all speeches from that chamber are carried nationwide and archived by C-SPAN, and in the age of YouTube, bits and pieces of political addresses reach many listeners. Former speechwriter and *Wall Street Journal* columnist Peggy Noonan was among those who caught Rubio's remarks and

As originally aired on C-SPAN2 on February 24 2014

blogged about them: "We have pressed in these parts for American political figures to speak clearly and with moral confidence about American sympathies in various international disputes. Rubio's speech is honest political indignation successfully deployed." You can watch the entire speech on C-SPAN's Web site (listed as "Rubio Speech on Venezuela") to see if you agree. And though Cuba and the United States did re-establish diplomatic relationships roughly ten months after the Harkin/Rubio exchange, issues raised by both senators — from health care to the immigration status of Cuban baseball players — will likely be argued for years to come.

RESPOND •

Working with a classmate, make a list of reasons why speakers in highly charged situations might need to use emotional appeals cautiously, even sparingly. What consequences might heightened emotional appeals lead to? What is at stake for the speaker in such situations, in terms of credibility and ethos? What are the advantages of evoking emotions in support of your claims or ideas?

Using Emotions to Build Bridges

You may sometimes want to use emotions to connect with readers to assure them that you understand their experiences or "feel their pain," to borrow a sentiment popularized by President Bill Clinton. Such a bridge is especially important when you're writing about matters that readers regard as sensitive. Before they'll trust you, they'll want assurances that you understand the issues in depth. If you strike the right emotional note, you'll establish an important connection. That's what Apple founder Steve Jobs does in a much-admired 2005 commencement address in which he tells the audience that he doesn't have a fancy speech, just three stories from his life:

> My second story is about love and loss. I was lucky. I found what I loved to do early in life. Woz [Steve Wozniak] and I started Apple in my parents' garage when I was twenty. We worked hard and in ten years, Apple had grown from just the two of us in a garage into a $2 billion company with over four thousand employees. We'd just released our finest creation, the Macintosh, a year earlier, and I'd just turned thirty, and then I got fired. How can you get fired from a company you started? Well, as Apple grew, we hired someone who I thought was very talented to run the company with me, and for the first year or so, things went well. But then our visions of the future began to diverge, and eventually we had a falling out. When we did, our board of directors sided with him, and so at thirty, I was out, and very publicly out. . . .
>
> I didn't see it then, but it turned out that getting fired from Apple was the best thing that could have ever happened to me. The heaviness of being successful was replaced by the lightness of being a beginner again, less sure about everything. It freed me to enter one of the most creative periods in my life. During the next five years I started a company named NeXT, another company named Pixar and fell in love with an amazing woman who would become my wife. Pixar went on to create the world's first computer-animated feature film, *Toy Story*, and is now the most successful animation studio in the world.
>
> —Steve Jobs, "You've Got to Find What You Love, Jobs Says"

In no obvious way is Jobs's recollection a formal argument. But it prepares his audience to accept the advice he'll give later in his speech, at least partly because he's speaking from meaningful personal experiences.

The excerpt from Shabana Mir's book *Muslim American Women on Campus* opens with comments that unify the undergraduate experience.

LINK TO P. 702

A more obvious way to build an emotional tie is simply to help readers identify with your experiences. If, like Georgina Kleege, you were blind and wanted to argue for more sensible attitudes toward blind people, you might ask readers in the first paragraph of your argument to confront their prejudices. Here Kleege, a writer and college instructor, makes an emotional point by telling a story:

> I tell the class, "I am legally blind." There is a pause, a collective intake of breath. I feel them look away uncertainly and then look back. After all, I just said I couldn't see. Or did I? I had managed to get there on my own—no cane, no dog, none of the usual trappings of blindness.

Eyeing me askance now, they might detect that my gaze is not quite focused. . . . They watch me glance down, or towards the door where someone's coming in late. I'm just like anyone else.

—Georgina Kleege, "Call It Blindness"

Given the way she narrates the first day of class, readers are as likely to identify with the students as with Kleege, imagining themselves sitting in a classroom, facing a sightless instructor, confronting their own prejudices about the blind. Kleege wants to put her audience on the edge emotionally.

Let's consider another rhetorical situation: how do you win over an audience when the logical claims that you're making are likely to go against what many in the audience believe? Once again, a slightly risky appeal to emotions on a personal level may work. That's the tack that Michael Pollan takes in bringing readers to consider that "the great moral struggle of our time will be for the rights of animals." In introducing his lengthy exploratory argument, Pollan uses personal experience to appeal to his audience:

The first time I opened Peter Singer's *Animal Liberation*, I was dining alone at the Palm, trying to enjoy a rib-eye steak cooked medium-rare.

A visual version of Michael Pollan's rhetorical situation. © Robert Mankoff/The New Yorker Collection/The Cartoon Bank

> If this sounds like a good recipe for cognitive dissonance (if not indigestion), that was sort of the idea. Preposterous as it might seem to supporters of animal rights, what I was doing was tantamount to reading *Uncle Tom's Cabin* on a plantation in the Deep South in 1852.
>
> —Michael Pollan, "An Animal's Place"

In creating a vivid image of his first encounter with Singer's book, Pollan's opening builds a bridge between himself as a person trying to enter into the animal rights debate in a fair and open-minded, if still skeptical, way and readers who might be passionate about either side of this argument.

Using Emotions to Sustain an Argument

You can also use emotional appeals to make logical claims stronger or more memorable. That is the way that photographs and other images add power to arguments. In a TV attack ad, the scowling cell phone video of a disheveled political opponent may do as much damage as the insinuation that he bought his home on the cheap from a financier convicted of fraud. In contrast, a human face smiling or showing honest emotion can sell just about any product—that's why indicted political figures now routinely smile for their mug shots. Using emotion is tricky, however. Lay on too much feeling—especially sentiments like outrage, pity, or shame, which make people uncomfortable—and you may offend the very audiences you hoped to convince.

Still, strong emotions can add energy to a passage or an entire argument, as they do when Walter Russell Mead, editor-at-large of the *American Interest*, argues about what *really* motivates Americans to donate lavishly to many colleges and universities. As you read the following excerpt, notice how the author paints vivid pictures of people at college sporting events, describes the emotions at those games, and then argues what schools really need to do to win contributions:

> But if you want to understand why so many generations of Americans have sent so much dough back to the campuses where they wasted some of the happiest years of their lives, watch the intensity of the tens of thousands of fans who attend these events. Look at the shirtless boys with faces and torsos painted in the school colors; look at the cheerleaders on the fields, the "waves" surging through the stands.
>
> American universities, those temples of reason (at their best), are tribes. The kids bond to each other and to their schools in the heat of

> the intense emotions that these contests generate. Those shirtless kids covered in paint, shivering in the November weather as they cheer their team on, will be prosperous, middle-aged alumni one day—and when they are, they will still be stirred by the memory of the emotions and the loyalty that brought them out to the field.
>
> If you want your alumni to give, you first have to make them fall in love with your school. This is not about having better chemistry programs or more faculty with higher name recognition than the school up the road. It is not about scoring higher on world indices of university quality. It is about competition, drama, intensity, about hope and fear, collective celebrations or collective disasters, seared into young and impressionable hearts where they will never be forgotten—and where they will be annually renewed as each sport in its season produces new highs and lows, new hopes and fears. Alumni watching their schools' games on TV, or celebrating or mourning their schools' results each week with friends, family and colleagues, are renewing their ties with their alma maters affirming that being an "Aggie" or a "Tar Heel" is an *identity*, not a line on the resume.
>
> This is why most of them give. It is irrational and tribal love. It is intense emotion, not a vague sense of obligation or philanthropy. They want to beat State.
>
> —Walter Russell Mead and *The American Interest* staff,
> "It All Begins with Football"

Mead's claim, emotional in itself, may not be exactly what college and university administrators and faculty want to hear. But in using language this evocative, he makes his argument memorable, hoping perhaps to make general readers admit how they have felt and acted themselves.

Kevin C. Cox/Getty Images

It's difficult to gauge how much emotion will work in a given argument. Some issues—such as racism, immigration, abortion, and gun control—provoke strong feelings and, as a result, are often argued on emotional terms. But even issues that seem deadly dull—such as reform of federal student loan programs—can be argued passionately when proposed changes in these programs are set in human terms: reduce support for college loans and Kai, Riley, and Jayden end up in dead-end, low-paying jobs; don't reform the program and we're looking at another Wall Street–sized loan bailout and subsequent recession. Both alternatives might scare people into paying enough attention to take political action.

Cartoonists Nick Anderson, Alfredo Martirena, and Larry Lambert make pointed arguments, even as they make audiences laugh.

LINK TO P. 751

Using Humor

Humor has always played an important role in argument, sometimes as the sugar that makes the medicine go down. You can slip humor into an argument to put readers at ease, thereby making them more open to a proposal you have to offer. It's hard to say *no* when you're laughing. Humor also makes otherwise sober people suspend their judgment and even their prejudices, perhaps because the surprise and naughtiness of wit are combustive: they provoke laughter or smiles, not reflection. Who can resist a no-holds-barred attack on a famous personality, such as this assessment of *Twilight* star Kristen Stewart:

> **The original scoffing, scowling, stammering, stuttering, gaping open mouth, temper-tantrum throwing, lip-biting, hair-flipping, plank of wood moody actress . . . A tape recorder in a mannequin could do her job.**

Humor deployed cleverly may be why TV shows like *South Park* and *Modern Family* became popular with mainstream audiences, despite their willingness to explore controversial themes. Similarly, it's possible to make a point through humor that might not work in more sober writing. People argue endlessly about eating the right foods, typically defined by diet gurus who favor locally sourced, organically grown, and profoundly dull vegetables. *Wall Street Journal* columnist Ron Rosenbaum will have none of that. With new research suggesting that fatty diets may have unanticipated health benefits, Rosenbaum deploys some high-calorie humor to argue for the pleasures of dining lavishly:

> **Preventing obesity is a laudable goal, but it has become the rationale for indiscriminate fat hunters. It can shade into a kind of bullying of**

the overweight, a badgering of anyone who likes butter or heavy cream. To the antifat crusaders, I say: Attack fatty junk food all you want. I'm with you. But you can deny me my roasted marrow bones when you pry them from my cold, dead hands.

I'm not suggesting that we embrace these life-changing food experiences just on grounds of pure pleasure (though there's much to be said for pure pleasure). As it turns out, the science on the matter is changing as well. We are discovering that fatty delights can actually be good for you: They allow Spaniards, Italians and Greeks to live longer, and they make us satisfied with eating less. I'm speaking up not for obesity-generating fat, then, but for the kind of fatty food that leads to swooning sensual satiety.

Roast goose, for instance, is a supremely succulent, mind-alteringly flavorful fatty food. In most of America, roast goose would be viewed as the raven of cardiac mortality, hoarsely honking "never more." And listening to the doctors on cable TV, you might think that it's better to cook up a batch of meth than to cook with butter.

Eating fatty foods has become the culinary version of *Breaking Bad*: a dangerous walk on the wild side for the otherwise timid consumers of tasteless butter substitutes and Lean Cuisine.

—Ron Rosenbaum, "Let Them Eat Fat"

Our laughter testifies to what some people have thought all along: people who want us to eat tofu are the real problem. Note the pleasure Rosenbaum takes in the emotive power of words themselves: *swooning sensual satiety*; *the raven of cardiac mortality, hoarsely honking "never more."*

A writer or speaker can even use humor to deal with sensitive issues. For example, sports commentator Bob Costas, given the honor of eulogizing the great baseball player Mickey Mantle, couldn't ignore problems in Mantle's life. So he argues for Mantle's greatness by admitting the man's weaknesses indirectly through humor:

It brings to mind a story Mickey liked to tell on himself and maybe some of you have heard it. He pictured himself at the pearly gates, met by St. Peter, who shook his head and said, "Mick, we checked the record. We know some of what went on. Sorry, we can't let you in. But before you go, God wants to know if you'd sign these six dozen baseballs."

—Bob Costas, "Eulogy for Mickey Mantle"

Similarly, politicians may use humor to deal with issues they couldn't acknowledge in any other way. Here, for example, is former president

George W. Bush at the 2004 Radio and TV Correspondents' Dinner discussing his much-mocked intellect:

> **Those stories about my intellectual capacity do get under my skin. You know, for a while I even thought my staff believed it. There on my schedule first thing every morning it said, "Intelligence briefing."**
>
> **—George W. Bush**

Not all humor is well-intentioned or barb-free. In fact, among the most powerful forms of emotional argument is ridicule—humor aimed at a particular target. Eighteenth-century poet and critic Samuel Johnson was known for his stinging and humorous put-downs, such as this comment to an aspiring writer: "Your manuscript is both good and original, but the part that is good is not original and the part that is original is not good." (Expect your own writing teachers to be kinder.) In our own time, the *Onion* has earned a reputation for its mastery of both ridicule and satire, the art of using over-the-top humor to making a serious point.

But because ridicule is a double-edged sword, it requires a deft hand to wield it. Humor that reflects bad taste discredits a writer completely, as does satire that misses its mark. Unless your target deserves riposte and you can be very funny, it's usually better to steer clear of such humor.

Using Arguments Based on Emotion

You don't want to play puppet master with people's emotions when you write arguments, but it's a good idea to spend some time early in your work thinking about how you want readers to feel as they consider your persuasive claims. For example, would readers of your editorial about campus traffic policies be more inclined to agree with you if you made them envy faculty privileges, or would arousing their sense of fairness work better? What emotional appeals might persuade meat eaters to consider a vegan diet—or vice versa? Would sketches of stage props on a Web site persuade people to buy a season ticket to the theater, or would you spark more interest by featuring pictures of costumed performers?

Consider, too, the effect that a story can have on readers. Writers and journalists routinely use what are called *human-interest stories* to give presence to issues or arguments. You can do the same, using a particular incident to evoke sympathy, understanding, outrage, or amusement. Take care, though, to tell an honest story.

RESPOND.

1. To what specific emotions do the following slogans, sales pitches, and maxims appeal?

   "Just do it." (ad for Nike)

   "Think different." (ad for Apple computers)

   "Reach out and touch someone." (ad for AT&T)

   "By any means necessary." (rallying cry from Malcolm X)

   "Have it your way." (slogan for Burger King)

   "The ultimate driving machine." (slogan for BMW)

   "It's everywhere you want to be." (slogan for Visa)

   "Know what comes between me and my Calvins? Nothing!" (tag line for Calvin Klein jeans)

   "Don't mess with Texas!" (anti-litter campaign slogan)

   "American by Birth. Rebel by Choice." (slogan for Harley-Davidson)

2. Bring a magazine to class, and analyze the emotional appeals in as many full page ads as you can. Then classify those ads by types of emotional appeal, and see whether you can connect the appeals to the subject or target audience of the magazine. Compare your results with those of your classmates, and discuss your findings. For instance, how exactly are the ads in publications such as *Cosmopolitan*, *Wired*, *Sports Illustrated*, *Motor Trend*, and *Smithsonian* adapted to their specific audiences?
3. How do arguments based on emotion work in different media? Are such arguments more or less effective in books, articles, television (both news and entertainment shows), films, brochures, magazines, email, Web sites, the theater, street protests, and so on? You might explore how a single medium handles emotional appeals or compare different media. For example, why do the comments pages of blogs seem to encourage angry outbursts? Are newspapers an emotionally colder source of information than television news programs? If so, why?
4. Spend some time looking for arguments that use ridicule or humor to make their point: check out your favorite Twitter feeds or blogs; watch for bumper stickers, posters, or advertisements; and listen to popular song lyrics. Bring one or two examples to class, and be ready to explain how the humor makes an emotional appeal and whether it's effective.

3
Arguments Based on Character: Ethos

Left to right: © Jon Arnold Images Ltd./Alamy; © Bernhard Classen/age fotostock; Richard Shotwell/Invision/AP

Whenever you read anything—whether it's a news article, an advertisement, a speech, or a text message—you no doubt subconsciously analyze the message for a sense of the character and credibility of the sender: *Is this someone I know and trust? Does the PBS reporter seem biased? Why should I believe an IRS official? Is this scholar really an authority on the subject?* Our culture teaches us to be skeptical of most messages, especially those that bombard us with slogans, and such reasonable doubt is a crucial skill in reading and evaluating arguments.

For that reason, people and institutions that hope to influence us do everything they can to establish their character and credibility, what ancient rhetors referred to as *ethos*. And sometimes slogans such as "All the News That's Fit to Print," "Fair & Balanced," or "Lean Forward" can be effective. At the very least, if a phrase is repeated often enough, it begins to sound plausible. Maybe CNN is the most trusted name in news!

But establishing character usually takes more than repetition, as marketers of all kinds know. It arises from credentials actually earned in some way. In the auto industry, for instance, companies such as Toyota, General Motors, and Nissan are hustling to present themselves as environmentally responsible producers of fuel-efficient, low-emission cars—the Prius, Volt, and Leaf. BMW, maker of "the ultimate driving machine," points to its fuel-sipping i3 and i8 cars as evidence of its commitment to "sustainable mobility." And Elon Musk (who builds rockets as well as Tesla cars) polishes his good-citizenship bona fides by sharing his electric vehicle patents with other manufacturers. All of these companies realize that their future success is linked to an ability to project a convincing ethos for themselves and their products.

If corporations and institutions can establish an ethos, consider how much character matters when we think about people in the public arena. Perhaps no individual managed a more exceptional assertion of personal ethos than Jorge Mario Bergoglio did after he became Pope Francis on March 13, 2013, following the abdication of Benedict XVI—a man many found scholarly, cold, and out of touch with the modern world. James Carroll, writing for the *New Yorker*, identifies the precise moment when the world realized that it was dealing with a new sort of pope:

> "Who am I to judge?" With those five words, spoken in late July [2013] in reply to a reporter's question about the status of gay priests in the Church, Pope Francis stepped away from the disapproving tone, the explicit moralizing typical of popes and bishops.
>
> —James Carroll, "Who Am I to Judge?"

Carroll goes on to explain that Francis quickly established his ethos with a series of specific actions, decisions, and moments of identification with ordinary people, marking him as someone even nonbelievers might listen to and respect:

> As pope, Francis has simplified the Renaissance regalia of the papacy by abandoning fur-trimmed velvet capes, choosing to live in a two-room apartment instead of the Apostolic Palace, and replacing the papal Mercedes with a Ford Focus. Instead of the traditional red slip-ons, Francis wears ordinary black shoes. . . . Yet Francis didn't criticize the choices of other prelates. "He makes changes without attacking people," a Jesuit official told me. In his interview with *La Civiltà Cattolica*, Francis said, "My choices, including those related to the day-to-day aspects of life, like the use of a modest car, are related to a spiritual discernment that responds to a need that arises from looking at things, at people, and from reading the signs of the times."

AP Photo/L'Osservatore Romano, Riccardo Aguiari

In that last sentence, Francis acknowledges that ethos is gained, in part, through identification with one's audience and era. And this man, movingly photographed embracing the sick and disfigured, also posed for selfies!

You can see, then, why Aristotle treats ethos as a powerful argumentative appeal. Ethos creates quick and sometimes almost irresistible connections between readers and arguments. We observe people, groups, or institutions making and defending claims all the time and inevitably ask ourselves, *Should we pay attention to them? Can we rely on them? Do we dare to trust them?* Consider, though, that the same questions will be asked about you and your work, especially in academic settings.

Thinking Critically about Arguments Based on Character

Put simply, arguments based on character (ethos) depend on *trust*. We tend to accept arguments from those we trust, and we trust them (whether individuals, groups, or institutions) in good part because of their reputations. Three main elements—credibility, authority, and unselfish or clear motives—add up to *ethos*.

To answer serious and important questions, we often turn to professionals (doctors, lawyers, engineers, teachers, pastors) or to experts (those with knowledge and experience) for good advice. Based on their backgrounds, such people come with their ethos already established.

Thus, appeals or arguments about character often turn on claims like these:

- A person (or group or institution) is or is not trustworthy or credible on this issue.
- A person (or group or institution) does or does not have the authority to speak to this issue.
- A person (or group or institution) does or does not have unselfish or clear motives for addressing this subject.

Establishing Trustworthiness and Credibility

Trustworthiness and credibility speak to a writer's honesty, respect for an audience and its values, and plain old likability. Sometimes a sense of humor can play an important role in getting an audience to listen to or "like" you. It's no accident that all but the most serious speeches begin with a joke or funny story: the humor puts listeners at ease and helps them identify with the speaker. Writer J. K. Rowling, for example, puts her audience (and herself) at ease early in the commencement address she delivered at Harvard in 2008 by getting real about such speeches:

> **Delivering a commencement address is a great responsibility; or so I thought until I cast my mind back to my own graduation. The commencement speaker that day was the distinguished British philosopher Baroness Mary Warnock. Reflecting on her speech has helped me enormously in writing this one, because it turns out that I can't remember a single word she said. This liberating discovery enables me to proceed without any fear that I might inadvertently influence you to abandon promising careers in business, the law, or politics for the giddy delights of becoming a gay wizard.**
>
> **You see? If all you remember in years to come is the "gay wizard" joke, I've come out ahead of Baroness Mary Warnock. Achievable goals: the first step to self improvement.**
>
> —J. K. Rowling, "The Fringe Benefits of Failure, and the Importance of Imagination"

In just a few sentences, Rowling pokes fun at herself, undercuts the expectation that graduation addresses change people's lives, slides in an allusion from her Harry Potter series, and then even offers a smidgen of advice. For an audience well disposed toward her already, Rowling has likely lived up to expectations.

In "Attention Whole Foods Shoppers," Robert Paarlberg cites research from respected organizations to support his stance on what makes food sustainable.

LINK TO P. 610

But using humor to enhance your credibility may be more common in oratory than in the kind of writing you'll do in school. Fortunately, you have many options, one being simply to make plausible claims and then back them up with evidence. Academic audiences appreciate a reasonable disposition; we will discuss this approach at greater length in the next chapter.

You can also establish trustworthiness by connecting your own beliefs to core principles that are well established and widely respected. This strategy is particularly effective when your position seems to be—at first glance, at least—a threat to traditional values. For example, when former Smith College president Ruth J. Simmons describes her professional self to a commencement audience she is addressing (see Chapter 1), she presents her acquired reputation in terms that align perfectly with contemporary values:

> **For my part, I was cast as a troublemaker in my early career and accepted the disapproval that accompanies the expression of unpopular views: unpopular views about disparate pay for women and minorities; unpopular views about sexual harassment; unpopular views about exclusionary practices in our universities.**
>
> —Ruth J. Simmons

It's fine to be a rebel when you are on the right side of history.

Writers who establish their credibility seem trustworthy. But sometimes, to be credible, you have to admit limitations, too, as *New York Times* columnist David Brooks does as he wrestles with a problem common in our time, an inability to focus on things that matter:

> **Like everyone else, I am losing the attention war. I toggle over to my emails when I should be working. I text when I should be paying attention to the people in front of me. I spend hours looking at mildly diverting stuff on YouTube. ("Look, there's a bunch of guys who can play 'Billie Jean' on beer bottles!")**
>
> **And, like everyone else, I've nodded along with the prohibition sermons imploring me to limit my information diet. Stop multitasking! Turn off the devices at least once a week!**
>
> **And, like everyone else, these sermons have had no effect. Many of us lead lives of distraction, unable to focus on what we know we should focus on.**
>
> —David Brooks, "The Art of Focus"

Making such concessions to readers sends a strong signal that you've looked critically at your own position and can therefore be trusted when you turn to arguing its merits. Speaking to readers directly, using *I* or *you* or *us*, can also help you connect with them, as can using contractions and everyday or colloquial language—both strategies employed by Brooks. In other situations, you may find that a more formal tone gives your claims greater credibility. You'll be making such choices as you search for the ethos that represents you best.

In fact, whenever you write a paper or present an idea, you are sending signals about your credibility, whether you intend to or not. If your ideas are reasonable, your sources are reliable, and your language is appropriate to the project, you suggest to academic readers that you're someone whose ideas *might* deserve attention. Details matter: helpful graphs, tables, charts, or illustrations may carry weight with readers, as will the visual attractiveness of your text, whether in print or digital form. Obviously, correct spelling, grammar, and mechanics are important too. And though you might not worry about it now, at some point you may need letters of recommendation from instructors or supervisors. How will they remember you? Often chiefly from the ethos you have established in your work. Think about that.

Claiming Authority

When you read or listen to an argument, you have every right to ask about the writer's authority: *What does he know about the subject? What experiences does she have that make her especially knowledgeable? Why should I pay attention to this person?* When you offer an argument yourself, you have to anticipate and be prepared to answer questions like these, either directly or indirectly.

How does someone construct an authoritative ethos? In examining what he describes as "the fundamental problem with President Obama's communications ethos," Ron Fournier, editorial director of *National Journal*, explains that authority cannot be taken for granted:

> **He and his advisers are so certain about their moral and political standing that they believe it's enough to make a declaration. *If we say it, the public should believe it.***
>
> **That's not how it works. A president must earn the public's trust. He must teach and persuade; speak clearly, and follow word with action; show empathy toward his rivals, and acknowledge the merits of a critique. A successful president pays careful attention to how his image is projected both to U.S. voters and to the people of the world.**

> He knows that to be strong, a leader must look strong. Image matters, especially in an era so dominated by them.
>
> —Ron Fournier, "Is the White House Lying, or Just Bad at Crisis Communications?"

Of course, writers establish their authority in various ways. Sometimes the assertion of ethos will be bold and personal, as it is when writer and activist Terry Tempest Williams attacks those who poisoned the Utah deserts with nuclear radiation. What gives her the right to speak on this subject? Not scientific expertise, but gut-wrenching personal experience:

> I belong to the Clan of One-Breasted Women. My mother, my grandmothers, and six aunts have all had mastectomies. Seven are dead. The two who survive have just completed rounds of chemotherapy and radiation.
>
> I've had my own problems: two biopsies for breast cancer and a small tumor between my ribs diagnosed as a "borderline malignancy."
>
> —Terry Tempest Williams, "The Clan of One-Breasted Women"

We are willing to listen to Williams because she has lived with the nuclear peril she will deal with in the remainder of her essay.

During her radio report about colleges and universities wanting to emphasize their diversity, Deena Prichep introduces guests by stating their professions—a sociologist and a college admissions director—to establish their ethos.

LINK TO P. 678

Other means of claiming authority are less dramatic. By simply attaching titles to their names, writers assert that they hold medical or legal or engineering degrees, or some other important credentials. Or they may mention the number of years they've worked in a given field or the distinguished positions they have held. As a reader, you'll pay more attention to an argument about global warming offered by a professor of atmospheric and oceanic science at the University of Minnesota than one by your Uncle Sid, who sells tools. But you'll prefer your uncle to the professor when you need advice about a reliable rotary saw.

When readers might be skeptical of both you and your claims, you may have to be even more specific about your credentials. That's exactly the strategy Richard Bernstein uses to establish his right to speak on the subject of "Asian culture." What gives a New York writer named Bernstein the authority to write about Asian peoples? Bernstein tells us in a sparkling example of an argument based on character:

> The Asian culture, as it happens, is something I know a bit about, having spent five years at Harvard striving for a Ph.D. in a joint program called History and East Asian Languages and, after that, living either as a student (for one year) or a journalist (six years) in China and Southeast Asia. At least I know enough to know there is no such thing as the "Asian culture." —Richard Bernstein, *Dictatorship of Virtue*

When you write for readers who trust you and your work, you may not have to make such an open claim to authority. But making this type of appeal is always an option.

Coming Clean about Motives

When people are trying to convince you of something, it's important (and natural) to ask: *Whose interests are they serving? How will they profit from their proposal?* Such suspicions go to the heart of ethical arguments.

In a hugely controversial essay published in the *Princeton Tory*, Tal Fortgang, a first-year student at the Ivy League school, argues that those on campus who used the phrase "Check your privilege" to berate white male students like him for the advantages they enjoy are, in fact, judging him according to gender and race, and not for "all the hard work I have done in my life." To challenge stereotypical assumptions about the "racist patriarchy" that supposedly paved his way to Princeton, Fortgang writes about the experiences of his ancestors, opening the paragraphs with a striking parallel structure:

> Perhaps it's the privilege my grandfather and his brother had to flee their home as teenagers when the Nazis invaded Poland, leaving their mother and five younger siblings behind, running and running. . . .
>
> Or maybe it's the privilege my grandmother had of spending weeks upon weeks on a death march through Polish forests in subzero temperatures, one of just a handful to survive. . . .
>
> Perhaps my privilege is that those two resilient individuals came to America with no money and no English, obtained citizenship, learned the language and met each other. . . .
>
> Perhaps it was my privilege that my own father worked hard enough in City College to earn a spot at a top graduate school, got a good job, and for 25 years got up well before the crack of dawn, sacrificing precious time he wanted to spend with those he valued most—his wife and kids—to earn that living.
>
> —Tal Fortgang, "Checking My Privilege: Character as the Basis of Privilege"

Fortgang thus attempts to establish his own ethos and win the argument against those who make assumptions about his roots by dramatizing the ethos of his ancestors:

> That's the problem with calling someone out for the "privilege" which you assume has defined their narrative. You don't know what their

> **struggles have been, what they may have gone through to be where they are. Assuming they've benefitted from "power systems" or other conspiratorial imaginary institutions denies them credit for all they've done, things of which you may not even conceive. You don't know whose father died defending your freedom. You don't know whose mother escaped oppression. You don't know who conquered their demons, or may still [be] conquering them now.**

As you might imagine, the pushback to "Checking My Privilege" was enormous, some of the hundreds of comments posted to an online version accusing Fortgang himself of assuming the very ethos of victimhood against which he inveighs. Peter Finocchiaro, a reviewer on *Slate*, is especially brutal: "Only a few short months ago he was living at home with his parents. His life experience, one presumes, is fairly limited. So in that sense, he doesn't really know any better. . . . He is an ignorant 19-year-old white guy from Westchester." You can see in this debate how ethos quickly raises issues of knowledge and motives. Fortgang tries to resist the stereotype others would impose on his character, but others regard the very ethos he fashions in his essay as evidence of his naïveté about race, discrimination, and, yes, privilege.

We all, of course, have connections and interests that bind us to other human beings. It makes sense that a young man would explore his social identity, that a woman might be concerned with women's issues, that members of minority groups might define social and cultural conditions on their own terms—or even that investors might look out for their investments. It's simply good strategy to let your audiences know where your loyalties lie when such information does, in fact, shape your work.

Using Ethos in Your Own Writing

- Establish your credibility by acknowledging your audience's values, showing respect for them, and establishing common ground where (and if) possible. How will you convince your audience you are trustworthy? What will you admit about your own limitations?
- Establish your authority by showing you have done your homework and know your topic well. How will you show that you know your topic well? What appropriate personal experience can you draw on?
- Examine your motives for writing. What, if anything, do you stand to gain from your argument? How can you explain those advantages to your audience?

CULTURAL CONTEXTS FOR ARGUMENT

Ethos

In the United States, students are often asked to establish authority by drawing on personal experiences, by reporting on research they or others have conducted, and by taking a position for which they can offer strong evidence. But this expectation about student authority is by no means universal.

Some cultures regard student writers as novices who can most effectively make arguments by reflecting on what they've learned from their teachers and elders—those who hold the most important knowledge and, hence, authority. When you're arguing a point with people from cultures other than your own, ask questions like:

- Whom are you addressing, and what is your relationship with that person?
- What knowledge are you expected to have? Is it appropriate or expected for you to demonstrate that knowledge—and if so, how?
- What tone is appropriate? And remember: politeness is rarely, if ever, inappropriate.

RESPOND•

1. Consider the ethos of these public figures. Then describe one or two products that might benefit from their endorsements as well as several that would not.

   Edward Snowden—whistleblower
   Kaley Cuoco-Sweeting—actress
   James Earl Jones—actor
   Michael Sam—athlete
   Megyn Kelly—TV news commentator
   Miley Cyrus—singer
   Seth Meyers—late-night TV host
   Cristiano Ronaldo—soccer player

2. Opponents of Richard Nixon, the thirty-seventh president of the United States, once raised doubts about his integrity by asking a single

ruinous question: *Would you buy a used car from this man?* Create your own version of the argument of character. Begin by choosing an intriguing or controversial person or group and finding an image online. Then download the image into a word-processing file. Create a caption for the photo that is modeled after the question asked about Nixon: *Would you give this woman your email password? Would you share a campsite with this couple? Would you eat lasagna that this guy fixed?* Finally, write a serious 300-word argument that explores the character flaws or strengths of your subject(s).

3. Take a close look at your Facebook page (or your page on any other social media site). What are some aspects of your character, true or not, that might be conveyed by the photos, videos, and messages you have posted online? Analyze the ethos or character you see projected there, using the advice in this chapter to guide your analysis.

4

Arguments Based on Facts and Reason: Logos

Left to right: Yui Mok/Press Association via AP Images; © NBC/Photofest, Inc.; © Frank Cotham/The New Yorker/The Cartoon Bank

These three images say a lot about the use and place of logic (*logos*) in Western and American culture. The first shows Benedict Cumberbatch from the BBC TV series *Sherlock*, just one of many actors to play Arthur Conan Doyle's much-loved fictional detective Sherlock Holmes, who solves perplexing crimes by using precise observation and impeccable logic. The second refers to an equally popular TV (and film) series character, Spock, the Vulcan officer in *Star Trek* who tries to live a life guided by reason alone—his most predicable observation being some version of "that would not be logical." The third is a cartoon spoofing a pseudo-logical argument (nine out of ten prefer X) made so often in advertising that it has become something of a joke.

These images attest to the prominent place that logic holds for most people: like Holmes, we want to know the facts on the assumption that they will help us make sound judgments. We admire those whose logic is, like Spock's, impeccable. So when arguments begin, "Nine out of ten authorities recommend," we respond favorably: those are good odds. But the three images also challenge reliance on logic alone: Sherlock Holmes and Spock are characters drawn in broad and often parodic strokes; the "nine out of ten" cartoon itself spoofs abuses of reason. Given a choice, however, most of us profess to respect and even prefer *appeals to logos*—that is, claims based on facts, evidence, and reason—but we're also inclined to read factual arguments within the context of our feelings and the ethos of people making the appeals.

Thinking Critically about Hard Evidence

Aristotle helps us out in classifying arguments by distinguishing two kinds:

Artistic Proofs	Arguments the writer/speaker creates	Constructed arguments	Appeals to reason; common sense
Inartistic Proofs	Arguments the writer/speaker is given	Hard evidence	Facts, statistics, testimonies, witnesses, contracts, documents

We can see these different kinds of logical appeals at work in a single paragraph from President Barack Obama's 2014 State of the Union address. Typically in such speeches—nationally televised and closely reviewed—the president assesses the current condition of the United States and then lays out an agenda for the coming years, a laundry list of commitments and goals. One of those items mentioned about halfway through the 2014 address focuses on the admirable objective of improving the conditions of working women:

> Today, women make up about half our workforce. But they still make 77 cents for every dollar a man earns. That is wrong, and in 2014, it's an embarrassment. A woman deserves equal pay for equal work. She deserves to have a baby without sacrificing her job. A mother deserves a day off to care for a sick child or sick parent without running into hardship—and you know what, a father does, too. It's time to do away with workplace policies that belong in a *Mad Men* episode. This year, let's all come together—Congress, the White House, and businesses from Wall Street to Main Street—to give every woman the opportunity she deserves. Because I firmly believe when women succeed, America succeeds.
>
> —Barack Obama, State of the Union address

As you see, Obama opens the paragraph with an important "inartistic" proof, that ratio of just 77 cents to a dollar representing what women earn in the United States compared to men. Beginning with that fact, he then offers a series of reasonable "artistic" appeals phrased as applause lines: *that is wrong*; *a woman deserves equal pay*; *a mother deserves a day off . . . a father does, too.*" Obama then concludes the paragraph by stating the core principle behind all these claims, what we'll later describe as the *warrant* in an argument (see Chapter 7): *when women succeed, America succeeds.*

Note, then, the importance of that single number the president puts forward. It is evidence that, despite decades of political commitment to pay equity and even federal laws banning gender discrimination in employment and compensation, much work remains to be done. Who can be satisfied with the status quo in the face of that damning number? But where did that statistic come from, and *what if it is wrong?*

Now, no one expects footnotes and documentation in a presidential address. The ethos of the office itself makes the public (at least some portion of it) willing to accept a president's factual claims, if only because his remarks have surely been vetted by legions of staffers. Yet some statistics and claims assume a life of their own, repeated so often that most people—even presidents and their speechwriters—assume that they are true. Add the problem of "confirmation bias," the tendency of most people to believe evidence that confirms their views of the world, and you have numbers that will not die.

We live, however, in an age of critics and fact-checkers. Writing for the *Daily Beast*, Christina Hoff Sommers, a former professor of philosophy and no fan of contemporary feminism, complains that the president is perpetuating an error: "What is wrong and embarrassing is the President of the United States reciting a massively discredited factoid." And in case you won't believe Sommers (and most feminists and those in the president's camp wouldn't), she directs skeptics to a more objective source, the *Washington Post*, which routinely fact-checks the State of the Union and other major addresses.

Like Sommers, that paper does raise questions about the 77/100 earnings ratio, and its detailed analysis of that number suggests just how complicated evidential claims can be. Here's a shortened version of the *Post*'s statement, which you'll note cites several government sources:

> **There is clearly a wage gap, but differences in the life choices of men and women—such as women tending to leave the workforce when they have children—make it difficult to make simple comparisons.**

Obama is using a figure (annual wages, from the Census Bureau) that makes the disparity appear the greatest. The Bureau of Labor Statistics, for instance, shows that the gap is 19 cents when looking at weekly wages. The gap is even smaller when you look at hourly wages—it is 14 cents—but then not every wage earner is paid on an hourly basis, so that statistic excludes salaried workers. . . .

Economists at the Federal Reserve Bank of St. Louis surveyed economic literature and concluded that "research suggests that the actual gender wage gap (when female workers are compared with male workers who have similar characteristics) is much lower than the raw

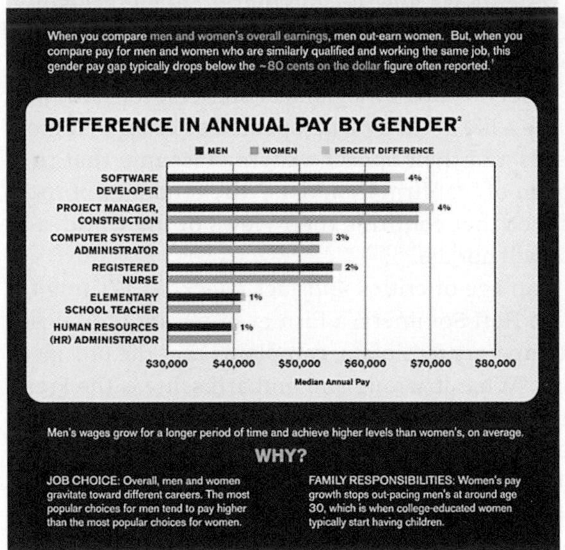

Factual arguments are often made or enhanced by charts, graphs, and infographics. Here PayScale, an online salary and wage information site, presents numbers to explain the pay equity issue: "Yes, men do earn more than women on average, but not that much more when they work the same job and they have similar experience and abilities." We reproduce here just a portion of the full infographic. PayScale, Inc., by permission

> **wage gap." They cited one survey, prepared for the Labor Department, which concluded that when such differences are accounted for, much of the hourly wage gap dwindled, to about 5 cents on the dollar.**

Is the entire paragraph of the president's address discredited because his hard evidence seems overstated or oversimplified? Not if we accept the *constructed* arguments he makes on the general principle of fairness for offering women—and men—more support as laborers in the job force. But he might have been more convincing at this point in a very lengthy speech if someone in the White House had taken a moment to check the government's own numbers, as the *Washington Post* did. This ongoing controversy over wage equity does, however, illustrate how closely logical arguments—whether artistic or inartistic—will be read and criticized. And so the connections between them matter.

RESPOND •

Discuss whether the following statements are examples of hard evidence or constructed arguments. Not all cases are clear-cut.

1. Drunk drivers are involved in more than 50 percent of traffic deaths.
2. DNA tests of skin found under the victim's fingernails suggest that the defendant was responsible for the assault.
3. A psychologist testified that teenage violence could not be blamed on video games.
4. An apple a day keeps the doctor away.
5. "The only thing we have to fear is fear itself."
6. Air bags ought to be removed from vehicles because they can kill young children and small-framed adults.

Facts

Gathering factual information and transmitting it faithfully practically define what we mean by professional journalism and scholarship. We'll even listen to people we don't agree with if their evidence is really good. Below, a reviewer for the conservative *National Review* praises William Julius Wilson, a liberal sociologist, because of how well he presents his case:

> **In his eagerly awaited new book, Wilson argues that ghetto blacks are worse off than ever, victimized by a near-total loss of low-skill jobs in and around inner-city neighborhoods. In support of this thesis, he**

> *musters mountains of data, plus excerpts from some of the thousands of surveys and face-to-face interviews that he and his research team conducted among inner-city Chicagoans.* It is a book that deserves a wide audience among thinking conservatives.
>
> —John J. DiIulio Jr., "When Decency Disappears" (emphasis added)

When your facts are compelling, they may stand on their own in a low-stakes argument, supported by little more than saying where they come from. Consider the power of phrases such as "reported by the *Wall Street Journal*" or "according to FactCheck.org." Such sources gain credibility if they have reported facts accurately and reliably over time. Using such credible sources in an argument can also reflect positively on you.

In scholarly arguments, which have higher expectations for accuracy, what counts is drawing sober conclusions from the evidence turned up through detailed research or empirical studies. The language of such material may seem dryly factual to you, even when the content is inherently interesting. But presenting new knowledge dispassionately is (ideally at least) the whole point of scholarly writing, marking a contrast between it and the kind of intellectual warfare that occurs in many media forums, especially news programs and blogs. Here for example is a portion of a lengthy opening paragraph in the "Discussion and Conclusions" section of a scholarly paper arguing that people who spend a great deal of time on Facebook often frame their lives by what they observe there:

> The results of this research support the argument that using Facebook affects people's perceptions of others. For those that have used Facebook longer, it is easier to remember positive messages and happy pictures posted on Facebook; these readily available examples give users an impression that others are happier. As expected in the first hypothesis, the results show that the longer people have used Facebook, the stronger was their belief that others were happier than themselves, and the less they agreed that life is fair. Furthermore, as predicted in the second hypothesis, this research found that the more "friends" people included on their Facebook whom they did not know personally, the stronger they believed that others had better lives than themselves. In other words, looking at happy pictures of others on Facebook gives people an impression that others are "always" happy and having good lives, as evident from these pictures of happy moments. In contrast to their own experiences of life events, which

are not always positive, people are very likely to conclude that others have better lives than themselves and that life is not fair.

—Hui-Tzu Grace Chou, PhD, and Nicholas Edge, BS, "'They Are Happier and Having Better Lives Than I Am': The Impact of Using Facebook on Perceptions of Others' Lives"

There are no fireworks in this conclusion, no slanted or hot language, no unfair or selective reporting of data, just a faithful attention to the facts and behaviors uncovered by the study. But one can easily imagine these facts being subsequently used to support overdramatized claims about the dangers of social networks. That's often what happens to scholarly studies when they are read and interpreted in the popular media.

Of course, arguing with facts can involve challenging even the most reputable sources if they lead to unfair or selective reporting or if the stories are presented or "framed" unfairly.

In an ideal world, good information—no matter where it comes from—would always drive out bad. But you already know that we don't live in an ideal world, so sometimes bad information gets repeated in an echo chamber that amplifies the errors.

Statistics

You've probably heard the old saying "There are three kinds of lies: lies, damned lies, and statistics," and, to be sure, it is possible to lie with numbers, even those that are accurate, because numbers rarely speak for themselves. They need to be interpreted by writers—and writers almost always have agendas that shape the interpretations.

Of course, just because they are often misused doesn't mean that statistics are meaningless, but it does suggest that you need to use them carefully and to remember that your careful reading of numbers is essential. Consider the attention-grabbing map on the next page that went viral in June 2014. Created by Mark Gongloff of the *Huffington Post* in the wake of a school shooting in Oregon, it plotted the location of all seventy-four school shootings that had occurred in the United States since the Sandy Hook tragedy in December 2012, when twenty elementary school children and six adults were gunned down by a rifle-wielding killer. For the graphic, Gongloff drew on a list assembled by the group Everytown for Gun Safety, an organization formed by former New York City mayor and billionaire Michael Bloomberg to counter the influence of the National Rifle Association (NRA). Both the map and Everytown's

Everytown for Gun Safety Action

sobering list of shootings received wide attention in the media, given the startling number of incidents it recorded.

It didn't take long before questions were raised about their accuracy. Were American elementary and secondary school children under such frequent assault as the map based on Everytown's list suggested? Well, yes and no. Guns were going off on and around school campuses, but the firearms weren't always aimed at children. The *Washington Post*, CNN, and other news outlets soon found themselves pulling back on their initial reporting, offering a more nuanced view of the controversial number. To do that, the *Washington Post* began by posing an important question:

> What constitutes a school shooting?
>
> That five-word question has no simple answer, a fact underscored by the backlash to an advocacy group's recent list of school shootings. The list, maintained by Everytown, a group that backs policies to limit gun violence, was updated last week to reflect what it identified as the 74 school shootings since the massacre in Newtown, Conn., a massacre that sparked a national debate over gun control.
>
> Multiple news outlets, including this one, reported on Everytown's data, prompting a backlash over the broad methodology used. As we wrote in our original post, the group considered any instance of a firearm discharging on school property as a shooting—thus casting a broad net that includes homicides, suicides, accidental discharges

and, in a handful of cases, shootings that had no relation to the schools themselves and occurred with no students apparently present.

—Niraj Chokshi, "Fight over School Shooting List Underscores Difficulty in Quantifying Gun Violence"

CNN followed the same path, re-evaluating its original reporting in light of criticism from groups not on the same page as Everytown for Gun Safety:

> Without a doubt, that number is startling.
>
> So . . . CNN took a closer look at the list, delving into the circumstances of each incident Everytown included. . . .
>
> CNN determined that 15 of the incidents Everytown included were situations similar to the violence in Newtown or Oregon—a minor or adult actively shooting inside or near a school. That works out to about one such shooting every five weeks, a startling figure in its own right.
>
> Some of the other incidents on Everytown's list included personal arguments, accidents and alleged gang activities and drug deals.
>
> —Ashley Fantz, Lindsey Knight, and Kevin Wang, "A Closer Look: How Many Newtown-like School Shootings since Sandy Hook?"

Other news organizations came up with their own revised numbers, but clearly the interpretation of a number can be as important as the statistic itself. And what were Mark Gongloff's Twitter reactions to these reassessments? They made an argument as well:

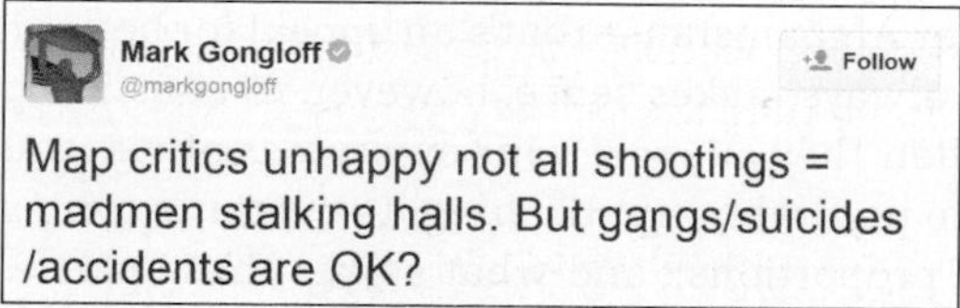

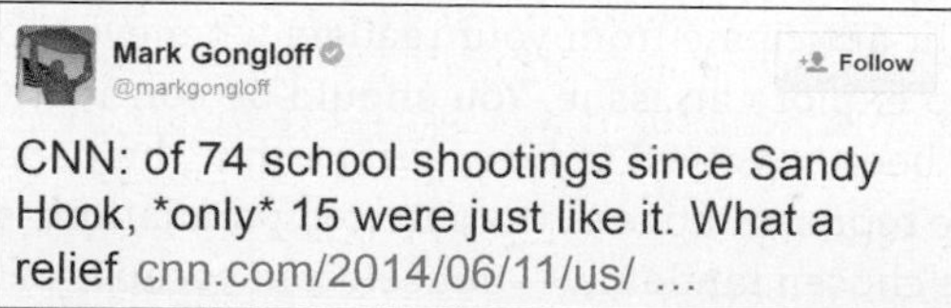

One lesson, surely, is that when you rely on statistics in your arguments, make sure you understand where they come from, what they mean, and what their limitations might be. Check and double-check them or get help in doing so: you don't want to be accused of using fictitious data based on questionable assumptions.

RESPOND•

Statistical evidence becomes useful only when interpreted fairly and reasonably. Go to the *USA Today* Web site and look for the daily graph, chart, or table called the "USA Today Snapshot." Pick a snapshot, and use the information in it to support three different claims, at least two of which make very different points. Share your claims with classmates. (The point is not to learn to use data dishonestly but to see firsthand how the same statistics can serve a variety of arguments.)

Surveys and Polls

When they verify the popularity of an idea or a proposal, surveys and polls provide strong persuasive appeals because they come as close to expressing the will of the people as anything short of an election—the most decisive poll of all. However, surveys and polls can do much more than help politicians make decisions. They can be important elements in scientific research, documenting the complexities of human behavior. They can also provide persuasive reasons for action or intervention. When surveys show, for example, that most American sixth-graders can't locate France or Wyoming on a map—not to mention Ukraine or Afghanistan—that's an appeal for better instruction in geography. It always makes sense, however, to question poll numbers, especially when they support your own point of view. Ask who commissioned the poll, who is publishing its outcome, who was surveyed (and in what proportions), and what stakes these parties might have in its outcome.

Are we being too suspicious? No. In fact, this sort of scrutiny is exactly what you might anticipate from your readers whenever you use (or create) surveys to explore an issue. You should be confident that enough subjects have been surveyed to be accurate, that the people chosen for the study were representative of the selected population as a whole, and that they were chosen randomly—not selected because of what they are likely to say. In a splendid article on how women can make research-based choices during their pregnancy, economist Emily Oster explores, for example, whether an expectant mother might in fact be able to drink responsibly. She researches not only the results of the data, but also who was surveyed, and how their participation might have influenced the results:

> **It is possible to unearth research that points to light drinking as a problem, but this work is deeply flawed. One frequently cited study from the journal *Pediatrics*, published in 2001, interviewed women about their drinking while they were pregnant and then contacted them for a child behavior assessment when their children were about 6. The researchers found some evidence that lighter drinking had an impact on behavior and concluded that even one drink a day could cause behavior problems.**
>
> **So what's wrong with this finding?**
>
> **In the study, 18% of the women who didn't drink at all and 45% of the women who had one drink a day reported using cocaine during pregnancy. Presumably your first thought is, really? Cocaine? Perhaps the problem is that cocaine, not the occasional glass of Chardonnay, makes your child more likely to have behavior problems.**
>
> **—Emily Oster, "Take Back Your Pregnancy"**

Clearly, polls, surveys, and studies need to be examined critically. You can't take even academic research at face value until you have explored its details.

The meaning of polls and surveys is also affected by the way that questions are posed. In the recent past, research revealed, for example, that polling about same-sex unions got differing responses according to how questions are worded. When people were asked whether gay and lesbian couples should be eligible for the same inheritance and partner health benefits that heterosexual couples receive, a majority of those polled said yes—unless the word *marriage* appeared in the question; then the responses are primarily negative. If anything, the differences here reveal how conflicted people may have been about the issue and how quickly opinions might shift—as they did. Remember, then, to be very careful in reviewing the wording of survey or poll questions.

Finally, always keep in mind that the date of a poll may strongly affect the results—and their usefulness in an argument. In 2010, for example, nearly 50 percent of California voters supported building more nuclear power plants. Less than a year later, that percentage had dropped to 37 percent after the meltdown of Japanese nuclear power plants in the wake of the March 2011 earthquake and tsunami. On public and political issues, you need to be sure that you are using timely information.

RESPOND.

Choose an important issue and design a series of questions to evoke a range of responses in a poll. Try to design a question that would make people strongly inclined to agree, another question that would lead them to oppose the same proposition, and a third that tries to be more neutral. Then try out your questions on your classmates.

Amy Stretten shares her personal experience with prejudice to strengthen her argument in "Appropriating Native American Imagery Honors No One but the Prejudice."

LINK TO P. 522

Testimonies and Narratives

Writers can support arguments by presenting human experiences in the form of narrative or testimony—particularly if those experiences are their own. In courts, judges and juries often take into consideration detailed descriptions and narratives of exactly what occurred. Look at this reporter's account of a court case in which a panel of judges decided, based on the testimony presented, that a man had been sexually harassed by another man. The narrative, in this case, supplies the evidence:

> The Seventh Circuit, in a 1997 case known as *Doe v. City of Belleville*, drew a sweeping conclusion allowing for same-sex harassment cases of many kinds. . . . This case, for example, centered on teenage twin brothers working a summer job cutting grass in the city cemetery of Belleville, Ill. One boy wore an earring, which caused him no end of grief that particular summer—including a lot of menacing talk among his coworkers about sexually assaulting him in the woods and sending him "back to San Francisco." One of his harassers, identified in court documents as a large former marine, culminated a verbal campaign by backing the earring-wearer against a wall and grabbing him by the testicles to see "if he was a girl or a guy." The teenager had been "singled out for this abuse," the court ruled, "because the way in which he projected the sexual aspect of his personality"—meaning his gender—"did not conform to his coworkers' view of appropriate masculine behavior."
>
> —Margaret Talbot, "Men Behaving Badly"

Personal perspectives can support a claim convincingly and logically, especially if a writer has earned the trust of readers. In arguing that Tea Party supporters of a government shutdown in 2011 had no business being offended when some opponents described them as "terrorists," Froma Harrop, one of the writers who used the term, argued logically and from experience why the characterization was appropriate:

> [T]he hurt the tea party writers most complained of was to their feelings. I had engaged in name-calling, they kept saying. One professing to want more civility in our national conversation, as I do, should not be flinging around the *terrorist* word.

> May I presume to disagree? Civility is a subjective concept, to be sure, but hurting people's feelings in the course of making solid arguments is fair and square. The decline in the quality of our public discourse results not so much from an excess of spleen, but a deficit of well-constructed arguments. Few things upset partisans more than when the other side makes a case that bats home.
>
> "Most of us know that effectively scoring on a point of argument opens us to the accusation of mean-spiritedness," writes Frank Partsch, who leads the National Conference of Editorial Writers' Civility Project. "It comes with the territory, and a commitment to civility should not suggest that punches will be pulled in order to avoid such accusations."
>
> —Froma Harrop, "Hurt Feelings Can Be a Consequence of Strong Arguments"

This narrative introduction gives a rationale for supporting the claim Harrop is making: we can expect consequences when we argue ineffectively. (For more on establishing credibility with readers, see Chapter 3.)

RESPOND•

Bring to class a full review of a recent film that you either enjoyed or did not enjoy. Using testimony from that review, write a brief argument to your classmates explaining why they should see that movie (or why they should avoid it), being sure to use evidence from the review fairly and reasonably. Then exchange arguments with a classmate, and decide whether the evidence in your peer's argument helps to change your opinion about the movie. What's convincing about the evidence? If it doesn't convince you, why doesn't it?

Using Reason and Common Sense

If you don't have "hard facts," you can turn to those arguments Aristotle describes as "constructed" from reason and common sense. The formal study of such reasoning is called *logic*, and you probably recognize a famous example of deductive reasoning, called a **syllogism**:

> All human beings are mortal.
>
> Socrates is a human being.
>
> Therefore, Socrates is mortal.

Logic: another thing that penguins aren't very good at.

In valid syllogisms, the conclusion follows logically—and technically—from the premises that lead up to it. Many have criticized syllogistic reasoning for being limited, and others have poked fun at it, as in the cartoon above.

But we routinely see something like syllogistic reasoning operating in public arguments, particularly when writers take the time to explain key principles. Consider the step-by-step reasoning Michael Gerson uses to explain why exactly it was wrong for the Internal Revenue Service in 2010–2011 to target specific political groups, making it more difficult for them to organize politically:

> Why does this matter deserve heightened scrutiny from the rest of us? Because crimes against democracy are particularly insidious. Representative government involves a type of trade. As citizens, we cede power to public officials for important purposes that require centralized power: defending the country, imposing order, collecting taxes to promote the common good. In exchange, we expect public institutions to be even-handed and disinterested. When the stewards of power—biased judges

RS officials—act unfairly,

ogant and Lawless IRS"

ptions and frag-
at help to make

ped out by the follow-

stem.

is n... ical beliefs is a

makes sense cur... dermine the

all this information on its ... soning when
ent, based on what audi- ... most people
... mostly on
... readers or

GUMENT

... may find
... ment. Here,
... ic in their
... the term
ed to draw on "hard facts" ... udes both
their claims: while ethi- ... t with an
cal appeals tend to hold ... hymemes
s speak volumes, as does ... umptions
as fairness and equity. In
mber that not all cultures
write to audiences across
d values in those cultures.
nd often indirect allusion
cooperation and commu-
s value religious texts as
ully about what you con- ... alize that
at counts as evidence to ... sider the
ons like:

dience: Facts? Concrete
s or philosophical texts? ... aker may

t precedents?
what kinds of experts are ... eather
... der of

Embedded in this brief argument are
ments of cultural information that are le
it persuasive:

Picnics are ordinarily held outdoors.

When the weather is bad, it's best to cancel pi

Rain is bad weather for picnics.

A 70 percent chance of rain means that rain
than not.

When rain is more likely to occur than not, i
picnics.

For most people, the original statement carries
own; the enthymeme is a compressed argum
ences know and will accept.

CULTURAL CONTEXTS FOR AR

Logos

In the United States, student writers are expect
and evidence as often as possible in supporting
cal and emotional appeals are important, logi
sway in academic writing. So statistics and fact
reasoning based on time-honored values such
writing to global audiences, you need to remem
value the same kinds of appeals. If you want to
cultures, you need to know about the norms an
Chinese culture, for example, values authority a
over "facts" alone. Some African cultures value
nity over individualism, and still other culture
providing compelling evidence. So think caref
sider strong evidence, and pay attention to w
others. You can begin by asking yourself questi

- What evidence is most valued by your a
examples? Firsthand experience? Religiou
Something else?
- Will analogies count as support? How abo
- Will the testimony of experts count? If so,
valued most?

But sometimes enthymemes aren't self-evident:

Be wary of environmentalism because it's religion disguised as science.

iPhones are undermining civil society by making us even more focused on ourselves.

It's time to make all public toilets unisex because to do otherwise is discriminatory.

In these cases, you'll have to work much harder to defend both the claim and the implicit assumptions that it's based on by drawing out the inferences that seem self-evident in other enthymemes. And you'll likely also have to supply credible evidence; a simple declaration of fact won't suffice.

Providing Logical Structures for Argument

Some arguments depend on particular logical structures to make their points. In the following pages, we identify a few of these logical structures.

Degree

Arguments based on degree are so common that people barely notice them, nor do they pay much attention to how they work because they seem self-evident. Most audiences will readily accept that *more of a good thing* or *less of a bad thing* is good. In her novel *The Fountainhead*, Ayn Rand asks: "If physical slavery is repulsive, how much more repulsive is the concept of servility of the spirit?" Most readers immediately comprehend the point Rand intends to make about slavery of the spirit because they already know that physical slavery is cruel and would reject any forms of slavery that were even crueler on the principle that *more of a bad thing is bad*. Rand still needs to offer evidence that "servility of the spirit" is, in fact, worse than bodily servitude, but she has begun with a logical structure readers can grasp. Here are other arguments that work similarly:

If I can get a ten-year warranty on an inexpensive Kia, shouldn't I get the same or better warranty from a more expensive Lexus?

The health benefits from using stem cells in research will surely outweigh the ethical risks.

Better a conventional war now than a nuclear confrontation later.

A demonstrator at an immigrants' rights rally in New York City in 2007. Arguments based on values that are widely shared within a society—such as the idea of equal rights in American culture—have an automatic advantage with audiences. AP Photo/Seth Wenig

Analogies

Analogies, typically complex or extended comparisons, explain one idea or concept by comparing it to something else.

Here, writer and founder of literacy project 826 Valencia, Dave Eggers, uses an analogy in arguing that we do not value teachers as much as we should:

> When we don't get the results we want in our military endeavors, we don't blame the soldiers. We don't say, "It's these lazy soldiers and their bloated benefits plans! That's why we haven't done better in Afghanistan!" No, if the results aren't there, we blame the planners. . . . No one contemplates blaming the men and women fighting every day in the trenches for little pay and scant recognition. And yet in education we do just that. When we don't like the way our students score on international standardized tests, we blame the teachers.
>
> —Dave Eggers and Nínive Calegari, "The High Cost of Low Teacher Salaries"

Precedent

Arguments from **precedent** and arguments of analogy both involve comparisons. Consider an assertion like this one, which uses a comparison as a precedent:

> If motorists in most other states can pump their own gas safely, surely the state of Oregon can trust its own drivers to be as capable. It's time for Oregon to permit self-service gas stations.

You could tease out several inferences from this claim to explain its reasonableness: people in Oregon are as capable as people in other states; people with equivalent capabilities can do the same thing; pumping gas is not hard; and so forth. But you don't have to because most readers get the argument simply because of the way it is put together.

Here is an excerpt from an extended argument by blogger Abby Phillip, in which she argues that the Ebola outbreak that began in 2014 may not follow the same pattern as past outbreaks:

> An idea long viewed as an unlikely possibility is now becoming increasingly real: Ebola might not go away for a very long time.
>
> It has never happened before in the thirty-eight-year history of the virus. Every other time Ebola has made the unlikely jump from the animal world to the human one, it has been snuffed out within days, weeks or, at most, months.
>
> This time, though, in Guinea, Sierra Leone and Liberia, the Ebola virus is raging like a forest fire, in the words of several public health officials. And some of them are raising the possibility that the outbreak-turned-full-fledged-epidemic could become fundamentally different from any other Ebola outbreak on record, in that it might stick around.
>
> "What's always worked before—contact tracing, isolation and quarantine—is not going to work, and it's not working now," said Daniel Lucey, a professor of microbiology and immunology at Georgetown University Medical Center, who spent three weeks treating Ebola patients in Sierra Leone and will soon travel to the Liberian capital of Monrovia for another five-week stint.
>
> "In my opinion," Lucey added, "a year from now, we won't have one or two cases; we'll have many cases of Ebola."
>
> Unlike past outbreaks, in which Ebola emerged in the sparsely populated countryside of central Africa, this outbreak has become an exponentially spreading urban menace.
>
> —Abby Phillip, "This Ebola Outbreak Could Be Here to Stay"

Christian Rudder discusses the precedents set by Facebook, Google, and his own company, OKCupid, in the interview "It's Not OK Cupid: Co-Founder Defends User Experiments."

LINK TO P. 763

Unfortunately, the prediction proved to be more accurate than Phillip might have preferred.

You'll encounter additional kinds of logical structures as you create your own arguments. You'll find some of them in Chapter 5, "Fallacies of Argument," and still more in Chapter 7 on Toulmin argument.

5 Fallacies of Argument

Left to right: Roy Delgado/www.Cartoonstock.com; © Bish/Cagle Cartoons, Inc.; © Eric Allie/Cagle Cartoons, Inc.

Do these editorial cartoons strike a chord with you? All three are complicated. The first panel pokes fun at slippery slope arguments, which aim to thwart action by predicting dire consequences: chase that Frisbee and you'll soon be pulling milk carts. The second item uses a scare tactic (a potential fallacy of argument) to raise opposition to the educational reform called "Common Core," suggesting ominously that the program's cookie-cutter approach will produce children who all think alike. And the third cartoon points to a fallacy of argument that a prominent politician has perhaps slipped into—the sentimental appeal; it alludes to Hillary Clinton's comment in a 2014 interview with Diane Sawyer that she and husband Bill "came out of the White House not only dead broke but in debt."

Fallacies are argumentative moves flawed by their very nature or structure. Because such tactics can make productive principled argument more difficult, they potentially hurt everyone involved, including the people responsible for them. The worst sorts of fallacies muck up the frank but civil conversations that people should be able to have, regardless of their differences.

Yet it's hard to deny the power in offering audiences a compelling either/or choice or a vulnerable straw man in an argument. For exactly that reason, it's important that you can recognize and point out fallacies in the work of others—and avoid them in your own writing. This chapter aims to help you meet these goals: here we'll introduce you to fallacies of argument classified according to the emotional, ethical, and logical appeals we've discussed earlier (see Chapters 2, 3, and 4).

Fallacies of Emotional Argument

Emotional arguments can be powerful and suitable in many circumstances, and most writers use them frequently. However, writers who pull on their readers' heartstrings or raise their blood pressure too often can violate the good faith on which legitimate argument depends.

Scare Tactics

Politicians, advertisers, and public figures sometimes peddle their ideas by frightening people and exaggerating possible dangers well beyond their statistical likelihood. Such ploys work because it's easier to imagine something terrible happening than to appreciate its rarity.

Scare tactics can also be used to stampede legitimate fears into panic or prejudice. Laborers who genuinely worry about losing their jobs can be persuaded to fear immigrants who might work for less money. Seniors living on fixed incomes can be convinced that minor changes to entitlement programs represent dire threats to their well-being. Such tactics have the effect of closing off thinking because people who are scared often act irrationally. Even well-intended fear campaigns—like those directed against smoking, unprotected sex, or the use of illegal drugs—can misfire if their warnings prove too shrill. People just stop listening.

Either/Or Choices

In "The Nothing-to-Hide Argument," Daniel J. Solove tries to dismantle the either-or fallacy in relation to our expectation of privacy.

LINK TO P. 734

Either/or choices can be well-intentioned strategies to get something accomplished. Parents use them all the time ("Eat your broccoli, or you won't get dessert"). But they become fallacious arguments when they

A false choice? © Adam Zyglis/Cagle Cartoons, Inc.

reduce a complicated issue to excessively simple terms or when they're designed to obscure legitimate alternatives. Here, for example, is Riyad Mansour, the Palestinian representative to the United Nations, offering the nation of Israel just such a choice in an interview with Charlie Rose in January 2014:

> It is up to them [the Israelis] to decide what kind of a state they want to be. Do they want to be a democratic state where Israel will be the state for all of its citizens? Or do they want to be a state for the Jewish people, therefore excluding 1.6 million Palestinian Arabs who are Israelis from their society? That debate is not our debate. That debate is their debate.

But Joel B. Pollak, writing for Breitbart News Network, describes Mansour's claim as a "false choice" since Israel already is a Jewish state that nonetheless allows Muslims to be full citizens. The either/or argument Mansour presents, according to Pollack, does not describe the realities of this complex political situation.

Slippery Slope

The **slippery slope** fallacy portrays today's tiny misstep as tomorrow's slide into disaster. Some arguments that aim at preventing dire consequences do not take the slippery slope approach (for example, the parent who corrects a child for misbehavior now is acting sensibly to prevent more serious problems as the child grows older). A slippery slope argument becomes wrongheaded when a writer exaggerates the likely consequences of an action, usually to frighten readers. As such, slippery slope arguments are also scare tactics. In recent years, the issue of gun ownership in America has evoked many slippery slope arguments. Here's one perspective on the tactic:

> The leadership of the NRA is exceptionally fond of the Slippery Slope argument. "Universal background checks will inevitably be followed by a national registry of gun-owners which will inevitably be followed by confiscation of all their guns." Or, "A ban on assault-style weapons and thirty+ round magazines will inevitably be followed by a ban on hand guns with ten-round magazines, that will inevitably be followed by bans on all guns, including antique dueling pistols inherited from our Founding Fathers."
>
> Problem number one with this slide down the fearsome slope is how much weaponry has changed since the days of militias with muskets. Even the NRA agrees that lines have to be drawn somewhere. They do not favor legalization of civilian use of rocket-propelled grenades, bazookas or stinger missiles. If there is a slippery slope we are starting approximately half-way down.
>
> —Michael Wolkowitz, "Slippery Slopes, Imagined and Real"

Social and political ideas and proposals do have consequences, but they aren't always as dire as writers fond of slippery slope tactics would have you believe.

Overly Sentimental Appeals

Overly **sentimental appeals** use tender emotions excessively to distract readers from facts. Often, such appeals are highly personal and individual and focus attention on heartwarming or heartrending situations that make readers feel guilty if they challenge an idea, a policy, or a proposal. Emotions become an impediment to civil discourse when they keep people from thinking clearly.

Such sentimental appeals are a major vehicle of television news, where tugging at viewers' heartstrings can mean high ratings. For example,

This image, taken from a gun control protest, is designed to elicit sympathy by causing the viewer to think about the dangers guns pose to innocent children and, thus, support the cause. Tim Boyle/Getty Images

when a camera documents the day-to-day sacrifices of a single parent trying to meet mortgage payments and keep her kids in college, the woman's on-screen struggles can seem to represent the plight of an entire class of people threatened by callous bankers and college administrators. But while such human interest stories stir genuine emotions, they seldom give a complete picture of complex social or economic issues.

Bandwagon Appeals

Bandwagon appeals urge people to follow the same path everyone else is taking. Such arguments can be relatively benign and seem harmless. But they do push people to take the easier path rather than think independently about what choices to make or where to go.

Many American parents seem to have an innate ability to refute bandwagon appeals. When their kids whine, *Everyone else is going camping without chaperones*, the parents reply, *And if everyone else jumps off a cliff (or a railroad bridge or the Empire State Building), you will too?* The children groan—and then try a different line of argument.

Some bandwagon appeals work better than others.

Unfortunately, not all bandwagon approaches are so transparent. In recent decades, bandwagon issues have included a war on drugs, the nuclear freeze movement, campaigns against drunk driving, campaigns for immigration reform, bailouts for banks and businesses, and *many* fads in education from high-stakes testing to MOOCs. All these issues are too complex to permit the suspension of judgment that bandwagon tactics require.

Fallacies of Ethical Argument

Because readers give their closest attention to authors they respect or trust, writers usually want to present themselves as honest, well-informed, likable, or sympathetic. But not all the devices that writers use to gain the attention and confidence of readers are admirable. (For more on appeals based on character, see Chapter 3.)

Appeals to False Authority

Many academic research papers find and reflect on the work of reputable authorities and introduce these authorities through direct quotations or citations as credible evidence. (For more on assessing the reliability of sources, see Chapter 19.) **False authority**, however, occurs when writers offer themselves or other authorities as sufficient warrant for believing a claim:

Claim	X is true because I say so.
Warrant	What I say must be true.
Claim	X is true because Y says so.
Warrant	What Y says must be true.

Though they are seldom stated so baldly, claims of authority drive many political campaigns. American pundits and politicians are fond of citing the U.S. Constitution and its Bill of Rights (Canadians have their Charter of Rights and Freedoms) as ultimate authorities, a reasonable practice when the documents are interpreted respectfully. However, the rights claimed sometimes aren't in the texts themselves or don't mean what the speakers think they do. And most constitutional matters are debatable—as volumes of court records prove. Likewise, religious believers often base arguments on books or traditions that wield great authority in a particular religious community. But the power of such texts is usually limited to that group and less capable of persuading others solely on the grounds of authority.

In short, you should pay serious attention to claims supported by respected authorities, such as the Centers for Disease Control, the National Science Foundation, or the *Globe and Mail*. But don't accept information simply because it is put forth by such offices and agencies. To quote a Russian proverb made famous by Ronald Reagan, "Trust, but verify."

Dogmatism

A writer who asserts or assumes that a particular position is the *only one* that is conceivably acceptable is expressing **dogmatism**, a fallacy of character that undermines the trust that must exist between those who make and listen to arguments. When people or organizations write dogmatically, they imply that no arguments are necessary: the truth is self-evident and needs no support. Here is an extreme example of such an appeal, quoted in an *Atlantic* story by Tracy Brown

Hamilton and describing an anti-smoking appeal made by the Third Reich:

> **"Brother national socialist, do you know that your Fuhrer is against smoking and thinks that every German is responsible to the whole people for all his deeds and omissions, and does not have the right to damage his body with drugs?"**
>
> **—From Tracy Brown Hamilton, "The Nazis' Forgotten Anti-Smoking Campaign"**

Subjects or ideas that can be defended with facts, testimony, and good reasons ought not to be off the table in a free society. In general, whenever someone suggests that even raising an issue for debate is totally unacceptable—whether on the grounds that it's racist, sexist, unpatriotic, blasphemous, insensitive, or offensive in some other way—you should be suspicious.

Ad Hominem Arguments

Ad hominem (Latin for "to the man") **arguments** attack the character of a person rather than the claims he or she makes: when you destroy the credibility of your opponents, you either destroy their ability to present reasonable appeals or distract from the successful arguments they may be offering. Such attacks, of course, aren't aimed at men only, as columnist Jamie Stiehm proved when she criticized Supreme Court Justice Sonia Sotomayor for delaying an Obamacare mandate objected to by the Little Sisters of the Poor, a Catholic religious order. Stiehm directly targets Sotomayor's religious beliefs:

> **Et tu, Justice Sonia Sotomayor? Really, we can't trust you on women's health and human rights? The lady from the Bronx just dropped the ball on American women and girls as surely as she did the sparkling ball at midnight on New Year's Eve in Times Square. Or maybe she's just a good Catholic girl.**
>
> **—Jamie Stiehm, "The Catholic Supreme Court's War on Women"**

Stiehm then widens her *ad hominem* assault to include Catholics in general:

> **Sotomayor's blow brings us to confront an uncomfortable reality. More than WASPs, Methodists, Jews, Quakers or Baptists, Catholics often try to impose their beliefs on you, me, public discourse and institutions. Especially if "you" are female.**

Arguably, *ad hominem* tactics like this turn arguments into two-sided affairs with good guys and bad guys (or gals), and that's unfortunate, since character often really *does* matter in argument. People expect the proponent of peace to be civil, a secretary of the treasury to pay his or her taxes, and the champion of family values to be a faithful spouse. But it's fallacious to attack an idea by uncovering the foibles of its advocates or by attacking their motives, backgrounds, or unchangeable traits.

Stacking the Deck

Just as gamblers try to stack the deck by arranging cards so they are sure to win, writers **stack the deck** when they show only one side of the story—the one in their favor. In a Facebook forum on the documentary film *Super Size Me* (which followed a 32-year-old man who ate three meals a day at McDonald's for thirty days with drastic health consequences), one student points out an example of stacking the deck:

> One of the fallacies was stacking the deck. Spurlock stated many facts and gave plenty of evidence of what can happen if you eat fast food in abundance. Weight gain, decline in health, habit forming, and a toll on your daily life. But he failed to show what could happen if you ate the fast food and participated in daily exercise and took vitamins. The fallacy is that he does not show us both sides of what can happen. Possibly you could eat McDonald's for three meals a day for thirty days and if you engaged in daily exercise and took vitamins maybe your health would be just fine. But we were not ever shown that side of the experiment.
>
> —Heather Tew Alleman, on a Facebook forum

In the same way, reviewers have been critical of documentaries by Michael Moore and Dinesh D'Souza that resolutely show only one side of a story or prove highly selective in their coverage. When you stack the deck, you take a big chance that your readers will react like Alleman and decide not to trust you: that's one reason it's so important to show that you have considered alternatives in making any argument.

Fallacies of Logical Argument

You'll encounter a problem in any argument when the claims, warrants, or proofs in it are invalid, insufficient, or disconnected. In theory, such problems seem easy enough to spot, but in practice, they can be camouflaged by a skillful use of words or images. Indeed, logical fallacies pose a challenge to civil argument because they often seem reasonable and natural, especially when they appeal to people's self-interests.

Hasty Generalization

A **hasty generalization** is an inference drawn from insufficient evidence: because *my* Fiat broke down, then *all* Fiats must be junk. It also forms the basis for most stereotypes about people or institutions: because *a few* people in a large group are observed to act in a certain way, *all* members of that group are inferred to behave similarly. The resulting conclusions are usually sweeping claims of little merit: *women are bad drivers*; *men are slobs*; *English teachers are nitpicky*; *computer jocks are* . . . , and on and on.

To draw valid inferences, you must always have sufficient evidence (see Chapter 18) and you must qualify your claims appropriately. After all, people do need generalizations to make reasonable decisions in life. Such claims can be offered legitimately if placed in context and tagged with sensible qualifiers—*some*, *a few*, *many*, *most*, *occasionally*, *rarely*, *possibly*, *in some cases*, *under certain circumstances*, *in my limited experience*.

Faulty Causality

In Latin, **faulty causality** is known as *post hoc, ergo propter hoc*, which translates as "after this, therefore because of this"—the faulty assumption that because one event or action follows another, the first causes the second. Consider a lawsuit commented on in the *Wall Street Journal* in which a writer sued Coors (unsuccessfully), claiming that drinking copious amounts of the company's beer had kept him from writing a novel.

Some actions do produce reactions. Step on the brake pedal in your car, and you move hydraulic fluid that pushes calipers against disks to create friction that stops the vehicle. In other cases, however, a supposed connection between cause and effect turns out to be completely wrong. For example, doctors now believe that when an elderly person falls and breaks a hip or leg, the injury usually caused the fall rather than the other way around.

That's why overly simple causal claims should always be subject to scrutiny. In summer 2008, writer Nicholas Carr posed a simple causal question in a cover story for the *Atlantic*: "Is Google Making Us Stupid?" Carr essentially answered yes, arguing that "as we come to rely on computers to mediate our understanding of the world, it is our own intelligence that flattens" and that the more one is online the less he or she is able to concentrate or read deeply.

But others, like Jamais Cascio (senior fellow at the Institute for Ethics and Emerging Technologies), soon challenged that causal connection: rather than making us stupid, Cascio argues, Internet tools like Google will lead to the development of "'fluid intelligence'—the ability to find meaning in confusion and to solve new problems, independent of acquired knowledge." The final word on this contentious causal relationship—the effects on the human brain caused by new technology—has yet to be written, and will probably be available only after decades of complicated research.

Begging the Question

Most teachers have heard some version of the following argument: *You can't give me a C in this course; I'm an A student.* A member of Congress accused of taking kickbacks can make much the same argument: *I can't be guilty of accepting such bribes; I'm an honest person.* In both cases, the claim is made on grounds that can't be accepted as true because those grounds themselves are in question. How can the accused bribe-taker defend herself on grounds of honesty when that honesty is in doubt? Looking at the arguments in Toulmin terms helps to see the fallacy:

Claim	You can't give me a C in this course . . .
Reason	. . . because I'm an A student.
Warrant	An A student is someone who can't receive Cs.
Claim	Representative X can't be guilty of accepting bribes . . .
Reason	. . . because she's an honest person.
Warrant	An honest person cannot be guilty of accepting bribes.

With the warrants stated, you can see why **begging the question**—assuming as true the very claim that's disputed—is a form of circular argument that goes nowhere. (For more on Toulmin argument, see Chapter 7.)

Equivocation

Equivocations—half truths or arguments that give lies an honest appearance—are usually based on tricks of language. Consider the plagiarist who copies a paper word for word from a source and then declares that "I wrote the entire paper myself"—meaning that she physically copied the piece on her own. But the plagiarist is using *wrote* equivocally and knows that most people understand the word to mean composing and not merely copying words.

Parsing words carefully can sometimes look like equivocation or be the thing itself. For example, early in 2014 Internal Revenue Service Commissioner John Koskinen promised to turn over to a committee of the House of Representatives all the relevant emails in a scandal involving the agency. Subsequently, the agency revealed that some of those requested emails had been destroyed by the failure of a computer's hard drive. But Koskinen defended his earlier promise by telling the chair of the committee, "I never said I would provide you emails we didn't have." A simple statement of fact or a slick equivocation?

Non Sequitur

A **non sequitur** is an argument whose claims, reasons, or warrants don't connect logically. You've probably detected a non sequitur when you react to an argument with a puzzled, "Wait, that doesn't follow." Children are adept at framing non sequiturs like this one: *You don't love me or you'd buy me a new bicycle!* It doesn't take a parental genius to realize that love has little connection with buying children toys.

Non sequiturs often occur when writers omit steps in an otherwise logical chain of reasoning. For example, it might be a non sequitur to argue that since postsecondary education now costs so much, it's time to move colleges and university instruction online. Such a suggestion *may* have merit, but a leap from brick-and-mortar schools to virtual ones is extreme. Numerous issues and questions must be addressed step-by-step before the proposal can be taken seriously.

Politicians sometimes resort to non sequiturs to evade thorny issues or questions. Here for example is presidential candidate Mitt Romney in a 2011 CNBC Republican primary debate turning moderator John Harwood's question about changing political positions into one about demonstrating personal integrity:

> *Harwood:* . . . Your opponents have said you switched positions on many issues. . . . What can you say to Republicans to persuade them

that the things you say in the campaign are rooted in something deeper than the fact that you are running for office?

Romney: John, I think people know me pretty well. . . . I think people understand that I'm a man of steadiness and constancy. I don't think you are going to find somebody who has more of those attributes than I do. I have been married to the same woman for . . . 42 years. . . . I have been in the same church my entire life.

Conservative writer Matt K. Lewis took Romney to task for this move, pointing out that a steady personal life is no guarantor of a consistent political philosophy:

> This, of course, is not to say that values and character do not matter—they *do*—but it is to say that Romney's answer was a non sequitur. Everyone knows Mitt Romney is a decent, respectable person. The question is whether or not he can be trusted to advance conservatism as president.

Straw Man

Those who resort to the **straw man** fallacy attack arguments that no one is really making or portray opponents' positions as more extreme or far less coherent than they actually are. The speaker or writer thus sets up an argument that is conveniently easy to knock down (like a man of straw), proceeds to do so, and then claims victory over an opponent who may not even exist.

Straw men are especially convenient devices for politicians who want to characterize the positions of their opponents as more extreme than they actually are: consider obvious memes such as "war on women" and "war on Christmas." But straw man arguments are often more subtle. For instance, Steven Novella of Yale University argues that political commentator Charles Krauthammer slips into the fallacy when he misconstrues the meaning of "settled science" in a column on climate change. Novella rebuts Krauthammer's assertion that "There is nothing more anti-scientific than the very idea that science is settled, static, impervious to challenge" by explaining why such a claim is deceptive:

> Calling something an established scientific fact means that it is reasonable to proceed with that fact as a premise, for further research or for policy. It does not mean "static, impervious to challenge." That is the straw man. Both evolution deniers and climate change deniers use this tactic to misinterpret scientific confidence as an anti-scientific resistance to new evidence or arguments. It isn't. It does mean that

> **the burden of proof has shifted to those opposing the theory that is now well-established (because it has already met a significant burden of proof).**
>
> **—Steven Novella, *NeuroLogica Blog*, February 25, 2014**

In other words, Krauthammer's definition of *science* is not one that most scientists use.

Red Herring

This fallacy gets its name from the old British hunting practice of dragging a dried herring across the path of the fox in order to throw the hounds off the trail. A **red herring** fallacy does just that: it changes the subject abruptly or introduces an irrelevant claim or fact to throw readers or listeners off the trail. For example, people skeptical about climate change will routinely note that weather is always changing and point to the fact that Vikings settled in Greenland one thousand years ago before harsher conditions drove them away. True, scientists will say, but the point is irrelevant to arguments about worldwide global warming caused by human activity.

The red herring is not only a device writers and speakers use in the arguments they create, but it's also a charge used frequently to undermine someone else's arguments. Couple the term "red herring" in a Web search to just about any political or social cause and you'll come up with numerous articles complaining of someone's use of the device.

> **climate change + red herring**
>
> **common core + red herring**
>
> **immigration reform + red herring**

"Red herring" has become a convenient way of saying "I disagree with your argument" or "your point is irrelevant." And perhaps making a too-easy rebuttal like that can itself be a fallacy?

Faulty Analogy

Comparisons can help to clarify one concept by measuring it against another that is more familiar. Consider the power and humor of this comparison attributed to Mark Twain, an implicit argument for term limits in politics:

> **Politicians and diapers must be changed often, and for the same reason.**

When comparisons such as this one are extended, they become *analogies*—ways of understanding unfamiliar ideas by comparing them with something that's better known (see p. 68). But useful as such comparisons are, they may prove false if either taken on their own and pushed too far, or taken too seriously. At this point, they turn into **faulty analogies**—inaccurate or inconsequential comparisons between objects or concepts. Economist Paul Krugman provides an eye-opening analysis of a familiar but, as he sees it, false analogy between personal and government debt:

> Deficit-worriers portray a future in which we're impoverished by the need to pay back money we've been borrowing. They see America as being like a family that took out too large a mortgage, and will have a hard time making the monthly payments.
>
> This is, however, a really bad analogy in at least two ways.
>
> First, families have to pay back their debt. Governments don't—all they need to do is ensure that debt grows more slowly than their tax base. The debt from World War II was never repaid; it just became increasingly irrelevant as the U.S. economy grew, and with it the income subject to taxation.
>
> Second—and this is the point almost nobody seems to get—an overborrowed family owes money to someone else; U.S. debt is, to a large extent, money we owe to ourselves.

Whether you agree with the Nobel laureate or not, his explanation offers insight into how analogies work (or fail) and how to think about them critically.

RESPOND.

1. Examine each of the following political slogans or phrases for logical fallacies.

   "Resistance is futile." (Borg message on *Star Trek: The Next Generation*)

   "It's the economy, stupid." (sign on the wall at Bill Clinton's campaign headquarters)

   "Make love, not war." (antiwar slogan popularized during the Vietnam War)

   "A chicken in every pot." (campaign slogan)

   "Guns don't kill, people do." (NRA slogan)

"Dog Fighters Are Cowardly Scum." (PETA T-shirt)

"If you can't stand the heat, get out of the kitchen." (attributed to Harry S Truman)

2. Choose a paper you've written for a college class and analyze it for signs of fallacious reasoning. Then find an editorial, a syndicated column, and a news report on the same topic and look for fallacies in them. Which has the most fallacies—and what kind? What may be the role of the audience in determining when a statement is fallacious?
3. Find a Web site that is sponsored by an organization (the Future of Music Coalition, perhaps), a business (Coca-Cola, Pepsi), or another group (the Democratic or Republican National Committee), and analyze the site for fallacious reasoning. Among other considerations, look at the relationship between text and graphics and between individual pages and the pages that surround or are linked to them.
4. Political blogs such as *Mother Jones* and *InstaPundit* typically provide quick responses to daily events and detailed critiques of material in other media sites, including national newspapers. Study one such blog for a few days to see whether and how the site critiques the articles, political commentary, or writers it links to. Does the blog ever point out fallacies of argument? If so, does it explain the problems with such reasoning or just assume readers will understand the fallacies? Summarize your findings in a brief oral report to your class.

6 Rhetorical Analysis

If you watched the 2013 Super Bowl between the Baltimore Ravens and the San Francisco 49ers, you may remember the commercial. For two solemn minutes, still photographs of rural America and the people who work there moved across the screen accompanied by the unmistakable voice of the late Paul Harvey reading words he had first delivered in 1978. Maria Godoy of NPR described it this way: "It may not have been as dramatic as the stadium blackout that halted play for more than a half-hour, or as extravagant as Beyonce's halftime show. But for many viewers of Super Bowl XLVII, one of the standout moments was a deceptively simple ad for the Dodge Ram called 'God Made a Farmer.'" It was a fourth quarter interrupted by cattle, churches, snowy farmyards, bales of hay, plowed fields, hardworking men, and a few sturdy women. Occasionally, a slide discreetly showed a Ram truck, sponsor of the video, but there were no overt sales pitches—only a product logo in the final frame. Yet visits to the Ram Web site spiked immediately, and sales of Ram pickups did too. (The official video has been viewed on YouTube more than 17 million times.)

So how to account for the appeal of such an unconventional and unexpected commercial? That would be the work of a **rhetorical analysis**, the close reading of a text or, in this case, a video commercial, to figure out exactly how it functions. Certainly, the creators of "God Made a Farmer" counted on the strong emotional appeal of the photographs they'd commissioned, guessing perhaps that the expert images and Harvey's spellbinding words would contrast powerfully with the frivolity and emptiness of much Super Bowl ad fare:

> God said, "I need somebody willing to sit up all night with a newborn colt. And watch it die. Then dry his eyes and say, 'Maybe next year.'"

They pushed convention, too, by the length of the spot and the muted product connection, doubtless hoping to win the goodwill of a huge audience suddenly all teary-eyed in the midst of a football game. And they surely gained the respect of a great many truck-buying farmers.

Rhetorical analyses can also probe the contexts that surround any argument or text—its impact on a society, its deeper implications, or even what it lacks or whom it excludes. Predictably, the widely admired Ram commercial (selected #1 Super Bowl XLVII spot by *Adweek*) acquired its share of critics, some attacking it for romanticizing farm life, others for ignoring the realities of industrial agriculture. And not a few writers noted what they regarded as glaring absences in its representation of farmers. Here, for instance, is copywriter and blogger Edye Deloch-Hughes, offering a highly personal and conflicted view of the spot in what amounts to an informal rhetorical analysis:

> . . . I was riveted by the still photography and stirring thirty-five-year-old delivery of legendary radio broadcaster Paul Harvey. But as I sat mesmerized, I waited to see an image that spoke to my heritage. What flashed before me were close-ups of stoic white men whose faces drowned out the obligatory medium shots of a minority token or two; their images minimized against the amber waves of grain.
>
> God made a Black farmer too. Where was my Grandpa, Grandma and Great Granny? My Auntie and Uncle Bolden? And didn't God make Hispanic and Native American farmers? They too were under-represented.
>
> I am the offspring of a century and a half of African-American caretakers of the land, from Arkansas, Mississippi and Louisiana, who experienced their toils and troubles, their sun ups and sun downs. Their injustices and beat-downs. I wrestled with my mixed emotions; loving the commercial and feeling dejected at the same time.

> **. . . Minimizing positive Black imagery and accomplishments is as American as wrestling cattle. We're often footnotes or accessories in history books, TV shows, movies and magazines as well as TV commercials. When content is exceptional, the omission is harder to recognize or criticize. Some friends of mine saw—or rather *felt*—the omission as I did. Others did not. I say be aware and vocal about how you are represented—if represented at all, otherwise your importance and relevance will be lost.**
>
> **—Edye Deloch-Hughes, "So God Made a Black Farmer Too"**

As this example suggests, whenever you undertake a rhetorical analysis, follow your instincts and look closely. Why does an ad for a cell phone or breakfast sandwich make people want one immediately? How does an op-ed piece in the *Washington Post* suddenly change your long-held position on immigration? A rhetorical analysis might help you understand. Dig as deep as you can into the context of the item you are analyzing, especially when you encounter puzzling, troubling, or unusually successful appeals—ethical, emotional, or logical. Ask yourself what strategies a speech, editorial, opinion column, film, or ad spot employs to move your heart, win your trust, and change your mind—or why, maybe, it fails to do so.

Composing a Rhetorical Analysis

You perform a rhetorical analysis by analyzing how well the components of an argument work together to persuade or move an audience. You can study arguments of any kind—advertisements (as we've seen), editorials, political cartoons, and even songs, movies, or photographs. In every case, you'll need to focus your rhetorical analysis on elements that stand out or make the piece intriguing or problematic. You could begin by exploring *some* of the following issues:

- What is the purpose of this argument? What does it hope to achieve?
- Who is the audience for this argument? Who is ignored or excluded?
- What appeals or techniques does the argument use—emotional, logical, ethical?
- What type of argument is it, and how does the genre affect the argument? (You might challenge the lack of evidence in editorials, but you wouldn't make the same complaint about bumper stickers.)

- Who is making the argument? What ethos does it create, and how does it do so? What values does the ethos evoke? How does it make the writer or creator seem trustworthy?
- What authorities does the argument rely on or appeal to?
- What facts, reasoning, and evidence are used in the argument? How are they presented?
- What claims does the argument make? What issues are raised—or ignored or evaded?
- What are the contexts—social, political, historical, cultural—for this argument? Whose interests does it serve? Who gains or loses by it?
- How is the argument organized or arranged? What media does the argument use and how effectively?
- How does the language or style of the argument persuade an audience?

In answering questions like these, try to show *how* the key devices in an argument actually make it succeed or fail. Quote freely from a written piece, or describe the elements in a visual argument. (Annotating a visual text is one option.) Let readers know where and why an argument makes sense and where it falls apart. If you believe that an argument startles, challenges, insults, or lulls audiences, explain why that is the case and provide evidence. Don't be surprised when your rhetorical analysis itself becomes an argument. That's what it should be.

Understanding the Purpose of Arguments You Are Analyzing

To understand how well any argument works, begin with its purpose: Is it to sell running shoes? To advocate for limits to college tuition? To push a political agenda? In many cases, that purpose may be obvious. A conservative blog will likely advance right-wing causes; ads from a baby food company will likely show happy infants delighted with stewed prunes.

But some projects may hide their persuasive intentions. Perhaps you've responded to a mail survey or telephone poll only to discover that the questions are leading you to switch your cable service or buy apartment insurance. Do such stealthy arguments succeed? Do consumers resent the intrusion? Answering questions like these provides material for useful rhetorical analyses that assess the strengths, risks, and ethics of such strategies.

Understanding Who Makes an Argument

Knowing *who* is claiming *what* is key to any rhetorical analysis. That's why persuasive appeals usually have a name attached to them. Remember the statements included in TV ads during the last federal election: "Hello, I'm X—and I approve this ad"? Federal law requires such statements so we can tell the difference between ads a candidate endorses and ones sponsored by groups not even affiliated with the campaigns. Their interests and motives might be very different.

But knowing a name is just a starting place for analysis. You need to dig deeper, and you could do worse than to Google such people or groups to discover more about them. What else have they produced? Who publishes them: the *Wall Street Journal*, the blog *The Daily Kos*, or even a LiveJournal celebrity gossip site such as *Oh No They Didn't*? Check out related Web sites for information about goals, policies, contributors, and funding.

Funny, offensive, or both? © Chris Maddaloni/CQ Roll Call

RESPOND •

Describe a persuasive moment that you can recall from a speech, an editorial, an advertisement, a YouTube clip, or a blog posting. Or research one of the following famous persuasive moments and describe the circumstances—the historical situation, the issues at stake, the purpose of the argument—that make it so memorable.

Abraham Lincoln's Gettysburg Address (1863)

Elizabeth Cady Stanton's Declaration of Sentiments at the Seneca Falls Convention (1848)

Chief Tecumseh's address to General William Henry Harrison (1810)

Winston Churchill's radio addresses to the British people during World War II (1940)

Martin Luther King Jr.'s "Letter from Birmingham Jail" (1963)

Ronald Reagan's tribute to the *Challenger* astronauts (1986)

Toni Morrison's speech accepting the Nobel Prize (1993)

Will.i.am's "Yes We Can" song/collage on YouTube (2008)

Identifying and Appealing to Audiences

The *Lebanon Daily News* explores how audiences reacted to an expensive marketing campaign in "Coca-Cola's Multilingual 'America' Ad Didn't Hit Any Wrong Notes."

LINK TO P. 570

Most arguments are composed with specific audiences in mind, and their success depends, in part, on how well their strategies, content, tone, and language meet the expectations of that audience. So your rhetorical analysis of an argumentative piece should identify its target readers or viewers (see "Appealing to Audiences," p. 21) if possible, or make an educated guess about the audience, since most arguments suggest whom they intend to reach and in what ways.

Both a flyer stapled to a bulletin board in a college dorm ("Why you shouldn't drink and drive") and a forty-foot billboard for Bud Light might be aimed at the same general population—college students. But each will adjust its appeals for the different moods of that group in different moments. For starters, the flyer will appeal to students in a serious vein, while the beer ad will probably be visually stunning and virtually text-free.

You might also examine how a writer or an argument establishes credibility with an audience. One effective means of building credibility is to show respect for your readers or viewers, especially if they may not agree with you. In introducing an article on problems facing African American women in the workplace, editor in chief of *Essence* Diane Weathers considers the problems that she faced with respecting all her potential readers:

> We spent more than a minute agonizing over the provocative cover line for our feature "White Women at Work." The countless stories we had heard from women across the country told us that this was a workplace issue we had to address. From my own experience at several major magazines, it was painfully obvious to me that Black and White women are not on the same track. Sure, we might all start out in the same place. But early in the game, most sisters I know become stuck—and the reasons have little to do with intelligence or drive. At some point we bump our heads against that ceiling. And while White women may complain of a glass ceiling, for us, the ceiling is concrete.
>
> So how do we tell this story without sounding whiny and paranoid, or turning off our White-female readers, staff members, advertisers and girlfriends? Our solution: Bring together real women (several of them highly successful senior corporate executives), put them in a room, promise them anonymity and let them speak their truth.
>
> —Diane Weathers, "Speaking Our Truth"

Retailers like Walmart build their credibility by simple "straight talk" to shoppers: our low prices make your life better. Beth Hall/Bloomberg News/Getty Images

Both paragraphs affirm Weathers's determination to treat audiences fairly *and* to deal honestly with a difficult subject. The strategy would merit attention in any rhetorical analysis.

Look, too, for signals that writers share values with readers or at least understand an audience. In the following passage, writer Jack Solomon is clear about one value that he hopes readers have in common—a preference for "straight talk":

> There are some signs in the advertising world that Americans are getting fed up with fantasy advertisements and want to hear some straight talk. Weary of extravagant product claims . . . , consumers trained by years of advertising to distrust what they hear seem to be developing an immunity to commercials.
>
> —Jack Solomon, "Masters of Desire: The Culture of American Advertising"

But straight talk still requires common sense. If ever a major television ad seriously misread its audience, it may have been a spot that ran during the 2014 Winter Olympics for Cadillac's pricey new plug-in hybrid, the ELR. The company seemed to go out of its way to offend a great many people, foreign and domestic. As is typical strategy in rhetorical analyses, *Huffington Post*'s Carolyn Gregoire takes care to describe in detail the item she finds offensive:

> The opening shot shows a middle-aged man, played by the actor Neal McDonough, looking out over his backyard pool, asking the question: "Why do we work so hard? For this? For stuff?"
>
> As the ad continues, it becomes clear that the answer to this rhetorical question is actually a big fat YES. And it gets worse. "Other countries, they work," he says. "They stroll home. They stop by the cafe. They take August off. Off."
>
> Then he reveals just what it is that makes Americans better than all those lazy, espresso-sipping foreigners.
>
> "Why aren't you like that?" he says. "Why aren't we like that? Because we're crazy, driven, hard-working believers, that's why."
>
> —Carolyn Gregoire, "Cadillac Made a Commercial about the American Dream, and It's a Nightmare"

Her conclusion then is blistering, showing how readily a rhetorical analysis becomes an argument—and subject to criticism itself:

> Cadillacs have long been a quintessentially American symbol of wealth and status. But as this commercial proves, no amount of

wealth or status is a guarantee of good taste. Now, the luxury car company is selling a vision of the American Dream at its worst: Work yourself into the ground, take as little time off as possible, and buy expensive sh*t (specifically, a 2014 Cadillac ELR).

Examining Arguments Based on Emotion: Pathos

Some emotional appeals are just ploys to win over readers with a pretty face, figurative or real. You've seen ads promising an exciting life and attractive friends if only you drink the right soda or wear a particular brand of clothes. Are you fooled by such claims? Probably not, if you pause to think about them. But that's the strategy—to distract you from thought just long enough to make a bad choice. It's a move worth commenting on in a rhetorical analysis.

How well does the emotional appeal here work?

Yet emotions can add real muscle to arguments, too, and that's worth noting. For example, persuading people not to drink and drive by making them fear death, injury, or arrest seems like a fair use of an emotional appeal. The public service announcement on page 95 uses an emotion-laden image to remind drivers to think of the consequences.

In a rhetorical analysis, you might note the juxtaposition of image with text, leading readers to connect casual notes left on windshields with the very serious consequences of drunk driving.

In analyzing emotional appeals, judge whether the emotions raised—anger, sympathy, fear, envy, joy, love, lust—advance the claims offered. Consider how columnist Ron Rosenbaum (whom we met in Chapter 2) makes the reasonable argument he offers for fatty foods all the more attractive by larding it with voluptuous language:

> **The foods that best hit that sweet spot and "overwhelm the brain" with pleasure are high-quality fatty foods. They discourage us from overeating. A modest serving of short ribs or Peking duck will be both deeply pleasurable and self-limiting. As the brain swoons into insensate delight, you won't have to gorge a still-craving cortex with mediocre sensations. "Sensory-specific satiety" makes a slam-dunk case (it's science!) for eating reasonable servings of superbly satisfying fatty foods.**
>
> **—Ron Rosenbaum, "Let Them Eat Fat"**

Does the use of evocative language ("swoons," "insensate delight," "superbly satisfying," "slam-dunk") convince you, or does it distract from considering the scientific case for "sensory-specific satiety"? Your task in a

Health food? Kittipojn Pravalpatkul/Shutterstock

rhetorical analysis is to study an author's words, the emotions they evoke, and the claims they support and then to make this kind of judgment.

RESPOND•

Browse YouTube or another Web site to find an example of a powerful emotional argument that's made visually, either alone or using words as well. In a paragraph, defend a claim about how the argument works. For example, does an image itself make a claim, or does it draw you in to consider a verbal claim? What emotion does the argument generate? How does that emotion work to persuade you?

Examining Arguments Based on Character: Ethos

It should come as no surprise: readers believe writers who seem honest, wise, and trustworthy. So in analyzing the effectiveness of an argument, look for evidence of these traits. Does the writer have the experience or authority to write on this subject? Are all claims qualified reasonably? Is evidence presented in full, not tailored to the writer's agenda? Are important objections to the author's position acknowledged and addressed? Are sources documented? Above all, does the writer sound trustworthy?

In his article "Are Engineered Foods Evil?" David H. Freedman examines the credibility of both advocates and critics of genetically modified food.

LINK TO P. 630

When a Norwegian anti-immigration extremist killed seventy-six innocent people in July 2011, Prime Minister Jens Stoltenberg addressed the citizens of Norway (and the world), and in doing so evoked the character or ethos of the entire nation:

> **We will not let fear break us! The warmth of response from people in Norway and from the whole world makes me sure of this one thing: evil can kill a single person, but never defeat a whole people. The strongest weapon in the world—that is freedom of expression and democracy.**

In analyzing this speech, you would do well to look at the way this passage deploys the deepest values of Norway—freedom of expression and democracy—to serve as a response to fear of terrorism. In doing so, Stoltenberg evokes ethical ideals to hold onto in a time of tragedy.

Or take a look at the following paragraph from a blog posting by Timothy Burke, a teacher at Swarthmore College and parent of a preschool child who is trying to think through the issue of homework for elementary school kids:

So I've been reading a bit about homework and comparing notes with parents. There is a lot of variation across districts, not just in the amount of homework that kids are being asked to do, but in the kind of homework. Some districts give kids a lot of time-consuming busywork; other districts try to concentrate on having homework assignments be substantive work that is best accomplished independently. Some give a lot from a very early point in K-12 education; some give relatively little. As both a professional educator and an individual with personal convictions, I'd tend to argue against excessive amounts of homework and against assigning busywork. But what has ultimately interested me more about reading various discussions of homework is how intense the feelings are swirling around the topic and how much that intensity strikes me as a problem in and of itself. Not just as a symptom of a kind of civic illness, an inability to collectively and democratically work through complex issues, but also in some cases as evidence of an educational failure in its own right.

Burke establishes his ethos by citing his reading and his talks with other parents.

He underscores his right to address the matter.

He expresses concern about immoderate arguments and implies that he will demonstrate an opposite approach.

In considering the role of ethos in rhetorical analyses, pay attention to the details right down to the choice of words or, in an image, the shapes and colors. The modest, tentative tone that Burke uses in his blog is an example of the kind of choice that can shape an audience's perception of ethos. But these details need your interpretation. Language that's hot and extreme can mark a writer as either passionate or loony. Work that's sober and carefully organized can paint an institution as competent or overly cautious. Technical terms and abstract phrases can make a writer seem either knowledgeable or pompous.

Examining Arguments Based on Facts and Reason: Logos

In analyzing most arguments, you'll have to decide whether an argument makes a plausible claim and offers good reasons for you to believe it. Not all arguments will package such claims in a single neat sentence, or **thesis**—nor should they. A writer may tell a story from which you have to infer the claim. Visual arguments may work the same way: viewers have to assemble the parts and draw inferences in order to get the point.

Some conventional arguments (like those on an editorial page) may be perfectly obvious: writers stake out a claim and then present reasons that you should consider, or they may first present reasons and lay out a case that leads you to accept a claim in the conclusion. Consider the following example. In a tough opinion piece in *Time*, political commentator John McWhorter argues that filmmaker Spike Lee is being racist when he rails against hipsters moving into Fort Greene, a formerly all-black neighborhood in Brooklyn, New York. Lee fears that the whites are raising housing prices, pushing out old-time residents and diminishing the African American character of Fort Greene. McWhorter, an African American like Lee, sees matters differently:

> Basically, black people are getting paid more money than they've ever seen in their lives for their houses, and a once sketchy neighborhood is now quiet and pleasant. And this is a bad thing . . . why?
>
> Lee seems to think it's somehow an injustice whenever black people pick up stakes. But I doubt many of the blacks now set to pass fat inheritances on to their kids feel that way. This is not the old story of poor blacks being pushed out of neighborhoods razed down for highway construction. Lee isn't making sense.
>
> —John McWhorter, "Spike Lee's Racism Isn't Cute"

When you encounter explicit charges like these, you analyze whether and how the claims are supported by good reasons and reliable evidence. A lengthy essay may, in fact, contain a series of claims, each developed to support an even larger point. Here's McWhorter, for instance, expanding his argument by suggesting that Lee's attitudes toward whites are irreconcilable.

> "Respect the culture" when you move in, Lee growls. But again, he isn't making sense. We can be quite sure that if whites "respected" the culture by trying to participate in it, Lee would be one of the first in line to call it "appropriation." So, no whites better open up barbecue joints or spoken word cafes or try to be rappers. Yet if whites walk on by the culture in "respectful" silence, then the word on the street becomes that they want to keep blacks at a distance.

An anti-fur protestor in London makes a rather specific claim.
© Charles Platiau/Reuters/Corbis

Indeed, every paragraph in an argument may develop a specific and related idea. In a rhetorical analysis, you need to identify all these separate propositions and examine the relationships among them: Are they solidly linked? Are there inconsistencies that the writer should acknowledge? Does the end of the piece support what the writer said (and promised) at the beginning?

You'll also need to examine the quality of the information presented in an argument, assessing how accurately such information is reported, how conveniently it's displayed (in charts or graphs, for example), and how well the sources cited represent a range of *respected* opinions on a topic. (For more information on the use of evidence, see Chapter 4.)

Knowing how to judge the quality of sources is more important now than ever before because the digital universe is full of junk. In some ways, the computer terminal has become the equivalent of a library reference room, but the sources available online vary widely in quality and have not been evaluated by a library professional. As a consequence, you must know the difference between reliable, firsthand, or fully documented sources and those that don't meet such standards. (For using and documenting sources, see Chapters 19, 20, and 22.)

Examining the Arrangement and Media of Arguments

Aristotle carved the structure of logical argument to its bare bones when he observed that it had only two parts:

- statement
- proof

You could do worse, in examining an argument, than to make sure that every claim a writer makes is backed by sufficient evidence. Some arguments are written on the fly in the heat of the moment. Most arguments that you read and write, however, will be more than mere statements followed by proofs. Some writers will lay their cards on the table immediately; others may lead you carefully through a chain of claims toward a conclusion. Writers may even interrupt their arguments to offer background information or cultural contexts for readers. Sometimes they'll tell stories or provide anecdotes that make an argumentative point. They'll qualify the arguments they make, too, and often pause to admit that other points of view are plausible.

In other words, there are no formulas or acceptable patterns that fit all successful arguments. In writing a rhetorical analysis, you'll have to assess the organization of a persuasive text on its own merits.

It's fair, however, to complain about what may be *absent* from an argument. Most arguments of proposal (see Chapter 12), for example, include a section that defends the feasibility of a new idea, explaining how it might be funded or managed. In a rhetorical analysis, you might fault an editorial that supports a new stadium for a city without addressing feasibility issues. Similarly, analyzing a movie review that reads like an off-the-top-of-the-head opinion, you might legitimately ask what criteria of evaluation are in play (see Chapter 10).

Rhetorical analysis also calls for you to look carefully at an argument's transitions, headings and subheadings, documentation of sources, and overall tone or voice. Don't take such details for granted, since all of them contribute to the strength—or weakness—of an argument.

Nor should you ignore the way a writer or an institution uses media. Would an argument originally made in a print editorial, for instance, work better as a digital presentation (or vice versa)? Would a lengthy paper have more power if it included more images? Or do these images distract from a written argument's substance?

Finally, be open to the possibility of new or nontraditional structures of arguments. The visual arguments that you analyze may defy conventional principles of logic or arrangement—for example, making juxtapositions rather than logical transitions between elements or using quick cuts, fades, or other devices to link ideas. Quite often, these nontraditional structures will also resist the neatness of a thesis, leaving readers to construct at least a part of the argument in their heads. As we saw with the "God Made a Farmer" spot at the beginning of this chapter, advertisers are growing fond of soft-sell multimedia productions that can seem like something other than what they really are—product pitches. We may be asked not just to buy a product but also to live its lifestyle or embrace its ethos. Is that a reasonable or workable strategy for an argument? Your analysis might entertain such possibilities.

Looking at Style

Even a coherent argument full of sound evidence may not connect with readers if it's dull, off-key, or offensive. Readers naturally judge the credibility of arguments in part by how stylishly the case is made—even when they don't know exactly what style is (for more on style, see Chapter 13). Consider how these simple, blunt sentences from the opening of an argument shape your image of the author and probably determine whether you're willing to continue to read the whole piece:

> **We are young, urban, and professional. We are literate, respectable, intelligent, and charming. But foremost and above all, we are unemployed.**
>
> **—Julia Carlisle, "Young, Privileged, and Unemployed"**

The strong, straightforward tone and the stark juxtaposition of being "intelligent" with "unemployed" set the style for this letter to the editor.

Now consider the brutally sarcastic tone of Nathaniel Stein's hilarious parody of the Harvard grading policy, a piece he wrote following up on a professor's complaint of out-of-control grade inflation at the school. Stein borrows the formal language of a typical "grading standards" sheet to mock the decline in rigor that the professor has lamented:

> **The A+ grade is used only in very rare instances for the recognition of truly exceptional achievement.**
>
> **For example: A term paper receiving the A+ is virtually indistinguishable from the work of a professional, both in its choice of paper**

> stock and its font. The student's command of the topic is expert, or at the very least intermediate, or beginner. Nearly every single word in the paper is spelled correctly; those that are not can be reasoned out phonetically within minutes. Content from Wikipedia is integrated with precision. The paper contains few, if any, death threats. . . .
>
> An overall course grade of A+ is reserved for those students who have not only demonstrated outstanding achievement in coursework but have also asked very nicely.
>
> Finally, the A+ grade is awarded to all collages, dioramas and other art projects.
>
> —Nathaniel Stein, "Leaked! Harvard's Grading Rubric"

Both styles probably work, but they signal that the writers are about to make very different kinds of cases. Here, style alone tells readers what to expect.

Manipulating style also enables writers to shape readers' responses to their ideas. Devices as simple as repetition, parallelism, or even paragraph length can give sentences remarkable power. Consider this passage from an essay by Sherman Alexie in which he explores the complex reaction of straight men to the announcement of NBA star Jason Collins that he is gay:

> Homophobic basketball fans will disparage his skills, somehow equating his NBA benchwarmer status with his sexuality. But let's not forget that Collins is still one of the best 1,000 basketball players in the world. He has always been better than his modest statistics would indicate, and his teams have been dramatically more efficient with him on the court. He is better at hoops than 99.9 percent of you are at anything you do. He might not be a demigod, but he's certainly a semi-demigod. Moreover, his basketball colleagues universally praise him as a physically and mentally tough player. In his prime, he ably battled that behemoth known as Shaquille O'Neal. Most of all, Collins is widely regarded as one of the finest gentlemen to ever play the game. Generous, wise, and supportive, he's a natural leader. And he has a degree from Stanford University.
>
> In other words, he's a highly attractive dude.
>
> —Sherman Alexie, "Jason Collins Is the Envy of Straight Men Everywhere"

In this passage, Alexie uses a sequence of short, direct, and roughly parallel sentences ("He is . . . He might . . . He ably battled . . . He has") to present evidence justifying the playful point he makes in a pointedly

Jason Collins © Gary A. Vasquez/USA Today Sports Images

emphatic, one-sentence paragraph. The remainder of his short essay then amplifies that point.

In a rhetorical analysis, you can explore such stylistic choices. Why does a formal style work for discussing one type of subject matter but not another? How does a writer use humor or irony to underscore an important point or to manage a difficult concession? Do stylistic choices, even something as simple as the use of contractions or personal pronouns, bring readers close to a writer, or do technical words and an impersonal voice signal that an argument is for experts only?

To describe the stylistic effects of visual arguments, you may use a different vocabulary and talk about colors, camera angles, editing, balance, proportion, fonts, perspective, and so on. But the basic principle is this: the look of an item—whether a poster, an editorial cartoon, or a film documentary—can support the message that it carries, undermine it, or muddle it. In some cases, the look will *be* the message. In a rhetorical analysis, you can't ignore style.

This poster, promoting travel to the bicycle-friendly city of Münster, Germany, demonstrates visually the amount of space needed to transport the same number of people by car, bicycle, and bus. Foto Presseamt Münster, City of Münster, Press Office

RESPOND.

Find a recent example of a visual argument, either in print or on the Internet. Even though you may have a copy of the image, describe it carefully in your paper on the assumption that your description is all readers may have to go on. Then make a judgment about its effectiveness, supporting your claim with clear evidence from the "text."

Examining a Rhetorical Analysis

On the following pages, well-known political commentator and columnist for the *New York Times* David Brooks argues that today's college graduates have been poorly prepared for life after school because of what he sees as a radical excess of supervision. Responding to his argument with a detailed analysis is Rachel Kolb, a student at Stanford University.

It's Not about You

DAVID BROOKS

© David Levene/eyevine/Redux Pictures

Over the past few weeks, America's colleges have sent another class of graduates off into the world. These graduates possess something of inestimable value. Nearly every sensible middle-aged person would give away all their money to be able to go back to age 22 and begin adulthood anew.

But, especially this year, one is conscious of the many ways in which this year's graduating class has been ill served by their elders. They enter a bad job market, the hangover from decades of excessive borrowing. They inherit a ruinous federal debt.

More important, their lives have been perversely structured. This year's graduates are members of the most supervised generation in American history. Through their childhoods and teenage years, they have been monitored, tutored, coached and honed to an unprecedented degree.

Yet upon graduation they will enter a world that is unprecedentedly wide open and unstructured. Most of them will not quickly get married, buy a home and have kids, as previous generations did. Instead, they will confront amazingly diverse job markets, social landscapes and lifestyle niches. Most will spend a decade wandering from job to job and clique to clique, searching for a role.

No one would design a system of extreme supervision to prepare people for a decade of extreme openness. But this is exactly what has emerged in modern America. College students are raised in an environment that demands one set of navigational skills, and they are then cast out into a different environment requiring a different set of skills, which they have to figure out on their own.

Worst of all, they are sent off into this world with the whole baby-boomer theology ringing in their ears. If you sample some of the commencement addresses being broadcast on C-Span these days, you see that many graduates are told to: Follow *your* passion, chart *your* own course, march to the beat of *your* own drummer, follow *your* dreams and find *your*self. This is the litany of expressive individualism, which is still the dominant note in American culture.

But, of course, this mantra misleads on nearly every front.

College grads are often sent out into the world amid rapturous talk of limitless possibilities. But this talk is of no help to the central business of adulthood, finding serious things to tie yourself down to. The successful young adult is beginning to make sacred commitments—to a spouse, a community and calling—yet mostly hears about freedom and autonomy.

Today's graduates are also told to find their passion and then pursue their dreams. The implication is that they should find themselves first and then go off and live their quest. But, of course, very few people at age 22 or 24 can take an inward journey and come out having discovered a developed self.

Most successful young people don't look inside and then plan a life. They look outside and find a problem, which summons their life. A relative suffers from Alzheimer's and a young woman feels called to help cure that disease. A young man works under a miserable boss and must develop management skills so his department can function. Another young woman finds herself confronted by an opportunity she never thought of in a job category she never imagined. This wasn't in her plans, but this is where she can make her contribution.

Most people don't form a self and then lead a life. They are called by a problem, and the self is constructed gradually by their calling.

The graduates are also told to pursue happiness and joy. But, of course, when you read a biography of someone you admire, it's rarely the things that made them happy that compel your admiration. It's the things they did to court unhappiness—the things they did that were arduous and miserable, which sometimes cost them friends and aroused hatred. It's excellence, not happiness, that we admire most.

Finally, graduates are told to be independent-minded and to express their inner spirit. But, of course, doing your job well often means suppressing yourself. As Atul Gawande mentioned during his countercultural address . . . at Harvard Medical School, being a good doctor often means being part of a team, following the rules of an institution, going down a regimented checklist.

Today's grads enter a cultural climate that preaches the self as the center of a life. But, of course, as they age, they'll discover that the tasks of a life are at the center. Fulfillment is a byproduct of how people engage their tasks, and can't be pursued directly. Most of us are egotistical and most are self-concerned most of the time, but it's nonetheless true that life comes to a point only in those moments when the self dissolves into some task. The purpose in life is not to find yourself. It's to lose yourself.

Understanding Brooks's Binaries

RACHEL KOLB

Courtesy of Rachel Kolb

As a high school and college student, I was given an incredible range of educational and extracurricular options, from interdisciplinary studies to summer institutes to student-organized clubs. Although today's students have more opportunities to adapt their educations to their specific personal goals, as I did, David Brooks argues that the structure of the modern educational system nevertheless leaves young people ill-prepared to meet the challenges of the real world. In his *New York Times* editorial "It's Not about You," Brooks illustrates excessive supervision and uncontrolled individualistic rhetoric as opposing problems that complicate young people's entry into adult life, which then becomes less of a natural progression than an outright paradigm shift. Brooks's argument itself mimics the pattern of moving from "perversely structured" youth to "unprecedentedly wide open" adulthood: it operates on the basis of binary oppositions, raising familiar notions about how to live one's life and then dismantling them. Throughout, the piece relies less on factual evidence than on Brooks's own authoritative tone and skill in using rhetorical devices.

Connects article to personal experience to create an ethical appeal.

Provides brief overview of Brooks's argument. States Brooks's central claim.

In his editorial, Brooks objects to mainstream cultural messages that sell students on individuality, but bases his conclusions more on general observations than on specific facts. His argument is, in itself, a loose form of rhetorical analysis. It opens by telling us to "sample some of the commencement addresses being broadcast on C-Span these days," where we will find messages such as: "Follow *your* passion, chart *your* own course, march to the beat of *your* own drummer, follow *your* dreams and find *your*self." As though moving down a checklist, it then scrutinizes the problems with this rhetoric of "expressive individualism." Finally, it turns to Atul Gawande's "countercultural address" about working collectively, en route to confronting the

Transition sentence.

individualism of modern America. C-Span and Harvard Medical School aside, however, Brooks's argument is astonishingly short on external sources. He cites no basis for claims such as "this year's graduates are members of the most supervised generation in American history" or "most successful young people don't look inside and then plan a life," despite the fact that these claims are fundamental to his observations. Instead, his argument persuades through painting a picture — first of "limitless possibilities," then of young men and women called into action by problems that "summon their life" — and hoping that we will find the illustration familiar.

Comments critically on author's use of evidence.

Instead of relying on the logos of his argument, Brooks assumes that his position as a baby boomer and *New York Times* columnist will provide a sufficient enough ethos to validate his claims. If this impression of age and social status did not enter our minds along with his bespectacled portrait, Brooks reminds us of it. Although he refers to the theology of the baby boomer generation as the "worst of all," from the beginning of his editorial he allots himself as another "sensible middle-aged person" and distances himself from college graduates by referring to them as "they" or as "today's grads," contrasting with his more inclusive reader-directed "you." Combined with his repeated use of passive sentence constructions that create a confusing sense of responsibility ("The graduates are sent off into the world"; "graduates are told"), this sense of distance could be alienating to the younger audiences for which this editorial seems intended. Granted, Brooks compensates for it by embracing themes of "excellence" and "fulfillment" and by opening up his message to "most of us" in his final paragraph, but nevertheless his self-defined persona has its limitations. Besides dividing his audience, Brooks risks reminding us that, just as his observations belong only to this persona, his arguments apply only to a subset of American society. More specifically, they apply only to the well-educated middle to upper class who might be more likely to fret after the implications of "supervision" and

Analyzes author's intended audience.

"possibilities," or the readers who would be most likely to flip through the *New York Times*.

Brooks overcomes his limitations in logos and ethos through his piece's greatest strength: its style. He effectively frames cultural messages in binaries in order to reinforce the disconnect that exists between what students are told and what they will face as full members of society. Throughout his piece, he states one assumption after another, then prompts us to consider its opposite. "Serious things" immediately take the place of "rapturous talk"; "look[ing] inside" replaces "look[ing] outside"; "suppressing yourself" becomes an alternative to being "independent-minded." Brooks's argument is consumed with dichotomies, culminating with his statement "It's excellence, not happiness, that we admire most." He frames his ideas within a tight framework of repetition and parallel structure, creating muscular prose intended to engage his readers. His repeated use of the phrase "but, of course" serves as a metronomic reminder, at once echoing his earlier assertions and referring back to his air of authority.

Closely analyzes Brooks's style.

Brooks illustrates the power of words in swaying an audience, and in his final paragraph his argument shifts beyond commentary. Having tested our way of thinking, he now challenges us to change. His editorial closes with one final binary, the claim that "The purpose in life is not to find yourself" but "to lose yourself." And, although some of Brooks's previous binaries have clanged with oversimplification, this one rings truer. In accordance with his adoption of the general "you," his concluding message need not apply only to college graduates. By unfettering its restrictions at its climax, Brooks liberates his argument. After all, only we readers bear the responsibility of reflecting, of justifying, and ultimately of determining how to live our lives.

Analyzes author's conclusion.

WORK CITED

Brooks, David. "It's Not about You." *Everything's an Argument*, 7th ed., by Andrea A. Lunsford and John J. Ruszkiewicz, Bedford/St. Martin's, 2016, pp. 106-8. Reprint of "It's Not about You," *The New York Times*, 30 May 2011.

GUIDE to writing a rhetorical analysis

Finding a Topic

A rhetorical analysis is usually assigned: you're asked to show how an argument works and to assess its effectiveness. When you can choose your own subject for analysis, look for one or more of the following qualities:

- a complex verbal or visual argument that challenges you—or disturbs or pleases you
- a text that raises current or enduring issues of substance
- a text that you believe should be taken more seriously

Look for arguments to analyze in the editorial and op-ed pages of any newspaper, political magazines such as the *Nation* or *National Review*, Web sites of organizations and interest groups, political blogs such as *Huffington Post* or *Power Line*, corporate Web sites that post their TV ad spots, videos and statements posted to YouTube, and so on.

Researching Your Topic

Once you've got a text to analyze, find out all you can about it. Use library or Web resources to explore:

- who the author is and what his or her credentials are
- if the author is an institution, what it does, what its sources of funding are, who its members are, and so on
- who is publishing or sponsoring the piece, and what the organization typically publishes
- what the leanings or biases of the author and publisher might be
- what the context of the argument is—what preceded or provoked it and how others have responded to it

Formulating a Claim

Begin with a hypothesis. A full thesis might not become evident until you're well into your analysis, but your final thesis should reflect the complexity of the piece that you're studying. In developing a thesis, consider questions such as the following:

- How can I describe what this argument achieves?
- What is the purpose, and is it accomplished?
- What audiences does the argument address and what audiences does it ignore, and why?
- Which of its rhetorical features will likely influence readers most: ethos of the author? emotional appeals? logical progression? style?
- What aspects of the argument work better than others?
- How do the rhetorical elements interact?

Here's the hardest part for most writers of rhetorical analyses: whether you agree or disagree with an argument usually doesn't matter in a rhetorical analysis. You've got to stay out of the fray and pay attention only to how—and to how well—the argument works.

Examples of Possible Claims for a Rhetorical Analysis

- Some people admire the directness and confidence of Hillary Clinton; others are put off by her bland and sometimes tone-deaf rhetoric. A close look at several of her speeches and public appearances will illuminate both sides of this debate.
- Today's editorial in the *Daily Collegian* about campus crimes may scare first-year students, but its anecdotal reporting doesn't get down to hard numbers—and for a good reason. Those statistics don't back the position taken by the editors.
- The imageboard 4chan has been called an "Internet hate machine," yet others claim it as a great boon to creativity. A close analysis of its home-page can help to settle this debate.
- The original design of New York's Freedom Tower, with its torqued surfaces and evocative spire, made a stronger argument about American values than its replacement, a fortress-like skyscraper stripped of imagination and unable to make any statement except "I'm 1,776 feet tall."

Preparing a Proposal

If your instructor asks you to prepare a proposal for your rhetorical analysis, here's a format you might use:

- Provide a copy of the work you're analyzing, whether it's a print text, a photograph, a digital image, or a URL, for instance.

- Offer a working hypothesis or tentative thesis.
- Indicate which rhetorical components seem especially compelling and worthy of detailed study and any connections between elements. For example, does the piece seem to emphasize facts and logic so much that it becomes disconnected from potential audiences? If so, hint at that possibility in your proposal.
- Indicate background information you intend to research about the author, institution, and contexts (political, economic, social, and religious) of the argument.
- Define the audience you'd like to reach. If you're responding to an assignment, you may be writing primarily for a teacher and classmates. But they make up a complex audience in themselves. If you can do so within the spirit of the assignment, imagine that your analysis will be published in a local newspaper, Web site, or blog.
- Conclude by briefly discussing the key challenges you anticipate in preparing a rhetorical analysis.

Considering Format and Media

Your instructor may specify that you use a particular format and/or medium. If not, ask yourself these questions to help you make a good choice:

- What format is most appropriate for your rhetorical analysis? Does it call for an academic essay, a report, an infographic, a brochure, or something else?
- What medium is most appropriate for your analysis? Would it be best delivered orally to a live audience? Presented as an audio essay or podcast? Presented in print only or in print with illustrations?
- Will you need visuals, such as moving or still images, maps, graphs, charts — and what function will they play in your analysis? Make sure they are not just "added on" but are necessary components of the analysis.

Thinking about Organization

Your rhetorical analysis is likely to include the following:

- Facts about the text you're analyzing: Provide the author's name; the title or name of the work; its place of publication or its location; the date it was published or viewed.

- Contexts for the argument: Readers need to know where the text is coming from, to what it may be responding, in what controversies it might be embroiled, and so on. Don't assume that they can infer the important contextual elements.
- A synopsis of the text that you're analyzing: If you can't attach the original argument, you must summarize it in enough detail so that a reader can imagine it. Even if you attach a copy of the piece, the analysis should include a summary.
- Some claim about the work's rhetorical effectiveness: It might be a simple evaluative claim or something more complex. The claim can come early in the paper, or you might build up to it, providing the evidence that leads toward the conclusion you've reached.
- A detailed analysis of how the argument works: Although you'll probably analyze rhetorical components separately, don't let your analysis become a dull roster of emotional, ethical, and logical appeals. Your rhetorical analysis should be an argument itself that supports a claim; a simple list of rhetorical appeals won't make much of a point.
- Evidence for every part of the analysis.
- An assessment of alternative views and counterarguments to your own analysis.

Getting and Giving Response: Questions for Peer Response

If you have access to a writing center, discuss the text that you intend to analyze with a writing consultant before you write the paper. Try to find people who agree with the argument and others who disagree, and take notes on their observations. Your instructor may assign you to a peer group for the purpose of reading and responding to one another's drafts; if not, share your draft with someone on your own. You can use the following questions to evaluate a draft. If you're evaluating someone else's draft, be sure to illustrate your points with examples. Specific comments are always more helpful than general observations.

The Claim

- Does the claim address the rhetorical effectiveness of the argument itself rather than the opinion or position that it takes?
- Is the claim significant enough to interest readers?

- Does the claim indicate important relationships between various rhetorical components?
- Would the claim be one that the creator of the piece would regard as serious criticism?

Evidence for the Claim

- Is enough evidence given to support all your claims? What evidence do you still need?
- Is the evidence in support of the claim simply announced, or are its significance and appropriateness analyzed? Is a more detailed discussion needed?
- Do you use appropriate evidence, drawn from the argument itself or from other materials?
- Do you address objections readers might have to the claim, criteria, or evidence?
- What kinds of sources might you use to explain the context of the argument? Do you need to use sources to check factual claims made in the argument?
- Are all quotations introduced with appropriate signal phrases (for instance, "As Áida Álvarez points out"), and do they merge smoothly into your sentences?

Organization and Style

- How are the parts of the argument organized? How effective is this organization? Would some other structure work better?
- Will readers understand the relationships among the original text, your claims, your supporting reasons, and the evidence you've gathered (from the original text and any other sources you've used)? If not, what could be done to make those connections clearer? Are more transitional words and phrases needed? Would headings or graphic devices help?
- Are the transitions or links from point to point, sentence to sentence, and paragraph to paragraph clear and effective? If not, how could they be improved?
- Is the style suited to the subject and appropriate to your audience? Is it too formal? Too casual? Too technical? Too bland or boring?
- Which sentences seem particularly effective? Which ones seem weakest, and how could they be improved? Should some short sentences be combined, or should any long ones be separated into two or more sentences?

- How effective are the paragraphs? Do any seem too skimpy or too long? Do they break the analysis at strategic points?
- Which words or phrases seem particularly effective, accurate, and powerful? Do any seem dull, vague, unclear, or inappropriate for the audience or your purpose? Are definitions provided for technical or other terms that readers might not know?

Spelling, Punctuation, Mechanics, Documentation, and Format

- Check the spelling of the author's name, and make sure that the name of any institution involved with the work is correct. Note that the names of many corporations and institutions use distinctive spelling and punctuation.
- Get the title of the text you're analyzing right.
- Are there any errors in spelling, punctuation, capitalization, and the like?
- Does the assignment require a specific format? Check the original assignment sheet to be sure.

RESPOND •

Find an argument on the editorial page or op-ed page in a recent newspaper. Then analyze it rhetorically, using principles discussed in this chapter. Show how it succeeds, fails, or does something else entirely. Perhaps you can show that the author is unusually successful in connecting with readers but then has nothing to say. Or perhaps you discover that the strong logical appeal is undercut by a contradictory emotional argument. Be sure that the analysis includes a summary of the original essay and basic publication information about it (its author, place of publication, and publisher).

PART 2

WRITING arguments

7 Structuring Arguments

I get hives after eating ice cream.
My mouth swells up when I eat cheese.
Yogurt triggers my asthma.
↓
Dairy products make me sick.

Dairy products make me sick.
Ice cream is a dairy product.
↓
Ice cream makes me sick.

These two sets of statements illustrate the most basic ways in which Western culture structures logical arguments. The first piles up specific examples and draws a conclusion from them: that's **inductive reasoning** and structure. The second sets out a general principle (the major premise of a syllogism) and applies it to a specific case (the minor premise) in order to reach a conclusion: that's **deductive reasoning** and structure. In everyday reasoning, we often omit the middle statement, resulting in what Aristotle called an *enthymeme*: "Since dairy products make me sick, I better leave that ice cream alone." (See p. 65 for more on enthymemes.)

But the arguments you will write in college call for more than just the careful critical thinking offered within inductive and deductive reasoning. You will also need to define claims, explain the contexts in which you are offering them, consider counterarguments fairly and carefully, defend your assumptions, offer convincing evidence, appeal to particular audiences, and more. And you will have to do so using a clear structure that moves your argument forward. This chapter introduces you to three helpful ways to structure arguments. Feel free to borrow from all of them!

The Classical Oration

The authors of this book once examined a series of engineering reports and found that—to their great surprise—these reports were generally structured in ways similar to those used by Greek and Roman rhetors two thousand years ago. Thus, this ancient structuring system is alive and well in twenty-first-century culture. The classical oration has six parts, most of which will be familiar to you, despite their Latin names:

Exordium: You try to win the attention and goodwill of an audience while introducing a topic or problem.

Narratio: You present the facts of the case, explaining what happened when, who is involved, and so on. The _narratio_ puts an argument in context.

Partitio: You divide up the topic, explaining what the claim is, what the key issues are, and in what order they will be treated.

Confirmatio: You offer detailed support for the claim, using both logical reasoning and factual evidence.

Refutatio: You carefully consider and respond to opposing claims or evidence.

Peroratio: You summarize the case and move the audience to action.

danah boyd and Kate Crawford provide a *narratio* that establishes a context for their argument when they examine the motivations behind Big Data in *Six Provocations for Big Data*.

LINK TO P. 754

That's Life used with the permission of Mike Twohy and The Cartoonist Group.

This structure is powerful because it covers all the bases: readers or listeners want to know what your topic is, how you intend to cover it, and what evidence you have to offer. And you probably need a reminder to present a pleasing *ethos* when beginning a presentation and to conclude with enough *pathos* to win an audience over completely. Here, in outline form, is a five-part updated version of the classical pattern, which you may find useful on many occasions:

Introduction

- gains readers' interest and willingness to listen
- establishes your qualifications to write about your topic
- establishes some common ground with your audience
- demonstrates that you're fair and even-handed
- states your claim

Background

- presents information, including personal stories or anecdotes that are important to your argument

Lines of Argument

- presents good reasons, including logical and emotional appeals, in support of your claim

Alternative Arguments

- carefully considers alternative points of view and opposing arguments
- notes the advantages and disadvantages of these views
- explains why your view is preferable to others

Conclusion

- summarizes the argument
- elaborates on the implications of your claim
- makes clear what you want the audience to think or do
- reinforces your credibility and perhaps offers an emotional appeal

Not every piece of rhetoric, past or present, follows the structure of the oration or includes all its components. But you can identify some of its elements in successful arguments if you pay attention to their design. Here are the words of the 1776 Declaration of Independence:

> When in the Course of human events, it becomes necessary for one people to dissolve the political bands which have connected them with another, and to assume among the powers of the earth, the separate and equal station to which the Laws of Nature and of Nature's God entitle them, a decent respect to the opinions of mankind requires that they should declare the causes which impel them to the separation.
>
> We hold these truths to be self-evident, that all men are created equal, that they are endowed by their Creator with certain unalienable Rights, that among these are Life, Liberty, and the pursuit of Happiness—that to secure these rights, Governments are instituted among Men, deriving their just powers from the consent of the governed—That whenever any Form of Government becomes destructive to these ends, it is the Right of the People to alter or to abolish it and to institute new Government, laying its Foundation on such principles and organizing its powers in such form, as to them shall seem most likely to effect their Safety and Happiness. Prudence, indeed, will dictate that Governments long established should not be changed for light and transient causes; and accordingly all experience hath shewn that mankind are more disposed to suffer, while evils are sufferable, than to right themselves by abolishing the forms to which they are accustomed. But when a long train of abuses and usurpations, pursuing invariably the same Object evinces a design to reduce them under absolute Despotism, it is their right, it is their duty, to throw off such Government and to

Opens with a brief *exordium* explaining why the document is necessary, invoking a broad audience in acknowledging a need to show "a decent respect to the opinions of mankind." Important in this case, the lines that follow explain the assumptions on which the document rests.

A *narratio* follows, offering background on the situation: because the government of George III has become destructive, the framers of the Declaration are obligated to abolish their allegiance to him.

> provide new Guards for their future security.—Such has been the patient sufferance of these Colonies; and such is now the necessity which constrains them to alter their former Systems of Government. The history of the present King of Great Britain is a history of repeated injuries and usurpations, all having in direct object the establishment of an absolute Tyranny over these States. To prove this, let Facts be submitted to a candid world.
>
> —Declaration of Independence, July 4, 1776

Arguably, the *partitio* begins here, followed by the longest part of the document (not reprinted here), a *confirmatio* that lists the "long train of abuses and usurpations" by George III.

The authors might have structured this argument by beginning with the last two sentences of the excerpt and then listing the facts intended to prove the king's abuse and tyranny. But by choosing first to explain the purpose and "self-evident" assumptions behind their argument and only then moving on to demonstrate how these "truths" have been denied by the British, the authors forge an immediate connection with readers and build up to the memorable conclusion. The structure is both familiar and inventive—as your own use of key elements of the oration should be in the arguments you compose.

IN CONGRESS. JULY 4, 1776.

The unanimous Declaration of the thirteen united States of America.

The Declaration of Independence National Archives

Rogerian and Invitational Arguments

In trying to find an alternative to confrontational and angry arguments like those that so often erupt in legislative bodies around the world, scholars and teachers of rhetoric have adapted the nonconfrontational principles employed by psychologist Carl Rogers in personal therapy sessions. In simple terms, Rogers argued that people involved in disputes should not respond to each other until they could fully, fairly, and even sympathetically state the other person's position. Scholars of rhetoric Richard E. Young, Alton L. Becker, and Kenneth L. Pike developed a four-part structure that is now known as Rogerian argument:

1. **Introduction:** You describe an issue, a problem, or a conflict in terms rich enough to show that you fully understand and respect any alternative position or positions.
2. **Contexts:** You describe the contexts in which alternative positions may be valid.
3. **Writer's position:** You state your position on the issue and present the circumstances in which that opinion would be valid.
4. **Benefits to opponent:** You explain to opponents how they would benefit from adopting your position.

The key to Rogerian argumentation is a willingness to think about opposing positions and to describe them fairly. In a Rogerian structure, you have to acknowledge that alternatives to your claims exist and that they might be reasonable under certain circumstances. In tone, Rogerian arguments steer clear of heated and stereotypical language, emphasizing instead how all parties in a dispute might gain from working together.

In the same vein, feminist scholars Sonja Foss and Cindy Griffin have outlined a form of argument they label "invitational," one that begins with careful attention to and respect for the person or the audience you are in conversation with. Foss and Griffin show that such listening—in effect, walking in the other person's shoes—helps you see that person's points of view more clearly and thoroughly and thus offers a basis for moving together toward new understandings. The kind of argument they describe is what another rhetorician, Krista Ratcliffe, calls "rhetorical listening," which helps to establish productive connections between people and thus helps enable effective cross-cultural communications.

Invitational rhetoric has as its goal not winning over opponents but getting people and groups to work together and identify with each other;

it strives for connection, collaboration, and the mutually informed creation of knowledge. As feminist scholar Sally Miller Gearhart puts it, invitational argument offers a way to disagree without hurting one another, to disagree with respect. This kind of argument is especially important in a society that increasingly depends on successful collaboration to get things done. In college, you may have opportunities to practice invitational rhetoric in peer-review sessions, when each member of a group listens carefully in order to work through problems and issues. You may also practice invitational rhetoric looking at any contested issue from other people's points of view, taking them into account, and engaging them fairly and respectfully in your own argument. Students we know who are working in high-tech industries also tell us how much such arguments are valued, since they fuel innovation and "out of the box" thinking.

Invitational arguments, then, call up structures that more resemble good two-way conversations or free-ranging dialogues than straight-line marches from thesis to conclusion. Even conventional arguments benefit from invitational strategies by giving space early on to a full range of perspectives, making sure to present them thoroughly and clearly. Remember that in such arguments your goal is enhanced understanding so that you can open up a space for new perceptions and fresh ideas.

Consider how Frederick Douglass tried to broaden the outlook of his audiences when he delivered a Fourth of July oration in 1852. Most nineteenth-century Fourth of July speeches followed a pattern of praising the Revolutionary War heroes and emphasizing freedom, democracy, and justice. Douglass, a former slave, had that tradition in mind as he delivered his address, acknowledging the "great principles" that the "glorious anniversary" celebrates. But he also asked his (white) listeners to see the occasion from another point of view:

> Fellow-citizens, pardon me, allow me to ask, why am I called upon to speak here today? What have I, or those I represent, to do with your national independence? Are the great principles of political freedom and natural justice, embodied in the Declaration of Independence, extended to us? And am I, therefore, called upon to bring our humble offering to the national altar, and to confess the benefits and express devout gratitude for the blessings resulting from your independence to us? . . . I say it with a sad sense of the disparity between us. I am not included within the pale of this glorious anniversary! Your high independence only reveals the immeasurable distance between us. The blessings in which you, this day, rejoice, are not enjoyed in common.

Frederick Douglass © World History Archive/Alamy

> The rich inheritance of justice, liberty, prosperity and independence, bequeathed by your fathers, is shared by you, not by me. The sunlight that brought life and healing to you, has brought stripes and death to me. This Fourth of July is yours, not mine. You may rejoice, I must mourn.
>
> —Frederick Douglass, "What to the Slave Is the Fourth of July?"

Although his speech is in some ways confrontational, Douglass is also inviting his audience to see a version of reality that they could have discovered on their own had they dared to imagine the lives of African Americans living in the shadows of American liberty. Issuing that invitation, and highlighting its consequences, points a way forward in the conflict between slavery and freedom, black and white, oppression and justice, although response to Douglass's invitation was a long time in coming.

In May 2014, First Lady Michelle Obama used elements of invitational argument in delivering a speech to high school graduates from several high schools in Topeka, Kansas. Since the speech occurred on the sixtieth anniversary of the Supreme Court's decision to disallow "separate but equal" schools in the landmark *Brown v. Board of Education* case, which was initiated in Topeka, Mrs. Obama invited the audience to experience the ups and downs of students before and after the decision, putting themselves in the places of the young African Americans who, in 1954, desperately wanted the freedom to attend well-funded schools open to white students. So she tells the stories of some of these young people, inviting those there to walk a while in their shoes. And she concludes her speech with a call for understanding and cooperation:

> Every day, you have the same power to choose our better history—by opening your hearts and minds, by speaking up for what you know is right, by sharing the lessons of *Brown v. Board of Education*, the lessons you learned right here in Topeka, wherever you go for the rest of our lives. I know you all can do it. I am so proud of all of you, and I cannot wait to see everything you achieve in the years ahead.

Michelle Obama speaking in Topeka, Kansas AP Photo/Orlin Wagner

In this speech, Mrs. Obama did not castigate audience members for failing to live up to the ideals of *Brown v. Board of Education* (though she could have done so), nor does she dwell on current ills in Topeka. Rather, she invokes "our better history" and focuses on the ways those in Topeka have helped to write that history. She identifies with her audience and asks them to identify with her—and she aims to inspire the young graduates to follow her example.

The use of invitational argument and careful listening in contemporary political life are rare, but in spite of much evidence to the contrary (think of the repeatedly demonstrated effectiveness of political attack ads), the public claims to prefer nonpartisan and invitational rhetoric to one-on-one, winner-take-all battles, suggesting that such an approach strikes a chord in many people, especially in a world that is increasingly open to issues of diversity. The lesson to take from Rogerian or invitational argument is that it makes good sense in structuring your own arguments to learn opposing positions well enough to state them accurately and honestly, to strive to understand the points of view of your opponents, to acknowledge those views fairly in your own work, and to look for solutions that benefit as many people as possible.

RESPOND.

Choose a controversial topic that is frequently in the news, and decide how you might structure an argument on the subject, using the general principles of the classical oration. Then look at the same subject from a Rogerian or invitational perspective. How might your argument differ? Which approach would work better for your topic? For the audiences you might want to address?

Toulmin Argument

In *The Uses of Argument* (1958), British philosopher Stephen Toulmin presented structures to describe the way that ordinary people make reasonable arguments. Because Toulmin's system acknowledges the complications of life—situations when we qualify our thoughts with words such as *sometimes*, *often*, *presumably*, *unless*, and *almost*—his method isn't as airtight as formal logic that uses syllogisms (see p. 121 in this chapter and p. 63 in Chapter 4). But for that reason, Toulmin logic has become a powerful and, for the most part, practical tool for understanding and shaping arguments in the real world.

Toulmin argument will help you come up with and test ideas and also figure out what goes where in many kinds of arguments. Let's take a look at the basic elements of Toulmin's structure:

Claim	the argument you wish to prove
Qualifiers	any limits you place on your claim
Reason(s)/ Evidence	support for your claim
Warrants	underlying assumptions that support your claim
Backing	evidence for warrant

If you wanted to state the relationship between them in a sentence, you might say:

> **My claim is true, to a qualified degree, because of the following reasons, which make sense if you consider the warrant, backed by these additional reasons.**

These terms—claim, evidence, warrants, backing, and qualifiers—are the building blocks of the Toulmin argument structure. Let's take them one at a time.

Making Claims

Toulmin arguments begin with **claims**, debatable and controversial statements or assertions you hope to prove.

A claim answers the question *So what's your point?* or *Where do you stand on that?* Some writers might like to ignore these questions and avoid stating a position. But when you make a claim worth writing about, then it's worth standing up and owning it.

Is there a danger that you might oversimplify an issue by making too bold a claim? Of course. But making that sweeping claim is a logical first step toward eventually saying something more reasonable and subtle. Here are some fairly simple, undeveloped claims:

> **Congress should enact legislation that establishes a path to citizenship for illegal immigrants.**
>
> **It's time for the World Health Organization (WHO) to exert leadership in coordinating efforts to stem the Ebola epidemic in West Africa.**
>
> **NASA should launch a human expedition to Mars.**
>
> **Veganism is the most responsible choice of diet.**
>
> **Military insurance should not cover the cost of sex change surgery for service men and women.**

Good claims often spring from personal experiences. You may have relevant work or military or athletic experience—or you may know a lot about music, film, sustainable agriculture, social networking, inequities in government services—all fertile ground for authoritative, debatable, and personally relevant claims.

RESPOND •

Claims aren't always easy to find. Sometimes they're buried deep within an argument, and sometimes they're not present at all. An important skill in reading and writing arguments is the ability to identify claims, even when they aren't obvious.

Collect a sample of six to eight letters to the editor of a daily newspaper (or a similar number of argumentative postings from a political blog). Read each item, and then identify every claim that the writer makes. When you've compiled your list of claims, look carefully at the words that the writer or writers use when stating their positions. Is there a common vocabulary? Can you find words or phrases that signal an impending claim? Which of these seem most effective? Which ones seem least effective? Why?

Offering Evidence and Good Reasons

You can begin developing a claim by drawing up a list of reasons to support it or finding **evidence** that backs up the point.

Evidence and Reason(s) → So Claim

Academic arguments such as "Playing with Prejudice: The Prevalence and Consequences of Racial Stereotypes in Video Games" by Melinda C. R. Burgess et al. often closely follow the Toulmin structure, making sure that their claims are well supported.

LINK TO P. 551

One student writer wanted to gather good reasons in support of an assertion that his college campus needed more official spaces for parking bicycles. He did some research, gathering statistics about parking-space allocation, numbers of people using particular designated slots, and numbers of bicycles registered on campus. Before he went any further, however, he listed his primary reasons for wanting to increase bicycle parking:

- **Personal experience:** At least twice a week for two terms, he was unable to find a designated parking space for his bike.
- **Anecdotes:** Several of his friends told similar stories. One even sold her bike as a result.
- **Facts:** He found out that the ratio of car to bike parking spaces was 100 to 1, whereas the ratio of cars to bikes registered on campus was 25 to 1.
- **Authorities:** The campus police chief told the college newspaper that she believed a problem existed for students who tried to park bicycles legally.

On the basis of his preliminary listing of possible reasons in support of the claim, this student decided that his subject was worth more research. He was on the way to amassing a set of good reasons and evidence that were sufficient to support his claim.

In shaping your own arguments, try putting claims and reasons together early in the writing process to create enthymemes. Think of these enthymemes as test cases or even as topic sentences:

> Bicycle parking spaces should be expanded because the number of bikes on campus far exceeds the available spots.
>
> It's time to lower the driving age because I've been driving since I was fourteen and it hasn't hurt me.
>
> National legalization of marijuana is long overdue since it is already legal in over twenty states, has shown to be less harmful than alcohol, and provides effective relief from pain associated with cancer.
>
> Violent video games should be carefully evaluated and their use monitored by the industry, the government, and parents because these games cause addiction and psychological harm to players.

As you can see, attaching a reason to a claim often spells out the major terms of an argument.

Anticipate challenges to your claims. © 2009 Charles Barsotti/The New Yorker Collection/The Cartoon Bank

But your work is just beginning when you've put a claim together with its supporting reasons and evidence—because readers are certain to begin questioning your statement. They might ask whether the reasons and evidence that you're offering really do support the claim: should the driving age really be changed just because you've managed to drive since you were fourteen? They might ask pointed questions about your evidence: exactly how do you know that the number of bikes on campus far exceeds the number of spaces available? Eventually, you've got to address potential questions about the quality of your assumptions and the quality of your evidence. The connection between claim and reason(s) is a concern at the next level in Toulmin argument.

Determining Warrants

Crucial to Toulmin argument is appreciating that there must be a logical and persuasive connection between a claim and the reasons and data supporting it. Toulmin calls this connection the **warrant**. It answers the question *How exactly do I get from the data to the claim?* Like the warrant in legal situations (a search warrant, for example), a sound warrant in an argument gives you authority to proceed with your case.

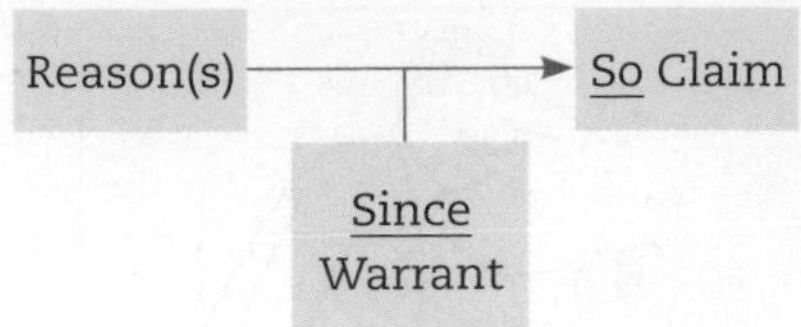

In "Little Girls or Little Women? The Disney Princess Effect," Stephanie Hanes interviews blogger and mom Mary Finucane, who believes that girls' princess obsession is harmful to their development as strong women. What warrants lie behind this claim?

LINK TO P. 509

The warrant tells readers what your (often unstated) assumptions are—for example, that any practice that causes serious disease should be banned by the government. If readers accept your warrant, you can then present specific evidence to develop your claim. But if readers dispute your warrant, you'll have to defend it before you can move on to the claim itself.

Stating warrants can be tricky because they can be phrased in various ways. What you're looking for is the general principle that enables you to justify the move from a reason to a specific claim—the bridge connecting them. The warrant is the assumption that makes the claim seem believable. It's often a value or principle that you share with your readers. Here's an easy example:

Don't eat that mushroom: it's poisonous.

The warrant supporting this enthymeme can be stated in several ways, always moving from the reason (*it's poisonous*) to the claim (*Don't eat that mushroom*):

Anything that is poisonous shouldn't be eaten.

If something is poisonous, it's dangerous to eat.

Here's the relationship, diagrammed:

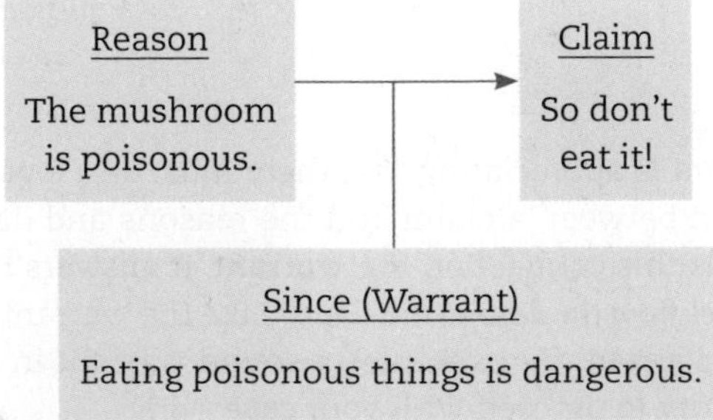

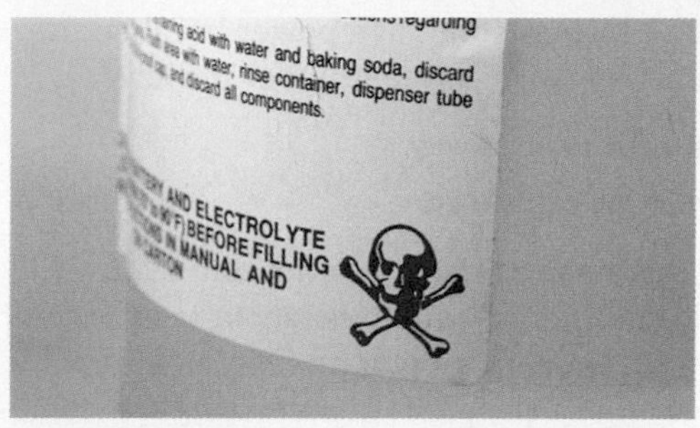

A simple icon—a skull and crossbones—can make a visual argument that implies a claim, a reason, and a warrant. PhotoLink/Getty Images

Perfectly obvious, you say? Exactly—and that's why the statement is so convincing. If the mushroom in question is a death cap or destroying angel (and you might still need expert testimony to prove that it is), the warrant does the rest of the work, making the claim that it supports seem logical and persuasive.

Let's look at a similar example, beginning with the argument in its basic form:

> **We'd better stop for gas because the gauge has been reading empty for more than thirty miles.**

In this case, you have evidence that is so clear (a gas gauge reading empty) that the reason for getting gas doesn't even have to be stated: the tank is almost empty. The warrant connecting the evidence to the claim is also pretty obvious:

> **If the fuel gauge of a car has been reading empty for more than thirty miles, then that car is about to run out of gas.**

Since most readers would accept this warrant as reasonable, they would also likely accept the statement the warrant supports.

Naturally, factual information might undermine the whole argument: the fuel gauge might be broken, or the driver might know that the car will go another fifty miles even though the fuel gauge reads empty. But in most cases, readers would accept the warrant.

Now let's consider how stating and then examining a warrant can help you determine the grounds on which you want to make a case. Here's a political enthymeme of a familiar sort:

> **Flat taxes are fairer than progressive taxes because they treat all tax-payers in the same way.**

Warrants that follow from this enthymeme have power because they appeal to a core American value—equal treatment under the law:

> **Treating people equitably is the American way.**
>
> **All people should be treated in the same way.**

You certainly could make an argument on these grounds. But stating the warrant should also raise a flag if you know anything about tax policy. If the principle is obvious and universal, then why do federal and many progressive state income taxes require people at higher levels of income to pay at higher tax rates than people at lower income levels? Could the warrant not be as universally popular as it seems at first glance? To explore the argument further, try stating the contrary claim and warrants:

> **Progressive taxes are fairer than flat taxes because people with more income can afford to pay more, benefit more from government, and shelter more of their income from taxes.**
>
> **People should be taxed according to their ability to pay.**
>
> **People who benefit more from government and can shelter more of their income from taxes should be taxed at higher rates.**

Now you see how different the assumptions behind opposing positions really are. If you decided to argue in favor of flat taxes, you'd be smart to recognize that some members of your audience might have fundamental reservations about your position. Or you might even decide to shift your entire argument to an alternative rationale for flat taxes:

> **Flat taxes are preferable to progressive taxes because they simplify the tax code and reduce the likelihood of fraud.**

Here, you have two stated reasons that are supported by two new warrants:

> **Taxes that simplify the tax code are desirable.**
>
> **Taxes that reduce the likelihood of fraud are preferable.**

Whenever possible, you'll choose your warrant knowing your audience, the context of your argument, and your own feelings.

Be careful, though, not to suggest that you'll appeal to any old warrant that works to your advantage. If readers suspect that your argument for progressive taxes really amounts to *I want to stick it to people who work harder than I*, your credibility may suffer a fatal blow.

Examples of Claims, Reasons, and Warrants

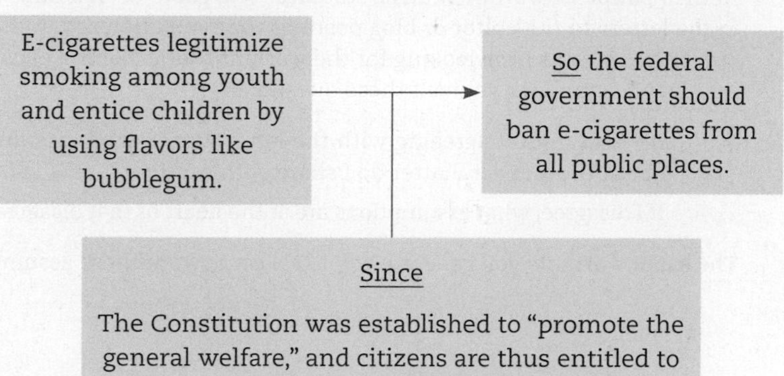

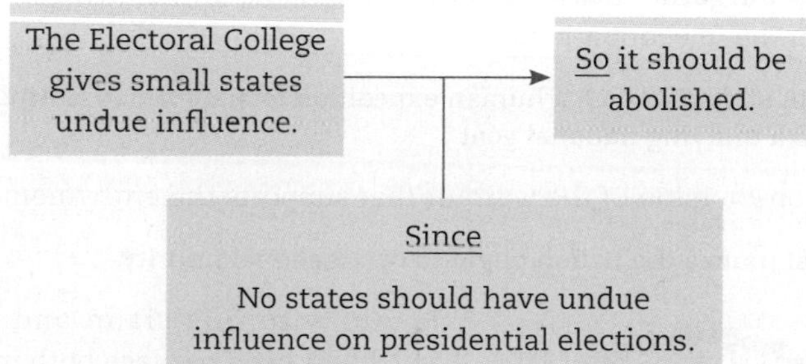

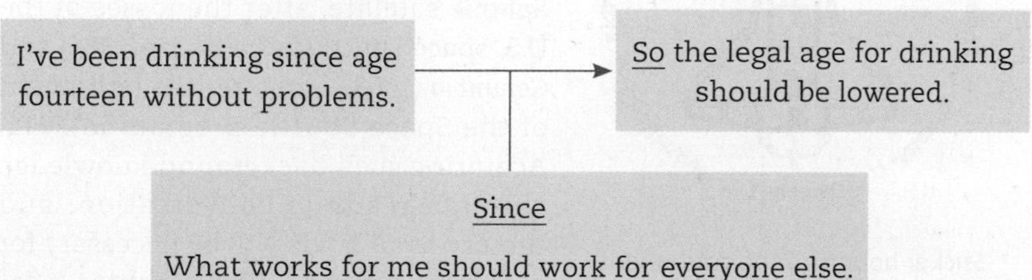

RESPOND.

At their simplest, warrants can be stated as "X is good" or "X is bad." Return to the letters to the editor or blog postings that you analyzed in the exercise on p. 131, this time looking for the warrant that is behind each claim. As a way to start, ask yourself these questions:

> If I find myself agreeing with the letter writer, what assumptions about the subject matter do I share with him/her?
>
> If I disagree, what assumptions are at the heart of that disagreement?

The list of warrants you generate will likely come from these assumptions.

Offering Evidence: Backing

The richest, most interesting part of a writer's work—backing—remains to be done after the argument has been outlined. Clearly stated claims and warrants show you how much evidence you will need. Take a look at this brief argument, which is both debatable and controversial, especially in tough economic times:

> **NASA should launch a human expedition to Mars because Americans need a unifying national goal.**

Here's one version of the warrant that supports the enthymeme:

> **What unifies the nation ought to be a national priority.**

Sticker honoring the retirement of the Space Shuttle program
© Steven Barrymore

To run with this claim and warrant, you'd first need to place both in context. Human space exploration has been debated with varying intensity following the 1957 launch of the Soviet Union's *Sputnik* satellite, after the losses of the U.S. space shuttles *Challenger* (1986) and *Columbia* (2003), and after the retirement of the Space Shuttle program in 2011. Acquiring such background knowledge through reading, conversation, and inquiry of all kinds will be necessary for making your case. (See Chapter 3 for more on gaining authority.)

There's no point in defending any claim until you've satisfied readers that questionable warrants on which the claim is based are defensible. In Toulmin argument, evidence you offer to support a warrant is called **backing**.

Warrant

What unifies the nation ought to be a national priority.

Backing

Americans want to be part of something bigger than themselves. (Emotional appeal as evidence)

In a country as diverse as the United States, common purposes and values help make the nation stronger. (Ethical appeal as evidence)

In the past, government investments such as the Hoover Dam and the *Apollo* moon program enabled many—though not all—Americans to work toward common goals. (Logical appeal as evidence)

In addition to evidence to support your warrant (backing), you'll need evidence to support your claim:

Argument in Brief (Enthymeme/Claim)

NASA should launch a human expedition to Mars because Americans now need a unifying national goal.

Evidence

The American people are politically divided along lines of race, ethnicity, religion, gender, and class. (Fact as evidence)

A common challenge or problem often unites people to accomplish great things. (Emotional appeal as evidence)

A successful Mars mission would require the cooperation of the entire nation—and generate tens of thousands of jobs. (Logical appeal as evidence)

A human expedition to Mars would be a valuable scientific project for the nation to pursue. (Appeal to values as evidence)

As these examples show, appeals to values and emotions can be just as appropriate as appeals to logic and facts, and all such claims will be stronger if a writer presents a convincing ethos. In most arguments, appeals work together rather than separately, reinforcing each other. (See Chapter 3 for more on ethos.)

Using Qualifiers

Experienced writers know that qualifying expressions make writing more precise and honest. Toulmin logic encourages you to acknowledge limitations to your argument through the effective use of **qualifiers**. You can save time if you qualify a claim early in the writing process. But you might not figure out how to limit a claim effectively until after you've explored your subject or discussed it with others.

Qualifiers

few	more or less	often
it is possible	in some cases	perhaps
rarely	many	under these conditions
it seems	typically	possibly
some	routinely	for the most part
it may be	most	if it were so
sometimes	one might argue	in general

Never assume that readers understand the limits you have in mind. Rather, spell them out as precisely as possible, as in the following examples:

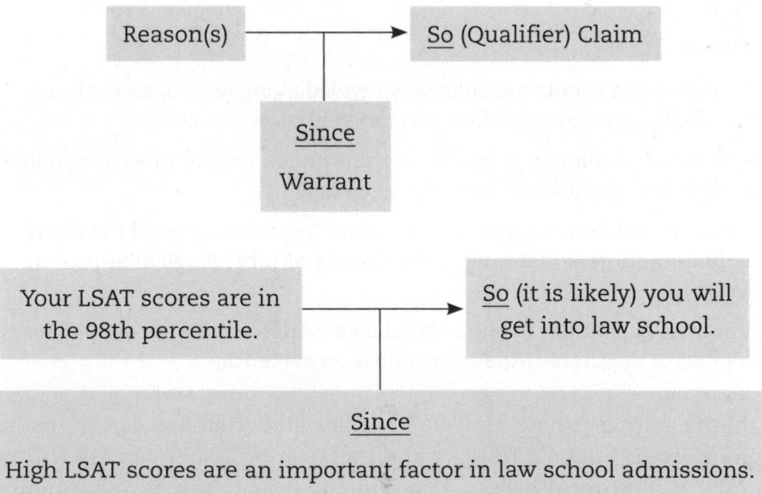

Unqualified Claim	**People who don't go to college earn less than those who do.**
Qualified Claim	***In most cases*, people who don't go to college earn less than those who do.**

Understanding Conditions of Rebuttal

In the Toulmin system, potential objections to an argument are called **conditions of rebuttal**. Understanding and reacting to these conditions are essential to support your own claims where they're weak and also to recognize and understand the reasonable objections of people who see the world differently. For example, you may be a big fan of the Public Broadcasting Service (PBS) and the National Endowment for the Arts (NEA) and prefer that federal tax dollars be spent on these programs. So you offer the following claim:

Claim	**The federal government should support the arts.**

You need reasons to support this thesis, so you decide to present the issue as a matter of values:

Argument in Brief	**The federal government should support the arts because it also supports the military.**

Now you've got an enthymeme and can test the warrant, or the premises of your claim:

Warrant	**If the federal government can support the military, then it can also support other programs.**

But the warrant seems frail: you can hear a voice over your shoulder saying, "In essence, you're saying that *Because we pay for a military, we should pay for everything!*" So you decide to revise your claim:

Revised Argument	**If the federal government can spend huge amounts of money on the military, then it can afford to spend moderate amounts on arts programs.**

Now you've got a new warrant, too:

Revised Warrant	**A country that can fund expensive programs can also afford less expensive programs.**

This is a premise that you can defend, since you believe strongly that the arts are just as essential as a strong military is to the well-being of the

The new NEA logo

country. Although the warrant now seems solid, you still have to offer strong grounds to support your specific and controversial claim. So you cite statistics from reputable sources, this time comparing the federal budgets for the military and the arts. You break them down in ways that readers can visualize, demonstrating that much less than a penny of every tax dollar goes to support the arts.

But then you hear those voices again, saying that the "common defense" is a federal mandate; the government is constitutionally obligated to support a military, and support for the arts is hardly in the same league! Looks like you need to add a paragraph explaining all the benefits the arts provide for very few dollars spent, and maybe you should suggest that such funding falls under the constitutional mandate to "promote the general welfare." Though not all readers will accept these grounds, they'll appreciate that you haven't ignored their point of view: you've gained credibility by anticipating a reasonable objection.

Dealing with conditions of rebuttal is an essential part of argument. But it's important to understand rebuttal as more than mere opposition. Anticipating objections broadens your horizons, makes you more open to alternative viewpoints, and helps you understand what you need to do to support your claim.

Within Toulmin argument, conditions of rebuttal remind us that we're part of global conversations: Internet newsgroups and blogs provide potent responses to positions offered by participants in discussions; instant messaging and social networking let you respond to and challenge others; links on Web sites form networks that are infinitely variable and open. In cyberspace, conditions of rebuttal are as close as your screen.

RESPOND.

Using an essay or a project you are composing, do a Toulmin analysis of the argument. When you're done, see which elements of the Toulmin scheme are represented. Are you short of evidence to support the warrant? Have you considered the conditions of rebuttal? Have you qualified your claim adequately? Next, write a brief revision plan: How will you buttress the argument in the places where it is weakest? What additional evidence will you offer for the warrant? How can you qualify your claim to meet the conditions of rebuttal? Then show your paper to a classmate and have him/her do a Toulmin analysis: a new reader will probably see your argument in different ways and suggest revisions that may not have occurred to you.

Outline of a Toulmin Argument

Consider the claim that was mentioned on p. 137:

Claim	The federal government should ban e-cigarettes.
Qualifier	The ban would be limited to public spaces.
Good Reasons	E-cigarettes have not been proven to be harmless. E-cigarettes legitimize smoking and also are aimed at recruiting teens and children with flavors like bubblegum and cotton candy.
Warrants	The Constitution promises to "promote the general welfare." Citizens are entitled to protection from harmful actions by others.
Backing	The United States is based on a political system that is supposed to serve the basic needs of its people, including their health.
Evidence	Analysis of advertising campaigns that reveal direct appeals to children Lawsuits recently won against e-cigarette companies, citing the link between e-cigarettes and a return to regular smoking Examples of bans on e-cigarettes already imposed in many public places
Authority	Cite the FDA and medical groups on effect of e-cigarette smoking.
Conditions of Rebuttal	E-cigarette smokers have rights, too. Smoking laws should be left to the states. Such a ban could not be enforced.
Responses	The ban applies to public places; smokers can smoke in private.

A Toulmin Analysis

You might wonder how Toulmin's method holds up when applied to an argument that is longer than a few sentences. Do such arguments really work the way that Toulmin predicts? In the following short argument, well-known linguist and author Deborah Tannen explores the consequences of a shift in the meaning of one crucial word: *compromise*. Tannen's essay, which originally appeared as a posting on Politico.com on June 15, 2011, offers a series of interrelated claims based on reasons, evidence, and warrants that culminate in the last sentence of the essay. She begins by showing that the word *compromise* is now rejected by both the political right and the political left and offers good reasons and evidence to support that claim. She then moves back to a time when "a compromise really was considered great," and offers three powerful pieces of evidence in support of that claim. The argument then comes back to the present, with a claim that the compromise and politeness of the nineteenth century have been replaced by "growing enmity." That claim is supported with reasoning and evidence that rest on an underlying warrant that "vituperation and seeing opponents as enemies is corrosive to the human spirit." The claims in the argument—that *compromise* has become a dirty word and that enmity and an adversarial spirit are on the rise—lead to Tannen's conclusion: rejecting compromise breaks the trust necessary for a democracy and thus undermines the very foundation of our society. While she does not use traditional qualifying words, she does say that the situation she describes is a "threat" to our nation, which qualifies the claim to some extent: the situation is not the "death" of our nation but rather a "threat." Tannen's annotated essay follows.

Photo: Stephen Voss, courtesy of Deborah Tannen

Why Is "Compromise" Now a Dirty Word?

DEBORAH TANNEN

When did the word "compromise" get compromised?

When did the negative connotations of "He was caught in a compromising position" or "She compromised her ethics" replace the positive connotations of "They reached a compromise"?

Contextual information leading up to initial claim

House Speaker John Boehner said it outright on *60 Minutes* last year. When talking about "compromise," Boehner said, "I reject the word."

"When you say the word 'compromise,'" he explained, ". . . a lot of Americans look up and go, 'Uh-oh, they're gonna sell me out.'" His position is common right now.

In the same spirit, Tony Perkins wrote in a recent CNN.com op-ed piece, "When it comes to conservative principles, compromise is the companion of losers."

The political right is particularly vehement when it comes to compromise. Conservatives are now strongly swayed by the tea party movement, whose clarion call is a refusal to compromise, regardless of the practical consequences.

But the rejection of compromise is more widespread than that. The left regularly savages President Barack Obama for compromising too soon, too much or on the wrong issues. Many who fervently sought universal health coverage, for example, could not celebrate its near accomplishment because the president gave up the public option.

Initial claim

The death of compromise has become a threat to our nation as we confront crucial issues such as the debt ceiling and that most basic of legislative responsibilities: a federal budget. At stake is the very meaning of what had once seemed unshakable: "the full faith and credit" of the U.S. government.

Reason

Evidence

Back when the powerful nineteenth-century senator Henry Clay was called "the great compromiser," achieving a compromise really was considered great. On three occasions, the Kentucky statesman helped the Senate preserve the Union by crafting compromises between the deadlocked slave-holding South and the Northern free states. In 1820, his Missouri Compromise stemmed the spread of slavery. In 1833, when the South was poised to defy federal tariff laws favored by the North and the federal government was about to authorize military action, Clay found a last-minute compromise. And his Compromise of 1850 averted civil war for at least a decade.

It was during an 1850 Senate debate that Clay stated his conviction: "I go for honorable compromise whenever it can be made." Something else he said then holds a key to how the dwindling respect for compromise is related to larger and more dangerous developments in our nation today.

Warrant

"All legislation, all government, all society," Clay said, "is formed upon the principle of mutual concession, politeness, comity, courtesy; upon these, everything is based."

Claim

Reason

Concession, politeness, comity, courtesy—none of these words could be uttered now with the assurance of listeners' approval. The word "comity" is rarely heard; "concession" sounds weak; "politeness" and "courtesy" sound quaint—much like the contemporary equivalent, "civility."

Evidence

That Clay lauded both compromise and civil discourse in the same speech reveals the link between, on the one hand, the word "compromise" falling into dispute, and, on the other, the glorification of aggression that I wrote about in my book, *The Argument Culture: Stopping America's War of Words.*

Claim

Today we have an increasing tendency to approach every task—and each other—in an ever more adversarial spirit. Nowhere is this more evident, or more destructive, than in the Senate.

Though the two-party system is oppositional by nature, there is plenty of evidence that a certain (yes) comity has been replaced by growing enmity. We don't have to look as far back as Clay for evidence. In 1996, for example, an unprecedented fourteen incumbent senators announced that they would not seek reelection. And many, in farewell essays, described an increase in vituperation and partisanship that made it impossible to do the work of the Senate.

Rebuttal

Evidence

"The bipartisanship that is so crucial to the operation of Congress," Howell Heflin of Alabama wrote, "especially the Senate, has been abandoned." J. James Exon of Nebraska described an "ever-increasing vicious polarization of the electorate" that had "all but swept aside the former preponderance of reasonable discussion."

Evidence

But this is not happening only in the Senate. There is a rising adversarial spirit among the people and the press. It isn't only the obvious invective on TV and radio. A newspaper story that criticizes its subject is praised as "tough"; one that refrains from criticism is scorned as a "puff piece."

Claim

The notion of "balance" today often leads to a search for the most extreme opposing views — so they can be presented as "both sides," leaving no forum for subtlety, multiple perspectives or the middle ground, where most people stand. Framing issues in this polarizing way reinforces the impression that Boehner voiced: that compromising is selling out.

Reason

Evidence

Being surrounded by vituperation and seeing opponents as enemies is corrosive to the human spirit. It's also dangerous to our democracy. The great anthropologist Margaret Mead explained this in a 1962 speech.

Warrant

Claim

"We are essentially a society which must be more committed to a two-party system than to either party," Mead said. "The only way you can have a two-party system is to belong to a party formally and to fight to the death . . ." not for your party to win but "for the right of the other party to be there too."

Reason

Today, this sounds almost as quaint as "comity" in political discourse.

Reason

Mead traced our two-party system to our unique revolution: "We didn't kill a king and we didn't execute a large number of our people, and we came into our own without the stained hands that have been associated with most revolutions."

With this noble heritage, Mead said, comes "the obligation to keep the kind of government we set up"—where members of each party may "disagree mightily" but still "trust in each other and trust in our political opponents."

Conclusion

Losing that trust, Mead concluded, undermines the foundation of our democracy. That trust is exactly what is threatened when the very notion of compromise is rejected.

What Toulmin Teaches

As Tannen's essay demonstrates, few arguments you read have perfectly sequenced claims or clear warrants, so you might not think of Toulmin's terms in building your own arguments. Once you're into your subject, it's easy to forget about qualifying a claim or finessing a warrant. But remembering what Toulmin teaches will always help you strengthen your arguments:

- Claims should be clear, reasonable, and carefully qualified.
- Claims should be supported with good reasons and evidence. Remember that a Toulmin structure provides the framework of an argument, which you fill out with all kinds of data, including facts, statistics, precedents, photographs, and even stories.
- Claims and reasons should be based on assumptions your audience will likely accept. Toulmin's focus on warrants can be confusing because it asks us to look at the assumptions that underlie our arguments—something many would rather not do. Toulmin pushes us to probe the values that support any argument and to think of how those values relate to particular audiences.
- Effective arguments respectfully anticipate objections readers might offer. Toulmin argument acknowledges that any claim can crumble under certain conditions, so it encourages a complex view that doesn't demand absolute or unqualified positions.

It takes considerable experience to write arguments that meet all these conditions. Using Toulmin's framework brings them into play automatically. If you learn it well enough, constructing good arguments can become a habit.

CULTURAL CONTEXTS FOR ARGUMENT

Organization

As you think about organizing your argument, remember that cultural factors are at work: patterns that you find persuasive are probably ones that are deeply embedded in your culture. In the United States, many people expect a writer to "get to the point" as directly as possible and to articulate that point efficiently and unambiguously. The organizational patterns favored by many in business hold similarities to the classical oration—a highly explicit pattern that leaves little or nothing unexplained—introduction and thesis, background, overview of the parts that follow, evidence, other viewpoints, and conclusion. If a piece of writing follows this pattern, American readers ordinarily find it "well organized."

So it's no surprise that student writers in the United States are expected to make their structures direct and their claims explicit, leaving little unspoken. Their claims usually appear early in an argument, often in the first paragraph.

But not all cultures take such an approach. Some expect any claim or thesis to be introduced subtly, indirectly, and perhaps at the end of a work, assuming that audiences will "read between the lines" to understand what's being said. Consequently, the preferred structure of arguments (and face-to-face negotiations, as well) may be elaborate, repetitive, and full of digressions. Those accustomed to such writing may find more direct Western styles overly simple, childish, or even rude.

When arguing across cultures, look for cues to determine how to structure your presentations effectively. Here are several points to consider:

- Do members of your audience tend to be very direct, saying explicitly what they mean? Or are they restrained, less likely to call a spade a spade? Consider adjusting your work to the expectations of the audience.
- Do members of your audience tend to respect authority and the opinions of groups? They may find blunt approaches disrespectful or contrary to their expectations.
- Consider when to state your thesis: At the beginning? At the end? Somewhere else? Not at all?
- Consider whether digressions are a good idea, a requirement, or an element to avoid.

8 Arguments of Fact

Left to right: Zoonar/N.Sorokin/age fotostock; Alfred Eisenstaedt/Getty Images; © David R. Frazier Photolibrary, Inc./Alamy

Many people believe that extensive use of the Internet, and especially social media, is harmful to memory and to learning, but recent research by scholars of literacy provides evidence suggesting that they are probably wrong.

In the past, female screen stars like Marilyn Monroe could be buxom and curvy, less concerned about their weight than actresses today. Or so the legend goes. But measuring the costumes worn by Monroe and other actresses reveals a different story.

When an instructor announces a tough new attendance policy for her course, a student objects that there is no evidence that students who regularly attend classes perform any better than those who do not. The instructor begs to differ.

Understanding Arguments of Fact

Factual arguments come in many varieties, but they all try to establish whether something is or is not so, answering questions such as *Is a historical legend true? Has a crime occurred?* or *Are the claims of a scientist accurate?* At first glance, you might object that these aren't arguments at all but just a matter of looking things up and then writing reports. And you'd be correct to an extent: people don't usually argue factual matters that are settled or undisputed (*The earth revolves around the sun*), that might be decided with simple research (*The Mendenhall Glacier has receded 1.75 miles since 1958*), or that are the equivalent of a rule (*One mile measures 5,280 feet*). Reporting facts, you might think, should be free of the friction of argument.

Yet facts become arguments whenever they're controversial on their own or challenge people's beliefs and lifestyles. Disagreements about childhood obesity, endangered species, or energy production ought to have a kind of clean, scientific logic to them. But that's rarely the case because the facts surrounding them must be interpreted. Those interpretations then determine what we feed children, where we can build a dam, or how we heat our homes. In other words, serious factual arguments almost always have consequences. *Can we rely on wind and solar power to solve our energy needs? Will the Social Security trust fund really go broke? Is it healthy to eat fatty foods?* People need well-reasoned factual arguments on subjects of this kind to make informed decisions. Such arguments educate the public.

For the same reason, we need arguments to challenge beliefs that are common in a society but held on the basis of inadequate or faulty information. Corrective arguments appear daily in the media, often based on studies written by scientists or researchers that the public would not encounter on their own. Many people, for example, believe that talking on a cell phone while driving is just like listening to the radio. But their intuition is not based on hard data: scientific studies show that using a cell phone in a car is comparable to driving under the influence of alcohol. That's a fact. As a result, fourteen states (and counting) have banned the use of handheld phones in cars.

Factual arguments also routinely address broad questions about how we understand the past. For example, are the accounts that we have of the American founding—or the Civil War, Reconstruction, or the heroics of the "Greatest Generation" in World War II—accurate? Or

do the "facts" that we teach today sometimes reflect the perspectives and prejudices of earlier times or ideologies? The telling of history is almost always controversial and rarely settled: the British and Americans will always tell different versions of what happened in North America in 1776.

The Internet puts mountains of information at our fingertips, but we need to be sure to confirm whether or not that information is fact, using what Howard Rheingold calls "crap detection," the ability to distinguish between accurate information and inaccurate information, misinformation, or disinformation. (For more on "crap detection," see Chapter 19, "Evaluating Sources.")

As you can see, arguments of fact do much of the heavy lifting in our world. They report on what has been recently discovered or explore the implications of that new information. They also add interest and complexity to our lives, taking what might seem simple and adding new dimensions to it. In many situations, they're the precursors to other forms of analysis, especially causal and proposal arguments. Before we can explore why things happen as they do or solve problems, we need to do our best to determine the facts.

RESPOND•

For each topic in the following list, decide whether the claim is worth arguing to a college audience, and explain why or why not.

Earthquakes are increasing in number and intensity.

Many people die annually of heart disease.

Fewer people would be obese if they followed the Paleo Diet.

Japan might have come to terms more readily in 1945 if the Allies in World War II hadn't demanded unconditional surrender.

Boys would do better in school if there were more men teaching in elementary and secondary classrooms.

The sharp drop in oil prices could lead drivers to go back to buying gas-guzzling trucks and SUVs.

There aren't enough high-paying jobs for college graduates these days.

Hydrogen may never be a viable alternative to fossil fuels because it takes too much energy to change hydrogen into a usable form.

Proponents of the Keystone Pipe Line have exaggerated the benefits it will bring to the American economy.

Characterizing Factual Arguments

Factual arguments are often motivated by simple human curiosity or suspicion: *Are people who earn college degrees happier than those who don't? If being fat is so unhealthy, why aren't mortality rates rising?* Researchers may notice a pattern that leads them to look more closely at some phenomenon or behavior, exploring questions such as *What if?* or *How come?* Or maybe a writer first notes something new or different or unexpected and wants to draw attention to that fact: *Contrary to expectations, suicide rates are much higher in rural areas than in urban ones.*

Such observations can lead quickly to **hypotheses**—that is, toward tentative and plausible statements of fact whose merits need to be examined more closely. *Maybe being a little overweight isn't as bad for people as we've been told? Maybe people in rural areas have less access to mental health services?* To support such hypotheses, writers then have to uncover evidence that reaches well beyond the casual observations that triggered an initial interest—like a news reporter motivated to see whether there's a verifiable story behind a source's tip.

For instance, the authors of *Freakonomics*, Stephen J. Dubner and Steven D. Levitt, were intrigued by the National Highway Traffic Safety Administration's claim that car seats for children were 54 percent effective in preventing deaths in auto crashes for children below the age of four. In a *New York Times* op-ed column entitled "The Seat-Belt Solution," they posed an important question about that factual claim:

> **But 54 percent effective compared with what? The answer, it turns out, is this: Compared with a child's riding completely unrestrained.**

Their initial question about that claim led them to a more focused inquiry, then to a database on auto crashes, and then to a surprising conclusion: for kids above age twenty-four months, those in car seats were statistically safer than those without any protection but weren't safer than those confined by seat belts (which are much simpler, cheaper, and more readily available devices). Looking at the statistics every which way, the authors wonder if children older than two years would be just as well off physically—and their parents less stressed and better off financially—if the government mandated seat belts rather than car seats for them.

What kinds of evidence typically appear in sound factual arguments? The simple answer might be "all sorts," but a case can be made that factual arguments try to rely more on "hard evidence" than do "constructed" arguments based on logic and reason (see Chapter 4). Even so, some pieces of evidence are harder than others!

Developing a Factual Argument

Entire Web sites are dedicated to finding and posting errors from news and political sources. Some, like Media Matters for America and Accuracy in Media, take overtly partisan stands. Here's a one-day sampling of headlines from Media Matters:

> **Hillary Clinton Overcompensates on Foreign Policy Because She's a Woman**
>
> **Fox Host Defends Calling Michelle Obama Fat**
>
> **Fox News Decries Granting Undocumented Children Their Right to Public Education**

And here's a listing from Accuracy in Media:

> **An Inside Look at How Democrats Rig the Election Game**
>
> **Why Obamacare Is Unfixable**
>
> **The American Left: Friends to Our Country's Enemies**

It would be hard to miss the blatant political agendas at work on these sites.

Other fact-checking organizations have better reputations when it comes to assessing the truths behind political claims and media presentations. Though both are also routinely charged with bias, Pulitzer Prize–winning PolitiFact.com and FactCheck.org at least make an effort to be fair-minded across a broader political spectrum. FactCheck, for example, provides a detailed analysis of the claims it investigates in relatively neutral and denotative language, and lists the sources its researchers used—just as if its writers were doing a research paper. At its best, FactCheck.org demonstrates what one valuable kind of factual argument can accomplish.

Any factual argument that you might compose—from how you state your claim to how you present evidence and the language you

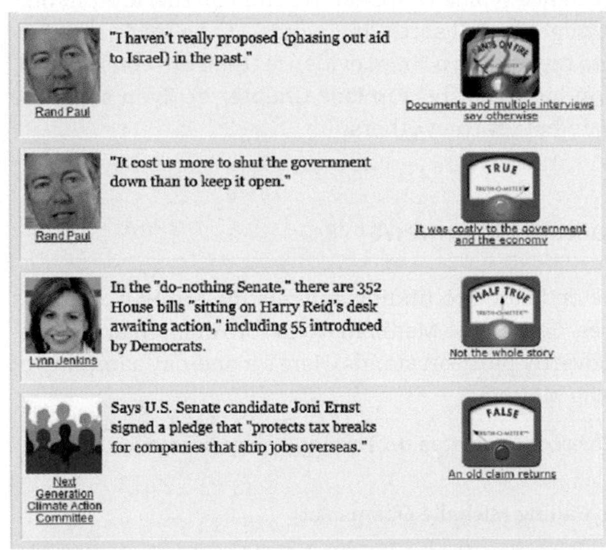

PolitiFact uses a meter to rate political claims from "True" to "Pants on Fire." Tampa Bay Times, all rights reserved

use—should be similarly shaped by the occasion for the argument and a desire to serve the audiences that you hope to reach. We can offer some general advice to help you get started.

RESPOND.

The Annenberg Public Policy Center at the University of Pennsylvania hosts FactCheck.org, a Web site dedicated to separating facts from opinion or falsehood in the area of politics. It claims to be politically neutral. Find a case that interests you, either a recent controversial item listed on its homepage or another from its archives. Carefully study the item. Pay attention to the devices that FactCheck uses to suggest or ensure objectivity and the way that it handles facts and statistics. Then offer your own brief *factual* argument about the site's objectivity.

Identifying an Issue

To offer a factual argument of your own, you need to identify an issue or problem that will interest you and potential readers. Look for situations or phenomena—local or national—that seem out of the ordinary in the expected order of things. For instance, you might notice that many people you know are deciding not to attend college. How widespread is this change, and who are the people making this choice?

Or follow up claims that strike you as at odds with the facts as you know them or believe them. Maybe you doubt explanations being offered for your favorite sport team's current slump or for the declining number of minority men in your college courses. Or you might give a local spin to factual questions that other people have already formulated on a national level. Do people in your town seem to be flocking to high-MPG vehicles or resisting bans on texting while driving or smoking in public places outdoors? You will likely write a better paper if you take on a factual question that genuinely interests you.

In fact, whole books are written when authors decide to pursue factual questions that intrigue them. But you want to be careful not to argue matters that pose no challenge for you or your audiences. You're not offering anything new if you just try to persuade readers that smoking is harmful to their well-being. So how about something fresh in the area of health?

Quick preliminary research and reading might allow you to move from an intuition to a hypothesis, that is, a tentative statement of your claim: *Having a dog is good for your health.* As noted earlier, factual

In their report "Student Veterans/Service Members' Engagement in College and University Life and Education," Young M. Kim and James S. Cole offer an argument of fact when they present data from the National Survey of Student Engagement.

LINK TO P. 688

arguments often provoke other types of analysis. In developing this claim, you'd need to explain what "good for your health" means, potentially an argument of definition. You'd also likely find yourself researching causes of the phenomenon if you can demonstrate that it is factual. As it turns out, your canine hypothesis would have merit if you defined "good for health" as "encouraging exercise." Here's the lead to a *New York Times* story reporting recent research:

> If you're looking for the latest in home exercise equipment, you may want to consider something with four legs and a wagging tail.
>
> Several studies now show that dogs can be powerful motivators to get people moving. Not only are dog owners more likely to take regular walks, but new research shows that dog walkers are more active overall than people who don't have dogs.
>
> One study even found that older people are more likely to take regular walks if the walking companion is canine rather than human.
>
> —Tara Parker-Pope, "Forget the Treadmill. Get a Dog," March 14, 2011

As always, there's another side to the story: what if people likely to get dogs are the very sort already inclined to be more physically active? You could explore that possibility as well (and researchers have) and then either modify your initial hypothesis or offer a new one. That's what hypotheses are for. They are works in progress.

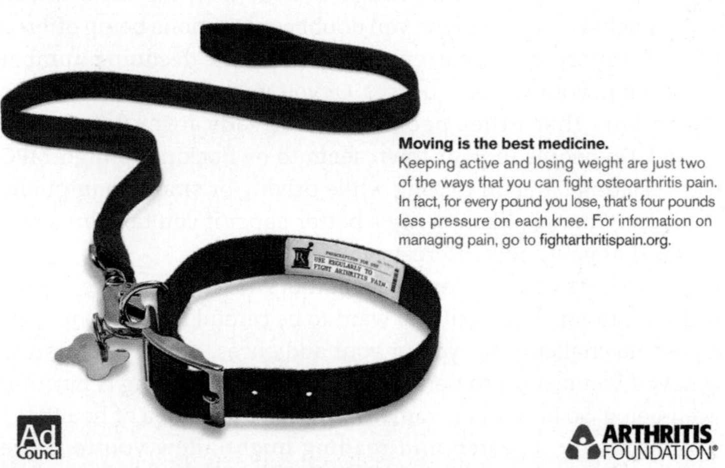

Here's an actual ad based on the claim that exercise (and dog ownership) is good for health.

RESPOND.

Working with a group of colleagues, generate a list of twenty favorite "mysteries" explored on TV shows, in blogs, or in tabloid newspapers. Here are three to get you started—the alien crash landing at Roswell, the existence of Atlantis, and the uses of Area 51. Then decide which—if any—of these puzzlers might be resolved or explained in a reasonable factual argument and which ones remain eternally mysterious and improbable. Why are people attracted to such topics? Would any of these items provide material for a noteworthy factual argument?

Researching Your Hypothesis

How and where you research your subject will depend, naturally, on your subject. You'll certainly want to review Chapter 18, "Finding Evidence," Chapter 19, "Evaluating Sources," and Chapter 20, "Using Sources," before constructing an argument of fact. Libraries and the Web will provide you with deep resources on almost every subject. Your task will typically be to separate the best sources from all the rest. The word *best* here has many connotations; some reputable sources may be too technical for your audiences; some accessible sources may be pitched too low or be too far removed from the actual facts.

Read the chapter from Scott L. Montgomery's book *Does Science Need a Global Language? English and the Future of Research.* What kinds of research does Montgomery use? Does the fact that much of the research is apparent only in his footnotes impact his argument?

LINK TO P. 577

You'll be making judgment calls like this routinely. But do use primary sources whenever you can. For example, when gathering a comment from a source on the Web, trace it whenever possible to its original site, and read the comment in its full context. When statistics are quoted, follow them back to the source that offered them first to be sure that they're recent and reputable. Instructors and librarians can help you appreciate the differences. Understand that even sources with pronounced biases can furnish useful information, provided that you know how to use them, take their limitations into account, and then share what you know about the sources with your readers.

Sometimes, you'll be able to do primary research on your own, especially when your subject is local and you have the resources to do it. Consider conducting a competent survey of campus opinions and attitudes, for example, or study budget documents (often public) to determine trends in faculty salaries, tuition, student fees, and so on. Primary research of this sort can be challenging because even the simplest surveys or polls have to be intelligently designed and executed in a way that samples a representative population (see Chapter 4). But the work could pay off in an argument that brings new information to readers.

Refining Your Claim

As you learn more about your subject, you might revise your hypothesis to reflect what you've discovered. In most cases, these revised hypotheses will grow increasingly complex and specific. Following are three versions of essentially the same claim, with each version offering more information to help readers judge its merit:

- Americans really did land on the moon, despite what some people think!
- Since 1969, when the *Eagle* supposedly landed on the moon, some people have been unjustifiably skeptical about the success of the United States' *Apollo* program.
- Despite plentiful hard evidence to the contrary—from *Saturn V* launches witnessed by thousands to actual moon rocks tested by independent labs worldwide—some people persist in believing falsely that NASA's moon landings were actually filmed on deserts in the American Southwest as part of a massive propaganda fraud.

'...And, of course, there are the conspiracy theorists who say that it was all a big hoax and I didn't jump over it at all.'

The additional details about the subject might also suggest new ways to develop and support it. For example, conspiracy theorists claim that the absence of visible stars in photographs of the moon landing is evidence that it was staged, but photographers know that the camera exposure needed to capture the foreground—astronauts in their bright space suits—would have made the stars in the background too dim to see. That's a key bit of evidence for this argument.

As you advance in your research, your thesis will likely pick up even more qualifying words and expressions, which help you to make reasonable claims. Qualifiers—words and phrases such as *some, most, few, for most people, for a few users, under specific conditions, usually, occasionally, seldom,* and so on—will be among your most valuable tools in a factual argument. (See p. 140 in Chapter 7 for more on qualifiers.)

Sometimes it is important to set your factual claim into a context that helps explain it to others who may find it hard to accept. You might have to concede some ground initially in order to see the broader picture. For instance, professor of English Vincent Carretta anticipated strong objections after he uncovered evidence that Olaudah Equiano—the author of *The Interesting Narrative* (1789), a much-cited autobiographical account of his Middle Passage voyage and subsequent life as a slave—may actually have been born in South Carolina and not in western Africa. Speaking to the *Chronicle of Higher Education* about why Equiano may have fabricated his African origins to serve a larger cause, Carretta explains:

> **"Whether [Equiano] invented his African birth or not, he knew that what that movement needed was a first-person account. And because they were going after the slave trade, it had to be an account of someone who had been born in Africa and was brought across the Middle Passage. An African American voice wouldn't have done it."**
>
> **—Jennifer Howard, "Unraveling the Narrative"**

Carretta asks readers to appreciate that the new facts that he has discovered about *The Interesting Narrative* do not undermine the work's historical significance. If anything, his research has added new dimensions to its meaning and interpretation.

Deciding Which Evidence to Use

In this chapter, we've blurred the distinction between factual arguments for scientific and technical audiences and those for the general public (in magazines, blogs, social media sites, television documentaries, and so on). In the former kind of arguments, readers will expect specific types of evidence arranged in a formulaic way. Such reports may include a hypothesis, a review of existing research on the subject, a description of methods, a presentation of results, and finally a formal discussion of the findings. If you are thinking "lab report," you are already familiar with an academic form of a factual argument with precise standards for evidence.

Less scientific factual arguments—claims about our society, institutions, behaviors, habits, and so on—are seldom so systematic, and they may draw on evidence from a great many different media. For instance, you might need to review old newspapers, scan videos, study statistics on government Web sites, read transcripts of congressional hearings, record the words of eyewitnesses to an event, glean information by following experts on Twitter, and so on. Very often, you will assemble your arguments from material found in credible, though not always concurring, authorities and resources—drawing upon the factual findings of scientists and scholars, but perhaps using their original insights in novel ways.

For example, you might be intrigued by a comprehensive report from the Kaiser Family Foundation (2010) providing the results of a study of more than 2,000 eight- to eighteen-year-old American children:

> **The study found that the average time spent reading books for pleasure in a typical day rose from 21 minutes in 1999 to 23 minutes in 2004, and finally to 25 minutes in 2010. The rise of screen-based media has not melted children's brains, despite ardent warnings otherwise: "It does not appear that time spent using screen media (TV, video games and computers) displaces time spent with print media," the report stated. Teens are not only reading more books, they're involved in communities of like-minded book lovers.**
>
> **—Hannah Withers and Lauren Ross, "Young People Are Reading More Than You"**

Reading about these results, however, may raise some new questions for you: Is twenty-five minutes of reading a day really something to be happy about? What is the quality of what these young people are reading? Such questions might lead you to do a new study that could challenge the conclusion of the earlier research by bringing fresh facts to the table.

Often, you may have only a limited number of words or pages in which to make a factual argument. What do you do then? You present your best evidence as powerfully as possible. But that's not difficult. You can make a persuasive factual case with just a few examples: three or four often suffice to make a point. Indeed, going on too long or presenting even good data in ways that make it seem uninteresting or pointless can undermine a claim.

Presenting Your Evidence

In *Hard Times* (1854), British author Charles Dickens poked fun at a pedagogue he named Thomas Gradgrind, who preferred hard facts before all things human or humane. When poor Sissy Jupe (called "girl number twenty" in his awful classroom) is unable at his command to define *horse*, Gradgrind turns to his star pupil:

> "Bitzer," said Thomas Gradgrind. "Your definition of a horse."
>
> "Quadruped. Graminivorous. Forty teeth, namely twenty-four grinders, four eyeteeth, and twelve incisive. Sheds coat in the spring; in marshy countries, sheds hoofs, too. Hoofs hard, but requiring to be shod with iron. Age known by marks in mouth." Thus (and much more) Bitzer.
>
> "Now girl number twenty," said Mr. Gradgrind. "You know what a horse is."
>
> —Charles Dickens, *Hard Times*

But does Bitzer? Rattling off facts about a subject isn't quite the same thing as knowing it, especially when your goal is, as it is in an argument of fact, to educate and persuade audiences. So you must take care how you present your evidence.

Factual arguments, like any others, take many forms. They can be as simple and pithy as a letter to the editor (or Bitzer's definition of a horse) or as comprehensive and formal as a senior thesis or even a dissertation. Such a thesis might have just two or three readers mainly interested in the facts you are presenting and the competence of your work. So your presentation can be lean and relatively simple.

But to earn the attention of readers in some more public forum, you may need to work harder to be persuasive. For instance, Pew Research Center's May 2014 formal report, *Young Adults, Student Debt, and Economic Well-Being*, which spends time introducing its authors and establishing their expertise, is twenty-three pages long, cites a dozen sources, and contains sixteen figures and tables. Like many such studies, it also includes a foreword, an overview, and a detailed table of contents. All these elements help readers find the facts they need while also establishing the ethos of the work, making it seem serious, credible, well conceived, and worth reading.

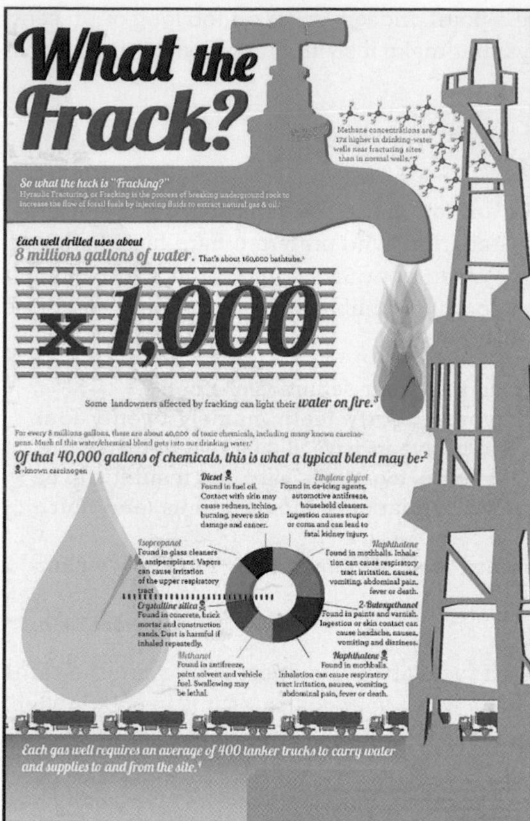

"What the Frack?" uses images to present its case against fracking.

For an example of how to use design and visuals in a factual argument, see the annotated metadata screenshot in "What Your Email Metadata Told the NSA about You" by Rebecca Greenfield. How does design reinforce the argument?

LINK TO P. 746

Considering Design and Visuals

When you prepare a factual argument, consider how you can present your evidence most effectively. Precisely because factual arguments often rely on evidence that can be measured, computed, or illustrated, they benefit from thoughtful, even artful presentation of data. If you have lots of examples, you might arrange them in a list (bulleted or otherwise) and keep the language in each item roughly parallel. If you have an argument that can be translated into a table, chart, or graph (see Chapter 14), try it. And if there's a more dramatic medium for your factual argument—a Prezi slide show, a multimedia mashup, a documentary video posted via a social network—experiment with it, checking to be sure it would satisfy the assignment.

Infographics like this one turn facts and data into arguments. USAID

Images and photos—from technical illustrations to imaginative re-creations—have the power to document what readers might otherwise have to imagine, whether actual conditions of drought, poverty, or a disaster like devastating typhoon Haiyan that displaced over 4 million people in the Philippines in 2013, or the dimensions of the Roman forum as it existed in the time of Julius Caesar. Readers today expect the arguments they read to include visual elements, and there's little reason not to offer this assistance if you have the technical skills to create them.

Consider the rapid development of the genre known as infographics—basically data presented in bold visual form. These items can be humorous and creative, but many, such as "Learning Out of Poverty" on the preceding page, make powerful factual arguments even when they leave it to viewers to draw their own conclusions. Just search "infographics" on the Web to find many examples.

GUIDE to writing an argument of fact

Finding a Topic

You're entering an argument of fact when you:

- make a claim about fact or existence that's controversial or surprising: *Climate change is threatening species in all regions by extending the range of non-native plants and animals.*
- correct an error of fact: *The overall abortion rate is not increasing in the United States, though rates are increasing in some states.*
- challenge societal myths: *Many Mexicans fought alongside Anglos in battles that won Texas its independence from Mexico.*
- wish to discover the state of knowledge about a subject or examine a range of perspectives and points of view: *The rationales of parents who homeschool their children reveal some surprising differences.*

Researching Your Topic

Use both a library and the Web to locate the information you need. A research librarian is often a valuable resource, as are experts or eyewitnesses. Begin research by consulting the following types of sources:

- scholarly books on your subject
- newspapers, magazines, reviews, and journals (online and print)
- online databases
- government documents and reports
- Web sites, blogs, social networking sites, and listservs or newsgroups
- experts in the field, some of whom might be right on your campus

Do field research if appropriate—a survey, a poll, or systematic observation. Or invite people with a stake in the subject to present their interpretations of the facts. Evaluate all sources carefully, making sure that each is authoritative and credible.

Formulating a Hypothesis

Don't rush into a thesis. Instead, begin with a hypothesis that expresses your beliefs at the beginning of the project but that may change as you learn more. It's OK to start with a question to which you don't have an answer or with a broad, general interest in a subject:

- **Question:** Have higher admissions standards at BSU reduced the numbers of entering first-year students from small, rural high schools?
- **Hypothesis:** Higher admissions standards at BSU are reducing the number of students admitted from rural high schools, which tend to be smaller and less well-funded than those in suburban and urban areas.
- **Question:** Have music sites like Pandora and Spotify reduced the amount of illegal downloading of music?
- **Hypothesis:** Services like Pandora and Spotify may have done more than lawsuits by record companies to discourage illegal downloads of music.
- **Question:** How dangerous is nuclear energy, really?
- **Hypothesis:** The danger posed by nuclear power plants is far less than that attributable to other viable energy sources.
- **Question:** Why can't politicians and citizens agree about the threat posed by the huge federal deficit?
- **Hypothesis:** People with different points of view read different threats into the budget numbers and so react differently.

Examples of Arguable Factual Claims

- A campus survey that shows that far more students have read *Harry Potter and the Prisoner of Azkaban* than *Hamlet* indicates that our current core curriculum lacks depth.
- Evidence suggests that the European conquest of the Americas may have had more to do with infectious diseases than any superiority in technology or weaponry.
- In the long run, dieting may be more harmful than moderate overeating.

Preparing a Proposal

If your instructor asks you to prepare a proposal for your project, here's a format that may help:

State your thesis or hypothesis completely. If you are having trouble doing so, try outlining it in Toulmin terms:

Claim:

Reason(s):

Warrant(s):

Alternatively, you might describe the complications of a factual issue you hope to explore in your project, with the thesis perhaps coming later.

- **Explain why the issue you're examining is important, and provide the context for raising the issue. Are you introducing new information, making available information better known, correcting what has been reported incorrectly, or complicating what has been understood more simply?**
- **Identify and describe those readers you most hope to reach with your argument. Why is this group of readers most appropriate for your project? What are their interests in the subject? How might you involve them in the paper?**
- **Discuss the kinds of evidence you expect to use in the project and the research the paper will require.**
- **Briefly discuss the key challenges you anticipate in preparing your argument.**

Considering Format and Media

Your instructor may specify that you use a particular format and/or medium. If not, ask yourself these questions to help you make a good choice:

- What format is most appropriate for your argument of fact? Does it call for an academic essay, a report, an infographic, a brochure, or something else?
- What medium is most appropriate for your argument? Would it be best delivered orally to a live audience? Presented as an audio essay or podcast? Presented in print only or in print with illustrations?

- Will you need visuals, such as moving or still images, maps, graphs, charts—and what function will they play in your argument? Make sure they are not just "added on" but are necessary components of the argument.

Thinking about Organization

The simplest structure for a factual argument is to make a claim and then prove it. But even a basic approach needs an introductory section that provides a context for the claim and a concluding section that assesses the implications of the argument. A factual argument that corrects an error or provides an alternative view of some familiar concept or historical event will also need a section early on explaining what the error or the common belief is. Be sure your opening section answers the *who*, *what*, *where*, *when*, *how*, and (maybe) *why* questions that readers will bring to the case.

Factual arguments offered in some academic fields follow formulas and templates. A format favored in the hard sciences and also in the social and behavioral sciences is known by its acronym, IMRAD, which stands for Introduction, Methods, Research, and Discussion. Another typical format calls for an abstract, a review of literature, a discussion of method, an analysis, and a references list. When you have flexibility in the structure of your argument, it makes sense to lead with a striking example to interest readers in your subject and then to conclude with your strongest evidence. Pay particular attention to transitions between key points.

If you are defending a specific claim, anticipate the ways people with different points of view might respond to your argument. Consider how to address such differences respectfully in the body of your argument. But don't let a factual argument with a persuasive thesis end with concessions or refutations, especially in pieces for the general public. Such a strategy leaves readers thinking about problems with your claim at precisely the point when they should be impressed by its strengths. On the other hand, if your factual argument becomes exploratory, you may find yourself simply presenting a range of positions.

Getting and Giving Response: Questions for Peer Response

Your instructor may assign you to a group for the purpose of reading and responding to each other's drafts. If not, ask for responses from serious readers or consultants at a writing center. Use the following questions to evaluate a colleague's draft. Since specific comments help more than general observations, be sure to illustrate your comments with examples. Some of the questions below assume a conventional, thesis-driven project, but more exploratory or invitational arguments of fact also need to be clearly phrased, organized, and supported with evidence.

The Claim

- Does the claim clearly raise a serious and arguable factual issue?
- Is the claim as clear and specific as possible?
- Is the claim qualified? If so, how?

Evidence for the Claim

- Is the evidence provided enough to persuade readers to believe your claim? If not, what additional evidence would help? Does any of the evidence seem inappropriate or ineffective? Why?
- Is the evidence in support of the claim simply announced, or do you explain its significance and appropriateness? Is more discussion needed?
- Are readers' potential objections to the claim or evidence addressed adequately? Are alternative positions understood thoroughly and presented fairly?
- What kinds of sources are cited? How credible and persuasive will they be to readers? What other kinds of sources might work better?
- Are all quotations introduced with appropriate signal phrases (such as "As Tyson argues, . . .") and blended smoothly into the writer's sentences?
- Are all visuals titled and labeled appropriately? Have you introduced them and commented on their significance?

Organization and Style

- How are the parts of the argument organized? Is this organization effective?
- Will readers understand the relationships among the claims, supporting reasons, warrants, and evidence? If not, how might those connections be clearer? Is the function of every visual clear? Are more transitions needed? Would headings or graphic devices help?
- Are the transitions or links from point to point, sentence to sentence, and paragraph to paragraph clear and effective? If not, how could they be improved?

- Are all visuals carefully integrated into the text? Is each visual introduced and commented on to point out its significance? Is each visual labeled as a figure or a table and given a caption as well as a citation?
- Is the style suited to the subject? Is it too formal, casual, or technical? Can it be improved?
- Which sentences seem effective? Which ones seem weaker, and how could they be improved? Should short sentences be combined, and any longer ones be broken up?
- How effective are the paragraphs? Too short or too long? How can they be improved?
- Which words or phrases seem effective? Do any seem vague or inappropriate for the audience or the writer's purpose? Are technical or unfamiliar terms defined?

Spelling, Punctuation, Mechanics, Documentation, and Format

- Are there any errors in spelling, punctuation, capitalization, and the like?
- Is an appropriate and consistent style of documentation used for parenthetical citations and the list of works cited or references? (See Chapter 22.)
- Does the paper or project follow an appropriate format? Is it appropriately designed and attractively presented? How could it be improved?

PROJECTS

1. Turn a database of information you find in the library or online into a traditional argument or, alternatively, into an infographic that offers a variety of potential claims. FedStats, a government Web site, provides endless data, but so can the sports or financial sections of a newspaper. Once you find a rich field of study, examine the data and draw your ideas from it, perhaps amplifying these ideas with material from other related sources of information. If you decide to create an infographic, you'll find good examples at VizWorld or Cool Infographics online. Software tools you can use to create infographics include Piktochart and Google Public Data. Have fun.
2. Write an argument about one factual matter you are confident—based on personal experience or your state of knowledge—that most people get wrong, time and again. Use your expertise to correct this false impression.
3. Tough economic and political times sometimes reinforce and sometimes undermine cultural myths. With your classmates, generate a list of common beliefs about education, employment, family life, marriage, social progress, technology, and so on that seem to be under unusual scrutiny today. *Does it still pay to invest in higher education? Do two-parent households matter as much as they used to? Can children today expect to do better than their parents? Is a home still a good investment?* Pick one area to explore in depth, narrow the topic as much as you can, and then gather facts that inform it by doing research, perhaps working collaboratively to expand your findings. Turn your investigation into a factual argument.
4. Since critic and writer Nicholas Carr first asked "Is Google Making Us Stupid?" many have answered with a resounding "yes," arguing that extensive time online is reducing attention spans and leaving readers less critical than ever. Others have disagreed, saying that new technologies are doing just the opposite—expanding our brain power. Do some research on this controversy, on the Web or in the library, and consult with a wide range of people interested in the subject, perhaps gathering them together for a discussion or panel discussion. Then offer a factual argument based on what you uncover, reflecting the range of perspectives and opinions you have encountered.

Readers will certainly notice the title.

Why You Should Fear Your Toaster More Than Nuclear Power

TAYLOR PEARSON

A recent nuclear disaster in Japan provides a challenging context for Pearson's claim: we need nuclear energy.

The first-person plural point of view (*we*) helps Pearson to connect with his audience.

For the past month or so, headlines everywhere have been warning us of the horrible crises caused by the damaged Japanese nuclear reactors. Titles like "Japan Nuclear Disaster Tops Scale" have fueled a new wave of protests against anything nuclear—namely, the construction of new nuclear plants or even the continued operation of existing plants. However, all this reignited fear of nuclear energy is nothing more than media sensationalism. We need nuclear energy. It's clean, it's efficient, it's economic, and it's probably the only thing that will enable us to quickly phase out fossil fuels.

Death Toll

First, let's address what is probably everyone's main concern about nuclear energy: the threat it poses to us and the likelihood of a nuclear power plant killing large numbers of people. The actual number of deaths caused by nuclear power plant accidents, even in worst-case scenarios, have been few. Take the Chernobyl accident—the worst and most lethal nuclear incident to date. As tragic

---

Taylor Pearson wrote "Why You Should Fear Your Toaster More Than Nuclear Power" while he was a sophomore at the University of Texas at Austin. The assignment asked for a public argument—one good enough to attract readers who could put it down if they lost interest. In other words, a purely academic argument wouldn't work. So Pearson allows himself to exercise his sense of humor. Nor did the paper have to be formally documented. However, Pearson was expected to identify crucial sources the way writers do in magazines and newspapers. The paper provides an example of a factual argument with a clear thesis: "We need nuclear energy."

as it was, the incident has killed only eighty-two people. More specifically, according to a 2005 release by the World Health Organization, thirty-two were killed in the effort to put out the fires caused by the meltdown and thirty-eight died within months of the accident as a result of acute radiation poisoning. Since the accident occurred in 1986, an additional twelve people have died from the radiation they were exposed to during the accident. Almost all deaths were highly exposed rescue workers. Other nuclear power accidents have been few and never resulted in more than ten deaths per incident. Still think that's too dangerous? To provide some perspective, let's consider an innocuous household appliance, the toaster: over three thousand people died from toaster accidents the first year the appliances were produced and sold in the 1920s, and they still cause around fifty accident-related deaths every year in the United States. So your toaster is far more likely to kill you than any nuclear power plant and subsequently give you a painfully embarrassing epitaph.

Pearson deflates fears by putting deaths caused by nuclear plants in perspective.

In fact, in comparison to the other major means of energy production in the United States, nuclear power is remarkably safe. According to the U.S. Department of Labor, coal mining currently causes about sixty-five deaths and eleven thousand injuries per year, while oil drilling is responsible for approximately 125 deaths per year in the United States. Annual death tolls fluctuate depending upon the demand for these resources and the subsequent drilling or mining required, but the human cost is still exponentially more than that of nuclear energy. However, in the decades that nuclear power has been used in the United States, there have been zero deaths caused by nuclear power accidents—none at all. That's much better than the thousands of lives coal, oil, and toasters have cost us. If you care about saving human lives, then you should like nuclear energy.

Radiation

Despite nuclear energy causing remarkably few deaths, people are also terrified of another aspect of nuclear power — radiation. Everyone's scared of developing a boulder-size tumor or our apples growing to similar size as a result of the awful radiation given off by nuclear power plants or their potential meltdowns. However, it should comfort you to know (or perhaps not) that you receive more radiation from a brick wall than from a nuclear power plant.

The argument uses technical terms but makes sure they are accessible to readers.

We live in a radioactive world — nearly everything gives off at least a trace amount of radiation; that includes brick walls. Yes, while such a wall emits about 3.5 millirems of radiation per year, a nuclear power plant gives off about .3 millirems per year. (Millirem is just a unit of radiation dosage.) Of course, this low level of emission is a result of the numerous safeguards set up around the reactors to suppress radiation. So what happens if those safeguards fail? Will everyone surrounding the plant turn into a mutant?

To answer that question, let's examine the reactor failures in the recent Japanese nuclear crisis following several devastating earthquakes. The damage from the quakes took out the power to several nuclear plants, which caused their core cooling systems to go offline. To prevent reactor meltdowns, workers had to douse the failing reactors in thousands of gallons of seawater to cool the fuel rods, which contain all the radioactive materials. Worries about the resulting radioactive seawater contaminating the ocean and sea life flared as a result. But just how radioactive is the water? Officials from Tokyo Electric Power Company said the water "would have to be drunk for a whole year in order to accumulate one millisievert." People are generally exposed to about 1 to 10 millisieverts each year from background radiation caused by substances in the air and soil. "You would have to eat or drink an awful lot to

The argument is full of data and statistics from what seem to be reputable authorities and sources.

get any level of radiation that would be harmful," said British nuclear expert Laurence Williams. You get exposed to 5 millisieverts during a coast-to-coast flight across the United States. According to the U.S. Food and Drug Administration, you receive between 5 and 60 millisieverts in a CAT scan, depending on the type. So drinking water for a year that was in direct contact with containers of radioactive material used in those Japanese nuclear plants will expose you to a fifth of the radiation you would get from the weakest CAT scan. How dangerous!

As the argument explores various aspects of nuclear energy, headings keep the reader on track.

WASTE

But even if we have little to fear from nuclear power plants themselves, what about the supposedly deadly by-products of these plants? Opponents of nuclear energy cite the fact that while nuclear power plants don't emit greenhouse gases, they do leave behind waste that remains radioactive for thousands of years. However, this nuclear waste problem is exaggerated. According to Professor Emeritus of Computer Science at Stanford University, John McCarthy, a 1,000-megawatt reactor produces only 1.5 cubic meters of waste after a year of operation. The current solution is to put the waste in protective containers and store them in caverns cut in granite. At the very least, with such a small amount of waste per reactor, the caverns don't have to be dug very fast.

Pearson strategically concedes a downside of nuclear energy.

Nuclear power plants do produce waste that needs to be kept away from living things, but the actual amount of waste produced is small and therefore manageable. If the United States got all its power from nuclear plants, the amount of waste produced would be equivalent to one pill of aspirin per person, per year—tiny compared to the amount of waste produced by plants that use fossil fuels; the U.S. Energy Information Administration notes that coal alone produces about 1.8 billion metric tons of CO_2 emissions per year.

Quantity is not the only factor that has been exaggerated—the amount of time the waste remains dangerously radioactive has also been inflated. After about five hundred years, the fission products' radiation levels drop to below the level at which we typically find them in nature; the thousands of years opponents of nuclear energy refer to are the years the waste will be radioactive, not excessively so. You don't want to stand right next to this material even after those first five hundred years, but if it can exist in nature without doing any noticeable damage, then it doesn't pose any serious threat. Essentially, everything is radioactive; to criticize something for being radioactive without specifying the level of radioactivity means nothing.

Meeting Our Energy Demands

Although I've done a lot here in an attempt to defend nuclear energy, I still acknowledge it's not perfect. While the nuclear waste problem isn't something to be too worried about, it would still be better if we could satisfy our demand for energy without producing waste, radioactive or otherwise. However, I believe nuclear energy is the only realistic option we have to one day achieve an entirely clean energy reality.

We live in an age dominated by energy—to power our cars, our homes, and our computers. Let's face it: we're not going to give up the lifestyle that energy gives us. But under the current means of energy production—primarily coal in the United States—we're pumping out billions of tons of greenhouse gases that will eventually destroy our planet. So we have a dilemma. While we want to do something about global warming, we don't want to change our high-energy-consumption way of life. What are our options?

The concluding paragraphs compare nuclear power to potential alternatives.

Currently, completely clean sources of energy haven't been developed enough to make them a realistic option to supply all our energy needs. For solar energy to match the energy production of nuclear power plants presently in use, we would have to cover an area the size of New Jersey with solar panels. That's not a realistic option; we're not going to build that many panels just to get ourselves off of our addiction to fossil fuels. The same is true of the other renewable energy sources: wind, geothermal, hydroelectric, etc. The technologies simply aren't mature enough.

However, nuclear power is realistic. We have the means and the technology to make enough nuclear power plants to satisfy our electricity demands. Nuclear plants produce a lot of power with relatively little waste. Moving from coal to nuclear plants could provide us with adequate power until we develop more efficient renewable sources of electricity.

So what's stopping us? Of course, those heavily invested in coal and other fossil fuels lobby the government to keep their industries profitable, but a large source of opposition is also the American public. Because of the atom bombs of World War II, the Cold War, and Chernobyl, we're scared of all things nuclear. Anytime we hear the word "radiation," images of mushroom clouds and fallout enter our minds. But nuclear power plants aren't bombs. No matter what happens to them, they will never explode. Strong as it might be, our fear of nuclear power is overblown and keeping us from using a source of energy that could literally save our planet. We need to stop the fearmongering before we burn our planet to a crisp.

Pearson ends his argument by asking readers to acknowledge that their fears of nuclear power aren't based in fact.

Of course, that's if our toasters don't kill us first.

What the Numbers Show about N.F.L. Player Arrests

NEIL IRWIN

Off-the-field violence by professional football players is coming under new focus this week after the release of a video involving the star Baltimore Ravens running back Ray Rice, followed by a bungled response by the National Football League.

But what do the numbers show about N.F.L. players' tangles with the law more broadly? Are some teams' players more likely to get into legal trouble? Are arrests rising or falling? What are the most common offenses?

USA Today maintains a database of arrests, charges, and citations of N.F.L. players for anything more serious than a traffic citation. Maintained by Brent Schrotenboer, it goes back to 2000 and covers, to date, 713 instances in which pro football players have had a run-in with the law that was reported by the news media.

The data set is imperfect; after all, it depends on news media outlets finding out about every time a third-string offensive lineman is pulled

Ray Rice was arraigned on domestic violence charges in May 2014. He was fired by the Baltimore Ravens in September 2014. AP Photo/The Philadelphia Inquirer, Tom Gralish, Pool

over for driving drunk, and so some arrests may well fall through the cracks. Moreover, arrests are included even if charges are dropped or the player is found not guilty, so it presumably includes legal run-ins in which the player did nothing wrong.

Finally, for purposes of these tabulations, a simple drug possession charge in which no one was hurt counts the same as a case like that of Mr. Rice, who is on tape punching his fiancée out cold (she is now his wife), or even that of the former New England Patriot Aaron Hernandez, who is in jail awaiting trial on murder charges.

But with those caveats aside, here's what the data show about how pro football players are interacting with the law. The numbers show a league in which drunk-driving arrests are a continuing problem and domestic violence charges are surprisingly common; in which the teams that have the most players getting in legal trouble don't always fit the impressions fans might have; and in which teams with high arrest rates tend to stay that way over time.

One N.F.L. player in 40 is arrested in a given year. There are 32 teams, each with 53 players on its roster plus another eight on its practice squad (plus more players who show up for training camp but do not make the team, but we didn't attempt to account for them). Thus over the nearly 15 years that the *USA Today* data goes back, the 713 arrests mean that 2.53 percent of players have had a serious run-in with the law in an average year. That may sound bad, but the arrest rate is lower than the national average for men in that age range.

Arrests peaked in the mid-2000s, and are way down this year. The peak year for arrests of N.F.L. players was 2006, followed closely by 2007 and 2008. (These are calendar years, not N.F.L. seasons.) One important caveat: The apparent increase could be a result of increased coverage of professional athletes' legal troubles by Internet media. In other words, we don't know for sure whether more N.F.L. players were being arrested in those years, or whether TMZ and other outlets were better positioned to find out about it.

Despite the Ray Rice episode, 2014 is on track to be the year with the fewest arrests of N.F.L. players on record. Through Sept. 10, there had only been 21. If the final four months of the year proceed at the same pace of arrests as the first eight, that will come to 28, well below the previous low of 36 in 2004.

The most common accusation is driving while drunk, but domestic violence is a big problem. Some 28 percent of the arrests in the database were for driving under the influence, with 202 incidents. Other frequent categories of charges include assault and battery (88 cases) and drug-related offenses (82). This data is also a reminder that domestic violence has been a problem among N.F.L. players since long before Ray and Janay Rice got on that Atlantic City elevator: There have been 85 charges for domestic violence and related offenses since 2000.

The Minnesota Vikings have had the most players arrested since 2000. The number of arrests by team range from a low of 11 (tie between the Arizona Cardinals and St. Louis Rams) versus a high of 44 (the Vikings), with the Cincinnati Bengals and Denver Broncos close behind. (The Houston Texans also have 11 but started playing in 2002.)

To look at it a different way, across the league from 2000 through 2013, 2.53 percent of players were arrested per year, but for the Vikings, that number is 5 percent. For the teams tied for fewest arrests, it is 1.3 percent.

The Ravens have received negative publicity over Rice, whom they fired, and over other players' legal troubles this year, but their 22 player

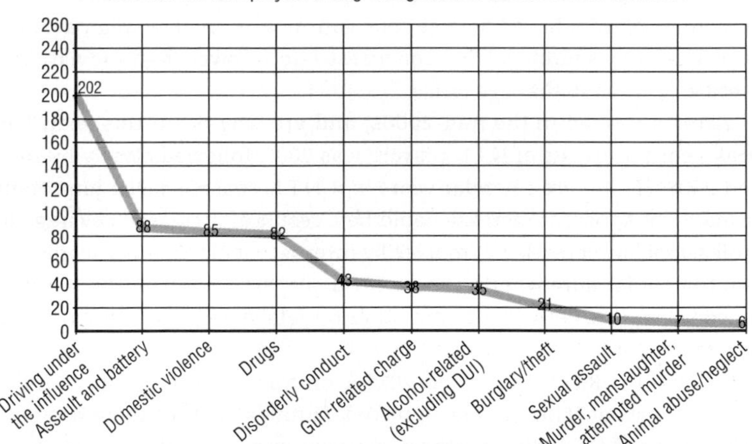

Although driving under the influence is the top reason NFL players ran into trouble with the law, the next three biggest reasons are very concerning.
Data from *USA Today*

arrests since 2000 make them right at the leaguewide average. The Oakland Raiders have cultivated an image of being a franchise for tough, rowdy bad boys. The team's players, however, have had 19 scrapes with the law since 2000, below average.

The frequency of arrests in a franchise tends to be consistent over time. One might imagine that the number of players from a given franchise who are arrested is a random phenomenon. Maybe, in the rankings above, for example, the Vikings and the Bengals were just unlucky and the Cardinals and Rams were just lucky.

But there's a simple way to test that. If the results were random, you would expect there to be no correlation between the number of player arrests in one time period with a subsequent time period. You could even imagine a negative correlation, if teams that had a run of players getting in trouble took extra care not to sign players reputed to have character issues.

But that is not what happened over the last 14 years. If you chart the number of arrests of players from each franchise in the first seven years of the data, 2000 to 2006, versus the number of arrests that franchise experienced from 2007 to 2013, the correlation is a pretty solid 53 percent. [This] shows a clear pattern in which those franchises with high numbers of arrests in the early years also tended to have high numbers of arrests in later years and vice versa.

The data don't tell us anything about why these patterns are so persistent, but there are two possibilities that seem to stand out. First, there could be club culture. The top management of a franchise may send a message to personnel scouts and coaches that they are either more or less tolerant of signing players who have had legal problems in the past. (One might imagine that the personal style of the coach could play a role as well, but coaches tend not to have long tenures in the modern N.F.L.; no coach has led his team continuously for the entirety of the time covered by this arrest data, though the Patriots' Bill Belichick misses that honor by only a few weeks, having been hired in late January 2000.)

Second, there is geography. Different cities have different patterns of living and different approaches to law enforcement. Perhaps players for the Jets and the Giants (both with persistently low arrest rates) are at less risk of arrest for D.U.I. because people are less likely to need to drive themselves to nightclubs in Manhattan. Or perhaps in some cities, young African-American men driving expensive cars attract more police attention than in others.

Regardless of the reasons, a handful of franchises have persistently higher numbers of players who end up being arrested, and may want to learn from their rivals in other cities as to why.

9 Arguments of Definition

Left to right: AP Photo/Seth Wenig; Bill Wight/Getty Images; Frederick M. Brown/Getty Images

A student writes a cookbook for her master's thesis, hoping to make it easier for people to eat good, healthy food for less money. Her work helps redefine current definitions of *thesis*.

A panel of judges must decide whether computer-enhanced images will be eligible in a contest for landscape photography. At what point is an electronically manipulated image no longer a *photograph*?

A conservative student group accuses the student government on campus of sponsoring a lecture series featuring a disproportionate number of "left-wing" writers and celebrities. A spokesperson for the student government defends its program by questioning the definition of *left-wing* used to classify some of the speakers.

Understanding Arguments of Definition

Definitions matter. Just ask a scientist, a mathematician, an engineer, a judge—or just an everyday person who wants to marry someone of the same sex. In 1996, the Congress passed, and President Clinton signed, the Defense of Marriage Act (DOMA), which defined marriage in federal law this way:

> **In determining the meaning of any Act of Congress, or of any ruling, regulation, or interpretation of the various administrative bureaus and agencies of the United States, the word "marriage" means only a legal union between one man and one woman as husband and wife, and the word "spouse" refers only to a person of the opposite sex who is a husband or a wife. 1 U.S.C. 7.**

This decision and its definitions of *marriage* and *spouse* have been challenged over and over again in the ensuing decades, leading eventually to another Supreme Court decision, in the summer of 2013, that declared DOMA unconstitutional. The majority opinion, written by Justice Kennedy, found that the earlier law was discriminatory and that it labeled same-sex unions as "less worthy than the marriage of others." In so ruling, the court affirmed that the federal government cannot differentiate between a "marriage" of heterosexuals and one of homosexuals. Laws regarding marriage—and thus attempting to define or redefine the term—are still ongoing, and you might want to check the status of such controversies in your own state.

In any case, such decisions demonstrate that arguments of definition aren't abstract academic exercises: they are contentious and very often have important consequences for ordinary people. That's because they wield the power to say what someone or something is or can be. Such arguments can both include or exclude: A wolf in Montana either is an endangered species or it isn't. An unsolicited kiss is or is not sexual harassment. A person merits official political refugee status in the United States or doesn't. Another way of approaching definitional arguments, however, is to think of what falls between is and *is not* in a definitional claim. In fact, many definitional disputes occur in that murky realm.

Consider the controversy over how to define *human intelligence*. Some argue that human intelligence is a capacity that is measured by tests of verbal and mathematical reasoning. In other words, it's defined by IQ and SAT scores. Others define *intelligence* as the ability to perform specific practical tasks. Still others interpret *intelligence* in emotional terms as a competence in relating to other people. Any of these positions could be defended reasonably, but perhaps the wisest approach would be to construct a definition of *intelligence* that is rich enough to incorporate all these perspectives—and maybe more.

The fact is that crucial political, social, and scientific terms—such as *intelligence*, *social justice*, *war*, or *marriage*—are reargued, reshaped, and updated for the times.

The use of drones in air strikes—and the loss of civilian lives involved—has led to a heated national controversy. Commenting in *The Daily Kos*, MinistryOfTruth wrote:

> **We all cringe when we hear of the innocent lives lost at war and civilians caught in the crossfire. These civilian deaths are always sad and tragic reminders of the cost of war. The Military/Industrial Complex doesn't like that. Reports of civilian deaths make the wars unpopular, and that's not the right way to continue to justify an ever growing military budget full of expensive drone missiles and the longest war in American history, is it? Nope. So what do they do? Re-define the dead civilians.**
>
> —**MinistryOfTruth, in** *The Daily Kos*

Blogger MinistryOfTruth goes on to quote from a lengthy article in the *New York Times* concluding that the administration "embraced a disputed method for counting civilian casualties that . . . in effect counts all military-age males in a strike zone as combatants, . . . unless there is explicit intelligence posthumously proving them innocent." As this example illustrates, during war times it is especially important to watch how definitions get shifted and changed to shape or change reality.

Red DaxLuma Gallery/
Shutterstock

The argument over how to define *militants* and *combatants* will not be settled simply by consulting a dictionary, no matter how up to date it is. In fact, dictionaries inevitably reflect the way that particular groups of people use words at a specified time and place. And like any form of writing, these reference books mirror the prejudices of their makers—as shown, perhaps most famously, in the entries of lexicographer Samuel Johnson (1709–1784), who gave the English language its first great dictionary. Johnson, no friend of the Scots, defined *oats* as "a grain which in England is generally given to horses, but in Scotland supports the people." (To be fair, he also defined *lexicographer* as "a writer of dictionaries, a harmless drudge.") Thus, it's possible to disagree with dictionary definitions or to regard them merely as starting points for arguments.

The *Dictionary for Landlubbers* defines words according to their point of view! Excerpted from *SAILING: A Dictionary for Landlubbers, Old Salts, & Armchair Drifters.* Copyright © 1981 by Henry Beard and Roy McKie. Used by permission of Workman Publishing Co., Inc., New York. All rights reserved.

RESPOND •

Briefly discuss how you might define the italicized terms in the following controversial claims of definition. Compare your definitions of the terms with those of your classmates.

Graphic novels are *serious literature*.

Burning a nation's flag is a *hate crime*.

Matt Drudge and Arianna Huffington aren't *journalists*.

College sports programs have become *big businesses*.

Plagiarism can be an act of *civil disobedience*.

Satanism is a *religion* properly protected by the First Amendment.

Campaign contributions are acts of *free speech* that should never be regulated.

The District of Columbia should not have all the privileges of an American *state*.

Polygamous couples should have the legal privileges of *marriage*.

Kinds of Definition

Because there are different kinds of definitions, there are also different ways to make a definition argument. Fortunately, identifying a particular type of definition is less important than appreciating when an issue of definition is at stake. Let's explore some common definitional issues.

Formal Definitions

Formal definitions are what you find in dictionaries. Such definitions place a term in its proper **genus** and **species**—first determining its class and then identifying the features or criteria that distinguish it from other members of that class. That sounds complicated, but a definition will help you see the principle. To define *hybrid car*, you might first place it in a general class—*passenger vehicles*. Then the formal definition would distinguish hybrid cars from other passenger vehicles: *they can move using two or more sources of power, either separately or in combination*. So the full definition might look like this: *a hybrid car is a passenger vehicle* (genus) *that can operate using two or more sources of power, separately or in combination* (species).

Many arguments involve deciding whether an object meets the criteria set by a formal definition. For instance, suppose that you are

2014 Honda Insight: fully hybrid or something else?
PHOTOEDIT/PhotoEdit, Inc.

considering whether a Toyota Prius and a Honda Insight are comparable hybrid vehicles. Both are clearly passenger cars, so the genus raises no questions. But not all vehicles that claim to be hybrids are powered by two sources: some of them are just electrically *assisted* versions of a regular gasoline car. That's the species question. Looking closely, you discover that a Prius can run on either gas or electric power alone. But does the Insight have that flexibility? Not quite. It has an electric motor that assists its small gas engine, but the vehicle never runs on electricity alone. So technically the Insight is labeled a *mild hybrid* whereas the Prius is called a *full hybrid*. This definitional distinction obviously has consequences for consumers concerned about CO_2 emissions.

How does Amy Zimmerman's piece "It Ain't Easy Being Bisexual on TV" add complexity to and challenge typical culturally reinforced operational definitions of sexuality?

LINK TO P. 561

Operational Definitions

Operational definitions identify an object or idea by what it does or by what conditions create it. For example, someone's offensive sexual imposition on another person may not meet the technical definition of *harassment* unless it is considered *unwanted*, *unsolicited*, and *repeated*. These three conditions then define what makes an act that might be acceptable in some situations turn into harassment. But they might also then become part of a highly contentious debate: were the conditions actually present in a given case? For example, could an offensive act really be harassment if the accused believed sexual interest was mutual and therefore solicited?

As you might imagine, arguments arise from operational definitions whenever people disagree about what the conditions define or whether these conditions have been fulfilled. Here are some examples of those types of questions:

Questions Related to Conditions

- Can institutional racism occur in the absence of specific and individual acts of racism?
- Can someone who is paid for their community service still be called a volunteer?
- Can an offensive act be termed harassment if the accused believed sexual interest was mutual and therefore solicited?

Questions Related to Fulfillment of Conditions

- Has an institution supported traditions or policies that have led to widespread racial inequities?
- Was the compensation given to a volunteer really "pay" or simply "reimbursement" for expenses?
- Should a person be punished for harassment if he or she believed the offensive action to be solicited?

Prince Charming considers whether an action would fulfill the conditions for an operational definition. Cartoonstock Ltd./www.CartoonStock.com

RESPOND.

This chapter opens with several rhetorical situations that center on definitional issues. Select one of these situations, and then, using the strategy of formal definition, set down some criteria of definition. For example, identify the features of a photograph that make it part of a larger class (*art, communication method, journalistic technique*). Next, identify the features that make it distinct from other members of that larger class. Then use the strategy of operational definition to establish criteria for the same object: what does it do? Remember to ask questions related to conditions (*Is a computer-scanned photograph still a photograph?*) and questions related to fulfillment of conditions (*Does a good photocopy of a photograph achieve the same effect as the photograph itself?*).

Definitions by Example

Resembling operational definitions are **definitions by example**, which define a class by listing its individual members. Such definitions can be helpful when it is easier to illustrate or show what related people or

An app like Discovr Music defines musical styles by example when it connects specific artists or groups to others who make similar sounds.
Discovr Music 2012

things have in common than to explain each one in precise detail. For example, one might define the broad category of *tablets* by listing the major examples of these products or define *heirloom tomatoes* by recalling all those available at the local farmers' market.

Arguments of this sort may focus on who or what may be included in a list that defines a category—*classic movies*, *worst natural disasters*, *groundbreaking painters*. Such arguments often involve comparisons and contrasts with the items that most readers would agree belong in this list. One could ask why Washington, D.C., is denied the status of a state: how does it differ from the fifty recognized American states? Or one might wonder why the status of planet is denied to asteroids, when both planets and asteroids are bodies that orbit the sun. A comparison between planets and asteroids might suggest that size is one essential feature of the eight recognized planets that asteroids don't meet. (In 2006, in a famous exercise in definitional argument, astronomers decided to deny poor Pluto its planetary classification.)

Developing a Definitional Argument

Definitional arguments don't just appear out of the blue; they often evolve out of daily life. You might get into an argument over the definition of *ordinary wear and tear* when you return a rental car with some soiled upholstery. Or you might be asked to write a job description for a new position to be created in your office: you have to define the job position in a way that doesn't step on anyone else's turf. Or maybe employees on your campus object to being defined as *temporary workers* when they've held their same jobs for years. Or someone derides one of your best friends as *just a nerd*. In a dozen ways every day, you encounter situations that are questions of definition. They're so frequent and indispensable that you barely notice them for what they are.

Formulating Claims

In addressing a question of definition, you'll likely formulate a *tentative claim*—a declarative statement that represents your first response to such situations. Note that such initial claims usually don't follow a single definitional formula.

Claims of Definition

> A person paid to do public service is not a *volunteer*.
>
> *Institutional racism* can exist—maybe even thrive—in the absence of overt civil rights violations.
>
> *Political bias* has been consistently practiced by the mainstream media.
>
> Theatergoers shouldn't confuse *musicals* with *operas*.
>
> *White lies* are hard to define but easy to recognize.

None of the statements listed here could stand on its own because it likely reflects a first impression and gut reaction. But that's fine because making a claim of definition is typically a starting point, a cocky moment that doesn't last much beyond the first serious rebuttal or challenge. Statements like these aren't arguments until they're attached to reasons, data, warrants, and evidence (see Chapter 7).

Finding good reasons to support a claim of definition usually requires formulating a general definition by which to explore the subject. To be persuasive, the definition must be broad and not tailored to the specific controversy:

> A volunteer is . . .
>
> Institutional racism is . . .
>
> Political bias is . . .
>
> A musical is . . . but an opera is . . .
>
> A white lie is . . .

Now consider how the following claims might be expanded with a general definition to become full-fledged definitional arguments:

Arguments of Definition

> Someone paid to do public service is not a volunteer because volunteers are people who . . .
>
> Institutional racism can exist even in the absence of overt violations of civil rights because, by definition, institutional racism is . . .
>
> Political bias in the media is evident when . . .
>
> Musicals focus on words first while operas . . .
>
> The most important element of a white lie is its destructive nature; the act of telling one hurts both the receiver and the sender.

Notice, too, that some of the issues can involve comparisons between things—such as operas and musicals.

Crafting Definitions

Imagine that you decide to tackle the concept of *paid volunteer* in the following way:

> **Participants in the federal AmeriCorps program are not really volunteers because they receive "education awards" for their public service. Volunteers are people who work for a cause without receiving compensation.**

In Toulmin terms, as explained in Chapter 7, the argument looks like this:

Claim	**Participants in AmeriCorps aren't volunteers . . .**
Reason	**. . . because they are paid for their service.**
Warrant	**People who are compensated for their services are, ordinarily, employees.**

As you can see, the definition of *volunteers* will be crucial to the shape of the argument. In fact, you might think you've settled the matter with this tight little formulation. But now it's time to listen to the readers over your shoulder (again, see Chapter 7), who are pushing you further. Do the terms of your definition account for all pertinent cases of volunteerism—in particular, any related to the types of public service AmeriCorps members might be involved in? What do you do with unpaid interns: how do they affect your definition of *volunteers*? Consider, too, the word *cause* in your original claim of the definition:

> **Volunteers are people who work for a cause without receiving compensation.**

Cause has political connotations that you may or may not intend. You'd better clarify what you mean by *cause* when you discuss its definition in your paper. Might a phrase such as *the public good* be a more comprehensive or appropriate substitute for *a cause?* And then there's the matter of *compensation* in the second half of your definition:

> **Volunteers are people who work for a cause without receiving compensation.**

Aren't people who volunteer to serve on boards, committees, and commissions sometimes paid, especially for their expenses? What about members of the so-called all-volunteer military? They're financially compensated during their years of service, and they enjoy benefits after they complete their tours of duty.

As you can see, you can't just offer up a definition as part of an argument and expect that readers will accept it. Every part of a definition has to be interrogated, critiqued, and defended. So investigate your subject in the library, on the Internet, and in conversation with others, including experts if you can. You might then be able to present your definition in a single paragraph, or you may have to spend several pages coming to terms with the complexity of the core issue.

After conducting research of this kind, you'll be in a better position to write an extended definition that explains to your readers what you believe makes a volunteer a volunteer, how to identify institutional racism, or how to distinguish between a musical and an opera.

Matching Claims to Definitions

Once you've formulated a definition that readers will accept—a demanding task in itself—you might need to look at your particular subject to see if it fits your general definition. It should provide evidence of one of the following:

- It is a clear example of the class defined.
- It clearly falls outside the defined class.
- It falls between two closely related classes or fulfills some conditions of the defined class but not others.
- It defies existing classes and categories and requires an entirely new definition.

How do you make this key move in an argument? Here's an example from an article by Anthony Tommasini entitled "Opera? Musical? Please Respect the Difference." Early in the piece, Tommasini argues that a key element separates the two musical forms:

> **Both genres seek to combine words and music in dynamic, felicitous and, to invoke that all-purpose term, artistic ways. But in opera, music is the driving force; in musical theater, words come first.**

His claim of definition (or of difference) makes sense because it clarifies aspects of the two genres.

> **This explains why for centuries opera-goers have revered works written in languages they do not speak. . . . As long as you basically know**

> what is going on and what is more or less being said, you can be swept away by a great opera, not just by music, but by visceral drama.
>
> In contrast, imagine if the exhilarating production of Cole Porter's *Anything Goes* now on Broadway . . . were to play in Japan without any kind of titling technology. The wit of the musical is embedded in its lyrics. . . .

But even after having found a distinction so perceptive, Tommasini (like most writers making arguments of definition) still has to acknowledge exceptions.

> Theatergoing audiences may not care much whether a show is a musical or an opera. But the best achievements in each genre . . . have been from composers and writers who grounded themselves in a tradition, *even while reaching across the divide*. [emphasis added]

If evidence you've gathered while developing an argument of definition suggests that similar limitations may be necessary, don't hesitate to modify your claim. It's amazing how often seemingly cut-and-dried matters of definition become blurry—and open to compromise and accommodation—as you learn more about them. That has proved to be the case as various campuses across the country have tried to define *hate speech* or *internship*—tricky matters. And even the Supreme Court has never said exactly what *pornography* is. Just when matters seem to be settled, new legal twists develop. Should virtual child pornography created with software be illegal, as is the real thing? Or is a virtual image—even a lewd one—an artistic expression that is protected (as other works of art are) by the First Amendment?

Considering Design and Visuals

In thinking about how to present your argument of definition, you may find a simple visual helpful, such as the Venn diagram on page 198 from Wikimedia Commons that defines *sustainability* as the place where our society and its economy intersect with the environment. Such a visual might even suggest a structure for an oral presentation.

Remember too that visuals like photographs, charts, and graphs can also help you make your case. Such items might demonstrate that the conditions for a definition have been met—as the widely circulated and horrific photographs from Abu Ghraib prison in Iraq helped to define *torture*. Or you might create a graphic yourself to illustrate a concept you are defining, perhaps through comparison and contrast.

Finally, don't forget that basic design elements — such as boldface and italics, headings, or links in online text — can contribute to (or detract from) the credibility and persuasiveness of your argument of definition. (See Chapter 14 for more on "Visual Rhetoric.")

See this diagram in context as one of the visuals supporting Christian R. Weisser's definitional argument in "Sustainability."

LINK TO P. 602

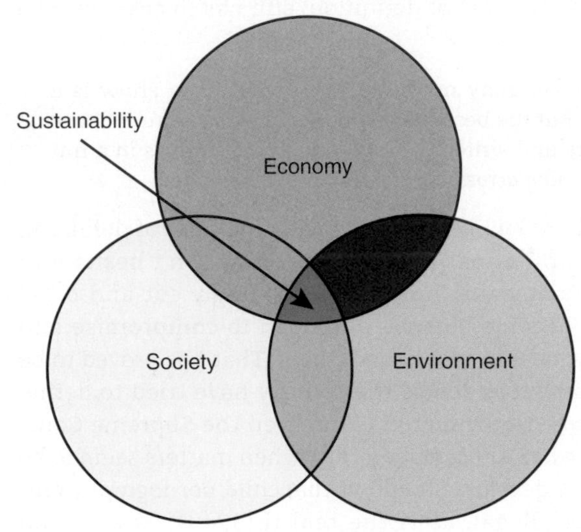

GUIDE to writing an argument of definition

Finding a Topic

You're entering an argument of definition when you:

- formulate a controversial or provocative definition: *The American Dream, which once meant a McMansion in a gated community, now has taken on a new definition.*
- challenge a definition: *For most Americans today, the American Dream involves not luxury but the secure pensions, cheap energy costs, and health insurance that workers in the 1950s and 1960s supposedly enjoyed.*
- try to determine whether something fits an existing definition: *Expanding opportunity is (or is not) central to the American Dream.*
- seek to broaden an existing definition or create a new definition to accommodate wider or differing perspectives: *In a world where information is easily and freely shared, it may be time to explore alternative understandings of the American Dream.*

Look for issues of definition in your everyday affairs—for instance, in the way that jobs are classified at work, that key terms are used in your academic major, that politicians characterize social issues that concern you, and so on. Be especially alert to definitional arguments that may arise when you or others deploy adjectives such as *true*, *real*, *actual*, or *genuine*: *a true patriot, real reform, authentic Mexican food.*

Researching Your Topic

You can research issues of definition by using the following sources:

- college dictionaries and encyclopedias
- unabridged dictionaries
- specialized reference works and handbooks, such as legal and medical dictionaries
- your textbooks (check their glossaries)
- newsgroups and blogs that focus on particular topics, especially political ones
- community or advocacy groups that are engaged in legal or social issues
- social media postings by experts you respect

Browse in your library reference room and use the electronic indexes and databases to determine how often disputed or contentious terms or phrases occur in influential online newspapers, journals, and Web sites.

When dealing with definitions, ask librarians about the most appropriate and reliable sources. For instance, to find the definition of a legal term, *Black's Law Dictionary* or a database such as FindLaw may help. Check USA.gov for how the government defines terms.

Formulating a Claim

After exploring your subject, try to formulate a thesis that lets readers know where you stand or what issues are at stake. Begin with the following types of questions:

- questions related to genus: *Is assisting in suicide a crime?*
- questions related to species: *Is marijuana a harmful addictive drug or a useful medical treatment?*
- questions related to conditions: *Must the imposition of sexual attention be both unwanted and unsolicited to be considered sexual harassment?*
- questions related to fulfillment of conditions: *Has our college kept in place traditions or policies that might constitute racial discrimination?*
- questions related to membership in a named class: *Can a story put together out of thirty-one retweets be called a novel, or even a short story?*

If you start with a thesis, it should be a complete statement that makes a claim of definition and states the reasons supporting it. You may later decide to separate the claim from its supporting reasons. But a working thesis should be a fully articulated thought that spells out all the details and qualifications: *Who? What? Where? When? How many? How regularly? How completely?*

However, since arguments of definition are often exploratory and tentative, an initial thesis (if you have one) may simply describe problems in formulating a particular definition: *What we mean by X is likely to remain unsettled until we can agree more fully about Y and Z; The key to understanding what constitutes X may lie in appreciating how different groups approach Y and Z.*

Examples of Definitional Claims

- Assisting a gravely ill person in committing suicide should not be considered *murder* when the motive for the act is to ease a person's suffering and not to benefit from the death.

- Although somewhat addictive, marijuana should not be classified as a *dangerous drug* because it damages individuals and society less than heroin or cocaine and because it helps people with life-threatening diseases live more comfortably.
- Giving college admission preference to all racial minorities can be an example of *class discrimination* because such policies may favor middle- and upper-class students who are already advantaged.
- Attempts to define the concept of *freedom* need to take into account the way the term is historically understood in cultures worldwide, not just in the countries of Western Europe and North America.

Preparing a Proposal

If your instructor asks you to prepare a proposal for your project, here's a format that may help:

State your thesis or hypothesis completely. If you're having trouble doing so, try outlining it in Toulmin terms:

Claim:

Reason(s):

Warrant(s):

Alternatively, you might describe the complications of a definitional issue you hope to explore in your project, with the thesis perhaps coming later.

- **Explain why this argument of definition deserves attention. What's at stake? Why is it important for your readers to consider?**
- **Identify whom you hope to reach through your argument and why these readers would be interested in it. How might you involve them in the paper?**
- **Briefly discuss the key challenges that you anticipate in preparing your argument.**
- **Determine what sources you expect to consult: Web? Databases? Dictionaries? Encyclopedias? Periodicals?**
- **Determine what visuals to include in your definitional argument.**

Considering Format and Media

Your instructor may specify that you use a particular format and/or medium. If not, ask yourself these questions to help you make a good choice:

- What format is most appropriate for your argument of definition? Does it call for an academic essay, a report, an infographic, a brochure, or something else?
- What medium is most appropriate for your argument? Would it be best delivered orally to a live audience? Presented as an audio essay or podcast? Presented in print only or in print with illustrations?
- Will you need visuals, such as moving or still images, maps, graphs, charts—and what function will they play in your argument? Make sure they are not just "added on" but are necessary components of the argument.

Thinking about Organization

Your argument of definition is likely to include some of the following parts:

- a claim involving a question of definition
- a general definition of some key concept
- a careful look at your subject in terms of that general definition
- evidence for every part of the argument, including visual evidence if appropriate
- a careful consideration of alternative views and counterarguments
- a conclusion drawing out the implications of the argument

It's impossible, however, to predict what emphasis each of those parts might receive or what the ultimate shape of an argument of definition will be. Try to account for the ways people with different points of view will likely respond to your argument. Then, consider how to address such differences civilly in the body of your argument.

Getting and Giving Response: Questions for Peer Response

Your instructor may assign you to a group for the purpose of reading and responding to each other's drafts. If not, ask for responses from serious readers or consultants at a writing center. Use the following questions to evaluate a colleague's draft. Be sure to illustrate your comments with examples; specific comments help more than general observations.

The Claim

- Is the claim clearly an issue of definition?
- Is the claim significant enough to interest readers?
- Are clear and specific criteria established for the concept being defined? Do the criteria define the term adequately? Using this definition, could most readers identify what's being defined and distinguish it from other related concepts?

Evidence for the Claim

- Is enough evidence furnished to explain or support the definition? If not, what kind of additional evidence is needed?
- Is the evidence in support of the claim simply announced, or are its significance and appropriateness analyzed? Is a more detailed discussion needed?
- Are all the conditions of the definition met in the concept being examined?
- Are any objections readers might have to the claim, criteria, evidence, or way the definition is formulated adequately addressed? Have you represented other points of view completely and fairly?
- What kinds of sources are cited? How credible and persuasive will they be to readers? What other kinds of sources might work better?
- Are all quotations introduced with appropriate signal phrases (such as "As Tyson argues, . . .") and blended smoothly into the writer's sentences?
- Are all visual sources labeled, introduced, and commented upon?

Organization and Style

- How are the parts of the argument organized? Is this organization effective?
- Will readers understand the relationships among the claims, supporting reasons, warrants, and evidence? If not, how might those connections be clearer? Is the function of every visual clear? Are more transitions needed? Would headings or graphic devices help?
- Are the transitions or links from point to point, sentence to sentence, and paragraph to paragraph clear and effective? If not, how could they be improved?
- Are all visuals (or other elements such as audio or video clips) carefully integrated into the text? Is each visual introduced and commented on to point out its significance? Is each visual labeled as a figure or a table and given a caption as well as a citation?
- Is the style suited to the subject? Is it too formal, casual, or technical? Can it be improved?
- Which sentences seem effective? Which ones seem weaker, and how could they be improved? Should short sentences be combined, and any longer ones be broken up?
- How effective are the paragraphs? Too short or too long? How can they be improved?
- Which words or phrases seem effective? Do any seem vague or inappropriate for the audience or the writer's purpose? Are technical or unfamiliar terms defined?

Spelling, Punctuation, Mechanics, Documentation, and Format

- Are there any errors in spelling, punctuation, capitalization, and the like?
- Is the documentation appropriate and consistent? (See Chapter 22.)
- Does the paper or project follow an appropriate format? Is it appropriately designed and attractively presented?

PROJECTS •

1. Write an argument of definition about a term such as *military combatants* or *illegal alien* that has suddenly become culturally significant or recently changed in some important way. Either defend the way the term has come to be defined or raise questions about its appropriateness, offensiveness, inaccuracy, and so on. Consider words or expressions such as *terrorism*, *marriage equality*, *racist*, *assisted suicide*, *enhanced interrogation*, *tea partier*, *collateral damage*, *forcible rape*, *net neutrality*, etc.
2. Write an essay in which you compare or contrast the meaning of two related terms, explaining the differences between them by using one or more methods of definition: formal definition, operational definition, definition by example. Be clever in your choice of the initial terms: look for a pairing in which the differences might not be immediately apparent to people unfamiliar with how the terms are used in specific communities. Consider terms such as *liberal/progressive*, *classy/cool*, *lead soprano/prima donna*, *student athlete/jock*, *highbrow /intellectual*, and so on.
3. In an essay at the end of this chapter, Natasha Rodriguez explores the adjective *underprivileged*, trying to understand why this label bothers her so much. She concludes that needing financial aid should not be conflated with being disadvantaged. After reading this selection carefully, respond to Rodriguez's argument in an argument of definition of your own. Or, alternatively, explore a concept similar to "underprivileged" with the same intensity that Rodriguez brings to her project. Look for a term to define and analyze either from your major or from an area of interest to you.
4. Because arguments of definition can have such important consequences, it helps to develop one by first getting input from lots of "stakeholders," that is, from people or groups likely to be affected by any change in the way a term is defined. Working with a small group, identify a term in your school or wider community that might need a fresh formulation or a close review. It could be a familiar campus word or phrase such as *nontraditional student*, *diversity*, *scholastic dishonesty*, or *social justice*; or it may be a term that has newly entered the local environment, perhaps reflecting an issue of law enforcement, safety, transportation, health, or even entertainment. Once you have settled on a significant term, identify a full range of stakeholders. Then, through some systematic field research (interviews, questionnaires) or by examining existing documents and materials (such as library sources, Web sites, pamphlets, publications), try to understand how the term currently functions in your community. Your definitional argument will, in effect, be what you can learn about the meanings that word or phrase has today for a wide variety of people.

Courtesy of Natasha Rodriguez

Who Are You Calling Underprivileged?

NATASHA RODRIGUEZ

I have come to loathe the word "underprivileged." When I filled out my college applications, I checked off the Latino/Hispanic box whenever I was asked to give my ethnicity. My parents in turn indicated their income, hoping that we would qualify for financial aid. But while I waited for acceptances and rejections, several colleges I was considering sent me material that made me feel worthless rather than excited about attending those institutions.

The author questions the connotations of *underprivileged.*

The first mailing I received was a brochure that featured a photograph of African-American, Asian, and Latino teens standing around in a cluster, their faces full of laughter and joy. The title of the brochure was "Help for Underprivileged Students." At first I was confused: "Underprivileged" was not a word that I associated with myself. But there was the handout, with my name printed boldly on the surface.

The text went on to inform me that, since I was a student who had experienced an underprivileged life, I could qualify for several kinds of financial aid and scholarships. While I appreciated the intent, I was turned off by that one word—"underprivileged."

I had never been called that before. The word made me question how I saw myself in the world. Yes, I needed financial aid, and I had received generous scholarships to help me attend a private high school on the Upper East Side of New York. Surely that didn't mean that I had

---

Natasha Rodriguez is a student at Sarah Lawrence College, where she edits the features section of her school newspaper, the *Phoenix*.

lived a less-privileged life than others. My upbringing had been very happy.

What does "underprivileged" actually mean? According to most dictionaries, the word refers to a person who does not enjoy the same standard of living or rights as a majority of people in a society. I don't fit that definition. Even though my family does not have a lot of money, we have always had enough to get by, and I have received an excellent education.

The author then gives a standard definition for *underprivileged* and explains why she refuses the label.

What angered me most about the label was why colleges would ever use such a term. Who wants to be called underprivileged? I'm sure that even those who have had no opportunities would not want their social status rubbed in their faces so blatantly. People should be referred to as underprivileged only if they're the ones who are calling themselves that.

Misfortune, like beauty, is in the eye of the beholder. It's not appropriate to slap labels on people that they might not like or even agree with. Social research has found that those who are negatively labeled usually have lower self-esteem than others who are not labeled in that way. So why does the label of "underprivileged" persist?

Most colleges brag about the diversity of their students. But I don't want to be bragged about if my ethnicity is automatically associated with "underprivileged." Several colleges that had not even received information on my parents' finances just assumed that I was underprivileged because I had checked "Latino/Hispanic" on their applications.

The author examines the assumptions colleges make based on ethnicity and income.

That kind of labeling has to stop. Brochures and handouts could be titled "Help for Students in Need" rather than "Help for Underprivileged Students." I am sure that many people, myself included, are more than willing to admit that they require financial aid, and would feel fine about a college that referred to them as a student in need.

That's a definition I can agree with. I am a student in need; I'm just not an underprivileged one.

The essay concludes with the author's own self-definition.

Friending: The Changing Definition of Friendship in the Social Media Era

JOYCE XINRAN LIU

March 6, 2014

In just two months, I boosted my LinkedIn connections from 300 to almost 500. I was proud of winning the numbers game. However, recently when I was trying to request an informational interview via LinkedIn, I was depressed that less than 5% actually responded to me. I think I know most of them, but I actually don't. Or they don't think so. Maybe this is social media's fault. It creates the illusion of intimacy and closeness that doesn't actually exist. Maybe I should blame myself. I rushed to think of my social media connections as true friends that I could rely on.

I forgot the rules of friendship. Social media is a new platform for communication that expands and accelerates the way we connect and engage people, but the old rules of thumb for building relationships are still there. To understand what makes a friend a "friend" in social media, we'd better step back and think about the chemistry needed in true friendship (sans social media).

To make a true friend, we first need to get to know the person well, such that we understand what she likes and dislikes, what experiences have made her who she is today, and what her values are in life. Yet knowing someone does not guarantee a lasting friendship. For example, some people know their boss pretty well, yet they may not define their boss as a friend. In addition to knowing each other well, building friendships takes time; it's necessary for both sides to have some investment in the relationship.

Now let's get back to the world of social media and reconsider the process of making friends. Facebook, Twitter, LinkedIn, and many other social

---

Joyce Xinran Liu is a graduate in Integrated Marketing Communications at Northwestern University's Medill School. She posted this piece on a blog called *Vitamin IMC*, a site developed by the graduate students in the program to "educate marketers, potential students and companies about integrated marketing communications—what it is, how it's applied and how it builds profit within organizations."

media platforms have provided tons of personal information—both ongoing and historical—about people we want to know. For example, we can gain insights into someone's social life and interests through Facebook, get up-to-the-minute status updates from Twitter, and read someone's full professional experience on LinkedIn. A five-minute search on a social media platform can make us feel that we are old friends of the person we want to make friends with. But this is only one side of the story since the person we are searching into may not feel the same way as we do. This is often the case. A one-way connection without reciprocal engagement can never be thought of as a friendship, even on social media.

When acquaintances share their joys, complaints or even private information on social media, does it mean that they deem all of these online connections as real friends? Probably not. But why share their private information then? My argument is that they sacrifice their privacy in exchange for intimacy. Some people may want to make more friends, attract more attention, or even enhance self-esteem with the inflated intimacy they receive from friends, acquaintances and mere strangers on social media. These shared social media updates make people feel close, but it doesn't always mean they are close.

It's not social media's fault that it helps us develop a wide net of connections, yet still leaves us wanting more. We've created the myth of building strong relationships via social media. It's possible to build friendship online, but more often we need to integrate online engagement with offline interaction. Overall, social media has changed ways people interact with each other, but it has not affected the rooted norms and socialization process of making friends either online or offline. And it's time to adjust our expectations for building relationships in this new media space.

10
Evaluations

Left to right: Mario Tama/Getty Images; Jonah Willihnganz, The Stanford Storytelling Project; Hulton Archive/Getty Images

"We don't want to go there for coffee. Their beans aren't fair trade, the drinks are high in calories, and the stuff is *way* overpriced."

The campus storytelling project has just won a competition sponsored by NPR, and everyone involved is thrilled. Then they realize that this year all but one of the leaders of this project will graduate and that they have very few new recruits. So they put their heads together to figure out what qualities they need in new recruits that will help maintain the excellence of their project.

Orson Welles's masterpiece *Citizen Kane* is playing at the Student Union for only one more night, but the new *Captain America* is featured across the street in 3-D. Guess which movie your roomie wants to see? You intend to set her straight.

Understanding Evaluations

Evaluations are everyday arguments. By the time you leave home in the morning, you've likely made a dozen informal evaluations: You've selected dressy clothes because you have a job interview with a law firm. You've chosen low-fat yogurt and fruit over the pancakes you really love. You've queued up the perfect playlist on your iPhone for your hike to campus. In each case, you've applied criteria to a particular problem and then made a decision. That's evaluating on the fly.

Some professional evaluations require more elaborate standards, evidence, and paperwork (imagine an aircraft manufacturer certifying a new jet for passenger service), but they don't differ structurally from the simpler choices that people make all the time. People love to voice their opinions, and they always have. In fact, a mode of ancient rhetoric—called the *ceremonial* or *epideictic* (see Chapter 1)—was devoted entirely to speeches of praise and blame.

Today, rituals of praise and blame are a significant part of American life. Adults who would choke at the notion of debating causal or definitional claims will happily spend hours appraising the Oakland Raiders, Boston Red Sox, or Tampa Bay Rays. Other evaluative spectacles in our culture include awards shows, beauty pageants, most-valuable-player presentations, lists of best-dressed or worst-dressed celebrities, "sexiest people" magazine covers, literary prizes, political opinion polls, consumer product magazines, and—the ultimate formal public gesture of evaluation—elections. Indeed, making evaluations is a form of entertainment in America and generates big audiences (think of *The Voice*) and revenues.

Arguments about sports are usually evaluations of some kind. Cal Sport Media via AP Images

RESPOND.

The last ten years have seen a proliferation of "reality" talent shows—*Dancing with the Stars*, *So You Think You Can Dance*, *American* (or *Canadian* or *Australian* or many other) *Idol*, *America's Got Talent*, *The Voice*, and so on. Write a short opinion piece assessing the merits of a particular "talent" show. What should a proper event of this kind accomplish? Does the event you're reviewing do so?

Criteria of Evaluation

Arguments of evaluation can produce simple rankings and winners or can lead to profound decisions about our lives, but they always involve standards. The particular standards we establish for judging anything—whether an idea, a work of art, a person, or a product—are called **criteria of evaluation**. Sometimes criteria are self-evident: a car that gets fifteen miles per gallon is a gas hog, and a piece of fish that smells even a little off shouldn't be eaten. But criteria get complicated when a subject is abstract: *What features make a song a classic? What constitutes a fair wage? How do we measure a successful foreign policy or college career?* Struggling to identify such difficult criteria of evaluation can lead to important insights into your values, motives, and preferences.

Why make such a big deal about criteria when many acts of evaluation seem effortless? We should be suspicious of our judgments especially when we make them casually. It's irresponsible simply to think that spontaneous and uninformed quips should carry the same weight as well-informed and well-reasoned opinions. Serious evaluations always require reflection, and when we look deeply into our judgments, we sometimes discover important questions that typically go unasked, many prefaced by *why*:

- You challenge the grade you received in a course, but you don't question the practice of grading.
- You argue passionately that a Republican Congress is better for America than a Democratic alternative, but you fail to ask why voters get only two choices.
- You argue that buying a hybrid car makes more sense than keeping an SUV, but you don't ask whether taking alternative forms of transportation (like the bus or a bike) makes the most sense of all.

Push an argument of evaluation hard enough and even simple judgments become challenging and intriguing.

In fact, for many writers, grappling with criteria is the toughest step in producing an evaluation. When you offer an opinion about a topic you know reasonably well, you want readers to learn something from your judgment. So you need time to think about and then justify the criteria for your opinion, whatever the subject.

Do you think, for instance, that you could explain what (if anything) makes a veggie burger good? Though many people have eaten veggie burgers, they probably haven't spent much time thinking about them. But it wouldn't be enough to claim merely that a proper one should be juicy or tasty—such trite claims are not even interesting. The following criteria offered on the *Cook's Illustrated* Web site show what happens when experts give the issue a closer look:

> **We wanted to create veggie burgers that even meat eaters would love. We didn't want them to taste like hamburgers, but we did want them to act like hamburgers, *having a modicum of chew, a harmonious blend of savory ingredients, and the ability to go from grill to bun without falling apart.* [emphasis added]**
>
> —*Cook's Illustrated*

After a lot of experimenting, *Cook's Illustrated* came up with a recipe that met these criteria.

What criteria of evaluation are embedded in this visual argument? © Ildi Papp/age fotostock

Criteria of evaluation aren't static, either. They differ according to time and audience. Much market research, for example, is designed to find out what particular consumers want now and may want in the future — what their criteria are for buying a product. In good times, people may demand homes with soaring entryways, lots of space, and premium appliances. In tougher times, they may care more about efficient use of space, quality insulation, and energy-efficient stoves and dishwashers. Shifts in values, attitudes, and criteria happen all the time.

RESPOND.

Choose one item from the following list that you understand well enough to evaluate. Develop several criteria of evaluation that you could defend to distinguish excellence from mediocrity in the area. Then choose an item that you don't know much about and explain the research you might do to discover reasonable criteria of evaluation for it.

smartwatches	U.S. vice presidents
NFL quarterbacks	organic vegetables
social networking sites	all-electric cars
TV journalists	spoken word poetry
video games	athletic shoes
graphic narratives	country music bands
Navajo rugs	sci-fi films

Characterizing Evaluation

One way of understanding evaluative arguments is to consider the types of evidence they use. A distinction explored in Chapter 4 between hard evidence and constructed arguments based on reason is helpful here: we defined **hard evidence** as facts, statistics, testimony, and other kinds of arguments that can be measured, recorded, or even found — the so-called smoking gun in a criminal investigation. We defined constructed arguments based on reason as those that are shaped by language and various kinds of logic.

We can talk about arguments of evaluation the same way, looking at some as quantitative and others as qualitative. **Quantitative arguments** of evaluation rely on criteria that can be measured, counted, or demonstrated in some mechanical fashion (something is taller, faster, smoother, quieter, or more powerful than something else). In contrast, **qualitative arguments** rely on criteria that must be explained through language and media, relying on such matters as values, traditions, and emotions (something is more ethical, more beneficial, more handsome, or more noble than something else). A claim of evaluation might be supported by arguments of both sorts.

Quantitative Evaluations

At first glance, quantitative evaluations seem to hold all the cards, especially in a society as enamored of science and technology as our own is. Making judgments should be easy if all it involves is measuring and counting—and in some cases, that's the way things work out. *Who's the tallest or heaviest or loudest person in your class?* If your classmates allow themselves to be measured, you could find out easily enough, using the right equipment and internationally sanctioned standards of measurement—the meter, the kilo, or the decibel.

But what if you were to ask, *Who's the smartest person in class?* You could answer this more complex question quantitatively, using IQ tests or college entrance examinations that report results numerically. In fact, almost all college-bound students in the United States submit to this kind of evaluation, taking either the SAT or the ACT to demonstrate their verbal and mathematical prowess. Such measures are widely accepted by educators and institutions, but they are also vigorously challenged. What do they actually measure? They predict likely academic success only in college, which is one kind of intelligence.

Quantitative measures of evaluation can be enormously useful, but even the most objective measures have limits. They've been devised by fallible people who look at the world from their own inevitably limited perspectives.

Qualitative Evaluations

Many issues of evaluation that are closest to people's hearts aren't subject to quantification. *What makes a movie great?* If you suggested a quantitative measure like length, your friends would probably hoot, "Get serious!" But what about box-office receipts, adjusted for inflation? Would films that made the most money—an easily quantifiable measure—be the "best pictures"? That select group would include movies such as *Star Wars*, *The Sound of Music*, *Gone with the Wind*, *Titanic*, *Avatar*, and *E.T.* An interesting group of films—but the best?

To define the criteria for "great movie," you'd more likely look for the standards and evidence that serious critics explore in their arguments, abstract or complicated issues such as their societal impact, cinematic technique, dramatic structures, intelligent casting, and so on. Most of these markers of quality could be defined and identified with some precision but not measured or counted. You'd also have to make your case rhetorically, convincing the audience to accept the markers of quality you are offering and yet appreciating that they might not. A movie reviewer making qualitative judgments might spend as much time defending criteria of evaluation as providing evidence that these standards are present in a particular film. But putting those standards into action can be what makes a review something worth reading. Consider how Roger Ebert, in writing about *Toy Story*, the first all-computer-made feature film, teaches his readers how to find evidence of quality in a great movie:

> *Toy Story* creates a universe out of a couple of kids' bedrooms, a gas station, and a stretch of suburban highway. Its heroes are toys, which come to life when nobody is watching. Its conflict is between an

Web sites such as Netflix and Rotten Tomatoes offer recommendations for films based on users' past selections and the ratings of other users and critics. Sometimes those judgments are at odds. Then whom do you trust? © Denis ALLARD/REA/Redux old-fashioned cowboy who has always been a little boy's favorite toy, and the new space ranger who may replace him. The villain is the mean kid next door who takes toys apart and puts them back together again in macabre combinations. And the result is a visionary roller-coaster ride of a movie.

For the kids in the audience, a movie like this will work because it tells a fun story, contains a lot of humor, and is exciting to watch. Older viewers may be even more absorbed, because *Toy Story*, the first feature made entirely by computer, achieves a three-dimensional reality and freedom of movement that is liberating and new. The more you know about how the movie was made, the more you respect it.

RESPOND.

For examples of powerful evaluation arguments, search the Web or your library for eulogies or obituaries of famous, recently deceased individuals. Try to locate at least one such item, and then analyze the types of claims it makes about the accomplishments of the deceased. What types of criteria of evaluation hold the obituary or eulogy together? Why should we respect or admire the person?

Developing an Evaluative Argument

Developing an argument of evaluation can seem like a simple process, especially if you already know what your claim is likely to be. To continue the movie theme for one more example:

Citizen Kane is the finest film ever made by an American director.

Having established a claim, you would then explore the implications of your belief, drawing out the reasons, warrants, and evidence that might support it:

Claim	*Citizen Kane* is the finest film ever made by an American director . . .
Reason	. . . because it revolutionizes the way we see the world.
Warrant	Great films change viewers in fundamental ways.
Evidence	Shot after shot, *Citizen Kane* presents the life of its protagonist through cinematic images that viewers can never forget.

The warrant here is, in effect, an implied statement of criteria—in this case, the quality that defines "great film" for the writer. It may be important for the writer to share that assumption with readers and perhaps to identify other great films that similarly make viewers appreciate new perspectives.

As you can see, in developing an evaluative argument, you'll want to pay special attention to criteria, claims, and evidence.

What criteria do Barbara Kingsolver and Steven L. Hopp use to distinguish heirloom tomatoes from those normally found in the grocery store? What arguments do their criteria support?

LINK TO P. 620

Formulating Criteria

Although even casual evaluations (*The band sucks!*) might be traced to reasonable criteria, most people don't defend their positions until they are challenged (*Oh yeah?*). Similarly, writers who address readers with whom they share core values rarely discuss their criteria in great detail. A film critic like the late Roger Ebert (see p. 216) isn't expected to restate all his principles every time he writes a movie review. Ebert assumes that his readers will—over time—come to appreciate his standards. Still, criteria can make or break a piece.

So spend time developing your criteria of evaluation. What exactly makes a shortstop an all-star? Why is a standardized test an unreliable measure of intelligence? Fundamentally, what distinguishes an inspired rapper from a run-of-the-mill one? List the possibilities and then pare them down to the essentials. If you offer vague, dull, or unsupportable principles, expect to be challenged.

You're most likely to be vague about your beliefs when you haven't thought (or read) enough about your subject. Push yourself at least as far as you imagine readers will. Anticipate readers looking over your shoulder, asking difficult questions. Say, for example, that you intend to argue that anyone who wants to stay on the cutting edge of personal technology will obviously want Apple's latest iPad because it does so many amazing things. But what does that mean exactly? What makes the device "amazing"? Is it that it gives access to email and the Web, has a high-resolution screen, offers an astonishing number of apps, and makes a good e-reader? These are particular features of the device. But can you identify a more fundamental quality to explain the product's appeal, such as an iPad user's experience, enjoyment, or feeling of productivity? You'll often want to raise your evaluation to a higher level of generality like this so that your appraisal of a product, book, performance, or political figure works as a coherent argument, and not just as a list of random observations.

Be certain, too, that your criteria of evaluation apply to more than just your topic of the moment. Your standards should make sense on their own merits and apply across the board. If you tailor your criteria to get the outcome you want, you are doing what is called "special pleading." You might be pleased when you prove that the home team is awesome, but it won't take skeptics long to figure out how you've cooked the books.

RESPOND.

Local news and entertainment magazines often publish "best of" issues or articles that catalog their readers' and editors' favorites in such categories as "best place to go on a first date," "best ice cream sundae," and "best dentist." Sometimes the categories are specific: "best places to say 'I was retro before retro was cool'" or "best movie theater seats." Imagine that you're the editor of your own local magazine and that you want to put out a "best of" issue tailored to your hometown. Develop ten categories for evaluation. For each category, list the evaluative criteria that you would use to make your judgment. Next, consider that because your criteria are warrants, they're especially tied to audience. (The criteria for "best dentist," for example, might be tailored to people whose major concern is avoiding pain, to those whose children will be regular patients, or to those who want the cheapest possible dental care.) For several of the evaluative categories, imagine that you have to justify your judgments to a completely different audience. Write a new set of criteria for that audience.

Making Claims

In evaluations, claims can be stated directly or, more rarely, strongly implied. For most writers, strong statements followed by reasonable qualifications work best. Consider the differences between the following three claims and how much greater the burden of proof is for the first claim:

> **Jessica Williams is the funniest "correspondent" ever on *The Daily Show*.**
>
> **Jessica Williams has emerged as one of the funniest of *The Daily Show*'s "correspondents."**
>
> **Jessica Williams may come to be regarded as one of the funniest and most successful of the "correspondents" on *The Daily Show*.**

The funniest of all? Jessica Williams reporting on *The Daily Show.*

Here's a second set of examples demonstrating the same principle, that qualifications generally make a claim of evaluation easier to deal with and smarter:

> **The Common Core Standards movement sure is a dumb idea.**
>
> **The Common Core Standards movement in educational reform is likely to do more harm than good.**
>
> **While laudable in their intentions to raise standards and improve student learning, the Common Core Standards adopted throughout the United States continue to put so high a premium on testing that they may well undermine the goals they seek to achieve.**

The point of qualifying a statement isn't to make evaluative claims bland but to make them responsible and reasonable. Consider how Reagan Tankersley uses the criticisms of a musical genre he enjoys to frame a claim he makes in its defense:

> **Structurally, dubstep is a simple musical form, with formulaic progressions and beats, something that gives a musically tuned ear little to grasp or analyze. For this reason, a majority of traditionally trained musicians find the genre to be a waste of time. These people have a legitimate position. . . . However, I hold that it is the simplicity of dubstep that makes it special: the primal nature of the song is what digs so deeply into fans. It accesses the most primitive area in our brains that connects to the uniquely human love of music.**
>
> **—Reagan Tankersley, "Dubstep: Why People Dance"**

Tankersley doesn't pretend that dubstep is something it's not, nor does he expect his argument to win over traditionally minded critics. Yet he still makes a claim worth considering.

Dubstep DJs Benga, Artwork, and Skream of Magnetic Man perform. Chiaki Nozu/Wire Image/Getty Images

One tip: Nothing adds more depth to an opinion than letting others challenge it. When you can, use the resources of the Internet or local discussion boards to get responses to your opinions or topic proposals. It can be eye opening to realize how strongly people react to ideas or points of view that you regard as perfectly normal. Share your claim and then, when you're ready, your first draft with friends and classmates, asking them to identify places where your ideas need additional support, either in the discussion of criteria or in the presentation of evidence.

Presenting Evidence

Generally, the more evidence in an evaluation the better, provided that the evidence is relevant. For example, in evaluating the performance of two laptops, the speed of their processors would be essential; the quality of their keyboards or the availability of service might be less crucial yet still worth mentioning. But you have to decide how much detail your readers want in your argument. For technical subjects, you might make your basic case briefly and then attach additional supporting documents at the end—tables, graphs, charts—for those who want more data.

Sheryll Cashin analyzes the implications of affirmative action in the introduction to her book *Place, Not Race: A New Vision of Opportunity in America*. What evidence does she use to support her stance that the system is broken?

LINK TO P. 712

Just as important as relevance in selecting evidence is presentation. Not all pieces of evidence are equally convincing, nor should they be treated as such. Select evidence that is most likely to influence your readers, and then arrange the argument to build toward your best material. In most cases, that best material will be evidence that's specific, detailed, memorable, and derived from credible sources. The details in these paragraphs from Sean Wilsey's review of *Fun Home: A Family Tragicomic*, a graphic novel by Alison Bechdel, tell you precisely what makes the work "lush," "absorbing," and well worth reading:

> It is a pioneering work, pushing two genres (comics and memoir) in multiple new directions, with panels that combine the detail and technical proficiency of R. Crumb with a seriousness, emotional complexity, and innovation completely its own. Then there are the actual words. Generally this is where graphic narratives stumble. Very few cartoonists can also write—or, if they can, they manage only to hit a few familiar notes. But *Fun Home* quietly succeeds in telling a story, not only through well-crafted images but through words that are equally revealing and well chosen. Big words, too! In 232 pages this memoir sent me to the dictionary five separate times (to look up "bargeboard," "buss," "scutwork," "humectant," and "perseverated").
>
> A comic book for lovers of words! Bechdel's rich language and precise images combine to create a lush piece of work—a memoir where concision and detail are melded for maximum, obsessive density. She has obviously spent years getting this memoir right, and it shows. You can read *Fun Home* in a sitting, or get lost in the pictures within the pictures on its pages. The artist's work is so absorbing you feel you are living in her world.
>
> —Sean Wilsey, "The Things They Buried"

The details in this passage make the case that Alison Bechdel's novel is one that pushes both comics and memoirs in new directions.

In evaluation arguments, don't be afraid to concede a point when evidence goes contrary to the overall claim you wish to make. If you're really skillful, you can even turn a problem into an argumentative asset, as Bob Costas does in acknowledging the flaws of baseball great Mickey Mantle in the process of praising him:

> None of us, Mickey included, would want to be held to account for every moment of our lives. But how many of us could say that our best moments were as magnificent as his?
>
> —Bob Costas, "Eulogy for Mickey Mantle"

RESPOND.

Take a close look at the cover of Alison Bechdel's graphic novel *Fun Home: A Family Tragicomic*. In what various ways does it make an argument of evaluation designed to make you want to read the work? Examine other books, magazines, or media packages (such as video game or software boxes) and describe any strategies they use to argue for their merit.

Fun Home: A Family Tragicomic by Alison Bechdel. Cover illustration © 2007 by Alison Bechdel. Reprinted by permission of Houghton Mifflin Harcourt Publishing Company.

Considering Design and Visuals

Visual components play a significant role in many arguments of evaluation, especially those based on quantitative information. As soon as numbers are involved in supporting a claim, think about ways to arrange them in tables, charts, graphs, or infographics to make the information more accessible to readers. Visual elements are especially helpful when comparing items. Indeed, a visual spread like the one in the federal government's comparison of electric and hybrid cars (see p. 224) becomes an argument in itself about the vehicles the government has analyzed for fuel economy. The facts seem to speak for themselves because they are presented with care and deliberation. In the same way, you will want to make sure that you use similar care when using visuals to inform and persuade readers.

But don't ignore other basic design features of a text—such as headings for the different criteria you're using or, in online evaluations, links to material related to your subject.

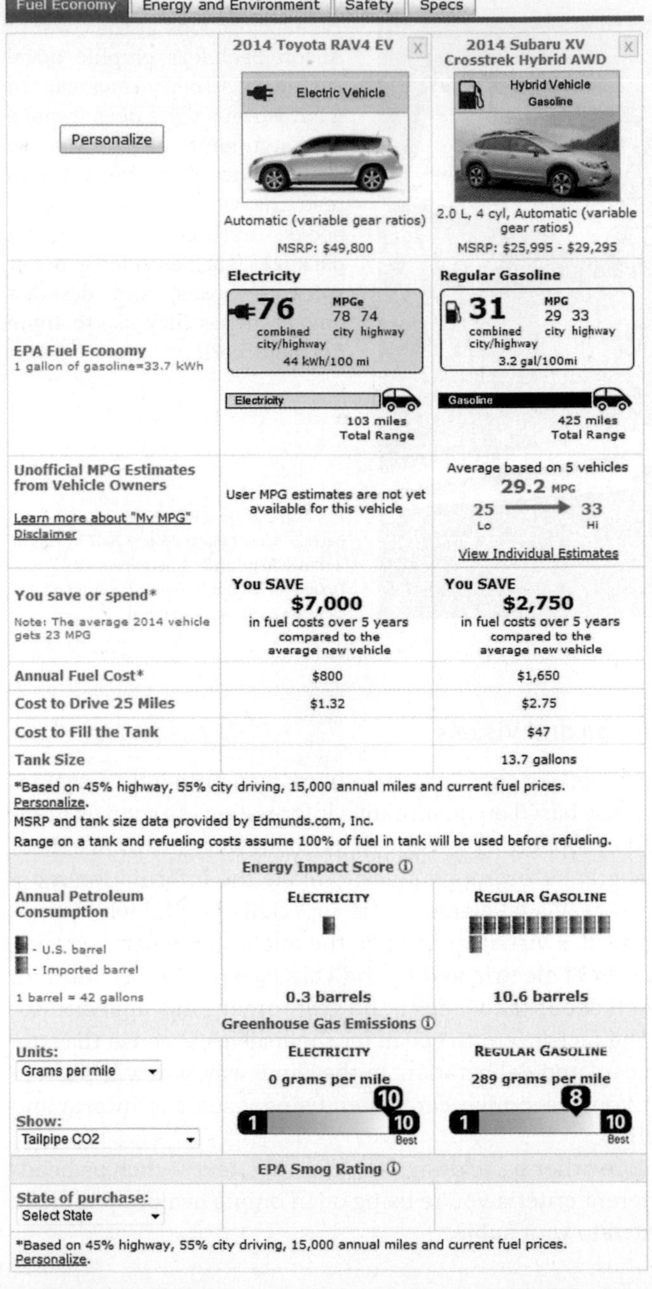

U.S. Department of Energy

GUIDE to writing an evaluation

Finding a Topic

You're entering an argument of evaluation when you:

- make a judgment about quality: Citizen Kane is *probably the finest film ever made by an American director*.
- challenge such a judgment: Citizen Kane is *vastly overrated by most film critics*.
- construct a ranking or comparison: Citizen Kane is *a more intellectually challenging movie than* Casablanca.
- explore criteria that might be used in making evaluative judgments: *Criteria for judging films are evolving as the production and audiences of films become ever more international*.

Issues of evaluation crop up everywhere—in the judgments you make about public figures or policies; in the choices you make about instructors and courses; in the recommendations you offer about books, films, or television programs; in the preferences you exercise in choosing products, activities, or charities. Evaluations typically use terms that indicate value or rank—*good/bad, effective/ineffective, best/worst, competent/incompetent, successful/unsuccessful*. When you can choose a topic for an evaluation, consider writing about something on which others regularly ask your opinion or advice.

Researching Your Topic

You can research issues of evaluation by using the following sources:

- journals, reviews, and magazines (for current political and social issues)
- books (for assessing judgments about history, policy, etc.)
- biographies (for assessing people)
- research reports and scientific studies
- books, magazines, and Web sites for consumers
- periodicals and Web sites that cover entertainment and sports
- blogs and social media sites that explore current topics

Surveys and polls can be useful in uncovering public attitudes: *What kinds of movies are young people seeing today? Who are the most admired people in the country? What activities or businesses are thriving or waning?* You'll discover that Web sites, newsgroups, and blogs thrive on evaluation. (Ever receive an invitation to "like" something on social media?) Browse these public forums for ideas, and, when possible, explore your own topic ideas there. But remember that all sources need to be evaluated themselves; examine each source carefully, making sure that it is legitimate and credible.

Formulating a Claim

After exploring your subject, try to draw up a full and specific claim that lets readers know where you stand and on what criteria you'll base your judgments. Come up with a thesis that's challenging enough to attract readers' attention. In developing a thesis, you might begin with questions like these:

- What exactly is my opinion? Where do I stand?
- Can I make my judgment more clear-cut?
- Do I need to narrow or qualify my claim?
- By what standards will I make my judgment?
- Will readers accept my criteria, or will I have to defend them, too? What criteria might others offer?
- What evidence or major reasons can I offer in support of my evaluation?

For a conventional evaluation, your thesis should be a complete statement. In one sentence, make a claim of evaluation and state the reasons that support it. Be sure your claim is specific. Anticipate the questions readers might have: *Who? What? Where? Under what conditions? With what exceptions? In all cases?* Don't expect readers to guess where you stand.

For a more exploratory argument, you might begin (and even end) with questions about the process of evaluation itself. *What are the qualities we seek—or ought to—in our political leaders? What does it say about our cultural values when we find so many viewers entertained by so-called reality shows on television? What might be the criteria for collegiate athletic programs consistent with the values of higher education?* Projects that explore topics like these might not begin with straightforward theses or have the intention to persuade readers.

Examples of Evaluative Claims

- Though they may never receive Oscars for their work, Tom Cruise and Keanu Reeves deserve credit as actors who have succeeded in a wider range of film roles than most of their contemporaries.
- People are returning to cities because they find life there more civilized than in the suburbs.
- Lena Dunham's writing and acting on *Girls* is the most honest presentation of the lives of twentysomething women today.
- Jimmy Carter has been highly praised for his work as a former president of the United States, but history may show that even his much-derided term in office laid the groundwork for the foreign policy and economic successes now attributed to later administrations.
- Young adults today are shying away from diving into the housing market because they no longer believe that homeownership is a key element in economic success.

Preparing a Proposal

If your instructor asks you to prepare a proposal for your project, here's a format that may help:

State your thesis completely. If you're having trouble doing so, try outlining it in Toulmin terms:

Claim:

Reason(s):

Warrant(s):

Alternatively, you might describe your intention to explore a particular question of evaluation in your project, with the thesis perhaps coming later.

- **Explain why this issue deserves attention. What's at stake?**
- **Identify whom you hope to reach through your argument and why these readers would be interested in it.**
- **Briefly discuss the key challenges you anticipate in preparing your argument.**
- **Determine what research strategies you'll use. What sources do you expect to consult?**

Considering Format and Media

Your instructor may specify that you use a particular format and/or medium. If not, ask yourself these questions to help you make a good choice:

- What format is most appropriate for your argument of evaluation? Does it call for an academic essay, a report, an infographic, a brochure, or something else?
- What medium is most appropriate for your argument? Would it be best delivered orally to a live audience? Presented as an audio essay or podcast? Presented in print only or in print with illustrations?
- Will you need visuals, such as moving or still images, maps, graphs, charts—and what function will they play in your argument? Make sure they are not just "added on" but are necessary components of the argument.

Thinking about Organization

Your evaluation will likely include elements such as the following:

- an evaluative claim that makes a judgment about a person, idea, or object
- the criterion or criteria by which you'll measure your subject
- an explanation or justification of the criteria (if necessary)
- evidence that the particular subject meets or falls short of the stated criteria
- consideration of alternative views and counterarguments

All these elements may be present in arguments of evaluation, but they won't follow a specific order. In addition, you'll often need an opening paragraph to explain what you're evaluating and why. Tell readers why they should care about your subject and take your opinion seriously.

Getting and Giving Response: Questions for Peer Response

Your instructor may assign you to a group for the purpose of reading and responding to each other's drafts. If not, ask for responses from serious readers or consultants at a writing center. Use the following questions to evaluate a colleague's draft. Be sure to illustrate your comments with examples; specific comments help more than general observations.

The Claim

- Is the claim an argument of evaluation? Does it make a judgment about something?
- Does the claim establish clearly what's being evaluated?
- Is the claim too sweeping? Does it need to be qualified?
- Will the criteria used in the evaluation be clear to readers? Do the criteria need to be defined more precisely?
- Are the criteria appropriate ones to use for this evaluation? Are they controversial? Should they be defended?

Evidence for the Claim

- Is enough evidence provided to show that what's being evaluated meets the established criteria? If not, what additional evidence is needed?
- Is the evidence in support of the claim simply announced, or are its significance and appropriateness analyzed? Is more detailed discussion needed?
- Are any objections readers might have to the claim, criteria, or evidence adequately addressed?
- What kinds of sources are cited? How credible and persuasive will they be to readers? What other kinds of sources might work better?
- Are all quotations introduced with appropriate signal phrases (such as "As Tyson argues, . . .") and blended smoothly into the writer's sentences?
- Are all visual sources labeled, introduced, and commented upon?

Organization and Style

- How are the parts of the argument organized? Is this organization effective?
- Will readers understand the relationships among the claims, supporting reasons, warrants, and evidence? If not, how might those connections be clearer? Is the function of every visual clear? Are more transitions needed? Would headings or graphic devices help?
- Are the transitions or links from point to point, sentence to sentence, and paragraph to paragraph clear and effective? If not, how could they be improved?

- Are all visuals carefully integrated into the text? Is each visual introduced and commented on to point out its significance? Is each visual labeled as a figure or a table and given a caption as well as a citation?
- Is the style suited to the subject? Is it too formal, casual, or technical? Can it be improved?
- Which sentences seem effective? Which ones seem weaker, and how could they be improved? Should short sentences be combined, and any longer ones be broken up?
- How effective are the paragraphs? Too short or too long? How can they be improved?
- Which words or phrases seem effective? Do any seem vague or inappropriate for the audience or the writer's purpose? Are technical or unfamiliar terms defined?

Spelling, Punctuation, Mechanics, Documentation, and Format

- Are there any errors in spelling, punctuation, capitalization, and the like?
- Is the documentation appropriate and consistent? (See Chapter 22.)
- Does the paper or project follow an appropriate format? Is it appropriately designed and attractively presented?

PROJECTS

1. What kinds of reviews or evaluations do you consult most often or read regularly—those of TV shows, sports teams, video games, fashions, fishing gear, political figures? Try composing an argument of evaluation in your favorite genre: make and defend a claim about the quality of some object, item, work, or person within your area of interest or special knowledge. Let the paper demonstrate an expertise you have gained by your reading. If it helps, model your evaluation upon the work of a reviewer or expert you particularly respect.
2. Prepare a project in which you challenge what you regard as a wrongheaded evaluation, providing sound reasons and solid evidence for challenging this existing and perhaps commonly held view. Maybe you believe that a classic novel you had to read in high school is overrated or that people who criticize video games really don't understand them. Explain why the topic of your evaluation needs to be reconsidered and provide reasons, evidence, and, if necessary, different criteria of evaluation for doing so. For an example of this type of evaluation, see Sean Kamperman's "The Wikipedia Game" on pp. 232–36.
3. Write an evaluation in which you compare or assess the contributions or achievements of two or three notable people working within the same field or occupation. They may be educators, entrepreneurs, artists, legislators, editorial cartoonists, fashion designers, programmers, athletes—you name it. While your first instinct might be to rank these individuals and pick a "winner," this evaluation will work just as well if you can help readers appreciate the different paths by which your subjects have achieved distinction.
4. Within this chapter, the authors claim that criteria of evaluation can change depending on times and circumstances: "In good times, people may demand homes with soaring entryways, lots of space, and premium appliances. In tougher times, they may care more about efficient use of space, quality insulation, and energy-efficient stoves and dishwashers." Working in a group, discuss several scenarios of change and then explore how those circumstances could alter the way we evaluate particular objects, activities, or productions. For example, what impact might global warming have upon the way we determine desirable places to live or vacation? How might a continued economic downturn change the criteria by which we judge successful careers or good educational paths for our children? If people across the globe continue to put on weight, how might standards of personal beauty or fashion alter? If government institutions continue to fall in public esteem, how might we modify our expectations for elected officials? Following the discussion, write a paper or prepare a project in which you explore how one scenario for change might revise customary values and standards of evaluation.

The Wikipedia Game: Boring, Pointless, or Neither?

SEAN KAMPERMAN

When most people think about Wikipedia — the self-styled "free, Web-based, collaborative, multilingual encyclopedia project" — they are likely reminded of the preliminary research they did for that term paper on post-structuralism, or of the idle minutes they may've spent exploring an interesting topic just for the heck of it — the neuroanatomy of purple-striped jellyfish, for example, or *Jersey Shore*. First and foremost a layman's tool, Wikipedia has struggled to find legitimacy alongside more reputable reference sources such as *Encyclopaedia Britannica*, even in spite of the outstanding quality of many of its entries. But fortunately for the makers of the Free Encyclopedia — and for the rest of us — Wikipedia's usefulness goes far beyond its intended "encyclopedic" purpose. Under the right circumstances, it can be as much a source of entertainment as one of knowledge and self-improvement.

Opening paragraph provides a context and a subtle evaluative thesis: "Wikipedia's usefulness goes far beyond its intended 'encyclopedic' purpose."

A prime example of this fact is a phenomenon identified as the Wikipedia game — or, as it's now known to users of Apple and Android smart phones, "WikiHunt." WikiHunt is a simple game whose rules draw upon the unique architectural features of wikis, in that players

WikiHunt is introduced as a cultural phenomenon.

Sean Kamperman wrote "The Wikipedia Game: Boring, Pointless, or Neither?" in spring 2010 for a lower-division course on rhetoric and media at the University of Texas at Austin. In his topic proposal he briefly described Wikipedia games familiar to many students and then indicated what he intended to explore: "A lot of scholars have been very critical of Wikipedia — some going so far as to discourage its use altogether, even for the purpose of gathering background info. Does the fact that games like these use Wikipedia detract from their educational value? Or do the games in some way rebut these criticisms, demonstrating that the practical uses of user-generated online encyclopedias go beyond traditional research and, by extension, considerations of factual correctness?" His paper is the answer to those questions.

perform "moves" by following the links that connect one Wikipedia entry to another. Driven by cultural conditions of dilettantism and the spurts of creativity that tend to come on in times of extreme boredom, dozens if not hundreds of Wikipedia users in high school computer labs, college dormitories, and professional workspaces around the globe have "discovered" the game on their own. Some have even gone so far as to claim sole proprietorship—as in the case of two of my friends, who swear they invented the game while sitting through a lecture on academic dishonesty. Questions of original authorship aside, the Wikipedia game would appear to be a bona fide grassroots phenomenon—and one well worth examining if we consider its possible implications for learning and education.

If you've never played the Wikipedia game, it's fun—educational—and, for the most part, free; indeed, all you'll need is one or more friends, two computers, and an Internet connection. To begin, navigate to the Wikipedia homepage and click the "Random article" link on the left-hand side of the screen. As advertised, this link will lead you and your friend to two randomly generated Wikipedia articles. The objective from here is to get from your article to your opponent's using nothing but links to other articles. These links, which appear within the text of the articles themselves, are bits of hypertext denoted in blue; click on any of them, and you'll be instantly transported to another article and another set of links. Depending on which version of the rules you're going by, either the player who finishes first or the one who gets to his or her opponent's page using the fewest number of links is the winner. Easy, right?

Understanding that not every reader will know WikiHunt, Kamperman offers a detailed explanation.

Not exactly. What makes the Wikipedia game hard—and coincidentally, what makes it so much fun—is the vastness of the Web site's encyclopedic content. Click the "Random article" button enough times, and you'll see a pattern emerge: the majority of articles that pop up are short ones covering extremely obscure topics, usually having to do with something related to European club soccer. Entries such as these, labeled "orphans" for their relative

The paper returns to its thesis when it notes how unexpectedly hard WikiHunt is.

paucity of length and links, in fact comprise the majority of Wikipedia articles. So the chances of you or your opponent hitting the randomly-generated-article jackpot and getting a "Jesus" or an "Adolf Hitler"—two pages with tons of links—are pretty slim. Rather, the task at hand usually requires that players navigate from orphan to orphan, as was the case in a game I played just last night with my friends David and Paige. They were unlucky enough to pull up an article on the summer village of Whispering Hills, Alberta, and I was no less unfortunate to get one on "blocking," an old 3D computer animation technique that makes characters and objects look like they're moving. Between these two pages, we were supplied with a total of nineteen links—they had nine doors to choose from, whereas I had ten. That's not a lot to work with. As you can probably surmise, games like this one take more than a few idle minutes—not to mention a heck of a lot of brainpower and spontaneous strategizing.

Kamperman uses his own experience to show precisely how WikiHunt tracks users' processes of thought and "knowledge sets."

Indeed, what makes the Wikipedia game interesting is that it welcomes comparison between the players' respective strategies and methods for getting from point A to point B, highlighting differences between their thought processes and respective knowledge sets. To elaborate using the aforementioned example, I initially knew nothing about either Whispering Hills, Alberta, or "Blocking (animation)." What I did know, however, was that in order to get to Canada, I'd have to go through the good old U.S. of A. So I clicked a link at the bottom of the page entitled "Categories: animation techniques," and from there looked for a well-known technique that I knew to be associated with an American software company. Selecting "PowerPoint animation," I was led from there to the article on Microsoft—which, thanks to the company's late '90s monopolistic indiscretions, furnished me with a link to the U.S. Department of Justice. Five clicks later and I was in Alberta, looking for a passageway to Whispering Hills, one of the province's smallest, obscurest villages. I finally found it in a series of lists on communities in Alberta—but not before my opponents beat me to the punch and got to my page on "blocking" first. David, a computer science major, had taken a different approach to clinch the win; rather than drawing upon his knowledge of a macroscopic, big-picture subject like geography, he skipped from the article on Canada to a page entitled "Canadian industrial research and development organizations," from which he quickly bored through twelve articles on various topics in the computer sciences before falling on "Blocking (animation)." In his case, specialized knowledge was the key to winning.

But did David and Paige really win? Perhaps—but in the wide world of the Wikipedia game, there are few hard-and-fast rules to go by. Whereas my opponents got to their destination quicker than I, my carefully planned journey down the funnel from big ("United States") to small ("List of summer villages in Alberta") got me to Whispering Hills using two fewer links than they. So in this example, one sees not a clear-cut lesson on how to win the game, but rather a study in contrasting styles. A player can rely on specialized knowledge, linking quickly to familiar domains and narrowing the possibilities from there; or, she/he may choose to take a slower, more methodical approach, employing abstract, top-down reasoning skills to systematically sift through broader categories of information. Ultimately, victory is possible in either case.

Its more casual, entertaining uses aside, Wikipedia gets a bad rap, especially in the classroom. Too many college professors and high school English teachers have simply written it off, some even going so far as to expressly forbid their students from using it while at school. These stances and attitudes are understandable. Teaching students how to find good sources and properly credit them is hard enough without the competing influence of the Wikipedia community, whose definition of an acceptably accurate source seems to extend not only to professionally or academically vetted articles, but to blogs as well, some obviously plagiarized. But to deny Wikipedia a place in the classroom is to deny both students and teachers alike the valuable experience of playing a game that shows us not only what we know, but

Acknowledging reservations about Wikipedia, the paper asserts that WikiHunt shows players "how we know."

how we know—how our brains work when posed with the everyday challenge of having to connect ostensibly unrelated pieces of information, and furthermore, how they work differently in that respect.

Knowledge building is a connective or associative process, as the minds behind Wikipedia well know. A casual perusal of any Wikipedia article reveals reams and reams of blue hypertext—bits of text that, when set in isolation, roughly correspond to discrete categories of information about the world. In a sense, the visual rhetoric of Wikipedia invokes the verbal rhetoric of exploration, prompting intrepid Web-using truth seekers to go sailing through a bright blue sea of information that is exciting by virtue of its seeming limitlessness. It should comfort teachers to know that, in quickly navigating through linked knowledge categories to reach their respective destinations, Wikipedia gamers aren't relying too much on their understanding of the articles themselves; rather, what they're relying on is their ability to understand relationships.

Argues that WikiHunt is about learning relationships between ideas.

The fact that so many people have independently found the fun at the heart of Wikipedia should be a heads-up. The Wikipedia game is a grassroots technological innovation that sheds new light on what it means to know—and, perhaps more importantly, one that reminds us that, yes, learning can be fun. It isn't too hard to imagine versions of the game that could be played by kids in school, and how teachers could then use the game to learn more about the stuff of their trade—namely, learning and how it works. So the next time you hear a friend, teacher, or coworker dismiss the Free Encyclopedia as "unreliable" or "unacademic," do knowledge a favor and challenge them to the following:

Defends Wikipedia as supporting a game that proves to be about "learning and how it works."

"Villa of Livia" to "List of Montreal Expos broadcasters" . . .

. . . no click-backs . . .

. . . twenty links or less.

Go.

My Awkward Week with Google Glass

HAYLEY TSUKAYAMA

The Washington Post/Getty Images

April 29, 2014

It's a Wednesday night, and I'm turning heads on the sidewalk. People are slowing halfway down the block as I approach. They're whispering about me as I walk through the room. Strangers are watching me, sometimes even stopping me on the street.

Why? Because I'm wearing Google Glass. And I hate it.

I shouldn't feel this way. I like new technology—I've been a tech reporter at the *Washington Post* for more than three years. And I admire the vision of technology that Google promises Glass can offer: a device that lets you keep track of e-mails, texts and other messages in a seamless way—all through a screen that's perched just over your right eye.

Headed into a week with Glass, on loan from a co-worker, I was prepared to review a buggy product. Glass, after all, is still in testing, and has only been released to developers, media and just a handful of "normal" people who were willing to spend $1,500 on an untested product. I expected tension headaches from constantly trying to focus on a floating screen above my line of vision. (I got only one headache, for what it's worth.) I even prepared myself to be comfortable talking aloud to the product in public because you can control Glass through voice commands.

What I wasn't prepared for was the attention I got. Sporting Glass put me among only a handful of people in Washington, and that meant getting a lot of looks. Most of it was good attention from curious people, but it still made me miserable. For wallflowers like me, wearing something that draws constant attention is more or less my personal idea of hell.

I've heard just about every privacy concern raised about Glass, but, as the one wearing the device, I wasn't expecting that the privacy most

---

Hayley Tsukayama covers consumer technology for the *Washington Post*.

invaded would be my own. That type of anxiety should lessen over time, particularly as Google works with designer labels such as Luxottica's Oakley and Ray-Ban to make prettier models. But anyone who opts to buy Glass should be ready and willing to become a constant topic of conversation and to answer questions from strangers. Wearing Google Glass in public is like wearing a sandwich-board that says "Talk to me!" And, given the rare but highly publicized fights, robberies and other major incidents some Glass users have experienced, I was a little wary about wearing the device in public.

In the name of fairness, though, I did wear them—nearly everywhere: to work, to the grocery store, out with friends, even to choir rehearsal. Here's a sample of what I heard (or overheard) from friends and strangers in the week I spent with Glass:

"Is she wearing Google Glass?" "Is that what I think that is?" "Are you recording, like, right now?" "You look ridiculous."

Or, my personal favorite, delivered deadpan, from a friend: "Oh, *Hayley*."

But beyond the personal privacy issues, I found that Google Glass is an intriguing device that has a lot of flaws. After more than two years in development, the number of remaining technical bugs is surprising.

On the hardware side, the problems ranged from the device becoming too warm—sometimes after just 10 minutes of use—to needing to be charged multiple times a day. The sensors on the device were far from perfect, and there were many times when I had to re-tap, re-swipe or (and maybe this was the worst part) jerk my head up repeatedly to wake up the device when it went dormant. I probably reset the device at least half a dozen times in the course of normal use because it wouldn't respond to my frantic taps, or refused to connect to my smartphone even when there were no other network problems.

Glass works better with Google's Android phones (in my case, an HTC One M8 on loan from HTC) than with the iPhone, if only because the integration between the Google systems is much smoother. As for software, developers have been smart about designing Glass apps to minimize the amount of data bombarding users. Big names such as Facebook, Twitter and CNN provide a strong app core for Glass. The CNN app, for example, will let you see headlines for top stories, or by subject, and serves headlines, photos and short video.

There are other apps that would be nice to have, however, particularly more photo apps to take advantage of the point-of-view vantage you get with the device.

The iPhone experience with Glass is improving. In fact, Google added a feature allowing Glass users to see iPhone text notifications during the week I wore the device. And some functions of Glass, such as the ability to project what a Glass user sees to a paired phone, were fantastic and useful in ways I didn't anticipate.

But though I tried, very hard, to make Glass a part of my life, I simply didn't feel comfortable with the screen hovering just out of my line of sight. I didn't get any direct challenges about filming others without their permission—not that I ever did film people without permission—but nearly every person who questioned me about Glass asked if I was filming.

What struck me most, however, was what happened when I let others try on the device, giving me a glimpse of how I appeared when I was wearing Glass: a conversation partner who was like a dinner guest who keeps looking at the door, as if to check if there's another person in the room they'd rather be talking to. Think of every person wearing earbuds or a Bluetooth headset who has annoyed you for the same reason. Now multiply it by a factor of 10.

All of which goes against what Glass is supposedly all about: the idea that you can avoid those awkward moments when you try to sneak a peek at your smartphone, which is always much more obvious than you think.

After a few earnest days of trying to make the thing work, I stopped trying to force the issue and used it as I would in real life—in situations when I needed to watch something hands-free, or when I wasn't required to actively engage with other people. In those cases, Glass worked as promised. It delivered updates to keep me informed without overwhelming me and acted as a useful second screen to my smartphone.

But that also meant that, more often than not, Glass ended up perched on the top of my head—the way you wear your sunglasses indoors—or discreetly tucked into my bag, in order to keep it from being the only subject of conversation.

Would I buy Google Glass? Not now, especially with that $1,500 price tag. The device has a lot of evolving to do before it's ready for the world. The world has some evolving to do before it's ready for Glass, too.

11
Causal Arguments

Left to right: c. byatt-norman/Shutterstock; Robyn Beck/AFP/Getty Images; AP Photo/Jeff Roberson

In spite of the fact that they have thrived for over fifty million years, around nine years ago colonies of bees started dying . . . and dying. Are pesticides the cause? Or perhaps it's the move agriculture has made from planting cover crops like alfalfa and clover that create natural fertilizers to using synthetic fertilizers that cater to crop monocultures but leave no food support for bees? Scientists believe a combination of these factors account for the current loss of bees.

Small business owners and big companies alike still seem reluctant to hire new employees. Is it because of complex government regulations, continuing uncertainties about health care costs, worries about debt, improvements in productivity—or all of the above? People needing jobs want to know.

Most state governments use high taxes to discourage the use of tobacco products. But when anti-smoking campaigns and graphic warning labels convince people to quit smoking, tax revenues decline, reducing support for health and education programs. Will raising taxes even higher restore that lost revenue?

Understanding Causal Arguments

Americans seem to be getting fatter, so fat in fact that we hear often about the "obesity crisis" in the United States. But what is behind this rise in weight? Rachel Berl, writing for *U.S. News and World Report*, points to unhealthy foods and a sedentary lifestyle:

> **"There is no single, simple answer to explain the obesity patterns" in America, says Walter Willett, who chairs the department of nutrition at the Harvard School of Public Health. "Part of this is due to lower incomes and education, which result in purchases of cheap foods that are high in refined starch and sugar. More deeply, this also reflects lower public investment in education, public transportation, and recreational facilities," he says. The bottom line: cheap, unhealthy foods mixed with a sedentary lifestyle have made obesity the new normal in America. And that makes it even harder to change, Willett says.**
>
> **—Rachel Pomerance Berl**

Many others agree that as processed fast food and other things such as colas have gotten more and more affordable, consumption of them has gone up, along with weight. But others offer different theories for the rise in obesity.

Whatever the reasons for our increased weight, the consequences can be measured by everything from the width of airliner seats to the rise of diabetes in the general population. Many explanations are offered

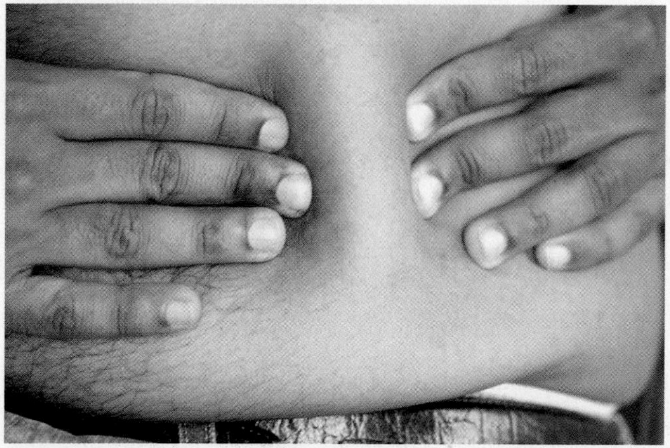

by scientists, social critics, and health gurus, and some are refuted. Figuring out what's going on is a national concern—and an important exercise in cause-and-effect argument.

Causal arguments—from the causes of poverty in rural communities to the consequences of ocean pollution around the globe—are at the heart of many major policy decisions, both national and international. But arguments about causes and effects also inform many choices that people make every day. Suppose that you need to petition for a grade change because you were unable to turn in a final project on time. You'd probably enumerate the reasons for your failure—the death of your cat, followed by an attack of the hives, followed by a crash of your computer—hoping that an associate dean reading the petition might see these explanations as tragic enough to change your grade. In identifying the causes of the situation, you're implicitly arguing that the effect (your failure to submit the project on time) should be considered in a new light. Unfortunately, the administrator might accuse you of faulty causality (see p. 80) and judge that failure to complete the project is due more to your procrastination than to the reasons you offer.

Causal arguments exist in many forms and frequently appear as part of other arguments (such as evaluations or proposals). It may help focus your work on causal arguments to separate them into three major categories:

Arguments that state a cause and then examine its effects

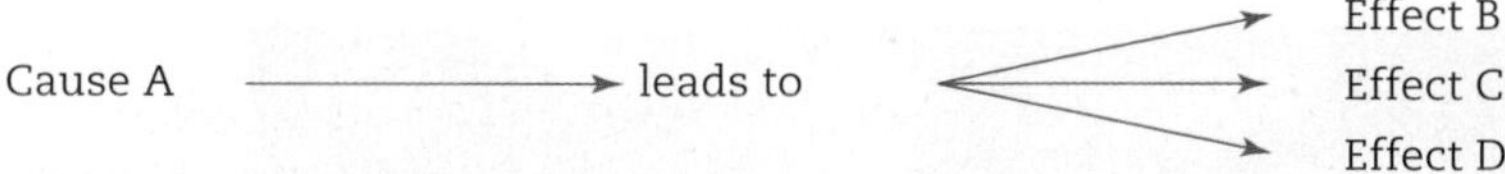

Arguments that state an effect and then trace the effect back to its causes

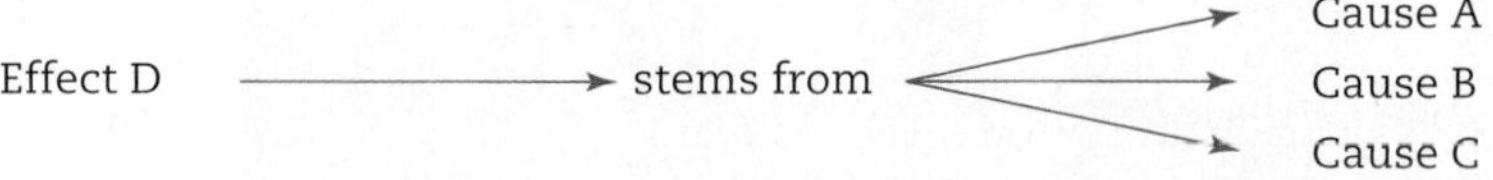

Arguments that move through a series of links: A causes B, which leads to C and perhaps to D

Cause A → leads to Cause B → leads to Cause C → leads to Effect D

Arguments That State a Cause and Then Examine Its Effects

What would happen if Congress suddenly came together and passed immigration reform that gave millions of people in the United States a legal pathway to citizenship? Before such legislation could be enacted, the possible effects of this "cause" would have to be examined in detail and argued intensely. Groups on various sides of this hot-button issue are actually doing so now, and the sides present very different scenarios. In this debate, you'd be successful if you could convincingly describe the consequences of such a change. Alternatively, you could challenge the causal explanations made by people you don't agree with. But speculation about causes and effects is always risky because life is complicated.

In her visual essay "Apples to Oranges," Claire Ironside depicts the striking effects that would result from the cause she is championing: a move to locally grown, organic food.

LINK TO P. 641

Consider the following passage from researcher Gail Tverberg's blog *Our Finite World*, from 2011, describing possible consequences of the commitment to increase the production of ethanol from corn:

> At the time the decision was made to expand corn ethanol production, we seemed to have an excess of arable land, and corn prices were low. Using some corn for ethanol looked like it would help farmers, and also help increase fuel for our vehicles. There was also a belief that cellulosic ethanol production might be right around the corner, and could substitute, so there would not be as much pressure on food supplies.
>
> Now the situation has changed. Food prices are much higher, and the number of people around the world with inadequate food supply

Paresh Nath, cartoonist for India's *National Herald*, personifies the causes for a world food crisis in this item from March 2011. © Paresh Nath, Cagle Cartoons, Inc.

> is increasing. The ethanol we are using for our cars is much more in direct competition with the food people around the world are using, and the situation may very well get worse, if there are crop failures.
>
> —Gail Tverberg, *Our Finite World*

Note that the researcher here begins by pointing out the cause-effect relationship that the government was hoping for and then points to the potential effects of that policy when circumstances change. As it turns out, using corn for fuel did have many unintended consequences, for example, inflating the price not only of corn but of wheat and soybeans as well, leading to food shortages and even food riots around the globe.

Arguments That State an Effect and Then Trace the Effect Back to Its Causes

This type of argument might begin with a specific effect (a catastrophic drop in sales of music CDs) and then trace it to its most likely causes (the introduction of MP3 technology, new modes of music distribution, a preference for single song purchases). Or you might examine the reasons that music executives offer for their industry's dip and decide whether their causal analyses pass muster.

Like other kinds of causal arguments, those tracing effects to a cause can have far-reaching significance. In 1962, for example, the scientist Rachel Carson seized the attention of millions with a famous causal argument about the effects that the overuse of chemical pesticides might have on the environment. Here's an excerpt from the beginning of her book-length study of this subject. Note how she begins with the effects before saying she'll go on to explore the causes:

> [A] strange blight crept over the area and everything began to change. Some evil spell had settled on the community: mysterious maladies swept the flocks of chickens; the cattle and sheep sickened and died. Everywhere was a shadow of death. The farmers spoke of much illness among their families. . . . There had been several sudden and unexplained deaths, not only among adults but even among children, who would be stricken suddenly while at play and die within a few hours. The roadsides, once so attractive, were now lined with browned and withered vegetation as though swept by fire. These, too, were silent, deserted by all living things. Even the streams were now lifeless. Anglers no longer visited them, for all the fish had died.

> **In the gutters under the eaves and between the shingles of the roofs, a white granular powder still showed a few patches; some weeks before it had fallen like snow upon the roofs and lawns, the fields and streams. No witchcraft, no enemy action had silenced the rebirth of new life in this stricken world. The people had done it themselves. . . . What has silenced the voices of spring in countless towns in America? This book is an attempt to explain.**
>
> —**Rachel Carson, *Silent Spring***

Today, one could easily write a causal argument of the first type about *Silent Spring* and the environmental movement that it spawned.

Arguments That Move through a Series of Links: A Causes B, Which Leads to C and Perhaps to D

In an environmental science class, for example, you might decide to argue that, despite reductions in acid rain, tightened national regulations regarding smokestack emissions from utility plants are still needed for the following reasons:

1. Emissions from utility plants in the Midwest still cause significant levels of acid rain in the eastern United States.
2. Acid rain threatens trees and other vegetation in eastern forests.
3. Powerful lobbyists have prevented midwestern states from passing strict laws to control emissions from these plants.
4. As a result, acid rain will destroy most eastern forests by 2030.

In this case, the first link is that emissions cause acid rain; the second, that acid rain causes destruction in eastern forests; and the third, that states have not acted to break the cause-and-effect relationship that is established by the first two points. These links set the scene for the fourth link, which ties the previous points together to argue from effect: unless X, then Y.

RESPOND.

The causes of some of the following events and phenomena are well known and frequently discussed. But do you understand these causes well enough to spell them out to someone else? Working in a group, see how well (and in how much detail) you can explain each of the following events or phenomena. Which explanations are relatively clear, and which seem more open to debate?

earthquakes/tsunamis

popularity of Lady Gaga or Taylor Swift or the band Wolf Alice

Cold War

Edward Snowden's leak of CIA documents

Ebola crisis in western Africa

popularity of the *Transformers* films

swelling caused by a bee sting

sharp rise in cases of autism or asthma

climate change

Characterizing Causal Arguments

Causal arguments tend to share several characteristics.

They Are Often Part of Other Arguments.

Many stand-alone causal arguments address questions that are fundamental to our well-being: *Why are juvenile asthma and diabetes increasing so dramatically in the United States? What are the causes of the rise in cases of malaria in Africa, and what can we do to counter this rise? What will happen to Europe if its birthrate continues to decline?*

But causal analyses often work to support other arguments—especially proposals. For example, a proposal to limit the time that children spend playing video games might first draw on a causal analysis to establish that playing video games can have bad results—such as violent behavior, short attention spans, and decreased social skills. The causal analysis provides a rationale that motivates the proposal. In this way, causal analyses can be useful in establishing good reasons for arguments in general.

They Are Almost Always Complex.

The complexity of most causal relationships makes it difficult to establish causes and effects. For example, in 2011 researchers at Northwestern University reported a startling correlation: youths who participated in church activities were far more likely to grow into obese adults than their counterparts who were not engaged in religious activities. How does one even begin to explain such a peculiar and unexpected finding? Too many church socials? Unhealthy food at potluck meals? More regular social engagement? Perhaps.

Or consider the complexity of analyzing the causes of food poisoning when they strike large populations: in 2008, investigators spent months trying to discover whether tomatoes, cilantro, or jalapeño peppers were the cause of a nationwide outbreak of salmonella. More than seventeen states were affected. But despite such challenges, whenever it is possible to demonstrate convincing causal connections between X and Y, we gain important knowledge and powerful arguments. That's why, for example, great effort went into establishing an indisputable link between smoking and lung cancer. Once proven, decisive legal action could finally be taken to warn smokers.

They Are Often Definition Based.

One reason that causal arguments are complex is that they often depend on careful definitions. Recent figures from the U.S. Department of Education, for example, show that the number of high school dropouts is rising and that this rise has caused an increase in youth unemployment. But exactly how does the study define *dropout*? A closer look may suggest that some students (perhaps a lot) who drop out later "drop back in" and complete high school or that some who drop out

"The rise in unemployment, however, which was somewhat offset by an expanding job market, was countered by an upturn in part-time dropouts, which, in turn, was diminished by seasonal factors, the anticipated summer slump, and, over-all, a small but perceptible rise in actual employment."

Causal arguments can also be confusing.

become successful entrepreneurs or business owners. Further, how does the study define *employment*? Until you can provide definitions for all key terms in a causal claim, you should proceed cautiously with your argument.

They Usually Yield Probable Rather Than Absolute Conclusions.

Because causal relationships are almost always complex or subtle, they seldom can yield more than a high degree of probability. Consequently, they are almost always subject to criticism or open to charges of false causality. (We all know smokers who defy the odds to live long, cancer-free lives.) Scientists in particular are wary when making causal claims.

Even after an event, proving precisely what caused it can be hard. During the student riots of the late 1960s, for example, a commission was charged with determining the causes of riots on a particular campus. After two years of work and almost a thousand pages of evidence and reports, the commission was unable to pinpoint anything but a broad network of contributing causes and related conditions. And how many years is it likely to take to unravel all the factors responsible for the extended recession and economic decline in the United States that began in 2008? After all, serious scholars are still arguing about the forces responsible for the Great Depression of 1929.

After exploring the effects of the mobile supermarket in an urban setting, Katherine Gustafson concludes that these markets aren't likely to be the best method of getting sustainable, affordable food into cities.

LINK TO P. 657

To demonstrate that X caused Y, you must find the strongest possible evidence and subject it to the toughest scrutiny. But a causal argument doesn't fail just because you can't find a single compelling cause. In fact, causal arguments are often most effective when they help readers appreciate how tangled our lives and landscapes really are.

Developing Causal Arguments

Exploring Possible Claims

To begin creating a strong causal claim, try listing some of the effects—events or phenomena—that you'd like to know the causes of:

- Why do college tuition costs routinely outstrip the rate of inflation?
- What's really behind the slow pace of development of alternative energy sources?
- Why are almost all the mothers in animated movies either dead to begin with or quickly killed off?

- Why is same-sex marriage more acceptable to American society than it was a decade ago?
- Why do so few younger Americans vote, even in major elections?

Or try moving in the opposite direction, listing some phenomena or causes you're interested in and then hypothesizing what kinds of effects they may produce:

- How will the growing popularity of e-readers change our relationships to books?
- What will happen as the result of efforts to repeal the Affordable Health Care Act?
- What will be the consequences if more liberal (or conservative) judges are appointed to the U.S. Supreme Court?
- What will happen as China and India become dominant industrialized nations?

Read a little about the causal issues that interest you most, and then try them out on friends and colleagues. They might suggest ways to refocus or clarify what you want to do or offer leads to finding information about your subject. After some initial research, map out the causal relationship you want to explore in simple form:

> **X might cause (or might be caused by) Y for the following reasons:**
>
> 1.
>
> 2.
>
> 3. **(add more as needed)**

Such a statement should be tentative because writing a causal argument should be an exercise in which you uncover facts, not assume them to be true. Often, your early assumptions (*Tuition was raised to renovate the stadium*) might be undermined by the facts you later discover (*Tuition doesn't fund the construction or maintenance of campus buildings*).

You might even decide to write a wildly exaggerated or parodic causal argument for humorous purposes. Humorist Dave Barry does this when he explains the causes of El Niño and other weather phenomena: "So we see that the true cause of bad weather, contrary to what they have been claiming all these years, is TV weather forecasters, who have also single-handedly destroyed the ozone layer via overuse of hair spray." Most of the causal reasoning you do, however, will take a serious approach to subjects that you, your family, and your friends care about.

RESPOND.

Working with a group, write a big *Why?* on a sheet of paper or computer screen, and then generate a list of *why* questions. Don't be too critical of the initial list:

Why

—*do people laugh?*

—*do swans mate for life?*

—*do college students binge drink?*

—*do teenagers drive fast?*

—*do babies cry?*

—*do politicians take risks on social media?*

Generate as lengthy a list as you can in fifteen minutes. Then decide which of the questions might make plausible starting points for intriguing causal arguments.

© Bill Coster/age fotostock

Defining the Causal Relationships

In developing a causal claim, you can examine the various types of causes and effects in play in a given argument and define their relationship. Begin by listing all the plausible causes or effects you need to consider. Then decide which are the most important for you to analyze or the easiest to defend or critique. The following chart on "Causes" may help you to appreciate some important terms and relationships.

Type of Causes	What It Is or Does	What It Looks Like
Sufficient cause	Enough for something to occur on its own	Lack of oxygen is sufficient to cause death Cheating on an exam is sufficient to fail a course
Necessary cause	Required for something to occur (but in combination with other factors)	Fuel is necessary for fire Capital is necessary for economic growth
Precipitating cause	Brings on a change	Protest march ignites a strike by workers Plane flies into strong thunderstorms
Proximate cause	Immediately present or visible cause of action	Strike causes company to declare bankruptcy Powerful wind shear causes plane to crash
Remote cause	Indirect or underlying explanation for action	Company was losing money on bad designs and inept manufacturing Wind shear warning failed to sound in cockpit
Reciprocal causes	One factor leads to a second, which reinforces the first, creating a cycle	Lack of good schools leads to poverty, which further weakens education, which leads to even fewer opportunities . . .

Even the most everyday causal analysis can draw on such distinctions among reasons and causes. What persuaded you, for instance, to choose the college you decided to attend? *Proximate* reasons might be the location of the school or the college's curriculum in your areas of interest. But what are the *necessary* reasons—the ones without which your choice of that college could not occur? Adequate financial support? Good test scores and academic record? The expectations of a parent?

Once you've identified a causal claim, you can draw out the reasons, warrants, and evidence that can support it most effectively:

Claim	Certain career patterns cause women to be paid less than men.
Reason	Women's career patterns differ from men's.
Warrant	Successful careers are made during the period between ages twenty-five and thirty-five.
Evidence	Women often drop out of or reduce work during the decade between ages twenty-five and thirty-five to raise families.

Claim	**Lack of community and alumni support caused the football coach to lose his job.**
Reason	**Ticket sales and alumni support have declined for three seasons in a row despite a respectable team record.**
Warrant	**Winning over fans is as important as winning games for college coaches in smaller athletic programs.**
Evidence	**Over the last ten years, coaches at several programs have been sacked because of declining support and revenues.**

RESPOND

Here's a schematic causal analysis of one event, exploring the difference among precipitating, necessary, and sufficient causes. Critique and revise the analysis as you see fit. Then create another of your own, beginning with a different event, phenomenon, incident, fad, or effect.

Event: Traffic fatality at an intersection

Precipitating cause: A pickup truck that runs a red light, totals a Prius, and injures its driver

Necessary cause: Two drivers who are navigating Friday rush-hour traffic (if no driving, then no accident)

Sufficient cause: A truck driver who is distracted by a cell-phone conversation

Supporting Your Point

In drafting your causal argument, you'll want to do the following:

- Show that the causes and effects you've suggested are highly probable and backed by evidence, or show what's wrong with the faulty causal reasoning you may be critiquing.
- Assess any links between causal relationships (what leads to or follows from what).
- Show that your explanations of any causal chains are accurate, or identify where links in a causal chain break down.
- Show that plausible cause-and-effect explanations haven't been ignored or that the possibility of multiple causes or effects has been considered.

In other words, you will need to examine your subject carefully and find appropriate ways to support your claims. There are different ways to accomplish that goal.

For example, in studying effects that are physical (as they would be with diseases or climate conditions), you can offer and test *hypotheses*, or theories about possible causes. That means researching such topics thoroughly because you'll need to draw upon authorities and research articles for your explanations and evidence. (See Chapter 17, "Academic Arguments," and Chapter 18, "Finding Evidence.") Don't be surprised if you find yourself debating which among conflicting authorities make the most plausible causal or explanatory arguments. Your achievement as a writer may be simply that you present these differences in an essay, leaving it to readers to make judgments of their own—as John Tierney does in "Can a Playground Be Too Safe?" at the end of this chapter (see p. 268).

But not all the evidence in compelling causal arguments needs to be strictly scientific or scholarly. Many causal arguments rely on **ethnographic observations**—the systematic study of ordinary people in their daily routines. How would you explain, for example, why some people step aside when they encounter someone head-on and others do not? In an argument that attempts to account for such behavior, investigators Frank Willis, Joseph Gier, and David Smith observed "1,038 displacements involving 3,141 persons" at a Kansas City shopping mall. In results that surprised the investigators, "gallantry" seemed to play a significant role in causing people to step aside for one another—more so than other causes that the investigators had anticipated (such as deferring to someone who's physically stronger or higher in status). Doubtless you've read of other such studies, perhaps in psychology courses. You may even decide to do a little fieldwork on your own—which raises the possibility of using personal experiences in support of a causal argument.

Indeed, people's experiences generally lead them to draw causal conclusions about things they know well. Personal experience can also help build your credibility as a writer, gain the empathy of listeners, and thus support a causal claim. Although one person's experiences cannot ordinarily be universalized, they can still argue eloquently for causal relationships. Listen to Sara Barbour, a recent graduate of Columbia University, as she draws upon her own carefully described experiences to bemoan what may happen when e-readers finally displace printed books:

> In eliminating a book's physical existence, something crucial is lost forever. Trapped in a Kindle, the story remains but the book can no longer be scribbled in, hoarded, burned, given, or received. We may be

able to read it, but we can't share it with others in the same way, and its ability to connect us to people, places, and ideas is that much less powerful.

I know the Kindle will eventually carry the day—an electronic reader means no more embarrassing coffee stains, no more library holds and renewals, no more frantic flipping through pages for a lost quote, or going to three bookstores in one afternoon to track down an evasive title. Who am I to advocate the doom of millions of trees when the swipe of a finger can deliver all 838 pages of *Middlemarch* into my waiting hands?

But once we all power up our Kindles something will be gone, a kind of language. Books communicate with us as readers—but as important, we communicate with each other through books themselves. When that connection is lost, the experience of reading—and our lives—will be forever altered.

—Sara Barbour, "Kindle vs. Books: The Dead Trees Society," *Los Angeles Times*, June 17, 2011

All these strategies—testing hypotheses, presenting experimental evidence, and offering personal experience—can help you support a causal argument or undermine a causal claim you regard as faulty.

RESPOND.

One of the fallacies of argument discussed in Chapter 5 is the *post hoc, ergo propter hoc* ("after this, therefore because of this") fallacy. Causal arguments are particularly prone to this kind of fallacious reasoning, in which a writer asserts a causal relationship between two entirely unconnected events. When Angelina Jolie gave birth to twins in 2008, for instance, the stock market rallied by nearly six hundred points, but it would be difficult to argue that either event is related to the other.

Because causal arguments can easily fall prey to this fallacy, you might find it instructive to create and defend an absurd connection of this kind. Begin by asserting a causal link between two events or phenomena that likely have no relationship: *The enormous popularity of* Doctor Who *is partially due to global warming.* Then spend a page or so spinning out an imaginative argument to defend the claim. It's OK to have fun with this exercise, but see how convincing you can be at generating plausibly implausible arguments.

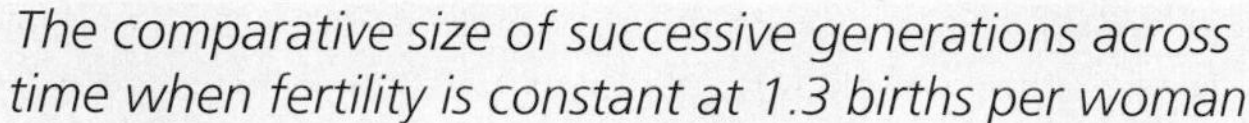

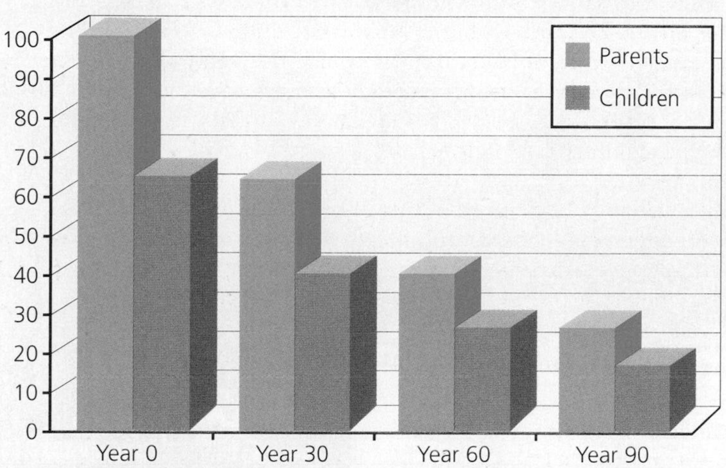

A simple graph can provide dramatic evidence for a causal claim—in this case, the effect of reduced fertility rates on a population. Data from Statistics Bureau, MIC; Ministry of Health, Labour and Welfare

Considering Design and Visuals

You may find that the best way to illustrate a causal relationship is to present it visually. Even a simple bar graph or chart can demonstrate a relationship between two variables that might be related to a specific cause, like the one above showing the dramatic effects of lowered birthrates. The report that uses this figure explores the effects that such a change would have on the economies of the world.

Or you may decide that the most dramatic way to present important causal information about a single issue or problem is via an infographic, cartoon, or public service announcement. Our arresting example on the next page is part of a campaign by People for the Ethical Treatment of Animals (PETA). An organization that advocates for animal rights, PETA promotes campaigns that typically try to sway people to adopt vegetarian diets by depicting the practices of the agriculture industry as cruel.

PETA's ad campaign expands its focus to environmentalists by explaining through causal links why they should consider vegetarian diets. Courtesy of People for the Ethical Treatment of Animals; peta.org

(Many of us have also seen their celebrity anti-fur campaigns; see p. 100 for one example.) Their "Meat's Not Green!" campaign, however, attempts to reach an audience that might not buy into the animal rights argument. Instead, it appeals to people who have environmentalist beliefs by presenting data that claims a causal link between animal farming and environmental destruction. How much of this data surprises you?

GUIDE to writing a causal argument

Finding a Topic

You're entering a causal argument when you:

- state a cause and then examine its effects: *The ongoing economic downturn has led more people to return to college to enhance their job market credentials.*
- describe an effect and trace it back to its causes: *There has been a recent surge in the hiring of part-time contract workers, likely due to the reluctance of businesses to hire permanent employees who would be subject to new health care regulations.*
- trace a string of causes to figure out why something happened: *The housing and financial markets collapsed in 2008 after government mandates to encourage homeownership led banks to invent questionable financial schemes in order to offer subprime mortgages to borrowers who bought homes they could not afford with loans they could not pay back.*
- explore plausible consequences (intended or not) of a particular action, policy, or change: *The ban on incandescent lightbulbs may draw more attention to climate change than any previous government action.*

Spend time brainstorming possibilities for causal arguments. Many public issues lend themselves to causal analysis and argument: browse the homepage of a newspaper or news source on any given day to discover plausible topics. Consider topics that grow from your own experiences.

It's fair game, too, to question the accuracy or adequacy of existing arguments about causality. You can write a strong paper by raising doubts about the facts or assumptions that others have made and perhaps offering a better causal explanation on your own.

Researching Your Topic

Causal arguments will lead you to many different resources:

- current news media—especially magazines and newspapers (online or in print)
- online databases
- scholarly journals

- books written on your subject (here you can do a keyword search, either in your library or online)
- blogs, Web sites, or social networking sites

In addition, why not carry out some field research? Conduct interviews with appropriate authorities on your subject, create a questionnaire aimed at establishing a range of opinions on your subject, or arrange a discussion forum among people with a stake in the issue. The information you get from interviews, questionnaires, or open-ended dialogue might provide ideas to enrich your argument or evidence to back up your claims.

Formulating a Claim

For a conventional causal analysis, try to formulate a claim that lets readers know where you stand on some issue involving causes and effects. First, identify the kind of causal argument that you expect to make (see pp. 241–45 for a review of these kinds of arguments) or decide whether you intend, instead, to debunk an existing cause-and-effect claim. Then explore your relationship to the claim. What do you know about the subject and its causes and effects? Why do you favor (or disagree with) the claim? What significant reasons can you offer in support of your position?

End this process by formulating a thesis—a complete sentence that says, in effect, *A causes (or does not cause or is caused by) B*, followed by a summary of the reasons supporting this causal relationship. Make your thesis as specific as possible and be sure that it's sufficiently controversial or intriguing to hold a reader's interest. Of course, feel free to revise any such claim as you learn more about a subject.

For causal topics that are more open-ended and exploratory, you may not want to take a strong position, particularly at the outset. Instead, your argument might simply present a variety of reasonable (and possibly competing) explanations and scenarios.

Examples of Causal Claims

- Right-to-carry gun laws have led to increased rates of crime in states that have approved such legislation.
- Sophisticated use of social media is now a must for any political candidate who hopes to win.
- Grade inflation is lowering the value of a college education.

- The proliferation of images in film, television, and computer-generated texts is changing the way we read and use information.
- Experts don't yet agree on the long-term impact that sophisticated use of social media will have on American political campaigns, though some effects are already evident.

Preparing a Proposal

If your instructor asks you to prepare a proposal for your project, here's a format that may help:

State your thesis completely. If you're having trouble doing so, try outlining it in Toulmin terms:

Claim:

Reason(s):

Warrant(s):

Alternatively, you might indicate an intention to explore a particular causal question in your project, with the thesis perhaps coming later.

- **Explain why this issue deserves attention. What's at stake?**
- **Identify whom you hope to reach through your argument and why this group of readers would be interested in it.**
- **Briefly discuss the key challenges you anticipate in preparing your argument.**
- **Determine what research strategies you'll use. What sources do you expect to consult?**
- **Briefly identify and explore the major stakeholders in your argument and what alternative perspectives you may need to consider as you formulate your argument.**

Considering Format and Media

Your instructor may specify that you use a particular format and/or medium. If not, ask yourself these questions to help you make a good choice:

- What format is most appropriate for your causal argument? Does it call for an academic essay, a report, an infographic, a brochure, or something else?

- What medium is most appropriate for your argument? Would it be best delivered orally to a live audience? Presented as an audio essay or podcast? Presented in print only or in print with illustrations?
- Will you need visuals, such as moving or still images, maps, graphs, charts—and what function will they play in your argument? Make sure they are not just "added on" but are necessary components of the argument.

Thinking about Organization

Your causal argument will likely include elements such as the following:

- a specific causal claim somewhere in the paper—or the identification of a significant causal issue
- an explanation of the claim's significance or importance
- evidence sufficient to support each cause or effect—or, in an argument based on a series of causal links, evidence to support the relationships among the links
- a consideration of other plausible causes and effects, and evidence that you have thought carefully about these alternatives before offering your own ideas

Getting and Giving Response: Questions for Peer Response

Your instructor may assign you to a group for the purpose of reading and responding to each other's drafts. If not, ask for responses from serious readers or consultants at a writing center. Use the following questions to evaluate a colleague's draft. Be sure to illustrate your comments with examples; specific comments help more than general observations.

The Claim

- Does the claim state a causal argument?
- Does the claim identify clearly what causes and effects are being examined?
- What about the claim will make it appeal to readers?
- Is the claim too sweeping? Does it need to be qualified? How might it be narrowed and focused?
- How strong is the relationship between the claim and the reasons given to support it? How could that relationship be made more explicit?

Evidence for the Claim

- What's the strongest evidence offered for the claim? What, if any, evidence needs to be strengthened?
- Is enough evidence offered to show that these causes are responsible for the identified effect, that these effects result from the identified cause, or that a series of causes and effects are linked? If not, what additional evidence is needed? What kinds of sources might provide this evidence?
- How credible will the sources be to potential readers? What other sources might be more persuasive?
- Is evidence in support of the claim analyzed logically? Is more discussion needed?
- Have alternative causes and effects been considered? Have objections to the claim been carefully considered and presented fairly? Have these objections been discussed?

Organization and Style

- How are the parts of the argument organized? Is this organization effective?
- Will readers understand the relationships among the claims, supporting reasons, warrants, and evidence? If not, how might those connections be clearer? Is the function of every visual clear? Are more transitions needed? Would headings or graphic devices help?
- Are the transitions or links from point to point, sentence to sentence, and paragraph to paragraph clear and effective? If not, how could they be improved?
- Are all visuals (or other elements such as audio or video clips) carefully integrated into the text? Is each visual introduced and commented on to point out its significance? Is each visual labeled as a figure or a table and given a caption as well as a citation?
- Is the style suited to the subject? Is it too formal, casual, or technical? Can it be improved?
- Which sentences seem effective? Which ones seem weaker, and how could they be improved? Should short sentences be combined, and any longer ones be broken up?
- How effective are the paragraphs? Too short or too long? How can they be improved?

- Which words or phrases seem effective? Do any seem vague or inappropriate for the audience or the writer's purpose? Are technical or unfamiliar terms defined?

Spelling, Punctuation, Mechanics, Documentation, and Format

- Are there any errors in spelling, punctuation, capitalization, and the like?
- Is the documentation appropriate and consistent? (See Chapter 22.)
- Does the paper or project follow an appropriate format? Is it appropriately designed and attractively presented?

PROJECTS

1. Develop an argument exploring one of the cause-and-effect topics mentioned in this chapter. Just a few of those topics are listed below:

   Disappearance of honeybees in the United States

   Causes of long-term unemployment or declining job markets

   Using the tax code to discourage/encourage specific behaviors (i.e., smoking, eating unhealthy foods, hiring more workers)

   Increasing numbers of obese children and/or adults

   Ramifications of increasing amounts of time spent on social media sites

   Results of failing to pass immigration reform legislation

   Repercussions of U.S. ethanol policy

   What is lost/gained as paper books disappear

2. Write a causal argument about a subject you know well, even if the topic does not strike you as particularly "academic": *What accounts for the popularity of* The Hunger Games *trilogy? What are the likely consequences of students living more of their lives via social media? How are video games changing the way students you know learn? Why do women love shoes?* In this argument, be sure to separate precipitating or proximate causes from sufficient or necessary ones. In other words, do a deep and revealing causal analysis about your subject, giving readers new insights.

3. John Tierney's essay "Can a Playground Be Too Safe?" (see p. 268) explores some unintended consequences of noble-minded efforts in recent decades to make children's playgrounds safer. After reading the Tierney piece, list any comparable situations you know of where unintended consequences may have undermined the good (or maybe even bad?) intentions of those who took action or implemented some change. Choose the most intriguing situation, do the necessary research, and write a causal argument about it.

4. Raven Jiang's "Dota 2: The Face of Professional Gaming" (see p. 264) argues that crowdfunding and netstreaming are two major causes in the rise of big-money professional gaming, which he sees as a phenomenon that is here to stay ("Watch out NFL, America's sport is about to change"). In a project of your own, describe the causes that have led to a particular effect on your campus or in your community or place of work. You may point out, as Jiang does, both advantages and disadvantages of the change brought about by the causes you analyze.

Dota 2: The Face of Professional Gaming

RAVEN JIANG

August 5, 2014

The introductory paragraph presents the "effect": a huge rise in professional online gaming.

Just over a week ago, history was made when a team of five young Chinese men left Seattle with $5 million in winnings. The game they were playing was not poker but "Dota 2," a multiplayer online game made by the Bellevue-based gaming company Valve. This year's annual "Dota 2" Internationals tournament, the fourth one since its creation, presented the largest prize pool ever seen in professional gaming—a total of $10.9 million. ESPN covered the matches and it seemed like every media outlet was trying to get in on the story, if only as a human interest piece. There is a sense that we are entering new uncharted territories.

A causal claim is stated.

Since the early 2000s, much has been written and said about the slow but steady rise of professional video gaming. What happened this month at Seattle is a coming-of-age story that we are all familiar with, but it is also so much more. A confluence of factors had brought the 2014 "Dota 2" Internationals into the mainstream consciousness and they represent an interesting microcosm of the technological forces that are shaping our future, gaming and otherwise.

The first cause is introduced: crowdfunding.

Kickstarter brought the idea of crowdfunding into our daily lives, but Valve made it addictive with "Dota 2." Unlike past video gaming tournaments that relied solely on sponsorships for prize money, which were often the first thing on the chopping boards when it came to corporate budget cuts, the Internationals were almost

---

Raven Jiang is an undergraduate at Stanford University, studying computer science. His piece was first published in the *Stanford Daily*, a student-produced newspaper founded in 1892.

entirely crowdfunded via in-game item purchases by online players. In the weeks leading up to the event, fans could purchase tournament-related in-game items to contribute to the prize pool and to eventually earn vanity visual effects that they could show off in-game on their characters. And just like a Kickstarter campaign, there was a counter tracking the amount raised, with final rewards that fans earn determined by the final total—think Kickstarter fundraising goals. For example, the reward for hitting $3.5 million this time was access to special chat emoticons. In this way, much like purchasing swag at an indie concert, fans not only contribute to the prize pool but feel like they get something back in return.

The benefits of crowdfunding are stated.

So, fans pay both to support the goal of having a more exciting tournament with bigger stakes and to gain per sonal items; Valve takes a cut as profits and professional Dota players get to make a career out of their passion. As Michael Scott once said, this is a win-win-win outcome. The final prize pool of $10.9 million was more than three times that of last year. To put that into perspective, the second placing team this year won more money than last year's winning team. That's a growth rate that would make Bernie Madoff jealous.

The author points out benefits to the winners as well as the viewers.

The successful use of crowdfunding by Valve is a great example of the value of crowdfunding as a whole. The reason why corporate sponsorships have historically been unreliable is because they are a poor indirect proxy for consumer demand. Much like the homemade gadgets that find their audience on Kickstarter, Valve is tapping into an underserved demand by getting the consumers to directly pay for the cost of production.

The other major force behind the modern "Dota 2" juggernaut is live game streaming. YouTube brought us video sharing and Netflix brought us the Internet's take on cable TV, but online gaming is helping to turn a very different form of visual entertainment into its own industry. Just like the Super Bowl, we now have the huge

The second major cause is presented to support the claim.

events that draw millions of viewers in the likes of the Internationals. But beyond that familiar format, there is also a burgeoning cottage industry of individual gamers who stream their gaming sessions live online and make money off of advertising and product placements. A popular full-time game streamer can take home a six-digit income doing what his parents say will never amount to much, probably right in their basement.

The prevalence of game streaming has created the interesting situation in which many fans of popular online games seldom ever actually feel the need to play them, because watching is so much less stressful, less time-consuming, and more readily accessible. In some sense, "Dota 2," a game notorious for its complex game mechanics, can probably thank the rise of stream watching for the success of its annual championship events, because let's face it: If every sports fan had to be able to play the game in order to understand and enjoy watching it, then college football would be bankrupt. With the professionalization of online gaming that parallels the paths taken by its traditional counterparts, it is no wonder Google recently decided to fork out a cool billion dollars to acquire the major game streaming site Twitch.tv.

The point is that online gaming is going to be a big deal. And it is a big deal not just because video gaming is becoming big money, but because its rise is symbolic of the same technological shifts that are changing all other aspects of our lives.

The author gives proof that online video gaming is already big time in South Korea and the United States.

The future is already here in South Korea, where professional "Starcraft" gamers are literally national celebrities. Significant milestones like the recent "Dota 2" Internationals suggest that the U.S. is on its way there. Watching the live stream of the Internationals with its extremely professional production value, the seasoned commentators throwing team and player stats at each other and the incredible amount of skill and concentration exhibited by the competitors, an alien visitor from Alpha Centauri would be hard-pressed to say what exactly differentiates "Dota 2" from sports. (I suppose there has not been any accusation of steroid abuse. Yet.)

That said, it is not all rainbows and unicorns. There is a general feeling that this year's matches at the Internationals have not been as exciting and eventful as last year's. Perhaps the unprecedented prize pool this year was causing players to be more risk-averse, leading to fewer clutch plays and comebacks from behind. Both of the teams in the final were also Chinese, who are known for being more methodological both in play style and training processes. The old fan favorite Na'Vi, the Eastern European past championship winners known for their dramatic comebacks and eccentric play styles, did not manage to get into the final four this year. Still, even if "Dota 2" does falter, it has already pushed the boundaries for professional gaming and paved the way for the future.

The downsides of the dramatic rise in online gaming are presented.

The concluding sentence assures readers that even if Dota 2 itself fails, what it represents has already had a major impact on the future of gaming.

Watch out NFL, America's sport is about to change.

Can a Playground Be Too Safe?

JOHN TIERNEY

A childhood relic: jungle gyms, like this one in Riverside Park in Manhattan, have disappeared from most American playgrounds in recent decades. © Dith Pran/The New York Times/Redux

When seesaws and tall slides and other perils were disappearing from New York's playgrounds, Henry Stern drew a line in the sandbox. As the city's parks commissioner in the 1990s, he issued an edict concerning the ten-foot-high jungle gym near his childhood home in northern Manhattan.

"I grew up on the monkey bars in Fort Tryon Park, and I never forgot how good it felt to get to the top of them," Mr. Stern said. "I didn't want to see that playground bowdlerized. I said that as long as I was parks commissioner, those monkey bars were going to stay."

John Tierney is a journalist and coauthor of the book *Willpower: Rediscovering the Greatest Human Strength* (2011). He writes the science column "Findings" for the *New York Times*, where this piece was originally published on July 18, 2011. You will note that, as a journalist, Tierney cites sources without documenting them formally. An academic version of this argument might offer both in-text citations and a list of sources at the end.

His philosophy seemed reactionary at the time, but today it's shared by some researchers who question the value of safety-first playgrounds. Even if children do suffer fewer physical injuries—and the evidence for that is debatable—the critics say that these playgrounds may stunt emotional development, leaving children with anxieties and fears that are ultimately worse than a broken bone.

"Children need to encounter risks and overcome fears on the playground," said Ellen Sandseter, a professor of psychology at Queen Maud University in Norway. "I think monkey bars and tall slides are great. As playgrounds become more and more boring, these are some of the few features that still can give children thrilling experiences with heights and high speed."

After observing children on playgrounds in Norway, England, and Australia, Dr. Sandseter identified six categories of risky play: exploring heights, experiencing high speed, handling dangerous tools, being near dangerous elements (like water or fire), rough-and-tumble play (like wrestling), and wandering alone away from adult supervision. The most common is climbing heights.

"Climbing equipment needs to be high enough, or else it will be too boring in the long run," Dr. Sandseter said. "Children approach thrills and risks in a progressive manner, and very few children would try to climb to the highest point for the first time they climb. The best thing is to let children encounter these challenges from an early age, and they will then progressively learn to master them through their play over the years."

Sometimes, of course, their mastery fails, and falls are the common form of playground injury. But these rarely cause permanent damage, either physically or emotionally. While some psychologists—and many parents—have worried that a child who suffered a bad fall would develop a fear of heights, studies have shown the opposite pattern: A child who's hurt in a fall before the age of nine is less likely as a teenager to have a fear of heights.

By gradually exposing themselves to more and more dangers on the playground, children are using the same habituation techniques developed by therapists to help adults conquer phobias, according to Dr. Sandseter and a fellow psychologist, Leif Kennair, of the Norwegian University for Science and Technology.

"Risky play mirrors effective cognitive behavioral therapy of anxiety," they write in the journal *Evolutionary Psychology*, concluding that this "anti-phobic effect" helps explain the evolution of children's fondness for thrill-seeking. While a youthful zest for exploring heights might not seem adaptive — why would natural selection favor children who risk death before they have a chance to reproduce? — the dangers seemed to be outweighed by the benefits of conquering fear and developing a sense of mastery.

"Paradoxically," the psychologists write, "we posit that our fear of children being harmed by mostly harmless injuries may result in more fearful children and increased levels of psychopathology."

The old tall jungle gyms and slides disappeared from most American playgrounds across the country in recent decades because of parental concerns, federal guidelines, new safety standards set by manufacturers and — the most frequently cited factor — fear of lawsuits.

Shorter equipment with enclosed platforms was introduced, and the old pavement was replaced with rubber, wood chips, or other materials designed for softer landings. These innovations undoubtedly prevented some injuries, but some experts question their overall value.

"There is no clear evidence that playground safety measures have lowered the average risk on playgrounds," said David Ball, a professor of risk management at Middlesex University in London. He noted that the risk of some injuries, like long fractures of the arm, actually increased after the introduction of softer surfaces on playgrounds in Britain and Australia.

"This sounds counterintuitive, but it shouldn't, because it is a common phenomenon," Dr. Ball said. "If children and parents believe they are in an environment which is safer than it actually is, they will take more risks. An argument against softer surfacing is that children think it is safe, but because they don't understand its properties, they overrate its performance."

Reducing the height of playground equipment may help toddlers, but it can produce unintended consequences among bigger children. "Older children are discouraged from taking healthy exercise on playgrounds because they have been designed with the safety of the very young in mind," Dr. Ball said. "Therefore, they may play in more dangerous places, or not at all."

Fear of litigation led New York City officials to remove seesaws, merry-go-rounds, and the ropes that young Tarzans used to swing from one platform to another. Letting children swing on tires became taboo because of fears that the heavy swings could bang into a child.

"What happens in America is defined by tort lawyers, and unfortunately that limits some of the adventure playgrounds," said Adrian Benepe, the current parks commissioner. But while he misses the Tarzan ropes, he's glad that the litigation rate has declined, and he's not nostalgic for asphalt pavement.

"I think safety surfaces are a godsend," he said. "I suspect that parents who have to deal with concussions and broken arms wouldn't agree that playgrounds have become too safe." The ultra-safe enclosed platforms of the 1980s and 1990s may have been an overreaction, Mr. Benepe said, but lately there have been more creative alternatives.

"The good news is that manufacturers have brought out new versions of the old toys," he said. "Because of height limitations, no one's building the old monkey bars anymore, but kids can go up smaller climbing walls and rope nets and artificial rocks."

Still, sometimes there's nothing quite like being ten feet off the ground, as a new generation was discovering the other afternoon at Fort Tryon Park. A soft rubber surface carpeted the pavement, but the jungle gym of Mr. Stern's youth was still there. It was the prime destination for many children, including those who'd never seen one before, like Nayelis Serrano, a ten-year-old from the South Bronx who was visiting her cousin.

When she got halfway up, at the third level of bars, she paused, as if that was high enough. Then, after a consultation with her mother, she continued to the top, the fifth level, and descended to recount her triumph.

"I was scared at first," she explained. "But my mother said if you don't try, you'll never know if you could do it. So I took a chance and kept going. At the top I felt very proud." As she headed back for another climb, her mother, Orkidia Rojas, looked on from a bench and considered the pros and cons of this unfamiliar equipment.

"It's fun," she said. "I'd like to see it in our playground. Why not? It's kind of dangerous, I know, but if you just think about danger you're never going to get ahead in life."

12
Proposals

Left to right: © Florian Kopp/agefotostock.com; spaxiax/Shutterstock; AP Photo/Eric Gay

A student looking forward to spring break proposes to two friends that they join a group that will spend the vacation helping to build a school in a Haitian village.

The members of a club for undergrad business majors talk about their common need to create informative, appealing, interactive résumés. After much talk, three members suggest that the club develop a résumé app especially for business majors looking for a first job.

A project team at a large architectural firm works for three months developing a response to an RFP (request for proposal) to convert a university library into a digital learning center.

Understanding and Categorizing Proposals

We live in an era of big proposals—complex programs for health care reform, bold dreams to privatize space exploration, multibillion-dollar designs for high-speed rail systems, ceaseless calls to improve education, and so many other such ideas brought down to earth by sobering proposals for budget reform and deficit reduction. As a result, there's often more talk than action because persuading people (or legislatures) to do something—or *anything!*—is always hard. But that's what *proposal arguments* do: they provide thoughtful reasons for supporting or sometimes resisting change.

Such arguments, whether national or local, formal or casual, are important not only on the national scene but also in all of our lives. How many proposals do you make or respond to in one day? A neighbor might suggest that you volunteer to help clean up an urban creek bed; a campus group might demand that students get better seats at football games; a supervisor might ask for ideas to improve customer satisfaction at a restaurant; you might offer an ad agency reasons to hire you as a summer intern—or propose to a friend that you take in the latest zombie film. In each case, the proposal implies that some action should take place and suggests that there are sound reasons why it should.

This cartoon, by Steve Breen, suggests that high-speed rail proposals are going to run into a major obstacle in California. By permission of Steve Breen and Creators Syndicate, Inc.

In their simplest form, proposal arguments look something like this:

A should do B because of C.

Our student government (A) **should endorse the Academic Bill of Rights** (B) **because students should not be punished in their courses for their personal political views.** (C)

Proposals come at us so routinely that it's not surprising that they cover a dizzyingly wide range of possibilities. So it may help to think of proposal arguments as divided roughly into two kinds—those that focus on specific practices and those that focus on broad matters of policy. Here are several examples of each kind:

Proposals about Practices

- The college should allow students to pay tuition on a month-by-month basis.
- Commercial hotels should stop opposing competitors like Airbnb.
- College athletes should be paid for the services they provide.

Proposals about Policies

- The college should adopt a policy guaranteeing that students in all majors can graduate in four years.
- The United Nations should make saving the oceans from pollution a global priority.
- Major Silicon Valley firms should routinely reveal the demographic makeup of their workforces.

RESPOND•

People write proposal arguments to solve problems and to change the way things are. But problems aren't always obvious: what troubles some people might be no big deal to others. To get an idea of the range of problems people face on your campus (some of which you may not even have thought of as problems), divide into groups, and brainstorm about things that annoy you on and around campus, including wastefulness in the cafeterias, 8:00 a.m. classes, and long lines for football or concert tickets. Ask each group to aim for at least a dozen gripes. Then choose three problems, and as a group, discuss how you'd prepare a proposal to deal with them.

Characterizing Proposals

Proposals have three main characteristics:

1. They call for change, often in response to a problem.
2. They focus on the future.
3. They center on the audience.

Proposals always call for some kind of action. They aim at getting something done—or sometimes at *preventing* something from being done. Proposals marshal evidence and arguments to persuade people to choose a course of action: *Let's build a completely green house. Let's oppose the latest Supreme Court ruling on Internet privacy. Let's create a campus organization for first-generation college students. Let's ban drones from campus airspace, especially at sporting events.* But you know the old saying, "You can lead a horse to water, but you can't make it drink." It's usually easier to *convince* audiences what a good course of action is than to *persuade* them to take it (or pay for it). Even if you present a cogent proposal, you may still have work to do.

What is Charles A. Riley II proposing in *Disability and the Media: Prescriptions for Change*? How does his argument center on the audience?

LINK TO P. 527

Proposal arguments must appeal to more than good sense. Ethos matters, too. It helps if a writer suggesting a change carries a certain gravitas earned by experience or supported by knowledge and research. If your word and credentials carry weight, then an audience is more likely to listen to your proposal. So when the commanders of three *Apollo* moon missions, Neil Armstrong, James Lovell, and Eugene Cernan, wrote an open letter to President Obama expressing their dismay at his administration's decision to cancel NASA's plans for advanced spacecraft and new lunar missions, they won a wide audience:

> **For The United States, the leading space faring nation for nearly half a century, to be without carriage to low Earth orbit and with no human exploration capability to go beyond Earth orbit for an indeterminate time into the future, destines our nation to become one of second or even third rate stature. While the President's plan envisages humans traveling away from Earth and perhaps toward Mars at some time in the future, the lack of developed rockets and spacecraft will assure that ability will not be available for many years.**
>
> **Without the skill and experience that actual spacecraft operation provides, the USA is far too likely to be on a long downhill slide to mediocrity. America must decide if it wishes to remain a leader in space. If it does, we should institute a program which will give us the very best chance of achieving that goal.**

But even their considerable ethos was not enough to carry the day with the space agency and the man who made the decision.

All that remains of the American space program?
Michael Williamson/The Washington Post/Getty Images

Yet, as the space program example obviously demonstrates, proposal arguments focus on the future—what people, institutions, or governments should do over the upcoming weeks, months, or, in the NASA moon-mission example, decades. This orientation toward the future presents special challenges, since few of us have crystal balls. Proposal arguments must therefore offer the best evidence available to suggest that actions we recommend will achieve what they promise.

In May 2014, Senator Elizabeth Warren introduced legislation aimed at reducing student loan debt, in part by allowing for refinancing. In an interview in *Rolling Stone*, Senator Warren explained:

> **Homeowners refinance their loans when interest rates go down. Businesses refinance their loans. But right now, there's no way for students to be able to do that. I've proposed that we reduce the interest rate on the outstanding loan debt to the same rate Republicans and Democrats came together last year to set on new loans [3.86 percent]. For millions of borrowers, that would cut interest rates in half or more.**

Yet Warren's proposal soon came under fire, particularly from senators who argued that the proposed bill did little to reduce borrowing or lower

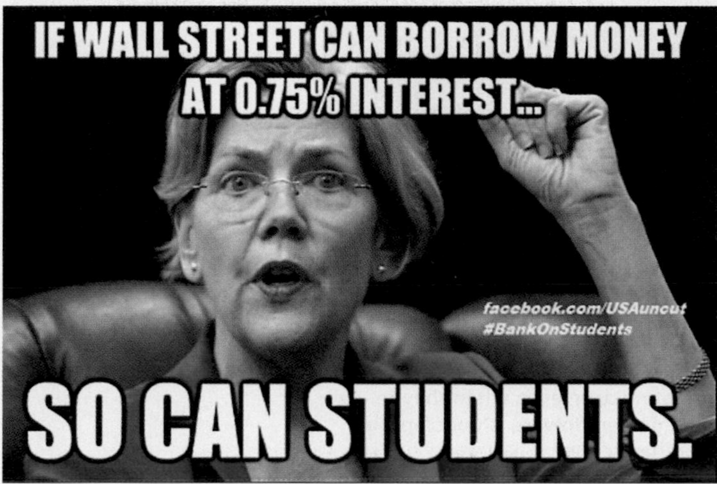

http://www.ClassWarfareExists.com

the cost of higher education. So despite the concerns of bankers and economists that the $1.1 trillion student loan debt is dampening the national economy, the bill was turned aside on June 11, 2014.

Which raises the matter of audiences, and we are left asking whether Senator Warren's bill spoke equally well to students, parents, bankers, and members of Congress. Some of those audiences failed to be convinced.

Some proposals are tailored to general audiences; consequently, they avoid technical language, make straightforward and relatively simple points, and sometimes use charts, graphs, and tables to make data comprehensible. You can find such arguments, for example, in newspaper editorials, letters to the editor, and political documents like Senator Warren's proposed legislation. And such appeals to a broad group make sense when a proposal—say, to finance new toll roads or build an art museum—must surf on waves of community support and financing.

But often proposals need to win the approval of specific groups or individuals (such as financiers, developers, public officials, and legislators) who have the power to make change actually happen. Such arguments will usually be more technical, detailed, and comprehensive than those aimed at the general public because people directly involved with an issue have a stake in it. They may be affected by it themselves and thus have in-depth knowledge of the subject. Or they may be responsible for implementing the proposal. You can expect them to have specific

Proposals have to take audience values into account. Shooting deer, even when they're munching on garden flowers, is unacceptable to most suburbanites. Ron Sanford/Science Source®/ Photo Researchers

questions about it and, possibly, formidable objections. So identifying your potential audiences is critical to the success of any proposal. On your own campus, for example, a plan to alter admissions policies might be directed both to students in general and (perhaps in a different form) to the university president, members of the faculty council, and admissions officers.

An effective proposal also has to be compatible with the values of the audience. Some ideas may make good sense but cannot be enacted. For example, many American towns and cities have a problem with expanding deer populations. Without natural predators, the deer are moving closer to homes, dining on gardens and shrubbery, and endangering traffic. Yet one obvious and feasible solution—culling the herds through hunting—is usually not saleable to communities (perhaps too many people remember *Bambi*).

RESPOND.

Work in a group to identify about half a dozen problems on your campus or in the local community, looking for a wide range of issues. (Don't focus on problems in individual classes.) Once you have settled on these issues, then use various resources—the Web, the phone book (if you can find one), a campus directory—to locate specific people, groups, or offices whom you might address or influence to deal with the issues you have identified.

Developing Proposals

In developing a proposal, you will have to do some or all of the following:

- Define a problem that needs a solution or describe a need that is not currently addressed.
- Make a strong claim that addresses the problem or need. Your solution should be an action directed at the future.
- Show why your proposal will fix the problem or address the need.
- Demonstrate that your proposal is feasible.

This might sound easy, but writing a proposal argument can be a process of discovery. At the outset, you think you know exactly what ought to be done, but by the end, you may see (and even recommend) other options.

Defining a Need or Problem

To make a proposal, first establish that a need or problem exists. You'll typically dramatize the problem that you intend to fix at the beginning of your project and then lead up to a specific claim. But in some cases, you could put the need or problem right after your claim as the major reason for adopting the proposal:

> **Let's ban cell phones on campus now. Why? Because we've become a school of walking zombies. No one speaks to or even acknowledges the people they meet or pass on campus. Half of our students are so busy chattering to people that they don't participate in the community around them.**

How can you make readers care about the problem you hope to address? Following are some strategies:

- Paint a vivid picture of the need or problem.
- Show how the need or problem affects people, both those in the immediate audience and the general public as well.
- Underscore why the need or problem is significant and pressing.
- Explain why previous attempts to address the issue may have failed.

For example, in proposing that the military draft be restored in the United States or that all young men and women give two years to national service (a tough sell!), you might begin by drawing a picture of a younger generation that is self-absorbed, demands instant gratification, and doesn't understand what it means to participate as a full member of society. Or you might note how many young people today fail to develop the life skills they need to strike out on their own. Or like congressional representative Charles Rangel (D-New York), who regularly proposes a Universal National Service Act, you could define the issue as a matter of fairness, arguing that the current all-volunteer army shifts the burden of national service to a small and unrepresentative sample of the American population. Speaking on CNN on January 26, 2013, Rangel said:

> **Since we replaced the compulsory military draft with an all-volunteer force in 1973, our nation has been making decisions about wars without worry over who fights them. I sincerely believe that reinstating the draft would compel the American public to have a stake in the wars we fight as a nation. That is why I wrote the Universal National Service Act, known as the "draft" bill, which requires all men and women between ages 18 and 25 to give two years of service in any capacity that promotes our national defense.**

Of course, you would want to cite authorities and statistics to prove that any problem you're diagnosing is real and that it touches your likely audience. Then readers *may* be ready to hear your proposal.

File this cartoon under "anticipate objections to your proposal." © Mike Keefe/Cagle Cartoons, Inc.

In describing a problem that your proposal argument intends to solve, be sure to review earlier attempts to fix it. Many issues have a long history that you can't afford to ignore (or be ignorant of). Understand too that some problems seem to grow worse every time someone tinkers with them. You might pause before proposing any new attempt to reform the current system of financing federal election campaigns when you discover that previous reforms have resulted in more bureaucracy, more restrictions on political expression, and more unregulated money flowing into the system. *"Enough is enough"* can be a potent argument when faced with such a mess.

RESPOND●

If you review "Let's Charge Politicians for Wasting Our Time" at the end of this chapter, a brief proposal by political and culture writer/blogger Virginia Postrel, you'll see that she spends quite a bit of time pointing out the irritation caused by unwanted political robocalls to her landline, even though she recognizes that such calls are illegal on cell phones. Does this focus on the landline take away from her proposal that the politicians should have to pay a fee for such calls as well as for unsolicited email messages they send, a proposal also put forward by technology guru Esther Dyson? Would you advise her to revise her argument—and if so, how?

Making a Strong and Clear Claim

After you've described and analyzed a problem, you're prepared to offer a fix. Begin with your claim (a proposal of what X or Y should do), followed by the reason(s) that X or Y should act and the effects of adopting the proposal:

Claim	**Communities should encourage the development of charter schools.**
Reason	**Charter schools are not burdened by the bureaucracy that is associated with most public schooling.**
Effects	**Instituting such schools will bring more effective education to communities and offer an incentive to the public schools to improve their programs.**

Having established a claim, you can explore its implications by drawing out the reasons, warrants, and evidence that can support it most effectively:

Claim	**In light of a recent U.S. Supreme Court decision that ruled that federal drug laws cannot be used to prosecute doctors who prescribe drugs for use in suicide, our state should immediately pass a bill legalizing physician-assisted suicide for patients who are terminally ill.**
Reason	**Physician-assisted suicide can relieve the suffering of those who are terminally ill and will die soon.**
Warrant	**The relief of suffering is desirable.**
Evidence	**Oregon voters have twice approved the state's Death with Dignity Act, which has been in effect since 1997, and to date the suicide rate has not risen sharply, nor have doctors given out a large number of prescriptions for death-inducing drugs. Several other states are considering ballot initiatives in favor of doctor-assisted suicide.**

The *reason* sets up the need for the proposal, whereas the *warrant* and *evidence* demonstrate that the proposal is just and could meet its objective. Your actual argument would develop each point in detail.

RESPOND.

For each problem and solution below, make a list of readers' likely objections to the solution offered. Then propose a solution of your own, and explain why you think it's more workable than the original.

Problem	**Future deficits in the Social Security system**
Solution	**Raise the age of retirement to seventy-two.**
Problem	**Severe grade inflation in college courses**
Solution	**Require a prescribed distribution of grades in every class: 10% A; 20% B; 40% C; 20% D; 10% F.**
Problem	**Increasing rates of obesity in the general population**
Solution	**Ban the sale of high-fat sandwiches and entrees in fast-food restaurants.**
Problem	**Inattentive driving because drivers are texting**
Solution	**Institute a one-year mandatory prison sentence for the first offense.**
Problem	**Increase in sexual assaults on and around campus**
Solution	**Establish a 10:00 p.m. curfew on weekends.**

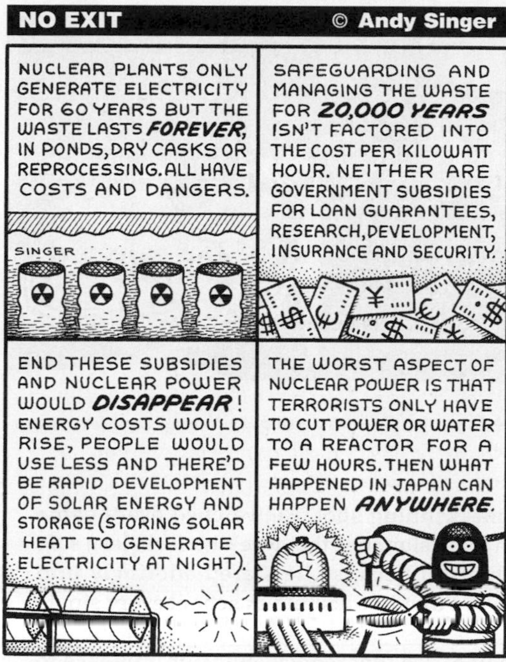

A proposal argument in four panels. You might compare this argument with Taylor Pearson's "Why You Should Fear Your Toaster More Than Nuclear Power" in Chapter 8. © Andy Singer/ Cagle Cartoons, Inc.

Showing That the Proposal Addresses the Need or Problem

An important but tricky part of making a successful proposal lies in relating the claim to the need or problem that it addresses. Facts and probability are your best allies. Take the time to show precisely how your solution will fix a problem or at least improve upon the current situation. Sometimes an emotional appeal is fair play, too. Here's former NBA player John Amaechi using that approach when he asks superstar Kobe Bryant of the L.A. Lakers not to appeal a $100,000 penalty he received for hurling an antigay slur at a referee:

> Kobe, stop fighting the fine. You spoke ill-advised words that shot out like bullets, and if the emails I received from straight and gay young people and sports fans in Los Angeles alone are anything to go by, you did serious damage with your outburst.
>
> A young man from a Los Angeles public school emailed me. You are his idol. He is playing up, on the varsity team, he has your posters all over his room, and he hopes one day to play in college and then in the NBA with you. He used to fall asleep with images of passing

Rose Eveleth explains how subtitled television and movies could help to preserve endangered languages in "Saving Languages through Korean Soap Operas."

LINK TO P. 596

Left: John Amaechi; right: Kobe Bryant. Left: Chris Goodney/Bloomberg News/Getty Images; right: © Lucy Nicholson/Reuters/LANDOV

> you the ball to sink a game-winning shot. He watched every game you played this season on television, but this week he feels less safe and less positive about himself because he stared adoringly into your face as you said the word that haunts him in school every single day.
>
> Kobe, stop fighting the fine. Use that money and your influence to set a new tone that tells sports fans, boys, men, and the society that looks up to you that the word you said in anger is not OK, not ever. Too many athletes take the trappings of their hard-earned success and leave no tangible legacy apart from "that shot" or "that special game."
>
> —John Amaechi, "A Gay Former NBA Player Responds to Kobe Bryant"

The paragraph describing the reaction of the schoolboy provides just the tie that Amaechi needs between his proposal and the problem it would address. The story also gives his argument more power.

Alternatively, if you oppose an idea, these strategies work just as well in reverse: if a proposal doesn't fix a problem, you have to show exactly why. Here are a few paragraphs from an editorial posting by Doug Bandow for *Forbes* in which he refutes a proposal for reinstating military conscription:

> All told, shifting to conscription would significantly weaken the military. New "accessions," as the military calls them, would be less

bright, less well educated, and less positively motivated. They would be less likely to stay in uniform, resulting in a less experienced force. The armed forces would be less effective in combat, thereby costing America more lives while achieving fewer foreign policy objectives.

Why take such a step?

One argument, most recently articulated by Thomas Ricks of the Center for a New American Security, is that a draft would save "the government money." That's a poor reason to impress people into service.

First, conscription doesn't save much cash. It costs money to manage and enforce a draft—history demonstrates that not every inductee would go quietly. Conscripts serve shorter terms and reenlist less frequently, increasing turnover, which is expensive. And unless the government instituted a Czarist lifetime draft, everyone beyond the first ranks would continue to expect to be paid.

Second, conscription shifts rather than reduces costs. Ricks suggested that draftees should "perform tasks currently outsourced at great cost to the Pentagon: paperwork, painting barracks, mowing lawns, driving generals around." Better to make people do grunt work than to pay them to do it? Force poorer young people into uniform in order to save richer old people tax dollars. Ricks believes that is a good reason to jail people for refusing to do as the government demands?

The government could save money in the same way by drafting FBI agents, postal workers, Medicare doctors, and congressmen. Nothing warrants letting old politicians force young adults to pay for Washington's profligacy. Moreover, by keeping some people who want to serve out while forcing others who don't want to serve in—creating a veritable evasion industry along the way—conscription would raise total social costs. It would be a bad bargain by any measure.

—Doug Bandow, "A New Military Draft Would Revive a Very Bad Old Idea"

Finally, if your own experience backs up your claim or demonstrates the need or problem that your proposal aims to address, then consider using it to develop your proposal (as John Amaechi does in addressing his proposal to Kobe Bryant). Consider the following questions in deciding when to include your own experiences in showing that a proposal is needed or will in fact do what it claims:

- Is your experience directly related to the need or problem that you seek to address or to your proposal about it?

- Will your experience be appropriate and speak convincingly to the audience? Will the audience immediately understand its significance, or will it require explanation?
- Does your personal experience fit logically with the other reasons that you're using to support your claim?

Be careful. If a proposal seems crafted to serve mainly your own interests, you won't get far.

Showing That the Proposal Is Feasible

To be effective, proposals must be *feasible*—that is, the action proposed can be carried out in a reasonable way. Demonstrating feasibility calls on you to present evidence—from similar cases, from personal experience, from observational data, from interview or survey data, from Internet research, or from any other sources—showing that what you propose can indeed be done with the resources available. "Resources available" is key: if the proposal calls for funds, personnel, or skills beyond reach or reason, your audience is unlikely to accept it. When that's the case, it's time to reassess your proposal, modify it, and test any new ideas against these revised criteria. This is also when you can reconsider proposals that others might suggest are better, more effective, or more workable than yours. There's no shame in admitting that you may have been wrong. When drafting a proposal, ask friends to think of counterproposals. If your own proposal can stand up to such challenges, it's likely a strong one.

Considering Design and Visuals

Because proposals often address specific audiences, they can take a number of forms—a letter, a memo, a Web page, a feasibility report, an infographic, a brochure, a prospectus, or even an editorial cartoon (see Andy Singer's "No Exit" item on p. 283). Each form has different design requirements. Indeed, the design may add powerfully to—or detract significantly from—the effectiveness of the proposal. Typically, though, proposals are heavy in photographs, tables, graphs, comparison charts, and maps, all designed to help readers understand the nature of a problem and how to solve it. Needless to say, any visual items should be handsomely presented: they contribute to your ethos.

Lengthy reports also usually need headings—or, in an oral report, slides—that clearly identify the various stages of the presentation. Those headings, which will vary, would include items such as Introduction, Nature of the Problem, Current Approaches or Previous Solutions,

Proposal/Recommendations, Advantages, Counterarguments, Feasibility, Implementation, and so on. So before you produce a final copy of any proposal, be sure its design enhances its persuasiveness.

A related issue to consider is whether a graphic image might help readers understand key elements of the proposal—what the challenge is, why it demands action, and what exactly you're suggesting—and help make the idea more attractive. That strategy is routinely used in professional proposals by architects, engineers, and government agencies.

For example, the artist rendering below shows the Bionic Arch, a proposed skyscraper in Taiwan designed by architect Vincent Callebaut. As a proposal, this one stands out because it not only suggests an addition to the city skyline, but it also offers architectural innovations to make the structure more environmentally friendly. If you look closely, you'll notice that each floor of the building includes suspended "sky gardens" that, according to the proposal, will help solve the problem of city smog by siphoning away toxic fumes. According to Callebaut, "The skyscraper reduces our ecological footprint in the urban area. It respects the environment and gives a new symbiotic ecosystem for the biodiversity of Taiwan. The Bionic Arch is the new icon of sustainable development." Who wouldn't support a building that looked great *and* helped clean the air?

The Bionic Arch proposes to do more than add retail and office space. AP/Wide World Photos

GUIDE to writing a proposal

Finding a Topic or Identifying a Problem

You're entering a proposal argument when you:

- make a claim that supports a change in practice: *Bottled water should carry a warning label describing the environmental impact of plastic.*
- make a claim that supports a change in policy: *Government workers, especially legislators and administrative officials, should never be exempt from laws or programs imposed on other citizens.*
- make a claim that resists suggested changes in practice or policy: *The surest way to guarantee that HOV lanes on freeways improve traffic flow is not to build any.*
- explore options for addressing existing issues or investigate opportunities for change: *Urban planners need to examine the long-term impact digital technologies may have on transportation, work habits, housing patterns, power usage, and entertainment opportunities in cities of the future.*

Since your everyday experience often calls on you to consider problems and to make proposals, begin your brainstorming for topics with practical topics related to your life, education, major, or job. Or make an informal list of proposals that you would like to explore in broader academic or cultural areas—problems you see in your field or in the society around you. Or do some freewriting on a subject of political concern, and see if it leads to a call for action.

Researching Your Topic

For many proposals, you can begin your research by consulting the following types of sources:

- newspapers, magazines, reviews, and journals (online and print)
- television or radio news reports
- online databases
- government documents and reports
- Web sites, blogs, social networking sites, listservs, or newsgroups
- books
- experts in the field, some of whom might be right on your campus

Consider doing some field research, if appropriate—a survey of student opinions on Internet accessibility, for example, or interviews with people who have experienced the problem you are trying to fix.

Finally, remember that your proposal's success can depend on the credibility of the sources you use to support it, so evaluate each source carefully (see Chapter 19).

Formulating a Claim

As you think about and explore your topic, begin formulating a claim about it. To do so, come up with a clear thesis that makes a proposal and states the reasons that this proposal should be adopted. To start formulating a claim, explore and respond to the following questions:

- What do I know about the proposal that I'm making?
- What reasons can I offer to support my proposal?
- What evidence do I have that implementing my proposal will lead to the results I want?

Rather than make a specific proposal, you may sometimes want to explore the range of possibilities for addressing a particular situation or circumstance. In that case, a set of open-ended questions might be a more productive starting point than a focused thesis, suggesting, for instance, what goals any plausible proposal might have to meet.

Examples of Proposal Claims

- Because lowering the amount of fuel required to be blended with ethanol would lower greenhouse gas emissions by millions of tons and decrease land use that is releasing unhealthy amounts of carbon into the atmosphere, the EPA proposal to reduce ethanol produced from corn should be adopted.
- Every home should be equipped with a well-stocked emergency kit that can sustain inhabitants for at least three days in a natural disaster.
- Congress should repeal the Copyright Extension Act, since it disrupts the balance between incentives for creators and the right of the public to information as set forth in the U.S. Constitution.
- To simplify the lives of consumers and eliminate redundant products, industries that manufacture rechargeable batteries should agree on a design for a universal power adapter.

- People from different economic classes, age groups, political philosophies, and power groups (government, Main Street, Wall Street) all have a stake in reforming current budget and tax policies. But how do we get them to speak and to listen to each other? That is the challenge we face if we hope to solve our national economic problems.

Preparing a Proposal

If your instructor asks you to prepare a proposal for your project, here's a format that may help:

State the thesis of your proposal completely. If you're having trouble doing so, try outlining it in Toulmin terms:

Claim:

Reason(s):

Warrant(s):

Alternatively, you might describe your intention to explore a particular problem in your project, with the actual proposal (and thesis) coming later.

- **Explain why this issue deserves attention. What's at stake?**
- **Identify and describe those readers whom you hope to reach with your proposal. Why is this group of readers appropriate? Can you identify individuals who can actually fix a problem?**
- **Briefly discuss the major difficulties that you foresee for your proposal. How will you demonstrate that the action you propose is necessary and workable? Persuade the audience to act? Pay for the proposal?**
- **Determine what research strategies you'll use. What sources do you expect to consult?**

Considering Format and Media

Your instructor may specify that you use a particular format and/or medium. If not, ask yourself these questions to help you make a good choice:

- What format is most appropriate for your proposal? Does it call for an academic essay, a report, an infographic, a brochure, or something else?
- What medium is most appropriate for your argument? Would it be best delivered orally to a live audience? Presented as an audio essay or podcast? Presented in print only or in print with illustrations?

- Will you need visuals, such as moving or still images, maps, graphs, charts—and what function will they play in your argument? Make sure they are not just "added on" but are necessary components of the argument.

Thinking about Organization

Proposals can take many different forms but generally include the following elements:

- a description of the problem you intend to address or the state of affairs that leads you to propose the action
- a strong and specific proposal, identifying the key reasons for taking the proposed action and the effects that taking this action will have
- a clear connection between the proposal and a significant need or problem
- a demonstration of ways in which the proposal addresses the need
- evidence that the proposal will achieve the desired outcome
- a consideration of alternative ways to achieve the desired outcome and a discussion of why these may not be feasible
- a demonstration that the proposal is feasible and an explanation of how it may be implemented

Getting and Giving Response: Questions for Peer Response

Your instructor may assign you to a group for the purpose of reading and responding to each other's drafts. If not, ask for responses from serious readers or consultants at a writing center. Use the following questions to evaluate a colleague's draft. Since specific comments help more than general observations, be sure to illustrate your comments with examples. Some of the questions below assume a conventional, thesis-driven project, but more exploratory, open-ended proposal arguments also need to be clearly phrased, organized, and supported with evidence.

The Claim

- Does the claim clearly call for action? Is the proposal as clear and specific as possible? Is it realistic or possible to accomplish?
- Is the proposal too sweeping? Does it need to be qualified? If so, how?

- Does the proposal clearly address the problem that it intends to solve? If not, how could the connection be strengthened?
- Is the claim likely to get the audience to act rather than just to agree? If not, how could it be revised to do so?

Evidence for the Claim

- Is enough evidence furnished to get the audience to support the proposal? If not, what kind of additional evidence is needed? Does any of the evidence provided seem inappropriate or otherwise ineffective? Why?
- Is the evidence in support of the claim simply announced, or are its significance and appropriateness analyzed? Is a more detailed discussion needed?
- Are objections that readers might have to the claim or evidence adequately and fairly addressed?
- What kinds of sources are cited? How credible and persuasive will they be to readers? What other kinds of sources might work better?
- Are all quotations introduced with appropriate signal phrases (such as "As Tyson argues, . . .") and blended smoothly into the writer's sentences?
- Are all visual sources labeled, introduced, and commented upon?

Organization and Style

- How are the parts of the argument organized? Is this organization effective?
- Will readers understand the relationships among the claims, supporting reasons, warrants, and evidence? If not, how might those connections be clearer? Is the function of every visual clear? Are more transitions needed? Would headings or graphic devices help?
- Are the transitions or links from point to point, sentence to sentence, and paragraph to paragraph clear and effective? If not, how could they be improved?
- Are all visuals carefully integrated into the text? Is each visual introduced and commented on to point out its significance? Is each visual labeled as a figure or a table and given a caption as well as a citation?
- Is the style suited to the subject? Is it too formal, casual, or technical? Can it be improved?

- Which sentences seem effective? Which ones seem weaker, and how could they be improved? Should short sentences be combined, and any longer ones be broken up?
- How effective are the paragraphs? Too short or too long? How can they be improved?
- Which words or phrases seem effective? Do any seem vague or inappropriate for the audience or the writer's purpose? Are technical or unfamiliar terms defined?

Spelling, Punctuation, Mechanics, Documentation, and Format

- Are there any errors in spelling, punctuation, capitalization, and the like?
- Is the documentation appropriate and consistent? (See Chapter 22.)
- Does the paper or project follow an appropriate format? Is it appropriately designed and attractively presented?

PROJECTS

1. Identify a proposal currently in the news or one advocated unrelentingly by the media that you *really* don't like. It may be a political initiative, a cultural innovation, a transportation alternative, or a lifestyle change. Spend time studying the idea more carefully than you have before. And then compose a proposal argument based on your deeper understanding of the proposal. You may still explain why you think it's a bad idea. Or you may endorse it, using your new information and your interesting perspective as a former dissenter.
2. The uses and abuses of technology and media—from smartphones and smartwatches to social networks—seem to be on everyone's mind. Write a proposal argument about some pressing dilemma caused by the digital screens that are changing (ruining?) our lives. You might want to explain how to bring traditional instructors into the digital age or establish etiquette for people who walk in traffic using handheld electronic devices. Or maybe you want to keep parents off of social networks. Or maybe you have a great idea for separating professional and private lives online. Make your proposal in some pertinent medium: print op-ed, cartoon, photo essay, infographic, set of PowerPoint or Prezi slides, podcast.
3. Write a proposal to yourself diagnosing some minor issue you would like to address, odd behavior you'd like to change, or obsession you'd like to curb. Explore the reasons behind your mania and the problems it causes you and others. Then come up with a plausible proposal to resolve the issue and prove that you can do it. Make the paper hilarious.
4. Working in a group initially, come up with a list of problems—local, national, or international—that seem just about insoluble, from persuading nations to cut down on their CO_2 emissions to figuring out how to keep tuition costs in check. After some discussion, focus on just one or two of these matters and then discuss not the issues themselves but the general reasons that the problems have proven intractable. What exactly keeps people from agreeing on solutions? Are some people content with the status quo? Do some groups profit from the current arrangements? Are alternatives to the status quo just too costly or not feasible for other reasons? Do people find change uncomfortable? Following the discussion, work alone or collaboratively on an argument that examines the general issue of *change*: What makes it possible in any given case? What makes it difficult? Use the problems you have discussed as examples to illustrate your argument. Your challenge as a writer may be to make such an open-ended discussion interesting to general readers.

A Call to Improve Campus Accessibility

MANASI DESHPANDE

Courtesy of Manasi Deshpande

Introduction

Wes Holloway, a sophomore at the University of Texas at Austin (UT), never considered the issue of campus accessibility during his first year on campus. But when an injury his freshman year left him wheelchair-bound, he was astonished to realize that he faced an unexpected challenge: maneuvering around the UT campus. Hills that he had effortlessly traversed became mountains; doors that he had easily opened became anvils; and streets that he had mindlessly crossed became treacherous terrain. Says Wes: "I didn't think about accessibility until I had to deal with it, and I think most people are the same way."

The paper opens with a personal example and dramatizes the issue of campus accessibility.

For the ambulatory individual, access for the mobility impaired on the UT campus is easy to overlook. Automatic door entrances and bathrooms with the universal handicapped symbol make the campus seem sufficiently accessible. But for many students and faculty at UT, including me, maneuvering the UT campus in a wheelchair is a daily experience of stress and frustration. Although the University has made a concerted and continuing effort to improve access, students and faculty with physical disabilities still suffer from discriminatory hardship, unequal opportunity to succeed, and lack of independence.

Both problem and solution are previewed here, with more details provided in subsequent sections of the paper.

Manasi Deshpande wrote a longer version of this essay for a course preparing her to work as a consultant in the writing center at the University of Texas at Austin. We have edited it to emphasize the structure of her complex proposal. Note, too, how she reaches out to a general audience to make an argument that might seem to have a narrow constituency. This essay is documented using MLA style.

The introduction's final paragraph summarizes the argument.

The University must make campus accessibility a higher priority and take more seriously the hardship that the campus at present imposes on people with mobility impairments. Better accessibility would also benefit the numerous students and faculty with temporary disabilities and help the University recruit a more diverse body of students and faculty.

Assessment of Current Efforts

The author's fieldwork (mainly interviews) enhances her authority and credibility.

The current state of campus accessibility leaves substantial room for improvement. There are approximately 150 academic and administrative buildings on campus (Grant). Eduardo Gardea, intern architect at the Physical Plant, estimates that only about nineteen buildings comply fully with the Americans with Disabilities Act (ADA). According to Penny Seay, PhD, director of the Center for Disability Studies at UT Austin, the ADA in theory "requires every building on campus to be accessible." However, as Bill Throop, associate director of the Physical Plant, explains, there is "no legal deadline to make the entire campus accessible"; neither the ADA nor any other law mandates that certain buildings be made compliant by a certain time. Though not bound by specific legal obligation, the University should strive to fulfill the spirit of the law and recognize campus accessibility as a pressing moral obligation.

The Benefits of Change

The paper uses several layers of headings to organize its diverse materials.

Benefits for People with Permanent Mobility Impairments

Improving campus accessibility would significantly enhance the quality of life of students and faculty with mobility impairments. The campus at present poses discriminatory hardship on these individuals by making daily activities such as getting to class and using the bathroom unreasonably difficult. Before Wes Holloway leaves home, he must plan his route carefully to avoid hills, use ramps that are easy to maneuver, and enter the side of the building with the accessible entrance. As he goes to class, Wes must go out of his way to avoid poorly paved sidewalks and roads. Sometimes he cannot avoid them and must take an uncomfortable and bumpy ride across potholes and uneven pavement. If his destination does not have an automatic door, he must wait for someone to open the door for him because it is too heavy for him to open himself. To get into Burdine Hall, he has to ask a stranger to push him through the heavy narrow doors because his fingers would get crushed if he pushed himself. Once in the classroom, Wes must find a suitable place to sit, often far away from his classmates because stairs block him from the center of the room.

The author outlines the challenges faced by a student with mobility impairment.

Accessibility issues are given a human face with examples of the problems that mobility-impaired people face on campus.

Other members of the UT community with mobility impairments suffer the same daily hardships as Wes. According to Mike Gerhardt, student affairs administrator of Services for Students with Disabilities (SSD), approximately eighty students with physical disabilities, including twenty to twenty-five students using wheelchairs, are registered with SSD. However, the actual number of students with mobility impairments is probably higher because some students choose not to seek services from SSD. The current state of campus accessibility discriminates against all individuals with physical disabilities in the unnecessary hardship it imposes and in the ways it denies them independence.

Benefits for People with Temporary Mobility Impairments

In addition to helping the few members of the UT campus with permanent mobility impairments, a faster rate of accessibility improvement would also benefit the much larger population of people with temporary physical disabilities. Many students and faculty will become temporarily disabled from injury at some point during their time at the University. They will encounter difficulties similar to those facing people with permanent disabilities, including finding accessible entrances, opening doors without

The author broadens the appeal of her proposal by showing how improved accessibility will benefit everyone on campus.

automatic entrances, and finding convenient classroom seating. And, according to Dr. Jennifer Maedgen, assistant dean of students and director of SSD, about 5 to 10 percent of the approximately one thousand students registered with SSD at any given time have temporary disabilities. By improving campus accessibility, the University would in fact reach out to all of its members, even those who have never considered the possibility of mobility impairment or the state of campus accessibility.

Numbers provide hard evidence for an important claim.

Benefits for the University

Better accessibility would also benefit the University as a whole by increasing recruitment of handicapped individuals and thus promoting a more diverse campus. When prospective students and faculty with disabilities visit the University, they might decide not to join the UT community because of poor access. On average, about one thousand students, or 2 percent of the student population, are registered with SSD. Mike Gerhardt reports that SSD would have about 1,500 to 3,000 registered students if the University reflected the community at large with respect to disability. These numbers suggest that the University can recruit more students with disabilities by taking steps to ensure that they have an equal opportunity to succeed.

The author offers a new but related argument: enhanced accessibility could bolster recruitment efforts.

Counterarguments

Arguments against devoting more effort and resources to campus accessibility have some validity but ultimately prove inadequate. Some argue that accelerating the rate of accessibility improvements and creating more efficient services require too much spending on too few people. However, this spending actually enhances the expected quality of life of all UT community members rather than just the few with permanent physical disabilities. Unforeseen injury can leave anyone with a permanent or temporary disability at any time. In making decisions about campus accessibility, administrators must realize that

The paper briefly notes possible objections to the proposal.

having a disability is not a choice and that bad luck does not discriminate. They should consider how their decisions would affect their campus experience if they became disabled. Despite the additional cost, the University should make accessibility a priority and accommodate more accessibility projects in its budget.

Recommendations

Foster Empathy and Understanding for Long-Term Planning

The University should make campus accessibility a higher priority and work toward a campus that not only fulfills legal requirements but also provides a user-friendly environment for the mobility impaired. It is difficult for the ambulatory person to empathize with the difficulties faced by these individuals. Recognizing this problem, the University should require the administrators who allocate money to ADA projects to use wheelchairs around the campus once a year. Administrators must realize that people with physical disabilities are not a small, distant, irrelevant group; anyone can join their ranks at any time. Administrators should ask themselves if they would find the current state of campus accessibility acceptable if an injury forced them to use a wheelchair on a permanent basis.

After establishing a case for enhanced campus accessibility, the author offers specific suggestions for action.

In addition, the University should actively seek student input for long-term improvements to accessibility. The University is in the process of creating the ADA Accessibility Committee, which, according to the office of the Dean of Students' Web site, will "address institutionwide, systemic issues that fall under the scope of the Americans with Disabilities Act." Students should play a prominent and powerful role in this new ADA Accessibility Committee. The Committee should select its student representatives carefully to make sure that they are driven individuals committed to working for progress and representing the interests of students with disabilities. The University should consider making Committee positions paid so that student representatives can devote sufficient time to their responsibilities.

Improve Services for the Mobility Impaired

The University should also work toward creating more useful, transparent, and approachable services for its members with physical disabilities by making better use of online technology and helping students take control of their own experiences.

First, SSD can make its Web site more useful by updating it frequently with detailed information on construction sites that will affect accessible routes. The site should delineate alternative accessible routes and approximate the extra time required to use the detour. This information would help people with mobility impairments to plan ahead and avoid delays, mitigating the stress of maneuvering around construction sites.

The University should also develop software for an interactive campus map. The software would work like MapQuest or Google Maps but would provide detailed descriptions of accessible routes on campus from one building to another. It would be updated frequently with new ADA improvements and information on construction sites that impede accessible routes.

Since usefulness of services is most important for students during their first encounters with the campus, SSD should hold one-on-one orientations for new students with mobility impairments. SSD should inform students in both oral and written format of their rights and responsibilities and make them aware of problems that they will encounter on the campus. Beyond making services more useful, these orientations would give students the impression of University services as open and responsive, encouraging students to report problems that they encounter and assume the responsibility of self-advocacy.

As a continuing resource for people with physical disabilities, the SSD Web site should include an anonymous forum for both general questions and specific complaints and needs. Many times, students notice problems but do not report them because they find visiting or calling SSD time-consuming or because they do not wish to be a burden. The anonymity and immediate feedback provided by the forum would allow for more freedom of expression and provide students an easier way to solve the problems they face.

Services for the mobility impaired should also increase their transparency by advertising current accessibility projects on their Web sites. The University should give its members with mobility impairments a clearer idea of its efforts to improve campus accessibility. Detailed online descriptions of ADA projects, including the cost of each project, would affirm its resolve to create a better environment for its members with physical disabilities.

Conclusion

Although the University has made progress in accessibility improvements on an old campus, it must take bolder steps to improve the experience of its members with mobility impairments. At present, people with permanent mobility impairments face unreasonable hardship, unequal opportunity to succeed, and lack of independence. To enhance the quality of life of all of its members and increase recruitment of disabled individuals, the University should focus its resources on increasing the rate of accessibility improvements and improving the quality of its services for the mobility impaired.

The writer reiterates her full proposal.

As a public institution, the University has an obligation to make the campus more inclusive and serve as an example for disability rights. With careful planning and a genuine desire to respond to special needs, practical and cost-effective changes to the University campus can significantly improve the quality of life of many of its members and prove beneficial to the future of the University as a whole.

Works Cited

Gardea, Eduardo. Personal interview, 24 Mar. 2005.

Gerhardt, Michael. Personal interview, 8 Apr. 2005.

Grant, Angela. "Making Campus More Accessible." *Daily Texan Online,* 14 Oct. 2003, www.dailytexanonline.com/2003/11/14/making-campus-more-accessible.

Holloway, Wesley Reed. Personal interview, 5 Mar. 2005.

Maedgen, Jennifer. Personal interview, 25 Mar. 2005.

Office of the Dean of Students. ADA Student Forum. *University of Texas at Austin*, 6 Apr. 2005, ddce.utexas.edu/disability/2005/04/april-6th-ada-student-forums/.

Seay, Penny. Personal interview, 11 Mar. 2005.

Throop, William. Personal interview, 6 Apr. 2005.

Let's Charge Politicians for Wasting Our Time

VIRGINIA POSTREL

There's an election today here in California, and that means my landline at home is ringing constantly with robocalls from assorted public figures whose recorded voices urge me to get out and vote for their favorite candidates. One called the other day while I was conducting an interview on the mobile phone I use for most purposes. I didn't answer, but it interrupted the flow of the conversation. Yesterday I picked up the receiver to find five voice mails, all from recorded political voices (including two identical messages from the same sheriff candidate).

Our phone number is on the National Do Not Call Registry, but those rules for telemarketers don't apply to political campaigns. The folks who make the laws aren't about to do away with a technique that works.

Political robocalls are illegal to mobile phones but OK to most landlines, as long as they meet disclosure requirements. Everyone I know hates such calls, and even political consultants know they're a problem. "Some voters get turned off by too many robocalls," cautions a political-strategy website. The cumulative annoyance, it warns, means that voters may resent yours even if they're rare. Yep.

Recorded, automatically dialed messages arguably constitute a legitimate and potentially important form of political speech. If I weren't so annoyed, I might actually like to know who's endorsing whom for sheriff. But it's ridiculous that the only way to limit the onslaught is to pay someone $24.99 to tell organizations, who may or may not listen, that I don't want them bothering me.

Here's a better idea: You should be able to set a charge for calling you. Every number that isn't on your "free" list would automatically be assessed a fee. The phone company would get a percentage of the revenue, and you'd be able to adjust the fee to different levels at different times of the day or for different seasons. (The nearer the election, the higher I'd make my charge.) If candidates really think it's valuable to call me, they should

---

Virginia Postrel posted this column on the Bloomberg View on June 3, 2014. She has also written for *Forbes*, the *Wall Street Journal*, the *New York Times*, and the *Atlantic*.

be willing to pay. Otherwise, they're just forcing me to subsidize their political efforts with my time and attention.

Technology investor Esther Dyson has for years been pushing a similar idea for e-mail. Unsolicited phone calls are much more annoying, and the technological challenges of "reversing the charges" should be much easier. Although you can't track down the true scamsters who break the do-not-call law and peddle fraudulent schemes from phony numbers, the politicians and charities that pester us for support aren't trying to hide. They're just trying to get something scarce and precious—our time and attention—for free.

PART 3

STYLE AND PRESENTATION IN arguments

13
Style in Arguments

The images above all reflect the notable styles of musicians from different times and musical traditions: Yo-Yo Ma, Count Basie, Kiss, and Rihanna. One could argue that these performers craft images to define their stage personalities, but how they present themselves also reflects the music they play and the audiences they perform for. Imagine Yo-Yo Ma appearing in Kiss makeup at Carnegie Hall. It doesn't work.

Writers, too, like to think of themselves as creating styles that express their ethos and life experiences—and they do. But in persuasive situations, style is also a matter of the specific choices they make—strategically and self-consciously—to influence audiences.

So it's not surprising that writers adapt their voices to a range of rhetorical situations, from very formal to very casual. At the formal and professional end of the scale, consider the opening paragraph of a dissent by Justice Sonia Sotomayor to a Supreme Court decision affecting affirmative action in Michigan public universities. Writing doesn't get much more consequential than this, and that earnestness is reflected in the justice's sober, authoritative, but utterly clear style:

> We are fortunate to live in a democratic society. But without checks, democratically approved legislation can oppress minority groups. For that reason, our Constitution places limits on what a majority of the people may do. This case implicates one such limit: the guarantee of equal protection of the laws. Although that guarantee is traditionally understood to prohibit intentional discrimination under existing laws, equal protection does not end there. Another fundamental strand of our equal protection jurisprudence focuses on process, securing to all citizens the right to participate meaningfully and equally in self-government. That right is the bedrock of our democracy, for it preserves all other rights.
>
> —Sonia Sotomayor, dissenting opinion, April 22, 2014

Contrast this formal style (perhaps the equivalent of Yo-Yo Ma's tuxedo?) to the more personal language Alexis C. Madrigal uses in an article for the *Atlantic* to argue that we are finally tiring of the relentless "stream" of information pouring down on us via social media. His subject is serious and his readers are too, but Madrigal employs a rougher style to express the resentment of people he sees as victimized by a once-promising technology that trivializes everything:

> Nowadays, I think all kinds of people see and feel the tradeoffs of the stream, when they pull their thumbs down at the top of their screens to receive a new update from their social apps.
>
> It is too damn hard to keep up. And most of what's out there is crap.
>
> When the half-life of a post is half a day or less, how much time can media makers put into something? When the time a reader spends on a story is (on the high end) two minutes, how much time should media makers put into something?
>
> —Alexis C. Madrigal, "2013: The Year 'the Stream' Crested"

Just a paragraph later, Madrigal again tunes his style to accommodate both high and low notes (maybe riffing like Count Basie?). First, he alludes to one of the toughest novels of the twentieth century, and then he chooses sentence structures—a fragment followed by two very short, emphatic, not-quite-parallel clauses—to mark the contrast between the formidable book and social media:

> I am not joking when I say: it is easier to read *Ulysses* than it is to read the Internet. Because at least *Ulysses* has an end, an edge. *Ulysses* can be finished. The Internet is never finished.

Far more casual in subject matter and style is a blog item by *Huffington Post* book editor Claire Fallon, arguing (tongue-in-cheek) that Shakespeare's Romeo is one of those literary figures readers just love to hate. The range of Fallon's vocabulary choices—from "most romantic dude" to "penchant for wallowing"—suggests the (Rihanna-like?) playfulness of the exercise. Style is obviously a big part of Fallon's game:

> **Romeo, Romeo, wherefore art thou such a wishy-washy doofus? Shakespeare himself would likely be baffled by the elevation of Romeo to the position of "most romantic dude in literature"—he spends his first scene in the play insisting he's heartbroken over a girl he goes on to completely forget about the second he catches a glimpse of Juliet! Poor Rosaline (or rather, nice bullet-dodging, Rosaline). Romeo's apparent penchant for wallowing in the romantic misery of unrequited love finds a new target in naive Juliet, who then dies for a guy who probably would have forgotten about her as soon as their honeymoon ended. Yes, Romeo is self-absorbed, fickle, and rather whiny, but we clearly love him anyway.**
>
> **—Claire Fallon, "11 Unlikeable Classical Book Characters We Love to Hate"**

As you might guess from these examples, style always involves making choices about language across a wide range of situations. Style can be public or personal, conventional or creative, and everything in between. When you write, you'll find that you have innumerable tools and options for expressing yourself exactly as you need to. This chapter introduces you to some of them.

Style and Word Choice

Words matter—and those you choose will define the style of your arguments.

For most academic arguments, what is called formal or professional style is appropriate. Such language sounds weighty because it usually is. It is not shy about employing highbrow terms, conventional vocabulary, or technical language because that's what readers of academic journals or serious magazines and newspapers expect. Formal writing typically avoids contractions, phrases that mimic speech, and sometimes even the pronoun *I*. But what may be most remarkable about the style is how little it draws attention to itself—and that's usually deliberate. Here's a levelheaded paragraph from the *Economist* arguing that digital education may yet have a huge impact on colleges and universities:

> **So demand for education will grow. Who will meet it? Universities face a new competitor in the form of massive open online courses, or MOOCs. These digitally-delivered courses, which teach students via the web or tablet apps, have big advantages over their established rivals. With low startup costs and powerful economies of scale, online courses dramatically lower the price of learning and widen access to it, by removing the need for students to be taught at set times or places. The low cost of providing courses—creating a new one costs about $70,000—means they can be sold cheaply, or even given away. Clayton Christensen of Harvard Business School considers MOOCs a potent "disruptive technology" that will kill off many inefficient universities. "Fifteen years from now more than half of the universities [in America] will be in bankruptcy," he predicted last year.**
>
> **—"The Future of Universities: The Digital Degree"**

The editors assume that readers of the *Economist* will understand technical terms such as "startup costs" and "economies of scale," though they do pause to explain "MOOCs"—a much-hyped innovation yet to catch on. Even as it delivers what seems like bad news for universities, the paragraph is efficient and cool in tone—modeling a style you'll often use in academic projects.

In an excerpt from his book *Whistling Vivaldi and Other Clues to How Stereotypes Affect Us*, Claude M. Steele presents a compelling example of the impact of subtle stylistic choices.

LINK TO P. 537

Colloquial words and phrases, *slang*, and even first- and second-person pronouns (*I*, *me*, *we*, *you*) can create relationships with audiences that feel much more intimate. When you use everyday language in arguments, readers are more likely to identify with you personally and, possibly, with the ideas you represent or advocate. In effect, such vocabulary choices lessen the distance between you and readers.

Admittedly, some colloquial terms simply bewilder readers not tuned in to them. A movie review in *Rolling Stone* or a music review in *Spin* might leave your parents (or some authors) scratching their heads. Jon Dolan, for example, has this to say about Drake's song "Draft Day":

> **Drake's latest statement-of-Drakeness casually big-ups his sports bros Johnny Manziel and Andrew Wiggins over a dreamy sample of Lauryn Hill's "Doo Wop (That Thing)," then drops a little Jennifer Lawrence fan fic: "On some *Hunger Games* sh–t/I would die for my district." It's baller brio with a characteristic light touch. May the odds be ever in your favor, son!**
>
> **—Jon Dolan, *Rolling Stone*, "Drake, 'Draft Day'"**

Huh, we say. But you probably get it.

Be alert, too, to the use of *jargon*, the special vocabulary of members of a profession, trade, or field. Although jargon serves as shorthand for experts, it can alienate readers who don't recognize technical words or acronyms.

Another verbal key to an argument's style is its control of **connotation**, the associations that surround many words. Consider the straightforward connotative differences among the following three statements:

> Students from the Labor Action Committee (LAC) carried out a hunger strike to call attention to the below-minimum wages that are being paid to campus temporary workers, saying, "The university must pay a living wage to all its workers."
>
> Left-wing agitators and radicals tried to use self-induced starvation to stampede the university into caving in to their demands.
>
> Champions of human rights put their bodies on the line to protest the university's tightfisted policy of paying temporary workers scandalously low wages.

The style of the first sentence is the most neutral, presenting facts and offering a quotation from one of the students. The second sentence uses loaded terms like "agitators," "radicals," and "stampede" to create a negative image of this event, while the final sentence uses other loaded words to create a positive view. As these examples demonstrate, the words you choose can change everything about a sentence.

But now watch how author Sherman Alexie, in an essay about Jason Collins, the first openly gay NBA star (see p. 103) makes the connotations surrounding three colloquial terms all meaning "beautiful" key to a controversial claim he intends to put forward:

> Cut. Shredded. Jacked. Those are violent straight-boy adjectives that mean "beautiful." But we straight boys aren't supposed to think of other men as beautiful. We're supposed to think of the most physically gifted men as warrior soldiers, as dangerous demigods.
>
> And there's the rub: When we're talking about professional athletes, we are mostly talking about males passionately admiring the physical attributes and abilities of other males. It might not be homosexual, but it certainly is homoerotic.

Here, words actually *become* the argument.

RESPOND •

Review the excerpts in this section and choose one or two words or phrases that you think are admirably selected or unusually interesting choices. Then explore the meanings and possibly the connotations of the word or words in a nicely developed paragraph or two.

Sentence Structure and Argument

Writers of effective arguments know that "variety is the spice of life" when it comes to stylish sentences. A strategy as simple as *varying sentence length* can keep readers attentive and interested. For instance, the paragraph from the *Economist* in the preceding section (p. 310) has sentences as short as four words and as lengthy as thirty-six. Its authors almost certainly didn't pause as they wrote and think, hmm, we need a little variation here. Instead, as experienced writers, they simply made sure that their sentences complemented the flow of their ideas and also kept readers engaged.

Sentences, you see, offer you more options and special effects than you can ever exhaust. To pull examples from selections earlier in this chapter, just consider how dramatic, punchy, or even comic short sentences can be:

> **The Internet is never finished. —Alexis C. Madrigal**
>
> **May the odds be ever in your favor, son! —Jon Dolan**

Longer sentences can explain ideas, build drama, or sweep readers along:

> **With low startup costs and powerful economies of scale, online courses dramatically lower the price of learning and widen access to it, by removing the need for students to be taught at set times or places.**
>
> **—*The Economist***

Meanwhile, sentences of medium length handle just about any task assigned without a fuss. They are whatever you need them to be: serviceable, discrete, thoughtful, playful. And they pair up nicely with companions:

> **But without checks, democratically approved legislation can oppress minority groups. For that reason, our Constitution places limits on what a majority of the people may do. —Sonia Sotomayor**

Balanced or parallel sentences, in which clauses or phrases are deliberately matched, as highlighted in the following examples, draw attention to ideas and relationships:

> *Ulysses* can be finished. The Internet is never finished.
>
> —Alexis C. Madrigal

> When we're talking about professional athletes, we are mostly talking about males passionately admiring the physical attributes and abilities of other males. It might not be homosexual, but it certainly is homoerotic.
>
> —Sherman Alexie

Sentences with especially complicated structures or interruptions make you pay attention to their motions and, therefore, their ideas:

> The low cost of providing courses—creating a new one costs about $70,000—means they can be sold cheaply, or even given away.
>
> *The Economist*

> Drake's latest statement-of-Drakeness casually big-ups his sports bros Johnny Manziel and Andrew Wiggins over a dreamy sample of Lauryn Hill's "Doo Wop (That Thing)," then drops a little Jennifer Lawrence fan fic: "On some *Hunger Games* sh–t/I would die for my district."
>
> —Jon Dolan

Even sentence fragments—which don't meet all the requirements for full sentence status—have their place when used for a specific effect:

> Because at least *Ulysses* has an end, an edge. —Alexis C. Madrigal

> Poor Rosaline (or rather, nice bullet-dodging, Rosaline). —Claire Fallon

> Cut. Shredded. Jacked. —Sherman Alexie

You see, then, that there's *much* more to the rhetoric of sentences than just choosing subjects, verbs, and objects—and far more than we can explain in one section. But you can learn a lot about the power of sentences simply by observing how the writers you admire engineer them—and maybe imitating some of those sentences yourself. You might also make it a habit to read and re-read your own sentences aloud (or in your head) as you compose them to gauge whether words and phrases are meshing with your ideas. And then tinker, tinker, tinker—until the sentences feel right.

RESPOND.

Working with a classmate, first find a paragraph you both admire, perhaps in one of the selections in Part 2 of this book. Then, individually write paragraphs of your own that imitate the sentences within it—making sure that both these new items are on subjects different from that of the original paragraph. When you are done, compare your paragraphs and pick out a few sentences you think are especially effective.

Punctuation and Argument

In a memorable comment, actor and director Clint Eastwood said, "You can show a lot with a look. . . . It's punctuation." He's certainly right about punctuation's effect, and it is important that as you read and write arguments, you consider punctuation closely.

Eastwood may have been talking about the dramatic effect of end punctuation: the finality of periods; the tentativeness of ellipses (. . .); the query, disbelief, or uncertainty in question marks; or the jolt in the now-appearing-almost-everywhere exclamation point! Yet even exclamations can help create tone if used strategically. In an argument about the treatment of prisoners at Guantánamo, consider how Jane Mayer evokes the sense of desperation in some of the suspected terrorists:

> As we reached the end of the cell-block, hysterical shouts, in broken English, erupted from a caged exercise area nearby. "Come here!" a man screamed. "See here! They are liars! . . . No sleep!" he yelled. "No food! No medicine! No doctor! Everybody sick here!"
>
> —Jane Mayer, "The Experiment"

Punctuation that works within sentences can also do much to enhance meaning and style. The *semicolon*, for instance, marks a pause that is stronger than a comma but not as strong as a period. Semicolons function like "plus signs"; used correctly, they join items that are alike in structure, conveying a sense of balance, similarity, or even contrast. Do you recall Nathaniel Stein's parody of grading standards at Harvard University (see p. 102)? Watch as he uses a semicolon to enhance the humor in his description of what an A+ paper achieves:

> Nearly every single word in the paper is spelled correctly; those that are not can be reasoned out phonetically within minutes.
>
> —Nathaniel Stein, "Leaked! Harvard's Grading Rubric"

"You can show a lot with a look. . . . It's punctuation." © Photofest, Inc.

In many situations, however, semicolons, with their emphasis on symmetry and balance, can feel stodgy, formal, and maybe even old-fashioned, and lots of writers avoid them, perhaps because they are very difficult to get right. Check a writing handbook before you get too friendly with semicolons.

Much easier to manage are colons, which function like pointers within sentences: they say *pay attention to this*. Philip Womack's London *Telegraph* review of *Harry Potter and the Deathly Hallows, Part 2* demonstrates how a colon enables a writer to introduce a lengthy illustration clearly and elegantly:

> **The first scene of David Yates's film picks up where his previous installment left off: with a shot of the dark lord Voldemort's noseless face in triumph as he steals the most powerful magic wand in the world from the tomb of Harry's protector, Professor Dumbledore.**
>
> **—Philip Womack**

And Paul Krugman shows how to use a colon to catch a reader's attention:

> **Recently two research teams, working independently and using different methods, reached an alarming conclusion: The West Antarctic ice sheet is doomed.**
>
> **—Paul Krugman, "Point of No Return"**

Colons can serve as lead-ins for complete sentences, complex phrases, or even single words. As such, they are versatile and potentially dramatic pieces of punctuation.

Like colons, dashes help readers focus on important, sometimes additional details. But they have even greater flexibility since they can be used singly or in pairs. Alone, dashes function much like colons to add information. Here's Eugene Washington commenting pessimistically on a political situation in Iraq, using a single dash to extend his thoughts:

> **The aim of U.S. policy at this point should be minimizing the calamity, not chasing rainbows of a unified, democratic, pluralistic Iraq—which, sadly, is something the power brokers in Iraq do not want.**
>
> **—Eugene Robinson, "The 'Ungrateful Volcano' of Iraq"**

And here are paired dashes used to insert such information in the opening of the Philip Womack review of *Deathly Hallows 2* cited earlier:

> ***Harry Potter and the Deathly Hallows, Part 2*—the eighth and final film in the blockbusting series—begins with our teenage heroes fighting for their lives, and for their entire world.**

And finally, notice how in an essay about President Obama's second term, writer Peggy Noonan surrounds a single word with dashes to emphasize it:

> **All this is weird, unprecedented. The president shows no sign—none—of being overwhelmingly concerned and anxious at his predicaments or challenges.**
>
> **—Peggy Noonan, "The Daydream and the Nightmare"**

As these examples illustrate, punctuation often enhances the rhythm of an argument. Take a look at how Maya Angelou uses a dash along with another punctuation mark—ellipsis points—to create a pause or hesitation, in this case one that builds anticipation:

> **Then the voice, husky and familiar, came to wash over us—"The winnah, and still heavyweight champeen of the world . . . Joe Louis."**
>
> **—Maya Angelou, "Champion of the World"**

RESPOND •

Try writing a brief movie review for your campus newspaper, experimenting with punctuation as one way to create an effective style. See if using a series of questions might have a strong effect, whether exclamation points would add or detract from the message you want to send, and so on. When you've finished the review, compare it to one written by a classmate, and look for similarities and differences in your choices of punctuation.

Special Effects: Figurative Language

You don't have to look hard to find examples of figurative language adding style to arguments. When a writing teacher suggests you take a weed whacker to your prose, she's using a figure of speech (in this case, a *metaphor*) to suggest you cut the wordiness. To indicate how little he trusts the testimony of John Koskinen, head of the Internal Revenue Service, political pundit Michael Gerson takes the metaphor of a "witch hunt" and flips it on the bureaucrat, relying on readers to recognize an *allusion* to Shakespeare's *Macbeth*:

> Democrats were left to complain about a Republican "witch hunt"—while Koskinen set up a caldron, added some eye of newt and toe of frog and hailed the Thane of Cawdor.
>
> —Michael Gerson, "An Arrogant and Lawless IRS"

Explore the meaning and effectiveness of figurative expressions such as "Gourmet Hay" and "'trail mix' for earthworms" in Eric Mortenson's "A Diversified Farm Prospers in Oregon's Willamette Valley by Going Organic and Staying Local."

LINK TO P. 653

John Koskinen Alex Wong/Getty Images

Figurative language like this — indispensable to writers — dramatizes ideas, either by clarifying or enhancing the thoughts themselves or by framing them in language that makes them stand out. As a result, figurative language makes arguments attractive, memorable, and powerful. An apt simile, a timely rhetorical question, or a wicked understatement might do a better job bringing an argument home than whole paragraphs of evidence.

Figures of speech are usually classified into two main types: **tropes**, which involve a change in the ordinary meaning of a word or phrase; and **schemes**, which involve a special arrangement of words. Here is a brief alphabetical listing — with examples — of some of the most familiar kinds.

Tropes

To create tropes, you often have to think of one idea or claim in relationship to others. Some of the most powerful — one might even say *inevitable* — tropes involve making purposeful comparisons between ideas: analogies, metaphors, and similes. Other tropes such as irony, signifying, and understatement are tools for expressing attitudes toward ideas: you might use them to shape the way you want your audience to think about a claim that you or someone else has made.

Allusion

An **allusion** is a connection that illuminates one situation by comparing it to another similar but usually more famous one, often with historical or literary connections. Allusions work with events, people, or concepts — expanding and enlarging them so readers better appreciate their significance. For example, a person who makes a career-ending blunder might be said to have met her *Waterloo*, the famous battle that terminated Napoleon's ambitions. Similarly, every impropriety in Washington brings up mentions of *Watergate*, the only scandal to lead to a presidential resignation; any daring venture becomes a *moon shot*, paralleling the ambitious program that led to a lunar landing in 1969. Using allusions can be tricky: they work only if readers get the connection. But when they do, they can pack a wallop. When on page 317 Michael Gerson mentions "eye of newt" and "toe of frog" in the same breath as IRS chief John Koskinen, he knows what fans of *Macbeth* are thinking. But other readers might be left clueless.

Analogy

Analogies compare two things, often point by point, either to show similarity or to suggest that if two concepts, phenomena, events, or even people are alike in one way, they are probably alike in other ways as well. Often extended in length, analogies can clarify or emphasize points of comparison, thereby supporting particular claims.

Here's the first paragraph of an essay in which a writer who is also a runner thinks deeply about the analogies between the two tough activities:

> When people ask me what running and writing have in common, I tend to look at the ground and say it might have something to do with discipline: You do both of those things when you don't feel like it, and make them part of your regular routine. You know some days will be harder than others, and on some you won't hit your mark and will want to quit. But you don't. You force yourself into a practice; the practice becomes habit and then simply part of your identity. A surprising amount of success, as Woody Allen once said, comes from just showing up.
>
> —Rachel Toor, "What Writing and Running Have in Common"

This cartoon draws a number of suggestive analogies (and one potent allusion) in the way it depicts the pope and personifies "economic inequality." © John Cole/Cagle Cartoons, Inc.

To be effective, an analogy has to make a good point and hold up to scrutiny. If it doesn't, it can be criticized as a faulty analogy, a fallacy of argument (see p. 84).

Antonomasia

Antonomasia is an intriguing trope that simply involves substituting a descriptive phrase for a proper name. It is probably most familiar to you from sports or entertainment figures: "His Airness" still means Michael Jordan; Aretha Franklin remains "The Queen of Soul," jazz singer Mel Torme was "The Velvet Fog," and Superman, of course, is "The Man of Steel." In politics, antonomasia is sometimes used neutrally (Ronald Reagan as "The Gipper"), sometimes as a backhanded compliment (Margaret Thatcher as "The Iron Lady"), and occasionally as a crude and sexist put-down (Sarah Palin as "Caribou Barbie"). As you well know if you have one, nicknames can pack potent arguments into just one phrase.

Hyperbole

Hyperbole is the use of overstatement for special effect, a kind of fireworks in prose. The tabloid gossip magazines that scream at you in the checkout line survive by hyperbole. Everyone has seen these overstated arguments and perhaps marveled at the way they sell.

Hyperbole can, however, serve both writers and audiences when very strong opinions need to be registered. One senses exasperation in the no-holds-barred opening of Rex Reed's review of the film *Tammy*—the paragraph ripples with hyperbole and other tropes:

> The good news is that *Tammy* is not a crappy remake of the 1957 *Tammy* movie with Debbie Reynolds that spawned three sequels and a TV comedy series. The bad news is that this one is much worse. It's a desperate and brainless vehicle for Melissa McCarthy, which she wrote herself, with her husband, Ben Falcone, who also directed, with all the efficiency and verve of an abandoned Volkswagen on the Jersey Turnpike. There isn't a single shred of evidence that either of them has one iota of talent in the world of filmmaking. *Tammy* is not just a celebration of everything vulgar and stupid in the dumbing down of American movies. It's a rambling, pointless and labored attempt to cash in on Ms. McCarthy's fan base without respect for any audience with a collective IQ of 10. And it's about as funny as a liver transplant.
>
> —Rex Reed, "Melissa McCarthy Gives 'Tammy' Her All, but It's Nowhere Near Enough"

Can you tell that Reed did not like the film?

Irony

Irony is a complex trope in which words convey meanings that are in tension with or even opposite to their literal meanings. Readers who catch the irony realize that a writer is asking them (or someone else) to think about all the potential connotations in their language. One of the most famous uses of satiric irony in literature occurs in Shakespeare's *Julius Caesar* when Antony punctuates his condemnation of Caesar's assassins with the repeated word "honourable." He begins by admitting, "So are they all, honourable men" but ends railing against "the honourable men / Whose daggers have stabb'd Caesar." Within just a few lines, Antony's funeral speech has altered the meaning of the term.

In popular culture, irony often takes a humorous bent in publications such as the *Onion* and the appropriately named *Ironic Times*. Yet even serious critics of society and politics use satiric devices to undercut celebrities and politicians, particularly when such powerful figures ignore the irony in their own positions. After Hillary Clinton argued that Americans don't regard her and her husband as part of the country's problem with income inequality "because we pay ordinary income tax . . . and we've done it through dint of hard work," *Washington Post* columnist and fellow liberal Ruth Marcus offered advice rich in sarcasm and irony:

> And for goodness' sake—*truly well-off? hard work?* You are truly well-off by anyone's definition of the term. And hard work is the guys tearing up my roof right now. It's not flying by private jet to pick up a check for $200,000 to stand at a podium for an hour. . . .
>
> —Ruth Marcus, "Hillary Clinton's Money Woes"

Metaphor

A bedrock of our language, **metaphor** creates or implies a comparison between two things, illuminating something unfamiliar by correlating it to something we usually know much better. For example, to explain the complicated structure of DNA, scientists Watson and Crick famously used items people would likely recognize: a helix (spiral) and a zipper. Metaphors can clarify and enliven arguments. In the following passage, novelist and poet Benjamin Sáenz uses several metaphors (highlighted) to describe his relationship to the southern border of the United States:

> It seems obvious to me now that I remained always a son of the border, a boy never quite comfortable in an American skin, and certainly not

> comfortable in a Mexican one. My entire life, I have lived in a liminal space, and that space has both defined and confined me. That liminal space wrote and invented me. It has been my prison, and it has also been my only piece of sky.
>
> —Benjamin Sáenz, "Notes from Another Country"

In another example from Andrew Sullivan's blog, he quotes an 1896 issue of *Munsey's Magazine* that uses a metaphor to explain what, at that time, the bicycle meant to women and to clarify the new freedom it gave women who weren't accustomed to being able to ride around on their own:

> To men, the bicycle in the beginning was merely a new toy, another machine added to the long list of devices they knew in their work and play. To women, it was a steed upon which they rode into a new world.

Metonymy

Metonymy is a rhetorical trope in which a writer uses a particular object to stand for a general concept. You'll recognize the move immediately in the expression "The *pen* is mightier than the *sword*"—which obviously is not about Bics and sabers. Metonyms are vivid and concrete ways of compacting big concepts into expressive packages for argument: the term *Wall Street* can embody the nation's whole complicated banking

It's not just a street; it's a metonym! Martin Lehmann/Shutterstock

and investment system, while all the offices and officials of the U.S. military become the *Pentagon*. You can quickly think of dozens of expressions that represent larger, more complex concepts: *Nashville*, *Hollywood*, *Big Oil*, *the Press*, *the Oval Office*, even perhaps *the electorate*.

Oxymoron

Oxymoron is a rhetorical trope that states a paradox or contradiction. John Milton created a classic example when he described Hell as a place of "darkness visible." We may be less poetic today, but we nevertheless appreciate the creativity (or arrogance) in expressions such as *light beer*, *sports utility vehicle*, *expressway gridlock*, or *negative economic growth*. You might not have much cause to use this figure in your writing, but you'll get credit for noting and commenting on oxymoronic ideas or behaviors.

Rhetorical Question

Rhetorical questions, which we use frequently, are questions posed by a speaker or writer that don't really require answers. Instead, an answer is implied or unimportant. When you say "Who cares?" or "What difference does it make?" you're using such questions.

Rhetorical questions show up in arguments for many reasons, most often perhaps to direct readers' attention to the issues a writer intends to explore. For example, Erin Biba asks a provocative, open-ended rhetorical question in her analysis of Facebook "friending":

> **So if we're spending most of our time online talking to people we don't even know, how deep can the conversation ever get?**
>
> **—Erin Biba, "Friendship Has Its Limits"**

Signifying

Signifying, in which a speaker or writer cleverly and often humorously needles another person, is a distinctive trope found extensively in African American English. In the following passage, two African American men (Grave Digger and Coffin Ed) signify on their white supervisor (Anderson), who has ordered them to discover the originators of a riot:

> **"I take it you've discovered who started the riot," Anderson said.**
> **"We knew who he was all along," Grave Digger said.**
> **"It's just nothing we can do to him," Coffin Ed echoed.**

"Why not, for God's sake?"

"He's dead," Coffin Ed said.

"Who?"

"Lincoln," Grave Digger said.

"He hadn't ought to have freed us if he didn't want to make provisions to feed us," Coffin Ed said. "Anyone could have told him that."

—Chester Himes, *Hot Day, Hot Night*

Coffin Ed and Grave Digger demonstrate the major characteristics of effective signifying—indirection, ironic humor, fluid rhythm, and a surprising twist at the end. Rather than insulting Anderson directly by pointing out that he's asked a dumb question, they criticize the question indirectly by ultimately blaming a white man for the riot (and not just any white man, but one they're supposed to revere). This twist leaves the supervisor speechless, teaching him something and giving Grave Digger and Coffin Ed the last word—and last laugh.

Take a look at the example of signifying from a *Boondocks* cartoon (see below). Note how Huey seems to be sympathizing with Jazmine and then, in two surprising twists, reveals that he has been needling her all along.

In these *Boondocks* strips, Huey signifies on Jazmine, using indirection, ironic humor, and two surprising twists.

Simile

A **simile** uses *like* or *as* to compare two things. Here's a simile from an essay on cosmology from the *New York Times*:

> **Through his general theory of relativity, Einstein found that space, and time too, can bend, twist, and warp, responding much as a trampoline does to a jumping child.**
>
> **—Brian Greene, "Darkness on the Edge of the Universe"**

And here is a series of similes, from an excerpt of a *Wired* magazine review of a new magazine for women:

> **Women's magazines occupy a special niche in the cluttered infoscape of modern media. Ask any *Vogue* junkie: no girl-themed Web site or CNN segment on women's health can replace the guilty pleasure of slipping a glossy fashion rag into your shopping cart. Smooth as a pint of chocolate Häagen-Dazs, feckless as a thousand-dollar slip dress, women's magazines wrap culture, trends, health, and trash in a single, decadent package. But like the diet dessert recipes they print, these slick publications can leave a bad taste in your mouth.**
>
> **—Tiffany Lee Brown, "En Vogue"**

Here, three similes—*smooth as a pint of chocolate Häagen-Dazs* and *feckless as a thousand-dollar slip dress* in the third sentence, and *like the diet dessert recipes* in the fourth—add to the image of women's magazines as a mishmash of "trash" and "trends."

Understatement

Understatement uses a quiet message to make its point. In her memoir, Rosa Parks—the civil rights activist who made history in 1955 by refusing to give up her bus seat to a white passenger—uses understatement so often that it becomes a hallmark of her style. She refers to her lifelong efforts to advance civil rights as just a small way of "carrying on."

Understatement can be particularly effective in arguments that might seem to call for its opposite. Outraged that New York's Metropolitan Opera has decided to stage *The Death of Klinghoffer*, a work depicting the murder by terrorists of a wheelchair-bound Jewish passenger on a cruise ship in 1985, writer Eve Epstein in particular points to an aria in which a terrorist named Rambo blames all the world's problems on Jews, and then, following an evocative dash, she makes a quiet observation:

> **Rambo's aria echoes the views of *Der Stürmer*, Julius Streicher's Nazi newspaper, without a hint of irony or condemnation. The leitmotif of the morally and physically crippled Jew who should be disposed of has been heard before—and it did not end well.**
>
> —Eve Epstein, "The Met's Staging of *Klinghoffer* Should Be Scrapped"

"It did not end well" alludes, of course, to the Holocaust.

RESPOND.

Use online sources (such as American Rhetoric's Top 100 Speeches at **americanrhetoric.com/top100speechesall.html**) to find the text of an essay or a speech by someone who uses figures of speech liberally. Pick a paragraph that is rich in figures and rewrite it, eliminating every bit of figurative language. Then read the original and your revised version aloud to your class. Can you imagine a rhetorical situation in which your pared-down version would be more appropriate?

Schemes

Schemes are rhetorical figures that manipulate the actual word order of phrases, sentences, or paragraphs to achieve specific affects, adding stylistic power or "zing" to arguments. The variety of such devices is beyond the scope of this work. Following are schemes that you're likely to see most often, again in alphabetical order.

Anaphora

Anaphora, or effective repetition, can act like a drumbeat in an argument, bringing the point home. Sometimes an anaphora can be quite obvious, especially when the repeated expressions occur at the beginning of a series of sentences or clauses. Here is President Lyndon Johnson urging Congress in 1965 to pass voting rights legislation:

> **There is no constitutional issue here. The command of the Constitution is plain.**
>
> **There is no moral issue. It is wrong—deadly wrong—to deny any of your fellow Americans the right to vote in this country.**

There is no issue of States rights or national rights. There is only the struggle for human rights.

I have not the slightest doubt what will be your answer.

Repetitions can occur within sentences or paragraphs as well. Here, in an argument about the future of Chicago, Lerone Bennett Jr. uses repetition to link Chicago to innovation and creativity:

> [Chicago]'s the place where organized Black history was born, where gospel music was born, where jazz and the blues were reborn, where the Beatles and the Rolling Stones went up to the mountaintop to get the new musical commandments from Chuck Berry and the rock'n'roll apostles. —Lerone Bennett Jr. "Blacks in Chicago"

Antithesis

Antithesis is the use of parallel words or sentence structures to highlight contrasts or opposition:

> Marriage has many pains, but celibacy has no pleasures.
>
> —Samuel Johnson

> Those who kill people are called murderers; those who kill animals, sportsmen.

Inverted Word Order

Inverted word order is a comparatively rare scheme in which the parts of a sentence or clause are not in the usual subject-verb-object order. It can help make arguments particularly memorable:

> Into this grey lake plopped the thought, I know this man, don't I?
>
> —Doris Lessing

> Hard to see, the dark side is. —Yoda

Parallelism

Parallelism involves the use of grammatically similar phrases or clauses for special effect. Among the most common of rhetorical effects, parallelism can be used to underscore the relationships between ideas in phrases, clauses, complete sentences, or even paragraphs. You probably recognize the famous parallel clauses that open Charles Dickens's *A Tale of Two Cities*:

> **It was the best of times,**
>
> **it was the worst of times . . .**

The author's paralleled clauses and sentences go on and on through more than a half-dozen pairings, their rhythm unforgettable. Or consider how this unattributed line from the 2008 presidential campaign season resonates because of its elaborate and sequential parallel structure:

> **Rosa sat so that Martin could walk. Martin walked so that Obama could run. Obama ran so that our children could fly.**

RESPOND•

Identify the figurative language used in the following slogans. Note that some slogans may use more than one device.

"A day without orange juice is like a day without sunshine." (Florida Orange Juice)

"Open happiness." (Coca-Cola)

"Be all that you can be." (U.S. Army)

"Breakfast of champions." (Wheaties)

"America runs on Dunkin'." (Dunkin' Donuts)

"Like a rock." (Chevrolet trucks)

CULTURAL CONTEXTS FOR ARGUMENT

Levels of Formality and Other Issues of Style

At least one important style question needs to be asked when arguing across cultures: what level of formality is most appropriate? In the United States, a fairly informal style is often acceptable and even appreciated. Many cultures, however, tend to value formality. If in doubt, err on the side of formality:

- Take care to use proper titles as appropriate (*Ms.*, *Mr.*, *Dr.*, and so on).
- Don't use first names unless you've been invited to do so.
- Steer clear of slang and jargon. When you're communicating with members of other cultures, slang may not be understood, or it may be seen as disrespectful.
- Avoid potentially puzzling pop cultural allusions, such as sports analogies or musical references.

When arguing across cultures or languages, another stylistic issue might be clarity. When communicating with people whose native languages are different from your own, analogies and similes almost always aid in understanding. Likening something unknown to something familiar can help make your argument forceful—and understandable.

14
Visual Rhetoric

To commemorate the two hundredth anniversary of "The Star-Spangled Banner," its lyrics composed by Francis Scott Key in September 1814 following the failed British bombardment of Fort McHenry outside Baltimore, the Smithsonian Institution asked a group of artists to reflect on what the American flag means today. Most of the artists expressed their ideas and opinions visually, through paintings, photographs, montages, sculptures, films, even a graphic "fantasy." Three of their items are reproduced above: left to right, a steel-and-aluminum flag by architect Daniel Libeskind; a figure in acrylic and watercolor by Anita Kunz; and a photo collage by graphic designer David Carson. Even so small a sampling of visual rhetoric underscores what you doubtless already know: images tease our imaginations, provoke responses from viewers, and, yes, make arguments. They have clout.

The Power of Visual Arguments

Even in everyday situations, images—from T-shirts to billboards to animated films and computer screens—influence us. Media analyst Kevin Kelly ponders the role screens and their images now play in our lives:

> Everywhere we look, we see screens. The other day I watched clips from a movie as I pumped gas into my car. The other night I saw a movie on the backseat of a plane. We will watch anywhere. Screens playing video pop up in the most unexpected places—like ATM machines and supermarket checkout lines and tiny phones; some movie fans watch entire films in between calls. These ever-present screens have created an audience for very short moving pictures, as brief as three minutes, while cheap digital creation tools have empowered a new generation of filmmakers, who are rapidly filling up those screens. We are headed toward screen ubiquity.
>
> —Kevin Kelly, "Becoming Screen Literate"

Of course, visual arguments weren't invented by YouTube, and their power isn't novel either. The pharaohs of Egypt lined the banks of the Nile River with statues of themselves to assert their authority, and there is no shortage of monumental effigies in Washington, D.C., today.

Not only the high and mighty: sculpture of a Great Depression–era breadline at the Franklin Delano Roosevelt Memorial in Washington, D.C. © Mel Longhurst/Photoshot

Still, the ease with which all of us make and share images is unprecedented: people are uploading a billion shots a *day* to Snapchat, a photo-messaging application that deletes items after only a brief viewing. And most of us have easily adjusted to instantaneous multichannel, multimedia connectivity (see Chapter 16). We expect it to be seamless too. The prophet of this era was Marshall McLuhan, who nearly fifty years ago proclaimed that "the medium is the massage," with the play on *message* and *massage* intentional. As McLuhan says, "We shape our tools and afterwards our tools shape us. . . . All media works us over completely."

RESPOND.

Find an advertisement, either print or digital, that uses both verbal and visual elements. Analyze its argument first by pointing out the claims the ad makes (or implies) and then by identifying the ways it supports them verbally and/or visually. (If it helps, go over the questions about multimedia texts offered in Chapter 16 on pp. 368–70.) Then switch ads with a classmate and discuss his/her analysis. Compare your responses to the two ads. If they're different—and they probably will be—how might you account for the differences?

Using Visuals in Your Own Arguments

Given the power of images, it's only natural that you would use them in your own composing. In fact, many college instructors now expect papers for their courses to be posted to the Web, where digital photos, videos, and design elements are native. Other instructors invite or even require students to do multimedia reports or to use videos, photo collages, cartoons, or other media to make arguments—an assignment not unlike that given to the artists in the Smithsonian's "Star-Spangled Banner" project. If using visual media still strikes you as odd in academic settings, just consider that such arguments can have all the reach and versatility of more conventional verbal appeals to pathos, ethos, and logos. Often even more.

Using Images and Visual Design to Create Pathos

Many advertisements, YouTube videos, political posters, rallies, marches, and even church services use visual images to trigger emotions. You can't flip through a magazine, watch a video, or browse the

Web without being cajoled or seduced by figures or design elements of all kinds—most of them fashioned in some way to attract your eye and attention.

Technology has also made it incredibly easy for you to create on-the-spot photographs and videos that you can use for making arguments of your own. With a GoPro camera strapped to your head, you could document transportation problems in and around campus and then present your visual evidence in a paper or an oral report. You don't have to be a professional these days to produce poignant, stirring, or even satirical visual texts.

Yet just because images are powerful doesn't mean they always work. When you compose visually, you have to be certain to generate impressions that support your arguments, not weigh against them.

Shape Visuals to Convey Appropriate Feelings

To appeal visually to your readers' emotions, think first of the goal of your writing: you want every image or use of multimedia to advance that purpose. Consider, for a moment, the iconic *Apollo 8* "earthrise" photograph of our planet hanging above the horizon of the moon. You could

Still striking almost fifty years later, this 1968 *Apollo 8* photograph of the earth shining over the moon can support many kinds of arguments. NASA

adapt this image to introduce an appeal for additional investment in the space program. Or it might become part of an argument about the need to preserve frail natural environments, or a stirring appeal against nationalism: *From space, we are one world.* Any of these claims might be supported successfully without the image, but the photograph—like most visuals—will probably touch members of your audience more strongly than words alone could.

Consider Emotional Responses to Color

As the "earthrise" photo demonstrates, color can have great power too: the beautiful blue earth floating in deep black space carries a message of its own. Indeed, our response to color is part of our biological and cultural makeup. So it makes sense to consider what shades are especially effective with the kinds of arguments you're making, whether they occur in images themselves or in elements such as headings, fonts, backgrounds, screens, banners and so on. And remember that a black-and-white image can also be a memorable design choice.

In most situations, let your selection of colors be guided by your own good taste, by designs you admire, or by the advice of friends or helpful professionals. Some design and presentation software will even help you choose colors by offering dependable "default" shades or an array of pre-existing designs and compatible colors (for example, of presentation slides). To be emotionally effective, the colors you choose for a design should follow certain commonsense principles. If you're using background colors on a political poster, Web site, or slide, the contrast between words and background should be vivid enough to make reading easy. For example, white letters on a yellow background are not usually legible. Similarly, bright background colors should be avoided for long documents because reading is easiest with dark letters against a light or white background. Avoid complex patterns; even though they might look interesting and be easy to create, they often interfere with other more important elements of a presentation.

When you use visuals in your college projects, test them on prospective readers. That's what professionals do because they appreciate how delicate the choices of visual and multimedia texts can be. These responses will help you analyze your own arguments and improve your success with them.

Eve Arnold took this powerful black-and-white photograph in 1958 at a party in Virginia for students being introduced to mixed-race schools. How might a full-color image have changed the impact of the scene? © Eve Arnold/Magnum Photos

Using Images to Establish Ethos

How does the image of the student from Mt. Holyoke impact your response to Sarah Fraas's piece "Trans Women at Smith: The Complexities of Checking 'Female'"?

LINK TO P. 683

If you are on Facebook, LinkedIn, or other social networking sites, you no doubt chose photographs for those sites with an eye to creating a sense of who you are, what you value, and how you wish to be perceived. You fashioned a self-image. So it shouldn't come as a surprise that you can boost your credibility as a writer by using visual design strategically: we know one person whose Facebook presentation of images and media so impressed a prospective employer that she got a job on the spot. So whether you are using photographs, videos, or other media on your personal pages or in your college work, it pays to attend to how they construct your ethos.

Understand How Images Enhance Credibility and Authority

You might have noticed that just about every company, organization, institution, government agency, or club now sports a logo or an emblem. Whether it's the Red Cross, the Canadian Olympic Committee, or perhaps the school you attend, such groups use carefully crafted images to

How does a photograph like this 1999 Bruce Davidson shot of President Bill Clinton shape your sense of Clinton's ethos? Based on this image alone, what words might you use to describe Clinton as a *politician*? © Bruce Davidson/Magnum Photos

signal their authority and trustworthiness. An emblem or a logo can also carry a wealth of cultural and historical implications. That's why university Web sites typically include the seal of the institution somewhere on the homepage (and always on its letterhead) or why the president of the United States travels with a presidential seal to hang on the speaker's podium.

Though you probably don't have a personal logo or trademark, your personal ethos functions the same way when you make an argument. You can establish it by offering visual evidence of your knowledge or competence. In an essay on safety issues in competitive biking, you might include a photo of yourself in a key race, embed a video showing how often serious accidents occur, or include an audio file of an interview with an injured biker. The photo proves that you have personal experience with biking, while the video and audio files show that you have done research and know your subject well, thus helping to affirm your credibility.

Predictably, your choice of *medium* also says something important about you. Making an appeal on a Web site sends signals about your technical skills, contemporary orientation, and personality. So if you direct people to a Facebook or Flickr page, be sure that any materials

Take a look at these three government logos, each of which intends to convey credibility, authority, and maybe more. Do they accomplish their goals? Why or why not? Left to right: NASA; Courtesy Internal Revenue Service; Courtesy Environmental Protection Agency

there present you favorably. Be just as careful in a classroom that any handouts or slides you use for an oral report demonstrate your competence. And remember that you don't always have to be high-tech to be effective: when reporting on a children's story that you're writing, the most sensible medium of presentation might be cardboard and paper made into an oversized book and illustrated by hand.

You demonstrate your ethos simply by showing an awareness of the basic design conventions for any kind of writing you're doing. It's no accident that lab reports for science courses are sober and unembellished. Visually, they reinforce the professional ethos of scientific work. The same is true of a college research paper. So whether you're composing a term paper, a résumé, a film, an animated comic, or a Web site, look for successful models and follow their design cues.

Consider How Details of Design Reflect Your Ethos

As we have just suggested, almost every design element you use in a paper or project sends signals about character and ethos. You might resent the tediousness of placing page numbers in the appropriate corner, aligning long quotations just so, and putting footnotes in the right place, but these details prove that you are paying attention. Gestures as simple as writing on official stationery (if, for example, you are representing a club or campus organization) or dressing up for an oral presentation matter too: suddenly you seem more mature and competent.

Even the type fonts that you select for a document can mark you as warm and inviting or as efficient and contemporary. The warm and inviting fonts often belong to a family called *serif*. The serifs are those little flourishes at the ends of the strokes that make the fonts seem handcrafted and artful:

warm and inviting (Bookman Old Style)

warm and inviting (Times New Roman)

warm and inviting (Georgia)

Cleaner, modern fonts go without those little flourishes and are called *sans serif*. These fonts are cooler, simpler, and, some argue, more readable on a computer screen (depending on screen resolution):

efficient and contemporary (Helvetica)

efficient and contemporary (Verdana)

efficient and contemporary (Comic Sans MS)

Other typographic elements send messages as well. The size of type can make a difference. If your text or headings are in boldface and too large, you'll seem to be shouting:

LOSE WEIGHT! PAY NOTHING!*

Tiny type, on the other hand, might make you seem evasive:

*Excludes the costs of enrollment and required meal purchases. Minimum contract: 12 months.

Consider the design choices made by the creators of the diversity posters in Chapter 26. Which ones are effective? Do any design choices get in the way of their messages?

LINK TO P. 670

Finally, don't ignore the signals you send through your choice of *illustrations* and *photographs* themselves. Images communicate your preferences, sensitivities, and inclusiveness—sometimes inadvertently. Conference planners, for example, are careful to create brochures that represent all participants, and they make sure that the brochure photos don't show only women, only men, or only members of one racial or ethnic group.

RESPOND.

Choose a project or an essay you have written recently and examine it for how well *visually* it establishes your credibility and how well it is designed. Ask a classmate or friend to look at it and describe the ethos you convey through the item. Then go back to the drawing board with a memo to yourself about how you might use images or media to improve it.

Who's missing in this picture of senior advisers to the president taken in December 2012? The *New York Times*, which published the item, pointed out that, if you looked very closely, you could see Valerie Jarrett's leg. The White House, photo by Pete Souza

Using Visual Images to Support Logos

Not that long ago, media critics ridiculed the colorful charts and graphs in newspapers like *USA Today*. Now, comparable features appear in even the most traditional publications because they work: they convey information efficiently *and* persuasively. We now expect evidence to be presented graphically and have learned to use and interact with multiple streams of data and information.

Organize Information Visually

Graphic presentation calls for design that enables readers and viewers to look at an item and understand what it does. A brilliant, much-copied example of such an intuitive design is a seat adjuster invented many years ago by Mercedes-Benz (see photo at left). It's shaped like a tiny seat. Push any element of the control, and the real seat moves in that direction — back and forth, up and down. No instructions are necessary.

Mercedes-Benz's seat adjuster © Ron Kimball/Kimball Stock

Good visual design can work the same way in an argument by conveying evidence, data, and other information without elaborate instructions. Titles, headings, subheadings, enlarged quotations, running heads, and boxes are some common visual signals:

- Use headings to guide your readers through your print or electronic document. For long and complex pieces, use subheadings as well, and make sure they are parallel.
- Use type font, size, and color to show related information among headings.
- Arrange headings or text on a page to enforce relationships among comparable items, ideas, or bits of evidence.
- Use a list or a box to set off material for emphasis or to show that it differs from the rest of the presentation. You can also use shading, color, and typography for emphasis.
- Place your images and illustrations strategically. What you position front and center will appear more important than items in less conspicuous places. Images of comparable size will be treated as equally important.

Remember, too, that design principles evolve and change from medium to medium. A printed text or presentation slide, for example, ordinarily works best when its elements are easy to read, simply organized, and surrounded by restful white space. But some electronic texts thrive on visual clutter, packing a grab bag of data into a limited space (See the "infographic of Infographics" on p. 342.) Look closely, though, and you'll probably find the logic in these designs.

Use Visuals to Convey Data Efficiently

Words are capable of great precision and subtlety, but some information is conveyed far more effectively by charts, graphs, drawings, maps, or photos—as several items in Chapter 4 illustrate. When making an argument, especially to a large group, consider what information might be more persuasive and memorable in nonverbal form.

A *pie chart* is an effective way of comparing parts to the whole. You might use a pie chart to illustrate the ethnic composition of your school, the percentage of taxes paid by people at different income levels, or the consumption of energy by different nations. Pie charts depict such information memorably.

A *graph* is an efficient device for comparing items over time or according to other variables. You could use a graph to trace the rise and fall of test scores over several decades, to show college enrollment by sex, race, and Hispanic origin, or to track bicycle usage in the United States, as in the bar graph on p. 342.

Diagrams or *drawings* are useful for attracting attention to details. Use drawings to illustrate complex physical processes or designs of all sorts. After the 2001 attack on the World Trade Center, for example, engineers prepared drawings and diagrams to help citizens understand precisely what led to the total collapse of the buildings.

You can use *maps* to illustrate location and spatial relationships—something as simple as the distribution of office space in your student union or as complex as poverty in the United States, as in the map on p. 343. In fact, scholars in many fields now use geographic information system (GIS) technology to merge maps with databases in all fields to offer new kinds of arguments about everything from traffic patterns and health care trends to character movements in literary works. Plotting data this way yields information far different from what might be offered in words alone. You can find more about GIS applications online.

Timelines allow you to represent the passage of time graphically, and online tools like Dipity can help you create them for insertion into your documents. Similarly, Web pages can make for valuable illustrations. Programs like ShrinkTheWeb let you create snapshots of Web sites that can then be inserted easily into your writing. And when you want to combine a variety of graphs, charts, and other texts into a single visual argument, you might create an *infographic* using software such as Google Public Data Explorer, Many Eyes, StatPlanet, and Wordle.

Follow Professional Guidelines for Presenting Visuals

Charts, graphs, tables, illustrations, timelines, snapshots of Web sites, and video clips play such an important role in many fields that professional groups have come up with guidelines for labeling and formatting these items. You need to become familiar with those conventions as you advance in a field. A guide such as the *Publication Manual of the American Psychological Association* (6th edition) or the *MLA Handbook for Writers of Research Papers* (7th edition) describes these rules in detail. See also Chapter 15, "Presenting Arguments."

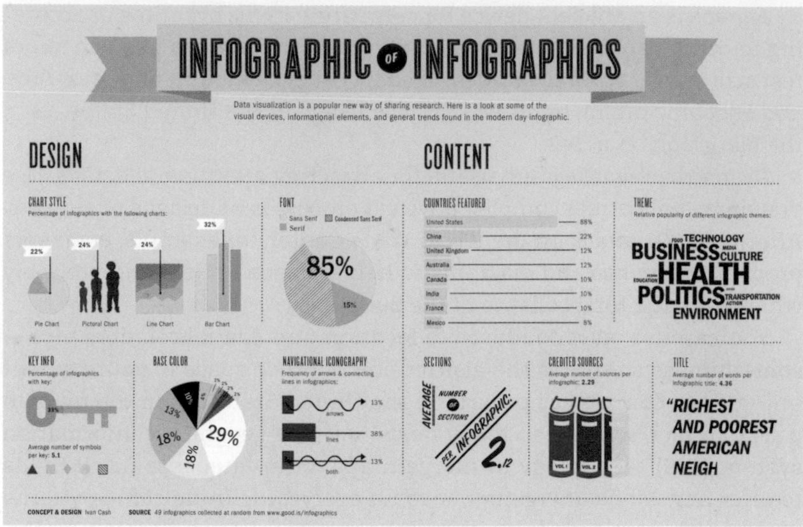

© Ivan Cash, CashStudios.com

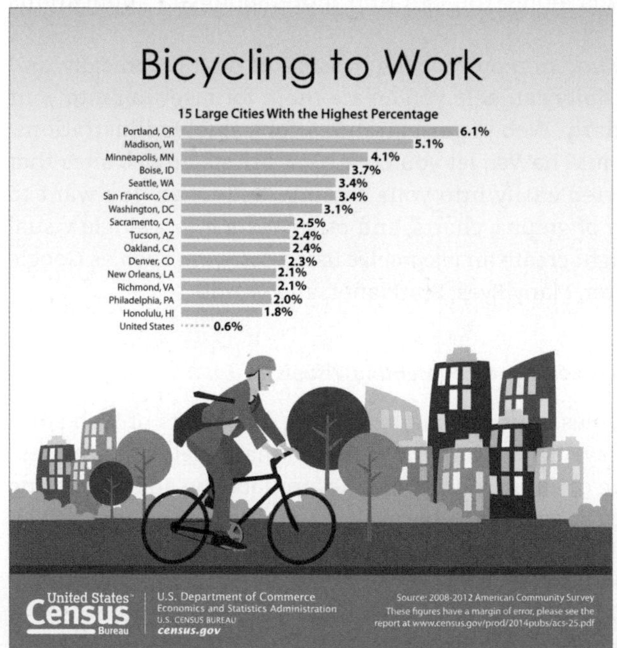

U.S. Census Bureau

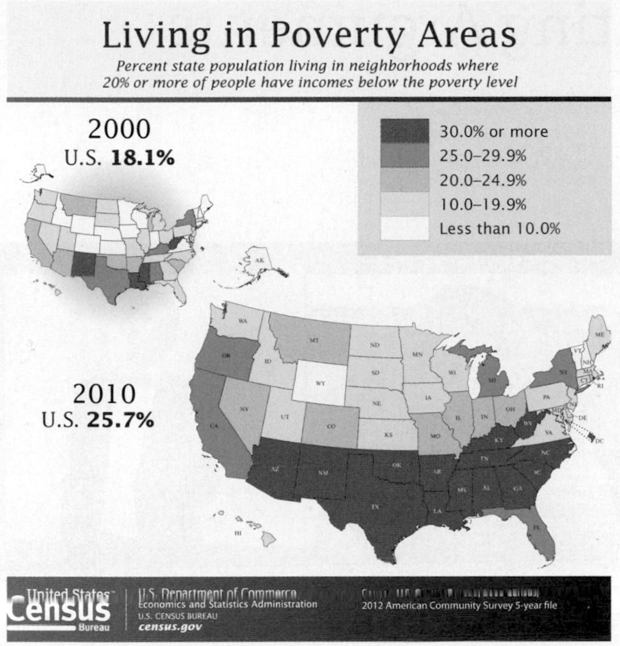

U.S. Census Bureau

Remember to Check for Copyrighted Material

You also must be careful to respect copyright rules when using visual items that were created by someone else. If you do introduce any borrowed items into academic work, be careful to document them fully. It's relatively easy these days to download visual texts of all kinds from the Web. Some of these items—such as clip art or government documents—may be in the *public domain*, meaning that you're free to use them without requesting permission or paying a royalty. But other visual texts may require permission, especially if you intend to publish your work or use the item commercially. Remember: anything you place on a Web site is considered "published." (See Chapter 21 for more on intellectual property and fair use.)

15
Presenting Arguments

Left to right: AP Photo/Paul Chiasson, CP; AP Photo/Andrew Medichini; Courtesy of George Chidiac

For many arguments you make in college, the format you've used since grade school is still a sensible choice — a traditional paper with double spacing, correct margins, MLA- or APA-style notes, and so on. Printed texts like these offer a methodical way to explain abstract ideas or to set down complicated chains of reasoning. Even spruced up with images or presented online (to enable color, media, and Web links), such conventional arguments — whether configured as essays, newsletters, or brochures — are cheap to create and easy to reproduce and share. You will find examples of printed texts throughout this book and especially in Part 4 on "Research and Arguments."

But print isn't your only medium for advancing arguments. Sometimes, you'll need to make a case orally, drawing on the visual or multimedia strategies discussed in previous chapters. Like Lawrence Lessig above, speaking about Internet gambling, you might need slides and Web tools to back up points in a lecture; or like Josette Sheeran, a panelist at a conference on world food security, you may find yourself engaged in serious discussions; or maybe like fellow student George Chidiac, you just need to deliver a first-rate oral report in class. Knowing how to speak eloquently to a point is a basic rhetorical skill.

Class and Public Discussions

No doubt you find yourself arguing all the time at school, maybe over a poem with a classmate in an English course or perhaps with a teaching assistant whose interpretation of economic trends you're sure is flat wrong. Or maybe you spoke up at a campus meeting against the administration's enforcement of "free speech zones"—*or wish you had*. The fact is, lots of people are shy about joining class discussions or public debates, even those that interest them. They find such occasions intimidating. Perhaps they don't want to tip their hands, or fear they know too little about a subject, or simply don't like the give-and-take of spirited debate.

You can improve your participation in such situations by observing both effective and ineffective speakers. Watch how the participants who enliven a discussion stay on topic, add new information or ideas, and pay attention to all members of the group. Notice, too, that less successful speakers often can't stop talking, somehow make all discussions about themselves, or just play the smart aleck when they don't know much about a topic. Surely, you can do better.

You can start just by joining in on conversations whenever you can. If speaking is a problem, take it slow at first—a comment or two, something as simple as "That's a really good idea!" or "I wonder how accurate this data is?" The more that you hear your own voice in discussions, the more comfortable you'll be offering your opinions in detail. Here are some more tips:

- Do the required reading in a class so that you know what you're talking about. That alone will give you a leg up in most groups.
- Listen carefully and purposefully, and jot down important points.
- Speak briefly to the point under discussion so that your comments are relevant. Don't do all the talking.
- Ask questions about issues that bother you: others probably have the same thoughts.
- Occasionally, summarize points that have already been made to make sure that everyone is "on the same page." Keep the summary brief.
- Respond to questions or comments by others in specific rather than vague terms.
- Try to learn the names of people in a discussion, and then use them.
- When you're already a player in a discussion, invite others to join in.

CULTURAL CONTEXTS FOR ARGUMENT

Speaking Up in Class

Speaking up in class is viewed as inappropriate or even rude in some cultures. In the United States and Canada, however, doing so is expected and encouraged. Some instructors even assign credit for such class participation.

Preparing a Presentation

Sooner or later, you'll be asked to deliver a presentation in a college class. That's because the ability to explain material clearly to an audience is a skill much admired by potential employers. Unfortunately, instructors sometimes give little practical advice about how to hone that talent, which is not a natural gift for most people. While it's hard to generalize here, capable presenters attribute their success to the following strategies and perceptions:

- They make sure they know their subjects thoroughly.
- They pay attention to the values, ideas, and needs of their listeners.
- They use patterns and styles that make their spoken arguments easy to follow.
- They realize that oral arguments are interactive. (Live audiences can argue back!)
- They appreciate that most oral presentations involve visuals, and they plan accordingly. (We'll address multimedia presentations in the next chapter.)
- They practice, practice—and then practice some more.

We suggest a few additional moves for when you are specifically required to make a formal argument or presentation in class (or on the job): assess the rhetorical situation you face, nail down the details of the presentation, fashion a script or plan, choose media to fit your subject, and then deliver a good show.

Assess the Rhetorical Situation

Whether asked to make a formal oral report in class, to speak to the general public, or to join a panel discussion, ask yourself the same questions about rhetorical choices that you face whenever you make an argument.

Understanding Purpose. Figure out the major purpose of the assignment or situation. Is it to inform and enlighten your audience? To convince or persuade them? To explore a concept or principle? To stimulate discussion? To encourage a decision? Something else? Very important in school, will you be speaking to share your expertise or to prove that you have it (as you might in a class report)?

Assessing the Audience. Determine who will be listening to your talk. Just an instructor and classmates? Interested observers at a public meeting? People who know more about the subject than you do—or less? Or will you be a peer of the audience members—typically, a classmate? What mix of age groups, of gender, of political affiliation, of rank, etc., will be in the group? What expectations will listeners bring to the talk, and what opinions are they likely to hold? Will this audience be invited to ask questions after the event?

Compare the Supreme Court ruling in Chapter 27 to the cartoons in the same chapter. Consider how audience has shaped the way these pieces address a similar topic.

LINK TO PP. 771 AND 751

Deciding on Content. What exactly is the topic for the presentation? What is its general scope? Are you expected to make a narrow and specific argument drawn from a research assignment? Are you expected to argue facts, definitions, causes and effects? Will you be offering an evaluation or perhaps a proposal? What degree of detail is necessary, and how much evidence should you provide for your claims?

Choosing Structure and Style. Will your instructor or audience expect a specific type of report? What "parts" must your presentation include: introduction, background information, thesis, evidence, refutation, discussion, conclusion? Can you model the talk after other reports you have heard or public events you have attended? Can you modify a conventional presentation to suit your topic better? Will the audience expect a serious presentation in academic style or can you be friendly and colloquial, perhaps even funny? Crucially, by what standards is your report likely to be assessed or graded?

Here's a live audience watching an HD broadcast of a performance inside the opera house right in front of them. Probably a grumpy group. Lonely Planet/Getty Images

Following are three excerpts from a detailed, three-page outline that sophomore George Chidiac worked up on his own to prepare for a fifteen-minute oral report on Thomas More's "Petition for Free Speech" (1523)—an important document on the path to establishing free speech as a natural right. Chidiac's outline of rhetorical issues and concerns prepped him well enough to deliver the entire report without notes. His thesis is highlighted, but also notice the question Chidiac asks at the very end: *So what?* He recognizes an obligation to explain why his report should matter to his audience.

Oral Report Outline

Requirements:

10 minutes

Share what I've learned in my research

Help colleagues appreciate the research I've done

Introduction

Introduce myself

Agenda—subject of presentation

Define free speech: the right to express any opinions without censorship or restraint

Set the stage and present a dilemma

Stage: From history of free speech, we are going to micro-focus to Renaissance, to 16th-century England, to April 18, 1523, in the House of Commons where I want to share insight on a pivotal point in the advancement of free speech in a political context.

Dilemma: The king called all his advisers and those able to enact legislation to raise funds to go to war. You are the intermediary between the main legislative body and the king. You have three obligations: one to truth, one to the king, and one to the body you're representing. The king wants money, the legislative body cannot object, and you want truth and the best outcome to win out. How do you *reconcile* this?

What

What's my message? What's the focal point of my presentation?

I want to provide a snapshot in time of the evolution of free speech.

Thomas More, in his *Petition for Free Speech*, incrementally advanced free speech as a duty and a right.

Who

Who made this happen? Who was involved?

Thomas More

Brief bio: Before he became Speaker → Chancellor of England, friend of King Henry VIII, theologian, poet, father

Henry VIII

William Roper (minor role)

Brief bio: son-in-law and chief biographer

* * *

Why

Why was More's Petition *"successful"? Why did Henry VIII accept the petition?*

Henry VIII's character

Humanist — or wished to subscribe to humanist principles

Resembled More

Rediscovery and reevaluation of classical civilization and application into modern intellectual and social culture

Spirit of *amicitia* — friendship with counsel — constancy, mutual loyalty, and concern for justice where the crux was "freedom of speech"

Parliamentary expectations

Relationship between king and Parliament

Still a matter of license, not true freedom — sufferance

Members of Parliament acting in goodwill

By accepting the petition, Henry acknowledged that while not all parliamentary speech should be *permitted*, not all speech critical of monarchy is *slanderous*

Oncoming war

* * *

SO WHAT?

What do I want my colleagues to take with them? Big lesson?

Freedom of speech we have today wasn't always enjoyed.

"A Campus More Colorful Than Reality: Beware That College Brochure" is a transcript of Deena Prichep's interview on NPR. The NPR Web site (and this textbook) contain a picture of the controversial campus brochure, but those listening on the radio would not have had this visual reference.

LINK TO P. 678

Nail Down the Specific Details

Big-picture rhetorical considerations are obviously important in an oral report, but so are the details. Pay attention to exactly how much time you have to prepare for an event, a lecture, or a panel session, and how long the actual presentation should be: *never* infringe on the time of other speakers. Determine what visual aids, slides, or handouts might make the presentation successful. Will you need an overhead projector, a flip chart, a whiteboard? Decide whether presentation software, such as PowerPoint, Keynote, or Prezi, will help you make a stronger report. Then figure out where to acquire the equipment as well as the expertise to use it. If you run into problems, especially with classroom reports, consider low-tech alternatives. Sometimes, speaking clearly or sharing effective handouts works better than a plodding slideshow.

If possible, check out where your presentation will take place. In a classroom with fixed chairs? A lecture or assembly hall? An informal sitting area? Will you have a lectern? Other equipment? Will you sit or stand? Remain in one place or move around? What will the lighting be, and can you adjust it? Take nothing for granted, and if you plan to use media equipment, be ready with a backup strategy if a projector bulb dies or a Web site won't load.

Not infrequently, oral presentations are group efforts. When that's the case, plan and practice accordingly. The work should be divvied up according to the strengths of the participants: you will need to work out who speaks when, who handles the equipment, who takes the questions, and so on.

Fashion a Script Designed to Be Heard by an Audience

Unless you are presenting a formal lecture (pretty rare in college), most oral presentations are delivered from notes. But even if you do deliver a live presentation from a printed text, be sure to compose a script that is designed to be *heard* rather than *read*. Such a text—whether in the form of note cards, an overhead list, or a fully written-out paper—should feature a strong introduction and conclusion, an unambiguous structure with helpful transitions and signposts, concrete diction, and straightforward syntax.

Strong Introductions and Conclusions. Like readers, listeners remember beginnings and endings best. Work hard, therefore, to make these elements of your spoken argument memorable and personable. Consider including a provocative or puzzling statement, opinion, or question; a memorable anecdote; a powerful quotation; or a strong visual image. If you can connect your report directly to the interests or experiences of your listeners in the introduction or conclusion, then do so.

Be sure that your introduction clearly explains what your presentation will cover, what your focus will be, and perhaps even how the presentation will be arranged. Give listeners a mental map of where you are taking them. If you are using presentation software, a bare-bones outline sometimes makes sense, especially when the argument is a straightforward academic presentation: thesis + evidence.

The conclusion should drive home and reinforce your main point. You can summarize the key arguments you have made (again, a simple slide could do some of the work), but you don't want to end with just a rehash, especially when the presentation is short. Instead, conclude by underscoring the *implications* of your report: what do you want your audience to be thinking and feeling at the end?

Clear Structures and Signposts. For a spoken argument, you want your organizational structure to be crystal clear. So make sure that you have a sharply delineated beginning, middle, and end and share the structure with listeners. You can do that by remembering to pause between major points of your presentation and to offer *signposts* marking your movement from one topic to the next. They can be transitions as obvious as *next*, *on the contrary*, or *finally*. Such words act as memory points in your spoken argument and thus should be explicit and concrete: *The second crisis point in the breakup of the Soviet Union occurred hard on the heels of the first*, rather than just *The breakup of the Soviet Union led to another crisis*. You can also keep listeners on track by repeating key words and concepts and by using unambiguous topic sentences to introduce each new idea. These transitions can also be highlighted as you come to them on a whiteboard or on presentation slides.

Straightforward Syntax and Concrete Diction. Avoid long, complicated sentences in an oral report and use straightforward syntax (subject-verb-object, for instance, rather than an inversion of that order). Remember, too, that listeners can grasp concrete verbs and nouns more easily than they can mentally process a steady stream of abstractions. When you need to deal with abstract ideas, illustrate them with concrete examples.

Take a look at the following text that student Ben McCorkle wrote about *The Simpsons*, first as he prepared it for an essay and then as he adapted it for a live oral and multimedia presentation:

Print Version

The Simpson family has occasionally been described as a *nuclear* family, which obviously has a double meaning: first, the family consists of two parents and three children, and, second, Homer works at a nuclear power plant with very relaxed safety codes. The overused label "dysfunctional," when applied to the Simpsons, suddenly takes on new meaning. Every episode seems to include a scene in which son Bart is being choked by his father, the baby is being neglected, or Homer is sitting in a drunken stupor transfixed by the television screen. The comedy in these scenes comes from the exaggeration of commonplace household events (although some talk shows and news programs would have us believe that these exaggerations are not confined to the madcap world of cartoons).

—Ben McCorkle, "*The Simpsons*: A Mirror of Society"

Oral Version (with a visual illustration)

What does it mean to describe the Simpsons as a *nuclear* family? Clearly, a double meaning is at work. First, the Simpsons fit the dictionary meaning—a family unit consisting of two parents and some children. The second meaning, however, packs more of a punch. You

Homer Simpson in a typical pose © Photofest, Inc.

> see, Homer works at a nuclear power plant [pause here] with *very* relaxed safety codes!
>
> Still another overused family label describes the Simpsons. Did everyone guess I was going to say *dysfunctional*? And like *nuclear*, when it comes to the Simpsons, *dysfunctional* takes on a whole new meaning.
>
> Remember the scene when Bart is being choked by his father?
>
> How about the many times the baby is being neglected?
>
> Or the classic view—Homer sitting in a stupor transfixed by the TV screen!
>
> My point here is that the comedy in these scenes often comes from double meanings—and from a lot of exaggeration of everyday household events.

Note that the second version presents the same information as the first, but this time it's written to be *heard*. The revision uses simpler syntax, so the argument is easy to listen to, and employs signposts, repetition, a list, and italicized words to prompt the speaker to give special emphasis where needed.

RESPOND.

Take three or four paragraphs from an essay that you've recently written. Then, following the guidelines in this chapter, rewrite the passage to be heard by a live audience. Finally, make a list of every change that you made.

Repetition, Parallelism, and Climactic Order. Whether they're used alone or in combination, repetition, parallelism, and climactic order are especially appropriate for spoken arguments that sound a call to arms or that seek to rouse the emotions of an audience. Perhaps no person in the twentieth century used them more effectively than Martin Luther King Jr., whose sermons and speeches helped to spearhead the civil rights movement. Standing on the steps of the Lincoln Memorial in Washington, D.C., on August 23, 1963, with hundreds of thousands of marchers before him, King called on the nation to make good on the "promissory note" represented by the Emancipation Proclamation.

Look at the way that King uses repetition, parallelism, and climactic order in the following paragraph to invoke a nation to action:

> It is obvious today that America has defaulted on this promissory note insofar as her citizens of color are concerned. Instead of honoring this sacred obligation, America has given the Negro people a bad *check* which has come back marked "*insufficient funds*." But *we* refuse to

> believe that the bank of justice is bankrupt. *We* refuse to believe that there are *insufficient funds* in the great vaults of opportunity of this nation. So *we have come* to cash this *check*—a *check* that will give us upon demand the riches of freedom and the security of justice. We *have also come* to this hallowed spot to remind America of the fierce urgency of now. There is no time to engage in the luxury of cooling off or to take the tranquillizing drug of gradualism. *Now* is the time *to rise* from the dark and desolate valley of segregation to the sunlit path of racial justice. *Now* is the time *to open* the doors of opportunity to all of God's children. *Now* is the time *to lift* our nation from the quicksands of racial injustice to the solid rock of brotherhood.
>
> —Martin Luther King Jr., "I Have a Dream" (emphasis added)

The italicized words highlight the way that King uses repetition to drum home his theme and a series of powerful verb phrases (*to rise*, *to open*, *to lift*) to build to a strong climax. These stylistic choices, together with the vivid image of the "bad check," help to make King's speech powerful, persuasive—and memorable.

You don't have to be as highly skilled as King to take advantage of the power of repetition and parallelism. Simply repeating a key word in your argument can impress it on your audience, as can arranging parts of sentences or items in a list in parallel order.

Choose Media to Fit Your Subject

Visual materials—charts, graphs, posters, and presentation slides—are major tools for conveying your message and supporting your claims. People are so accustomed to visual (and aural) texts that they genuinely expect to see them in most oral reports. And, in many cases, a picture, video, or graph can truly be worth a thousand words. (For more about visual argument, see Chapter 14.)

Successful Use of Visuals. Be certain that any visuals that you use are large enough to be seen by all members of your audience. If you use slides or overhead projections, the information on each frame should be simple, clear, and easy to process. For slides, use 24-point type for major headings, 18 point for subheadings, and at least 14 point for other text. Remember, too, to limit the number of words per slide. The same rules of clarity and simplicity hold true for posters, flip charts, and whiteboards. (Note that if your presentation is based on source materials—either text or images—remember to include a slide that lists all those sources at the end of the presentation.)

Four simple and evocative slides from a presentation entitled "We Learn through Stories." Imagine the commentary that might accompany them. *Photo:* Fotovika/Shutterstock; *Diagrams:* Darren Kuropatwa; Robot designed by Simon Child from the Noun Project-Creative Commons — Attribution (CC BY 3.0)

Use presentation software to furnish an overview for a report or lecture and to give visual information and signposts to listeners. Audiences will be grateful to see the people you are discussing, the key data points you are addressing, the movement of your argument as it develops. But if you've watched many oral presentations, you're sure to have seen some bad ones. Perhaps nothing is deadlier than a speaker who stands up and just reads from each screen. Do this and you'll just put people to sleep. Also remember not to turn your back on your audience when you refer to these visuals. And if you prepare supplementary materials (such as bibliographies or other handouts), don't distribute them until the audience actually needs them, or wait until the end of the presentation so that they don't distract listeners from your spoken arguments. (For advice on creating multimedia arguments, see Chapter 16.)

The best way to test the effectiveness of any images, slides, or other visuals is to try them out on friends, family members, classmates, or roommates. If they don't get the meaning of the visuals right away, revise and try again.

Accommodations for Everyone. Remember that visuals and accompanying media tools can help make your presentation accessible but that some members of your audience may not be able to see your presentation or may have trouble seeing or hearing them. Here are a few key rules to remember:

- Use words to describe projected images. Something as simple as "That's Eleanor Roosevelt in 1944" can help even sight-impaired audience members appreciate what's on a screen.
- If you use video, take the time to label sounds that might not be audible to audience members who are hearing impaired. (Be sure your equipment is caption capable and use the captions; they can be helpful to everyone when audio quality is poor.)
- For a lecture, consider providing a written handout that summarizes your argument or putting the text on an overhead projector—for those who learn better by reading *and* listening.

Deliver a Good Show

In spite of your best preparation, you may feel some anxiety before a live presentation. This is natural. (According to one Gallup poll, Americans often identify public speaking as a major fear—scarier than possible attacks from outer space.) Experienced speakers say that they have strategies for dealing with anxiety, and even suggest that a little nervousness — and its accompanying adrenaline — can work to a speaker's advantage.

The most effective strategy seems to be simply knowing your topic and material thoroughly. Confidence in your own knowledge goes a long way toward making you an eloquent speaker. In addition to being well prepared, you may want to try some of the following strategies:

- Practice a number of times, running through every part of the presentation. Leave nothing out, even audio or video clips. Work with the equipment you intend to use so that you are familiar with it. It also may help to visualize your presentation, imagining the scene in your mind as you run through your materials.
- Time your presentation to make sure you stay within your allotted slot.
- Tape yourself (video, if possible) at least once so that you can listen to your voice. Tone of voice and body language can dispose audiences for — or against — speakers. For most oral arguments, you want to develop a tone that conveys commitment to your position as well as respect for your audience.
- Think about how you'll dress for your presentation, remembering that audience members notice how a speaker looks. Dressing for a presentation depends on what's appropriate for your topic, audience, and setting, but experienced speakers choose clothes that are comfortable, allow easy movement, and aren't overly casual. Dressing up indicates that you take pride in your appearance, have confidence in your argument, and respect your audience. (Notice George Chidiac's bow tie on p. 344.)
- Get some rest before the presentation, and avoid consuming too much caffeine.
- Relax! Consider doing some deep-breathing exercises. Then pause just before you begin, concentrating on your opening lines.
- Maintain eye contact with members of your audience. Speak to them, not to your text or to the floor.
- Interact with the audience whenever possible; doing so will often help you relax and even have some fun.

- Most speakers make a stronger impression standing than sitting, so stand if you have that option. Moving around a bit may help you maintain good eye contact.
- Remember to allow time for audience responses and questions. Keep your answers brief so that others may join the conversation.
- Finally, at the very end of your presentation, thank the audience for its attention to your arguments.

A Note about Webcasts: Live Presentations over the Web

This discussion of live oral presentations has assumed that you'll be speaking before an audience in the same room with you. Increasingly, though—especially in business, industry, and science—the presentations you make will be live, but you won't occupy the same physical space as the audience. Instead, you might be in front of a camera that will capture your voice and image and relay them via the Web to attendees who might be anywhere in the world. In another type of Webcast, participants can see only your slides or the software that you're demonstrating, using a screen-capture relay without cameras: you're not visible but still speaking live.

In either case, most of the strategies that work well for oral presentations with an in-house audience will continue to serve in Webcast environments. But there are some significant differences.

- Practice is even more important in Webcasts, since you need to be able to access online any slides, documents, video clips, names, dates, and sources that you provide during the Webcast.
- Because you can't make eye contact with audience members, it's important to remember to look into the camera (if you are using one), at least from time to time. If you're using a stationary Webcam, perhaps one mounted on your computer, practice standing or sitting without moving out of the frame and yet without looking stiff.
- Even though your audience may not be visible to you, assume that if you're on camera, the Web-based audience can see you. If you slouch, they'll notice. Assume too that your microphone is always live. Don't mutter under your breath, for example, when someone else is speaking or asking a question.

RESPOND.

Attend a presentation on your campus, and observe the speaker's delivery. Note the strategies that the speaker uses to capture and hold your attention (or not). What signpost language and other guides to listening can you detect? How well are visuals integrated into the presentation? What aspects of the speaker's tone, dress, eye contact, and movement affect your understanding and your appreciation (or lack of it)? What's most memorable about the presentation, and why? Finally, write up an analysis of this presentation's effectiveness.

16
Multimedia Arguments

Left to right: Iain Masterton/age fotostock/Superstock; imageBROKER/Superstock; Yoko Aziz/Superstock

The very first paragraph in this edition of *Everything's an Argument* features a tweet by Michelle Obama focusing on political kidnapping in Nigeria. And elsewhere in the book, we draw on examples from a wide range of media and genres, including online news sources, blog posts and comments, editorial cartoons, ads, maps, infographics, bumper stickers, even a selfie—and of the pope, no less. In one way or another, all of these items illustrate principles of persuasion. And while much of this book is about more conventional forms of argument—essays, extended articles, and academic papers—the fact is that many arguments are now shaped, distributed, and connected in ways that no one imagined a generation ago.

Online sources used daily such as *Gawker* and *Huffington Post* and social networks such as Facebook and Twitter have virtually redefined the nature of influence and persuasion. The cascade of information you take for granted, the 24-hour news cycle, the incessant connectivity of screens simply amazes anyone old enough to remember when newspapers were flung on doorsteps by kids on bicycles. More to the point here:

all this online and onscreen activity is rhetorical in both its aims and its methods. We want to spend a chapter exploring new media, teasing out some connections between traditional modes of persuasion and those currently reshaping our social and political lives.

Old Media Transformed by New Media

Civic arguments and opinions used to be delivered orally, typically in speeches, debates, and dialogues and often at public forums. Later, especially after the development of printing, they arrived via paper, and then through other media such as film and over-the-air broadcasting. Some of these traditional channels of communication were actual physical objects distributed one by one: books, journals, newspapers, fliers, photographs. Other "old media" such as movies, TV news, or radio shows were more like performances that could not be distributed or shared readily, at least not until audio- and videotape became cheap. Yet these media were all-powerful, handy, and relatively inexpensive shapers of opinion: books and serious magazines appealed to readers accustomed to intellectual challenges; well-staffed newspapers provided professional (if sometimes sensational) coverage of local and world affairs; nightly, the three national TV networks reached large and relatively undistracted audiences, establishing some degree of cultural consensus.

At least that's the romantic side of old media. We all recognize today the remarkable limitations of paper books and journals or celluloid film and print photographs. But we didn't appreciate quite how clumsy, hard to locate, hard to distribute, hard to search, and hard to archive analog objects could be until they went digital.

Fortunately, to one degree or another, electronic media have made peace with all these genres and formats and transformed them—though almost always with some compromises. Books on e-readers have become like ancient scrolls again, handy for sequential reading, but not so great for moving back and forth or browsing. Magazine articles or newspaper editorials (when not blocked by paywalls) can be found instantly online (or in databases), complete with updates and corrections, links that help establish their context, and, usually, lots and lots of comments. The downside? Lots and lots of inane, offensive, and bitter comments. And of course films and music are now accessible everywhere. You can experience *Lawrence of Arabia*—with its awesome horizons and desert landscapes—on your iPhone while in line at McDonald's. Or maybe you can't.

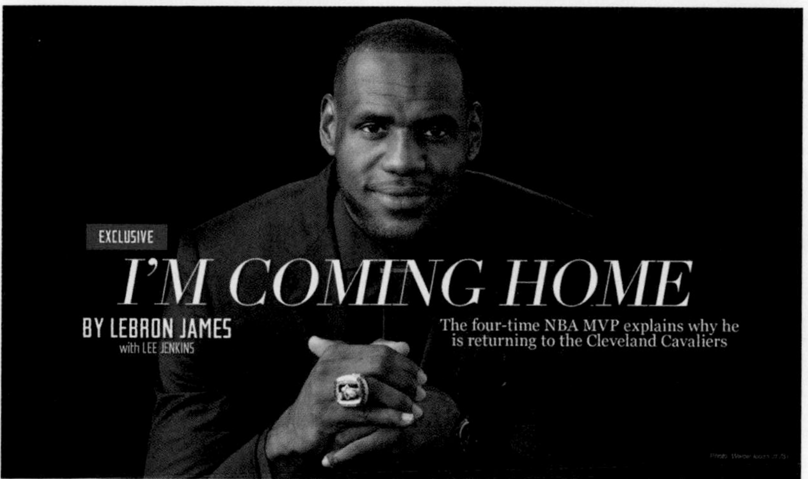

NBA superstar LeBron James chose a traditional genre to announce his return to the Cleveland Cavaliers in 2014, explaining, "I'm doing this *essay* because I want an opportunity to explain myself *uninterrupted*" (emphasis added). Of course, his essay appeared online at SportsIllustrated.com. Walter Iooss Jr./Sports Illustrated/ Contour by Getty Images; Graphics: si.com

The bigger point is that the serious, attentive, and carefully researched arguments that represent the best of old media are in no danger of disappearing. Books, research articles, and serious pieces of journalism are still being ground out—and read attentively—in the new media world because they play an essential role there. They provide the logos (see Chapter 4) for innumerable Web sites and Web 2.0 networks, the full-bodied arguments, research studies, and no-nonsense science propping up all those links in tighter, punchier new media features. They give clout and credibility to the quick blog post, the Facebook status, even the trending Twitter hashtag.

New Content in New Media

As you well know, new media represent a vast array of interconnected, electronic platforms where ideas and arguments (and a great deal else) can be introduced and shared. In these "environments," the content is almost anything that can be delivered digitally—words, pictures, movement, and sounds. Perhaps the first Web capability that writers and

The ubiquitous hashtag is liable to turn up anywhere. knape/Getty Images

thinkers appreciated was the distribution of traditional printed texts via online databases; it made possible huge advances in speed, accuracy, and efficiency. (Consider, for a moment, the professional databases in every field and discipline that are available through your school library.)

Online content quickly evolved once it became apparent that just about anyone could create a Web site—and they did. Soon valuable sites emerged, covering every imaginable topic, many of them focusing on serious social and political concerns. Today, such blogs range from those that collect short items and links to promote a topic or point of view (*Instapundit*, *The Daily Kos*) to slick, full-featured magazines with original content and extensive commentary (*Salon*, *Gawker*). Social, political, and cultural sites such as Slate, Drudge, and Politico have become powerful shapers of opinion by showcasing a wide variety of writers and arguments. Right from the beginning, blogs demonstrated that interactive online sites could create virtual communities and audiences, enabling people (sometimes acting as citizen journalists) to find allies for their causes and concerns.

Enter Web 2.0 social media and the wildly diverse worlds they now represent. Consider the vast difference among platforms and environments such as Facebook, YouTube, Reddit, Flickr, Pinterest, Yelp, and, of course, Twitter. Reviews on Yelp are by nature evaluative arguments,

"Like" is easy; contributing is hard. (See Chapter 1 on the difference between convincing and persuading.)

and many Facebook postings have a persuasive bent, though they may not go much beyond observations, claims, or complaints supported by links or images. Both services are hugely influential because of their vast reach, as is Twitter—despite (or, maybe, *because of*) its 140-character limit. Indeed, the frameworks of these self-selected environments encourage posting and, to varying degrees, opinion making and sharing. And what gets posted in social media? Everything allowed—especially stuff already available in digital form on other online sites: cool pictures, funny people and pets, outrageous videos, trendy performers, and, yes, lots of links to serious talk about politics, culture, and social issues.

New Audiences in New Media

When it comes to making arguments, perhaps the most innovative aspect of new media is its ability to summon audiences. Since ancient times (see p. 21), rhetoricians have emphasized the need to frame arguments to influence people, but new media and social networks now create places for specific audiences to emerge and make the arguments themselves, assembling them in bits and pieces, one comment or supporting link at a time. Audiences muster around sites that represent their perspectives on politics or mirror their social conditions and interests.

"It's Not OK Cupid: Co-Founder Defends User Experiments" is aimed at an audience made possible by technology: those interested in the phenomenon of online dating.

LINK TO P. 763

Here's what Twitter's audience looked like when the government of Turkey tried to ban the service. Adem Altam/Getty Images

It seems natural. Democrats engage with different blog sites than do Libertarians; champions of immigration or gun rights advocates have their favored places too. Within social networks themselves, supporters of causes can join existing activist communities or create new alliances among people with compatible views. And then all those individuals contribute to the never-ending newsfeeds: links, favorite books and authors, preferred images or slogans, illustrative videos, and so on. They stir the pot and generate still more energy, concern, and emotion. It can be very exciting or begin to sound like an echo chamber. But activity within virtual communities itself is potent and powerful. Some have attributed President Obama's second-term electoral victory, in part, to the buzz his campaign generated within social media. These days, assembling an audience may be just as important as making or winning arguments.

That principle may help account for the Twitter phenomenon. There, celebrities and political figures alike, for a wide variety of reasons, attract "followers" cued into their occasional 140-character musings (Hillary Clinton: 1.6M followers; Pope Francis: 4.2M; Taylor Swift: 40M+). In some respects, "following" becomes a measure of ethos, the trust and connection people have in the person offering a point of view (see Chapter 3). Sometimes that ethos is largely just about media fame, but in other cases it may measure genuine influence that public figures have earned by virtue of their ideas or opinions. People who sign on as their followers signal their willingness to listen to their Twitter commentary—ideas they probably agree with already.

But logos would seem to have little chance of emerging in a platform like Twitter: can you do much more than make a bare claim or two in the few words and symbols allowed? That's where hashtags come in. Hashtags are words prefixed with a # sign in a Twitter posting to identify a topic and place around which an audience may gather. It provides a way of linking related comments within the vast environment or, just as important, drawing audiences to specific ideas. This is the point, for instance, of Mrs. Obama holding up a card with the #BringBackOurGirls hashtag (see p. 3)—using her ethos to attract an even larger audience to the issue she and many others support. So, once again, the audience in new media becomes a tangible object—its political power evident in the sheer number of people weighing in on controversies, expressing their sentiments succinctly, but also accumulating a sense of direction, solidarity, and gravity. It's also why political journalists or print publications now routinely identify trending hashtags in their reporting or even direct audiences to Twitter to track breaking stories or social movements as they unfold there.

It's a kind of suasion Aristotle could not have imagined.

No comment necessary.

Analyzing Multimedia Arguments

As the previous section suggests, a multimedia argument can be complex. But you can figure it out by giving careful attention to its key components: the creators and distributors; the medium it uses; the viewers and readers it hopes to reach; its content and purpose; its design. Following are some questions to ask when you want to understand the rhetorical strategies in arguments and interactions you encounter in social media or on blogs, Web sites, or other nontraditional media. It's worth noting that the questions here don't differ entirely from those you might ask about books, journal articles, news stories, or print ads when composing a rhetorical analysis (see Chapter 6).

Questions about Creators and Distributors

- Who is responsible for this multimedia text? Did someone else distribute, repurpose, or retweet the item?
- What can you find out about these people and any other work they might have done?
- What does the creator's attitude seem to be toward the content: serious, ironic, emotionally charged, satiric, comic? What is the attitude of the distributor, if different from the creator?
- What do the creator and the distributor expect the effects of the text or posting to be? Do they share the same intentions? (Consider, for example, that someone might post an item in order to mock or criticize it.)

Questions about the Medium

- Which media are used by this text? Images only? Words and images? Sound, video, animation, graphs, charts? Does the site or environment where the text appears suggest a metaphor: photo album, pinup board, message board, chat room?
- In what ways is this text or its online environment interactive? Who can contribute to or comment on it? Where can an item be sent or redirected? How did it get to where you encountered it?
- How do various texts work together in the site? Do they make arguments? Accumulate evidence? Provide readers with examples and illustrations?
- What effect does the medium have on messages or items within it? How would a message, text, or item be altered if different media were used?

- Do claims or arguments play an explicit role in the medium? How are they presented, clarified, reinforced, connected, constrained, or commented upon?

Questions about Audience and Viewers

- What are the likely audiences for the text or medium? How are people invited into the text or site? Who might avoid the experience?
- How does the audience participate in the site or platform? Does the audience respond to content, create it, or something else? What audience interactions or connections occur there? Can participants interact with each other?
- How does the text or media site evoke or reward participation? Are audience members texted or emailed about events or interactions in the site?

Questions about Content and Purpose

- What purpose does the multimedia text achieve? What is it designed to convey?
- What social, cultural, or political values does the text or site support? Cultural Interaction? Power? Resistance? Freedom?
- Does the text, alone or in reaction to others, reinforce these values or question them? Does the text constitute an argument in itself or contribute to another claim in some way—as an illustration, example, exception, metaphor, analogy?
- What emotions does the multimedia site or text evoke? Are these the emotions that it intends to raise? How does it do it?

Questions about Design

- How does the site present itself? What draws you to it? How easy is the environment to sign up for, learn, or use?
- How is the multimedia text or environment structured? Does the structure enhance its purpose or functionality? If it presents data, is the information easy to understand? (See also Chapter 14, "Visual Rhetoric.")
- How are arguments, concepts, or ideas presented or framed within the text or environment? How are ideas identified? How are they amplified or connected to other supporting texts and ideas?
- What details are emphasized in the text or media environment? What details are omitted or de-emphasized? To what effect? Is

anything downplayed, ambiguous, confusing, distracting, or obviously omitted? Why?

- What, if anything, is surprising about the design of the text or environment? What do you think is the purpose of that surprise?
- How are you directed to move within the text or site? Are you encouraged to read further? Click on links? Contribute links and information?

RESPOND.

Using the discussion of multimedia arguments in this chapter and the questions about multimedia texts and platforms above, find a multimedia text that makes an intriguing argument *or* a social media platform where you sometimes encounter debates about political and social issues. Then write a brief rhetorical analysis of the text or the site, focusing more on the way the messages are conveyed than on the messages that are in play.

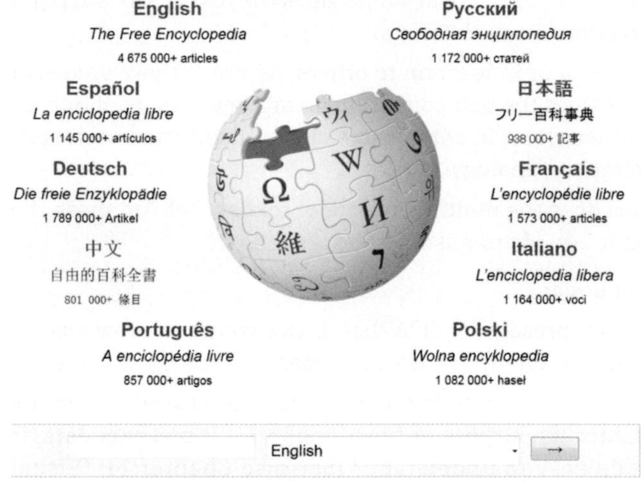

This is the central image on the homepage of Wikipedia, a collaborative nonprofit encyclopedia project. Since its launch (as Nupedia) in 2000, Wikipedia has grown to include 31 million articles in 285 languages (4.5 million articles in English), all of them authored by volunteers around the world. This central image acts as a logo, a portal to access the site's content, and, in a way, a mission statement for the organization. How does your eye construct this logo? What do you notice first, and how do your eyes move around the page? Do the parts make sense when you put them together? Creative Commons

Making Multimedia Arguments

Though you have likely been active in new media platforms for quite some time—browsing Web sites, checking Facebook, sending text messages, following "Texas Humor" on Twitter—you may not have thought of these activities as rhetorical. But they certainly can be, especially those that might have classroom or extracurricular connections. Here we discuss just a few such situations. In other chapters in this section, we talk in more detail about visual rhetoric (often a component in new media) and oral presentations, which now almost always have a digital component.

Web Sites

It's likely you have already created Web sites for a class or for an organization to which you belong. In planning any Web site, pay careful attention to your rhetorical situation (see Chapter 1)—the purpose of your site, its intended audience, and the overall impression that you want to make. To get started, you may want to study several sites that you admire, looking for effective design ideas or ways of organizing navigation and information. Creating a map or storyboard for your site will help you to think through the links from page to page.

Experienced Web designers such as Robin Williams cite several important principles for Web-based presentations. The first of these is *contrast*, which is achieved through the use of color, icons, boldface, and so on; contrast helps guide readers through the site (see also Chapter 14). The second principle, *proximity*, calls on you to keep together the parts of a page that are closely related, again for ease of reading. *Repetition* means using a consistent design throughout the site for the elements (such as headings and links) that help readers move smoothly through the environment. Finally, designers concentrate on an *overall impression* or mood for the site, which means that the colors and visuals on the pages should help to create that impression rather than challenge or undermine it.

Here are some additional tips that may help you design your site:

- The homepage should be informative, eye-catching, and inviting (see Chapter 14)—especially when making an argument. Use titles and illustrations to make clear what the site is about.
- Think carefully about two parts of every page—the navigation area (menus or links) and the content areas. You want to make these two areas distinct from one another. And make sure you *have* a navigation

area for every page, including links to the key sections of the site and a link back to the homepage. Ease of navigation is one key to a successful Web site.

- Either choose a design template that is provided by Web-writing tools or create a template of your own that ensures that the elements of each page are consistent.
- Consider how to balance claims and evidence on a page. Claims might be connected to supporting links, or they can be enhanced by images or videos that dramatize a position you want to champion.
- Remember to include Web contact information on every page, but not your personal address or phone number.

Videos

When is a video the best medium for delivering a message? Given the ease with which competent digital films can be produced, the answer is certainly more often than ever before. You will see videos routinely now, for example, on college and university sites, showcasing distinguished students and faculty or explaining programs. It is an effective way to enhance the ethos of a group or institution. Videos can also document public events or show how to do practical things such as registering to vote or navigating an unfamiliar campus. So whenever a video fits well with the purpose of the message, consider creating one.

You can, of course, shoot a video with your smartphone. But more sophisticated software might be needed to edit your film and get it ready for prime time: iMovie, Movie Maker, Blender (for animation) or Animoto, Camtasia, and Soundslides (for combining media such as digital video, photos, music, and text).

Wikis

To make working on group projects easier, many classes use wikis, which are Web-based sites that enable writers to collaborate in the creation of a single project or database. The most famous group effort of this kind is, of course, Wikipedia, but software such as DokuWiki, MediaWiki, or Tiki Wiki helps people to manage similar, if less ambitious, efforts of their own, whether it be exploring questions raised in academic courses or examining and supporting needs within a community. Wiki projects can be argumentative in themselves, or they might furnish raw data and evidence for subsequent projects.

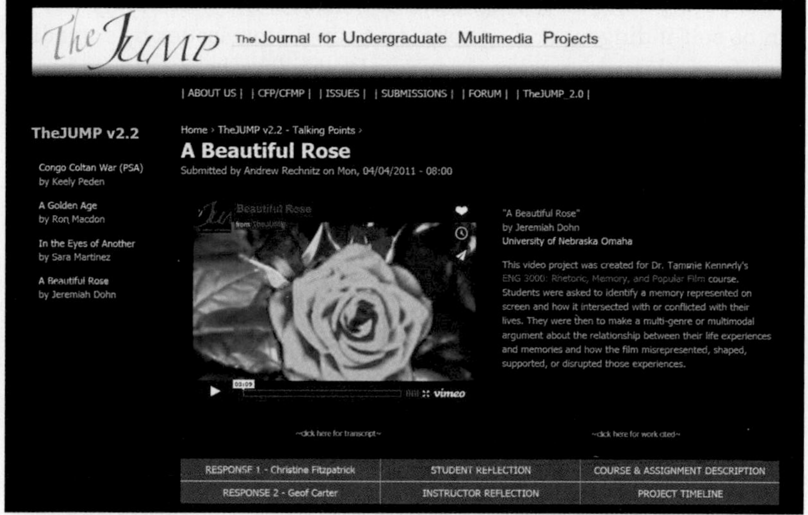

Here is an example of a video entitled "A Beautiful Rose," created by Jeremiah Dohn for a class assignment and subsequently accepted by the online journal *The Jump.* The Journal for Undergraduate Multimedia Projects

If asked to participate in a wiki, you should, naturally, learn how to use the assigned software and follow course or project guidelines for entering and documenting the material you contribute. Just as you will expect your colleagues to use reliable sources or make accurate observations, they will depend on you to do your part in shaping the project. Within the wiki, participants will be able to draw upon each other's strengths and, ideally, to compensate for any weaknesses. So take your responsibilities seriously.

Blogs

Perhaps no Web texts have been more instrumental in advancing political, social, and cultural issues than blogs, which are now too numerous to count. Blogs open an ideal space for building interactive communities, engaging in arguments, and giving voice to views and opinions of ordinary citizens. Today, just about all major news media, including the most prestigious newspapers and journals, feature the functionality of blogs or sponsor blogs themselves as part of their electronic versions.

Like everything else, blogs have downsides: they are idiosyncratic, can be self-indulgent and egoistic, and can distort issues by spreading misinformation *very* quickly. If you're a fan of blogs, be sure to read carefully, remembering that information on blogs hasn't been critically reviewed in the way that traditional print sources edit their stories. But also remember that blogs have reported many instances of the mainstream news sources failing to live up to their own standards.

Activist blogs of all kinds get plenty of attention, and you can easily join in on the conversation there, sharing your arguments in the comments section. If you do blog yourself, or comment on others' postings, remember to follow commonsense good manners: be respectful and think carefully about what you are saying and about the impression you want to leave with those who read you. Blogging software, in case you want to open shop yourself, includes Blogger, Tumblr, and WordPress.

Social Media

You likely know a great deal already about the strengths and weaknesses of social media such as Facebook, Twitter, Snapchat, Pinterest, or whatever platforms you use—especially their remarkable ability to absorb big chunks of time.

But do consider how these media may be influencing your political and cultural views, and pay attention to how arguments there are made, supported, and connected. Think about how people with similar views come together in social media and perhaps what role these platforms now play in shaping current social and political activism. What audience roles have you assumed, what causes do you follow or champion, what ethos have you fashioned for yourself in these environments?

Then consider opportunities for using these platforms in your academic work. Social media provide tools for connecting with experts in a field, collaborating on projects with classmates, or sharing your insights with people around the world. Twitter will keep you up-to-date on news and events in almost every field and discipline. And platforms like Facebook or Kickstarter can help you find people who share your ideas and are even willing to support them financially. Social media offer potent (if occasionally risky) tools for expanding all the worlds you live in—including the academic one.

RESPOND.

Go to a blog that you admire or consult frequently. Then answer the following questions:

Why is a blog—a digital presentation—the best way to present this material?

What advantages over a print text or a live oral and multimedia presentation does the blog have?

How could you "translate" the argument(s) of this site into print format, oral format, or social media platform? What might be gained or lost in the process?

PART 4

RESEARCH AND arguments

17
Academic Arguments

Left to right: Imaginechina via AP Images; AP/Invision/Charles Sykes; © Javier Larrea/age fotostock

Much of the writing you will do in college (and some of what you will no doubt do later in your professional work) is generally referred to as *academic discourse* or *academic argument*. Although this kind of writing has many distinctive features, in general it shares these characteristics:

- It is based on research and uses evidence that can be documented.
- It is written for a professional, academic, or school audience likely to know something about its topic.
- It makes a clear and compelling point in a fairly formal, clear, and sometimes technical style.
- It follows agreed-upon conventions of format, usage, and punctuation.
- It is documented, using some professional citation style.

Academic writing is serious work, the kind you are expected to do whenever you are assigned a term essay, research paper, or capstone project. Manasi Deshpande's proposal "A Call to Improve Campus Accessibility" in Chapter 12 is an example of an academic argument of the kind you may write in college. You will find other examples of such work throughout this book.

Understanding What Academic Argument Is

Academic argument covers a wide range of writing, but its hallmarks are an appeal to reason and a faith in research. As a consequence, such arguments cannot be composed quickly, casually, or off the top of one's head. They require careful reading, accurate reporting, and a conscientious commitment to truth. But academic pieces do not tune out all appeals to ethos or emotion: today, we know that these arguments often convey power and authority through their impressive lists of sources and their immediacy. But an academic argument crumbles if its facts are skewed or its content proves to be unreliable.

Look, for example, how systematically Susannah Fox and Lee Rainie, director and codirector of the Pew Internet Project, present facts and evidence in arguing that the Internet has been, overall, a big plus for society and individuals alike.

> [Today,] 87% of American adults now use the Internet, with near-saturation usage among those living in households earning $75,000 or more (99%), young adults ages 18–29 (97%), and those with college degrees (97%). Fully 68% of adults connect to the Internet with mobile devices like smartphones or tablet computers.
>
> The adoption of related technologies has also been extraordinary: Over the course of Pew Research Center polling, adult ownership of cell phones has risen from 53% in our first survey in 2000 to 90% now. Ownership of smartphones has grown from 35% when we first asked in 2011 to 58% now.
>
> Impact: Asked for their overall judgment about the impact of the Internet, toting up all the pluses and minuses of connected life, the public's verdict is overwhelmingly positive: 90% of Internet users say the Internet has been a good thing for them personally and only 6% say it has been a bad thing, while 3% volunteer that it has been some of both. 76% of Internet users say the Internet has been a good thing for society, while 15% say it has been a bad thing and 8% say it has been equally good and bad.
>
> —Susannah Fox and Lee Rainie, "The Web at 25 in the U.S."

Note, too, that these writers draw their material from research and polls conducted by the Pew Research Center, a well-known and respected organization. Chances are you immediately recognize that this paragraph is an example of a researched academic argument.

You can also identify academic argument by the way it addresses its audiences. Some academic writing is clearly aimed at specialists in a field who are familiar with both the subject and the terminology that surrounds it. As a result, the researchers make few concessions to general readers unlikely to encounter or appreciate their work. You see that single-mindedness in this abstract of an article about migraine headaches in a scientific journal: it quickly becomes unreadable to nonspecialists.

Nicholas Ostler's conference paper "Is It Globalization That Endangers Languages?" meets the criteria listed here for academic argument and provides a potential model for your own writing.

LINK TO P. 589

Abstract

> **Migraine is a complex, disabling disorder of the brain that manifests itself as attacks of often severe, throbbing head pain with sensory sensitivity to light, sound and head movement. There is a clear familial tendency to migraine, which has been well defined in a rare autosomal dominant form of familial hemiplegic migraine (FHM). FHM mutations so far identified include those in CACNA1A (P/Q voltage-gated Ca(2+) channel), ATP1A2 (N(+)-K(+)-ATPase) and SCN1A (Na(+) channel) genes. Physiological studies in humans and studies of the experimental correlate—cortical spreading depression (CSD)—provide understanding of aura, and have explored in recent years the effect of migraine preventives in CSD. . . .**
>
> —Peter J. Goadsby, "Recent Advances in Understanding Migraine Mechanisms, Molecules, and Therapeutics," *Trends in Molecular Medicine* (January 2007)

Yet this very article might later provide data for a more accessible argument in a magazine such as *Scientific American*, which addresses a broader (though no less serious) readership. Here's a selection from an article on migraine headaches from that more widely read journal (see also the infographic on p. 382):

> **At the moment, only a few drugs can prevent migraine. All of them were developed for other diseases, including hypertension, depression and epilepsy. Because they are not specific to migraine, it will come as no surprise that they work in only 50 percent of patients—and, in them, only 50 percent of the time—and induce a range of side effects, some potentially serious.**
>
> **Recent research on the mechanism of these antihypertensive, antiepileptic and antidepressant drugs has demonstrated that one of their effects is to inhibit cortical spreading depression. The drugs' ability to prevent migraine with and without aura therefore supports the school**

of thought that cortical spreading depression contributes to both kinds of attacks. Using this observation as a starting point, investigators have come up with novel drugs that specifically inhibit cortical spreading depression. Those drugs are now being tested in migraine sufferers with and without aura. They work by preventing gap junctions, a form of ion channel, from opening, thereby halting the flow of calcium between brain cells.

—David W. Dodick and J. Jay Gargus, "Why Migraines Strike," ***Scientific American*** **(August 2008)**

Such writing still requires attention, but it delivers important and comprehensible information to any reader seriously interested in the subject and the latest research on it.

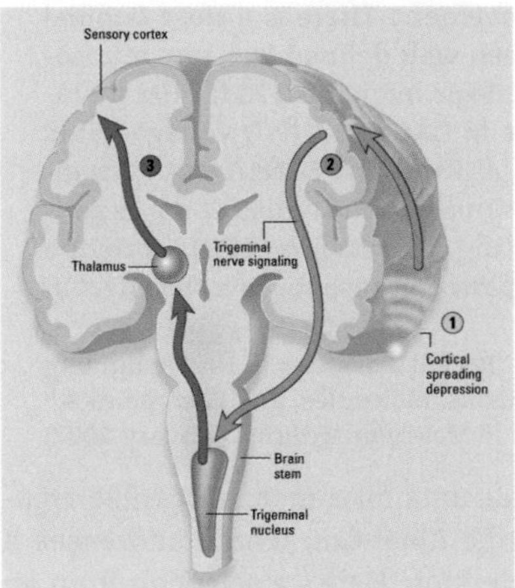

Infographic: The Root of Migraine Pain © Tolpa Studios, Inc.

Even when academic writing is less technical and demanding, its style will retain a degree of formality. In academic arguments, the focus is on the subject or topic rather than the authors, the tone is straightforward, the language is largely unadorned, and all the i's are dotted and t's crossed. Here's an abstract for an academic paper written by a scholar of communications on the Burning Man phenomenon, demonstrating those qualities:

Every August for more than a decade, thousands of information technologists and other knowledge workers have trekked out into a barren

> stretch of alkali desert and built a temporary city devoted to art, technology, and communal living: Burning Man. Drawing on extensive archival research, participant observation, and interviews, this paper explores the ways that Burning Man's bohemian ethos supports new forms of production emerging in Silicon Valley and especially at Google. It shows how elements of the Burning Man world—including the building of a socio-technical commons, participation in project-based artistic labor, and the fusion of social and professional interaction—help shape and legitimate the collaborative manufacturing processes driving the growth of Google and other firms. The paper thus develops the notion that Burning Man serves as a key cultural infrastructure for the Bay Area's new media industries.
>
> —Fred Turner, "Burning Man at Google: A Cultural Infrastructure for New Media Production"

You might imagine a different and far livelier way to tell a story about the annual Burning Man gathering in Nevada, but this piece respects the conventions of its academic field.

Another way you likely identify academic writing—especially in term papers or research projects—is by the way it draws upon sources and builds arguments from research done by experts and reported in journal articles and books. Using an evenhanded tone and dealing with all points of view fairly, such writing brings together multiple voices and

A scene from Burning Man Mike Nelson/AFP/Getty Images

intriguing ideas. You can see these moves in just one paragraph from a heavily documented student essay examining the comedy of Chris Rock:

> **The breadth of passionate debate that [Chris] Rock's comedy elicits from intellectuals is evidence enough that he is advancing discussion of the foibles of black America, but Rock continually insists that he has no political aims: "Really, really at the end of the day, the only important thing is being funny. I don't go out of my way to be political" (qtd. in Bogosian 58). His unwillingness to view himself as a black leader triggers Justin Driver to say, "[Rock] wants to be caustic and he wants to be loved" (32). Even supporters wistfully sigh, "One wishes Rock would own up to the fact that he's a damned astute social critic" (Kamp 7).**
>
> **—Jack Chung, "The Burden of Laughter: Chris Rock Fights Ignorance His Way"**

Readers can quickly tell that author Jack Chung has read widely and thought carefully about how to support his argument.

As you can see even from these brief examples, academic arguments cover a broad range of topics and appear in a variety of media—as a brief note in a journal like *Nature*, for example, a poster session at a conference on linguistics, a short paper in *Physical Review Letters*, a full research report in microbiology, or an undergraduate honors thesis in history. What do all these projects have in common? One professor we know defines academic argument as "carefully structured research," and that seems to us to be a pretty good definition.

Conventions in Academic Argument Are Not Static.

Far from it. In fact, the rise of new technologies and the role that blogs, wikis, social media sites, and other digital discourses play in all our lives are affecting academic writing as well. Thus, scholars today are pushing the envelope of traditional academic writing in some fields. Physicians, for example, are using narrative (rather than charts) more often in medicine to communicate effectively with other medical personnel. Professional journals now sometimes feature serious scholarly work in new formats—such as comics (as in legal scholar Jamie Boyle's work on intellectual property, or Nick Sousanis's Columbia University PhD dissertation, which is entirely in comic form). And student writers are increasingly producing serious academic arguments using a wide variety of modalities, including sound, still and moving images, and more.

Developing an Academic Argument

In your first years of college, the academic arguments you make will probably include the features and qualities we've discussed above—and which you see demonstrated in the sample academic arguments at the end of this chapter. In addition, you can make a strong academic argument by following some time-tested techniques.

Choose a topic you want to explore in depth. Unless you are assigned a topic (and remember that even assigned topics can be tweaked to match your interests), look for a subject that intrigues you—one you *want* to learn more about. One of the hardest parts of producing an academic argument is finding a topic narrow enough to be manageable in the time you have to work on it but also rich enough to sustain your interest over the same period. Talk with friends about possible topics and explain to them why you'd like to pursue research on this issue. Look through your Twitter feeds and social network postings to identify themes or topics that leap out as compelling. Browse through books and articles that interest you, make a list of potential subjects, and then zero in on one or two top choices.

Get to know the conversation surrounding your topic. Once you've chosen a topic, expect to do even more reading and browsing—a lot more. Familiarize yourself with what's been said about your subject and especially with the controversies that currently surround it. Where do scholars agree, and where do they disagree? What key issues seem to be at stake? You can start by exploring the Internet, using key terms that are associated with your topic. But you may be better off searching the more specialized databases at your library with the assistance of a librarian who can help you narrow your search and make it more efficient. Library databases will also give you access to materials not available via Google or other online search engines—including, for example, full-text versions of journal articles. For much more on identifying appropriate sources, see Chapter 18, "Finding Evidence."

Assess what you know and what you need to know. As you read about your topic and discuss it with others, keep notes on what you have learned, including what you already know about it. Such notes should soon reveal where the gaps are in your knowledge. For instance, you may discover a need to learn about legal issues and thus end up doing research in a law school library. Or perhaps talking with experts about your topic might be helpful. Instructors on your campus may have the knowledge you need, so explore your school's Web site to find faculty or staff to talk with. Make an appointment to visit them during office hours and bring the sorts of questions to your meeting that show you've done basic work on the subject. And remember that experts are now only a click away: a student we know, working on Internet privacy concerns, wrote a brief message to one of the top scholars in the field asking for help with two particular questions—and got a response within two days!

Come up with a claim about your topic. The chapters in Part 2, "Writing Arguments," offer instruction in formulating thesis statements, which most academic arguments must have. Chapters 8–12, in particular, explain how to craft claims tailored to individual projects ranging from arguments of fact to proposals. Remember here, though, that good claims are controversial. After all, you don't want to debate something that everyone already agrees upon or accepts.

In addition, your claim needs to say something consequential about that important or controversial topic and be supported with strong evidence and good reasons (see Chapter 18). Here, for example, is the claim that student Charlotte Geaghan-Breiner makes after observing the alienation of today's children from the natural world and arguing for the redesign of schoolyards that invite children to interact with nature: "As a formative geography of childhood, the schoolyard serves as the perfect place to address nature deficit disorder." Charlotte develops her claim and supports it with evidence about the physical, psychological, academic, and social benefits of interacting with the natural world. She includes images illustrating the contrast between traditional schoolyards and "biophilic," or nature-oriented, schoolyards and establishes guidelines for creating natural play landscapes. (See Charlotte's complete essay, reprinted at the end of this chapter.)

Consider your rhetorical stance and purpose. Once you have a claim, ask yourself where you stand with respect to your topic and how you want to represent yourself to those reading your argument:

- You may take the stance of a reporter: you review what has been said about the topic; analyze and evaluate contributions to the conversation surrounding it; synthesize the most important strands of that conversation; and finally draw conclusions based on them.
- You may see yourself primarily as a critic: you intend to point out the problems and mistakes associated with some view of your topic.

- You may prefer the role of an advocate: you present research that strongly supports a particular view on your topic.

Whatever your perspective, remember that in academic arguments you want to come across as fair and evenhanded, especially when you play the advocate. Your stance will always be closely tied to your purpose, which in most of your college writing will be at least twofold: to do the best job in fulfilling an assignment for a course and to support the claim you are making to the fullest extent possible. Luckily, these two purposes work well together.

Think about your audience(s). Here again, you will often find that you have at least two audiences—and maybe more. First, you will be writing to your instructor, so take careful notes when the assignment is given and, if possible, set up a conference to nail down your teacher's expectations: what will it take to convince this audience that you have done a terrific job of writing an academic argument? Beyond your instructor, you should also think of your classmates as an audience—informed, intelligent peers who will be interested in what you have to say. Again, what do you know about these readers, and what will they expect from your project?

Finally, consider yet another important audience—people who are already discussing your topic. These will include the authors whose work you have read and the larger academic community of which they are now a part. If your work appears online or in some other medium, you will reach more people than you initially expect, and most if not all of them will be unknown to you. As a result, you need to think carefully about the various ways your argument could be read—or misread—and plan accordingly.

Concentrate on the material you are gathering. Any academic argument is only as good as the evidence it presents to support its claims. Give each major piece of evidence (say, a lengthy article that addresses your subject directly) careful scrutiny:

- Summarize its main points.
- Analyze how those points are pertinent.
- Evaluate the quality of the supporting evidence.
- Synthesize the results of your analysis and evaluation.
- Summarize what you think about the article.

In other words, test each piece of evidence and then decide which to keep—and which to throw out. But do not gather only materials that favor your take on the topic. You want, instead, to look at all legitimate perspectives on your claim, and in doing so, you may even change your mind. That's what good research for an academic argument can do: remember the "conscientious commitment to truth" we mentioned earlier? Keep yourself open to discovery and change. (See Chapter 19, "Evaluating Sources," and Chapter 20, "Using Sources.")

Give visual and nonprint materials the same scrutiny you would to print sources, since these days you will likely be gathering or creating such materials in many fields. Remember that the graphic representation of data always involves an interpretation of that material: numbers can lie and pictures distort. (For more information on evaluating visuals, see Chapter 14.) In addition, infographics today often make complex academic arguments in a visual form. (See p. 164 for one such example.)

Take special care with documentation. As you gather materials for your academic argument, record where you found each source so that you can cite it accurately. For print sources, develop a working bibliography either on your computer or in a notebook you can carry with you. For each book, write the name of the author, the title of the book, the city of publication, the publisher, the date of publication, and the place that you found it (the section of the library, for example, and the call number for the book). For each print article, write the name of the author, the title of the article, the title of the periodical, and the volume, issue, publication date, and exact page numbers. Include any other information you may later need in preparing a works cited list or references list.

For electronic sources, keep a careful record of the information you'll need in a works cited list or references list. Write the author and title information, the name of the database or other online site where you found the source, the full URL, the date the document was first produced, the date it was published on the Web or most recently updated, and the date you accessed and examined it. The simplest way to ensure that you have this information is to print a copy of the source, highlight source information, and write down any other pertinent information.

Remember, too, that different academic fields use different systems of documentation, so if your instructor has not recommended a style of documentation to you, ask in class about it. Scholars have developed these systems over long periods of time to make research in an area reliable and routine. Using documentation responsibly shows that you understand the conventions of your field or major and that you have paid your dues, thereby establishing your position as a member of the academic community. (For more detailed information, see Chapter 22, "Documenting Sources.")

Think about organization. As you review the research materials you have gathered, you are actually beginning the work of drafting and designing your project. Study the way those materials are organized, especially any from professional journals, whether print or digital. You may need to include in your own argument some of the sections or features you find in professional research:

- Does the article open with an abstract, summarizing its content?
- Does the article give any information about the author or authors and their credentials?
- Is there a formal introduction to the subject or a clear statement of a thesis or hypothesis?
- Does the article begin with a "review of literature," summarizing recent research on its topic?
- Does the piece describe its methods of research?
- How does the article report its results and findings?
- Does the article use charts and graphs or other visuals to report data?
- Does the piece use headings and subheadings?
- How does the work summarize its findings or how does it make recommendations?
- Does the essay offer a list of works cited or references?

Anticipate some variance in the way materials are presented from one academic field to another.

As you organize your own project, check with your instructor to see if there is a recommended pattern for you to follow. If not, create a scratch outline or storyboard to describe how your essay will proceed. In reviewing your evidence, decide which pieces support specific points in the argument. Then try to position your strongest pieces of evidence in key places—near the beginning of paragraphs, at the end of the introduction, or toward a powerful conclusion. In addition, strive to achieve a balance between, on the one hand, your own words and argument and, on the other hand, the sources that you use or quote in support of the argument. The sources of evidence are important supports, but they shouldn't overpower the structure of your argument itself. Finally, remember that your organization needs to take into account the placement of visuals—charts, tables, photographs, and so on. (For specific advice on structuring arguments, review the "Thinking about Organization" sections in the "Guides to Writing" for Chapters 8–12.)

The Trouble with Diversity: How We Learned to Love Identity and Ignore Inequality by Walter Benn Michaels exemplifies a clear and direct academic style. Even though the author makes a complex argument, addressing a broad and difficult issue, his writing remains straightforward and readable.

LINK TO P. 725

Consider style and tone. Most academic argument adopts the voice of a reasonable, fair-minded, and careful thinker who is interested in coming as close to the truth about a topic as possible. A style that achieves that tone may have some of the following features:

- It strives for clarity and directness, though it may use jargon appropriate to a particular field.
- It favors denotative rather than connotative language.
- It is usually impersonal, using first person (*I*) sparingly.
- In some fields, it may use the passive voice routinely.
- It uses technical language, symbols, and abbreviations for efficiency.
- It avoids colloquialisms, slang, and sometimes even contractions.

The examples at the end of this chapter demonstrate traditional academic style, though there is, as always, a range of possibilities in its manner of expression.

Consider genre, design, and visuals. Most college academic arguments look more like articles in professional journals than like those one might find in a glossier periodical like *Scientific American*—that is, they are still usually black on white, use a traditional font size and type (like 11-point Times New Roman), and lack any conscious design other than inserted tables or figures. But such conventions are changing.

Indeed, student writers today can go well beyond print, creating digital documents that integrate a variety of media and array data in strikingly original ways. But always consider what genres best suit your topic, purpose, and audience and then act accordingly. As you think about the design possibilities for your academic argument, you may want to consult your instructor—and to test your ideas and innovations on friends or classmates.

In choosing visuals to include in your argument, be sure each one makes a strong contribution to your message and is appropriate and fair to your topic and your audience. Treat visuals as you would any other sources and integrate them into your text. Like quotations, paraphrases, and summaries, visuals need to be introduced and commented on in

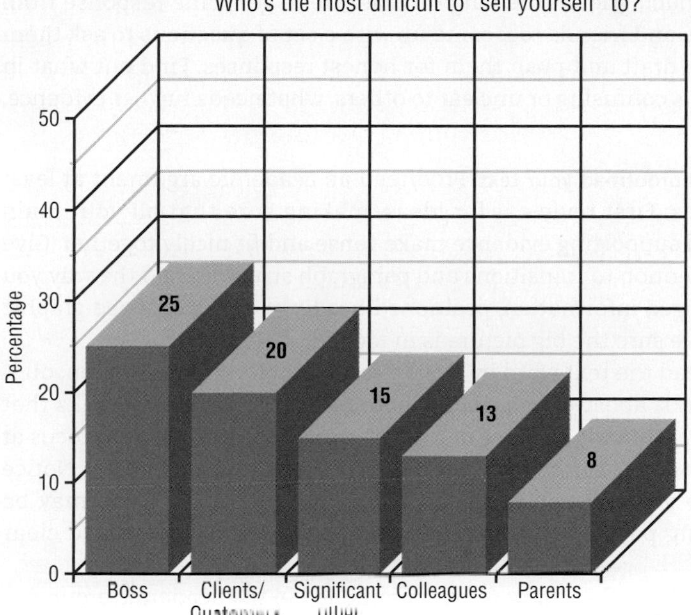

This bar chart, based on data from a Sandler Training survey of 1,053 adults, would be listed in your works cited or references under the authors' names. Data from Sandler Training survey of 1,053 adults.

some way. In addition, label and number ("Figure 1," "Table 2," and so on) each visual, provide a caption that includes source information and describes the visual, and cite the source in your references page or works cited list. Even if you create a visual (such as a bar graph) by using information from a source (the results, say, of a Gallup poll), you must cite the source. If you use a photograph you took yourself, cite it as a personal photograph.

Reflect on your draft and get responses. As with any important piece of writing, an academic argument calls for careful reflection on your draft. You may want to do a "reverse outline" to test whether a reader can pull a logical and consistent pattern out of the paragraphs or sections you have written. In addition, you can also judge the effectiveness of your overall argument, assessing what each paragraph contributes and what may be missing. Turning a critical eye to your own work at the draft stage can save much grief in the long run. Be sure to get some response from classmates and friends too: come up with a set of questions to ask them about your draft and push them for honest responses. Find out what in your draft is confusing or unclear to others, what needs further evidence, and so on.

Edit and proofread your text. Proofread an academic argument at least three times. First review it for ideas, making sure that all your main points and supporting evidence make sense and fit nicely together. Give special attention to transitions and paragraph structure and the way you have arranged information, positioned headings, and captioned graphic items. Make sure the big picture is in focus.

Then read the text word by word to check spelling, punctuation, quotation marks, apostrophes, abbreviations—in short, all the details that can go wrong simply because of a slip in attention. To keep their focus at this level, some readers will even read an entire text backwards. Notice too where your computer's spelling and grammar checkers may be underlining particular words and phrases. Don't ignore these clear signals.

Finally, check that every source mentioned in the academic argument appears in the works cited or references list and that every citation is correct. This is also the time to make any final touchups to your overall design. Remember that how the document looks is part of what establishes its credibility.

RESPOND •

1. Look closely at the following five passages, each of which is from an opening of a published work, and decide which ones provide examples of academic argument. How would you describe each one, and what are its key features? Which is the most formal and academic? Which is the least? How might you revise them to make them more—or less—academic?

   During the Old Stone Age, between thirty-seven thousand and eleven thousand years ago, some of the most remarkable art ever conceived was etched or painted on the walls of caves in southern France and northern Spain. After a visit to Lascaux, in the Dordogne, which was discovered in 1940, Picasso reportedly said to his guide, "They've invented everything." What those first artists invented was a language of signs for which there will never be a Rosetta stone; perspective, a technique that was not rediscovered until the Athenian Golden Age; and a bestiary of such vitality and finesse that, by the flicker of torchlight, the animals seem to surge from the walls, and move across them like figures in a magic-lantern show (in that sense, the artists invented animation). They also thought up the grease lamp—a lump of fat, with a plant wick, placed in a hollow stone—to light their workplace; scaffolds to reach high places; the principles of stenciling and Pointillism; powdered colors, brushes, and stumping cloths; and, more to the point of Picasso's insight, the very concept of an image. A true artist reimagines that concept with every blank canvas—but not from a void.

—Judith Thurman, "First Impressions," *The New Yorker*

I stepped over the curb and into the street to hitchhike. At the age of ten I'd put some pretty serious mileage on my thumb. And I knew how it was done. Hold your thumb up, not down by your hip as though you didn't much give a damn whether you got a ride or not. Always hitch at a place where a driver could pull out of traffic and give you time to get in without risking somebody tailgating him.

—Harry Crews, "On Hitchhiking," *Harper's*

Coral reef ecosystems are essential marine environments around the world. Host to thousands (and perhaps millions) of diverse organisms, they are also vital to the economic well-being of an estimated 0.5 billion people, or 8% of the world's population who live on tropical coasts (Hoegh-Guldberg 1999). Income from tourism and fishing industries, for instance, is essential to the economic prosperity of many countries, and the various plant and animal species present in reef ecosystems are sources for different natural products and medicines. The degradation of coral reefs can therefore have a devastating impact on coastal populations, and it is estimated that between 50% and 70% of all reefs around the world are currently threatened (Hoegh-Guldberg). Anthropogenic influences are cited as the major cause of this degradation, including sewage, sedimentation, direct trampling of reefs, over-fishing of herbivorous fish, and even global warming (Umezawa et al. 2002; Jones et al. 2001; Smith et al. 2001).

—Elizabeth Derse, "Identifying the Sources of Nitrogen to Hanalei Bay, Kauai, Utilizing the Nitrogen Isotope Signature of Macroalgae," *Stanford Undergraduate Research Journal*

While there's a good deal known about invertebrate neurobiology, these facts alone haven't settled questions of their sentience. On the one hand, invertebrates lack a cortex, amygdala, as well as many of the other major brain structures routinely implicated in human emotion. And unsurprisingly, their nervous systems are quite minimalist compared to ours: we have roughly a hundred thousand bee brains worth of neurons in our heads. On the other hand, some invertebrates, including insects, do possess the rudiments of our stress response system. So the question is still on the table: do they experience emotion in a way that we would recognize, or just react to the world with a set of glorified reflexes?

—Jason Castro, "Do Bees Have Feelings?" *Scientific American*

> Bambi's mother, shot. Nemo's mother, eaten by a barracuda. Lilo's mother, killed in a car crash. Koda's mother in *Brother Bear*, speared. Po's mother in *Kung Fu Panda 2*, done in by a power-crazed peacock. Ariel's mother in the third *Little Mermaid*, crushed by a pirate ship. Human baby's mother in *Ice Age*, chased by a saber-toothed tiger over a waterfall. . . . The mothers in these movies are either gone or useless. And the father figures? To die for!
>
> —Sarah Boxer, "Why Are All the Cartoon Mothers Dead?" *The Atlantic*

2. Working with another student in your class, find examples from two or three different fields of academic arguments that strike you as being well written and effective. Spend some time looking closely at them. Do they exemplify the key features of academic arguments discussed in this chapter? What other features do they use? How are they organized? What kind of tone do the writers use? What use do they make of visuals? Draw up a brief report on your findings (a list will do), and bring it to class for discussion.

3. Read the following three paragraphs, and then list changes that the writer might make to convert them into an academic argument:

> The book—the physical paper book—is being circled by a shoal of sharks, with sales down 9 percent this year alone. It's being chewed by the e-book. It's being gored by the death of the bookshop and the library. And most importantly, the mental space it occupied is being eroded by the thousand Weapons of Mass Distraction that surround us all. It's hard to admit, but we all sense it: it is becoming almost physically harder to read books.
>
> In his gorgeous little book *The Lost Art of Reading—Why Books Matter in a Distracted Time*, the critic David Ulin admits to a strange feeling. All his life, he had taken reading as for granted as eating—but then, a few years ago, he "became aware, in an apartment full of books, that I could no longer find within myself the quiet necessary to read." He would sit down to do it at night, as he always had, and read a few paragraphs, then find his mind was wandering, imploring him to check his email, or Twitter, or Facebook. "What I'm struggling with," he writes, "is the encroachment of the buzz, the sense that there's something out there that merits my attention."
>
> I think most of us have this sense today, if we are honest. If you read a book with your laptop thrumming on the other side of the room, it can be like trying to read in the middle of a party, where everyone is shouting to each other. To read, you need to slow down. You need mental silence except for the words. That's getting harder to find.
>
> —Johann Hari, "How to Survive the Age of Distraction"

4. Choose two pieces of your college writing, and examine them closely. Are they examples of strong academic writing? How do they use the key features that this chapter identifies as characteristic of academic arguments? How do they use and document sources? What kind of tone do you establish in each? After studying the examples in this chapter, what might you change about these pieces of writing, and why?
5. Go to a blog that you follow, or check out one on the *Huffington Post* or *Ricochet*. Spend some time reading the articles or postings on the blog, and look for ones that you think are the best written and the most interesting. What features or characteristics of academic argument do they use, and which ones do they avoid?

Title begins with a reference many readers will recognize (Sendak) and then points to the direction the argument will take.

Where the Wild Things Should Be: Healing Nature Deficit Disorder through the Schoolyard

CHARLOTTE GEAGHAN-BREINER

Background information introduces a claim that states an effect and traces it back to its various causes.

Considerable evidence supports the claim.

The developed world deprives children of a basic and inalienable right: unstructured outdoor play. Children today have substantially less access to nature, less free range, and less time for independent play than previous generations had. Experts in a wide variety of fields cite the rise of technology, urbanization, parental over-scheduling, fears of stranger-danger, and increased traffic as culprits. In 2005 journalist Richard Louv articulated the causes and consequences of children's alienation from nature, dubbing it "nature deficit disorder." Louv is not alone in claiming that the widening divide between children and nature has distressing health repercussions, from obesity and attention disorders to depression and decreased cognitive functioning. The dialogue surrounding nature deficit disorder deserves the attention and action of educators, health professionals, parents, developers, environmentalists, and conservationists alike.

Presents a solution to the problem and foreshadows full thesis

The most practical solution to this staggering rift between children and nature involves the schoolyard. The schoolyard habitat movement, which promotes the "greening" of school grounds, is quickly gaining international recognition and legitimacy. A host of organizations, including the National Wildlife Federation, the American Forest Foundation, and the Council for Environmental Education, as well as their international counterparts, have committed themselves to this cause. However, while many recognize the need for "greened

---

Charlotte Geaghan-Breiner wrote this academic argument for her first-year writing class at Stanford University.

school grounds," not many describe such landscapes beyond using adjectives such as "lush," "green," and "natural." The literature thus lacks a coherent research-based proposal that both asserts the power of "natural" school grounds *and* delineates what such grounds might look like.

The author identifies a weakness in the proposed solution.

My research strives to fill in this gap. I advocate for the schoolyard as the perfect place to address nature deficit disorder, demonstrate the benefits of greened schoolyards, and establish the tenets of natural schoolyard design in order to further the movement and inspire future action.

Ending paragraph of the introduction presents the full thesis and outlines the entire essay.

Asphalt Deserts: The State of the Schoolyard Today

Author uses subheads to help guide readers through the argument.

As a formative geography of childhood, the schoolyard serves as the perfect place to address nature deficit disorder. Historian Peter Stearns argues that modern childhood was transformed when schooling replaced work as the child's main social function (1041). In this contemporary context, the schoolyard emerges as a critical setting for children's learning and play. Furthermore, as parental traffic and safety concerns increasingly constrain children's free range outside of school, the schoolyard remains a safe haven, a protected outdoor space just for children.

Explains why it's valuable to focus on the schoolyard

Despite the schoolyard's major significance in children's lives, the vast majority of schoolyards fail to meet children's needs. An outdated theoretical framework is partially to blame. In his 1890 *Principles of Psychology*, psychologist Herbert Spencer championed the "surplus energy theory": play's primary function, according to Spencer, was to burn off extra energy (White). Play, however, contributes to the social, cognitive, emotional, and physical growth of the child (Hart 136); "[l]etting off steam" is only one of play's myriad functions. Spencer's theory thus constitutes a serious oversimplification, but it still continues to inform the design of children's play areas.

Most US playgrounds conform to an equipment-based model constructed implicitly on Spencer's surplus energy theory (Frost and Klein 2). The sports fields, asphalt courts, swing sets, and jungle gyms common to schoolyards relegate nature to the sidelines and prioritize gross motor play at the expense of dramatic play or exploration. An eight-year-old in England says it best: "The space outside feels boring. There's nothing to do. You get bored with just a square of tarmac" (Titman 42). Such an environment does not afford children the chance to graduate to new, more complex challenges as they develop. While play equipment still deserves a spot in the schoolyard, equipment-*dominated* playscapes leave the growing child bereft of stimulating interactions with the environment.

Quotations by children provide evidence to support the claim and bring in a personal touch. Note that the writer is following MLA style for in-text citations.

Also to blame for the failure of school grounds to meet children's needs are educators' and developers' adult-centric aims. Most urban schoolyards are sterile environments with low biodiversity (see fig. 1). While concrete, asphalt, and synthetic turf may be easier to maintain and supervise, they exacerbate the "extinction

Presents reasons why schoolyards continue to be poorly designed

Fig. 1: Addison Elementary in Palo Alto, CA, conforms to the traditional playground model, dominated by synthetic landcover and equipment. Photo by Charlotte Geaghan-Breiner

Note that the figure is introduced in the text and has a caption.

of experience," a term that Pyle has used to describe the disappearance of children's embodied, intuitive experiences in nature. Asphalt deserts are major instigators of this "cycle of impoverishment" (Pyle 312). Loss of biodiversity begets environmental apathy, which in turn allows the process of extinction to persist. Furthermore, adults' preference for manicured, landscaped grounds does little to enhance children's creative outdoor play. Instead of rich, stimulating play environments for children, such highly ordered schoolyards are constructed with adults' convenience in mind.

The Greener, the Better: The Benefits of Greened School Grounds

A great body of research documents the physiological, cognitive, psychological, and social benefits of contact with nature. Health experts champion outdoor play as an antidote to two major trends in children of the developed world: the Attention Deficit Disorder and obesity epidemics. A 2001 study by Taylor, Kuo, and Sullivan indicates that green play settings decrease the severity of symptoms in children with ADD. They also combat inactivity in children by diversifying the "play repertoire" and providing for a wider range of physical activity than traditional playgrounds. In the war against childhood obesity, health advocates must add the natural schoolyard to their arsenal.

Author cites research that discusses the health benefits of interacting with nature.

The schoolyard also has the ability to influence the way children play. Instead of being prescribed a play structure with a clear purpose (e.g., a swing set), children in natural schoolyards must discover the affordances of their environment—they must imagine what could be. In general, children exhibit more prosocial behavior and higher levels of inclusion in the natural schoolyard (Dyment 31). A 2006 questionnaire-based study of a greening initiative in Toronto found that the naturalization of the school grounds yielded a decrease in aggressive actions and disciplinary problems and a

Social benefits of interacting with nature

corresponding increase in civility and cooperation (Dyment 28). The greened schoolyard offers benefits beyond physical and mental health; it shapes the character and quality of children's play interactions.

The schoolyard also has the potential to shape the relationship between children and the natural world. In the essay "Eden in a Vacant Lot," Pyle laments the loss of vacant lots and undeveloped spaces in which children can play and develop intimacy with the land. However, Pyle overlooks the geography of schoolyards, which can serve as enclaves of nature in an increasingly urbanized and developed world. Research has shown that school ground naturalization fosters nature literacy and intimacy just as Pyle's vacant lots do. For instance, a school ground greening program in Toronto dramatically enhanced children's environmental awareness, sense of stewardship, and curiosity about their local ecosystem (Dyment 37). When integrated with nature, the schoolyard can mitigate the effects of nature deficit disorder and reawaken children's innate biophilia, or love of nature.

Biophilic Design: Establishing the Tenets of Natural Schoolyard Design

The need for naturalized schoolyards is urgent. But how might theory actually translate into reality? Here I will propose four principles of biophilic schoolyard design, or landscaping that aims to integrate nature and natural systems into the man-made geography of the schoolyard.

The author establishes four guidelines for redesigning schoolyards.

The first is biodiversity. Schools should strive to incorporate a wide range of greenery and wildlife on their grounds (see fig. 2). Native plants should figure prominently so as to inspire children's interest in their local habitats. Inclusion of wildlife in school grounds can foster meaningful interactions with other species. Certain plants and flowers, for example, attract birds, butterflies, and other insects; aquatic areas can house fish, frogs,

Fig. 2: A seating area at Ohlone School in Palo Alto, CA, features a healthy range of plant species. Photo by Charlotte Geaghan-Breiner

tadpoles, and pond bugs. School pets and small-scale farms also serve to teach children important lessons about responsibility, respect, and compassion for animals. Biodiversity, the most vital feature of biophilic design, transforms former "asphalt deserts" into realms teeming with life.

The second principle that schoolyard designers should keep in mind is sensory stimulation. The greater the degree of sensory richness in an environment, the more opportunities it affords the child to imagine, learn, and discover. School grounds should feature a range of colors, textures, sounds, fragrances, and in the case of the garden, tastes. Such sensory diversity almost always accompanies natural environments, unlike concrete, which affords comparatively little sensory stimulation.

Diversity of topography constitutes another dimension of a greened schoolyard (Fjortoft and Sageie 83). The best school grounds afford children a range of places to climb, tunnel, frolic, and sit. Natural elements function as "play equipment": children can sit on stumps, jump over logs, swing on trees, roll down grassy mounds, and climb on boulders. The playscape should also offer nooks and crannies for children to seek shelter and refuge. While asphalt lots and play structures are still fun for children, they should not dominate the school grounds (see fig. 3).

A figure illustrates a specific point about play structures.

Last but not least, naturalized schoolyards must embody the theory of loose parts proposed by architect Simon Nicholson. "In any environment," he writes, "both the degree of inventiveness and the possibility of discovery are directly proportional to the number and kinds of variables in it" (qtd. in Louv 87). Loose parts—sand, water, leaves, nuts, seeds, rocks, and sticks—are abundant in the natural world. The detachability of loose parts makes them ideal for children's construction projects.

Fig. 3: Peninsula School in Menlo Park, CA, has integrated traditional equipment, such as a playhouse and slide, into the natural setting. Photo by Charlotte Geaghan-Breiner

While some might worry about the possible hazards of loose parts, conventional play equipment is far from safe: more than 200,000 of children's emergency room visits every year in the United States are linked to these built structures (Frost 217). When integrated into the schoolyard through naturalization, loose parts offer the child the chance to gain ever-increasing mastery of the environment.

The four tenets proposed provide a concrete basis for the application of biophilic design to the schoolyard. Such design also requires a frame-shift away from adult preferences for well-manicured grounds and towards children's needs for wilder spaces that can be constructed, manipulated, and changed through play (Lester and Maudsley 67; White and Stoecklin). Schoolyards designed according to the precepts of biodiversity, sensory stimulation, diversity of topography, and loose parts will go a long way in healing the rift between children and nature, a rift that adult-centric design only widens.

Grounds for Change

In conclusion, I have shown that natural schoolyard design can heal nature deficit disorder by restoring free outdoor play to children's lives in the developed world. Successful biophilic schoolyards challenge the conventional notion that natural and man-made landscapes are mutually exclusive. Human-designed environments, and especially those for children, should strive to integrate nature into the landscape. All schools should be designed with the four tenets of natural schoolyard design in mind.

Author restates her claim.

Though such sweeping change may seem impractical given limitations on school budgets, greening initiatives that use natural elements, minimal equipment, and volunteer work can be remarkably cost-effective. Peninsula School in Menlo Park, California, has minimized maintenance costs through the inclusion of hardy native species; it is essentially "designed for neglect" (Dyment 44).

Offers examples of successful biophilic schoolyard design

Gardens and small-scale school farms can also become their own source of funding, as they have for Ohlone Elementary School in Palo Alto, California. Ultimately, the cognitive, psychological, physiological, and social benefits of natural school grounds are priceless. In the words of author Richard Louv, "School isn't supposed to be a polite form of incarceration, but a portal to the wider world" (Louv 226). With this in mind, let the schoolyard restore to children their exquisite intimacy with nature: their inheritance, their right.

Works Cited

Dyment, Janet. "Gaining Ground: The Power and Potential of School Ground Greening in the Toronto District School Board." *Evergreen*, 2006, www.evergreen.ca/downloads/pdfs/Gaining-Ground.pdf.

Fjortoft, Ingunn, and Jostein Sageie. "The Natural Environment as a Playground for Children." *Landscape and Urban Planning*, vol. 48, no. 2, Winter 2001, pp. 83-97.

Frost, Joe L. *Play and Playscapes*. Delmar, 1992.

Frost, Joe L., and Barry L. Klein. *Children's Play and Playgrounds*. Allyn and Bacon, 1979.

Hart, Roger. "Containing Children: Some Lessons on Planning for Play from New York City." *Environment and Urbanization*, vol. 14, no. 2, October 2002, pp. 135-48, eau.sagepub.com/content/14/2/135.full.pdf.

Lester, Stuart, and Martin Maudsley. *Play, Naturally: A Review of Children's Natural Play*. Play England, National Children's Bureau, 2007.

Louv, Richard. *Last Child in the Woods: Saving Our Children from Nature-Deficit Disorder*. Algonquin of Chapel Hill, 2005.

Nicholson, S. "How Not to Cheat Children: The Theory of Loose Parts." *Landscape Architecture*, vol. 62, October 1971, pp. 30-35.

Pyle, Robert M. "Eden in a Vacant Lot: Special Places, Species, and Kids in the Neighborhood of Life." *Children and Nature: Psychological, Sociocultural, and Evolutionary Investigations*, edited by Peter H. Kahn and Stephen R. Kellert, MIT Press, 2002, pp. 305-27.

Stearns, Peter N. "Conclusion: Change, Globalization and Childhood." *Journal of Social History,* vol. 38, no. 4, 2005, pp. 1041-46.

Taylor, Andrea F., et al. "Coping with ADD: The Surprising Connection to Green Play Settings." *Environment and Behavior,* vol. 33, no. 1, 2001, pp. 54-77.

Titman, Wendy. *Special Places; Special People: The Hidden Curriculum of Schoolgrounds*. World Wide Fund for Nature, 1994, files.eric.ed.gov/fulltext/ED430384.pdf.

White, Randy. "Young Children's Relationship with Nature: Its Importance to Children's Development & the Earth's Future." *Taproot*, vol. 16, no. 2, Fall/Winter 2006, *White Hutchinson Leisure and Learning Group*, www.whitehutchinson.com/children/articles/childrennature.shtml.

White, Randy, and Vicki Stoecklin. "Children's Outdoor Play & Learning Environments: Returning to Nature." *Early Childhood News,* Mar. 1998, *White Hutchinson Leisure and Learning Group*, www.whitehutchinson.com/children/articles/outdoor.shtml.

GrAI/Shutterstock

China: The Prizes and Pitfalls of Progress

LAN XUE

Abstract

Pushes to globalize science must not threaten local innovations in developing countries, argues Lan Xue.

Developing countries such as China and India have emerged both as significant players in the production of high-tech products and as important contributors to the production of ideas and global knowledge. China's

This article was written by Lan Xue, a faculty member in the School of Public Policy and Management and the director of the China Institute for Science and Technology Policy, both at Tsinghua University in Beijing, China. It was published in the online edition of *Nature* in July 2008.

rapid ascent as a broker rather than simply a consumer of ideas and innovation has made those in the "developed" world anxious. A 2007 report by UK think tank Demos says that "U.S. and European pre-eminence in science-based innovation cannot be taken for granted. The centre of gravity for innovation is starting to shift from west to east."[1]

But the rapid increase in research and development spending in China—of the order of 20% per year since 1999—does not guarantee a place as an innovation leader. Participation in global science in developing countries such as China is certainly good news for the global scientific community. It offers new opportunities for collaboration, fresh perspectives, and a new market for ideas. It also presents serious challenges for the management of innovation in those countries. A major discovery in the lab does not guarantee a star product in the market. And for a country in development, the application of knowledge in productive activities and the related social transformations are probably more important than the production of the knowledge itself. By gumming the works in information dissemination, by misplacing priorities, and by disavowing research that, although valuable, doesn't fit the tenets of modern Western science, developing countries may falter in their efforts to become innovation leaders.

Vicious Circle

China's scientific publications (measured by articles recorded in the Web of Science) in 1994 were around 10,000, accounting for a little more than 1% of the world total. By 2006, the publications from China rose to more than 70,000, increasing sevenfold in 12 years and accounting for almost 6% of the world total (see graph, next page). In certain technical areas, the growth has been more dramatic. China has been among the leading countries in nanotechnology research, for example, producing a volume of publications second only to that of the United States.

The publish-or-perish mentality that has arisen in China, with its focus on Western journals, has unintended implications that threaten to obviate the roughly 8,000 national scientific journals published in Chinese. Scientists in developing countries such as China and India pride themselves on publishing articles in journals listed in the Science Citation Index (SCI) and the Social Science Citation Index (SSCI) lists. In some top-tier research institutions in China, SCI journals have become the required outlet for research.

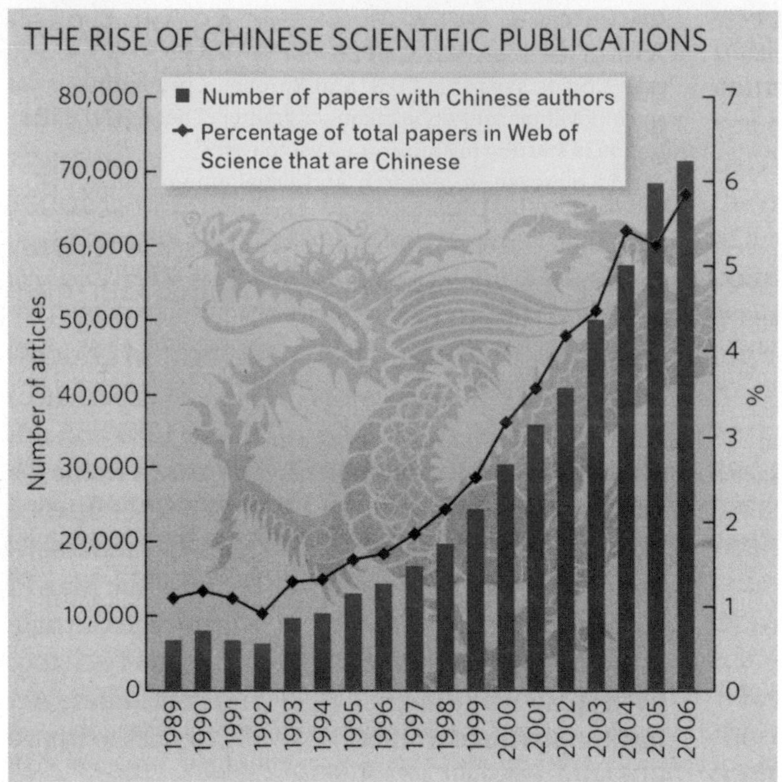

Nature Publishing Group. Illustration by D. Parkins.

A biologist who recently returned to China from the United States was told by her colleague at the research institute in the prestigious Chinese Academy of Sciences (CAS) that publications in Chinese journals don't really count toward tenure or promotion. Moreover, the institute values only those SCI journals with high impact factors. Unfortunately, the overwhelming majority of the journals in SCI and SSCI lists are published in developed countries in English or other European languages. The language requirement and the high costs of these journals mean that few researchers in China will have regular access to the content. Thus as China spends more and publishes more, the results will become harder to find for Chinese users. This trend could have a devastating impact on the local scientific publications and hurt China's ability to apply newly developed knowledge in an economically useful way.

Several members of the CAS expressed their concerns on this issue recently at the 14th CAS conference in Beijing. According to Molin Ge, a theoretical physicist at the Chern Institute of Mathematics, Nankai University, Tianjin, as more high-quality submissions are sent to overseas journals, the quality of submissions to local Chinese journals declines, which lowers the impact of the local Chinese journals. This becomes a vicious circle because the lower the impact, the less likely these local journals are to get high-quality submissions.[2]

Setting Agendas

Research priorities in developing countries may be very different from those in developed nations, but as science becomes more globalized, so too do priorities. At the national level, developing countries' research priorities increasingly resemble those of the developed nations, partly as a result of international competitive pressures. For example, after the United States announced its National Nanotechnology Initiative (NNI) in 2001, Japan and nations in Europe followed suit, as did South Korea, China, India, and Singapore. According to a 2004 report by the European Union,[3] public investment in nanotechnology had increased from €400 million (U.S. $630 million) in 1997 to more than €3 billion in 2004.

Part of the pressure to jump on the international bandwagon comes from researchers themselves. Scientists in the developing world maintain communications with those elsewhere. It is only natural that they want to share the attention that their colleagues in the developed Western world and Japan are receiving by pursuing the same hot topics. The research is exciting, fast-moving, and often easier to publish. At the same time, there are many other crucial challenges to be met in developing countries. For example, public health, water and food security, and environmental protection all beg for attention and resources. If people perceive these research areas as less intellectually challenging and rewarding, the issues will fail to receive the resources, support, and recognition they require. Without better agenda-setting practices, the scientific community will continue to face stinging criticism. It can send a satellite to Mars but not solve the most basic problems that threaten millions of lives in the developing world.

The introduction of Western scientific ideals to the developing world can generate an environment that is hostile to the indigenous research that prima facie does not fit those ideals. The confrontation between Western medicine and traditional Chinese medicine dates back to the early days of the twentieth century when Western medicine was first introduced in China. The debate reached a peak last year when a famous actress, Xiaoxu Chen, died from breast cancer. She allegedly insisted on treatment by Chinese traditional medicine, raising the hackles of some who claimed it to be worthless. Many Chinese still support traditional medicine and say that the dominance of Western medicine risks endangering China's scientific and cultural legacy.

A similar row erupted around earthquake prediction. In the 1960s and 1970s, China set up a network of popular earthquake-prediction stations, using simple instruments and local knowledge. For the most part, the network was decommissioned as China built the modern earthquake-monitoring system run by the China Earthquake Administration. When the system failed to predict the recent Sichuan earthquake, several people claimed that non-mainstream approaches had predicted its imminence. Scientists in the agency have tended to brush off such unofficial and individual predictions. To many this seems arrogant and bureaucratic.

It would be foolish and impossible to stop the globalization of science. There are tremendous benefits to science enterprises in different countries being integrated into a global whole. One should never think of turning back the clock. At the same time, it is possible to take some practical steps to minimize the harmful effects of this trend on local innovation.

Prioritizing for the People

First of all, there is a need to re-examine the governance of global science in recognition of the changing international geography of science. Many international norms and standards should be more open and accommodating to the changing environment in developing countries. For example, there is a need to re-evaluate the SCI and SSCI list of journals to include quality journals in the developing countries. In the long run, the relevant scientific community could also think about establishing an international panel to make decisions on the selection of journals for these indices, given their important influence. The recent move by Thomson Reuters, the parent company of ISI, to expand its coverage of the SCI list by adding 700 regional academic journals is a step in the right direction.[4]

English has become the de facto global language of science. Developing countries should invest in public institutions to provide translation services so that global scientific progress can be disseminated quickly. Developing countries can learn from Japan, a world leader in collecting scientific information and making it available to the public in the local language. At the same time, there should also be international institutions to provide similar services to the global science community so that "results and the knowledge generated through research should be freely accessible to all," as advocated by Nobel Laureates John Sulston and Joseph Stiglitz.[5]

When setting agendas, governments in developing countries must be careful in allocating their resources for science to achieve a balance between following the science frontier globally and addressing crucial domestic needs. A balance should also be struck between generating knowledge and disseminating and using knowledge. In addition, the global science community has a responsibility to help those developing countries that do not have adequate resources to solve problems themselves.

Finally, special efforts should be made to differentiate between pseudoscience and genuine scientific research. For the latter, one should tolerate or even encourage such indigenous research efforts in developing countries even if they do not fit the recognized international science paradigm. After all, the real advantage of a globalized scientific enterprise is not just doing the same research at a global scale, but doing new and exciting research in an enriched fashion.

Notes

1. Charles Leadbeater and James Wilsdon, *The Atlas of Ideas: How Asian Innovation Can Benefit Us All* (Demos, 2007).
2. Y. Xie et al., "Good Submissions Went Overseas—Chinese S&T Journals Could Not Keep Up with Their Overseas Peers," *Chinese Youth Daily*, June 25, 2008.
3. http://ec.europa.eu/nanotechnology/pdf/nano_com_en_new.pdf
4. http://scientific.thomsonreuters.com/press/2008/8455931/
5. Joseph Stiglitz and John Sulston, "Science is Being Held Back by Outdated Laws," *The Times*, July 5, 2008.

18
Finding Evidence

Left to right: © Wavebreakmedia, Ltd./age fotostock; www.CartoonStock.com; © Zoonar M Kang/age fotostock

In making and supporting claims for academic arguments, writers use all kinds of evidence: data from journal articles; scholarly books; records from archives; blogs, wikis, social media sites, and other digital sources; personal observations and fieldwork; surveys; and even DNA. But such evidence doesn't exist in a vacuum. Instead, the quality of evidence — how and when it was collected, by whom, and for what purposes — may become part of the argument itself. Evidence may be persuasive in one time and place but not in another; it may convince one kind of audience but not another; it may work with one type of argument but not with the kind you are writing. The point is that finding "good" evidence for a research project is rarely a simple matter.

Considering the Rhetorical Situation

To be most persuasive, evidence should match the time and place in which you make your argument — that is to say, your rhetorical situation.

For example, arguing that government officials in the twenty-first century should use the same policies to deal with economic troubles that were employed in the middle of the twentieth might not be convincing on its own. After all, almost every aspect of the world economy has changed in the past fifty years. In the same way, a writer may achieve excellent results by citing a detailed survey of local teenagers as evidence for education reform in her small rural hometown, but she may have less success using the same evidence to argue for similar reforms in a large inner-city community.

College writers also need to consider the fields that they're working in. In disciplines such as experimental psychology or economics, **quantitative data**—the sort that can be observed and counted—may be the best evidence. In many historical, literary, or philosophical studies, however, the same kind of data may be less appropriate or persuasive, or even impossible to come by. As you become more familiar with a discipline, you'll gain a sense of what it takes to support a claim. The following questions will help you understand the rhetorical situation of a particular field:

- What kinds of data are preferred as evidence? How are such data gathered and presented?
- How are definitions, causal analyses, evaluations, analogies, and examples used as evidence?
- How does the field use firsthand and secondhand sources as evidence? What kinds of data are favored?
- How are statistics or other numerical information used and presented as evidence? Are tables, charts, or graphs commonly used? How much weight do they carry?
- What or who counts as an authority in this field? How are the credentials of authorities established?
- What weight do writers in the field give to **precedence**—that is, to examples of similar actions or decisions made in the past?
- Is personal experience allowed as evidence? When?
- How are quotations used as part of evidence?
- How are still or moving images or sound(s) used as part of evidence, and how closely are they related to the verbal parts of the argument being presented?

As these questions suggest, evidence may not always travel well from one field to another. Nor does it always travel easily from culture to culture. Differing notions of evidence can lead to arguments that go nowhere fast. For instance, when Italian journalist Oriana Fallaci interviewed Ayatollah Khomeini, Iran's supreme leader, in 1979, she argued in a way that's common in North American and Western European cultures: she presented claims that she considered to be adequately backed up with facts ("Iran denies freedom to people. . . . Many people have been put in prison and even executed, just for speaking out in opposition"). In response, Khomeini relied on very different kinds of evidence—analogies ("Just as a finger with gangrene should be cut off so that it will not destroy the whole body, so should people who corrupt others be pulled out like weeds so they will not infect the whole field") and, above all, the authority of the Qur'an. Partly because of these differing beliefs about what counts as evidence, the interview ended unsuccessfully.

The need for evidence depends a lot on the rhetorical situation. © Mick Stevens/The New Yorker Collection/The Cartoon Bank

CULTURAL CONTEXTS FOR ARGUMENT

The Rhetorical Situation

To take another example, a *Harvard Business Review* blog post from December 4, 2013, on "How to Argue across Cultures" recounts the story of a Western businessperson who was selling bicycles produced in China to a buyer in Germany. When the business owner went to pick up the bicycles, he noticed that they rattled. In considering how to bring up this defect with the Chinese supplier, the businessperson could have confronted him directly, relying on physical evidence to support his claim. He rejected this form of evidence, however, because he knew that such a confrontation would result in loss of face for the supplier and very likely lead to an undesirable outcome. So instead, he suggested that he and the Chinese supplier take a couple of bikes out for a ride, during which the bikes rattled away. At the end of the ride, the Western businessperson quietly mentioned that he "thought his bike had rattled" and then departed, leaving the Chinese supplier to consider his subtle presentation of evidence. And it worked: when the Germans received the bicycle delivery, the rattle had been repaired.

It's always good to remember, then, that when arguing across cultural divides, whether international or more local, you need to think carefully about how you're accustomed to using evidence—and about what counts as evidence to other people (without surrendering your own intellectual principles).

Using Data and Evidence from Research Sources

The evidence you will use in most academic arguments—books, articles, videos, documents, photographs and other images—will likely come from sources you locate in libraries, in databases, or online. How well you can navigate these complex territories will determine the success of many of your academic and professional projects. Research suggests that most students overestimate their ability to manage these tools and, perhaps more important, don't seek the help they need to find the best materials for their projects. We can't cover all the nuances of doing academic research here, but we can at least point you in the right directions.

Explore library resources: printed works and databases. Your college library has printed materials (books, periodicals, reference works) as well as terminals that provide access to its electronic catalogs, other libraries' catalogs via the Internet, and numerous proprietary databases (such as *Academic Search Complete*, *Academic OneFile*, *JSTOR*) not available publicly on the Web. Crucially, libraries also have librarians whose job it is to guide you through these resources, help you identify reputable materials, and show you how to search for materials efficiently. The best way to begin a serious academic argument then is often with a trip to the library or a discussion with your professor or librarian. Also be certain that you know your way around the library. If not, ask the staff there to help you locate the following tools: general and specialized encyclopedias; biographical resources; almanacs, yearbooks, and atlases; book and periodical indexes; specialized indexes and abstracts; the circulation computer or library catalog; special collections; audio, video, and art collections; and the interlibrary loan office.

At the outset of a project, determine what kinds of sources you will need to support your project. (You might also review your assignment to see whether you're required to consult different kinds of sources.) If you'll use print sources, find out whether they're readily available in your library or whether you must make special arrangements (such as an interlibrary loan) to acquire them. For example, your argument for a senior thesis might benefit from material available mostly in old newspapers and magazines: access to them might require time and ingenuity. If you need to locate other nonprint sources (such as audiotapes, videotapes, artwork, or photos), find out where those are kept and whether you need special permission to examine them.

Most academic resources, however, will be on the shelves or available electronically through databases. Here's when it's important to understand the distinction between library databases and the Internet/Web. Your library's computers hold important resources that aren't on the Web or aren't available to you except through the library's system. The most important of these resources is the library's catalog of its holdings (mostly books), but college libraries also pay to subscribe to *scholarly databases*—for example, guides to journal and magazine articles, the *Academic Search Complete* database (which holds the largest collection of multidisciplinary journals), the *LexisNexis* database of news stories and legal cases, and compilations of statistics—that you can use for free.

You should consult these electronic sources through your college library, perhaps even before turning to the Web. But using these professional databases isn't always easy or intuitive, even when you can reach them on your own computer. You likely need to learn how to focus and narrow your searches (by date, field, types of material, and so on) so that you don't generate unmanageable lists of irrelevant items. That's when librarians or your instructor can help, so ask them for assistance. They expect your questions.

For example, librarians can draw your attention to the distinction between subject headings and keywords. The Library of Congress Subject Headings (LCSH) are standardized words and phrases that are used to classify the subject matter of books and articles. Library catalogs and databases usually use the LCSH headings to index their contents by author, title, publication date, and subject headings. When you do a subject search of the library's catalog, you need to use the exact wording of the LCSH headings. On the other hand, searches with *keywords* use the computer's ability to look for any term in any field of the electronic record. So keyword searching is less restrictive, but you'll have to think hard about your search terms to get usable results and to learn how to limit or expand your search.

Determine, too, early on, how current your sources need to be. If you must investigate the latest findings about, say, a new treatment for malaria, check very recent periodicals, medical journals, and the Web. If you want broader, more detailed coverage and background information, look for scholarly books. If your argument deals with a specific time period, newspapers, magazines, and books written during that period may be your best assets.

How many sources should you consult for an academic argument? Expect to look over many more sources than you'll end up using, and be sure to cover all major perspectives on your subject. Read enough sources to feel comfortable discussing it with someone with more knowledge than you. You don't have to be an expert, but your readers should sense that you are well informed.

Explore online resources. Chances are your first instinct when you need to find information is to do a quick keyword search on the Web, which in many instances will take you to a source in Wikipedia, the free encyclopedia launched by Jimmy Wales in 2001. For years, many teachers and institutions argued that the information on Wikipedia was suspect and could not be used as a reliable source. Times have changed, however, and many serious research efforts now include a stop at Wikipedia. As always, however, let the buyer beware: you need to verify the credibility of all of your sources! If you intend to support a serious academic argument, remember to approach the Web carefully and professionally.

Like the catalogs and databases in your college library, the Internet offers two ways to search for sources related to an argument—one using subject categories and one using keywords. A subject directory organized by categories (such as you might find at About.com) allows you to choose a broad category like "entertainment" or "science," and then click on increasingly narrow categories like "movies" or "astronomy," and then "thrillers" or "the solar system," until you reach a point where you're given a list of Web sites or the opportunity to do a keyword search.

With the second kind of Internet search option, a search engine, you start right off with a keyword search—filling in a blank, for example, on Google's homepage. Because the Internet contains vastly more material than even the largest library catalog or database, exploring it with a search engine requires careful choices and combinations of keywords. For an argument about the fate of the antihero in contemporary films, for example, you might find that *film* and *hero* produce far too many possible matches, or hits. You might further narrow the search by adding a third keyword—say, *American* or *current*. In doing such searches, you'll need to observe the search logic that is followed by a particular database. Using *and* between keywords (*movies and heroes*) usually indicates that both terms must appear in a file for it to be called up. Using *or* between keywords usually instructs the computer to locate every file in which either one word or the other shows up, and using *not* tells the computer to exclude files containing a particular word from the search results (*movies not heroes*).

More crucial with a tool like Google is to discover how the resources of the site itself can refine your choice or direct you to works better suited to academic argument. When you search for any term, you can click "Advanced Search" at the bottom of the results page and bring up a full screen of options to narrow your search in important ways.

But that's not the end of your choices. With an *academic* argument, you might want to explore your topic in either Google Books or Google Scholar. Both resources send you to the level of materials you might need for a term paper or professional project. And Google offers other options as well: it can direct you to images, photographs, blogs, and so on. The lesson is simple. If your current Web searches typically involve no more than using the first box that a search engine offers, you aren't close to using all the power available to you. Explore that tool you use all the time and see what it can really do.

search.com

Advanced Search

include **all** of these words:

include this **exact phrase**:

include **at least one** of these words:

exclude these words:

language: any language

file type: any format

last updated: anytime

limit domain to:

that link to:

related to:

Cancel Search

Most search engines offer many kinds of research tools like this "Advanced Search" page from search.com. Explore them from the "More" and "Even More" menus on search pages.

SEARCHING ONLINE OR IN DATABASES

- Don't rely on simple Web searches only.
- Find library databases targeted to your subject.
- Use advanced search techniques to focus your search.
- Learn the difference between *subject heading* and *keyword* searches.
- Understand the differences between academic and popular sources.
- Admit when you don't know how to find material—you won't be alone!
- *Routinely* ask for help from librarians and instructors.

Collecting Data on Your Own

Not all your supporting materials for an academic argument must come from print or online sources. You can present research that you have carried out or been closely involved with; this kind of research usually requires that you collect and examine data. Here, we discuss the kinds of firsthand research that student writers do most often.

Perform experiments. Academic arguments can be supported by evidence you gather through experiments. In the sciences, data from experiments conducted under rigorously controlled conditions is highly valued. For other kinds of writing, more informal experiments may be acceptable, especially if they're intended to provide only part of the support for an argument.

If you want to argue, for instance, that the recipes in *Bon Appétit* magazine are impossibly tedious to follow and take far more time than the average person wishes to spend preparing food, you might ask five or six people to conduct an experiment—following two recipes from a recent issue and recording and timing every step. The evidence that you gather from this informal experiment could provide some concrete support—by way of specific examples—for your contention.

But such experiments should be taken with a grain of salt (maybe organic in this case). They may not be effective with certain audiences. And if your experiments can easily be attacked as skewed or sloppily done ("The people you asked to make these recipes couldn't cook a Pop-Tart"), then they may do more harm than good.

Make observations. "What," you may wonder, "could be easier than observing something?" You just choose a subject, look at it closely, and record what you see and hear. But trained observers say that recording an observation accurately requires intense concentration and mental agility. If observing were easy, all eyewitnesses would provide reliable stories. Yet experience shows that when several people observe the same phenomenon, they generally offer different, sometimes even contradictory, accounts of those observations.

Before you begin an observation yourself, decide exactly what you want to find out, and anticipate what you're likely to see. Do you want to observe an action that is repeated by many people—perhaps how people behave at the checkout line in a grocery store? Or maybe you want to study a sequence of actions—for instance, the stages involved in student registration, which you want to argue is far too complicated. Or maybe you are motivated to examine the interactions of a notoriously contentious campus group. Once you have a clear sense of what you'll analyze and what questions you'll try to answer through the observation, use the following guidelines to achieve the best results:

- Make sure that the observation relates directly to your claim.
- Brainstorm about what you're looking for, but don't be rigidly bound to your expectations.

- Develop an appropriate system for collecting data. Consider using a split notebook page or screen: on one side, record the minute details of your observations; on the other, record your thoughts or impressions.
- Be aware that the way you record data will affect the outcome, if only in respect to what you decide to include in your observational notes and what you leave out.
- Record the precise date, time, and place of the observation(s).

You may be asked to prepare systematic observations in various science courses, including anthropology or psychology, where you would follow a methodology and receive precise directions. But observation can play a role in other kinds of arguments and use various media: a photo essay, for example, might serve as an academic argument in some situations.

Conduct interviews. Some evidence is best obtained through direct interviews. If you can talk with an expert—in person, on the phone, or online—you might obtain information you couldn't have gotten through any other type of research. In addition to an expert opinion, you might ask for firsthand accounts, biographical information, or suggestions of other places to look or other people to consult. The following guidelines will help you conduct effective interviews:

- Determine the exact purpose of the interview, and be sure it's directly related to your claim.
- Set up the interview well in advance. Specify how long it'll take, and if you wish to record the session, ask permission to do so.
- Prepare a written list of both factual and open-ended questions. (Brainstorming with friends can help you come up with good questions.) Leave plenty of space for notes after each question. If the interview proceeds in a direction that you hadn't expected but that seems promising, don't feel that you have to cover every one of your questions.
- Record the subject's full name and title, as well as the date, time, and place of the interview.
- Be sure to thank those people whom you interview, either in person or with a follow-up letter or email message.

A serious interview can be eye-opening when the questions get a subject to reveal important experiences or demonstrate his or her knowledge or wisdom.

In his article "Immigrants Who Speak Indigenous Languages Encounter Isolation," Kirk Semple draws on several different surveys to provide the necessary factual grounding for his argument.

LINK TO P. 573

Use questionnaires to conduct surveys. Surveys usually require the use of questionnaires. Questions should be clear, easy to understand, and designed so that respondents' answers can be easily analyzed. Questions that ask respondents to say "yes" or "no" or to rank items on a scale (1 to 5, for example, or "most helpful" to "least helpful") are particularly easy to tabulate. Because tabulation can take time and effort, limit the number of questions you ask. Note also that people often resent being asked to answer more than about twenty questions, especially online.

Here are some other guidelines to help you prepare for and carry out a survey:

- Ask your instructor if your college or university requires that you get approval from the local Institutional Review Board (IRB) to conduct survey research. Many schools waive this requirement if students are doing such research as part of a required course, but you should check to make sure. Securing IRB permission usually requires filling out a series of online forms, submitting all of your questions for approval, and asking those you are surveying to sign a consent form saying they agree to participate in the research.
- Write out your purpose in conducting the survey, and make sure that its results will be directly related to your purpose.
- Brainstorm potential questions to include in the survey, and ask how each relates to your purpose and claim.
- Figure out how many people you want to contact, what the demographics of your sample should be (for example, men in their twenties or an equal number of men and women), and how you plan to reach these people.
- Draft questions that are as free of bias as possible, making sure that each calls for a short, specific answer.
- Think about possible ways that respondents could misunderstand you or your questions, and revise with these points in mind.
- Test the questions on several people, and revise those questions that are ambiguous, hard to answer, or too time-consuming to answer.
- If your questionnaire is to be sent by mail or email or posted on the Web, draft a cover letter explaining your purpose and giving a clear deadline. For mail, provide an addressed, stamped return envelope.

- On the final draft of the questionnaire, leave plenty of space for answers.
- Proofread the final draft carefully. Typos will make a bad impression on those whose help you're seeking.
- After you've done your tabulations, set out your findings in clear and easily readable form, using a chart or spreadsheet if possible.

"Next question: I believe that life is a constant striving for balance, requiring frequent tradeoffs between morality and necessity, within a cyclic pattern of joy and sadness, forging a trail of bittersweet memories until one slips, inevitably, into the jaws of death. Agree or disagree?"

A key requirement of survey questions is that they be easy to understand. © George Price/The New Yorker Collection/The Cartoon Bank

Wes Anderson, film's primary advocate of Twee, and *Moonrise Kingdom* Indian Paintbrush/The Kobal Collection

Draw upon personal experience. Personal experience can serve as powerful evidence when it's appropriate to the subject, to your purpose, and to the audience. If it's your only evidence, however, personal experience usually won't be sufficient to carry the argument. Your experiences may be regarded as merely "anecdotal," which is to say possibly exceptional, unrepresentative, or even unreliable. Nevertheless, personal experience can be effective for drawing in listeners or readers, as James Parker does in the following example. His full article goes on to argue that—in spite of his personal experience with it—the "Twee revolution" has some good things going for it, including an "actual moral application":

> Eight years ago or so, the alternative paper I was working for sent me out to review a couple of folk-noise-psych-indie-beardie-weirdie bands. I had a dreadful night. The bands were bad enough—"fumbling," I scratched in my notebook, "infantile"—but what really did me in was the audience. Instead of baying for the blood of these lightweights . . . the gathered young people—behatted, bebearded, besmiling—obliged them with patters of validating applause. I had seen it before, this fond curiosity, this acclamation of the undercooked, but never so much of it in

one place: the whole event seemed to exult in its own half-bakedness. *Be as crap as you like* was the message to the performers. *The crapper, the better. We're here for you.* I tottered home, wrote a homicidally nasty nervous breakdown of a review, and decided I should take myself out of circulation for a while. No more live reviews until I calmed down. A wave of Twee—as I now realize—had just broken over my head.

—James Parker, *The Atlantic*, July/August 2014, p. 36

RESPOND.

1. The following is a list of general topic ideas from the Yahoo! Directory's "Issues and Causes" page. Narrow one or two of the items down to a more specific subject by using research tools in the library or online such as scholarly books, journal articles, encyclopedias, magazine pieces, and/or informational Web sites. Be prepared to explain how the particular research resources influenced your choice of a more specific subject within the general subject area. Also consider what you might have to do to turn your specific subject into a full-blown topic proposal for a research paper assignment.

Age discrimination	Poverty
Child soldiers	Racial profiling
Climate change	Solar power
Corporal punishment	Sustainable agriculture
Drinking age	Tax reform
Educational equity	Urban sprawl
Immigration reform	Video games
Media ethics and accountability	Violence in the NFL
Military use of drones	Whistleblowing
Pornography	Zoos

2. Go to your library's online catalog page and locate its list of research databases. You may find them presented in various ways: by subject, by field, by academic major, by type—even alphabetically. Try to identify three or four databases that might be helpful to you either generally in college or when working on a specific project, perhaps one you identified in the previous exercise. Then explore the library catalog to see how much you can learn about each of these resources: What fields do they report on? What kinds of data do they offer? How do they present the content of their materials (by abstract, by full text)? What years do they cover? What search strategies do they support (keyword, advanced search)? To find such information, you might look

for a help menu or an "About" link on the catalog or database homepages. Write a one-paragraph description of each database you explore and, if possible, share your findings via a class discussion board, blog, or wiki.

3. What counts as evidence depends in large part on the rhetorical situation. One audience might find personal testimony compelling in a given case, whereas another might require data that only experimental studies can provide. Imagine that you want to argue that advertisements should not include demeaning representations of chimpanzees and that the use of primates in advertising should be banned. You're encouraged to find out that a number of companies such as Honda and Puma have already agreed to such a ban, so you decide to present your argument to other companies' CEOs and advertising officials. What kind of evidence would be most compelling to this group? How would you rethink your use of evidence if you were writing for the campus newspaper, for middle-schoolers, or for animal-rights group members? What can you learn about what sort of evidence each of these groups might value—and why?
4. Finding evidence for an argument is often a discovery process. Sometimes you're concerned not only with digging up support for an already established claim but also with creating and revising tentative claims. Surveys and interviews can help you figure out what to argue, as well as provide evidence for a claim.

   Interview a classmate with the goal of writing a brief proposal argument about the career that he/she should pursue. The claim should be something like *My classmate should be doing X five years from now.* Limit yourself to ten questions. Write them ahead of time, and don't deviate from them. Record the results of the interview (written notes are fine; you don't need to tape the interview). Then interview another classmate with the same goal in mind. Ask the same first question, but this time let the answer dictate the next nine questions. You still get only ten questions.

   Which interview gave you more information? Which one helped you learn more about your classmate's goals? Which one better helped you develop claims about his/her future?

19
Evaluating Sources

Left to right: © Bartomeu Amengual/age fotostock; © Terry Harris/Alamy; © Zoonar/pzAxe/age fotostock

As many examples in this text have shown, the effectiveness of an argument often depends on the quality of the sources that support or prove it. You'll need to carefully evaluate and assess all your sources, including those that you gather in libraries, from other print sources, in online searches, or in your own field research.

Remember that different sources can contribute in different ways to your work. In most cases, you'll be looking for reliable sources that provide accurate information or that clearly and persuasively express opinions that might serve as evidence for a case you're making. At other times, you may be seeking material that expresses ideas or attitudes—how people are thinking and feeling at a given time. You might need to use a graphic image, a sample of avant-garde music, or a controversial YouTube clip that doesn't fit neatly into categories such as "reliable" or "accurate" yet is central to your argument. With any and all such sources and evidence, your goals are to be as knowledgeable about them and as responsible in their use as you can be and to share honestly what you learn about them with readers.

Might a tattle-tale ever be a reliable source?
www.Cartoonstock.com

"I'm *not* being a tattle-tale! — I'm being a reliable source!"

No writer wants to be naïve in the use of source material, especially since most of the evidence that is used in arguments on public issues — even material from influential and well-known sources — comes with considerable baggage. Scientists and humanists alike have axes to grind, corporations have products to sell, politicians have issues to promote, journalists have reputations to make, publishers and media companies have readers, listeners, viewers, and advertisers to attract and to avoid offending. All of these groups produce and use information to their own benefit, and it's not (usually) a bad thing that they do so. You just have to be aware that when you take information from a given source, it will almost inevitably carry with it at least some of the preferences, assumptions, and biases — conscious or not — of the people who produce and disseminate it. Teachers and librarians are not exempted from this caution: even when we make every effort to be clear and comprehensive in reporting information, we cannot possibly see that information from every single angle. So even the most honest and open observer can deliver only a partial account of an event.

To correct for these biases, draw on as many reliable sources as you can handle when you're preparing to write. You shouldn't assume that all arguments are equally good or that all the sides in a controversy can

When might a blogger actually be a reliable source—and how would you know? © Adam Zyglis/Cagel Cartoons, Inc.

be supported by the same weight of evidence and good reasons. But you want to avoid choosing sources so selectively that you miss essential issues and perspectives. That's easy to do when you read only sources that agree with you or when the sources that you read all seem to carry the same message. In addition, make sure that you read each source thoroughly enough that you understand its overall points: national research conducted for the Citation Project indicates that student writers often draw from the first paragraph or page of a source and then simply drop it, without seeing what the rest of the source has to say about the topic at hand.

Especially when writing on political subjects, be aware that the sources you're reading or citing almost always support particular beliefs and goals. That fact has been made apparent in recent years by bloggers—from all parts of the political spectrum—who put the traditional news media under daily scrutiny, exposing errors, biases, and omissions. Even so, these political bloggers (mostly amateur journalists, although many are professionals in their own fields) have their own agendas and so must be read with caution themselves.

Assessing Print Sources

Since you want information to be reliable and persuasive, it pays to evaluate each potential source thoroughly. The following principles can help you evaluate print sources:

- **Relevance.** Begin by asking what a particular source will add to your argument and how closely the source is related to your argumentative claim. For a book, the table of contents and the index may help you decide. For an article, look for an abstract that summarizes its content. If you can't think of a good reason for using the source, set it aside. You can almost certainly find something better.
- **Credentials of the author.** Sometimes the author's credentials are set forth in an article, in a book, or on a Web site, so be sure to look for them. Is the author an expert on the topic? To find out, you can gather information about the person on the Internet using a search engine like Yahoo! or Ask.com. Another way to learn about the credibility of an author is to search Google Groups for postings that mention the author or to check the Citation Index to find out how others refer to this author. If you see your source cited by other sources you're using, look at how they cite it and what they say about it, which could provide clues to the author's credibility.
- **Stance of the author.** What's the author's position on the issue(s) involved, and how does this stance influence the information in the source? Does the author's stance support or challenge your own views?

Consider the differences in a publisher's credentials by comparing Daniel J. Solove's book excerpt, which was published by Yale University Press, and Amy Zimmerman's engaging article from the *Daily Beast*. Do your expectations differ?

LINK TO PP. 734 AND 561

- **Credentials of the publisher or sponsor.** If your source is from a newspaper, is it a major one (such as the *Wall Street Journal* or the *Washington Post*) that has historical credentials in reporting, or is it a tabloid? Is it a popular magazine like *O: The Oprah Magazine* or a journal sponsored by a professional group, such as the *Journal of the American Medical Association*? If your source is a book, is the publisher one you recognize or that has its own Web site? When you don't know the reputation of a source, ask several people with more expertise: a librarian, an instructor, or a professional in the field.
- **Stance of the publisher or sponsor.** Sometimes this stance will be obvious: a magazine called *Save the Planet!* will take a pro-environmental position, whereas one called *America First!* will probably take a conservative stance. But other times, you need to read carefully between the

lines to identify particular positions and see how the stance affects the message the source presents. Start by asking what the source's goals are: what does the publisher or sponsoring group want to make happen?

- **Currency.** Check the date of publication of every book and article. Recent sources are often more useful than older ones, particularly in the sciences. However, in some fields (such as history and literature), the most authoritative works may well be the older ones.
- **Accuracy.** Check to see whether the author cites any sources for the information or opinions in the article and, if so, how credible and current they are.
- **Level of specialization.** General sources can be helpful as you begin your research, but later in the project you may need the authority or currency of more specialized sources. Keep in mind that highly specialized works on your topic may be difficult for your audience to understand.
- **Audience.** Was the source written for a general readership? For specialists? For advocates or opponents?

Note the differences between the cover of the *Journal of Abnormal Psychology* and *The How of Happiness*, a book about psychology. *Journal of Abnormal Psychology* cover reproduced with permission. Copyright © 2013 by the American Psychological Association. No further reproduction or distribution is permitted without written permission from the American Psychological Association.

- **Length.** Is the source long enough to provide adequate details in support of your claim?
- **Availability.** Do you have access to the source? If it isn't readily accessible, your time might be better spent looking elsewhere.
- **Omissions.** What's missing or omitted from the source? Might such exclusions affect whether or how you can use the source as evidence?

Assessing Electronic Sources

You'll probably find working with digital media both exciting and frustrating, for even though these tools (the Web, social networks, Twitter, and so on) are enormously useful, they offer information of widely varying quality—and mountains and mountains of it. Because Web sources are mostly open and unregulated, careful researchers look for corroboration before accepting evidence they find online, especially if it comes from a site whose sponsor's identity is unclear.

Every man [and woman] should have a built-in automatic crap detector operating inside him.
—Ernest Hemingway, during a 1954 interview with Robert Manning
Alfred Eisenstadt/The Life Picture Collection/Getty Images

Practicing Crap Detection

In such an environment, you must be the judge of the accuracy and trustworthiness of particular electronic sources. This is a problem all researchers face, and one that led media critic Howard Rheingold to develop a system for detecting "crap," that is, "information tainted by ignorance, inept communication, or deliberate deception." To avoid such "crap," Rheingold recommends a method of triangulation, which means finding three separate credible online sources that corroborate the point you want to make. But how do you ensure that these sources are credible? One tip Rheingold gives is to use sites like FactCheck.org to verify information, or to use the search term "whois" to find out about the author or sponsor of a site. Try googling Martin Luther King Jr., he says, and somewhere in the top ten "hits" you'll see something called "Martin Luther King, Jr.—a True Historical Examination," which sounds like it should be credible. Check by typing "whois" and the URL of the True Historical Examination, however, and you will find that it is sponsored by a group called Stormfront. Check out *that* site and you'll find that it is a white supremacist group. Hardly a fair, unbiased, and credible source.

In making judgments about online sources, then, you need to be especially mindful and to rely on the same criteria and careful thinking that you use to assess print sources. In addition, you may find the following questions helpful in evaluating online sources:

- Who has posted the document or message or created the site/medium? An individual? An interest group? A company? A government agency? For Web sites, does the URL offer any clues? Note especially the final suffix in a domain name—*.com* (commercial), *.org* (nonprofit organization), *.edu* (educational institution), *.gov* (government agency), *.mil* (military), or *.net* (network). Also note the geographical domains that indicate country of origin—as in *.ca* (Canada) or *.ar* (Argentina). Click on some links of a Web site to see if they lead to legitimate and helpful sources or organizations.
- What can you determine about the credibility of the author or sponsor? Can the information in the document or site be verified in other sources? How accurate and complete is it? On a blog, for example, look for a link that identifies the creator of the site (some blogs are managed by multiple authors).
- Who can be held accountable for the information in the document or site? How well and thoroughly does it credit its own sources? On a wiki, for example, check its editorial policies: who can add to or edit its materials?
- How current is the document or site? Be especially cautious of undated materials. Most reliable sites are refreshed or edited regularly and should list the date.
- What perspectives are represented? If only one perspective is represented, how can you balance or expand this point of view? Is it a straightforward presentation, or could it be a parody or satire?

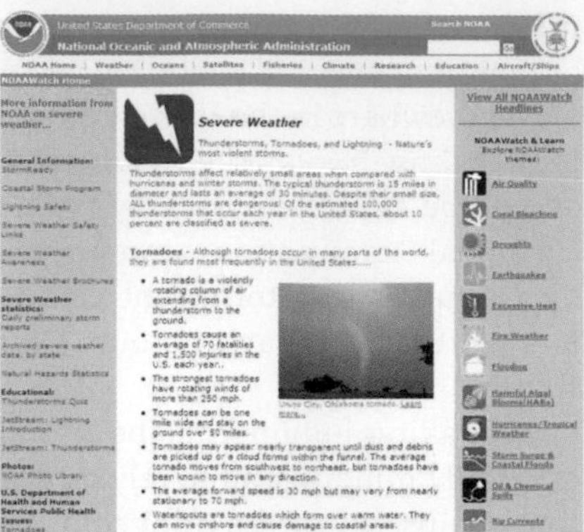

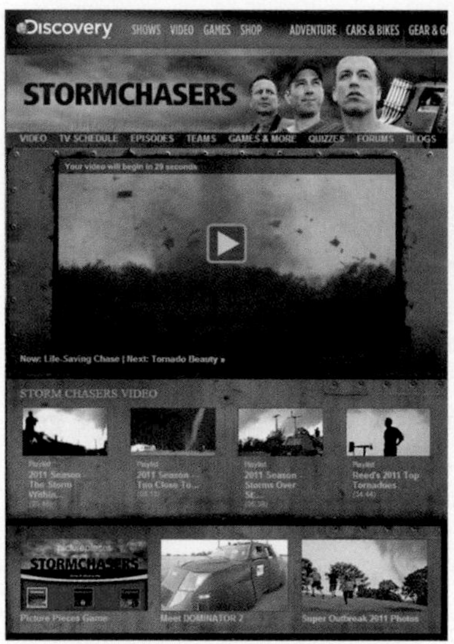

What are the kinds and levels of information available on these Web sites—a commercial site about the TV show *Stormchasers* and a federal site on tornadoes and severe weather?
Left: Discovery Communications, Inc.; right: NOAA

Assessing Field Research

If you've conducted experiments, surveys, interviews, observations, or any other field research in developing and supporting an argument, make sure to review your results with a critical eye. The following questions can help you evaluate your own field research:

- Have you rechecked all data and all conclusions to make sure they're accurate and warranted?
- Have you identified the exact time, place, and participants in all your field research?
- Have you made clear what part you played in the research and how, if at all, your role could have influenced the results or findings?

- If your research involved other people, have you gotten their permission to use their words or other materials in your argument? Have you asked whether you can use their names or whether the names should be kept confidential?
- If your research involved interviews, have you thanked the person or persons you interviewed and asked them to verify the words you have attributed to them?

RESPOND.

1. The chapter claims that "most of the evidence that is used in arguments on public issues . . . comes with considerable baggage" (p. 428). Find an article in a journal, newspaper, or magazine that uses evidence to support a claim of some public interest. It might be a piece about new treatments for malaria, Internet privacy, dietary recommendations for schoolchildren, proposals for air-quality regulation, the rise in numbers of campus sexual assaults, and so on. Identify several specific pieces of evidence, information, or data presented in the article and then evaluate the degree to which you would accept, trust, or believe those statements. Be prepared to explain specifically why you would be inclined to trust or mistrust any claims based on the data.
2. Check out Goodreads (you can set up an account for free) and see what people there are recommending—or search for "common reading programs" or "common reading lists." Then choose one of the recommended books, preferably a work of nonfiction, and analyze it by using as many of the principles of evaluation for printed books listed in this chapter as you can without actually reading the book: Who is the author, and what are his/her credentials? Who is the publisher, and what is its reputation? What can you find out about the book's relevance and popularity: why might the book be on the list? Who is the primary audience for the book? How lengthy is it? How difficult? Finally, consider how likely it is that the book you have selected would be used in an academic paper. If you do choose a work of fiction, might the work be studied in a literature course?
3. Choose a news or information Web site that you visit routinely. Then, using the guidelines discussed in this chapter, spend some time evaluating its credibility. You might begin by comparing it with Google News or Arts & Letters Daily, two sites that have a reputation for being reliable.

20
Using Sources

Left to right: © imageBROKER/age fotostock; kstudija/Shutterstock; Paul Faith/PA Wire URN:9724483 (Press Association via AP Images)

You may gather an impressive amount of evidence on your topic—from firsthand interviews, from careful observations, and from intensive library and online research. But until that evidence is thoroughly understood and then woven into the fabric of your own argument, it's just a stack of details. You still have to turn that data into credible information that will be persuasive to your intended audiences.

Practicing Infotention

Today it's a truism to say that we are all drowning in information, that it is pouring out at us like water from a never-ending fire hose. Such a situation has its advantages: it's never been easier to locate information on any imaginable topic. But it also has distinct disadvantages: how do you identify useful and credible sources among the millions available to you, and how do you use them well once you've found them? We addressed the first of these questions in Chapter 18, "Finding Evidence." But finding good sources is only the first step. Experts on technology and information like professors Richard Lanham and Howard Rheingold point to the next challenge: managing *attention*. Lanham points out that our age of information calls on us to resist the allure of every single thing vying for our attention and to discriminate among what deserves notice and what doesn't. Building on this insight, Rheingold has coined the term "infotention," which he says "is a word I came up with to describe a mind-machine combination of brain-powered attention skills and computer-powered information filters" (Howard Rheingold, "Infotention," http://www.rheingold.com).

Practicing infotention calls for synthesizing and thinking critically about the enormous amount of information available to us from the "collective intelligence" of the Web. And while some of us can learn to be mindful while multitasking (a fighter pilot is an example Rheingold gives of those who must learn to do so), most of us are not good at it and need to train ourselves, literally, to pay attention to attention (and intention as well), to be aware of what we are doing and thinking, to take a deep breath and notice where we are directing our focus. In short, writers today need to learn to focus their attention, especially online, and learn to avoid distractions. So just how do you put all these skills together to practice infotention?

Building a Critical Mass

Throughout the chapters in Part 4, "Research and Arguments," we've stressed the need to discover as much evidence as possible in support of your claim and to read and understand it as thoroughly as you can. If you can find only one or two pieces of evidence — only one or two reasons or illustrations to back up your thesis — then you may be on unsteady ground. Although there's no definite way of saying just how much evidence is enough, you should build toward a critical mass by having several pieces of evidence all pulling in the direction of your claim. Begin by putting Rheingold's triangulation into practice: find at least three credible sources that support your point.

And remember that **circumstantial evidence** (that is, indirect evidence that *suggests* that something occurred but doesn't prove it directly) may not be enough if it is the only evidence that you have. In the

© Cog Design, Ltd.

infamous case of Jack the Ripper, the murderer who plagued London's East End in 1888, nothing but circumstantial evidence ever surfaced and hence no one was charged with or convicted of the crimes. In 2007, however, amateur detective Russell Edwards bought a shawl at auction—a shawl found at one of the murder sites. After consulting with a number of scientific experts and using DNA evidence, Edwards identified Jack the Ripper as Aaron Kosminski, who eventually died in an asylum.

If your evidence for a claim relies solely on circumstantial evidence, on personal experience, or on one major example, you should extend your search for additional sources and good reasons to back up your claim—or modify the argument. Your initial position may simply have been wrong.

Synthesizing Information

As you gather information, you must find a way to make all the facts, ideas, points of view, and quotations you have encountered work with and for you. The process involves not only reading information and recording data carefully (paying "infotention"), but also pondering and synthesizing it—that is, figuring out how the sources you've examined come together to support your specific claims. Synthesis, a form of critical thinking highly valued by business, industry, and other institutions—especially those that reward innovation and creative thinking—is hard work. It almost always involves immersing yourself in your information or data until it feels familiar and natural to you.

At that point, you can begin to look for patterns, themes, and commonalities or striking differences among your sources. Many students use highlighters to help with this process: mark in blue all the parts of sources that mention point A; mark in green those that have to do with issue B; and so on. You are looking for connections among your sources, bringing together what they have to say about your topic in ways you can organize to help support the claim you are making.

You typically begin this process by paraphrasing or summarizing sources so that you understand exactly what they offer and which ideas are essential to your project. You also decide which, if any, sources offer materials you want to quote directly or reproduce (such as an important graph or table). Then you work to introduce such borrowed materials so that readers grasp their significance, and organize them to highlight important relationships. Throughout this review process, use "infotention" strategies by asking questions such as the following:

- Which sources help to set the context for your argument? In particular, which items present new information or give audiences an incentive for reading your work?
- Which items provide background information that is essential for anyone trying to understand your argument?
- Which items help to define, clarify, or explain key concepts of your case? How can these sources be presented or sequenced so that readers appreciate your claims as valid or, at a minimum, reasonable?
- Which of your sources might be used to illustrate technical or difficult aspects of your subject? Would it be best to summarize such technical information to make it more accessible, or would direct quotations be more authoritative and convincing?
- Which sources (or passages within sources) furnish the best support or evidence for each claim or sub-claim within your argument? Now is the time to group these together so you can decide how to arrange them most effectively.
- Which materials do the best job outlining conflicts or offering counterarguments to claims within a project? Which sources might help you address any important objections or rebuttals?

Remember that yours should be the dominant and controlling voice in an argument. You are like the conductor of an orchestra, calling upon separate instruments to work together to create a rich and coherent sound. The least effective academic papers are those that mechanically walk through a string of sources—often just one item per paragraph—without ever getting all these authorities to talk to each other or with the author. Such papers go through the motions but don't get anywhere. You can do better.

Paraphrasing Sources You Will Use Extensively

In a **paraphrase**, you put an author's ideas—including major and minor points—into your own words and sentence structures, following the order the author has given them in the original piece. You usually paraphrase sources that you expect to use heavily in a project. But if you compose your notes well, you may be able to use much of the paraphrased material directly in your paper (with proper citation) because all of the language is your own. A competent paraphrase proves you have read material or data carefully: you demonstrate not only that you know what a source contains but also that you appreciate what it means. There's an important difference.

Here are guidelines to help you paraphrase accurately and effectively in an academic argument:

- Identify the source of the paraphrase, and comment on its significance or the authority of its author.
- Respect your sources. When paraphrasing an entire work or any lengthy section of it, cover all its main points and any essential details, following the same order the author uses. If you distort the shape of the material, your notes will be less valuable, especially if you return to them later.

Backing up your claims with well-chosen sources makes almost any argument more credible. © Ed Fisher/The New Yorker Collection/The Cartoon Bank

- If you're paraphrasing material that extends over more than one page in the original source, note the placement of page breaks since it is highly likely that you will use only part of the paraphrase in your argument. You will need the page number to cite the specific page of material you want to cite.
- Make sure that the paraphrase is in your own words and sentence structures. If you want to include especially memorable or powerful language from the original source, enclose it in quotation marks. (See "Using Quotations Selectively and Strategically" on p. 443.)
- Keep your own comments, elaborations, or reactions separate from the paraphrase itself. Your report on the source should be clear, objective, and free of connotative language.
- Collect all the information necessary to create an in-text citation as well as an item in your works cited list or references list. For online materials, be sure you know how to recover the source later.
- Label the paraphrase with a note suggesting where and how you intend to use it in your argument.
- Recheck to make sure that the words and sentence structures are your own and that they express the author's meaning accurately.

Here is a passage from linguist David Crystal's book *Language Play*, followed by a student's paraphrase of the passage.

> **Language play, the arguments suggest, will help the development of pronunciation ability through its focus on the properties of sounds and sound contrasts, such as rhyming. Playing with word endings and decoding the syntax of riddles will help the acquisition of grammar. Readiness to play with words and names, to exchange puns and to engage in nonsense talk, promotes links with semantic development. The kinds of dialogue interaction illustrated above are likely to have consequences for the development of conversational skills. And language play, by its nature, also contributes greatly to what in recent years has been called metalinguistic awareness, which is turning out to be of critical importance to the development of language skills in general and literacy skills in particular (180).**

Paraphrase of the Passage from Crystal's Book

In *Language Play*, David Crystal argues that playing with language—creating rhymes, figuring out riddles, making puns, playing with names, using inverted words, and so on—helps children figure out a great deal, from the basics of pronunciation and grammar to how to carry on a conversation. This kind of play allows children to understand the overall concept of how language works, a concept that is key to learning to use—and read—language effectively (180).

In the excerpt from his book *Does Science Need a Global Language? English and the Future of Research*, Scott L. Montgomery uses a bulleted list to summarize the major conclusions of leading language scholars.

LINK TO P. 577

Summarizing Sources

Unlike a paraphrase, a **summary** records just the gist of a source or a key idea—that is, only enough information to identify a point you want to emphasize. Once again, this much-shortened version of a source puts any borrowed ideas into your own words. At the research stage, summaries help you identify key points you want to make and, just as important, provide a record of what you have read. In a project itself, a summary helps readers understand the sources you are using.

Here are some guidelines to help you prepare accurate and helpful summaries:

- Identify the thesis or main point in a source and make it the heart of your summary. In a few detailed phrases or sentences, explain to yourself (and readers) what the source accomplishes.
- If your summary includes a comment on the source (as it might in the summaries used for annotated bibliographies), be sure that you won't later confuse your comments with what the source itself asserts.
- When using a summary in an argument, identify the source, state its point, and add your own comments about why the material is significant for the argument that you're making.
- Include just enough information to recount the main points you want to cite. A summary is usually much shorter than the original. When you need more information or specific details, you can return to the source itself or prepare a paraphrase.
- Use your own words in a summary and keep the language objective and denotative. If you include any language from the original source, enclose it in quotation marks.
- Collect all the information necessary to create an in-text citation as well as an item in your works cited list or references list. For online sources without page numbers, record the paragraph, screen, or section number(s) if available.
- Label the summary with a note that suggests where and how you intend to use it in your argument.
- Recheck the summary to make sure that you've captured the author's meaning accurately and that the wording is entirely your own.

Following is a summary of the David Crystal passage:

> In *Language Play*, David Crystal argues that playing with language helps children figure out how language works, a concept that is key to learning to use—and read—language effectively (180).

Notice that the summary is shorter than the paraphrase shown on p. 441–42.

Using Quotations Selectively and Strategically

To support your argumentative claims, you'll want to quote (that is, to reproduce an author's precise words) in at least three kinds of situations:

1. when the wording expresses a point so well that you cannot improve it or shorten it without weakening it,
2. when the author is a respected authority whose opinion supports your own ideas powerfully, and/or
3. when an author or authority challenges or seriously disagrees with others in the field.

Consider, too, that charts, graphs, and images may also function like direct quotations, providing convincing evidence for your academic argument.

In an argument, quotations from respected authorities will establish your ethos as someone who has sought out experts in the field. Just as important sometimes, direct quotations (such as a memorable phrase in your introduction or a detailed eyewitness account) may capture your readers' attention. Finally, carefully chosen quotations can broaden the appeal of your argument by drawing on emotion as well as logic, appealing to the reader's mind and heart. A student who is writing on the ethical issues of bullfighting, for example, might introduce an argument that bullfighting is not a sport by quoting Ernest Hemingway's comment that "the formal bull-fight is a tragedy, not a sport, and the bull is certain to be killed" and then accompany the quotation with an image such as the one on the next page.

The following guidelines can help you quote sources accurately and effectively:

- Quote or reproduce materials that readers will find especially convincing, purposeful, and interesting. You should have a specific reason for every quotation.

A tragedy, not a sport? Juan Castillo/AFP/Getty Images

- Don't forget the double quotation marks [" "] that must surround a direct quotation in American usage. If there's a quote within a quote, it is surrounded by a pair of single quotation marks [' ']. British usage does just the opposite, and foreign languages often handle direct quotations much differently.
- When using a quotation in your argument, introduce its author(s) and follow the quotation with commentary of your own that points out its significance.
- Keep quoted material relatively brief. Quote only as much of a passage as is necessary to make your point while still accurately representing what the source actually said.
- If the quotation extends over more than one page in the original source, note the placement of page breaks in case you decide to use only part of the quotation in your argument.

- In your notes, label a quotation you intend to use with a note that tells you where you think you'll use it.
- Make sure you have all the information necessary to create an in-text citation as well as an item in your works cited list or references list.
- Copy quotations carefully, reproducing the punctuation, capitalization, and spelling exactly as they are in the original. If possible, copy the quotation from a reliable text and paste it directly into your project.
- Make sure that quoted phrases, sentences, or passages fit smoothly into your own language. Consider where to begin the quotation to make it work effectively within its surroundings or modify the words you write to work with the quoted material.
- Use square brackets if you introduce words of your own into the quotation or make changes to it ("And [more] brain research isn't going to define further the matter of 'mind'").
- Use ellipsis marks if you omit material ("And brain research isn't going to define . . . the matter of 'mind'").
- If you're quoting a short passage (four lines or less in MLA style; forty words or less in APA style), it should be worked into your text, enclosed by quotation marks. Longer quotations should be set off from the regular text. Begin such a quotation on a new line, indenting every line a half inch or five to seven spaces. Set-off quotations do not need to be enclosed in quotation marks.
- Never distort your sources or present them out of context when you quote from them. Misusing sources is a major offense in academic arguments.

Framing Materials You Borrow with Signal Words and Introductions

Because source materials are crucial to the success of arguments, you need to introduce borrowed words and ideas carefully to your readers. Doing so usually calls for using a signal phrase of some kind in the sentence to introduce or frame the source. Often, a signal phrase will precede a quotation. But you need such a marker whenever you introduce borrowed material, as in the following examples:

> According to noted primatologist Jane Goodall, the more we learn about the nature of nonhuman animals, the more ethical questions we face about their use in the service of humans.

> The more we learn about the nature of nonhuman animals, the more ethical questions we face about their use in the service of humans, according to noted primatologist Jane Goodall.

> The more we learn about the nature of nonhuman animals, according to noted primatologist Jane Goodall, the more ethical questions we face about their use in the service of humans.

In each of these sentences, the signal phrase tells readers that you're drawing on the work of a person named Jane Goodall and that this person is a "noted primatologist."

Now look at an example that uses a quotation from a source in more than one sentence:

> In *Job Shift*, consultant William Bridges worries about "dejobbing and about what a future shaped by it is going to be like." Even more worrisome, Bridges argues, is the possibility that "the sense of craft and of professional vocation . . . will break down under the need to earn a fee" (228).

The signal verbs *worries* and *argues* add a sense of urgency to the message Bridges offers. They also suggest that the writer either agrees with—or is neutral about—Bridges's points. Other signal verbs can have a more negative slant, indicating that the point being introduced by the quotation is open to debate and that others (including the writer) might disagree with it. If the writer of the passage above had said, for instance, that Bridges *unreasonably contends* or that he *fantasizes*, these signal verbs would carry quite different connotations from those associated with *argues*.

In some cases, a signal verb may require more complex phrasing to get the writer's full meaning across:

> Bridges recognizes the dangers of changes in work yet refuses to be overcome by them: "The real issue is not how to stop the change but how to provide the necessary knowledge and skills to equip people to operate successfully in this New World" (229).

As these examples illustrate, the signal verb is important because it allows you to characterize the author's or source's viewpoint as well as your own—so choose these verbs with care.

David H. Freedman quotes scientists and biology experts in his article "Are Engineered Foods Evil?" Explore how he uses signal verbs. Where might he incorporate more of them?

LINK TO P. 630

Some Frequently Used Signal Verbs

acknowledges	claims	emphasizes	remarks
admits	concludes	expresses	replies
advises	concurs	hypothesizes	reports

agrees	confirms	interprets	responds
allows	criticizes	lists	reveals
argues	declares	objects	states
asserts	disagrees	observes	suggests
believes	discusses	offers	thinks
charges	disputes	opposes	writes

Note that in APA style, these signal verbs should be in a past tense: *Blau (1992) claimed*; *Clark (2001) has concluded*.

Using Sources to Clarify and Support Your Own Argument

The best academic arguments often have the flavor of a hearty but focused intellectual conversation. Scholars and scientists create this impression by handling research materials strategically and selectively. Here's how some college writers use sources to achieve their own specific goals within an academic argument.

Establish context. Taylor Pearson, whose essay "Why You Should Fear Your Toaster More Than Nuclear Power" appears in Chapter 8, sets the context for his argument in the first two sentences, in which he cites a newspaper source ("Japan Nuclear Disaster Tops Scale") as representative of "headlines everywhere" warning of nuclear crises and the danger of existing nuclear plants. Assuming that these sentences will remind readers of other warnings and hence indicate that this is a highly fraught argument with high emotional stakes, Pearson connects those fears to his own argument by shifting, in the third sentence, into a direct rebuttal of the sources (such fears are "nothing more than media sensationalism") before stating his thesis: "We need nuclear energy. It's clean, it's efficient, it's economic, and it's probably the only thing that will enable us to quickly phase out fossil fuels." It will be up to Pearson in the rest of the essay to explain how, even in a context of public fear, his thesis is defensible:

> For the past month or so, headlines everywhere have been warning us of the horrible crises caused by the damaged Japanese nuclear reactors. Titles like "Japan Nuclear Disaster Tops Scale" have fueled a new wave of protests against anything nuclear—namely, the construction of new nuclear plants or even the continued operation of existing plants. However, all this reignited fear of nuclear energy is nothing more than media sensationalism. We need nuclear energy. It's clean, it's efficient, it's economic, and it's probably the only thing that will enable us to quickly phase out fossil fuels.

When using Web sources such as blogs, take special care to check authors' backgrounds and credentials. © Roz Chast/The New Yorker Collection/The Cartoon Bank

Review the literature on a subject. You will often need to tell readers what authorities have already written about your topic, thus connecting them to your own argument. So, in a paper on the effectiveness of peer editing, Susan Wilcox does a very brief "review of the literature" on her subject, pointing to three authorities who support using the method in writing courses. She quotes from the authors and also puts some of their ideas in her own words:

> Bostock cites one advantage of peer review as "giving a sense of ownership of the assessment process" (1). Topping expands this view, stating that "peer assessment also involves increased time on task: thinking, comparing, contrasting, and communicating" (254). The extra time spent thinking over the assignment, especially in terms of helping someone else, can draw in the reviewer and lend greater importance to taking the process seriously, especially since the reviewer knows that the classmate is relying on his advice. This also adds an extra layer of accountability for the student; his hard work—or lack thereof—will be seen by peers, not just the instructor. Cassidy notes, "[S]tudents work harder with the knowledge that they will be assessed by their

> peers" (509): perhaps the knowledge that peer review is coming leads to a better-quality draft to begin with.

The paragraph is straightforward and useful, giving readers an efficient overview of the subject. If they want more information, they can find it by consulting Wilcox's works cited page.

Introduce a term or define a concept. Quite often in an academic argument, you may need to define a term or explain a concept. Relying on a source may make your job easier *and* enhance your credibility. That is what Laura Pena achieves in the following paragraph, drawing upon two authorities to explain what teachers mean by a "rubric" when it comes to grading student work:

> To understand the controversy surrounding rubrics, it is best to know what a rubric is. According to Heidi Andrade, a professor at SUNY-Albany, a rubric can be defined as "a document that lists criteria and describes varying levels of quality, from excellent to poor, for a specific assignment" ("Self-Assessment" 61). Traditionally, rubrics have been used primarily as grading and evaluation tools (Kohn 12), meaning that a rubric was not used until after students handed their papers in to their teacher. The teacher would then use a rubric to evaluate the students' papers according to the criteria listed on the rubric.

Note that the first source provides the core definition while information from the second offers a detail important to understanding when and how rubrics are used—a major issue in Pena's paper. Her selection of sources here serves her thesis while also providing readers with necessary information.

Present technical material. Sources can be especially helpful, too, when material becomes technical or difficult to understand. Writing on your own, you might lack the confidence to handle the complexities of some subjects. While you should challenge yourself to learn a subject well enough to explain it in your own words, there will be times when a quotation from an expert serves both you and your readers. Here is Natalie San Luis dealing with some of the technical differences between mainstream and Black English:

> The grammatical rules of mainstream English are more concrete than those of Black English; high school students can't check out an MLA handbook on Ebonics from their school library. As with all dialects, though, there are certain characteristics of the language that most Black English scholars agree upon.

> According to Samy Alim, author of *Roc the Mic Right,* these characteristics are the "[h]abitual *be* [which] indicates actions that are continuing or ongoing. . . . Copula absence. . . . Stressed *been*. . . . *Gon* [indicating] the future tense. . . . *They* for possessive. . . . Postvocalic *-r*. . . . [and] *Ank* and *ang* for 'ink' and 'ing'" (115). Other scholars have identified "[a]bsence of third-person singular present-tense *s*. . . . Absence of possessive *'s*," repetition of pronouns, and double negatives (Rickford 111-24).

Note that using ellipses enables San Luis to cover a great deal of ground. Readers not familiar with linguistic terms may have trouble following the quotation, but remember that academic arguments often address audiences comfortable with some degree of complexity.

Develop or support a claim. Even academic audiences expect to be convinced, and one of the most important strategies for a writer is to use sources to amplify or support a claim.

Here is Manasi Deshpande, whose proposal argument appears in Chapter 12 (pp. 295–302), making the following claim: "Although the University has made a concerted and continuing effort to improve access, students and faculty with physical disabilities still suffer from discriminatory hardship, unequal opportunity to succeed, and lack of independence." See how she weaves sources together in the following paragraph to help support that claim:

> The current state of campus accessibility leaves substantial room for improvement. There are approximately 150 academic and administrative buildings on campus (Grant). Eduardo Gardea, intern architect at the Physical Plant, estimates that only about nineteen buildings comply fully with the Americans with Disabilities Act (ADA). According to Penny Seay, PhD, director of the Center for Disability Studies at UT Austin, the ADA in theory "requires every building on campus to be accessible."

Highlight differences or counterarguments. The sources you encounter in developing a project won't always agree with each other or you. In academic arguments, you don't want to hide such differences, but instead point them out honestly and let readers make judgments based upon actual claims. Here is a paragraph in which Laura Pena again presents two views on the use of rubrics as grading tools:

> Some naysayers, such as Alfie Kohn, assert that "any form of assessment that encourages students to keep asking, 'How am I doing?' is likely to change how they look at themselves and what they're learning, usually for the worse."

> Kohn cites a study that found that students who pay too much attention to the quality of their performance are more likely to chalk up the outcome of an assignment to factors beyond their control, such as innate ability, and are also more likely to give up quickly in the face of a difficult task (14). However, Ross and Rolheiser have found that when students are taught how to properly implement self-assessment tools in the writing process, they are more likely to put more effort and persistence into completing a difficult assignment and may develop higher self-confidence in their writing ability (sec. 2). Building self-confidence in elementary-age writers can be extremely helpful when they tackle more complicated writing endeavors in the future.

In describing Kohn as a "naysayer," Pena may tip her hand and lose some degree of objectivity. But her thesis has already signaled her support for rubrics as a grading tool, so academic readers will probably not find the connotations of the term inappropriate.

These examples suggest only a few of the ways that sources, either summarized or quoted directly, can be incorporated into an academic argument to support or enhance a writer's goals. Like these writers, you should think of sources as your copartners in developing and expressing ideas. But you are still in charge

Avoiding "Patchwriting"

When using sources in an argument, writers —and especially those new to research-based writing— may be tempted to do what Professor Rebecca Moore Howard terms "**patchwriting**": stitching together material from Web or other sources without properly paraphrasing or summarizing and with little or no documentation. Here, for example, is a patchwork paragraph about the dangers wind turbines pose to wildlife:

> Scientists are discovering that technology with low carbon impact does not mean low environmental or social impacts. That is the case especially with wind turbines, whose long, massive fiberglass blades have been chopping up tens of thousands of birds that fly into them, including golden eagles, red-tailed hawks, burrowing owls, and other raptors in California. Turbines are also killing bats in great numbers. The 420 wind turbines now in use across Pennsylvania killed more than 10,000 bats last year—mostly in the late summer months, according to the State Game Commission. That's an average of 25 bats per turbine per year, and the Nature Conservancy predicts as many as 2,900 turbines will be set up across the state by 2030. It's not the spinning blades that kill the bats; instead, their lungs effectively blow up from the

> rapid pressure drop that occurs as air flows over the turbine blades. But there's hope we may figure out solutions to these problems because, since we haven't had too many wind turbines heretofore in the country, we are learning how to manage this new technology as we go.

The paragraph reads well and is full of details. But it would be considered plagiarized (see Chapter 21) because it fails to identify its sources and because most of the material has simply been lifted directly from the Web. How much is actually copied? We've highlighted the borrowed material:

> Scientists are discovering that technology with low carbon impact does not mean low environmental or social impacts. That is the case especially with wind turbines, whose long, massive fiberglass blades have been chopping up tens of thousands of birds that fly into them, including golden eagles, red-tailed hawks, burrowing owls, and other raptors in California. Turbines are also killing bats in great numbers. The 420 wind turbines now in use across Pennsylvania killed more than 10,000 bats last year—mostly in the late summer months, according to the State Game Commission. That's an average of 25 bats per turbine per year, and the Nature Conservancy predicts as many as 2,900 turbines will be set up across the state by 2030. It's not the spinning blades that kill the bats; instead, their lungs effectively blow up from the rapid pressure drop that occurs as air flows over the turbine blades. But there's hope we may figure out solutions to these problems because, since we haven't had too many wind turbines heretofore in the country, we are learning how to manage this new technology as we go.

But here's the point: an academic writer who has gone to the trouble of finding so much information will gain more credit and credibility just by properly identifying, paraphrasing, and quoting the sources used. The resulting paragraph is actually more impressive because it demonstrates how much reading and synthesizing the writer has actually done:

> Scientists like George Ledec of the World Bank are discovering that technology with low carbon impact "does not mean low environmental or social impacts" (Tracy). That is the case especially with wind turbines. Their massive blades spinning to create pollution-free electricity are also killing thousands of valuable birds of prey, including eagles, hawks, and owls in California (Rittier). Turbines are also killing bats in great numbers (Thibodeaux). The *Pittsburgh Post-Gazette* reports that 10,000 bats a year are killed by the 420 turbines currently in Pennsylvania. According to the state game commissioner, "That's an average of 25 bats per turbine per year, and the Nature Conservancy predicts as

many as 2,900 turbines will be set up across the state by 2030" (Schwartzel). It's not the spinning blades that kill the animals; instead, *DiscoveryNews* explains, "the bats' lungs effectively blow up from the rapid pressure drop that occurs as air flows over the turbine blades" (Marshall). But there's hope that scientists can develop turbines less dangerous to animals of all kinds. "We haven't had too many wind turbines heretofore in the country," David Cottingham of the Fish and Wildlife Service points out, "so we are learning about it as we go" (Tracy).

Works Cited

Marshall, Jessica. "Wind Turbines Kill Bats without Impact." *Discovery News,* 25 Aug. 2008, news.discovery.com/20111112-turbinebats/.

Rittier, John. "Wind Turbines Taking Toll on Birds of Prey." *USA Today,* 4 Jan. 2005, usatoday30.usatoday.com/news/nation/2005-01-04-windmills-usat_x.htm.

Schwartzel, Erich. "Pa. Wind Turbines Deadly to Bats, Costly to Farmers." *Post-Gazette.com*, 17 July 2011, www.post-gazette.com/business/businessnews/2011/07/17/Pa-wind-turbines-deadly-to-bats-costly-to-farmers/stories/201107170197.

Thibodeaux, Julie. "Bats Getting Caught in Texas Wind Turbines." *PegasusNews.com*, 9 Nov. 2011, www.pegasusnews.com/2011/11/09/bats-getting-caught-in-texas-wind-turbines/.

Tracy, Ryan. "Wildlife Slows Wind Power." *The Wall Street Journal,* 10 Dec. 2011, www.wsj.com/articles/SB10001424052970203501304577088593307132850.

RESPOND •

1. Select one of the essays from Chapters 8–12 or 17. Following the guidelines in this chapter, write a paraphrase of the essay that you might use subsequently in an academic argument. Be careful to describe the essay accurately and to note on what pages specific ideas or claims are located. The language of the paraphrase should be entirely your own—though you may include direct quotations of phrases, sentences, or longer passages you would likely use in a paper. Be sure these quotations are introduced and cited in your paraphrase: *Pearson claims that nuclear power is safe, even asserting that "your toaster is far more likely to kill you than any nuclear power plant" (175).* When you are done, trade your paraphrase with a partner to get feedback on its clarity and accuracy.

2. Summarize three readings or fairly lengthy passages from Parts 1–3 of this book, following the guidelines in this chapter. Open the item with a correct MLA or APA citation for the piece (see Chapter 22). Then provide the summary itself. Follow up with a one- or two-sentence evaluation of the work describing its potential value as a source in an academic argument. In effect, you will be preparing three items that might appear in an annotated bibliography. Here's an example:

   Pearson, Taylor. "Why You Should Fear Your Toaster More Than Nuclear Power." *Everything's an Argument*, by Andrea A. Lunsford and John J. Ruszkiewicz, 7th ed., Bedford/St. Martin's, 2016, pp. 174-79. Argues that since the dangers of nuclear power (death, radiation, waste) are actually less than those of energy sources we rely on today, nuclear plants represent the only practical way to generate the power we need and still reduce greenhouse gases. The journalistic piece provides many interesting facts about nuclear energy, but is informally documented and so does not identify its sources in detail or include a bibliography.

3. Working with a partner, agree upon an essay that you will both read from Chapters 8–12 or 17, examining it as a potential source for a research argument. As you read it, choose about a half-dozen words, phrases, or short passages that you would likely quote if you used the essay in a paper and attach a frame or signal phrase to each quotation. Then compare the passages you selected to quote with those your partner culled from the same essay. How do your choices of quoted material create an image or ethos for the original author that differs from the one your partner has created? How do the signal phrases shape a reader's sense of the author's position? Which set of quotations best represents the author's argument? Why?

4. Select one of the essays from Chapters 8–12 or 17 to examine the different ways an author uses source materials to support claims. Begin by highlighting the signal phrases you find attached to borrowed ideas or direct quotations. How well do they introduce or frame this material? Then categorize the various ways the author actually uses particular sources. For example, look for sources that provide context for the topic, review the scholarly literature, define key concepts or terms, explain technical details, furnish evidence, or lay out contrary opinions. When you are done, write a paragraph assessing the author's handling of sources in the piece. Are the borrowed materials integrated well with the author's own thoughts? Do the sources represent an effective synthesis of ideas?

21
Plagiarism and Academic Integrity

Left to right: © imagineasia/age fotostock; Jutta Kuss/Getty Images; Dimitri Otis/Getty Images

In many ways, "nothing new under the sun" is more than just a cliché. Most of what you think or write is built on what you've previously read or experienced or learned from others. Luckily, you'll seldom be called on to list every influence on your life. But you do have responsibilities in school and professional situations to acknowledge any intellectual property you've made use of when you create arguments of your own. If you don't, you may be accused of **plagiarism**—claiming as your own the words, research, or creative work of others.

What is intellectual property? It's complicated. But, for academic arguments in Western culture, it is the *expression* of ideas you find in works produced by others that you then use to advance and support your own claims. You have to document not only when you use or reproduce someone's exact words, images, music, or other creations (in whole or in part), but also when you borrow the framework others use to put ideas together in original or creative ways. Needless to say, intellectual property rights have always been contentious, but never more so than today, when new media make it remarkably easy to duplicate and share

The FBI has warned consumers for decades about the penalties for violating copyright. Your school no doubt has its own policies for handling such violations, including plagiarism. www.cartoonsbysheila.com

all sorts of materials. Accustomed to uploading and downloading files, cutting and pasting passages, you may be comfortable working with texts day-to-day in ways that are considered inappropriate, or even dishonest, in school. You may, for example, have patched together sources without putting them in your own words or documenting them fully, practices that will often be seen as plagiarism (see p. 451).

So it is essential that you read and understand any policies on academic integrity that your school has set down. In particular, pay attention to how those policies define, prosecute, and punish cheating, plagiarism, and collusion. Some institutions recognize a difference between intentional and unintentional plagiarism, but you don't want the honesty of anything you write to be questioned. You need to learn the rules and understand that the penalties for plagiarism are severe not only for students but for professional writers as well.

But don't panic! Many student writers today are so confused or worried about plagiarism that they shy away from using sources—or end up with a citation for almost every sentence in an essay. There's no reason to go to such extremes. As a conscientious researcher and writer, you simply need to give your best effort in letting readers know what sources you have used. Being careful in such matters will have a big payoff: when you give full credit to your sources, you enhance your ethos in academic arguments—which is why "Academic Integrity" appears in this chapter's title. Audiences will applaud you for saying thanks to those who've helped you. Crediting your sources also proves that you have done your homework: you demonstrate that you understand what others have written about the topic and encourage others to join the intellectual conversation. Finally, citing sources reminds you to think critically about how to use the evidence you've collected. Is it timely and reliable? Have you referenced authorities in a biased or overly selective way? Have you double-checked all quotations and paraphrases? Thinking through such questions helps to guarantee the integrity of your academic work.

DOONESBURY **BY GARRY TRUDEAU**

A Doonesbury cartoon on intellectual property pokes fun at best-selling historian and presidential biographer Stephen Ambrose, who was found to have plagiarized passages from at least twelve authors in at least six of his books—and in his doctoral dissertation.

Proper acknowledgment of sources is crucial in academic writing. Check out danah boyd and Kate Crawford's extensive references for an example of how to do it right.

LINK TO P. 754

Giving Credit

The basic principles for documenting materials are relatively simple. Give credit to all source materials you borrow by following these three steps: (1) placing quotation marks around any words you quote directly, (2) citing your sources according to the documentation style you're using, and (3) identifying all the sources you have cited in a list of references or works cited. Materials to be cited in an academic argument include all of the following:

- direct quotations
- facts that are not widely known
- arguable statements
- judgments, opinions, and claims that have been made by others
- images, statistics, charts, tables, graphs, or other illustrations that appear in any source
- collaboration — that is, the help provided by friends, colleagues, instructors, supervisors, or others

However, three important types of evidence or source material do not need to be acknowledged or documented. They are the following:

1. Common knowledge, which is a specific piece of information most readers in your intended audience will know (that Barack Obama won the 2012 presidential election, for instance)
2. Facts available from a wide variety of sources (that the Japanese bombed Pearl Harbor on December 7, 1941, for example). If, for instance, you search for a piece of information and find the same information on hundreds of different reputable Web sites, you can be pretty sure it is common knowledge.
3. Your own findings from field research (observations, interviews, experiments, or surveys you have conducted), which should be clearly presented as your own

For the actual forms to use when documenting sources, see Chapter 22.

Of course, the devil is in the details. For instance, you may be accused of plagiarism in situations like the following:

- if you don't indicate clearly the source of an idea you obviously didn't come up with on your own

- if you use a paraphrase that's too close to the original wording or sentence structure of your source material (*even* if you cite the source)
- if you leave out the parenthetical in-text reference for a quotation (*even* if you include the quotation marks themselves)

And the accusation can be made even if you didn't intend to plagiarize.

But what about all the sampling and mashups you see all the time online and in popular culture? And don't some artistic and scholarly works come close to being "mashups"? Yes and no. It's certainly fair to say, for example, that Shakespeare's plays "mash up" a lot of material from *Holinshed's Chronicles*, which he used without acknowledgment. But it's also true that Shakespeare's works are "transformative"—that is, they are made new by Shakespeare's art. Current copyright law protects such works that qualify as transformative and exempts them from copyright violations. But the issues swirling around the debate over sampling, mashups, and other uses of prior materials are far from clear, and far from over. Perhaps Jeff Shaw (in a posting that asks, "Is Mashup Music Protected by Fair Use?") sums up the current situation best:

> **Lest we forget, the purpose of copyright law is to help content creators and to enhance creative expression. Fair use is an important step toward those ends, and further legislative work could solidify the step forward that fair use represents.**
>
> **—Jeff Shaw, "Is Mashup Music Protected by Fair Use?"**

Getting Permission for and Using Copyrighted Internet Sources

When you gather information from Internet sources and use it in your own work, it's subject to the same rules that govern information gathered from other types of sources.

A growing number of online works, including books, photographs, music, and video, are published under the Creative Commons license, which often eliminates the need to request permission. These works—marked with a Creative Commons license—are made available to the public under this alternative to copyright, which grants permission to reuse or remix work under certain terms if credit is given to the work's creator.

Even if the material does not include a copyright notice or symbol ("© 2016 by Andrea A. Lunsford and John J. Ruszkiewicz," for example),

it's likely to be protected by copyright laws, and you may need to request permission to use part or all of it. "Fair use" legal precedents allow writers to quote brief passages from published works without permission from the copyright holder if the use is for educational or personal, noncommercial reasons and if full credit is given to the source. For blog postings or any serious professional uses (especially online), however, you should ask permission of the copyright holder before you include any of his/her ideas, text, or images in your own argument.

If you do need to make a request for permission, here is an example:

From: sanchez.32@stanford.edu
To: litman@mindspring.com
CC: lunsford.2@stanford.edu
Subject: Request for permission

Dear Professor Litman:

I am writing to request permission to quote from your essay "Copyright, Owners' Rights and Users' Privileges on the Internet: Implied Licenses, Caching, Linking, Fair Use, and Sign-on Licenses." I want to quote some of your work as part of an article I am writing for the *Stanford Daily* to explain the complex debates over ownership on the Internet and to argue that students at my school should be participating in these debates. I will give full credit to you and will cite the URL where I first found your work (msen.com/~litman/dayton.htm).

Thank you very much for considering my request.

Raul Sanchez

Acknowledging Your Sources Accurately and Appropriately

While artists, lawyers, and institutions like the film and music industries sort out fair use laws, the bottom line in your academic work is clear: document sources accurately and fully and do not be careless about this very important procedure.

Here, for example, is the first paragraph from a print essay by Russell Platt published in the *Nation*:

> **Classical music in America, we are frequently told, is in its death throes: its orchestras bled dry by expensive guest soloists and greedy musicians' unions, its media presence shrinking, its prestige diminished, its educational role ignored, its big record labels dying out or merging into faceless corporate entities. We seem to have too many well-trained musicians in need of work, too many good composers going without commissions, too many concerts to offer an already satiated public.**
>
> **—Russell Platt, "New World Symphony"**

To cite this passage correctly in MLA documentation style, you could quote directly from it, using both quotation marks and some form of note identifying the author or source. Either of the following versions would be acceptable:

> Russell Platt has doubts about claims that classical music is "in its death throes: its orchestras bled dry by expensive guest soloists and greedy musicians unions" ("New World").

> But is classical music in the United States really "in its death throes," as some critics of the music scene suggest (Platt)?

You might also paraphrase Platt's paragraph, putting his ideas entirely in your own words but still giving him due credit by ending your remarks with a simple in-text note:

> A familiar story told by critics is that classical music faces a bleak future in the United States, with grasping soloists and unions bankrupting orchestras and classical works vanishing from radio and television, school curricula, and the labels of recording conglomerates. The public may not be willing to support all the talented musicians and composers we have today (Platt).

All of these sentences with citations would be keyed to a works cited entry at the end of the paper that would look like the following in MLA style:

> Platt, Russell. "New World Symphony." *The Nation*, 3 Oct. 2005, www.thenation.com/article/new-world-symphony/.

How might a citation go wrong? As we indicated, omitting either the quotation marks around a borrowed passage or an acknowledgment of the source is grounds for complaint. Neither of the following sentences provides enough information for a correct citation:

> But is classical music in the United States really in its death throes, as some critics of the music scene suggest, with its prestige diminished, its educational role ignored, and its big record labels dying (Platt)?
>
> But is classical music in the United States really in "its death throes," as some critics of the music scene suggest, with "its prestige diminished, its educational role ignored, [and] its big record labels dying"?

Just as faulty is a paraphrase such as the following, which borrows the words or ideas of the source too closely. It represents plagiarism, despite the fact that it identifies the source from which almost all the ideas—and a good many words—are borrowed:

> In "New World Symphony," Russell Platt observes that classical music is thought by many to be in bad shape in America. Its orchestras are being sucked dry by costly guest artists and insatiable unionized musicians, while its place on TV and radio is shrinking. The problem may be that we have too many well-trained musicians who need employment, too many good composers going without jobs, too many concerts for a public that prefers *The Real Housewives of Atlanta*.

Even the fresh idea not taken from Platt at the end of the paragraph doesn't alter the fact that the paraphrase is mostly a mix of Platt's original words, lightly stirred.

Acknowledging Collaboration

Writers generally acknowledge all participants in collaborative projects at the beginning of the presentation, report, or essay. In print texts, the acknowledgment is often placed in a footnote or brief prefatory note.

The eighth edition of the *MLA Handbook* (2016) calls attention to the shifting landscape of collaborative work, noting that:

> **Today academic work can take many forms other than the research paper. Scholars produce presentations, videos, and interactive Web projects, among other kinds of work...but the aims will remain the same: providing the information that enables a curious reader, viewer, or other user to track down your sources and giving credit to those whose work influenced yours.**

RESPOND.

1. Define *plagiarism* in your own terms, making your definition as clear and explicit as possible. Then compare your definition with those of two or three other classmates, and write a brief report on the similarities and differences you noted in the definitions. You might research terms such as *plagiarism*, *academic honesty*, and *academic integrity* on the Web. Also be certain to check how your own school defines the words.
2. Spend fifteen or twenty minutes jotting down your ideas about intellectual property and plagiarism. Where do you stand, for example, on the issue of music file sharing? On downloading movies free of charge? Do you think these forms of intellectual property should be protected under copyright law? How do you define your own intellectual property, and in what ways and under what conditions are you willing to share it? Finally, come up with your own definition of *academic integrity*.
3. Not everyone agrees that intellectual material is property that should be protected. The slogan "information wants to be free" has been showing up in popular magazines and on the Internet for a long time, often with a call to readers to take action against protection such as data encryption and further extension of copyright.

   Using a Web search engine, look for pages where the phrase "free information" appears. Find several sites that make arguments in favor of free information, and analyze them in terms of their rhetorical appeals. What claims do the authors make? How do they appeal to their audience? What's the site's ethos, and how is it created? After you've read some arguments in favor of free information, return to this chapter's arguments about intellectual property. Which arguments do you find most persuasive? Why?
4. Although this book is concerned principally with ideas and their written expression, other forms of intellectual property are also legally

protected. For example, scientific and technological developments are protectable under patent law, which differs in some significant ways from copyright law.

Find the standards for protection under U.S. copyright law and U.S. patent law. You might begin by visiting the U.S. copyright Web site (copyright.gov). Then imagine that you're the president of a small high-tech corporation and are trying to inform your employees of the legal protections available to them and their work. Write a paragraph or two explaining the differences between copyright and patent, and suggest a policy that balances employees' rights to intellectual property with the business's needs to develop new products.

22
Documenting Sources

Left to right: Seregram/Shutterstock; © Zero Creatives/Image/age fotostock; Iculig/Shutterstock

What does documenting sources have to do with argument? First, the sources that a writer chooses form part of any argument, showing that he/she has done some research, knows what others have said about the topic, and understands how to use these items as support for a claim. Similarly, the list of works cited or references makes a statement, saying, "Look at how thoroughly this essay has been researched" or "Note how up-to-date I am!"

Writers working in digital spaces sometimes simply add hotlinks so that their readers can find their sources. If you are writing a multimodal essay that will appear on the Web, such links will be appreciated. But for now, college assignments generally call for full documentation rather than simply a link. You'll find the information you need to create in-text citations and works cited/references lists in this chapter.

Documentation styles vary from discipline to discipline, with one format favored in the social sciences and another in the natural sciences, for example. Your instructor will probably assign a documentation style for you to follow. If not, you can use one of the two covered in this chapter. But note that even the choice of documentation style makes an argument in a subtle way. You'll note in the instructions that follow, for example, that the Modern Language Association (MLA) style requires putting the date of publication of a print source at or near the end of a works cited list entry, whereas the American Psychological Association (APA) style places that date near the beginning of a references list citation. Such positioning suggests that in MLA style, the author and title are of greater importance than the date for humanities scholars, while APA puts a priority on the date—and timeliness—of sources. Pay attention to such fine points of documentation style, always asking what these choices suggest about the values of scholars and researchers who use a particular system of documentation.

MLA Style

Widely used in the humanities, MLA style is fully described in the *MLA Handbook* (8th edition, 2016). In this discussion, we provide guidelines drawn from the *MLA Handbook* for in-text citations, notes, and entries in the list of works cited.

In-Text Citations

MLA style calls for in-text citations in the body of an argument to document sources of quotations, paraphrases, summaries, and so on. For in-text citations, use a signal phrase to introduce the material, often with the author's name (*As Geneva Smitherman explains, . . .*). Keep an in-text citation short, but include enough information for readers to locate the source in the list of works cited. Place the parenthetical citation as near to the relevant material as possible without disrupting the flow of the sentence, as in the following examples.

1. Author Named in a Signal Phrase

Ordinarily, use the author's name in a signal phrase to introduce the material, and cite the page number(s) in parentheses.

> Ravitch chronicles how the focus in education reform has shifted toward privatizing school management rather than toward improving curriculum, teacher training, or funding (36).

2. Author Named in Parentheses

When you don't mention the author in a signal phrase, include the author's last name before the page number(s) in the parentheses.

> Oil from shale in the western states, if it could be extracted, would be equivalent to six hundred billion barrels, more than all the crude so far produced in the world (McPhee 413).

3. Two Authors

Use all authors' last names.

> Gortner and Nicolson maintain that "opinion leaders" influence other people in an organization because they are respected, not because they hold high positions (175).

4. Three or More Authors

When there are three or more authors, brevity (and the MLA) suggests you use the first author's name with *et al.* (in regular type, not italicized).

> Similarly, as Goldberger et al. note, their new book builds on their collaborative experiences to inform their description of how women develop cognitively (xii).

5. Organization as Author

Give the full name of a corporate author if it's brief or a shortened form if it's long.

> Many global economists assert that the term "developing countries" is no longer a useful designation, as it ignores such countries' rapid economic growth (Gates Foundation 112).

6. Unknown Author

Use the full title of the work if it's brief or a shortened form if it's long.

> "Hype," by one analysis, is "an artificially engendered atmosphere of hysteria" ("Today's Marketplace" 51).

7. Author of Two or More Works

When you use two or more works by the same author, include the title of the work or a shortened version of it in the citation.

> Gardner presents readers with their own silliness through his description of a "pointless, ridiculous monster, crouched in the shadows, stinking of dead men, murdered children, and martyred cows" (*Grendel* 2).

8. Authors with the Same Last Name

When you use works by two or more authors with the same last name, include each author's first initial in the in-text citation.

> Public health officials agree that the potential environmental risk caused by indoor residual spraying is far lower than the potential risk of death caused by malaria-carrying mosquitoes (S. Dillon 76).

9. Multivolume Work

Note the volume number first and then the page number(s), with a colon and one space between them.

> Aristotle's "On Plants" is now available in a new translation edited by Barnes (2: 1252).

10. Literary Work

Because literary works are often available in many different editions, you need to include enough information for readers to locate the passage in any edition. For a prose work such as a novel or play, first cite the page number from the edition you used, followed by a semicolon; then indicate the part or chapter number (114; ch. 3) or act or scene in a play (42; sc. 2).

> In Ben Jonson's *Volpone,* the miserly title character addresses his treasure as "dear saint" and "the best of things" (1447; act 1).

For a poem, cite the stanza and line numbers. If the poem has only line numbers, use the word *line(s)* in the first reference (lines 33–34) and the number(s) alone in subsequent references.

> On dying, Whitman speculates, "All that goes onward and outward, nothing collapses, / And to die is different from what any one supposed, and luckier" (6.129-30).

For a verse play, omit the page number, and give only the act, scene, and line numbers, separated by periods.

> Before he takes his own life, Othello says he is "one that loved not wisely but too well" (5.2.348).

> As *Macbeth* begins, the witches greet Banquo as "Lesser than Macbeth, and greater" (1.3.65).

11. Works in an Anthology

For an essay, short story, or other short work within an anthology, use the name of the author of the work, not the editor of the anthology; but use the page number(s) from the anthology.

> In the end, if the black artist accepts any duties at all, that duty is to express the beauty of blackness (Hughes 1271).

12. Sacred Text

To cite a sacred text, such as the Qur'an or the Bible, give the title of the edition you used, the book, and the chapter and verse (or their equivalent), separated by a period. In your text, spell out the names of books. In a parenthetical reference, use an abbreviation for books with names of five or more letters (for example, *Gen.* for Genesis).

> He ignored the admonition "Pride goes before destruction, and a haughty spirit before a fall" (*New Oxford Annotated Bible*, Prov. 16.18).

13. Indirect Source

Use the abbreviation *qtd. in* to indicate that what you're quoting or paraphrasing is quoted (as part of a conversation, interview, letter, or excerpt) in the source you're using.

> As Catherine Belsey states, "to speak is to have access to the language which defines, delimits and locates power" (qtd. in Bartels 453).

14. Two or More Sources in the Same Citation

Separate the information for each source with a semicolon.

> Adefunmi was able to patch up the subsequent holes left in worship by substituting various Yoruba, Dahomean, or Fon customs made available to him through research (Brandon 115-17; Hunt 27).

15. Entire Work or One-Page Article

Include the citation in the text without any page numbers or parentheses.

> Kazuo Ishiguro's dystopian novel *Never Let Me Go* explores questions of identity and authenticity.

16. Nonprint or Electronic Source

Give enough information in a signal phrase or parenthetical citation for readers to locate the source in the list of works cited. Usually give the author or title under which you list the source. If the work isn't numbered by page but has numbered sections, parts, or paragraphs, include the name and number(s) of the section(s) you're citing. (For paragraphs, use the abbreviation *par.* or *pars.*; for section, use *sec.*; for part, use *pt.*)

> In his film version of *Hamlet*, Zeffirelli highlights the sexual tension between the prince and his mother.
>
> Zora Neale Hurston is one of the great anthropologists of the twentieth century, according to Kip Hinton (par. 2).
>
> Describing children's language acquisition, Pinker explains that "what's innate about language is just a way of paying attention to parental speech" (qtd. in Johnson, sec. 1).

17. Visual Included in the Text

Number all figures (photos, drawings, cartoons, maps, graphs, and charts) and tables separately.

> This trend is illustrated in a chart distributed by the College Board as part of its 2014 analysis of aggregate SAT data (see fig. 1).

Include a caption with enough information about the source to direct readers to the works cited entry. (For an example of an image that a student created, see the sample page from an MLA-style essay on p. 485 in this chapter.)

Explanatory and Bibliographic Notes

We recommend using explanatory notes for information or commentary that doesn't readily fit into your text but is needed for clarification, further explanation, or justification. In addition, bibliographic notes will allow you to cite several sources for one point and to offer thanks to, information about, or evaluation of a source. Use a superscript number in your text at the end of a sentence to refer readers to the notes, which usually appear as endnotes (with the heading *Notes*, not underlined or italicized) on a separate page before the list of works cited. Indent the first line of each note five spaces, and double-space all entries.

Text with Superscript Indicating a Note

> Stewart emphasizes the existence of social contacts in Hawthorne's life so that the audience will accept a different Hawthorne, one more attuned to modern times than the figure in Woodberry.[3]

Note

[3] Woodberry does, however, show that Hawthorne was often unsociable. He emphasizes the seclusion of Hawthorne's mother, who separated herself from her family after the death of her husband, often even taking meals alone (28). Woodberry seems to imply that Mrs. Hawthorne's isolation rubbed off on her son.

List of Works Cited

A list of works cited is an alphabetical listing of the sources you cite in your essay. The list appears on a separate page at the end of your argument, after any notes, with the heading *Works Cited* centered an inch from the top of the page; don't underline or italicize it or enclose it in quotation marks. Double-space between the heading and the first entry, and double-space the entire list. (If you're asked to list everything you've read as background—not just the sources you cite—call the list *Works Consulted*.) The first line of each entry should align on the left; subsequent lines indent one-half inch or five spaces. See p. 486 for a sample works cited page.

Print Books

The basic information for a book includes four elements:

- the author's name, last name first (for a book with multiple authors, only the first author's name is inverted)
- the title and subtitle, italicized
- the publication information, including the publisher's name (such as Harvard UP) followed by a comma, and the publication date

1. One Author

Larsen, Erik. *Dead Wake: The Last Crossing of the* Lusitania. Crown Publishers, 2015.

2. Two or More Authors

Jacobson, Sid, and Ernie Colón. *The 9/11 Report: A Graphic Adaptation*. Farrar, Straus, and Giroux, 2006.

3. Organization as Author

American Horticultural Society. *The Fully Illustrated Plant-by-Plant Manual of Practical Techniques*. DK, 1999.

4. Unknown Author

National Geographic Atlas of the World. National Geographic, 2004.

5. Two or More Books by the Same Author

List the works alphabetically by title. Use three hyphens for the author's name for the second and subsequent works by that author.

Lorde, Audre. *A Burst of Light*. Firebrand Books, 1988.

---. *Sister Outsider*. Crossings Press, 1984.

6. Editor

Rorty, Amelie Oksenberg, editor. *Essays on Aristotle's Poetics*. Princeton UP, 1992.

7. Author and Editor

Shakespeare, William. *The Tempest*. Edited by Frank Kermode, Routledge, 1994.

8. Selection in an Anthology or Chapter in an Edited Book

List the author(s) of the selection or chapter; its title; the title of the book in which the selection or chapter appears; *Ed.* and the name(s) of the editor(s); the publication information; and the inclusive page numbers of the selection or chapter.

Brown, Paul. "'This thing of darkness I acknowledge mine': *The Tempest* and the Discourse of Colonialism." *Political Shakespeare: Essays in Cultural Materialism*, edited by Jonathan Dollimore and Alan Sinfield, Cornell UP, 1985, pp. 48-71.

9. Two or More Works from the Same Anthology

Include the anthology itself in the list of works cited.

Gates, Henry Louis, Jr., and Nellie McKay, editors. *The Norton Anthology of African American Literature*, Norton, 1997.

Then list each selection separately by its author and title, followed by a cross-reference to the anthology.

Karenga, Maulana. "Black Art: Mute Matter Given Force and Function." Gates and McKay, pp. 1973-77.

Neal, Larry. "The Black Arts Movement." Gates and McKay, pp. 1960-72.

10. Translation

Hietamies, Laila. *Red Moon over White Sea*. Translated by Borje Vahamaki, Aspasia Books, 2000.

11. Edition Other Than the First

Lunsford, Andrea A., et al. *Everything's an Argument with Readings*. 7th ed., Bedford/St. Martin's, 2016.

12. Graphic Narrative

If the words and images are created by the same person, cite a graphic narrative just as you would a book (see item 1 on p. 472).

Bechdel, Alison. *Are You My Mother?* Houghton Mifflin Harcourt, 2012.

If the work is a collaboration, indicate the author or illustrator who is most important to your research before the title. Then list other contributors in order of their appearance on the title page. Label each person's contribution to the work.

Stavans, Ilan, writer. *Latino USA: A Cartoon History*. Illustrated by Lalo Arcaraz, Basic Books, 2000.

13. One Volume of a Multivolume Work

Byron, Lord George. *Byron's Letters and Journals*. Edited by Leslie A. Marchand, vol. 2, John Murray, 1973. 12 vols.

14. Two or More Volumes of a Multivolume Work

Byron, Lord George. *Byron's Letters and Journals*. Edited by Leslie A. Marchand, John Murray, 1973-82. 12 vols.

15. Preface, Foreword, Introduction, or Afterword

Dunham, Lena. Foreword. *The Liars' Club*, by Mary Karr, Penguin Classics, 2015, pp. xi-xiii.

16. Article in a Reference Work

Robinson, Lisa Clayton. "Harlem Writers Guild." *Africana: The Encyclopedia of the African and African American Experience,* 2nd ed., Oxford UP, 2005.

17. Book That Is Part of a Series

Include the title and number of the series after the publication information.

Moss, Beverly J. *A Community Text Arises*. Hampton, 2003. Language and Social Processes Ser. 8.

18. Republication

Trilling, Lionel. *The Liberal Imagination*. 1950. Introduction by Louis Menand, New York Review of Books, 2008.

19. Government Document

Canada, Minister of Aboriginal Affairs and Northern Development. *2015-16 Report on Plans and Priorities*. Minister of Public Works and Government Services Canada, 2015.

20. Pamphlet

The Legendary Sleepy Hollow Cemetery. Friends of Sleepy Hollow Cemetery, 2008.

21. Published Proceedings of a Conference

Meisner, Marx S., et al., editors. *Communication for the Commons: Revisiting Participation and Environment*. Proceedings of Twelfth Biennial Conference on Communication and the Environment, 6-11 June 2015, Swedish U of Agricultural Sciences, International Environmental Communication Association, 2015.

22. Title within a Title

Shanahan, Timothy. *Philosophy and* Blade Runner. Palgrave Macmillan, 2014.

Print Periodicals

The basic entry for a periodical includes three elements:

- the author's name, last name first, followed by a period
- the article title, in quotation marks, followed by a period

- the publication information, including the periodical title (italicized), the volume and issue numbers (if any, not italicized), the date of publication, and the page number(s), all followed by commas, with a period at the end of the page numbers

For works with multiple authors, only the first author's name is inverted. Note that the period following the article title goes inside the closing quotation mark.

23. Article in a Print Journal

Give the issue number, if available.

Matchie, Thomas. "Law versus Love in *The Round House*." *Midwest Quarterly*, vol. 56, no. 4, Summer 2015, pp. 353-64.

Fuqua, Amy. "'The Furrow of His Brow': Providence and Pragmatism in Toni Morrison's *Paradise*." *Midwest Quarterly*, vol. 54, no. 1, Autumn 2012, pp. 38-52.

24. Article That Skips Pages

Seabrook, John. "Renaissance Pears." *The New Yorker,* 5 Sept. 2005, pp. 102+.

25. Article in a Print Monthly Magazine

Kunzig, Robert. "The Will to Change." *National Geographic*, Nov. 2015, pp. 32-63.

26. Article in a Print Weekly Magazine

Grossman, Lev. "A Star Is Born." *Time*, 2 Nov. 2015, pp. 30-39.

27. Article in a Print Newspaper

Bray, Hiawatha. "As Toys Get Smarter, Privacy Issues Emerge." *The Boston Globe,* 10 Dec. 2015, p. C1.

28. Editorial or Letter to the Editor

Posner, Alan. "Colin Powell's Regret." *The New York Times,* 9 Sept. 2005, p. A20.

29. Unsigned Article

"Court Rejects the Sale of Medical Marijuana." *The New York Times,* 26 Feb. 1998, late ed., p. A21.

30. Review

Walton, James. "Noble, Embattled Souls." Review of *The Bone Clocks* and *Slade House*, by David Mitchell, *The New York Review of Books*, 3 Dec. 2015, pp. 55-58.

Digital Sources

Most of the following models are based on the MLA's guidelines for citing electronic sources in the *MLA Handbook* (8th edition, 2016), as well as on up-to-date information available at its Web site (mla.org). The MLA advocates the use of URLs but prefers a Digital Object Indicator (DOI) where available. A DOI is a unique number assigned to a selection, and does not change regardless of where the item is located online. The basic MLA entry for most electronic sources should include the following elements:

- name of the author, editor, or compiler
- title of the work, document, or posting
- publication information (volume, issue, year or date). List page numbers (or *n. pag.*, not italicized, if none are listed).
- name of database, italicized
- DOI or URL

31. Document from a Web Site

Begin with the author, if known, followed by the title of the work, title of the Web site, publisher or sponsor (if it is notably different from the title of the Web site), date of publication or last update, and the Digital Object Identifier or URL. If no publication or update date is available, please include a date of access at the end.

"Social and Historical Context: Vitality." *Arapesh Grammar and Digital Language Archive Project*, Institute for Advanced Technology in the Humanities, www.arapesh.org/socio_historical_context_vitality.php. Accessed 22 Mar. 2016.

32. Entire Web Site

Include the name of the person or group who created the site, if relevant; the title of the site, italicized; the publisher or sponsor of the site; the date of publication or last update; and the URL.

Railton, Stephen. *Mark Twain in His Times*. Stephen Railton / U of Virginia Library, 2012, twain.lib.virginia.edu/.

Halsall, Paul, editor. *Internet Modern History Sourcebook*. Fordham U, 4 Nov. 2011, legacy.fordham.edu/halsall/index.asp.

33. Course, Department, or Personal Web Site

For a course Web site, include the instructor's name; the title of the site, italicized; a description of the site (such as *Course home page*, *Department home page*, or *Home page*—not italicized); the sponsor of the site (academic department and institution); dates of the course or last update to the page; and the URL. Note that the MLA spells *home page* as two separate words. For an academic department, list the name of the department; a description; the academic institution; the date the page was last updated; and the URL.

Film Studies. Department home page. *Wayne State University, College of Liberal Arts and Sciences*, 2016, clas.wayne.edu/FilmStudies/.

Masiello, Regina. 355:101: Expository Writing. *Rutgers School of Arts and Sciences*, 2016, wp.rutgers.edu/courses/55-355101.

34. Online Book

Cite an online book as you would a print book. After the print publication information (if any), give the title of the Web site or database in which the book appears, italicized; and the DOI or URL.

Riis, Jacob A. *How the Other Half Lives: Studies among the Tenements of New York*. Edited by David Phillips, Scribner's, 1890. *The Authentic History Center*, www.authentichistory.com/1898-1913/2-progressivism/2-riis/.

Treat a poem, essay, or other short work within an online book as you would a part of a print book. After the print publication information (if any), give the title of the Web site or database, italicized; and the DOI or URL.

Milton, John. *Paradise Lost: Book I. Poetry Foundation*, 2014, www.poetryfoundation.org/poem/174987.

35. Article in a Journal on the Web

For an article in an online journal, cite the same information that you would for a print journal. Then add the DOI or URL.

Bryson, Devin. "The Rise of a New Senegalese Cultural Philosophy?" *African Studies Quarterly*, vol. 14, no. 3, Mar. 2014, pp. 33-56, asq.africa.ufl.edu/files/Volume-14-Issue-3-Bryson.pdf.

36. Article in a Magazine or Newspaper on the Web

For an article in an online magazine or newspaper, cite the author; the title of the article, in quotation marks; the name of the magazine or newspaper, italicized; the date of publication; and the URL of the page you accessed.

Leonard, Andrew. "The Surveillance State High School." *Salon*, 27 Nov. 2012, www.salon.com/2012/11/27/the_surveillance_state_high_school/.

Crowell, Maddy. "How Computers Are Getting Better at Detecting Liars." *The Christian Science Monitor*, 12 Dec. 2015, www.csmonitor.com/Science/Science-Notebook/2015/1212/How-computers-are-getting-better-at-detecting-liars.

37. Entry in a Web Reference Work

Cite the entry as you would an entry from a print reference work (see item 16). Follow with the name of the Web site, the date of publication, and the URL of the site you accessed.

Duranto, Amy M. "Finn Mac Cumhail." *Encyclopedia Mythica*, 17 Apr. 2011, www.pantheon.org/articles/f/finn_mac_cumhail.html.

38. Post or Comment on a Web Site

Begin with the author's name; the title of the posting, in quotation marks (if there is no title, use the description *Weblog post* or *Weblog comment*, not italicized); the name of the blog, italicized; the sponsor of the blog; the date of the most recent update; and the URL of the page you accessed.

mitchellfreedman. Comment on "*Cloud Atlas's* Theory of Everything," by Emily Eakin. *NYR Daily*, NYREV, 3 Nov. 2012, www.nybooks.com/daily/2012/11/02/ken-wilber-cloud-atlas/.

39. Entry in a Wiki

Since wikis are collectively edited, do not include an author. Treat a wiki as you would a work from a Web site (see item 31). Include the title of the entry; the name of the wiki, italicized; the date of the latest update; and the URL of the page you accessed.

House Music." *Wikipedia*, 16 Nov. 2015, en.wikipedia.org/wiki/House_music.

40. Posting on a Social Networking Site

To cite a posting on Facebook or another social networking site, include the writer's name, a description of the posting, the date of the posting, and the URL of the page you accessed.

Bedford English. "Stacey Cochran explores Reflective Writing in the classroom and as a writer: http://ow.ly/YkjVB." *Facebook*, 15 Feb. 2016, www.facebook.com/BedfordEnglish/posts/10153415001259607.

41. Email or Message on a Social Networking Site

Include the writer's name; the subject line, in quotation marks (for email); *Received by* (not italicized or in quotation marks) followed by the recipient's name; and the date of the message. You do not need to include the medium, but may if you are concerned there will be confusion.

Thornbrugh, Caitlin. "Coates Lecture." Received by Rita Anderson, 20 Oct. 2015.

42. Tweet

Include the writer's real name, if known, with the user name (if different) in parentheses. If you don't know the real name, give just the user name. Include the entire tweet, in quotation marks. Include the publisher (Twitter) in italics, follow by the date and time of the message and the URL.

Curiosity Rover. "Can you see me waving? How to spot #Mars in the night sky: https://youtu.be/hv8hVvJlcJQ." *Twitter*, 5 Nov. 2015, 11:00 a.m., twitter.com/marscuriosity/status/672859022911889408.

43. Work from an Online Database or a Subscription Service

For a work from an online database, list the author's name; the title of the work, in quotation marks; any print publication information; the name of the database, italicized; and the DOI or URL.

Goldsmith, Oliver. *The Vicar of Wakefield: A Tale*. Philadelphia, 1801. *America's Historical Imprints*, infoweb.newsbank.com.ezproxy.bpl.org/.

For a work from an online service to which your library subscribes, include the same information as for an online database. After the information about the work, give the name of the database, italicized; and the DOI or URL.

Coles, Kimberly Anne. "The Matter of Belief in John Donne's Holy Sonnets." *Renaissance Quarterly*, vol. 68, no. 3, Fall 2015, pp. 899-931. *JSTOR*, doi:10.1086/683855.

"The Road toward Peace." *The New York Times*, 15 Feb. 1945, p. 18. Editorial. *ProQuest Historical Newspapers: The New York Times*, search.proquest.com/hnpnewyorktimes.

44. Computer Software or Video Game

Include the title, italicized; the version number (if given); and publication information. If you are citing material downloaded from a Web site, include the title and version number (if given), but instead of publication information, add the publisher or sponsor of the Web site; the date of publication; and the URL.

Edgeworld. Atom Entertainment, 1 May 2012, www.kabam.com/games/edgeworld.

Words with Friends. Version 5.84. Zynga, 2013.

Other Sources (Including Online Versions)

45. Unpublished Dissertation

Abbas, Megan Brankley. "Knowing Islam: The Entangled History of Western Academia and Modern Islamic Thought." Dissertation, Princeton U, 2015.

46. Published Dissertation

Kidd, Celeste. *Rational Approaches to Learning and Development*. Dissertation, U of Rochester, 2013.

47. Article from a Microform

Sharpe, Lora. "A Quilter's Tribute." *The Boston Globe*, 25 Mar. 1989, p. 13. Microform. *NewsBank*: Social Relations 12, 1989, fiche 6, grids B4-6.

48. Personal, Published, or Broadcast Interview

For a personal interview, list the name of the person interviewed, the label Personal interview (not italicized), and the date of the interview.

Ashdown, Audrey. Personal interview, 1 Jan. 2015.

For a published interview, list the name of the person interviewed and the title (if any), or if there is no title, use the label *Interview by* [*interviewer's name*] (not italicized); then add the publication information, including the URL if there is one.

Weddington, Sarah. "Sarah Weddington: Still Arguing for *Roe*." Interview by Michele Kort, *Ms.*, Winter 2013, pp. 32-35.

Jaffrey, Madhur. "Madhur Jaffrey on How Indian Cuisine Won Western Taste Buds." Interview by Shadrach Kabango, *Q*, CBC Radio, 29 Oct. 2015, www.cbc.ca/1.3292918.

For a broadcast interview, list the name of the person interviewed, the label *Interview* (not italicized), and the name of the interviewer (if relevant); then list information about the program, the date of the interview, and the URL, if applicable.

Fairey, Shepard. "Spreading the Hope: Street Artist Shepard Fairey." Interview by Terry Gross, *Fresh Air*, National Public Radio, WBUR, Boston, 20 Jan. 2009.

Putin, Vladimir. Interview by Charlie Rose. *Charlie Rose: The Week*, PBS, 19 June 2015.

49. Letter

Treat a published letter like a work in an anthology, but include the date of the letter.

Jacobs, Harriet. "To Amy Post." 4 Apr. 1853. *Incidents in the Life of a Slave Girl*, edited by Jean Fagan Yellin, Harvard UP, 1987, pp. 234-35.

50. Film

For films, ordinarily begin with the title, followed by the director and major performers. If your essay or project focuses on a major person related to the film, such as the director, you can begin with that name or names, followed by the title and performers.

Birdman or (The Unexpected Virtue of Ignorance). Directed by Alejandro González Iñárritu, performances by Michael Keaton, Emma Stone, Zach Galifianakis, Edward Norton, and Naomi Watts, Fox Searchlight, 2014.

Scott, Ridley, director. *The Martian*. Performances by Matt Damon, Jessica Chastain, Kristen Wiig, and Kate Mara, Twentieth Century Fox, 2015.

51. Television or Radio Program

"Free Speech on College Campuses." *Washington Journal*, narrated by Peter Slen, C-SPAN, 27 Nov. 2015.

"Take a Giant Step." *Prairie Home Companion*, narrated by Garrison Keillor, American Public Media, 27 Feb. 2016, prairiehome.publicradio.org/listen/full/?name=phc/2016/02/27/phc_20160227_128.

52. Online Video Clip

Cite a short online video as you would a work from a Web site (see item 31).

Nayar, Vineet. "Employees First, Customers Second." *YouTube*, 9 June 2015, www.youtube.com/watch?v=cCdu67s_C5E.

53. Sound Recording

Blige, Mary J. "Don't Mind." *Life II: The Journey Continues (Act 1)*, Geffen, 2011.

54. Work of Art or Photograph

List the artist or photographer; the work's title, italicized; and the date of composition. Then cite the name of the museum or other location and the city.

Bradford, Mark. *Let's Walk to the Middle of the Ocean*. 2015, Museum of Modern Art, New York.

Feinstein, Harold. *Hangin' Out, Sharing a Public Bench, NYC*. 1948, Panopticon Gallery, Boston.

To cite a reproduction in a book, add the publication information.

O'Keeffe, Georgia. *Black and Purple Petunias*. 1925, private collection. *Two Lives: A Conversation in Paintings and Photographs*, edited by Alexandra Arrowsmith and Thomas West, HarperCollins, 1992, p. 67.

To cite artwork found online, add the title of the database or Web site, italicized; and the URL of the site you accessed.

Clough, Charles. *January Twenty-First*. 1988-89, Joslyn Art Museum, Omaha, www.joslyn.org/collections-and-exhibitions/permanent-collections/modern-and-contemporary/charles-clough-january-twenty-first/.

55. Lecture or Speech

Smith, Anna Deavere. "On the Road: A Search for American Character." National Endowment for the Humanities, John F. Kennedy Center for the Performing Arts, Washington, 6 Apr. 2015. Address.

56. Performance

The Draft. By Peter Snoad, directed by Diego Arciniegas, Hibernian Hall, Boston, 10 Sept. 2015.

57. Map or Chart

"Map of Sudan." *Global Citizen*, Citizens for Global Solutions, 2011, globalsolutions.org/blog/bashir#.VthzNMfi_FI.

58. Cartoon

Zyglis, Adam. "City of Light." *Buffalo News*, 8 Nov. 2015, adamzyglis .buffalonews.com/2015/11/08/city-of-light/. Cartoon.

59. Advertisement

Banana Republic. *Wired,* Sept. 2009, p. 13. Advertisement.

On p. 485, note the formatting of the first page of a sample essay written in MLA style. On p. 486, you'll find a sample works cited page written for the same student essay.

Sample First Page for an Essay in MLA Style

Author name and page number in upper right corner of each page

Name, instructor, course, date aligned at left

Title centered

Lesk 1

Emily Lesk

Professor Arraéz

Electric Rhetoric

15 November 2014

Red, White, and Everywhere

America, I have a confession to make: I don't drink Coke. But don't call me a hypocrite just because I am still the proud owner of a bright red shirt that advertises it. Just call me an American. Even before setting foot in Israel three years ago, I knew exactly where I could find one. The tiny T-shirt shop in the central block of Jerusalem's Ben Yehuda Street did offer other designs, but the one with a bright white "Drink Coca-Cola Classic" written in Hebrew cursive across the chest was what drew in most of the dollar-carrying tourists. While waiting almost twenty minutes for my shirt (depicted in fig. 1), I watched nearly every customer ahead of me ask for "the Coke shirt, *todah rabah* [thank you very much]."

Fig. 1. Hebrew Coca-Cola T-shirt. Personal photograph. Despite my dislike for the beverage, I bought this Coca-Cola T-shirt in Israel.

Figure number and caption noting the source of the photo

At the time, I never thought it strange that I wanted one, too. After having absorbed sixteen years of Coca-Cola propaganda through everything from NBC's Saturday morning cartoon lineup to the concession stand at Camden Yards (the Baltimore Orioles' ballpark), I associated the shirt with singing along to the "Just for the Taste of It" jingle and with America's favorite pastime, not with a brown fizzy beverage I refused to consume.

Sample List of Works Cited for an Essay in MLA Style

Lesk 7

Heading centered

Works Cited

Subsequent lines of each entry indented

List is alphabetized by authors' last names (or by title when there is no author)

Coca-Cola Santa pin. Personal photograph by the author, 9 Nov. 2008.

"The Fabulous Fifties." *Beverage Industry,* vol. 87, no. 6, 1996, p. 16. *General OneFile,* go.galegroup.com/.

"Fifty Years of Coca-Cola Television Advertisements." *American Memory*. Motion Picture, Broadcasting and Recorded Sound Division, Library of Congress, memory.loc.gov/ammem/ccmphtml/colahome.html. Accessed 5 Nov. 2014.

"Haddon Sundblom and Coca-Cola." *Thehistoryofchristmas.com,* 10 Holidays, 2004, www.thehistoryofchristmas.com/sc/coca_cola.htm.

Hebrew Coca-Cola T-shirt. Personal photograph by the author, 8 Nov. 2014.

Ikuta, Yasutoshi, editor. *'50s American Magazine Ads.* Graphic-Sha, 1987.

Pendergrast, Mark. *For God, Country, and Coca-Cola: The Definitive History of the Great American Soft Drink and the Company That Makes It.* 2nd ed., Basic Books, 2000.

APA Style

The *Publication Manual of the American Psychological Association* (6th edition, 2010) provides comprehensive advice to student and professional writers in the social sciences. Here we draw on the *Publication Manual*'s guidelines to provide an overview of APA style for in-text citations, content notes, and entries in the list of references.

In-Text Citations

APA style calls for in-text citations in the body of an argument to document sources of quotations, paraphrases, summaries, and so on. These in-text citations correspond to full bibliographic entries in the list of references at the end of the text.

1. Author Named in a Signal Phrase

Generally, give the author's name in a signal phrase to introduce the cited material, using the past tense for the signal verb. Place the date, in parentheses, immediately after the author's name. For a quotation, the page number, preceded by *p.* (not italicized), appears in parentheses after the quotation. For electronic texts or other works without page numbers, paragraph numbers may be used instead, preceded by the abbreviation *para.* For a long, set-off quotation, position the page reference in parentheses one space after the punctuation at the end of the quotation.

> According to Brandon (1993), Adefunmi opposed all forms of racism and believed that black nationalism should not be a destructive force (p. 29).

> As Johnson (2005) demonstrated, contemporary television dramas such as *ER* and *Lost* are not only more complex than earlier programs but "possess a quality that can only be described as subtlety and discretion" (p. 83).

2. Author Named in Parentheses

When you don't mention the author in a signal phrase, give the name and the date, separated by a comma, in parentheses at the end of the cited material.

> *The Sopranos* has achieved a much wider viewing audience than ever expected, spawning a cookbook and several serious scholarly studies (Franklin, 2002).

3. Two Authors

Use both names in all citations. Use *and* in a signal phrase, but use an ampersand (&) in parentheses.

Associated with purity and wisdom, Obatala is the creator of human beings, whom he is said to have formed out of clay (Edwards & Mason, 1985).

4. Three to Five Authors

List all the authors' names for the first reference. In subsequent references, use just the first author's name followed by *et al.* (in regular type, not underlined or italicized).

Lenhoff, Wang, Greenberg, and Bellugi (1997) cited tests that indicate that segments of the left brain hemisphere are not affected by Williams syndrome, whereas the right hemisphere is significantly affected (p. 1641).

Shackelford (1999) drew on the study by Lenhoff et al. (1997).

5. Six or More Authors

Use only the first author's name and *et al.* (in regular type, not underlined or italicized) in every citation, including the first.

As Flower et al. (2003) demonstrated, reading and writing involve both cognitive and social processes.

6. Organization as Author

If the name of an organization or a corporation is long, spell it out the first time, followed by an abbreviation in brackets. In later citations, use the abbreviation only.

First Citation	(Federal Bureau of Investigation [FBI], 2002)
Subsequent Citations	(FBI, 2002)

7. Unknown Author

Use the title or its first few words in a signal phrase or in parentheses. (In the example below, a book's title is italicized.)

The school profiles for the county substantiate this trend (*Guide to secondary schools*, 2003).

8. Authors with the Same Last Name

If your list of references includes works by different authors with the same last name, include the authors' initials in each citation.

> G. Jones (1998) conducted the groundbreaking study of retroviruses, whereas P. Jones (2000) replicated the initial trials two years later.

9. Two or More Sources in the Same Citation

List sources by the same author chronologically by publication year. List sources by different authors in alphabetical order by the authors' last names, separated by semicolons.

> While traditional forms of argument are warlike and agonistic, alternative models do exist (Foss & Foss, 1997; Makau, 1999).

10. Specific Parts of a Source

Use abbreviations (*p.*, *pt.*, and so on) in a parenthetical citation to name the part of a work you're citing. However, *chapter* is not abbreviated.

> Pinker (2003) argued that his research yielded the opposite results (p. 6).

> Pinker (2003) argued that his research yielded the opposite results (Chapter 6).

11. Online Document

To cite a source found on the Internet, use the author's name and date as you would for a print source, and indicate the chapter or figure of the document, as appropriate. If the source's publication date is unknown, use *n.d.* ("no date"). To document a quotation, include paragraph numbers if page numbers are unavailable. If an online document has no page or paragraph numbers, provide the heading of the section and the number of the paragraph that follows.

> Werbach (2002) argued convincingly that "despite the best efforts of legislators, lawyers, and computer programmers, spam has won. Spam is killing email" (p. 1).

12. Email and Other Personal Communication

Cite any personal letters, email messages, electronic postings, telephone conversations, or personal interviews by giving the person's initial(s) and last name, the identification, and the date. Do not list email in the references list, and note that APA style uses a hyphen in the word *e-mail*.

> E. Ashdown (personal communication, March 9, 2015) supported these claims.

Content Notes

The APA recommends using content notes for material that will expand or supplement your argument but otherwise would interrupt the text. Indicate such notes in your text by inserting superscript numerals. Type the notes themselves either at the bottom of the page or on a separate page headed *Footnotes* (not italicized or in quotation marks), centered at the top of the page. Double-space all entries. Indent the first line of each note one-half inch or five spaces, and begin subsequent lines at the left margin.

Text with Superscript Indicating a Note

> Data related to children's preferences in books were instrumental in designing the questionnaire.[1]

Note

> [1]Rudine Sims Bishop and members of the Reading Readiness Research Group provided helpful data.

List of References

The alphabetical list of sources cited in your text is called *References*. (If your instructor asks you to list everything you've read as background—not just the sources you cite—call the list *Bibliography*.) The list of references appears on a separate page or pages at the end of your paper, with the heading *References* (not underlined, italicized, or in quotation marks) centered one inch from the top of the page. Double-space after the heading, and begin your first entry. Double-space the entire list. For print sources, APA style specifies the treatment and placement of four basic elements: author, publication date, title, and publication information. Each element is followed by a period.

- **Author:** List all authors with last name first, and use only initials for first and middle names. Separate the names of multiple authors with commas, and use an ampersand (&) before the last author's name.
- **Publication date:** Enclose the publication date in parentheses. Use only the year for books and journals; use the year, a comma, and the

month or month and day for magazines and newspapers. Do not abbreviate the month. If a date is not given, put *n.d.* ("no date," not italicized) in the parentheses. Put a period after the parentheses.

- **Title:** Italicize titles and subtitles of books and periodicals. Do not enclose titles of articles in quotation marks. For books and articles, capitalize only the first word of the title and subtitle and any proper nouns or proper adjectives; also capitalize the first word following a colon. Capitalize all major words in the title of a periodical.
- **Publication information:** For a book published in the United States, list the city of publication and state abbreviation. For books published outside the United States, identify the city and country. Provide the publisher's name, dropping *Inc.*, *Co.*, or *Publishers*. If the state is already included within the publisher's name, do not include the postal abbreviation for the state. For a periodical, follow the periodical title with a comma, the volume number (italicized), the issue number (if provided) in parentheses and followed by a comma, and the inclusive page numbers of the article. For newspaper articles and for articles or chapters in books, include the abbreviation *p.* ("page") or *pp.* ("pages").

The following APA style examples appear in a "hanging indent" format, in which the first line aligns on the left and the subsequent lines indent one-half inch or five spaces.

Print Books

1. One Author

Fraser, S. (2015). *The age of acquiescence: The life and death of American resistance to organized wealth and power.* New York, NY: Little, Brown.

2. Two or More Authors

Steininger, M., Newell, J. D., & Garcia, L. (1984). *Ethical issues in psychology*. Homewood, IL: Dow Jones-Irwin.

3. Organization as Author

Use the word *Author* (not italicized) as the publisher when the organization is both the author and the publisher.

Linguistics Society of America. (2002). *Guidelines for using sign language interpreters*. Washington, DC: Author.

4. Unknown Author

National Geographic atlas of the world. (2010). Washington, DC: National Geographic Society.

5. Book Prepared by an Editor

Hardy, H. H. (Ed.). (1998). *The proper study of mankind*. New York, NY: Farrar, Straus.

6. Selection in a Book with an Editor

Villanueva, V. (1999). An introduction to social scientific discussions on class. In A. Shepard, J. McMillan, & G. Tate (Eds.), *Coming to class: Pedagogy and the social class of teachers* (pp. 262-277). Portsmouth, NH: Heinemann.

7. Translation

Pérez-Reverte, A. (2002). *The nautical chart* (M. S. Peden, Trans.). New York, NY: Harvest. (Original work published 2000)

8. Edition Other Than the First

Bok, D. (2015). *Higher education in America* (Rev. ed.). Princeton, NJ: Princeton University Press.

9. One Volume of a Multivolume Work

Will, J. S. (1921). *Protestantism in France* (Vol. 2). Toronto, Canada: University of Toronto Press.

10. Article in a Reference Work

Chernow, B., & Vattasi, G. (Eds.). (1993). Psychomimetic drug. In *The Columbia encyclopedia* (5th ed., p. 2238). New York, NY: Columbia University Press.

If no author is listed, begin with the article title, followed by the year, and the rest of the citation as shown here.

11. Republication

Sharp, C. (1978). *History of Hartlepool.* Hartlepool, United Kingdom: Hartlepool Borough Council. (Original work published 1816)

12. Graphic Narrative

If the words and images are created by the same person, cite a graphic narrative just as you would a book with one author (see item 1 on p. 491).

Bechdel, A. (2012). *Are you my mother?* New York, NY: Houghton Mifflin Harcourt.

If the work is a collaboration, indicate the author or illustrator who is most important to your research, followed by other contributors in order of their appearance on the title page. Label each person's contribution to the work.

Stavans, I. (Writer), & Arcaraz, L. (Illustrator). (2000). *Latino USA: A cartoon history*. New York, NY: Basic.

13. Government Document

U.S. Bureau of the Census. (2001). *Survey of women-owned business enterprises*. Washington, DC: Government Printing Office.

14. Two or More Works by the Same Author

List the works in chronological order of publication. Repeat the author's name in each entry.

Lowin, S. (2006). *The making of a forefather: Abraham in Islamic and Jewish exegetical narratives*. Leiden, The Netherlands: Brill.

Lowin, S. (2013). *Arabic and Hebrew love poems in Al-Andalus*. New York, NY: Routledge.

Print Periodicals

15. Article in a Journal Paginated by Volume

Bowen, L. M. (2011). Resisting age bias in digital literacy research. *College Composition and Communication, 62*, 586-607.

16. Article in a Journal Paginated by Issue

Carr, S. (2002). The circulation of Blair's Lectures. *Rhetoric Society Quarterly, 32*(4), 75-104.

17. Article in a Monthly Magazine

Baker, C. (2008, September). Master of the universe. *Wired, 16*(9), 134-141.

18. Article in a Newspaper

Nagourney, A. (2002, December 16). Gore rules out running in '04. *The New York Times*, pp. A1, A8.

19. Letter to the Editor or Editorial

Erbeta, R. (2008, December). Swiftboating George [Letter to the editor]. *Smithsonian, 39*(9), 10.

20. Unsigned Article

Guidelines issued on assisted suicide. (1998, March 4). *The New York Times*, p. A15.

21. Review

Avalona, A. (2008, August). [Review of the book *Weaving women's lives: Three generations in a Navajo family*, by L. Lamphere]. *New Mexico, 86*(8), 40.

22. Published Interview

Shor, I. (1997). [Interview with A. Greenbaum]. *Writing on the Edge, 8*(2), 7-20.

23. Two or More Works by the Same Author in the Same Year

List two or more works by the same author published in the same year alphabetically by title (excluding *A*, *An*, or *The*), and place lowercase letters (*a*, *b*, etc.) after the dates.

Murray, F. B. (1983a). Equilibration as cognitive conflict. *Developmental Review, 3*, 54-61.

Murray, F. B. (1983b). Learning and development through social interaction. In L. Liben (Ed.), *Piaget and the foundations of knowledge* (pp. 176-201). Hillsdale, NJ: Erlbaum.

Digital Sources

The following models are based on the APA's *Publication Manual* (6th edition). A change for handling electronic sources involves the use of a digital object identifier (DOI) when available (instead of a URL) to locate an electronic source. The DOI is a unique number assigned to an electronic text (article, book, or other item) and intended to give reliable access to it. A second change is that a date of retrieval is no longer necessary unless a source changes very frequently. The basic APA entry for most electronic sources should include the following elements:

- name of the author, editor, or compiler
- date of electronic publication or most recent update
- title of the work, document, or posting
- publication information, including the title, volume or issue number, and page numbers
- the DOI (digital object identifier) of the document, if one is available
- a URL, only if a DOI is not available, with no angle brackets and no closing punctuation

24. Web Site

To cite a whole site, give the address in a parenthetical reference. To cite a document from a Web site, include information as you would for a print document, followed by a note on its retrieval. Provide a date of retrieval only if the information is likely to change frequently.

American Psychological Association. (2013). Making stepfamilies work. Retrieved from http://www.apa.org/helpcenter/stepfamily.aspx

Mullins, B. (1995). Introduction to Robert Hass. Readings in contemporary poetry at Dia Center for the Arts. Retrieved from http://www.diacenter.org/prg/poetry/95_96/intrhass.html

25. Article from a Periodical on the Web

For an article you read online, provide either the URL of the periodical's homepage, preceded by *Retrieved from* (not italicized) or a DOI.

Haines, R. (2015, February 27). The problem with separate toys for boys and girls. *The Boston Globe*. Retrieved from http://www.bostonglobe.com

Lambert, N. M., Graham, S. M., & Fincham, F. D. (2009). A prototype analysis of gratitude: Varieties of gratitude experiences. *Personality and Social Psychology Bulletin, 35*, 1193-1207. doi:10.1177/0146167209338071

26. Article or Abstract from a Database

For an article you find on a database, provide a DOI if one is available. If the online article does not have a DOI, locate the homepage for the journal in which the article appears and provide that URL. You need not identify the database you have used.

Strully, K. (2014). Racially and ethnically diverse schools and adolescent romantic relationships. *American Journal of Sociology*, *120*(3), 750-757. doi:10.1086/679190

Hayhoe, G. (2001). The long and winding road: Technology's future. *Technical Communication, 48*(2), 133-145. Retrieved from techcomm.stc.org

27. Software or Computer Program

OS X Lion (Version 10.7) [Computer operating system]. (2011). Cupertino, CA: Apple.

28. Online Government Document

Cite an online government document as you would a printed government work, adding the URL. Note that the APA spells *website* as one word.

Finn, J. D. (1998, April). *Class size and students at risk: What is known? What is next?* Retrieved from United States Department of Education website: http://www.ed.gov/pubs/ClassSize/title.html

29. Entry in a Web Reference Work

Cite the entry as you would an entry from a print reference work (see item 10). Follow with the date of publication, the name of the Web site, and the URL.

Tour de France. (2006). In *Encyclopaedia Britannica Online*. Retrieved from http://www.britannica.com/EBchecked/topic/600732/Tour-de-France

30. Posting or Comment on a Web Site

Begin with the author's name; the date of the most recent update; the title of the posting (if there is no title, use the description *Blog post* or *Blog comment*, not italicized); the name of the blog, italicized, and the URL.

Marcotte, A. (2012). Rights without perfection. *Pandagon*. Retrieved from http://www.rawstory.com/rs/2010/05/pandagon-rights_without_perfection/

31. Entry in a Wiki

Since wikis are collectively edited, do not include an author. Include the title of the entry; the date of the latest update; the name of the wiki, italicized; and the URL of the source.

Fédération Internationale de Football Association. (2014). In *Wikipedia*. Retrieved May 11, 2014 from http://en.wikipedia.org/wiki/FIFA

32. Posting on a Social Networking Site

To cite a posting on Facebook or another social networking site, include the writer's name, the date of the post, a description of the item in brackets, and the URL of the source.

Ferguson, S. (2014, March 6). Status update [Facebook post]. Retrieved from https://www.facebook.com/sarah.ferguson?fref=nf

33. Posting on a Public Facebook Page

When citing a posting on a public Facebook page or another social networking site that is visible to anyone, include the writer's name as it appears in the post. Give a few words from the post, and add an identifying label. Include the date you retrieved the post and the URL for the public page. Do not include a page on the list of references if your readers will not be able to access the source; instead, cite it as a personal communication in the text.

American Psychological Association (2014, April 24). Why do many people do their best thinking while walking? [Facebook post]. Retrieved April 24, 2014, from https://www.facebook.com/AmericanPsychologicalAssociation

34. Tweet

Include the writer's Twitter handle; the date of the tweet; the entire text of the tweet with no end punctuation, followed by *Tweet* in brackets; the words *Retrieved from*; and the full Twitter account URL with no end punctuation.

Aalrhetorician. (2014, August 27). Just read (again) about demise of the apostrophe. Argument getting a bit old [Tweet]. Retrieved from https://twitter.com/aalrhetorician

35. Newsgroup Posting

Include the author's name, the date and subject line of the posting, and the name of the newsgroup.

Wittenberg, E. (2001, July 11). Gender and the Internet [Msg 4]. Retrieved from news://comp.edu.composition

36. Email Message or Synchronous Communication

Because the APA stresses that any sources cited in your list of references must be retrievable by your readers, you shouldn't include entries for email messages or synchronous communications (MOOs, MUDs); instead, cite these sources in your text as forms of personal communication (see item 12 on p. 489). And remember that you shouldn't quote from other people's email without asking their permission to do so.

Other Sources

37. Technical or Research Reports and Working Papers

Kinley-Horn and Associates. (2011). *ADOT bicycle safety action plan* (Working Paper No. 3). Phoenix: Arizona Department of Transportation.

38. Unpublished Paper Presented at a Meeting or Symposium

Welch, K. (2002, March). *Electric rhetoric and screen literacy*. Paper presented at the meeting of the Conference on College Composition and Communication, Chicago, IL.

39. Unpublished Dissertation

Seward, D. E. (2008). *Civil voice in Elizabethan parliamentary oratory: The rhetoric and composition of speeches delivered at Westminster in 1566* (Unpublished doctoral dissertation). University of Texas at Austin, Austin, TX.

40. Poster Session

Mensching, G. (2002, May). *A simple, effective one-shot for disinterested students*. Poster session presented at the National LOEX Library Instruction Conference, Ann Arbor, MI.

41. Motion Picture, Video, or DVD

Bigelow, K. (Director). (2009). *The hurt locker* [Motion picture]. United States: Summit Entertainment.

42. Television Program, Single Episode

Burnett, A. (Writer), & Attias, D. (Director). (2014, March 26). The deal [Television series episode]. In J. Weisberg (Executive producer), *The Americans.* Los Angeles, CA: DreamWorks Television.

43. Online Video Clip

Weber, J. (2012). *As we sow, part I: Where are the farmers?* [Video file]. Retrieved from http://www.youtube.com/watch?v=_cdcDpMf6qE

44. Sound Recording

Begin with the writer's name, followed by the date of copyright. Give the recording date at the end of the entry (in parentheses, after the period) if it's different from the copyright date.

Ivey, A., Jr., & Sall, R. (1995). Rollin' with my homies [Recorded by Coolio]. On *Clueless* [CD]. Hollywood, CA: Capitol Records.

Sample Title Page for an Essay in APA Style

Running head (fifty characters or fewer) appears flush left on first line of title page

Page number appears flush right on first line of every page

Running Head: MOOD MUSIC 1

Title, name, and affiliation centered and double-spaced

Mood Music: Music Preference and the Risk for Depression and Suicide in Adolescents

Tawnya Redding

Oregon State University

Author Note

This paper was prepared for Psychology 480, taught by Professor Ede.

Sample First Text Page for an Essay in APA Style

MOOD MUSIC 3

Full title centered

Mood Music: Music Preference and the Risk for Depression and Suicide in Adolescents

Paragraphs indented

Music is a significant part of American culture. Since the explosion of rock and roll in the 1950s, there has been a concern for the effects that music may have on listeners, and especially on young people. The genres most likely to come under suspicion in recent decades have included heavy metal, country, and blues. These genres have been suspected of having adverse effects on the mood and behavior of young listeners. But can music really alter the disposition and create self-destructive behaviors in listeners? And if so, which genres and aspects of those genres are responsible? The following review of the literature will establish the correlation between potentially problematic genres of music such as heavy metal and country and depression and suicide risk. First, correlational studies concerning music preference and suicide risk will be discussed, followed by a discussion of the literature concerning the possible reasons for this link. Finally, studies concerning the effects of music on mood will be discussed. Despite the link between genres such as heavy metal and country and suicide risk, previous research has been unable to establish the causal nature of this link.

Boldface headings help organize review

The Correlation Between Music and Depression and Suicide Risk

A large portion of studies over the past two decades have focused on heavy metal and country music as the main genre culprits associated with youth suicidality and depression (Lacourse, Claes, & Villeneuve, 2001; Scheel & Westefeld, 1999; Stack & Gundlach, 1992). Stack and Gundlach (1992) examined the radio airtime devoted to country music in 49 metropolitan areas and found that the

Parenthetical references follow APA style

Sample References List for an Essay in APA Style

References begin on new page

Heading is centered

MOOD MUSIC 9

References

Baker, F., & Bor, W. (2008). Can music preference indicate mental health status in young people? *Australasian Psychiatry, 16*(4), 284-288. Retrieved from http://www3.interscience.wiley.com/journal/118565538/home

George, D., Stickle, K., Rachid, F., & Wopnford, A. (2007). The association between types of music enjoyed and cognitive, behavioral, and personality factors of those who listen. *Psychomusicology, 19*(2), 32-56.

Lacourse, E., Claes, M., & Villeneuve, M. (2001). Heavy metal music and adolescent suicidal risk. *Journal of Youth and Adolescence, 30*(3), 321-332.

Lai, Y. (1999). Effects of music listening on depressed women in Taiwan. *Issues in Mental Health Nursing, 20,* 229-246. doi:10.1080/016128499248637

Martin, G., Clark, M., & Pearce, C. (1993). Adolescent suicide: Music preference as an indicator of vulnerability. *Journal of the American Academy of Child and Adolescent Psychiatry, 32,* 530-535.

Scheel, K., & Westefeld, J. (1999). Heavy metal music and adolescent suicidality: An empirical investigation. *Adolescence, 34*(134), 253-273.

Siedliecki, S., & Good, M. (2006). Effect of music on power, pain, depression and disability. *Journal of Advanced Nursing, 54*(5), 553-562. doi:10.1111/j.1365-2648.2006.03860

Smith, J. L., & Noon, J. (1998). Objective measurement of mood change induced by contemporary music. *Journal of Psychiatric & Mental Health Nursing, 5,* 403-408.

RESPOND •

1. The MLA and APA styles differ in several important ways, both for in-text citations and for lists of sources. You've probably noticed a few: the APA uses lowercase letters for most words in titles and lists the publication date right after the author's name, whereas the MLA capitalizes most words and puts the publication date at the end of the works cited entry. More interesting than the details, though, is the reasoning behind the differences. Placing the publication date near the front of a citation, for instance, reveals a special concern for that information in the APA style. Similarly, the MLA's decision to capitalize titles isn't arbitrary: that style is preferred in the humanities for a reason. Working in a group, find as many consistent differences between the MLA and APA styles as you can. Then, for each difference, speculate about the reasons these groups organize or present information in that way. The MLA and APA style manuals themselves may be of help. You might also begin by determining which academic disciplines subscribe to the APA style and which to the MLA.
2. Working with another person in your class, look for examples of the following sources: an article in a journal, a book, a film, a song, and a TV show. Then make a references page or works cited list (five entries in all), using either MLA or APA style.

PART 5

arguments

23

How Does Popular Culture Stereotype *You*?

Left to right: Megan Haaga, for Open Gates, by permission; © Frank Fell/age fotostock; AP Photo/Kin Cheung

Check the dictionary, and you'll learn that the term *stereotype* originally referred to a printing plate cast in metal from the mold of a page of set type. Although English borrowed the word from French, its parts are ultimately of Greek origin: *stereo* means "solid" or "three-dimensional" while *type* means "model." By extension, the word has come to mean a widely held image that is fixed, allowing for little individuality among a group's members. Ironic, isn't it, that a term that originally referred to a three-dimensional printing plate has come to refer to a one-dimensional representation of an entire group?

The selections in this chapter focus on stereotyping in popular culture, including the media, challenging you to analyze what many would consider to be unsavory or unfair stereotypes of various groups found there. The chapter opens with a selection about stereotypes and little girls. "Little Girls or Little Women? The Disney Princess Effect," an article from 2011, examines the ways that, once little girls discover Disney Princesses, a line of merchandise based on the animated films, their understanding of themselves often changes in ways many parents and social scientists find troubling.

The chapter's selection focusing on making a visual argument examines stereotypes about gender (including Barbie dolls), generational differences, gun control, and racial profiling of African American men that are simultaneously mocked and perpetuated in recent cartoons. As you study these cartoons carefully, give some thought to the ways that humorous arguments like these permit our society to deal indirectly with controversial issues. You will likewise want to consider the stereotypes that don't show up here, whether they are simply too potentially explosive or whether the editors may not have felt comfortable reproducing them for fear of unwanted controversy.

In the third selection, Amy Stretten, a Native American, argues that appropriating Native American imagery honors little more than prejudice itself. It's worth noting that public attitudes about this topic continue to shift away from the acceptability of such imagery, reminding us that attitudes toward stereotypes change—and can change in a short period of time.

The fourth selection, the preface to a book by Charles A. Riley II, focuses passionately on how people with disabilities are—and aren't—represented in the media and popular culture. In addition to his take on these problems, we include a set of guidelines from the National Center on Disability and Journalism that offers advice about how media might do a better job than they currently do in this regard. We've found this advice helpful in our writing.

Next, a selection from Claude M. Steele's important 2010 book *Whistling Vivaldi and Other Clues to How Stereotypes Affect Us* examines what researchers term "stereotype threat," the way that our fear of being stereotyped often influences our actions. Steele, a psychologist, coined this term.

In the sixth selection, an excerpt from a research study, psychologist Melinda C. R. Burgess and four colleagues investigate the prevalence and consequences of racial stereotyping in video games.

The chapter closes with Amy Zimmerman's discussion of the stereotyped ways that television represents individuals who identify as bisexual, a topic we wouldn't have considered a few editions back, partly because bisexuals weren't represented, even in stereotyped ways, on TV.

Originally, stereotypes were part of a printer's trade, enabling the printer to disseminate information quickly and cheaply. No less a part of popular culture today, stereotypes of a different sort still disseminate information. You'll have to evaluate how much that information is worth.

▼ *Stephanie Hanes, a freelance journalist, has written for a number of U.S. publications, including the* Christian Science Monitor, *where this article first appeared,* Smithsonian Magazine, *and* USA Today. *She also lived for four years in South Africa and continues to write frequently about topics related to southern Africa and areas in the developing world where there are crises of various sorts. In this cover story from the* Christian Science Monitor *published October 3, 2011, Hanes examines in some detail a trend that many find disturbing: the growing sexualization of very young girls. As you read, pay special attention to the kinds of evidence that Hanes uses to support her analysis and to the ways she uses statistics in particular. (By the way, if you're not already familiar with the Disney Princesses, take the time to Google the term; what you learn will be especially useful background as you read the article.)*

Little Girls or Little Women? The Disney Princess Effect

STEPHANIE HANES

In today's highly sexualized environment — where 5-year-olds wear padded bras — some see the toddlers-and-tiaras Disney Princess craze leading to the preteen pursuit of "hot" looks. Do little girls become little women too soon?

A few years ago, Mary Finucane started noticing changes in the way her 3-year-old daughter played. The toddler had stopped running and jumping, and insisted on wearing only dresses. She sat on the front step quietly — waiting, she said, for her prince. She seemed less imaginative, less spunky, less interested in the world.

Mary Finucane and her daughter, dressed like a princess. Melanie Stetson Freeman/© 2011 The Christian Science Monitor (www.CSMonitor.com). Reprinted with permission.

Ms. Finucane believes the shift began when Caoimhe (pronounced Keeva) discovered the Disney Princesses, that omnipresent, pastel packaged franchise of slender-waisted fairy-tale heroines. When Finucane mentioned her suspicions to other parents, they mostly shrugged.

"Everyone seemed to think it was inevitable," Finucane says. "You know, it was Disney Princesses from [ages] 2 to 5, then Hannah Montana, then

High School Musical. I thought it was so strange that these were the new trajectories of female childhood."

She decided to research the princess phenomenon, and what she found worried her. She came to believe that the $4 billion Disney Princess empire was the first step down a path to scarier challenges, from self-objectification° to cyberbullying to unhealthy body images. Finucane, who has a background in play therapy, started a blog — *Disney Princess Recovery: Bringing Sexy Back for a Full Refund* — to chronicle her efforts to break the grip of Cinderella, Belle, Ariel, et al. on her household.

5 Within months she had thousands of followers.

"It was validating, in a sense, that a lot of parents were experiencing it," she says. "It was this big force entering our lives so early, with such strength. It concerned me for what was down the road."

Finucane's theory about Disney Princesses is by no means universal. Many parents and commentators defend Happily Ever After against what some critics call a rising "feminist attack," and credit the comely ladies with teaching values such as kindness, reading, love of animals, and perseverance.

If there's any doubt of the controversy surrounding the subject, journalist Peggy Orenstein mined a whole book (*Cinderella Ate My Daughter*) out of the firestorm she sparked in 2006 with a *New York Times* essay ("What's Wrong With Cinderella?").

Disney, for its part, repeated to the *Monitor* its standard statement on the topic: "For 75 years, millions of little girls and their parents around the world have adored and embraced the diverse characters and rich stories featuring our Disney princesses. . . . [L]ittle girls experience the fantasy and imagination provided by these stories as a normal part of their childhood development."

10 And yet, the Finucane and Orenstein critique does resonate with many familiar with modern American girlhood as "hot" replaces pretty in pink, and getting the prince takes on a more ominous tone. Parents and educators regularly tell researchers that they are unable to control the growing onslaught of social messages shaping their daughters and students.

"Parents are having a really hard time dealing with it," says Diane Levin, an early childhood specialist at Wheelock College in Boston who recently co-wrote the book *So Sexy So Soon*. "They say that things they used to do aren't working; they say they're losing control of what happens to their girls at younger and younger ages."

It only takes a glance at some recent studies to understand why parents are uneasy:

- A University of Central Florida poll found that 50 percent of 3- to 6-year-old girls worry that they are fat.
- One-quarter of 14- to 17-year-olds of both sexes polled by The Associated Press and MTV in 2009 reported either sending naked pictures of themselves or receiving naked pictures of someone else.
- The marketing group NPD Fashionworld reported in 2003 that more than $1.6 million is spent annually on thong underwear for 7- to 12-year-olds.
- Children often come across Internet pornography unintentionally: University of New Hampshire researchers found in 2005 that one-third of Internet users ages 10 to 17 were exposed to unwanted sexual material, and a London School of Economics study in 2004 found that 60 percent of children who use the Internet regularly come into contact with pornography.

And on, and on. It's enough, really, to alarm the most relaxed parent.

But as Professor Levin, Finucane, and Orenstein show, there is another trend today, too — one that gets far less press, but is much more hopeful.

Trying to make a safer, healthier environment for girls, an ever-stronger group of educators, parents, institutions, and girls themselves are pushing back against growing marketing

self-objectification: turning one's self into an object, seeing oneself through the eyes of others.

More and more girls begin wearing eye makeup early in life. Melanie Stetson Freeman/© 2011 The Christian Science Monitor (www.CSMonitor.com). Reprinted with permission.

pressure, new cyberchallenges, and sexualization, which the American Psychological Association (APA) defines in part as the inappropriate imposition of sexuality on children.

Many are trying to intervene when girls are younger, like Finucane, who doesn't advocate banning the princesses but taking on the ways that they narrow girls' play (advocating more color choices, suggesting alternative story plotlines). Some tap into the insight and abilities of older girls — with mentoring, for example. Still others take their concerns into the public sphere, lobbying politicians and executives for systemic change such as restricting sexualized advertising targeting girls.

Together, they offer some insights for how, as Finucane says, to bring sexy back for a refund.

Soccer Heading Makes a Bad Hair Day

The first step, some say, is to understand why any of this matters.

15 By many measures, girls are not doing badly. According to the Washington-based Center on Education Policy, high school girls perform as well as boys on math and science tests and do better than their male peers in reading. Three women now graduate from college for every two men. Far more women play sports, which is linked to better body image, lower teen pregnancy rates, and higher scholastic performance.

And opportunities for girls today are much broader than 50 years ago when, for example, schools didn't even allow girls to wear pants or to raise and lower the flag, notes Stephanie Coontz, co-chair of the nonprofit Council on Contemporary Families. "It is important to keep all of this in perspective," she says.

Still, there are signs of erosion of the progress in gender equity. Take athletics. 20

"Girls are participating in sports at a much increased level in grade school," says Sharon Lamb, a professor of education and mental health at the University of Massachusetts, Boston. But, she adds, they start to drop out of sports at the middle school level when they start to believe that sports are unfeminine and unsexy.

The Women's Sports Foundation found that 6 girls drop out of sports for every 1 boy by the end of high school, and a recent Girl Scout study found that 23 percent of girls between the ages of 11 and 17 do not play sports because they do not think their bodies look good doing so.

And looking good, Ms. Lamb says, is increasingly tied to what it means to play. Star female athletes regularly pose naked or seminaked for men's magazines; girls see cheerleaders (with increasingly sexualized routines) on TV far more than they see female basketball players or other athletes.

The effects are felt in academia as well. Earlier this year, a Princeton University study found a growing leadership gap among male and female undergraduates. Nannerl Keohane, who chaired the Princeton steering committee, wrote in an e-mail interview that "the climate was different in the late 1990s and the past decade." And she linked the findings to shifts in popular culture such as "the receding of second-wave feminist° excitement and commitment, a backlash in some quarters, a reorientation of young women's expectations based on what they had seen of their mothers' generation, a profound reorientation of popular culture which now glorifies sexy babes consistently, rather than sometimes showing an accomplished woman without foregrounding her sexuality."

This "sexy babes" trend is a big one. 25

"For young women, what has replaced the feminine mystique is the hottie mystique," Ms. Coontz says. "Girls no longer feel that there is anything they must not do or cannot do because they're female, but they hold increasingly strong beliefs that if you are going to attempt these other things, you need to look and be sexually hot."

In television shows, for instance, women are represented in far more diverse roles — they are lawyers, doctors, politicians. But they are always sexy. A woman might run for high political office, but there is almost always analysis about whether she is sexy, too.

In 2010, the APA released a report on the sexualization of girls, which it described as portraying a girl's value as coming primarily from her sexual appeal. It found increased sexualization in magazines, by marketers, in music lyrics, and on television — a phenomenon that includes "harm to the sexualized individuals themselves, to their interpersonal relationships, and to society."

Sexualization, it reported, leads to lower cognitive performance and greater body dissatisfaction. One study cited by the report, for instance, compared the ability of college-age women to solve math problems while trying on a sweater (alone in a dressing room) with that of those trying on swimsuits. Sweater wearers far outperformed the scantily dressed.

Research also connects sexualization to eating disorders, depression, 30 and physical health problems. Even those young women — and experts say there are growing numbers of them — who claim that it is empowering to be a sex object often suffer the ill effects of sexualization.

Girls' shoes increasingly resemble those worn by adult women. Melanie Stetson Freeman/© 2011 The Christian Science Monitor (www.CSMonitor.com). Reprinted with permission.

"The sexualization of girls may not only reflect sexist attitudes, a society tolerant of sexual violence, and the exploitation of girls and women but may also contribute to these phenomena," the APA said.

Objectifying women is not new, of course.

"What's different is just the sheer amount of messaging that girls are

second-wave feminist: feminism associated with the period from the 1960s until the early 1990s in contrast to first-wave feminism (nineteenth and early twentieth century), which focused on getting the vote for women, or third-wave feminism (feminism since the mid-1980s), which is much more international and much more concerned with the diversity of experiences among women from different backgrounds within a society.

hypersexualized: extremely or excessively sexualized.

getting, and the effective way that these images are used to market to younger and younger girls," says Lyn Mikel Brown, an education professor at Colby College in Waterville, Maine. "They're getting it relentlessly. And in this busy world it's somehow harder for parents to stop and question it. It's like fish in water — it's the water. It's in the air. It's easy for it to get by us."

Help Girls to See the Problem

So what to do? To start, girls can become media critics, says Professor Brown's high school–age daughter, Maya Brown. The younger Brown serves on the Girls' Advisory Board of Hardy Girls Healthy Women, an organization based in Maine that develops girl-friendly school curricula and runs a variety of programs for girls.

"There are so many images of girls, and they are always objectifying — it's hard to make that go away," Maya says. "What you really need is for the girls to be able to see it."

She knows this firsthand. Her mother would regularly pause television shows or movies to talk about female stereotypes; when she read to Maya, she would often change the plotlines to make the female characters more important. (It was only when Maya got older that she realized that Harry Potter was far more active than Hermione.)

"It would get kind of annoying," Maya, now 16, says with a laugh. "When we were watching a movie and she'd pause it and say, 'You know, this isn't a good representation,' I'd be like, 'Yeah, yeah, yeah, I caught that. Can we watch our show now?'"

Professor Brown had many opportunities to intervene. According to the Kaiser Family Foundation, the percentage of television shows with sexual content — from characters talking about their sexual exploits to actual intercourse — increased from 54 percent in 1998 to 70 percent in 2005.

In her book, Levin says that the numbers would be even higher if advertisements were included. And reality television, which has ballooned during the past decade, is particularly sexualizing. Scholars point out that the most popular reality shows either have harem-style plots, with many women competing to please one man, or physical-improvement goals.

Young girls get similarly sexualizing messages in their own movies and television shows. The Geena Davis Institute on Gender and Media found recently that fewer than 1 in 3 speaking characters (animal or human) in G-rated family films are female, and even animated female characters tend to wear sexualized attire: Disney's Jasmine, for instance, has a sultry off-the-shoulder look, while even Miss Piggy shows cleavage.

Given this backdrop, many child development experts say the best way to handle the media onslaught for younger girls is for parents to simply opt out.

The American Academy of Pediatrics recommends no screen time — television, movies, and Internet — for infants under 2 years of age; for older children, the AAP suggests only one to two hours a day. This would be a significant change for most American families. In 2003, the Kaiser Family Foundation found that 36 percent of children under 6 live in a house where the TV is on all or almost all of the time; 43 percent of children ages 4 to 6 have a TV in their bedroom. In 2010 the foundation reported that, on average, children ages 8 to 18 consume 10 hours, 45 minutes' worth of screen media content a day.

Even if parents limited TV and movies, though, the sexualization of women would still get through on the radio, in magazines at grocery store checkout lines, on billboards, and in schools, not to mention on the all-powerful Internet. Those images, as in television, have become far more sexualized.

In one recent study, University of Buffalo sociologists Erin Hatton and Mary Nell Trautne examined the covers of *Rolling Stone* magazine between 1967 and 2009. They found a "dramatic increase in hypersexualized° images of women," to the point that by 2009, nearly every woman to grace the magazine's cover was conveyed in a blatantly sexual way, as compared with 17 percent of the men. (Examples include a tousled-haired Jennifer Aniston lying naked on a bed, or a topless Janet Jackson with an unseen man's hands covering her breasts.)

With no way to get away from the sexualized images, Maya says, it's better to recognize and co-opt them.

She and other young women helped develop the website powered bygirl.org on which girls blog, comment, and share ideas about female sexualization in the media. The site includes an app that lets users graffiti advertisements and then post the altered images — one recent post, for instance, takes a Zappos magazine advertisement showing a naked woman covered only by the caption "more than shoes!" and adds, "Yet no creativity" to the slogan.

"Once it's brought to light in a satirical way, it loses its power," says

Jackie Dupont, the programs director at Hardy Girls Healthy Women. "The ridiculousness about what the advertisements are trying to say about women becomes more apparent."

Sexy's Not about Sex, It's about Shopping

Media images, though, are only a part of the sexualization problem. More invasive, Levin and others say, is marketing.

Since the deregulation movement of the 1980s, the federal government has lost most oversight of advertising to children. This has encouraged marketers to become increasingly brazen, says Levin. Marketers are motivated to use the sexualization of women to attract little girls, or violence to attract little boys, because developmentally children are drawn to things they don't understand, or find unnerving, Levin says.

50 In this context, she says, sexy is not about sex, but about shopping. If girls can be convinced to equate "sexy" with popularity and girlness itself, and if "sexy" requires the right clothes, makeup, hairdo, accessories, and shoes, then marketers have a new bunch of consumers.

"Age compression," the phenomenon of younger children adopting patterns once reserved for older youths, helps with sales. If girls start wearing lip gloss when they are 6 years old (as almost half of them do, according to Experian Simmons national consumer research) and mascara when they are 8 (the percentage of 8- to 12-year-olds wearing mascara doubled between 2007 and 2009, to almost 1 in 5, according to market research from the NPD Group), then it's clearly better for cosmetic companies. This is also why, Levin speculates, thong underwear is now sold to 7-year-olds, and padded bras show up on the racks for 5-year-olds.

A Disney Princess hosting a tea party. Ben Hider/Getty Images

Meanwhile, there are deepening gender divisions in toys, clothing, and play activities. Orenstein explores in *Cinderella Ate My Daughter* how the color pink has become increasingly ubiquitous to the point where many young girls police each other with a pink radar — if that tricycle, for instance, isn't pink, well then, you shouldn't be riding it.

Brown points out in her book that there is no pink equivalent for boys. Although the color blue, sports equipment, and fire engines grace much of their décor, boys still have far more options of how to define themselves.

"In unprecedented levels, girls are being presented with a very narrow image of girlhood," Brown says.

55 One of the best ways to keep girls from falling into rigid gender roles is to broaden their horizons.

"If we are bombarded with thousands of images a day that give the illusion of choice, but are in fact really simplistic and repetitive, it's important to not just say girls can do anything, but to give them the actual experience," said Ms. Dupont from Hardy Girls Healthy Women, where the Adventure Girls program for second- to sixth-graders connects girls with women who have excelled in nontraditional fields, from construction and rugby to chemistry and dog-sledding.

This is what Finucane tried to do with her daughter. She did not want to crush Caoimhe's fantasies, but she also wanted her to see more of the possibilities open to girls. So although Caoimhe wanted to read only Disney Princess books — titles such as *Cinderella: My Perfect Wedding* — Finucane insisted on sharing stories about Amelia Earhart° and other powerful women. She bought native American dress-up clothes and a Princess Presto outfit to go with the frothy pink Disney gowns.

Amelia Earhart (1897–1937): famous American pilot and author who disappeared over the Pacific Ocean while trying to fly around the world. Earhart, the first woman to fly across the Atlantic, set a number of aviation records. She was also the first woman to receive the Distinguished Flying Cross.

Trying to Stay One Step Ahead

Finucane says that Caoimhe, now 5, is pretty much free of the princess obsession. These days she is entranced by *James and the Giant Peach* and *The Wizard of Oz*.

"I try to stay maybe one step ahead," Finucane says. "The grip they had is lost. She's still into characters and theatrical production, but she no longer believes that you can't leap if you're a princess, or female."

Parents' involvement is key, Levin says, but they do not have to act alone. Over the past few years, a growing group of advocacy organizations have formed to help fight against marketing pressure and sexualization.

Levin and others have campaigned for new regulations on how advertisers can approach children; groups such as truechild.org and Campaign for a Commercial Free Childhood have also pushed for marketing restrictions and have held summits about countering the consumer culture and sexualization. The organization TRUCE — Teachers Resisting Unhealthy Children's Entertainment — publishes media and play guides in which they review toys, check marketers' claims, and recommend age-appropriate activities. Recently, actress Geena Davis joined Sen. Kay Hagan (D) of North Carolina and Rep. Tammy Baldwin (D) of Wisconsin to lobby for a bill that would support efforts to improve the image of women and girls in the media.

Girls themselves have joined different advocacy efforts, including organizing and participating in the SPARK (Sexualization Protest: Action, Resistance, Knowledge) Summit in New York City, a gathering of girls and adults who hold forums on media awareness, sexuality, and fighting stereotypes.

Schools can also share the burden. Catherine Steiner-Adair, a therapist and educational consultant, has worked with school systems across the country for 30 years to develop curriculum that will increase social and emotional intelligence among boys and girls. She says that programs where girls are encouraged to create and then delve into their own projects are often successful.

"Girls discover what it means to take their own interests seriously and to pursue them deeply and vigorously," she says. She says that schools that can start focusing on these issues earliest have the best success. In a four-year study published in 2007 by the Collaborative for Academic, Social, and Emotional Learning, researchers found that students who participate in these sorts of programs show more empathy, self-confidence, and more academic success than their peers without social-emotional curriculum.

"Given today's culture and the access people have and the lack of boundaries between home and school and between people and technology, you have to begin this work in first grade," she says. "The schools that are doing it in first grade are very different cultures — they're kinder, they're more respectful, they're less bullying."

Girls Stuck in the Social-Feedback Loop

Ms. Steiner-Adair's point about technology is the elephant in the chat room.

In any conversation about the sexualization of girls, the Internet is always mentioned as a huge new challenge. Not only does the Web allow easy — and often unwanted — access to sexual images (in terms of numbers of websites and views, porn is king of the Web), it offers a social-feedback loop that is heavy on appearance and superficiality, and low on values that scholars say might undermine sexualization, such as intelligence and compassion.

Girls — and boys — encourage each other to embrace sexualization. Teens who post sexy pictures of themselves on Facebook, for instance, are rewarded with encouraging comments. Educator and author Rachel Simmons, who recently rereleased *Odd Girl Out*, her book about girl aggression, with new chapters on the Internet, tells of a 13-year-old who posted a photo of herself in tight leggings, her behind lifted toward the camera.

"She posts it on Facebook and gets 10 comments underneath it telling her how great her butt looks," Ms. Simmons says.

"Girls are using social media to get feedback in areas that they've been told by the culture that they need to express or work on. That's not girls being stupid. . . . Many girls post or send provocative images because they're growing up in a culture that places a lot of value in their sexuality."

The answer is not for parents to cancel the Wi-Fi, Simmons and others say. There are many ways that girls can use the Internet and social media for good. But the technology does require monitoring — and self-evaluation.

It's hard to criticize a girl for delving into social media, for instance, when her parents are constantly checking their own iPhones.

"We can't sit there and say, 'Oh, the kids are so messed up,'" she says. "We have to look at ourselves."

RESPOND •

1. As Hanes represents the "Disney Princess Effect," what is it, and why does it matter? What other cultural trends is it related to? According to Hanes's characterization of the situation, who or what might be responsible for the increasing sexualization of little girls?
2. In its online form, the original article included a link to an online photo gallery: **http://bit.ly/t8qkxP**. Examine these photos and their captions. Do they merely illustrate the article, or are they providing particular kinds of support for the claims it makes? Which photo(s) and caption(s) do you find most effective? Why? (Chapter 14, which discusses visual arguments, may help you think systematically about these questions.)
3. Hanes uses statistics along with other kinds of evidence in interesting ways to support her claims. (Often arguments about this topic in the media rely primarily on personal experience or analyses of a few cases.) Find three or four statistics Hanes cites that gave you pause—that surprised you a bit—and be prepared to share these, to talk about your response, and to explain the value of using statistics effectively when discussing topics that are often discussed only in terms of personal experience.
4. Visit Mary Finucane's blog, *Disney Princess Recovery: Bringing Sexy Back for a Full Refund*: **http://bit.ly/gIwa2H**. Pay special attention to the "Welcome" information on the right-hand side of the page. How accurately has Hanes characterized and represented Finucane's stance or position toward sexualization? What evidence can you provide for your evaluation?
5. Another especially interesting aspect of this article is the process by which Hanes defines the notion of *sexualization*. Rather than giving a single definition at the first mention of the term, she builds up a definition across the course of the article. Skim the article again, noting every place that she provides or more indirectly suggests a definition for *sexualization*. Once you have collected and listed these instances of definition, **write a formal definition** of the sort you might use in a paper on this topic. Then **create an operational definition** of the term. Finally, **give a definition by example**. (See Chapter 9 for information on kinds of definitions. To complete this assignment, you may decide that you need to consult other sources; if you do, be sure to credit them properly, using information provided in Chapter 22.)

Steve Kelley has been drawing cartoons since he was a college student at Dartmouth, and he held positions as the staff cartoonist at the *San Diego Union Tribune* and the *New Orleans Times-Picayune*. With Jeff Parker, he created the award-winning cartoon strip *Dustin*. Kelley also does stand-up comedy. How do you think Kelley might respond to the first selection in this chapter, Stephanie Hanes's "Little Girls or Little Women? The Disney Princess Effect"? *Steve Kelley Editorial Cartoon* used with the permission of Steve Kelley and Creators Syndicate.

Making a Visual Argument: Cartoons and Stereotypes

▲ *A well-known anthropologist claims that if he were dropped into a strange culture and had only an afternoon to figure out the nature of social organization there, he'd ask local people to tell him jokes because jokes ultimately reveal the fault lines in a society; that is, they indirectly indicate where the social divisions are. Jokes frequently treat topics that are taboo or nearly so; thus, they likewise reveal perspectives on controversial issues as understood within a given society. Of course, jokes are a genre of the spoken language while cartoons are their multimodal print equivalent. By combining image and text in some way, cartoons present arguments that critique some aspect of the social order, whether a controversy that has simmered for quite a while or some recent event that was the hot topic of yesterday's talk shows and Twitter feeds. The arguments cartoons present, often mocking in nature, are profoundly local. A major reason humor, including jokes and cartoons, doesn't translate well is that the things each society (and subgroups within any given society) considers funny and the topics it considers appropriate to make light of vary widely. As you study the cartoons in this selection, examine each from these perspectives. Is the cartoon concerned with a long-standing controversy or some specific event or situation? What social divisions in American society does the cartoon acknowledge, and what is the basis for those divisions — political affiliation, age, ethnicity, sex or gender, sexual identity, region of birth, or some combination of these? As noted in the introductory note to the chapter, you will also want to consider which common stereotypes you don't see represented in these cartoons and whether it is because they are too potentially incendiary or explosive to find their way into print in mainstream publications or in textbooks like this one. In other words, what social taboos can't be violated, at least not in these contexts, when the medium is cartoons? Finally, think about the cultural knowledge required to understand each of these cartoons; as you'll see, in some cases, that knowledge is quite complex.*

Adam Zyglis is editorial cartoonist for the *Buffalo News*. Like Kelley, he drew cartoons for his college paper at Canisius College, where he majored in computer science, minored in math, took a concentration in studio art, and wrote his honors thesis on editorial cartooning. (How is that for calling stereotypes into question?) Consider how Zyglis comments on generational differences in attitudes and experiences in this cartoon. (It's fairly easy to guess which generation Zyglis belongs to!) © Adam Zyglis/Cagle Cartoons, Inc.

Harley Schwadron has been publishing cartoons as a freelancer in a range of newspapers for over a quarter of a century; his cartoons and illustrations have also appeared in a number of books. As you analyze this cartoon, seek to place it in the context of debates about gun control in American society. www.CartoonStock.com

Barry Deutsch is an award-winning Portland-based cartoonist and a graduate of Portland State University. He creates *Ampersand*, which he characterizes as having "a generally progressive sensibility." His work appears regularly in *Dollars and Sense* magazine, which is subtitled *Real World Economics*, and he's currently working on a comic book featuring an eleven-year-old Orthodox Jewish girl as protagonist. Once you've studied the cartoon, imagine whether you might have interpreted it differently had you not known the cartoonist is a man. In other words, would you understand its message differently if you assumed a female cartoonist had drawn it? B. Deutsch, leftycartoons.com

Pulitzer Prize–winning syndicated cartoonist Clay Bennett draws editorial cartoons for the *Chattanooga Times Free Press*. He has worked at the *Pittsburgh Post-Gazette*, the *Fayetteville* (NC) *Times*, and the *St. Petersburg Times*. Bennett lost his job at the St. Petersburg paper, he and supporters contend, because of his political views. As he notes, "Obviously, expressing your point of view can cost you your job," a reminder that cartoons are anything but innocent fun. This cartoon appeared in 2014, after the shooting of Michael Brown by a police officer in Ferguson, Missouri. How do you imagine Americans with different sets of political convictions might respond to it? What about Americans from different ethnic backgrounds? *Clay Bennett Editorial Cartoon* used with the permission of Clay Bennett, the Washington Post Writers Group, and the Cartoonist Group. All rights reserved.

John Deering serves as chief editorial cartoonist at the *Arkansas Democrat-Gazette*, a post he has held for over fifteen years. His cartoons are syndicated in publications across the country. Like the other cartoonists featured in this section, he has won numerous awards. Like the previous cartoon, this one is a response to the events in Ferguson, Missouri, during 2014. Do you think the message of the cartoon would have been different had the two young gentlemen on the right side of the cartoon been portrayed as members of ethnic minority groups and especially as African American? Why or why not? *John Deering Editorial Cartoon* used with the permission of John Deering and Creators Syndicate. All rights reserved.

RESPOND.

1. How would you state the argument each cartoon is making? In particular, what position or stance is the cartoonist taking with respect to the topic of the cartoon? What evidence can you cite for your claim?
2. Cartoonists who create single-panel cartoons like these face great challenges: they have limited resources and space to make their argument clear, and they must do so in a humorous way. A key way they succeed is by paying careful attention to visual and verbal detail. Choose two of these cartoons you think are especially effective in this regard, and be prepared to explain to your classmates how the cartoonists have used visual images and words effectively in ways that support each cartoon's argument.
3. A common source of humor is the juxtaposition of things that normally do not occur together. Where do we see evidence of this strategy in each of these cartoons?
4. How does each cartoonist rely on stereotypes to make his point? In other words, which stereotypes common in American society do we see represented in these cartoons, and how does each cartoonist represent them so that they are immediately identifiable by readers?
5. How do the last two cartoons respond to the events in Ferguson during 2014? Do you consider either an especially appropriate response to those events? Collect several cartoons about these events or a similar event that has divided the country along various lines of social difference, and **write a rhetorical analysis** of them. (See Chapter 6 on writing rhetorical analyses.) We'd encourage you to collect cartoons from different kinds of sources. Both of these cartoons are from major newspapers in the South. Do cartoons in other regions treat the issue differently? And what about cartoons in newspapers produced for the African American community?
6. As noted in the introduction to this selection, understanding humor requires a great deal of local contextual information. Imagine that a newly arrived international student asked you to explain one of these cartoons to her/him. In several healthy paragraphs, **write a description and an explanation** of the cartoon you find most interesting. Begin by describing what readers see when they read the cartoon; then move on to explain what the cartoon means. Be sure to deal with the issues raised in questions 1–4. Conclude by explaining what Americans would likely find humorous about the cartoon and what the cartoon tells us about American society.

Amy Stretten, a member of the Chickahominy Tribe of Virginia, is a Florida-based bilingual (Spanish/English) multimedia consultant and producer whose focus is helping public and private entities successfully deal with the challenges of being part of a diverse, multicultural country and world. This technology-enriched essay appeared on the Web site Fusion in late 2013. As you'll note, much of Stretten's evidence for her claims is only a click away; we've provided a URL (p. 524, paragraph 13) to help you find the evidence she is drawing on as she makes her argument. As you read Stretten's essay, consider the interesting ways in which she combines personal experience with artistic and inartistic proofs to support her claims. (If these terms are unfamiliar to you, check out Chapter 4 on arguments based on fact and reason.)

Appropriating Native American Imagery Honors No One but the Prejudice

AMY STRETTEN

Sept. 18, 2013

I was a sophomore in high school, about fifteen years old, when a rather hostile group of cheerleaders and football players cornered me, yelling, as I sat on a bench in the quad between classes. "Don't you have school pride?" a cheerleader shouted. "You should feel proud! We're honoring your people!" one football player hollered.

I was the only Native American (as far as I knew) at Woodbridge High School in Irvine, California. Irvine is a planned city in Southern California and one of the safest cities in the United States, but I didn't feel safe that day.

I had met one-on-one with the principal, my guidance counselor, a few teachers, and several students to share my negative feelings toward our school's mascot—an anonymous Native American "warrior" with long, flowing, jet-black hair, a large nose, and huge muscles. I guess I thought if I made it known that I felt appropriating Native American imagery was offensive, they'd stop. I was outnumbered, though, and my personal feelings didn't matter. But that's the thing: as Native people, especially as urban Natives (what we Indigenous people living in urban centers call ourselves), we are almost always outnumbered. So, we go unnoticed and unheard. Our opinions never really matter.

Students wore goofy, cartoonish costumes of our mascot (and his equally tasteless "warrior princess" girlfriend) at pep rallies and games. The pair would dance and do occasional acrobatic moves, as they made their grand entrance to the deafening sounds of the school's marching band, playing the quintessential° Hollywood fight song that, for me at least, conjures up images of a scene from an old Western movie: "savage" Indians on horseback approaching a village of settlers . . . Uh-oh, there must be trouble.

quintessential: of or relating to the perfect example of something.

Spectators always stood for the song and sliced the air with their arms. I'm sure 5
you've seen it, or done it yourself—the tomahawk chop. Every now and then you'd hear a distant war whoop. And if you were lucky, you'd get to see an imitation of war paint on game day.

You likely won't be surprised to learn that this Associated Press photo went viral in April 2014, shortly after a Cleveland Indians game where local American Indians protested the continuing use by sports teams of Native nicknames and logos. Sportswriters contend that the team uses its Chief Wahoo logo far less than in the past, a claim disputed by some and a move that the team's management has yet to acknowledge—if it is, in fact, a matter of policy. Obviously, some fans continue to dress in "red face." The Associated Press identifies the person on the left as Robert Roche, an Apache. © Peter Pattakos

I didn't understand how face paint purchased from a drug store and a faux headdress made of brown construction paper and dyed arts & crafts feathers was respect. How does celebrating Native people with war imagery honor a living people? Well, it doesn't. It saddens me that this is all we are to you: people who speak in broken English ("How.") and the only thing we do is engage in battle with bows, arrows, and tomahawks. Oh, and perform an occasional rain dance when we hear a repetitive drum beat.

Racial stereotyping, inaccurate racial portrayals, and cultural appropriation do not honor a living breathing people. Plain and simple, cultural appropriation—especially when members of the culture protest the appropriation—is not respectful.

It's beyond me why people are okay with this. With any other culture, people would be up in arms.

Maybe the Woodbridge High School community and others don't understand how this type of bullying—yes, it's bullying—affects young people. Native American and Alaskan Native youth have the highest rates of suicide-related fatalities, according to the Centers for Disease Control and Prevention. The lack of positive images of Native Americans doesn't help self-esteem.

I'm not the only one who thinks that racist mascots don't belong in sports. Just 10
ask a psychologist.

The American Psychology Association (APA) recommends retiring American Indian mascots altogether. First of all, the organization found that the stereotypical images were harmful for the development and self-esteem of American Indian students. That wasn't all. The portrayals had a negative effect on all students.

The problem, according to the APA, is that American Indian mascots are "undermining the educational experiences of members of all communities – especially those who have had little or no contact with Indigenous peoples." And, it "establishes an unwelcome and often times hostile learning environment for American Indian students that affirms negative images/ stereotypes that are promoted in mainstream society."

One of the best films on the subject that I've seen is the documentary film *In Whose Honor?*. The film focuses on Charlene Teters (Spokane) and her campaign against "Chief Illiniwek," the mascot of University of Illinois. Other highly publicized Native American mascot battles are described here: http://abcnews.go.com/US/sports-mascots-stir-controversy/story?id=20194389.

Unfortunately, this racial insensitivity extends beyond U.S. borders. Ian Campeau, an Ojibway father and member of the DJ group, A Tribe Called Red, has filed a human rights complaint with the Ontario Human Rights Tribunal against an amateur football club, the Nepean "Redskins," in hopes of eradicating the use of the term altogether. The team is based in Canada's capital city, Ottawa, and uses a cartoon image of a red-faced Indian man with a large nose, a long, black braid, and two feathers in his hair as their mascot.

"The players call each other 'redskins' on the field," said Campeau in a press 15
release. "How are they going to differentiate the playing field from the school yard? What's going to stop them from calling my daughter a redskin in the schoolyard? That's as offensive as using the n-word."

If Campeau's request is granted, the Human Rights Tribunal would order the National Capital Amateur Football Association to change the name and logo. His complaint also requests that the Tribunal draft a policy on the use of Indigenous imagery in sports, which could have an impact on teams of various levels that use the Redskins name in Canada.

The most in-your-face examples of racist mascots are in professional sports, including the football team of our nation's capital, the Washington Redskins. The team's owner, Dan Snyder, refuses to change the team's name despite the obvious offensive nature of the imagery and name itself. Snyder has been quoted as saying, "We'll never change it. It's that simple. NEVER—you can use caps."

Well, to anyone else who believes in turning a marginalized group of people into a goofy caricature, I'd like to ask: Who asked you to honor me? Let alone in this way? Cultural exploitation for profit in the name of respect is not how you honor a minority group. You honor someone important with a building named in their honor, a street named after them, a scholarship fund in their name, or a key to the city—not a sports mascot.

In 2001, after facing increased pressure from the Southern California Indian Center and others, Irvine Unified School District decided to retire Woodbridge High School's Warrior mascot and imagery. The school would paint over the huge mural on the side of the gym of the anonymous Native American warrior and they would remove it from the gym floor. The *L.A. Times* reported on it.

But racism dies hard. In 2009, eight years later, my mother was forced to contact 20
the school district due to cyber-bullying my sister, who is nine years younger, faced while a student at Woodbridge. A group of students who were in favor of the Warrior mascot created a Facebook campaign called "Save Our Warrior Mascot" and several members of the group wanted to find out who the sophomore girl opposed to the mascot was and "teach her a lesson." (Their words.)

Last year was my ten-year high school reunion, and despite making close friendships with some classmates, I decided not to attend primarily because one former classmate suggested they get together to repaint the warrior face on the exterior of the gym.

The name Redskins is offensive to many, but my beef is not just with the name. It's with the imagery. When can we let go of our need to own Native American imagery?

RESPOND •

1. Stretten makes a complex argument that does not mince words, claiming that Native mascots are harmful to both Native Americans and Americans who are not Native. In particular, she links mascots with bullying in schools—a hot topic in 2013—and raises what are ultimately profound questions about ownership of images. Did Stretten challenge you to think about this issue in new ways? Why or why not?

2. How and where does Stretten use personal experience to good effect in this essay? Reread the essay, marking the passages where Stretten relies on personal experience. How would the essay be different if those passages were omitted? (If you find this question challenging, look up "personal experience" in the book's index, and you'll find discussions in several chapters of its use and power.)
3. As the headnote points out, Stretten does not rely uniquely on personal experience, however. What other sorts of evidence does she present? (Again, Chapter 4 may help you out here.) Visit the URL link in paragraph 13 of this article to determine whether Stretten uses online sources in fair and appropriate ways. (Chapters 18–20, which deal with aspects of finding, evaluating, and using sources appropriately, may be helpful here.)
4. Stretten's essay raises complex questions about who owns or should own the past and the present. Characterize her position on these questions, making explicit as best you can her reasoning for her position. Where, exactly, do stereotypes play into these questions? (Chapter 7 on structuring arguments may prove useful here.)
5. **Write an extended dialogue** between the two Americans pictured in the photo accompanying this article: Robert Roche, a Native American who is Apache, and the sports fan, who is not Native American (or, certainly, that is the assumption that everyone who reposted or retweeted this image made, and it is likely a safe one for many reasons). In the dialogue, you'll obviously want to construct an argument, likely a proposal argument. You will need to determine whether your goal is to construct a Rogerian or an invitational argument, one that builds on common ground (see Chapter 7) or one that offers no room for compromise.
6. **Write a proposal essay** in which you tackle the issues Stretten raises but with a focus on another debate about stereotypical representations. The mascots for college football teams have often been controversial, but there are certainly other issues: the statues that do (and do not) grace the campuses of colleges across the country; the Confederate flag; the presence of crosses, statues representing the Ten Commandments, or menorahs; the Muslim call to prayer played over loudspeakers; and the representation of various groups in television cartoons or programs. As in all strong proposal arguments, you'll need to acknowledge and discuss perspectives other than the one you put forward. (See Chapter 12 on proposal arguments for assistance with this assignment.)

▼ *Charles A. Riley II is a professor of journalism at Baruch College, part of the City University of New York. He also served as editor in chief of* WE, *a now-defunct national bimonthly magazine that focused on disability issues. During his career, he has received several awards for his writing on issues relating to disability. (Riley is able-bodied, a fact that he believes has important consequences for his writing on these issues.) Among his books are* Aristocracy and the Modern Imagination *(1980);* Disability and Business: Best Practices and Strategies for Inclusion *(1980);* Color Codes: Modern Theories of Color in Philosophy, Painting and Architecture, Literature, Music, and Psychology *(1995);* Small Business, Big Politics: What Entrepreneurs Need to Know to Use Their Growing Political Power *(1996); and* The Jazz Age in France *(2004). The selections featured here come from* Disability and the Media: Prescriptions for Change *(2005). These selections include the opening pages of Riley's preface as well as an appendix created by the National Center on Disability and Journalism in 2002 that offers guidelines for portraying people with disabilities in the media. As you read, note ways in which Riley marshals evidence to demonstrate a need for change and how the appendix constitutes a set of proposals to create that change.*

Disability and the Media: Prescriptions for Change

CHARLES A. RILEY II

Every time Aimee Mullins sees her name in the papers she braces herself for some predictable version of the same headline followed by the same old story. Paralympian, actress, and fashion model, Mullins is a bilateral, below-the-knee amputee, who sprints a hundred meters in less than sixteen seconds on a set of running prostheses called Cheetahs because they were fashioned after the leg form of the world's fastest animal. First, there are the headlines: "Overcoming All Hurdles" (she is not a hurdler, although she is a long jumper) or "Running Her Own Race," "Nothing Stops Her," or the dreaded overused "Profile in Courage." Then come the clichés and stock scenes, from the prosthetist's office to the winner's podium. Many of the articles dwell on her success as the triumph of biomechanics, a "miracle of modern medicine,"

Aimee Mullins at the sixth annual L'Oréal Paris Women of Worth awards ceremony in 2011.
Eugene Gologursky/Wire Image/Getty Images

turning her fairy tale into a *Coppélia*° narrative (or a *Six Million Dollar Woman*° movie sequel). From the local paper where she grew up (Allentown, Pennsylvania), to national exposure in *Esquire* and *People* and guest spots on *Oprah*, Mullins's "inspiring" saga is recycled almost verbatim by well-meaning journalists for audiences who never seem to get enough of its feel-good message even if they never actually find out who Mullins is.

This is the patronizing, trivializing, and marginalizing ur-narrative° of disability in the media today. The mainstream press finds it irresistible, but this steady diet of sugar has its dangers. The cliché has excluded the mature, fully realized coverage that people with disabilities have long deserved. For Mullins, it has translated into well over her Warholian° fifteen minutes of fame, bringing her the financial rewards of sponsorships, motivational speaking gigs, and modeling contracts at the expense of being turned into a latter-day poster child.° Stories about her rarely get around to mentioning that she was a Pentagon intern while making the dean's list as an academic star in history and diplomacy at Georgetown, or that she is one of the actresses in Matthew Barney's avant-garde *Cremaster* film series.

Mullins is not the only celebrity with a disability to be steamrolled out of three-dimensional humanity into allegorical° flatness. All the branches of

Coppélia: a nineteenth-century French comic and sentimental opera in which Dr. Coppélius creates a dancing doll that is so lifelike that a young man falls in love with her.

Six Million Dollar Woman: an allusion to *Six Million Dollar Man*, a late 1970s ABC television program about an astronaut who was "rebuilt" after a crash to become a cyborg, part human and part machine.

ur-narrative: the prefix *ur-* refers to the earliest, original, or most primitive or basic. Hence, the ur-narrative is the source narrative on which all others are based.

Warholian: a reference to Andy Warhol (1928–1987), American avant-garde artist who commented in 1968, "In the future, everyone will be famous for fifteen minutes," a critique of how modern media create instant celebrities.

Early examples of poster children.
AP/Wide World Photos

poster child: a perfect representative. The source of the phrase is the image of a disabled child or one with a visible medical condition whose photo is used on posters to elicit sympathy and donations.

allegorical: the adjectival form of *allegory*, a moral story in which the characters, always one-dimensional in nature, suggest a meaning beyond the story. Thus, in Aesop's fable about the ant and the grasshopper, listeners are to understand that the wise person prepares for future needs, as the ant did, rather than wasting time, as did the grasshopper.

Before he offers his proposal, Riley first explains how stereotyping causes problems for the disabled. For more on causal arguments, see Chapter 11.

LINK TO P. 240

the media considered here, from print to television, radio and the movies (including advertisements) to multimedia and the Internet, are guilty of the same distillation of stories to meet their own, usually fiscal, ends. For example, even though her autobiography is remarkably ahead of its time in its anticipation of disability culture, by the time Helen Keller° had been sweetened for movie audiences in Patty Duke's° version of her life, little was left out of the fiery trailblazer. In much the same way, Christopher Reeve° and Michael J. Fox° have been pigeonholed by print and television hagiographers° as lab experiments and tragic heroes. Packaged to raise philanthropic or advertising dollars, they perform roles no less constrained than the pretty-boy parts they played on screen earlier in their lives.

What is wrong with this picture? By jamming Mullins and the others into prefabricated stories — the supercrip, the medical miracle, the object of pity — writers and producers have outfitted them with the narrative equivalent of an ill-fitting set of prostheses. Each of these archetypal narratives has its way of reaching mass audiences, selling products (including magazines and movie tickets), and financially rewarding both the media outlet and the featured subject. In some ways, as optimists point out, this represents an improvement. We have had millennia of fiction and nonfiction depicting

Helen Keller (1880–1968): the first American who was both deaf and blind to graduate from college, Keller was an author and activist for progressive causes.

Patty Duke (1946–): an American actress who played Helen Keller in the 1959 play *The Miracle Worker* and in the 1962 film version of the story.

Christopher Reeve (1952–2004): an American actor who is best known for his four Superman films. In 1995, he was paralyzed in a riding accident and used a wheelchair for the rest of his life. After his accident, he became an activist for public issues related to spinal-cord injuries and stem-cell research.

Michael J. Fox (1961–): an award-winning Canadian-born actor. Diagnosed with Parkinson's disease in 1991, he revealed the condition to the public in 1998 and partially retired in 2000.

hagiographer: technically, one who studies saints. Here, hagiography is used to refer to the ways in which able-bodied individuals often portray people with disabilities as saints, thereby refusing to let them be fully human.

Patty Duke (center) as Helen Keller in The Miracle Worker. Everett Collection

Michael J. Fox, an actor and a Parkinson's disease activist. Hubert Boesi DPA/LANDOV angry people with disabilities as villains, from Oedipus° to Ahab° to Dr. Strangelove.° The vestigial° traces of that syndrome still occasionally recur, although with far less frequency, in current movies or television series and in journalists' fixation on the mental instability of violent criminals. However, today's storytellers, including those in the disability media, are more likely to make people with disabilities into "heroes of assimilation," to borrow a phrase from Erving Goffman's° seminal work on disability, *Stigma: Notes on the Management of Spoiled Identity*.

As Goffman knew too well, just as the stigmatization of the villain had its 5
dilatory effects° on societal attitudes, so too does relentless hagiography, particularly by transforming individuals into symbols and by playing on an audience's sympathy and sense of superiority. Those who labor in the field of disability studies point out that disability culture and its unique strengths are absent from this story of normalization. Others would simply note that the individual is lost in the fable, an all-American morality tale that strikes one of the most resonant chords in the repertoire: redemption. Like the deathless Horatio Alger° tale, the story of the hero of assimilation emphasizes many of the deepest values and beliefs of the Puritan tradition, especially the notion that suffering makes us stronger and better. An able-bodied person falls from grace (often literally falling or crashing, as in the case of many spinal cord injuries), progresses through the shadows of rehabilitation and

Oedipus: the mythical Greek king who unknowingly fulfills a prophecy that he will kill his father and marry his mother. After realizing what he has done, he blinds himself.

Ahab: the captain of the whaling ship in Herman Melville's 1851 novel *Moby-Dick*. After losing a leg in an earlier effort to kill the whale Moby-Dick, Ahab is obsessed with harpooning the creature. His actions lead to the loss of the ship and the lives of all onboard with the exception of Ishmael, whose narrative opens the novel.

Ahab from Moby-Dick. Everett Collection

Dr. Strangelove: the title character in the 1964 film comedy *Dr. Strangelove or: How I Learned to Stop Worrying and Love the Bomb*. Strangelove, played by Peter Sellers, uses a wheelchair and suffers from alien hand syndrome. He is often used to represent the stereotype of a "mad scientist."

vestigial: adjectival form of *vestige*, a more basic or rudimentary structure that no longer has any useful function; therefore, a useless leftover.

Erving Goffman (1922–1982): a highly influential Canadian-born sociologist who taught in the United States. His work was much concerned with the nature of the social organization of everyday life.

dilatory effects: effects that delay or cause delay, here of positive changes in societal attitudes.

Horatio Alger Jr. (1832–1899): the prolific author of popular "rags to riches" tales in which hardworking, virtuous poor boys rise to stable and productive lives at the lower edges of the middle class.

depression, and by force of willpower along with religious belief pulls through to attain a quality of life that is less disabled, more normal, basking in the glow of recognition for beating the odds.

This pervasive narrative can be found in print, on television, in movies, in advertisements, and on the Web. Its corrosive effect on understanding and attitudes is as yet unnoticed. It is impossible to know the full degree of damage wreaked by the demeaning and wildly inaccurate portrayal of people with disabilities, nor is it altogether clear whether much current progress is being made. Painful as it is for me as an advocate to report the bad news, I cannot help but point out that the "movement" has slowed to a crawl in terms of political and economic advancement for 54 million Americans. The stasis° that threatens is at least partly to be blamed on a reassuring, recurring image projected by the media that numbs nondisabled readers and viewers into thinking that all is well.

stasis: here, inactivity or lack of movement.

This study aims to expose the extent of the problem while pinpointing how writers, editors, photographers, filmmakers, advertisers, and the executives who give them their marching orders go wrong, or occasionally get it right. Through a close analysis of the technical means of representation, in conjunction with the commentary of leading voices in the disability community, I hope to guide future coverage to a more fair and accurate way of putting the disability story on screen or paper. Far from another stab at the political correctness target, the aim of this content analysis° of journalism, film, advertising, and Web publishing is to cut through the accumulated clichés and condescension to find an adequate vocabulary that will finally represent the disability community in all its vibrant and fascinating diversity. Nothing like that will ever happen if the press and advertisers continue to think, write, and design as they have in the past.

content analysis: a family of research methodologies used in the humanities and social sciences that focus on the content of "messages"—books, articles, movies, paintings, research interviews—to study recurring themes or patterns across time or at a given time. For example, we could use content analysis to trace the shift from the use of *crippled* to *disabled* in newspaper articles or the ways that people with disabilities were portrayed in early twentieth-century American novels.

Appendix A

Guidelines for Portraying People with Disabilities in the Media

Fear of the unknown. Inadequate experience. Incorrect or distorted information. Lack of knowledge. These shape some of the attitudinal barriers that people with disabilities face as they become involved in their communities.

People working in the media exert a powerful influence over the way people with disabilities are perceived. It's important to the 54 million Americans with disabilities that they be portrayed realistically and that their disabilities are explained accurately.

Awareness is the first step toward change. 10

TIPS FOR REPORTING ON PEOPLE WITH DISABILITIES

- When referring to individuals with disabilities use "disability," not "handicapped."
- Emphasize the person, not the disability or condition. Use "people with disabilities" rather than "disabled persons," and "people with epilepsy" rather than "epileptics."
- Omit mention of an individual's disability unless it is pertinent to the story.
- Depict the typical achiever with a disability, not just the super-achiever.
- Choose words that are accurate descriptions and have non-judgmental connotations.
- People with disabilities live everyday lives and should be portrayed as contributing members of the community. These portrayals should:

  Depict people with disabilities experiencing the same pain/pleasure that others derive from everyday life, e.g., work, parenting, education, sports and community involvement.

  Feature a variety of people with disabilities when possible, not just someone easily recognized by the general public.

  Depict employees/employers with disabilities working together.
- Ask people with disabilities to provide correct information and assistance to avoid stereotypes in the media.
- Portray people with disabilities as people, with both strengths and weaknesses.

APPROPRIATE WORDS WHEN PORTRAYING PEOPLE WITH DISABILITIES

Never Use

victim—use: person who has/experienced/with.
[the] cripple[d]—use: person with a disability.
afflicted by/with—use: person has.
invalid—use: a person with a disability.
normal—most people, including people with disabilities, think they are.
patient—connotes sickness. Use: person with a disability.

Avoid Using

wheelchair bound/confined—use: uses a wheelchair or wheelchair user.
homebound employment—use: employed in the home.

Use with Care

courageous, brave, inspirational and similar words routinely used to describe persons with disabilities. Adaption to a disability does not necessarily mean someone acquires these traits.

Interviewing People with Disabilities

When interviewing a person with a disability, relax! Conduct your interview as you would with anyone. Be clear and candid in your questioning and ask for clarification of terms or issues when necessary. Be upfront about deadlines, the focus of your story, and when and where it will appear.

Interviewing Etiquette

- Shake hands when introduced to someone with a disability. People with limited hand use or artificial limbs do shake hands.
- Speak directly to people with disabilities, not through their companions.
- Don't be embarrassed using such phrases as "See you soon," "Walk this way" or "Got to run." These are common expressions, and are unlikely to offend.
- If you offer to help, wait until the offer is accepted.
- Consider the needs of people with disabilities when planning events.
- Conduct interviews in a manner that emphasizes abilities, achievements and individual qualities.
- Don't emphasize differences by putting people with disabilities on a pedestal.

When Interviewing People with Hearing Disabilities

- Attract the person's attention by tapping on his or her shoulder or waving.
- If you are interviewing someone with a partial hearing loss, ask where it would be most comfortable for you to sit.
- If the person is lip-reading, look directly at him/her and speak slowly and clearly. Do not exaggerate lip movements or shout. Do speak expressively, as facial expressions, gestures and body movements will help him/her understand you.
- Position yourself facing the light source and keep hands and food away from your mouth when speaking.

This appendix offers a set of clear guidelines but sometimes does not explain the reasoning behind particular guidelines. Practice identifying the warrants, as described in Chapter 7, that lie behind these claims.

LINK TO P. 133

When Interviewing People with Vision Disabilities

- Always identify yourself and anyone else who might be present.
- When offering a handshake, say, "Shall we shake hands?"
- When offering seating, place the person's hand on the back or arm of the seat.
- Let the person know if you move or need to end the conversation.

When Interviewing People with Speech Disabilities

- Ask short questions that require short answers when possible.
- Do not feign understanding. Try rephrasing your questions, if necessary.

When Interviewing People Using a Wheelchair or Crutches

- Do not lean on a person's wheelchair. The chair is part of his/her body space.
- Sit or kneel to place yourself at eye level with the person you are interviewing.
- Make sure the interview site is accessible. Check for:
  Reserved parking for people with disabilities
  A ramp or step-free entrance
  Accessible restrooms
  An elevator if the interview is not on the first floor
  Water fountains and telephones low enough for wheelchair use

Be sure to notify the interviewee if there are problems with the location. Discuss what to do and make alternate plans.

Writing about Disability

One of the first and most significant steps to changing negative stereotypes and attitudes toward people with disabilities begins when we rethink the way written and spoken images are used to portray people with disabilities. The following is a brief, but important, list of suggestions for portraying people with disabilities in the media.

People with disabilities are not "handicapped," unless there are physical or attitudinal barriers that make it difficult for them to participate in everyday activities. An office building with steps and no entry ramp creates a "handicapping" barrier for people who use wheelchairs. In the same way, a hotel that does not have a TTY/telephone (teletypewriter) creates a barrier for someone who is hearing disabled. It is important to focus on the person, not necessarily the disability. In writing, name the person first and then, if necessary, explain his or her disability. The same rule applies when speaking. Don't focus on someone's disability unless it's crucial to the point being made.

In long, written materials, when many references have been made to persons with disabilities or someone who is disabled, it is acceptable for later references to refer to "disabled persons" or "disabled individuals."

Because a person is not a condition or a disease, avoid referring to some- 15
one with a disability by his or her disability alone. For example, don't say someone is a "post-polio" or a "C.P." or an "epileptic." Refer instead to someone who has post-polio syndrome, or has cerebral palsy, or has epilepsy.

Don't use "disabled" as a noun because it implies a state of separateness. "The disabled" are not a group apart from the rest of society. When writing or speaking about people with disabilities, choose descriptive words and portray people in a positive light.

Avoid words with negative connotations:

- Avoid calling someone a "victim."
- Avoid referring to people with disabilities as "cripples" or "crippled." This is negative and demeaning language.
- Don't write or say that someone is "afflicted."
- Avoid the word "invalid" as it means, quite literally, "not valid."
- Write or speak about people who use wheelchairs. Wheelchair users are not "wheelchair-bound."
- Refer to people who are not disabled as "non-disabled" or "able-bodied." When you call non-disabled people "normal," the implication is that people with disabilities are not normal.
- Someone who is disabled is only a patient to his or her physician or in a reference to medical treatment.
- Avoid cliches. Don't use "unfortunate," "pitiful," "poor," "dumb," "crip," "deformed," "retard," "blind as a bat" or other patronizing and demeaning words.
- In the same vein, don't glamorize or make heroes of people with disabilities simply because they have adapted to their disabilities.

Your concerted efforts to use positive, non-judgmental respectful language when referring to people with disabilities in writing and in everyday speaking can go a long way toward helping to change negative stereotypes.

RESPOND •

1. In what ways does Riley contend that the media and popular culture wrongly stereotype people with disabilities? What negative consequences follow from this stereotyping for such people? For those who do not have disabilities? Why?
2. How convincingly has Riley defined a problem or need, which is the first step in a proposal argument? (For a discussion of proposal arguments, see Chapter 12.)
3. What is your response to "Appendix A: Guidelines for Portraying People with Disabilities in the Media"? Are you familiar with the practices that these guidelines seek to prevent? Do you find the guidelines useful or necessary? Why or why not? What justification might be offered for why specific guidelines are important? (Here, you will want to choose three or four of the guidelines and make explicit the arguments in support of each of them.)
4. Look for some specific representations of people with disabilities in current media and popular culture—in advertisements, television programs, or movies. To what extent do these representations perpetuate the stereotypes that Riley discusses, "the supercrip, the medical miracle, the object of pity" (paragraph 4)? **Write an argument of fact** in which you present your findings. (For a discussion of arguments of fact, see Chapter 8.) If you do not find representations of people with disabilities in various media or in popular culture, that absence is significant and merits discussion and analysis.
5. **Write an evaluative essay** in which you assess the value of these guidelines. In other words, if the media follow these guidelines, what will the consequences be for the media? For society at large? To what extent will following these guidelines likely influence negative stereotypes about people with disabilities? (For a discussion of evaluative arguments, see Chapter 10.)

Aimee Mullins practices her jumps. © Lynn Johnson/Aurora/Getty Images

▼ *Claude M. Steele (1946–) is currently executive chancellor and provost at the University of California at Berkeley. He held earlier administrative appointments at Stanford and Columbia and taught at several universities before becoming an administrator. Steele is a social psychologist, that is, a psychologist whose research focuses on the ways in which other people influence us; these other people may be people we know or those we imagine, and their influence on us can shape what we think, what we feel, or how we behave. An example might be our fears about how others—our best friends or strangers on the street—might respond to something we wear or say or do. Steele is best known for his work on what is called stereotype threat, the topic of this selection. In fact, this selection is the opening chapter of Steele's 2010 book,* Whistling Vivaldi and Other Clues to How Stereotypes Affect Us, *which appeared in the very important series of books* Issues of Our Times. *You'll immediately note that Steele is not writing for other psychologists; rather, he is writing for a general educated audience. Thus, the kinds of evidence he uses are not limited to the kinds of evidence—quantitative data from experiments—that he would use in a research article intended for other social psychologists. As you read, pay attention to the kinds of evidence Steele uses to support his argument; likewise pay close attention to your own response to his claims about how stereotypes ultimately affect us all.*

An Introduction: At the Root of Identity, from *Whistling Vivaldi and Other Clues to How Stereotypes Affect Us*

CLAUDE M. STEELE

1.

I have a memory of the first time I realized I was black. It was when, at seven or eight, I was walking home from school with neighborhood kids on the last day of the school year—the whole summer in front of us—and I learned that we "black" kids couldn't swim at the pool in our area park, except on Wednesday afternoons. And then on those summer Wednesdays, with our swimming suits wrapped tightly in our towels, we filed, caravan-style, out of our neighborhood toward the hallowed pool in the adjoining white neighborhood. It was a strange weekly pilgrimage. It marked the racial order of the time and place—Chicagoland, the 1950s and early 1960s. For me it was what the psychologist William Cross calls an "encounter"—with the very fact that there was a racial order. The implications of this order for my life seemed massive—a life of swimming only on Wednesday afternoons? Why? Moreover, it turned out to be a portent of things to come. I next found out that we black kids—who, by the way, lived in my neighborhood and who had been, until these encounters, just kids—couldn't go to the roller rink, except on Thursday nights. We could be regular people but only in the middle of the week? These segregations were hard to ignore. And mistakes were costly, as when, at thirteen, after arriving at six in the morning, I waited all day to be hired as a caddy at an area golf course, only to be told at the end of the day that they didn't hire Negroes. This is how I became aware I was black. I didn't know what being black meant, but I was getting the idea that it was a big deal.

With decades of hindsight, I now think I know what was going on. I was recognizing nothing less than a condition of life—most important, a condition of life tied to my race, to my being black in that time and place. The condition was simple enough: *if* I joined the caravan and went to the pool on Wednesday afternoons, *then* I got in; *if* I went to the pool any other time, *then* I didn't get in. To my seven- or eight-year-old self, this was a bad condition of life. But the condition itself wasn't the worst of it. For example, had my parents imposed it on me for not taking out the garbage, I wouldn't have been so upset. What got me was that it was imposed on me because I was black. There was nothing I could do about that, and if being black was reason enough to restrict my swimming, then what else would happen because of it?

In an interview many years later, a college student . . . would describe for me an experience that took a similar form. He was one of only two whites in an African American political science class composed of mostly black and other minority students. He, too, described a condition of life: if he said something that revealed an ignorance of African American experience, or a confusion about how to think about it, then he could well be seen as racially insensitive, or . . . worse; if he said nothing in class, then he could largely escape the suspicion of his fellow students. His condition, like my swimming pool condition, made him feel his racial identity, his whiteness, in that time and place—something he hadn't thought much about before.

From experiences like these, troubling questions arise. Will there be other conditions? How many? In how many areas of life? Will they be about important things? Can you avoid them? Do you have to stay on the lookout for them?

5 When I encountered my swimming pool restriction, it mystified me. Where did it come from? Conditions of life tied to identity like that still mystify me. But now I have a working idea about where they come from. They come from the way a society, at a given time, is organized around an identity like race. That organization reflects the history of a place, as well as the ongoing individual and group competition for opportunity and the good life. The way Chicagoland was organized around race in the late 1950s and early 1960s—the rigid housing segregation, the de facto° school segregation, the employment discrimination, and so on—meant that black people in that time and place had many restrictive conditions of life tied to their identity, perhaps the least of which was the Wednesday afternoon swimming restriction that so worried my seven- or eight-year-old self.

de facto: a Latin expression meaning "concerning fact"; in modern English, it refers to something that is the case because of practice, that is, because of what people do. It stands in contrast to *de jure*, which means "concerning law." Steele's point is that even though school segregation may not have been legal, it was the day-to-day reality for schoolchildren at that time with rare exception.

This book is about what my colleagues and I call *identity contingencies*—the things you have to deal with in a situation because you have a given social identity, because you are old, young, gay, a white male, a woman, black, Latino, politically conservative or liberal, diagnosed with bipolar disorder, a cancer patient, and so on. Generally speaking, contingencies are circumstances you have to deal with in order to get what you want or need in a situation. In the Chicagoland of my youth, in order to go swimming I had to restrict my pool going to Wednesday afternoons. That's a contingency. In his African American political science class, my interviewee had the added pressure that his ignorance could cause him serious disapproval. That, too, is a contingency. What makes both of these contingencies identity contingencies is that the people involved had to deal with them because they had a particular social identity in the situation. Other people in the situation didn't have to deal with them, just the people who had the same identity he had. This book examines the role these *identity contingencies* play in our lives, in the broader society, and in some of society's most tenacious problems.

Now, of course, ours is an individualistic society. We don't like to think that conditions tied to our social identities have much say in our lives, especially if we don't want them to. We have a creed. When barriers arise, we're supposed to march through the storm, picking ourselves up by our bootstraps. I have to count myself a subscriber to this creed. But this book offers an important qualification to this creed: that by imposing on us certain conditions of life, our social identities can strongly affect things as important as our performances in the classroom and on standardized tests, our memory capacity, our athletic performance, the pressure we feel to prove ourselves, even the comfort level we have with people of different groups—all things we typically think of as being determined by individual talents, motivations, and preferences.

The purpose of this book is nothing less than to bring this poorly understood part of social reality into view. I hope to convince you that ignoring it—allowing our creed of individualism, for example, to push it into the shadows—is costly, to our own personal success and development, to the quality of life in an identity-diverse society and world, and to our ability to fix some of the bad ways that identity still influences the distribution of outcomes in society.

How do identity contingencies influence us? Some constrain our behavior down on the ground, like restricted access to a public swimming pool. Others, just as powerful, influence us more subtly, not by constraining behavior on the ground but by putting a threat in the air.

2.

At the center of this book is a particular kind of identity contingency, that of 10
stereotype threat. I believe stereotype threat is a standard predicament of life. It springs from our human powers of intersubjectivity—the fact that as members of society we have a pretty good idea of what other members of our society think about lots of things, including the major groups and identities in society. We could all take out a piece of paper, write down the major stereotypes of these identities, and show a high degree of agreement in what we wrote. This means that whenever we're in a situation where a bad stereotype about one of our own identities could be applied to us—such as those about being old, poor, rich, or female—we know it. We know what "people could think." We know that anything we do that fits the stereotype could be taken as confirming it. And we know that, for that reason, we could be judged and treated accordingly. That's why I think it's a standard human predicament. In one form or another—be it through the threat of a stereotype about having lost memory capacity or being cold in relations with others—it happens to us all, perhaps several times a day.

It is also a threat that, like the swimming pool restriction, is tied to an identity. It is present in any situation to which the stereotype is relevant. And this means that it follows members of the stereotyped group into these situations like a balloon over their heads. It can be very hard to shake.

Consider the experience of Brent Staples, now a columnist for the *New York Times*, but then a psychology graduate student at the University of Chicago, a young African American male dressed in informal student clothing walking down the streets of Chicago's Hyde Park° neighborhood. In his own words:

> I became an expert in the language of fear. Couples locked arms or reached for each other's hand when they saw me. Some crossed to the other side of the street. People who were carrying on conversations went mute and stared straight ahead, as though avoiding my eyes would save them. . . .
>
> I'd been a fool. I'd been walking the streets grinning good evening at people who were frightened to death of me. I did violence to them by just being. How had I missed this? . . .
>
> I tried to be innocuous but didn't know how. . . . I began to avoid people. I turned out of my way into side streets to spare them the sense that they were being stalked. . . . Out of nervousness I began to whistle and discovered I was good at it. My whistle was pure and sweet—and also in tune. On the street at night I whistled popular tunes from the Beatles and Vivaldi's° *Four Seasons*. The tension drained from people's bodies when they heard me. A few even smiled as they passed me in the dark. (pp. 202–203)

Staples was dealing with a phantom, a bad stereotype about his race that was in the air on the streets of Hyde Park—the stereotype that young African American males in this neighborhood are violence prone. People from other groups in other situations might face very different stereotypes—about lacking math ability rather than being violence prone for example—but their

Hyde Park: the affluent neighborhood where the University of Chicago and several other educational institutions are located on the South Side of the city. It is adjacent to some of Chicago's poorest neighborhoods, which are overwhelmingly African American.

Antonio Vivaldi (1678–1741): prolific Italian Baroque composer, violinist, and priest. Among the best known of his works is a set of four violin concertos, *The Four Seasons*, each of which tries to paint a sound picture of the season it represents.

Antonio Vivaldi. Civico Museo Bibliografico Musicale, Bologna, Italy/Alinari/Bridgeman Images

The Algonquin Apartments in Hyde Park, Chicago, in a 1951 photo. Hedrich Blessing Collection/Chicago History Museum/Getty Images

predicaments would be the same. When they were in situations where those stereotypes could apply to them, they understood that one false move could cause them to be reduced to that stereotype, to be seen and treated in terms of it. That's stereotype threat, a contingency of their identity in these situations.

Unless, as Staples discovered, they devised a way to deflect it. Staples whistled Vivaldi, by his own account a very good version of it. What would that do for him? Would it improve his attitude toward others on the street, make him more understanding? Probably not. What it did for sure was change the situation he was dealing with. And how it did this illustrates nicely the nature of stereotype threat. In a single stroke, he made the stereotype about violence-prone African American males less applicable to him personally. He displayed knowledge of white culture, even "high white culture." People on the street may not have recognized the Vivaldi he was whistling, but they could tell he was whistling classical music. This caused him to be seen differently, as an educated, refined person, not as a violence-prone African American youth. Such youths don't typically walk down the street whistling classical music. While hardly being aware of it, people drop the stereotype of violence-proneness as the lens through which they see him. He seems less threatening. People don't know who he is; but they know he isn't someone to fear. Fear fades from their demeanor.° Staples himself relaxes. The stereotype in the air that threatened him is fended off. And the change in the behavior of those on the street, and in his own behavior, reveals the power that a mere stereotype—floating in the air like a cloud gathering the nation's history—was having on everyone all along.

demeanor: behavior or appearance.

Whistling Vivaldi is about the experience of living under such a cloud—an 15
experience we all have—and the role such clouds play in shaping our lives and society.

3.

Suppose you are invited into a psychology laboratory and asked to play ten holes of golf on a miniature course that has been set up in a small room. Suppose also that you are a white college student, reasonably athletically inclined. Now suppose that just as you are getting the feel of the golf clubs, you are told that the golf task is part of a standardized sports psychology measure called the Michigan Athletic Aptitude Test (MAAT), which measures "natural athletic ability." How well do you think you'd do? Would being told that the golf task measures natural athletic ability make a difference?

A group of social psychologists at Princeton University led by Jeff Stone did exactly this experiment several years ago. They found something very interesting: white students who were told the golf task measured natural athletic ability golfed a lot worse than white students who were told nothing about the task. They tried just as hard. But it took them, on average, three strokes more to get through the course.

What was it about thinking of the task as a measure of natural athletic ability that so strikingly undermined their performance?

Jeff and his colleagues reasoned that it had something to do with their being white. In the terms I have been using, it had to do with a contingency of white identity that comes to bear in situations where natural athletic ability is being evaluated. This contingency comes from a broadly known stereotype in this society that, compared with blacks at least, whites may have less natural athletic ability. Participants in Jeff's experiment would know this stereotype simply by being members of this society. They might not believe it. But being told that the golfing task measured the very trait their group was stereotyped as lacking, just before they began the task, could put them in a quandary: their frustration on the task could be seen as confirming the stereotype, as a characterization both of themselves and of their group. And this, in turn, might be upsetting and distracting enough to add an average of three strokes to their scores.

The stereotype about their group, and the threatening interpretation of 20
their golf frustration that it posed, is not a contingency like the swimming pool restriction of my youth that directly affected behavior. It imposed no extra restrictions on their golfing, or any material° impediments. But it was nonetheless a contingency of their identity during the golf task. *If* they experienced frustration at golf, *then* they could be confirming, or be seen to be confirming, the unsavory stereotype. *If* they didn't experience frustration at golf, *then* they didn't confirm the racial stereotype. This was an extra pressure they had to deal with during the golfing task, for no other reason than that they were white. It hung over them as a threat in the air, implying that one false move could get them judged and treated as a white kid with no natural athletic ability. (You will learn later in the book how my colleagues and I came to call this kind of threat in the air simply *stereotype threat*.)

material: here, concrete or actual (in contrast to psychological or imagined).

With this reasoning in tow, Jeff and colleagues started asking more questions.

If the mere act of telling white Princeton students that their golfing measured natural athletic ability had caused them to golf poorly by distracting them with the risk of being stereotyped, then telling black Princeton students the same thing should have no effect on their golfing, since their group isn't stereotyped in that way. And it didn't. Jeff and his colleagues had put a group

How do what Steele calls stereotype threats *show how stereotypes about groups of people are culturally ingrained?* Jeff Siner/Charlotte Observer/MCT/Getty Images

of black Princeton students through the same procedure they'd put the white students through. And, lo and behold, their golfing was unaffected. They golfed the same whether or not they'd been told the task measured natural athletic ability.

Here was more evidence that what had interfered with white students' golfing, when it was seen to measure natural athletic ability, was a distracting sense of threat arising from how whites are stereotyped in the larger society.

But Jeff and his research team weren't satisfied. They devised a still cleverer way to make their argument.

They reasoned that if group stereotypes can really set up threats in the 25
air that are capable of interfering with actions as concrete as golfing for entire groups of people—like the stereotype threat Staples had to contend with on the streets of Hyde Park—then it should be possible to set up a stereotype threat that would interfere with black students' golfing as well. All they'd have to do was represent the golfing task as measuring something related to a bad stereotype of blacks. Then, as black participants golfed, they'd have to fend off, like whites in the earlier experiment, the bad stereotype about their group. This added pressure might hurt their golfing.

They tested this idea in a simple way. They told new groups of black and white Princeton students that the golf task they were about to begin was a measure of "sports strategic intelligence." This simple change of phrase had a powerful effect. It now put black students at risk, through their golfing, of confirming or being seen to confirm the ancient and very bad stereotype of blacks as less intelligent. Now, as they tried to sink their putts, any mistake could make them feel vulnerable to being judged and treated like a less intelligent black kid. That was a heavy contingency of identity in this situation indeed, which might well cause enough distraction to interfere with their golfing. Importantly, this same instruction freed white students of stereotype threat in this situation, since whites aren't stereotyped as less intelligent.

The results were dramatic. Now the black students, suffering their form of stereotype threat during the golfing task, golfed dramatically worse than the white students, for whom this instruction had lifted stereotype threat. They took, on average, four strokes more to get through the course.

Neither whites, when the golfing task was represented as a test of natural athletic ability, nor blacks, when it was represented as a test of sports strategic intelligence, confronted a directly interfering contingency of identity in these experiments—nothing that directly affected their behavior like a swimming pool restriction. The contingencies they faced were threats in the air—the threat that their golfing could confirm or be seen to confirm a bad group stereotype as a characterization of their group and of themselves. Still, it was a threat with a big effect. On a course that typically took between twenty-two and twenty-four strokes to complete, it led whites to take three more strokes to complete it, and blacks to take five more strokes to complete it.

At first glance, one might dismiss the importance of something "in the air" like stereotype threat. At second glance, however, it's clear that this threat can be a tenacious force in our lives. Staples had to contend with it every time he walked down the streets of his own neighborhood. White athletes have to contend with it in each competition, especially against black athletes. Think of the white athlete in a sport with heavy black competition. To reach a high level of performance, say, to make it into the National Basketball Association, which is dominated by black players, the white athlete would have to survive and prosper against a lifelong gauntlet° of performance situations loaded with this extra race-linked threat. No single good athletic performance would put the stereotype to rest. The effort to disprove it would be Sisyphean,° reemergent at each important new performance.

The aim of this book is not to show that stereotype threat is so powerful 30
and persistent that it can't be overcome. Quite the contrary. Its goal is to show how, as an unrecognized factor in our lives, it can contribute to some of

gauntlet: an earlier military punishment where the soldier punished had to run between a row of soldiers who struck him from either side as he passed.

Sisyphean: endless and futile; the term comes from Greek mythology, where Sisyphus, a king of Corinth who had repeatedly sought to outsmart the gods, was condemned in the afterlife to roll a large boulder up a steep hill, only to watch it roll to the bottom of the hill again, at which point Sisyphus had to begin the task again. The image below represents Sisyphus rolling the stone.

Leemage/Universal Images Group/Getty Images

our most vexing personal and societal problems, but that doing quite feasible things to reduce this threat can lead to dramatic improvements in these problems.

4.

Now suppose it wasn't miniature golf that you were asked to perform when you arrived at a psychology experiment, and suppose it wasn't your group's athletic ability that was negatively stereotyped in the larger society. Suppose it was difficult math problems that you were asked to solve on a timed standardized test, and suppose that it was your group's math ability that was negatively stereotyped in the larger society. In other words, suppose you were an American woman showing up for an experiment involving difficult math.

Would the stereotype threat that is a contingency of your gender identity in math-related settings be enough to interfere with your performance on the test? Would you be able to just push through this threat of being seen stereotypically and perform well anyway? Or would the very effort to push hard on a timed test be distracting enough to impair your performance despite the extra effort? Would you experience this threat, this contingency of identity, every time you tried difficult math in settings with males around? Would this contingency of identity in math settings become frustrating enough to make you avoid math-related college majors and careers? Would women living in a society where women's math ability is not negatively stereotyped experience this threat? Would their scores be better?

Or suppose the test you were asked to take wasn't the Michigan Athletic Aptitude Test but was the SAT, and suppose the negative stereotype about your group wasn't about athletic ability, or even about math ability, alone, but about scholastic ability in general. Again, would the stereotype threat you experience as a contingency of your identity in scholastic settings be enough to interfere with your performance on this test? Does the threat cause this interference by diverting mental resources away from the test and onto your worries? Would the stereotype threat you experience in scholastic settings affect other experiences as well, such as your classroom performance and your comfort interacting with teachers, professors, teaching assistants, and even other students not in your group? Would this contingency of identity make these settings so frustrating for you that you might try to avoid them in choosing a walk of life?

The purpose of this book is to describe the journey that my colleagues and I have taken in formulating these and related questions and then in systematically trying to answer them over the past twenty years. The experience has been like trying to solve a mystery. And the approach of the book is to give you an over-the-shoulder view of how that mystery has unfolded, of the progression of ideas and revelations, often from the research itself, about the surprising ways that stereotypes affect us — our intellectual functioning, our stress reactions, the tension that can exist between people from different groups, and the sometimes very surprising strategies that alleviate these effects and thereby help solve some of society's worst problems. And because science is rarely a solitary activity anymore — something long true for me — the story also describes many of the people who have done this research, as well as how they work. You will also meet many interesting people who have experienced this threat — including a famous journalist, an African American expatriate in Paris, a person who rose from sharecropping to wealth in rural North Carolina, students at some of America's most elite universities, and students in some of America's most wanting K through 12 schools.

Although the book deals with issues that can have a political charge, nei- 35
ther it nor the work it reports is propelled by an ideological orientation — to the best of my and my colleagues' ability. One of the first things one learns as a social psychologist is that everyone is capable of bias. We simply are not, and cannot be, all knowing and completely objective. Our understandings and views of the world are partial, and reflect the circumstances of our particular lives. This is where a discipline like science comes in. It doesn't purge us of bias. But it extends what we can see and understand, while constraining bias. That is where I would stake my claim, at any rate. The constant back-and-forth between ideas and research results hammers away at bias and, just as important, often reveals aspects of reality that surpass our original ideas and insights. When that has happened — and it has — that is the direction our research goes in. I would like to see my strongest convictions as arising from that kind of revelation, not from prior belief, and I hope you will get a view of that experience as you read along.

Arising this way, several general patterns of findings have persistently emerged in this research. Seeing these patterns, more than any ideas or hunches I began this research with, has convinced me of the importance of identity contingencies and identity threat in our lives.

The first pattern is that despite the strong sense we have of ourselves as autonomous individuals, evidence consistently shows that contingencies tied to our social identities do make a difference in shaping our lives, from the way we perform in certain situations to the careers and friends we choose. As the white world-class sprinter takes the starting blocks in the 100-meter dash at the Olympic trials, he is as autonomous an individual as the black sprinters next to him. And they all face precisely the same 100 meters of free and open track. Nonetheless, in order to do well in that situation, research suggests that he may have to surmount a pressure tied to his racial identity that the black sprinters don't face.

The second dimension of reality, long evident in our research, is that identity threats—and the damage they can do to our functioning—play an important role in some of society's most important social problems. These range from the racial, social class, and gender achievement gaps that persistently plague and distort our society to the equally persistent intergroup tensions that often trouble our social relations.

Third, also coming to light in this research is a general process—involving the allocation of mental resources and even a precise pattern of brain activation—by which these threats impair a broad range of human functioning. Something like a unifying understanding of how these threats have their effect is emerging.

Finally, a set of things we can do as individuals to reduce the impact of 40
these threats in our own lives, as well as what we as a society can do to reduce their impact in important places like schools and workplaces, has come to light. There is truly inspirational news here: evidence that often small, feasible things done to reduce these threats in schools and classrooms can dramatically reduce the racial and gender achievement gaps that so discouragingly characterize our society.

These findings have convinced me of the importance of understanding identity threat to our personal progress, in areas of great concern like achievement and better group relations, and to societal progress, in achieving the identity-integrated civil life and equal opportunity that is a founding dream of this society. This book presents the journey that my colleagues and I have taken in getting to this conviction.

Let's begin the journey where it began—Ann Arbor, Michigan, 1987.

References

Staples, B. (1986, December). Black men and public space. *Harper's Magazine*.

Stone, J., Lynch, C. I., Sjomeling, M., & Darley, J. M. (1999). Stereotype threat effects on Black and White athletic performance. *Journal of Personality and Social Psychology*, 77, 1213–1227.

RESPOND •

1. How does Steele define *stereotype threat* and its importance for all of us? What specific conclusions does he draw from his research and that of others on stereotype threat and stereotypes more broadly?
2. What specific functions does the lengthy quotation from an essay by Brent Staples (paragraph 12) play in Steele's argument? Why could Steele simply not paraphrase or summarize Staples's discussion? What value is there for Steele in using a first-person example here? In using an example from someone else, rather than using another example of his own? If Steele had been writing an essay of five hundred words, how might he have used this quotation or information from it? Why? (See Chapter 20 for a discussion of using sources.)
3. As noted in the headnote, if Steele were writing only for social psychologists, his primary support would come from quantitative evidence based on experiments. Here, however, Steele uses many sorts of evidence. What kinds of evidence does he use to support his claims? (See Chapter 18 for information on what counts as evidence in different contexts.) How effective are they and why? (For example, is any of his evidence particularly memorable? What makes it so?)
4. Steele also uses definitions in very interesting and effective ways. Explain how Steele goes about defining the following abstract notions: *encounter* (paragraph 1), *condition of life* (paragraph 2), *contingency* (paragraph 6), *threat in the air* (paragraph 9), and *intersubjectivity* (paragraph 10). (We've listed the first occurrence of each term; you may need to track a term's recurrence throughout the piece to understand how Steele works to define it. You may want to consult Chapter 9 on arguments of definition to get a clear picture of how writers can go about offering definitions.) How does each of these definitions contribute to the effectiveness of Steele's selection?
5. Even though Steele is writing for a general audience, he is adamant that he is writing as a social scientist, and one of the major arguments of the selection is the importance of scientific ways of creating knowledge. In this regard, he sees himself as constructing an argument based on facts. Study the selection from this perspective, paying special attention to his discussions of qualifications to our society's creed (paragraph 7), how psychologists develop hypotheses and then refine them by doing additional experiments (paragraph 22 and following), and the value of science (paragraph 35). **Write an argument of fact** based on Steele's understanding of the value of science, specifically how and why science is necessary if we are to understand what it means to be human. (Chapter 8 discusses arguments of fact in detail.)

6. The selections in this chapter focus on how society stereotypes you in ways you may not even have been aware of. This chapter adds an additional notion—stereotype threat—to our discussion. **Write an essay** in which you apply this notion to your own life or that of someone you know well. The essay could take any of several forms; for example, it could be primarily factual, definitional, evaluative, or causal in nature, or it might make a proposal. (Chapters 8–12 treat these categories of arguments.)

▼ *This selection is an excerpt from a 2011 research article that appeared in* Media Psychology. *As the abstract notes, the study uses content analysis of video game magazines to make claims about the perpetuation of racial stereotypes in the world of video gaming and about the possible consequences of such stereotypes.*

In excerpting this article, we have retained the abstract, the introduction (including the literature review), and part of Study 1, specifically, the discussion of the method used, the content variables analyzed, the first part of the results section, the discussion section, and the conclusion. We have omitted the technical part of the results section, which reports the statistical analyses of the data presented in Table 1; we also omitted Studies 2 and 3. We found the authors' discussion of the theoretical importance of stereotyped portrayals—part of the literature review—especially relevant for this chapter.

At the time of the article's publication, its authors were teaching or conducting research at Southwestern Oklahoma State University (Burgess and Burgess), UC–Santa Barbara (Dill), Oklahoma State University (Stermer), and UNC–Wilmington (Brown).

In their general discussion at the end of the study, the authors wrote, "Whereas schools are teaching children to tolerate and even celebrate diversity, this research demonstrates that some forms of popular media are sending opposing signals with troubling effects" (pp. 308–309). As you read, consider how these researchers provide evidence to back up this claim and give serious thought to the ways other kinds of popular media perpetuate, rather than challenge, stereotypes of various sorts.

Playing with Prejudice: The Prevalence and Consequences of Racial Stereotypes in Video Games

MELINDA C. R. BURGESS, KAREN E. DILL, S. PAUL STERMER, STEPHEN R. BURGESS, AND BRIAN P. BROWN

Abstract

A content analysis of top-selling video game magazines (Study 1) and of 149 video game covers (Study 2) demonstrated the commonality of overt racial stereotyping. Both studies revealed that minority females are virtually absent in game representations. Study 1 revealed that, in video game magazines, minority males, underrepresented generally, were more likely to be portrayed as athletes or as aggressive, and less likely to be depicted in military combat or using technology, than White males. Study 2 also showed evidence of the "dangerous" minority male stereotype in video game covers. Again, underrepresented overall, minority males were overrepresented as thugs, using extreme guns, and also as athletes. Study 3, an experiment, exposed players to both violent and nonviolent games with both White and Black characters. Participants were faster at classifying violent stimuli following games with Black characters and at classifying nonviolent stimuli following games with White characters, indicating that images of popular video game characters evoke racial stereotypes.

Introduction

Emerging in recent years as one of the most ubiquitous° forms of entertainment, video games have become a media giant with U.S. sales recently reaching a record high of over $21 billion (Ortutay, 2009). Children between 8 and 17 years old make up the group that plays the most video games (Gentile, Saleem, & Anderson, 2007), with approximately 90% of this age group being regular players (Walsh et al., 2005). There is a sizeable effects literature° demonstrating that games influence behaviors, thoughts, feelings, and attitudes (Anderson, Berkowitz, et al., 2003; Anderson, Gentile, & Buckley, 2007; Dill, Brown, & Collins, 2008; Konijn, Bijvank, & Bushman, 2007). Recent brain research even demonstrates differences in the brain's empathic° responding based on differential video game exposure (Bartholow, Bushman, & Sestir, 2006).

Only recently has gaming research begun to concern itself with the portrayals of game characters, and this research has often focused on the portrayal of women in games (e.g., Burgess, Stermer, & Burgess, 2007; Dill & Thill, 2007). Two initial investigations of race in video games (Dill, Gentile, Richter, & Dill, 2005; Glaube, Miller, Parker, & Espejo, 2001) revealed a pattern of infrequent appearance for minority characters and stereotyped depictions when minorities were present. Glaube et al.'s (2001) examination of 70 console games (such as PlayStation) found that some minorities (e.g., Latina women and Native American men) were never present, and that children's games included only White and nonhuman characters. This pattern was echoed in a sample of 20 computer games examined by Dill, Gentile, et al. (2005), which revealed only a few Black and Latino men in the role of main characters and not a single Latino or Latina secondary character. Beyond this, both investigations found frequent stereotyping of minority characters. Glaube et al. (2001) found that Latino characters were only present in sports games, that Asian characters were largely consigned to a wrestling or fighting role, and that Black characters were typically depicted as unaffected by violence through a lack of pain or physical suffering. Interestingly, even in games created before the terror attacks of 9/11, targets of violence were disproportionately likely to be portrayed as Middle Eastern (Dill, Gentile, et al., 2005).

Other content analyses have focused specifically on portrayals of aggression related to gender and race. Smith, Lachlan, and Tamborini (2003) found that, across all game types, 71% of perpetrators of violence and 65% of targets were White, and that 79% of perpetrators and 77% of targets were male. In a further investigation, these same authors classified the ethnicity of violent characters as White, Black, Hispanic, Native American, Asian/Pacific Islander, Middle Eastern, or undefined. Results showed that the majority of characters were White (40.5%) with the next largest group being Asian/Pacific Islander, at only 8%. Interestingly, whereas mild violence was the most common form of violence, Asian/Pacific Islanders was the ethnicity most

---

ubiquitous: present everywhere.

effects literature: a body of research in a particular discipline focusing on the effects of some phenomenon (e.g., stereotypes in the media, eating too much sugar, exercising, praying).

empathic: showing evidence of understanding others' feelings or life situations.

likely to engage in extreme violence, defined in part by large scale bloodshed and disfiguring injuries.

Whereas the portrayal of game characters has been a concern, there is also a growing body of research examining the social effects of media images, from video game as well as other outlets, on young adults (Dill, Brown, et al., 2008; Johnson, Bushman, & Dovidio, 2008). Dill, Brown, et al. (2008) exposed participants to images of women and men that were either stereotypical sex-typed images from video games or professional images from press photographs. Then participants gave their reactions to a real-life account of the sexual harassment of a female college student by her male professor. Results demonstrated that men who were exposed to the video game images (female sex objects and powerful males) were more tolerant of sexual harassment. This research suggests that exposure to stereotypical imagery in the media can alter social judgments, such as deciding that a case of sexual harassment is less serious or requires less action against the perpetrator. The larger meaning is that stories we glean from mass media can change how we behave in the real world.

In one study dealing with racial stereotypes (Dill & Burgess, 2011), White students saw either video game images of Black men who fit the aggressive criminal or "dangerous minority" stereotype or media images of esteemed Black leaders such as Barack Obama alongside analogous White images. Next, in a purportedly unrelated study, participants evaluated the Web site of a political candidate named Peter Smith who was either Black or White. Results revealed interactive effects of the exemplar prime° (negative or positive) on favorability and capability ratings of this candidate. Those who saw the negative (Black video game) exemplars rated the Black candidate as less favorable and capable than the White candidate. In a reversal, those who saw the positive (Black leader) exemplars rated the Black candidate as more favorable and capable than the White candidate.

Whereas there is a sufficient body of literature to appreciate the damage inherent in repeated negative and stereotyped portrayals of minorities and women, there has been a paucity° of research on racial portrayals in video games. At the same time, there has been public interest in these portrayals, centering on a sample of blatantly stereotypical portrayals. Perhaps most notably, *Grand Theft Auto: Vice City* was criticized for depicting Haitians and Cubans as criminals and for potentially inciting hate crimes (Haitian, Cuban leaders denounce GTA, 2003). The game's producer, Rockstar, responded to public protest about game content by removing the lines "Kill the Haitians" and "Kill the Cubans" from the game.

Theoretical Importance of Stereotyped Portrayals

Stereotypes have both cognitive° (e.g., generalizations) and affective° (e.g., fear) components (Amodio

---

interactive effects of the exemplar prime: the priming image here was the initial video game image—"Black men who fit the aggressive criminal or 'dangerous minority' stereotype or media images of esteemed Black leaders"—while the interactive effects refer to the consequences of the first images seen on the evaluation of the candidate, Peter Smith, when presented as Black or White. In other words, the researchers were examining whether there is an interaction between the image research subjects were first exposed to and their subsequent evaluations of the fictitious character, Peter Smith.

paucity: only a limited amount.

cognitive: relating to thought.

affective: relating to feelings or emotions.

& Devine, 2006). Repeated exposure to a particular portrayal of a group teaches that this cultural view is a relevant schema° for processing members of that particular group. For example, exposure to the schema of the violent Black man teaches that it is appropriate to experience apprehension° when approached by a Black male. Further, exposure to these stereotypical images triggers access to thoughts, preferences, and evaluations, ultimately predicting discriminatory behavior (Amodio & Devine, 2006).

Stereotypes may sometimes be consciously processed, but stereotypes can also provoke thoughtless, non-conscious, impulsive reactions. In an update of his cognitive neoassociation theory° of aggression, Berkowitz (2008) underlined the theoretical importance of these automatic processes, and the role of classical conditioning in inciting hostility and aggression. Negative ideas and feelings associated with a group are applied to other group members. These negative associations can trigger negative affect which, in turn, prompts impulsive aggressive reactions that preempt more conscious reasoning. "My cognitive-neoassociationistic analysis . . . suggests what kinds of external stimuli have this relatively compelling capacity to elicit aggressive reactions: primarily situational features that are associated with aggression and those that are linked to decidedly negative experiences" (Berkowitz, 2008, p. 120).

10 Berkowitz (2008) noted that African Americans are commonly stereotyped as aggressive, hostile, and criminal (see also Devine, 1989), and that these are devalued social identities. He wrote, ". . . those people who are associated with aggression generally and/or with gratifications° for aggression in particular or who are associated with negative affect are especially likely to be the victims of aggression" (p. 128). Again, for aggression to be evoked, the perpetrator need not engage in a conscious cognitive appraisal (of the stereotype or situation) because aggression can be provoked through an automatic, impulsive route. Berkowitz cited research — particularly that of Devine (1989) and of Bargh, Chen, and Burrows (1996) — as examples of how even unconscious exposure to images of Blacks and words associated with Black stereotypes evoke hostility and aggression. He noted that aggressive portrayals activate hostility toward African Americans, which in turn makes aggression toward them more likely. ". . . [N]on-conscious activation of the African American stereotype can promote hostile-aggressive behavior towards others" (Berkowitz, 2008, p. 122).

Relating this explicitly to mass media, imagery that associates African American men with the negative stereotypes of aggression, hostility, and criminality conditions viewers to associate this constellation of negativity with African American men in general. Subsequently, unrelated Black men will trigger this association, which can, in turn, provoke increased aggression and hostility.

It is important to note that the stereotypical images of Black video game characters are not even real

---

schema: pattern of thought that influences how we process new information.

apprehension: fear or anxiety.

cognitive neoassociation theory: psychological theory developed by Berkowitz to explain the link between negative feelings and anger or hostile behavior toward some group or situation.

gratifications: sources of pleasure.

people, but they can still provide fodder for negative social judgments and negative reactions to real Black men. Support for this notion comes from Slusher and Anderson (1987), who found that even when people are simply asked to imagine stereotypes such as a rich lawyer, they do not distinguish between what they have imagined and what they have seen in reality. Slusher and Anderson call this a failure of reality monitoring. People treat their imaginary vision as they would a real-life image and it supports their stereotypes. If this is true, then it follows logically that seeing another type of imaginary or fantasy image — a picture of a video game character — might also be treated as confirmation of a stereotype. There will be little difference from seeing a Black thug in a video game and seeing a real Black criminal — both will be taken as evidence confirming the culturally held stereotype of the Black male criminal.

Given the large body of violent video game research (see Anderson, Berkowitz, et al., 2003), we expected portrayals of aggression. We were also aware of the racially charged discussions surrounding games like *Grand Theft Auto* (Leonard, 2009) and wanted to explore whether or not the portrayal of aggression differed as a function of the race of characters. A theoretically relevant way of characterizing this portrayal of violence is whether or not it is socially sanctioned (Lachlan, Tamborini, et al., 2009). We were interested in whether Whites would be more likely to be portrayed as engaged in socially sanctioned violence compared to minorities.

Study 1

Method

Study 1 is an exploratory° content analysis° designed to investigate how Black males are portrayed in imagery from top-selling video game magazines. The variables, described below (and the percent agreement between the two raters), are: race (.98), hypermasculinity (.99), aggression (.99), war/military aggression (.96), fighting (1.00), athletics (.91), and use of technology (.94). The sample used in the present study included images taken from the six top-selling game magazines on sale in January 2006. One issue from each magazine was selected, and the largest male and female images on every page from each issue were included. This produced a sample of 482 images (362 male images and 120 female images), which were then coded by one White male and one White female undergraduate research assistant. For details about magazine and image selection, and for rating procedures, see Dill and Thill (2007).

Content Variables

15 For each image, the following races were coded following Dill and Thill (2007): White, Black, Hispanic, Asian, other, and humanoid. The other category was reserved for characters who appeared to be human and who appeared to be of a non-White race that was not always determinable. Only three races (Native American, Egyptian, and undeterminable) were listed by coders under the other category.

---

exploratory (study): a study that seeks to explore some topic in a new way rather than directly continuing an existing research tradition.

content analysis: in the social sciences, a method of analyzing texts with a focus on their content.

Hypermasculinity was defined as exaggerated male characteristics such as unnaturally large muscles or expressions of dominance. Hypermasculinity relates to features of extreme dominance, power, and aggression (Dill & Thill, 2007; Scharrer, 2004, 2005).

Aggression was defined as being engaged in behavior intended to harm another living being (Aronson, Wilson, & Akert, 2007). Of the violence categories used in Study 1, we categorized war and military aggression as socially sanctioned and fighting as not socially sanctioned. We argue that military violence should be considered relatively more socially sanctioned than fighting because military aggression is legal and, thus, sanctioned by governments and often respected by citizens. In contrast, violence in the form of non-sports fighting is most often considered criminal activity and thus, by definition, is not socially sanctioned. Therefore, aggressive images were further coded as war/military aggression or fighting (no identifiable military rationale). Some images did not fit either category, such as a violent athlete. These images were simply coded as aggressive and not included in the subcategorical analysis.

In the initial stages of this exploratory investigation, we remarked that computer and technology use were regularly portrayed in gaming magazines. We were also aware that sports games have ranked consistently among the top sellers. We, therefore, coded computer and technology use and athletics by race of character.

Results

The data were coded using the variables described above. Frequency data were calculated for each race on the variables described above (see Table 1).

The authors of this article gathered evidence by analyzing the images in gaming magazines. Chapter 4 offers other examples of "hard evidence" used in arguments based on fact.

LINK TO P. 54

Table 1. Character portrayals as a function of race in video game magazines (%)

	White	*Black*	*Asian*	*Hispanic*	*Other*
Frequency (*N*) of males	223	37	6	5	21
Frequency (%) of males	76.4	12.7	2.1	1.7	7.2
U.S. population (%)	66.9	12.8	4.3	14.4	2.7
Gamers (%)	59	15	3	18	5
Frequency (*N*) of females	91	3	5	2	5
Frequency (%) of females	85.8	2.8	4.7	1.9	4.7
U.S. population (%)—whites vs. all minorities	66.9	12.8	4.3	14.4	2.7
Gamers (%)—whites vs. all minorities	59	15	3	18	5
Hypermasculine—males	21.2	29.8	0	20	38.1
Aggressive (males)—yes	66.4	73	66.6	80	85.7
Socially sanctioned (military) (out of aggressive)	8.1	0	0	0	0
Fighting (out of aggressive)	37.8	48.1	25	75	55.5
Aggressive (males)—no	33.6	27	33	20	14.3
Armor (males) (out of aggressive)	48	22.2	0	0	77.7
Posing with weapons (males)—(out of aggressive)	39.2	18.5	0	25	66.6
Athlete (males)	8.1	29.7	0	0	9.5
Violent and/or athletic	74.4	100	75	80	95
Technology use (males)	13.9	2.7	33.3	20	0

Discussion

20 The results of this content analysis illustrate that, although by no means were all minorities portrayed stereotypically, portrayals of race in video game magazines did differ across racial lines in a manner that was consistent with stereotypes. First, from a simple perspective of frequency, minority characters were underrepresented as compared to U.S. Census statistics, even when using the comparison group of gamers. It is interesting to note that humanoid (alien) characters were depicted more often than minority humans. Minority females were particularly underrepresented.

From the perspective of pedagogy° it is useful to consider actual frequency of nonviolent character portrayals, as opposed to relative frequency. Minority male characters were generally infrequent (constituting only 23.6% of the total male images), and nonviolent minorities were even more infrequent (only 5.5% of the total male images). In fact, nonviolent White males (25.6% of the total male images) were as common as all minority males.

Finally, results of exploratory analysis revealed that minority males were more than twice as likely as White males to be portrayed as athletic. Computer and technology use was almost exclusively limited to White males with White males being more than twice as likely as Black males to be depicted using technology. These data are possibly consistent with stereotypes about minorities, for example, that Black males are more athletic and less intelligent than Whites (Berkowitz, 2008). However, because these are exploratory data, we will be conservative when speculating on reasons for these patterns.

pedagogy: teaching.

Following APA style, Burgess and her coauthors included a list of references at the end of the essay. Chapter 22 provides detailed examples of citations in APA style.

LINK TO P. 487

Conclusions

Research has shown that those exposed to false information in fictional stories are persuaded by it and that persuasion persists over time (Appel & Richter, 2007). Furthermore, Slusher and Anderson (1987) demonstrated that people fail to distinguish between stereotyped associations they imagine and those they have actually seen. The results of this content analysis of gaming magazines illustrates that there are consistent racial stereotypes in video game magazines and that representations of race do not match with reality. The problem with this is that the magazines may shape reality by being a source of social information to those who are exposed to them. In other words, after seeing negative racial stereotypes in video game magazines, players may experience failures in reality monitoring and may believe that they have had actual stereotype-confirming experiences. Furthermore, given what we know about the persuasive power of false information in fiction (Appel & Richter, 2007), it is likely that this information could alter gamers' thoughts, feelings, and behaviors.

References

Amodio, D. M., & Devine, P. G. (2006). Stereotyping and evaluation in implicit race bias: Evidence for independent constructs and unique effects on behavior. *Journal of Personality and Social Psychology, 91*(4), 652–661.

Anderson, C. A., Berkowitz, L., Donnerstein, E., Huesmann, R. L., Johnson, J., Linz, D., . . . Wartella, E. (2003). The influence of media violence on youth. *Psychological Science in the Public Interest, 4,* 81–110.

Anderson, C. A., Gentile, D. A., & Buckley, K. E. (2007). *Violent video game effects on children and adolescents: Theory, research, and public policy.* New York, NY: Oxford University Press.

Appel, M., & Richter, T. (2007). Persuasive effects of fictional narratives increase over time. *Media Psychology, 10,* 113–134.

Aronson, E., Wilson, T. D., & Akert, R. M. (2007). *Social psychology* (6th ed.). Upper Saddle River, NJ: Pearson Prentice Hall.

Bargh, J. A., Chen, M., & Burrows, L. (1996). Automaticity of social behavior: Direct effects of trait construct and stereotype activation on action. *Journal of Personality and Social Psychology, 71,* 230–244.

Bartholow, B. D., Bushman, B. J., & Sestir, M. A. (2006). Chronic violent video game exposure and desensitization to violence: Behavioral and event-related brain potential data. *Journal of Experimental Social Psychology, 42,* 532–539.

Berkowitz, L. (2008). On the consideration of automatic as well as controlled psychological processes in aggression. *Aggressive Behavior, 34,* 117–129.

Burgess, M. C. R., Stermer, S. P., & Burgess, S. R. (2007). Sex, lies, and video games: The portrayal of male and female characters on video game covers. *Sex Roles, 57,* 419–433.

Department of Defense. (2002). *Population representation in the military services.* Retrieved from http://www.defenselink.mil/prhome/poprep2002/summary/summary.htm

Devine, P. G. (1989). Stereotyping and prejudice: Their automatic and controlled components. *Journal of Personality and Social Psychology, 56,* 5–18.

Dill, K. E., Brown, B. P., & Collins, M. A. (2008). Effects of exposure to sex-stereotyped video game characters on tolerance of sexual harassment. *Journal of Experimental Social Psychology, 44,* 1402–1408.

Dill, K. E., & Burgess, M. C. R. (2011). *Media images as positive and negative exemplars of race: Evoking Obama or video game characters changes outcomes for black men.*

Dill, K. E., Gentile, D. A., Richter, W. A., & Dill, J. C. (2005). Violence, sex, age and race in popular video games: A content analysis. In E. Cole & J. Henderson-Daniel (Eds.), *Featuring females: Feminist analyses of media* (pp. 115–130). Washington, DC: American Psychological Association.

Dill, K. E., & Thill, K. P. (2007). Video game characters and the socialization of gender roles: Young people's perceptions mirror sexist media depictions. *Sex Roles, 57,* 851–864.

Funk, J. B. (2005). Children's exposure to violent video games and desensitization to violence. *Child and Adolescent Psychiatric Clinics of North America, 14,* 387–403.

Gentile, D. A., Saleem, M., & Anderson, C. A. (2007). Public policy and the effects of media violence on children. *Social Issues and Policy Review, 1,* 15–61.

Glaube, C. R., Miller, P., Parker, M. A., & Espejo, E. (2001). *Fair play? Violence, gender, and race in video games.* Retrieved from http://publications.childrennow.org/publications/media/fairplay_2001b.cfm

Haitian, Cuban leaders denounce. (2003, December). *Grand Theft Auto.* Retrieved from http://www.nbc6.net/entertainment/2706043/detail.html

Johnson, J. D., Bushman, B. J., & Dovidio, J. F. (2008). Support for harmful treatment and reduction of empathy toward Blacks: Remnants of stereotype activation involving Hurricane Katrina and L'il Kim. *Journal of Experimental Social Psychology, 44,* 1506–1513.

Lachlan, K., Tamborini, R., Weber, R., Westerman, D., Skalski, P., & Davis, J. (2009). The spiral of violence: Equity of violent reprisal in professional wrestling and its dispositional and motivational features. *Journal of Broadcasting & Electronic Media, 53,* 56–75.

Leonard, D. (2009). Young, black (& brown) and don't give a fuck: Virtual gangstas in the era of state violence. *Cultural Studies/Critical Methodologies, 9,* 248–272. doi:10.1177/1532708608325938

Ortutay, B. (2009). *Video game sales top $21 billion in 2008.* Retrieved from http://www.msnbc.msn.com/id/28682836/ns/technology_and_science-games/t/video-game-sales-top-billion/

Scharrer, E. (2004). Virtual violence: Gender and aggression in video game advertisements. *Mass Communication & Society, 7,* 393–412.

Scharrer, E. (2005). Hypermasculinity, aggression, and television violence: An experiment. *Media Psychology, 7,* 353.

Slusher, M. P., & Anderson, C. A. (1987). When reality monitoring fails: The role of imagination in stereotype maintenance. *Journal of Personality and Social Psychology, 52,* 653–662.

RESPOND

1. How do Burgess and her coauthors use data to support their claims **(a)** that the representations of minorities found in gaming magazines correspond to stereotypes, rather than reality, and **(b)** that such stereotyping is far from innocent in its consequences? In other words, what sorts of evidence do Burgess et al. provide for their claims?
2. What are the benefits of using the careful and clearly stated methods of analyzing quantifiable data that are associated with a field like psychology when dealing with a topic as complex and controversial as the one Burgess et al. are tackling?
3. As you no doubt noted, Burgess et al. define the variables in their study—race, hypermasculinity, aggression (both socially sanctioned and unsanctioned), and the use of technology—in the section "Content Variables." What kind of definition do they provide for each of these variables? (See Chapter 9 on kinds of definitions.) Do you think you could code data from a gaming magazine appropriately and consistently based on these definitions? Why or why not? (The answer to this question illustrates something important about this kind of definition.) How do these variables and the definitions of them map onto the categories used in Table 1 of the article? Why might the list of portrayals be more detailed than the list of variables that are defined?
4. Research studies in fields like psychology and in the social, natural, and applied sciences all have a similar format, often referred to as IMRAD (introduction, methods, results, analysis, and discussion), and the sections are often labeled by their function. What are the advantages of having such a standardized format for writers? For readers?
5. Both this selection and the previous one, Claude M. Steele's "An Introduction: At the Root of Identity," are written by psychologists. Steele's chapter is from a book written for an educated audience while this excerpt is written for peers—other psychologists. Compare and contrast the two in terms of format, kinds of evidence presented, and the general shape of the argument. What do your answers tell you about writing for different audiences? (Chapters 1 and 6 may help you here.)
6. Carefully reread the discussion and conclusions sections of this study to be sure you understand the logic of the authors' claims in the conclusion, including the ways the researchers qualify their claims. (It may also be useful to review the section on the theoretical importance of stereotyped portrayals.) **Write an essay** in which you evaluate these claims by describing the stereotyped portrayal of some group in a specific example of popular culture—a movie, a television series, or a

video game. (For a discussion of evaluative arguments, see Chapter 10.) To complete this assignment, you'll obviously need to study the example you are analyzing with some care, and you may well wish to code instances of certain stereotyped portrayals, as the authors of this research study did. At the end of your essay, be sure to speculate about how the stereotyped portrayal may, in light of the study excerpted here, be harmful for the individuals who consume it and for society at large.

The Kobal Collection at Art Resource, NY

Amy Zimmerman writes about entertainment for the Daily Beast, a popular Web site devoted to reporting news and opinion. In this piece, she analyzes and critiques the media's portrayal of bisexuals and bisexuality. As you read, pay special attention to the way Zimmerman describes the stereotypes she is critiquing and offers specific examples of them.

It Ain't Easy Being Bisexual on TV

AMY ZIMMERMAN

Aug. 14, 2014

> *Game of Thrones* had an overly sensual libertine while *House of Cards* had a manipulative psychopath. And then there's Piper Chapman. It isn't easy being vaguely bisexual on TV.

In a recent interview with Anna Paquin,° Larry King° asked the actress, who is currently married to a man, if she is a "non-practicing bisexual." In a perfect world, Paquin would have been able to cite multiple examples of well-known, "out" bisexuals to help illustrate how sexuality isn't a button you can turn on and off, or a naughty habit that goes away once you find the right man.

Unfortunately, the television and film industries aren't going out of their way to showcase bisexual role models. *Game of Thrones*° and *House of Cards*° are two of the only shows in recent years to have heavily featured male bisexual characters, and these men are portrayed respectively as an overly sensual libertine° and a manipulative psychopath. While male bisexuality is routinely dismissed as a tool, an indulgence, or a fallacy, female bisexuality is almost exclusively trotted out to fulfill a male fantasy. No wonder Larry King didn't have his facts straight.

Anna Paquin (1982–): Canadian-born actress who has been winning awards since the age of eleven, when she won an Academy Award for Best Supporting Actress for her role in *The Piano*.

Larry King (1933–): prominent American host of radio and television interview programs.

Game of Thrones: an internationally acclaimed HBO drama based on the fantasy novels of George R. R. Martin (1948–) that first came on the air in 2011.

House of Cards: American adaptation of a BBC series released by Netflix; its focus is the power-hungry nature of politics. It was the first Web-only series to receive nominations for major Emmy awards.

libertine: a person, usually a man, who behaves with no sense of responsibility or morality, especially with regard to sex.

In the GLAAD° "Where We Are on TV" report for the 2013–2014 television season, the organization noted an overall decrease in the number of LGBT characters slated for broadcast. More specifically, they counted forty-six LGBT characters in total, out of which there were only ten bisexual characters. Out of that minuscule number of bisexual roles, only two were male characters.

Of course, homogeny° is an irritating yet omnipresent aspect of the television experience, much like Simon Cowell or infomercials. The world inside our television sets is nothing like the diverse world we live in, and it would take many more words to explore the ways in which people of color, trans individuals, and women are under- or misrepresented time and time again.

Despite the growing acceptance of certain agreed upon queer lifestyles (namely, 5
loving monogamous relationships between two people who share one gender), it's important to note that a number of individuals have been left out of the conversation. The absence of bisexuals in the media, particularly bisexual men, is an issue that's less commonly discussed and acknowledged.

Our mainstream media reinforces the notion that bisexuality is either a fun, voluntary act of experimentation or a mere myth through two tried and true tactics: misrepresenting and oversimplifying bisexual characters until they are either punchlines or wet dream fodder, or simply refusing to portray bisexual characters in the first place. Bisexual erasure — or the tendency to blot out bisexuality and deny its existence entirely — on film and television highlights the way that certain types of queerness are undermined and erased in popular narratives, while others are increasingly caricaturized and/or celebrated.

Part of the problem is simply a lack of daring and imagination. After all, television and film rely heavily on predictable scripts. Known characters result in familiar products, for which there is a pre-established and reliable audience. We are left with stalwart° genres (action, rom com) and classic roles (prude, seductress, jock, backstory-less best friend). As homosexuality has become more and more prevalent and acceptable in the national conversation, the media has responded in the only way it knows how: boiling down a complex sexual identity into a recyclable, stereotypical character. While any other character's (hetero)sexuality is taken for granted, a gay character's sexual orientation is key to his or her characterization.

Most homosexual male characters are reduced to the *Clueless* definition of "a disco-dancing, Oscar Wilde°-reading, Streisand° ticket-holding friend of

GLAAD: a U.S.-based media advocacy organization focused on lesbian, gay, bisexual, and transgender (LGBT) issues. Founded in 1985 as the Gay and Lesbian Alliance Against Defamation in response to media coverage of what we now know as HIV/AIDS, it dropped this name and has used only the acronym since 2013 as its focus has clearly shifted to issues related to the broader LGBT community and its allies.

homogeny: similarity of structure, a variant of *homogeneity*.

stalwart: here, firmly established and uncompromising in their content.

Oscar Wilde (1854–1900): Irish novelist (*The Picture of Dorian Gray*), playwright (*The Importance of Being Earnest*), and poet. He was tried and convicted of homosexual behavior; he never recovered from his time in prison and died in Paris in poverty.

Barbara Streisand (1942–): award-winning Jewish American singer, songwriter, actress, producer, and director; said to be the best-selling female singer/recording artist of all time. Streisand is much beloved by gay men of a certain generation.

Dorothy,"° a man for whom gayness is an all-encompassing personality. One need look no further than *Queer Eye for the Straight Guy*,° a show that not-very-subtly reinforced the notion that a gay man's most important job is honoring his god-given aesthetic eye; while the straight "projects" on the show were given backstories and motivations, the gay men, who were actually recurring characters, were simply trotted out for their gay abilities, and denied any sort of complexity or realistic characterization in the process.

Of course, there are examples of "good" gay characters, role models who play authentic, fully realized roles. Max from *Happy Endings*,° the women of *The L Word*,° and *Will & Grace*'s° beloved Will are a few notable examples. However, this doesn't change the fact that most gay characters are more shtick than substance, butch women brought in for a laugh, or a sassy gay friend who gives our beloved female lead a makeover or some advice on how to snare a man.

10 These characters have their pre-established roles, and they serve a handful of very specific purposes. But television and film don't have an equivalent stereotypical "personality" for the bisexual man or woman. While we know all the markers for a gay man or woman in mainstream media, what would a bisexual one look or sound like? Would a bisexual man be half as sassy as a gay one, or half as well dressed? Would we even know how to recognize or differentiate him from his "normal" straight counterparts?

Because bisexuals, particularly bisexual men, are so absent from the agreed upon narrative of acceptable queerness, they are their own particular brand of illegible, much in the same way that no one seems to know how to write a female character who isn't a sex object or a maternal Madonna.° Of course, someone could attempt to simply write a complex, able, interesting character who is a woman, or who is attracted to both men and women. But so far, the mainstream media attempts to portray bisexuality have almost uniformly missed the mark.

Game of Thrones's Oberyn Martell is a fantastic, nuanced character that has sex with men and women. However, he also lives in George R. R. Martin's magical, man-made realm. Young boys can watch *Will & Grace* reruns and dream of being a successful, social, young gay professional. Meanwhile, it seems as though in order to be a sexually appealing, confidently masculine bisexual man one must travel back in time to a place that doesn't even exist, throw on a sumptuous tunic with a deep V-neck, and go into extensive spear training.

friend of Dorothy: gay slang for a gay man. Several decades ago, a gay man could use the question "Are you a friend of Dorothy?" to ask another man if he was gay in a discreet manner. Although the origin of the term is uncertain, the expression is popularly linked with Dorothy in *The Wizard of Oz*, who was accepting of various sorts of difference. (Like Streisand, *The Wizard of Oz* was quite popular among gay men of an earlier generation.)

Queer Eye for the Straight Guy: American television series that ran from 2003 to 2007, in which five gay men ("The Fab Five") offered advice about clothes, decorating, grooming, and food, among other topics, to a different heterosexual man each week. It gave rise to the creation of similar shows in at least a dozen countries, mostly in Europe.

Max from* Happy Endings*: Max Blum, a character played by Adam Pally in *Happy Endings*, an ABC sitcom that ran from 2011 to 2013. Because he did not fit the stereotype many people have of gay men, another character in the series referred to him as a "straight dude who likes dudes."

But The Red Viper's° sexual philosophy is even more problematic than his otherworldliness. Commenting on his character's bisexuality, Pedro Pascal° explained that Oberyn "does not discriminate in his pleasures. This is the way he understands life, to live it to its fullest. And to limit yourself in terms of experience doesn't make any sense to him – what's beautiful is beautiful." This, in and of itself, is a form of bisexual erasure. Martell is not presented as a man who was born with a particular sexual orientation, who goes on to honor his identity in the face of hardships and doubt. Rather, he is portrayed not as someone who happens to be bisexual, but as a man with an insatiable appetite. His sexuality, therefore, is simply a means of characterization – this is a character that wants every pleasure, be it sexual, physical, or academic. In this way, bisexual is code for libertine, which is something else altogether. This convenient coding turns bisexuality, a potential source of questioning and shame, into a masculine asset: the capacity for pure, unbridled desire and acquisition.

House of Cards's Frank Underwood is another prime example of this phenomenon. Underwood has sex with men and women. But instead of presenting Frank's bisexuality as another layer of this complex character, the show wraps Underwood's sexuality up with his ethos. In Underwood's words, "Sex is power," and power is everything. In this way, the question of Underwood's sexuality is quietly pushed back into the closet; we are supposed to be content with the explanation that Frank is a man who denies himself nothing, who must control everyone. Bisexuality is one of his tools, but the show stops just short of saying that it is part of his identity. *House of Cards* isn't afraid of sex, but sexuality is another matter.

While many of these depictions play into bisexual erasure, others reinforce 15 harmful bisexual stereotypes. More often than not, the use of one of these tactics over the other follows the gender divide; bisexual men are largely unseen and uncelebrated, while bisexual women are trapped in oversimplified roles, their sexuality transformed by a misogynistic industry into another means of sexual objectification.

To understand the ideology that these bisexual stock characters reinforce, we must examine the pervasive stereotypes that surround female bisexuality. In his interview with Anna Paquin, Larry King unwittingly went through a checklist of bisexual lady myths, casually outlining the many stereotypes still left to debunk. When Paquin said that she was merely in a monogamous relationship with a man, the clearly befuddled host responded, "But you were bisexual?" King is alluding

The L Word: a Showtime TV drama from 2007 to 2008, now syndicated through various on-demand services, centered on a group of young people from West Hollywood, CA. The program was among the first to represent lesbians and to do so in ways that did not pander to common stereotypes. Because it was created for a cable channel, it could deal frankly with issues of sex and sexuality in ways that network television could not—and does not even now. (The "L-word" is, of course, *lesbian*.)

Will & Grace: an NBC sitcom that ran from 1998 to 2006. Set in New York City, the show focused on the relationship between Will Truman, a gay attorney, and his best friend, Grace Adler, an interior designer who is Jewish. Despite criticism of its frequently stereotypical portrayal of gay men, the program is often credited with educating the general American public about a host of LGBT issues.

Madonna: here, Mary, who, as Christianity teaches, miraculously gave birth to Jesus, her first-born son, while still a virgin. She is thus seen as the perfect symbol of purity and motherhood. Feminist critics have long pointed out that images of women tend to fall into two categories: the Madonna or the prostitute.

to the widely held belief that a "bisexual" woman is simply a misinformed girl who hasn't settled down yet. Once this experimental floozy finally finds monogamy with a man, her bisexuality will be relegated to the mythologized realm of experimental adolescence. According to this false theory, bisexuality is nothing more than a phase.

It doesn't take a rocket scientist to unpack the appeal of this falsified narrative of bisexuality. The concept of a bisexual or lesbian woman who needs to be "saved" from her own sexuality is essentially a revamping of the classic damsel in distress narrative, with the male character's conquering masculinity cast in the role of hero. The character of the bisexual woman offers the potential for a killer combination of girl-on-girl action paired with the possibility of heterosexual redemption.

Look no further than *Dodgeball*'s° Kate Veatch, whose cold attitude and softball skills make her the butt of lesbian jokes throughout the film. Since Kate is a beautiful blonde, it makes sense to have her passionately make out with a girl at the end of the movie—that's hot! But instead of leaving Kate with her lesbian happy ending, the film insists on going a step further when Kate declares that she's actually bisexual, which makes her finally available to the movie's male protagonist. Through this clever device, "bisexuality" comes to describe a girl who hooks up with other girls (and lets you watch), but will still eventually acquiesce and be your girlfriend. This isn't an attempt to represent a group of women—it's a male fantasy. Because we all know that the sexual gratification of the off-screen male viewer is valued more than an accurate portrayal of female sexual gratification.

From *Orange Is the New Black*'s° Piper Chapman,° who describes herself as a "former lesbian" who has only ever been interested in one woman, to Kurt Hummel° on *Glee*,° who smugly informs his boyfriend that "Bisexual's a term that gay guys in high school use when they wanna hold hands with girls and feel like a normal person for a change," pop culture is quick to perpetuate confusing and destructive narratives of bisexuality. When even a show like *Glee*, which claims to recognize and empower all the freaks and underdogs, makes fun of the "myth" of bisexuality, it's clear that bisexual representation, at least on network television, is still stuck in the dark ages.

The act of erasure through mis- or underrepresentation is an insidious one. 20
Regardless of sexual orientation, everyone should have the right to envision a

Red Viper: a nickname for Oberyn Martell, a character in *Game of Thrones*, resulting from the claim that his weapons are poisoned. Note that this nickname is an example of antonomasia (see discussion in Chapter 13).

Pedro Pascal: Chilean actor who portrays Oberyn Martell in *Game of Thrones*.

Dodgeball: 2004 movie; among its characters was Kate Veatch, an attorney. Near the end of the movie, after a volleyball game in which Kate plays on the winning side, a girlfriend who has been watching the game passionately kisses her. Peter, a male character who is interested in Kate, is distressed. Kate simply announces that she is bisexual and kisses Peter as well.

Orange Is the New Black: award-winning television series from Netflix first broadcast in 2013 and concerned with life in a women's prison.

Piper Chapman: bisexual fictional character on *Orange Is the New Black* based on the life of Piper Kerman.

Kurt Hummel: fictional gay male lead and countertenor in *Glee*.

Glee: Fox musical comedy-drama first broadcast in 2009 that focused on the glee club at a fictional high school.

future for themselves; to engage with popular culture as an aspirational means of self-discovery. Just as every young girl should be able to see a reflection of her future self in a blockbuster female superhero or a powerful network TV executive, so should children of all sexual orientations be able to imagine lives for themselves inspired by the images they see in movies, television, and magazines.

For those who are growing up in families, institutions, or regions that do not accept their desires or lifestyles, this positive media reinforcement could become an invaluable inspiration, as essential to continued life as food or air. Pop culture has a responsibility to these children, just as it has a responsibility to accurately depict, to the best of its ability, the world in which we live. While not every show is, or should be, reality television, hundreds of channels filled to the brim with white, traditionally beautiful, heterosexual characters is a manufactured unreality; a deliberate denial of authentic diversity that could result in or contribute to self-hatred and denial for anyone whose desires differ from the glorified norm.

RESPOND.

1. Despite the validity of Zimmerman's claims, how does the existence of her essay stand as evidence that the media have, in fact, made progress in representing bisexuality and other sexual minorities in the past decade? How does her essay give you new ways of thinking about stereotypes in the media generally and how stereotypes of underrepresented groups often change across time?
2. Zimmerman uses a range of kinds of evidence as she seeks to support her argument. Reread her essay carefully, noting the kinds of evidence she uses and characterizing each. (Chapter 4 on arguments based on facts and reason and Chapter 7 on structuring arguments should help you with these tasks.)
3. In the course of her essay, Zimmerman lists a number of stereotypes of bisexuals generally and some stereotypes associated specifically with female and male bisexuals. She also describes several processes that perpetuate the stereotyping of bisexuals in and by the media. Make a list of these examples and processes. In what sense do these constitute arguments of definition? What kinds of definition are they? (See Chapter 9 for a discussion of arguments of definition.)
4. In writing this essay, Zimmerman describes in some detail many of the stereotypes she is so vehemently critiquing. In some sense, then, she reproduces the very stereotypes that she dislikes and that moved

her to write this article for the *Daily Beast*. Does she have alternatives, or are those who wish to critique stereotypes doomed to repeat them even as they criticize them? Are there advantages to reproducing such stereotypes in the context of critique, or does reproducing them inevitably contribute to the problem of continued stereotyping?

5. Zimmerman's style is quite informal, and it is laced with references to popular culture that she assumes will be familiar to her readers. (How many, in fact, were new for you?) Let's assume you decided to use a summary of this article in an essay you were writing for a course you are taking. **Write the summary**, being sure to include both paraphrase and direct quotations. Note that you will also need to unpack the popular culture references Zimmerman uses that provide support for her claims; in other words, you'll need to give your readers more background than she does because academic writing generally requires a kind of explicitness of background that journalistic writing does not. (Chapter 20 on using sources and Chapter 21 on plagiarism and academic integrity will help you with this question.)
6. Zimmerman offers a strong proposal near the end of her article: "children of all sexual orientations [should] be able to imagine lives for themselves inspired by the images they see in movies, television, and magazines" (paragraph 20)—even as she acknowledges that the media fall far short of reaching this goal. Choose another group that you believe the media stereotypes, and **write an evaluative argument** in which you critique the treatment of that group by the media generally, a particular television program, or a specific movie. Like Zimmerman, you will want to provide evidence for your claims from one or more television programs or movies. (You may wish to review Chapter 8 on arguments of fact and Chapter 9 on arguments of definition as you prepare this assignment.) As noted in the previous question, you'll also want to include more background than Zimmerman does. You may or may not wish to end your evaluation with a call for action, a proposal, as Zimmerman has.

24
What's Globalization Doing to Language?

Left to right: Megan Haaga, for Open Gates, by permission; © Frank Fell/age fotostock; AP Photo/Kin Cheung

Globalization, or the deepening connections among nations, governments, companies, and individuals, is having an impact on all kinds of things—the food we eat, the people whom we end up with in class, and even the language(s) we speak. In this chapter, you'll read selections investigating some of the many ways that globalization has consequences for language. Most of the time, we take language for granted. We treat it much like a glass windowpane, not even realizing it's there until, of course, we meet someone who speaks a markedly different dialect or who doesn't speak the language well or at all. In those situations, we're reminded that language is much more than a mere medium of communication. It reflects who we are and aren't and how we do and don't want to be identified.

The chapter's opening selection, an editorial from the *Lebanon* (PA) *Daily News*, comments on that most American of events, the Super Bowl. It focuses specifically on a commercial broadcast during the 2014 game, an ad for Coca-Cola that featured "America the Beautiful." As you may recall, the lines of the song were sung in a variety of languages now found across the United States. The Twittersphere went wild, and this editorial responds to the controversy, asking some profound questions about what makes for a successful commercial and a successful country, especially where language and attitudes toward language are concerned.

The second selection, Kirk Semple's newspaper article "Immigrants Who Speak Indigenous Languages Encounter Isolation," considers the situation of immigrants to the United States from Spanish-speaking Latin America whose first language is not Spanish but, rather, an indigenous language. Because of where they live, they often find learning Spanish helps them integrate in the United States more quickly than would learning English. Obviously, these languages are adding to the complexity of our country's linguistic mosaic.

Scott L. Montgomery focuses on a very different consequence of globalization—the use of English as the global language in the field of science. Because the most prestigious scientific journals are published in English-speaking countries, scientists around the world who want to share their research with colleagues must do so in English. While such a situation encourages the exchange of ideas and information, it also has its downsides, as Montgomery discusses. Interestingly, he argues that the biggest losers may be those of us who speak English as our first and often only language.

"Infographic: Speak My Language" by Santos Henarejos presents a visual argument that highlights some of the side effects of globalization for language, such as the ways that the availability of technology influences how we communicate, including the languages we use.

Picking up a topic mentioned by Montgomery, Nicholas Ostler asks whether globalization is the reason many "small" languages are disappearing. Depending on whom you ask, you'll hear that there are some six thousand languages spoken in the world today, but given the growing influence of more widely spoken languages, as few as six hundred of them will likely still be spoken a century from now. Many are quick to blame globalization as the reason for this loss; Ostler, who is chair of the Foundation for Endangered Languages, contends that globalization alone is not the culprit.

Finally, Rose Eveleth's "Saving Languages through Korean Soap Operas" investigates what at first seems like a wacky idea: crowdsourcing the subtitling of television programs into these small languages as a way of encouraging their maintenance and use—that is, creating reasons for people to learn them. These last two articles remind us that mutually reinforcing, complex forces like technology and globalization can work in amazing and unpredictable ways.

▼ *Even if you're not a football fan, you likely know that Super Bowl commercials are big business—thirty seconds will set you back about $4 million. They are also seen as important barometers of American culture in complex ways. Likely the most controversial of the 2014 Super Bowl ads was an ad for a product that, around the world, is synonymous with America: Coca-Cola: http://bit.ly/1ibf7P1. The ad centered on the song "America the Beautiful," and the issue was language or, more properly, languages. As you'll learn in this selection, during halftime, tweets began flying about the commercial, and the following day, conservative commentators in particular were highly critical of it.*

This unsigned editorial appeared on February 3, 2014, the day after Super Bowl XLVIII. The Lebanon Daily News *is the local newspaper of Lebanon, Pennsylvania, and it has a circulation of up to 50,000. The city itself has a population of just over 25,000, 74 percent of whom are White, 32 percent of whom identify as Hispanic or Latino, 6 percent of whom are African American, 3.2 percent of whom identify as multiracial, and 1 percent of whom identify as Asian American. As you read, consider why and how language quickly becomes such a powerful symbol for many things—in this case, a particular understanding of nationalism as patriotism defined for many by the language in which one sings.*

Coca-Cola's Multilingual "America" Ad Didn't Hit Any Wrong Notes

FROM THE *LEBANON DAILY NEWS*

When spending more than $4 million for 30 seconds of America's attention, one's first job is to assure that whatever is put in front of it is remembered 30 seconds later; ideally, days later.

For Coca-Cola, call it mission accomplished.

One of Coca-Cola's Super Bowl ads featured "America the Beautiful" sung in eight different languages. They were: English, Tagalog,° Senegalese-French, Hebrew, Mandarin, Keres Pueblo,° Arabic, and Spanish.

Well done. We'll defend that stance in just a moment.

5 Before that, it's worth noting that portions of the Twitter universe lost their collective mind after the commercial aired. The hashtag #f---coke started trending hot as irrational 'Murricans utterly misplaced their patriotism and, ape-like, started heaving poop at one of America's iconic brands.

Freedom means the right to make an ass of oneself, allowing others as gently as possible, to point out the fact.

America: English! That's what some Twitterers were saying; that's what they wanted. A patriotic song rendered in America's language.

There are, according to statistics cited in a *Huffington Post* article (see

Tagalog: the most widely spoken language of the Philippines.

Keres Pueblo: a language indigenous to the United States, spoken in New Mexico with some 13,000 native speakers.

http://huff.to/1nJc0Sn), 381 languages spoken in these United States. That is a potent passel° of patois° in which we Americans freely engage. One of those used in the commercial, Keres Pueblo, is a Native American tongue that was used in this nation before there was a hint of a nation.

We can't fathom that the argument should gather much traction here in the Lebanon Valley, steeped as we are in our Pennsylvania German° traditions. Yes, our forebears learned English, but PA Dutch° still gets trotted out for occasional use in church services and when watching stuffed groundhogs predict winter weather, as happened just this weekend.

10 There is nothing wrong with multilingualism. If anything, we don't spend nearly enough time learning at least a second language. That is both an American-centric and educational failure.

The first thing the commercial proved is that the song sounds pretty good regardless of the language in which it is sung. The second thing it proved is that there are individuals who believe in the words even if the language in which it was originally written is not the one that came first for them.

Yes, we believe those living in the United States should learn English. It is not the official language° but it has

---

passel: a large group of undetermined number.

patois: a term of French origin, which is used to mean any unstandardized language variety. It is used to refer to the historically spoken regional languages that were largely replaced by French as well as the pidgins and creoles that grew up in French colonies. The word has the patronizing connotations of *quaint*, *uncultivated*, and even *vulgar*. Here, the term is used to alliterative effect—"potent passel of patois"—three of the four words beginning with the same consonant sound.

Pennsylvania German: culture associated with the descendants of the German speakers who settled parts of Pennsylvania. Although most now speak only English, they maintain certain cultural traditions and practices, and the variety of English they speak is influenced by the German widely spoken in the area until World War II.

PA Dutch: the name commonly used for the variety of German spoken in Pennsylvania. At a much earlier time in the history of English, which belongs to the family of Germanic languages, terms related to *Dutch* referred to the Germanic people generally; only much later did the term come to refer to the speakers of a Germanic language who live in what is today the Netherlands.

official language: a language whose use is mandated by law. As noted here, the United States has no official language, although English serves as the national language, that is, the most widely used language in the country.

been, since the nation's inception, the accepted common tongue, and it will continue to be. Our inclusive society requires some desire on the part of others to be included. Learning English is a part of that inclusivity.

But it does not mean that we are forced to unlearn those things that defined us before we came to be Americans. We can be just as patriotic, and we can act just as freely, if we sing those words in English or in any of the languages listed above and any of the others that were not.

In the final analysis, for Coca-Cola, this was money well spent. Here we are, still talking about that ad.

RESPOND •

1. As this editorial acknowledges, it is making two arguments simultaneously, one about what makes a commercial successful and one about what makes a country successful—or doesn't. Summarize each as a definitional argument. (See Chapter 9 for more on definitional arguments.) What role, if any, does or might language play in this second argument? Why or how?
2. Watch a video related to this commercial, "Coca-Cola—It's Beautiful—Behind the Scenes," at **http://bit.ly/1fAb3rN**. How does this second video provide additional background or context for the first? Do you imagine that critics of the original ad also viewed this second video? What do you think their response would have been? Why? Did it change your response to the first video? If so, in what ways?
3. One of the most interesting aspects of this editorial is its use of language, particularly informal language that one might associate with humor and even mockery and that might not be appropriate in many contexts. Make a list of these uses, and be prepared to explain what function they serve in creating the tone of the editorial and in supporting its argument. (Chapter 13 discusses style in arguments.)
4. The controversy about the Coca-Cola Super Bowl commercial focuses on the uses of languages other than English, particularly in a song associated specifically with the United States. While it is not uncommon for a certain strand of conservatives to object to the use of languages other than English in public life, their complaint in such cases is usually that they cannot understand what is being said. In this case, since all the critics know the lyrics to this song by heart, the issue cannot be that they do not understand the meaning of what is being sung even though they likely cannot understand the words themselves. What, then, do you imagine the basis for the complaints was? Were the complaints about language, or was language a symbol for other things? What other things? Why does language have this power?
5. The Coca-Cola Super Bowl commercial is memorable for many reasons. **Write an analysis** of this advertisement as a multimedia argument. (See Chapter 16 for information on multimedia arguments and analyses of them.)

▼ *This article discusses an increasingly common situation in cities and towns across the United States: the presence of immigrants from Mexico or Central America whose first language is not Spanish and who may speak little, if any, Spanish. While many readers might assume that this situation would immediately lead the immigrants to learn English, in fact, the reality is more complicated. For many reasons, learning Spanish is easier for them than learning English, and Spanish is often more useful in daily life, given the circumstances of these immigrants. As the article notes, the number of classes in Spanish or English for immigrants is insufficient to meet the needs of learners. Kirk Semple has worked since 2003 at the* New York Times, *where this article first appeared in July 2014. An English/Spanish bilingual, he reports on issues related to immigration and immigrant life in the New York City region in particular. He has also been a correspondent for the paper in Miami, Haiti, Iraq, and Afghanistan. As you read this article, seek to be aware of the assumptions you may be quick to make about the linguistic situation of Mexico and immigrants from Mexico as well as the challenges, especially linguistic ones, immigrants might face.*

Immigrants Who Speak Indigenous Languages Encounter Isolation

KIRK SEMPLE

Laura is a Mexican immigrant who lives in East Harlem, a neighborhood with one of the largest Latino populations in New York City. Yet she understands so little of what others are saying around her that she might just as well be living in Siberia.

Laura, 27, speaks Mixtec, a language indigenous° to Mexico. But she knows little Spanish and no English. She is so scared of getting lost on the subway and not being able to find her way home that she tends to spend her days within walking distance of her apartment.

"I feel bad because I can't communicate with people," she said, partly in Spanish, partly in Mixtec. "I can't do anything."

Laura, who asked that her last name not be revealed because she does not have legal immigration status, is among hundreds if not thousands of indigenous people from Latin America living in the New York region who speak neither the dominant language of the city, English, nor

indigenous: native to a place. Indigenous languages are those that were spoken in an area before later waves of settlers, often colonizers, arrived and became the dominant group; not surprisingly, indigenous languages that have managed to survive are disappearing quickly in the contemporary world. The heritage languages of Native Americans would be the indigenous languages of the United States.

the dominant language of the broader Latino community, Spanish.

5 These language barriers, combined with widespread illiteracy, have posed significant challenges to their survival, from finding work to gaining access to health care, seeking help from the police, and getting legal redress in the courts.

The phenomenon, sometimes called linguistic isolation, affects many immigrant populations to varying degrees. But its prevalence among the fast-growing population of newly arrived immigrants from Latin America, many of working and childbearing age, has made them an increasing concern to local service providers and government agencies.

Partly as a result of this population's isolation, there are no reliable estimates of its size, experts said.

In recent years, the Mexican Consulate in New York, seeking to learn more about the local indigenous Mexican population, has surveyed the Mexican citizens who seek the consulate's services. As of the end of 2013, more than 17 percent of respondents spoke an indigenous language, with Mixtec and Nahuatl being the most popular among a total of sixteen. (Scores of indigenous languages with hundreds of variants are spoken in Mexico alone.)

According to the latest data from the Census Bureau, about 8,700 immigrants from Central America and over the age of 4 in the United States speak an indigenous language and do not speak English very well or at all.

10 But the Census Bureau's major surveys do not gauge Spanish proficiency, an equally critical measure for the community of indigenous Latin Americans.

Indeed, for many, not knowing Spanish is as big an impediment as not knowing English. Spanish is the lingua franca° among immigrants from Latin America and dominates conversation in neighborhoods like East Harlem; Corona, Queens; and Hunts Point, in the Bronx.

After arriving in New York, most indigenous Latin Americans will learn Spanish before they learn English — if they ever learn English at all. The need has driven demand for Spanish language classes around the city. About a decade ago, the staff at Little Sisters of the Assumption° Family Health Service, an organization in East Harlem that provides services to the poor, noticed that an increasing number of the students enrolling in its English as a second language classes were not only indigenous language speakers from Latin America but were also illiterate.

Reasoning that it would be easier to teach the newcomers Spanish, which they were beginning to pick up at home and on the street, the organization turned the English classes into Spanish classes.

Beyond the critical language and literacy instruction the classes provided, they also helped the newcomers build "a much-needed social support network," said Rosemary Siciliano, head of communications for Little Sisters of the Assumption. In 2012, however, the organization had to cut the program because of budget shortfalls.

15 For those immigrants who have less than a working knowledge of Spanish and English, even basic services can often remain out of reach. While New York City has a progressive language access policy, it guarantees the provision of interpretation and translation services for city business in only the six most-used non-English languages, which do not include any of the indigenous languages spoken by Latin American immigrants.

Sometimes the struggle of these immigrants is simply to get others to recognize that they are somehow different from the Latin Americans who speak Spanish. They are often mistaken for Spanish speakers because of their nationality and appearance and

---

lingua franca: a widely used language; more specifically, a language used among individuals or groups that may not speak the same language. In many business contexts, English serves as a lingua franca (or shared language) for people who might speak a range of languages natively and have no language in common otherwise.

Little Sisters of the Assumption: a Catholic religious institute, or society, that assists the poor.

are addressed in Spanish, but may be too shy or confused to interrupt, advocates said.

"They may nod when they don't know what's going on," said Lucia Russett, director of advocacy at Little Sisters of the Assumption.

Several years ago, Juan Carlos Aguirre, executive director of Mano a Mano,° a Mexican cultural organization based in New York, received a call from a hospital official in Manhattan. The official was having trouble communicating with a Mexican family. "She said, 'I need your help,'" Mr. Aguirre recalled. "'I think they're all mentally challenged.'"

Mr. Aguirre asked the caller if she had asked the family what language they spoke. "They're Mexican, so they speak Spanish," the woman replied matter-of-factly. It turned out that the family spoke Mixtec.

20 The isolation, their advocates said, is particularly widespread among women, many of whom stay at home with young children while their husbands go to work on construction sites and in restaurant kitchens, where they can pick up Spanish more quickly.

"Monolingual women can end up completely dependent on their husbands for communication with the outside world," said Daniel Kaufman, executive director of the Endangered Language Alliance, a nonprofit organization based in New York.

In the seven years she has lived in New York, Carmen, who is from the state of Guerrero in Mexico and speaks Mixtec, has learned a smattering of Spanish. But, she said, beyond running simple errands, she is not able to do much without the help of her husband, Juan Manuel, who learned Spanish from co-workers at a restaurant where he works as a prep cook. Neither attended school in Mexico as children.

The power imbalance in their relationship was evident in a recent interview with the couple in the East Harlem headquarters of Little Sisters of the Assumption, where they participate in parenting and childhood development programs. He answered most of the questions posed to them, even those directed specifically at Carmen. "If she goes to the store to buy clothes or whatever, she doesn't know how to buy," Juan Manuel said in Spanish. "I always go with her."

Laura, the woman who avoids the subways, arrived in New York in 2010, joining her husband, who had emigrated from Mexico. They had a son, now 2 years old.

25 But recently, she said, their marriage took a downward turn. Her husband assaulted her, she said, and a neighbor, hearing the noise, called the police. Her husband was imprisoned and is now facing deportation, she said.

His absence has thrown Laura's linguistic challenges into sharp relief. Insecure about her ability to navigate the city using her rudimentary Spanish, she has relied heavily on her cousin, Catalina, to accompany her to her appointments, including meetings with the prosecutors who are handling her husband's case. But Catalina, who has a family of her own, is not always available.

Laura, who has not been able to find a job, said she wished it had not come to this. "He's not a bad person," she said. She now fears being left entirely alone, with her young son, in New York City.

Mano a Mano: a not-for-profit organization in New York City that supports the appreciation of Mexican culture in the United States. Its name means "hand to hand" in Spanish, here in the sense of "from hand to hand."

RESPOND •

1. What specific challenges does not speaking Spanish present for immigrants from Mexico and Central America? In what ways are these challenges gendered (that is, in what ways do women and men generally experience them differently)? What specific challenges does this situation present for social services agencies of various sorts here in the United States?

2. According to this article, why is it more logical for these immigrants to learn Spanish rather than English? What functions do Spanish as a Second Language classes serve for these immigrants? What situations arise when no language classes are available?

3. What sorts of evidence does Semple use in this argument of fact? How and how successfully does he combine short narratives of individual experience with other sorts of evidence? (See Chapter 8 on arguments of fact and Chapter 18 on kinds of evidence.)

4. How would you characterize the ethos that Semple creates in this argument of fact? How does he create this ethos? Is it appropriate for an argument of fact? Why or why not? (See Chapter 3 on ethos and Chapter 8 on arguments of fact.)

5. **Write an essay based on fact** regarding immigrants and language issues in your area, whether defined as your neighborhood, your community, your town or city, or your state. Obviously, you'll need to do some research to find out which language groups are present, how many of them there are, what their specific needs are, and how they might be changing. The census is a good place to begin your research: **http://www.census.gov**. Use the search terms "foreign-born" and "language" to help you find relevant data. You may also find useful information using the pull-down menus: TOPICS>POPULATION, where you will see links for both "foreign-born" and "language." At the same time, be aware that censuses rely on self-report data — someone in the household reports on the language abilities of all who live there, a notoriously unreliable measure of language ability. Many communities have nonprofit organizations that work with immigrants, and a number of houses of worship also have programs to assist immigrants; these institutions may be sources of information as well. (See Chapter 8 on arguments of fact.)

▼ *Scott L. Montgomery is an independent scholar who teaches at the University of Washington in Seattle. Trained as a geologist, Montgomery has interests that span the sciences and the humanities, as the titles of some of his books demonstrate:* Minds for the Making: The Role of Science in American Education, 1750–1990 *(1994),* The Chicago Guide to Communicating Science *(2002),* Science in Translation: Movements of Knowledge through Cultures and Time *(2002), and* Does Science Need a Global Language? English and the Future of Research *(2013), from which this selection is excerpted. Montgomery's perspective on the spread of English as the lingua franca, or shared language, among scientists globally is especially interesting because he is a practicing scientist. As Montgomery notes, "What has happened to modern science is remarkable, revolutionary." He later comments, "It is this ability of scientists throughout the world to speak and write to each other, to read each other's work directly, and to collaborate without mediators of any kind that defines the new era." As you read, you'll notice that Montgomery's approach to this topic is anything but naïve. He is quick to criticize some common assumptions people make about English and why it is widely used today, and he is quick to point out some of the limitations of the continuing monolingualism of many people who are born as native speakers of English. In reading this excerpt, pay special attention to the ways that Montgomery combines facts with personal experience to make this point.*

Chapter 4: Impacts

A DISCUSSION OF LIMITATIONS AND ISSUES FOR A GLOBAL LANGUAGE

SCOTT L. MONTGOMERY

During the summer of 2010, I spent three weeks in northwestern Australia as part of a geology seminar run by the University of Washington. Our travels took us through a sizable portion of the Kimberleys, a wild, remote, and pellucid° region of low-ridge mountains, sandstone gorges, and small towns encased by vast savannah° ranches and bordered by tiny Aboriginal° communities. In August, near the end of "the Dry," the area overflows with pitiless sun. The heat falls with a physical weight that can leave the visitor from higher latitudes breathless.

pellucid: completely clear.

savannah: plain with trees far enough apart that grasses can cover the ground.

Aboriginal: the indigenous groups of Australia.

Native languages in Northern Australia are being lost at a disturbing rate. Long-standing conflict with white settlers destroyed many Aboriginal groups, forcing others into enclaves caught between a hunter-gatherer past now largely gone and a modern present yet to be fulfilled. One evening, during a rare, merciful breeze in the town of Timber Creek, I fell into conversation with Roger, an Aboriginal man perhaps in his late thirties, who had flashed me a friendly smile outside the grocery store and asked me where I was from. "I knew you wasn't from around here," he said. It emerged that he is a father of two boys, just as I am, and so we first traded tales of sibling relations and discipline problems. Then I mentioned the language issue; he nodded.

His boys, he said, knew three languages, none of them completely. It worried him. Roger's own birth tongue was Warimajarri,° and he also knew Gurindji pretty well; but his wife came from over Tennant Creek way and spoke Warumungu and also Warlpiri. Both parents knew Kriol,° a pidgin° blending English and several Aboriginal tongues, used by white settlers and natives since the early twentieth century as a lingua franca° across much of the region. The boys spoke their father's language fairly well, their mother's first tongue, Warumungu, better still, and Kriol best of all, because both parents and the extended family often used it at home. When the boys spoke Warumungu they might mix in some English words, too, since this was seen as status speech. At school, Kriol was used by the other children, and some of the teachers knew it. Roger noted that his sons and their friends typically switched back and forth between all three languages, depending on who was talking and whether or not a nearby adult might understand what they were saying. A big problem, he said, was that Kriol contains a lot of English words. "The white fellas always thought me boys could speak English fine, but they can't. They had terrible time in school. Now the government change everything in school to English, so I think they learn it better. I think this might be good for them. Good for their future."

I asked Roger how he had learned his English. "I learned well at school—me mum made me study hard!" he laughed. "Later, I worked at a cattle station. Had to use it there. Now I been working in a store about ten year, using English every day." It was time for me to get back to camp, so I shook Roger's hand, wished his family well, and began to leave. "Hang on," he said suddenly. "Your boys in school, right? What they want to be?" "Well," I began, "one wants to be a doctor, the other a scientist, I think, to study the oceans." "You a lucky man." Roger shook his head and smiled, looking down. Then he looked up: "How many tongues your boys speak?" I replied, "Well, just one for now, though they're studying another in school." He gave me a humorous but pitying look. "Got to do better, mate! One never enough!"

Warimajarri, Gurindji, Warumungu, Warlpiri: These are all related languages native to northwestern Australia. Spoken by the Aboriginal groups there, they continue to disappear as a result of the spread of English.

Kriol: a creole language of Australia that developed out of language contact between Aboriginal Australians, who spoke many languages; English-speaking settlers of Australia; and settlers from China and other parts of Asia. A creole is a natural (i.e., human) language that develops out of a pidgin as children begin to speak it as their native language. (In fact, Montgomery errs in referring to Kriol as a pidgin.)

pidgin: a simplified contact language that develops when more than two groups interact but do not share a language. Pidgins have no native speakers; are used for a limited range of purposes, such as trade; and, hence, have very limited structure and vocabulary.

lingua franca: a language systematically used to permit people who otherwise do not share a language to communicate. Increasingly, English is the lingua franca of business and tourism, for example; thus, a French tourist visiting Vietnam may use English

Perspective

5 It is common to extol the benefits of using a global tongue for science. Such benefits are perceived to include not merely those of a short-term, practical nature, such as expanded collegiality and more immediate dissemination of findings, but those that will profit science in the long term through the globalization of knowledge. There is, too, the symbolic capital° of a "global scientific community" embodied in a shared global tongue. Most researchers around the world, therefore, if asked to comment, would be unlikely to find the status of English problematic or controversial.*

Yet international tongues, past and present, have not been universally kind to their foreign users. Such a language inevitably requires adoption, adaptation, and accommodation, none of which happen overnight, all of which involve difficulty and inequity. Former lingua francas of science—Greek, Latin, Arabic, Chinese among them—did not attain their authority by consensus, but arrived on the back of conquest and empire-building. The impacts they had, for example on tongues that existed before their arrival, were often mixed. They could bring extinction to native languages in conquered territories, but also the creation of new tongues over time, such as the dozens of Romance languages that eventually emerged from Latin. Historically, a dominant language has had profound impacts on any preexisting intellectual community. It has altered many institutions of scholarly practice—education, literacy, practices of reading and writing, the definition of acceptable scholarship, the mobility of scholars themselves.[1] Overall, this has involved loss as well as gain. There are thus limits and drawbacks to be considered when a powerful lingua franca gains authority.

To what degree might this be the case with the use of English in the natural sciences? Are there important disadvantages that stand out, and if so, how serious are they? Given the many years of training and the intense competition for resources and rewards in contemporary science, can any such problems be addressed in some way? In truth, these are important, even central questions for the future of scientific endeavor, since they involve the capabilities of researchers themselves.

Scholars of language have paid some attention to these realities and questions.[2] The role of English specifically and the issues it presents have been taken up or touched upon by specialists in the field of applied linguistics, yielding much that is valuable. Some of these authors are highly critical

*My own discussions with many scientists over the past decade, at international meetings and other encounters, show this to be the case.

with a Vietnamese waitress when ordering a meal, or an Arab businesswoman may use English when negotiating a contract with a counterpart in China.

symbolic capital: resources that afford someone recognition or prestige, for example, wearing certain brands of clothing or driving a particular make of car. Speaking a language, and especially being able to speak it "without an accent," is likewise a form of symbolic capital in many circumstances. Similarly, speaking some languages—(e.g., French)—brings more symbolic capital than speaking others—(e.g., Spanish)—even though in the United States, a knowledge of Spanish may be far more practically useful than a knowledge of French.

of English dominance in the sciences (seeing it, for example, as a loss of diversity); others are more drawn to its linguistic and social aspects. Be that as it may, a number of important conclusions emerge from this work. Here are the main ones relevant to our discussion:

- The global role of English in science has nothing to do with inherent qualities in the language. There is no wondrous "fit" between English and things scientific. The rise of this language is due to historical developments.
- English dominance is especially strong in the physical and life sciences and biomedicine. It is less pervasive in applied sciences and less (but increasing) in the social sciences and humanities.
- Such dominance is expanding because scientists want broad recognition, desire more opportunities, and understand that these now depend on publishing papers and citations° in international journals, where English dominates.
- Since English is the native tongue for certain countries, researchers, universities, and companies from those places gain immediate advantage. Most anglophone° researchers are monolingual and cite only papers in English.
- Poorer, developing nations have less capability to teach and learn English, so their scientists are at a strong disadvantage. This inequity can be understood as a situation of "haves" and "have-nots," or a type of core-periphery° division, with wealthy nations at the center and developing nations at the margins.
- In many countries, most science is published in the native tongue. This work is internationally unknown, as it is not cited outside the domestic language community. Its scientific value may be local or it may not; we can't tell. Important work may go unnoticed, to the disadvantage of science and scientists everywhere.
- Many nonnative speakers of English suffer from low confidence when they use this language. There is much struggle, failure, and inefficiency attached to such use.
- Bibliographic databases such as SCI° and *Scopus*,° as a key part of the evolving "memory" of science, are biased toward publications written in English, though this has changed to a certain degree. Global visibility for any journal accepted into these databases is hugely increased; as a result, there is a powerful incentive for them to publish in English, creating a type of "feedback loop"° for the further spread of this language in scientific publication.

citations: references to a text, most often a research article or book. The works listed in a bibliography or reference list in an academic work represent cases of citation. The more a work is cited, the more influential or significant it is assumed to be.

anglophone: a speaker of English (here with the presupposition that the person is a monolingual speaker of English).

core-periphery: a metaphor from systems theory that divides the world's countries into core countries—those that are highly industrialized and benefit from the global market system, including the United States, Canada, Europe, Australia, and New Zealand—and the periphery, those that are less economically developed and, hence, peripheral or at the margins of the world economic system.

SCI (Science Citation Index): the major citation index for science, which enables researchers to determine how often an article has been cited, a measure of the article's impact or importance. When a journal's articles are indexed in *SCI*, that fact is taken as evidence of the journal's legitimacy. As Montgomery notes, *SCI* and similar databases favor English-language publications.

- No imperial policy° is at work to spread scientific English. Non-anglophone scientists are urged to use this language by historical realities, the policies of their research departments, universities, and companies, and the influence of their ambitions.

Each of these points, and others as well, will be taken up in what follows. The question of this book can't be adequately answered unless some of these conclusions are interrogated themselves.

[. . .]

A Final Story, and an Idea

Toward the end of my stay in the Kimberleys, a remarkable event occurred. 10
Driving back to the Gibbs River Road from Tunnel Creek (a kilometer-long walk through a magnificent limestone cavern), the left back wheel of our jeep suddenly flew off, bounding into the bush like a frightened wallaby. The vehicle ground to a stop in the red dirt. Pieces of broken metal lay about, like shrapnel in the dust.

Within a short time, several cars and jeeps had stopped, and we found ourselves surrounded by friendly voices. We were plied with water, beer, bananas, energy bars, and a flow of encouraging words. Two men proved to be mechanics, and conceived a repair that took the better part of two hours. The sun drove the rest of us into the miserly shade of a boab tree,° where I ended up talking with a leathery-faced young woman wearing a broad sunhat who was a grad student in environmental science at the Australian National University. I remarked on the kindness shown, and was told that this was typical in the outback. People like a gathering, she said, and also stop because a breakdown can be fatal in such a remote area. The Aboriginals, she noted, had many ways to find water in the Dry. Their territory was like a secret text; they knew hidden watering holes, rainwater gouges in granite, the hollows of certain trees, hand-dug wells in hidden, shady places. In times of drought, they used plants and could find new water by observing the movements of birds. Early in the era of white settlement, men or boys were sometimes kidnapped and forced to show where water could be found. This was especially true of expeditions to the interior, but not those of Donald Thomson.

Thomson was an anthropologist, perhaps the most famous champion of Aboriginal causes in Australian history, who led a series of ethnographic trips between 1957 and 1965 to the Bindibu people in the Great Sandy Desert. Even at this date, many of the Bindibu had never seen a white face and lived the

Scopus: another important bibliographic database of academic journal articles.

feedback loop: part of a self-regulating system where the output or result of some process is fed back into the system, perpetuating it.

imperial policy: the (language) policy of a colonial power, which encourages or enforces the use of its language in the areas it dominates. During the last century, Britain, France, Germany, Japan, the Soviet Union, and the United States all enforced such policies in certain areas of the world at various times.

boab (also baobab) tree: a tree indigenous to northwestern Australia; it is characterized by a very broad, bottle-shaped trunk.

hunter-gatherer life as they had for tens of millennia. To the whites, the Great Sandy was "the land where men perish," the harshest desert on the continent. The first to cross it was Colonel Peter Warburton in 1873; his expedition fell into legendary difficulties of heat, thirst, and incompetence, and members were forced to survive by eating their much-abused camels and by relying on their Aboriginal tracker, Charley. Several subsequent crossings by later explorers all suffered greatly from lack of water. Thomson, despite many preparations, did not avoid this challenge. Though he had only a single companion plus two trackers, they promptly lost one of the jeeps, and lost the second one before long in the midst of a raging sandstorm.

Thus stranded, Thomson was soon befriended by a group of the Bindibu. They showed absolutely no fear of him or anything he did, and this extended to the children, who would come over and squat to watch whatever task he was engaged in. Learning a portion of their language, teaching them some of his, Thomson was allowed to live and hunt with this group for several months. He found the people not merely sociable but complex, witty, ingenious. He saw that their lives and songs revolved around water. "It soon became apparent," he says in his account, "[they] had a practical knowledge of the ecology of the desert in advance of any white man. . . . There was certainly a great deal more water . . . than had been assumed."[3]

Eventually, a replacement axle for the second jeep arrived. Thomson decided it was time to return. On the eve of his departure, the people gave him a gift. It was a type of life-giving knowledge. Carved on the back of a wooden atlatl° was a design of lines connecting a set of spirals that the leader, Tjappanongo, showed to him.

atlatl: an apparatus that enables its user to throw a spear at a far faster speed than would be possible using his or her arm alone. (Interestingly, *atlatl* is from Nahuatl, a Meso-American language; *woomera* is a term used by Aboriginal Australians.)

> Sometimes with a stick, or with his finger, he would point to each well or rock hole in turn and recite its name, waiting for me to repeat it after him. Each time, the group of old men listened intently and grunted in approval "Eh!"? or repeated the name again and listened once more. This process continued with the name of each water until they were satisfied with my pronunciation. . . . I realized that here was the most important discovery of the expedition—that what Tjappanongo and the old men had shown to me was really a map . . . of the waters of the vast terrain over which the Bindibu hunted.[4]

15 Thomson's journey can be read as an example and as a parable.° A more capable society will be one that is able to utilize directly the knowledge of others. In the future, knowing English alone will not be enough. As more of humanity learns this language, and therefore becomes still more multilingual (in many cases), monolingual speakers will increasingly find themselves approaching the edges of a desert where they have less access to a greater part of the outside world. The greatest long-term danger coming from the global spread of English—could it be to its own native speakers?

parable: a story that functions as an analogy, teaching a lesson by drawing a parallel between the characters or situation depicted in the story and the context in which the story is told.

Notes

1. Scott L. Montgomery, *Science in Translation: Movements of Knowledge through Cultures and Time* (Chicago: University of Chicago Press, 2002).
2. A significant literature has come to surround this idea of language inequality or, in some writings, "injustice." One branch of this literature has tended to take a highly critical position toward English as a global tongue for science and advocates major changes in language planning and policy for the whole of international scientific publishing. While these writings are mostly by nonscientists and do not much consider, in any consistent manner, the opinions of researchers themselves, they nonetheless raise a number of issues that can be neither avoided nor ignored in any balanced view of the larger situation. A selection would include Ulrich Ammon, "Global English and the Non-Native Speaker: Overcoming Disadvantage," in *Language in the 21st Century*, ed. Humphrey Tonkin and Timothy Reagan (Amsterdam: Benjamins, 2003), 23–34; Ulrich Ammon, "Language Planning for International Scientific Communication: An Overview of Questions and Potential Solutions," *Current Issues in Language Planning* 7 (2006): 1–31; A. Suresh Canagarajah, *A Geopolitics of Academic Writing* (Pittsburgh: University of Pittsburgh Press, 2002); Bonnie Lee La Madeleine, "Lost in Translation," *Nature* 445 (2007): 454–55; R. E. Hamel, "The Dominance of English in the International Scientific Periodical Literature and the Future of Language Use in Science," *AILA Review* 20 (2008): 53–71; Humphrey Tonkin, "Language and the Ingenuity Gap," *Scientist* 22, no. 4 (2008): 1–10; Erin Bidlake, "Whose Voice Gets Read? English as the International Language of Scientific Publication," *E-pisteme* 1, no. 1 (2008): 3–21; Miguel Clavero, "'Awkward wording. Rephrase': Linguistic Injustice in Ecological Journals," *Trends in Ecology and Evolution* 25, no. 10 (2010): 552; and Charles Durand, *La Mise en Place des Monopoles du Savoir* (Paris: L'Harmattan, 2001). A second branch of the relevant literature focuses less on issues of policy and intervention and more on the attitudes of researchers, as well as giving a more fine-grained analysis of nonnative speakers' experiences in working with English. Some representative publications here include Gibson Ferguson, Carmen Pérez-Llantada, and Ramón Plo, "English as an International Language of Scientific Publication: A Study of Attitudes," *World Englishes* 30, no. 1 (2011): 41–59; Diane Belcher, "Seeking Acceptance in an English-Only Research World," *Journal of Second Language Writing* 16 (2007): 1–22; Mary Curry and Theresa Lillis, "Multilingual Scholars and the Imperative to Publish in English: Negotiating Interests, Demands and Rewards," *TESOL Quarterly* 38, no. 4 (2007): 663–88; John Flowerdew, "The Non-Anglophone Scholar at the Periphery of Scientific Communication," *AILA Review* 20 (2008): 14–27; Laura Landa, "Academic Language Barriers and Language Freedom," *Current Issues in Language Planning* 7 (2006): 61–81; and Ragnhild Ljosland, "English in Norwegian Academia: A Step toward Diglossia," *World Englishes* 26, no. 4 (2007): 395–410.
3. Donald F. Thomson, "The Bindibu Expedition III," *Geographical Journal* 128, no. 3 (September 1962): 262–78; quotation is from p. 274.
4. Ibid., 274.

RESPOND.

1. How does this selection challenge you to think about English and its use in the world in new ways? What are some of the advantages and disadvantages of any global language, according to Montgomery?
2. The "Perspective" section of this excerpt does a very good job of summarizing many of the claims made about the dominance of English as the global language of science. (Later in this chapter, before the closing section, "A Final Story, and an Idea," Montgomery examines these claims in greater detail; this section of the chapter is omitted here.) How does this list of claims form an argument? In other words, how does the strategic ordering of the list of claims become an argument? What sort of argument is it—an argument of fact, an argument of definition, an evaluative argument, a proposal argument? How do you know?
3. Can parts of the "Perspective" section be analyzed as Toulmin arguments? Which ones? Why? (See Chapter 7 for information on Toulmin's method of analyzing arguments.)
4. Montgomery uses personal experience narratives as bookends to this chapter, beginning and ending with a story about something that happened to him. How do these stories influence the way you read and understand the "Perspective" section of the selection, which is based on different kinds of evidence?
5. An interesting aspect of this selection is the way that Montgomery represents the speech of Roger, the Aboriginal Australian with whom he speaks in the opening section of the text. As is clear, English is not Roger's first or only language, and the variety of English he would have been exposed to is obviously not American English but some variety found in Australia. Study Roger's speech carefully. Do you see patterns to the language that differ from those a native speaker might use? Do you see any words you associate with Australian English? It is quite easy to represent the speech of speakers like Roger in ways that are patronizing or mocking. Do you think Montgomery avoided doing so? Do you think he set out to do so? Why or why not?
6. **Write an evaluative argument** in which you consider the claims Montgomery makes in the closing section of this essay. Are there perils to being monolingual for individuals? For countries? In other words, are there ways in which monolingualism is limiting for individuals or countries? In contrast, what costs come with the challenges of multilingualism? Taking a clue from Montgomery in responding to this question, don't fall prey to much of what you might hear about these issues. In other words, focus on the findings of research rather than opinions that may not be backed up by fact. You'll likely need to do some research if you want your opinions on these topics to be taken seriously. (See Chapter 10 for information on evaluative arguments and the chapters in Part 4 for help with research.)

▼ *Santos Henarejos is a graphic designer who lives in Madrid, Spain. With Gemma Navarro, he is co-founder of the international design firm We Are Rifle; both serve as art directors for* Makeshift, *where we found this selection.* Makeshift *is a magazine that seeks to be a "field guide to hidden creativity," and you can visit it online at http://mkshft.org/. The idiom "speak my language" can mean to communicate in a way that someone else understands, often because of shared worldview* (Janet speaks Alissa's language. They get along just fine.) *or to express a strong positive feeling for something* (Chocolate cake? Now you're speaking my language!). *In this visual argument, Henarejos offers an infographic, a genre for presenting data and text that, when done well, does not misrepresent the information displayed but encourages readers to see new relationships between the phenomena illustrated. As you study Henarejos's infographic, spend time thinking about whether and how its various parts add up to a single argument or several possible arguments.*

Infographic: Speak My Language

SANTOS HENAREJOS

INFOGRAPHIC

Speak My Language

From submarine fiber to towering transmitters, technology has laid the piping for us to connect across vast distances. And more nodes are in more hands: there are nine mobile subscriptions for every 10 people. But how does this affect *how* we communicate? Western influence in technology and politics has bred three times as many non-native English speakers as native ones, boosting the language mortality rate to a record high. But not to fear—recognizing that English isn't a suitable conveyor of every cultural nuance, new pidgins and dialects are cropping up and evolving each day. Here's a look at our ever-changing chatter.

THE WORLD'S TOP LANGUAGES

NATIVE SPEAKERS

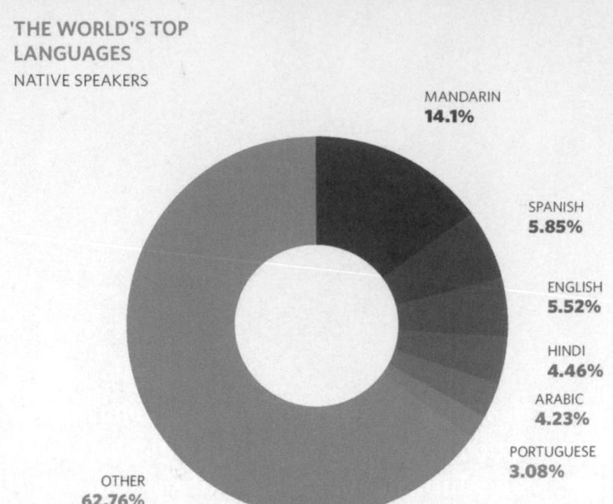

GLOBAL BANDWIDTH

REGIONAL BANDWIDTH CAPACITY AND TRANSFER

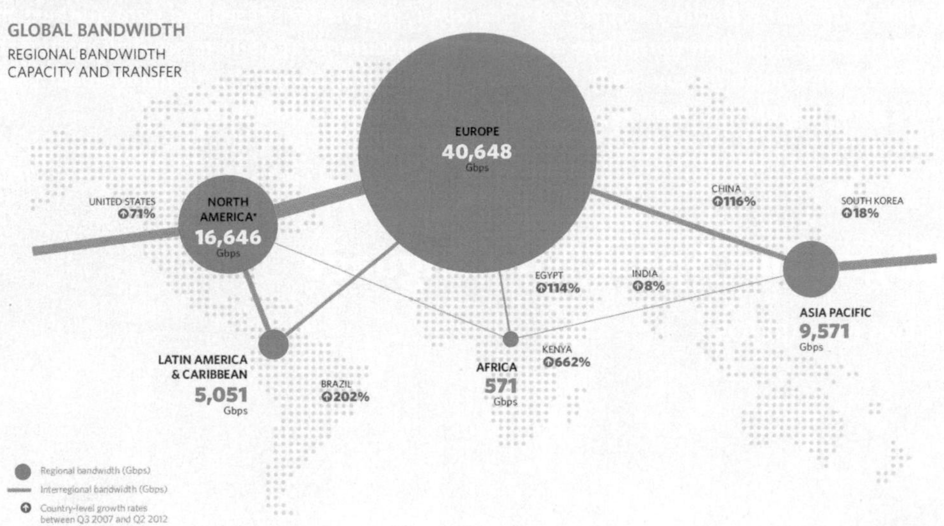

94%
percent of languages spoken by 6% of the world

6%
percent of languages spoken by 94% of the world

7,000
living languages in the world today

50-90%
of living languages expected to "die" by 2100

1.5 billion
speakers of English around the world

3:1
the ratio of nonnative to native English speakers

*North America excludes Mexico and Caribbean

Sources: Akamai, British Council, Ethnologue, ITU, Nationalencyklopedin, Portio Research, Telegeography, World Bank

MOBILE DATA

COST AND DEMAND
OF MOBILE DATA

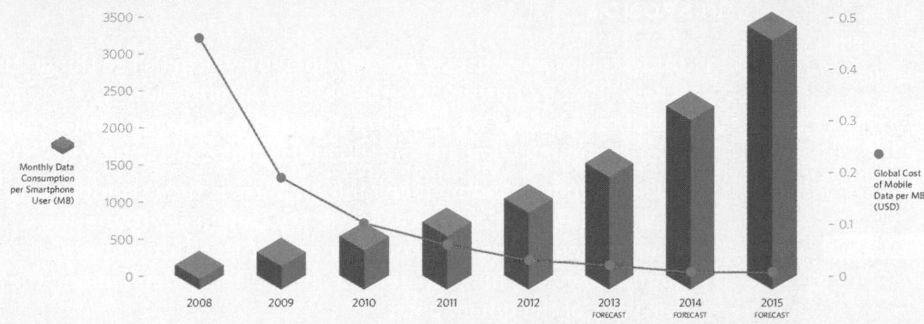

LANGUAGE CONTACT

HOW GLOBALIZATION CHANGES LANGUAGES

Borrowing. Borrowing words from another language to fill lexical gaps and modifying them to fit the language's rules. Japanese. コップ [/kop:u/] (From Portuguese *copo*)

Code-switching. Multilinguals may switch between languages during the course of their speech, using elements of each. Spanglish. Me voy *a wake up*. (I'm going to wake up)

Interference. Influence of a native language results in common mistakes among new language learners, breeding a local dialect. Indian English. Doubt: a question or query (e.g. I have a doubt)

SPEECH VARIETIES

FORMS OF SPEECH

Dialect. A local variant of a language, by geography or class, distinguished by vocabulary, grammar, or pronunciation.

Slang. Use of informal expressions not considered standard. Argot slang is a secret language used to exclude others.

Patois. Any language considered nonstandard, sometimes referring to pidgin or creole combinations of languages.

HOW WE COMMUNICATE

SUBSCRIPTIONS TO COMMUNICATION TECHNOLOGIES (PER 100 INHABITANTS)

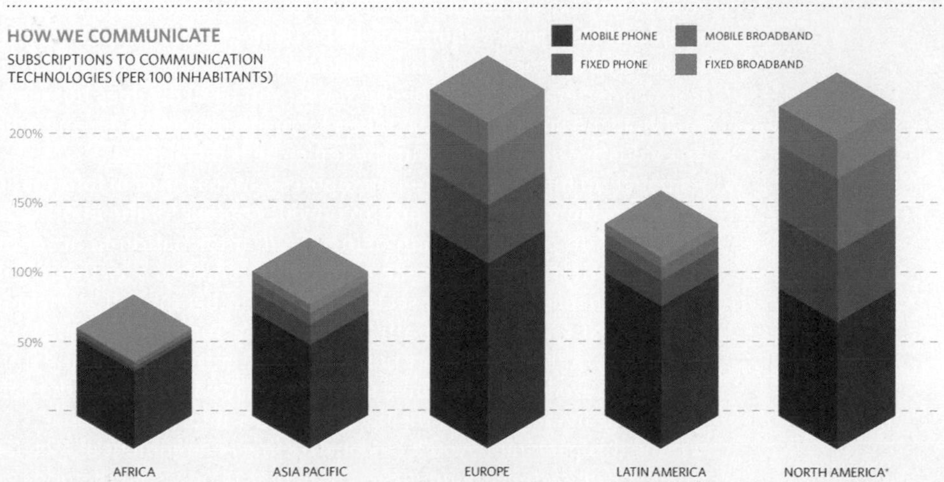

Consider the organization of this infographic. What other ways might Santos Henarejos have chosen to convey this information? Chapter 14 discusses how different types of visuals transmit information clearly and effectively.

LINK TO P. 339

RESPOND.

1. Infographics are most successful when they help us see things in new ways, often by putting together bits of information we hadn't seen juxtaposed before. What information about language (rather than cellular communication and broadband) in this chart is new to you?
2. A key to understanding many infographics is the accompanying text. How does Henarejos's text "Speak My Language" frame the way we read and consume the various parts of this infographic? In other words, how does his text create a context for understanding the various parts of the infographic?
3. As you'll note, there are no marginal glosses for this selection. Why would we expect a successful infographic for a general audience not to need glosses? (Chapter 14 on visual rhetoric may be helpful here.)
4. From a linguistic point of view, one instance of Henarejos's word choice is especially interesting. Find the two places in the infographic where Henarejos uses a form of the verb *breed*. What are the connotations of this verb in English? (In other words, who or what breeds or is bred? Is the term usually used in ways that are positive or negative?) Someone trained in linguistics would likely have used a verbal phrase like *give rise to* in these cases. What difference is communicated by the choice of *give rise to* instead of *breed*? If we assume that Henarejos knows about this distinction and consciously chose to use *breed*, what argument is he making by using that word rather than other alternatives? (See Chapter 13 for a discussion of word choice.) By the way, we wonder if Henarejos's choice might be related to the fact that his first language is Spanish; if so, this would be an instance of the phenomenon of interference, which he discusses, and he likely does not realize that in using *breed*, he will be taken by many readers as having made an evaluative argument about the topics he is discussing.
5. As noted, an infographic often juxtaposes various kinds of information while providing limited remarks to provide context for the information presented. In contrast, when using visual information in academic writing, writers need to make explicit the point of any figure they include. Choose one of the sections of this infographic that includes limited text (e.g., the diagram "The World's Top Languages: Native Speakers") and **write a short paragraph** that might accompany it if it were to be used in an academic essay. You may wish to begin the paragraph "The figure [name of the figure] provides information about . . ." In writing this paragraph, you'll be constructing an argument of fact. (See Chapter 8 on factual arguments and Chapter 14 on visual rhetoric.)

▼ *Linguist Nicholas Ostler is author of* Empires of the Word: A Language History of the World *(2005), which examines the spread of various major languages across history, and* Ad Infinitum: A Biography of Latin *(2007), which focuses specifically on Latin and its spread. Currently, he chairs the Foundation for Endangered Languages (http://www.ogmios.org/), a non-governmental organization in Britain that supports the documentation, preservation, and promotion of endangered languages, that is, languages that are at risk of disappearing as those who speak them natively die while younger members of the community shift to speaking other languages. "Is It Globalization That Endangers Languages?" was presented at a 2008 conference on "Globalization and Languages: Building Our Rich Heritage" jointly sponsored by the United Nations Educational, Scientific, and Cultural Organization (UNESCO) and the United Nations University in Tokyo, Japan, where the conference took place. Thus, it represents a special type of written text, one constructed to be read aloud to an audience in a formal setting. As you read this selection, consider both the argument Ostler makes regarding the role of globalization in language endangerment and the ways in which he writes his text so that he can easily read it aloud instead of writing it so that readers can read it silently.*

Written texts that originated as oral presentations, like this article by Nicholas Ostler, often have a distinct tone or emphasize audience in particular ways. Oral presentations are just one type of presentation discussed in Chapter 15.

LINK TO P. 351

Is It Globalization That Endangers Languages?

NICHOLAS OSTLER (F.E.L.)°

F.E.L.: Foundation for Endangered Languages

Globalization, meaning the increasingly active and conscious interaction of human activities in different parts of the Earth, has a very long history—at least by the standards of the term's modern usage.

The spread of a single species of hominids° round the world, starting in east Africa 65,000 years ago and completed in the Americas fifty millennia later, is the founding achievement for all later globalization, but its extent totally exceeded the means for different communities to go on interacting. This had to await the advent of trade routes, from the fifth millennium BCE in southwest Asia, second millennium BCE in Central Asia, and which jointly seem to have reached Egypt by 1070 BCE, to judge from some silk found in the tomb of an Egyptian pharaoh.

hominids: the primate family that includes humans.

After this, the first large-scale regional empires were founded, in the Middle East, China, and latterly India and Europe. This meant there were fewer, larger units to get to know about, but knowledge about life in widely distant parts of the globe spread more slowly than goods. Merchants, however, were also spreading knowledge of religions, initially Buddhism. And empires, local accumulations of power and wealth, gradually found that they could extend their reach too: notable early successes in this were the Arabs in the seventh century CE, the Mongols in the twelfth, and the Russians in the sixteenth. Globalized epidemics became possible, firstly the Black Death,° an unintended present to the west from the Mongol Empire.

Black Death (1346–1353): plague originating in Asia that traveled to Europe, likely via fleas on the rats in ships, and killed 30 to 60 percent of the continent's population.

The combinations of trade, religion and power began to be conveyed overseas from Europe in the sixteenth century too, and this is when globalization achieves a recognizably modern form. At last everyone in the world had a known address, so to speak, and a self-consciously global world-system was born. It was left to the empires of the nineteenth and twentieth centuries to improve the technology of communications, so that it is now literally possible for any nation to speak unto nation, either with a direct visit, or more typically, without leaving home at all.

This then is globalization, where messages can now travel the world 5
instantly and reliably enough to sustain real-time conversations. What is more, that power is increasingly diffused, so it is not just the summits of the power hierarchies who are in touch, but the vast majority of the world's people.

Since globalization is about human contact, it has naturally been accompanied by language effects throughout, from the original peopling of the world with an efflorescence° of languages at the beginning of reconstructible history, to the immoderate° spread of English in the nineteenth and twentieth centuries. Indeed, the continental, and later global, spread of certain languages is the clearest long-term evidence of what global contacts have been achieved.

efflorescence: flowering.
immoderate: unrestrained or excessive.

But this brings us, at last, to the question I want to address in this talk. We all know that in this modern world, alongside the languages that have become global, there are others—the vast majority—which have remained local in size and scope. There are close to seven thousand languages in the world, and half of them have fewer than seven thousand speakers each, less than a village. What is more, 80% of the world's languages have fewer than one hundred thousand speakers, the size of a small town. These smaller languages are increasingly thought of as endangered, since all over the world they are failing to be taken up by young people.

Now the question: Is it globalization, and the consequent spread of the global languages—above all at present, English—which is responsible for the endangerment of these other languages?

I have dwelt at some length on the historical background of globalization, so that we can remember that this situation has been a long time in the making; and also to remember that there may be evidence about cause and effect which is not just from the last few decades when globalization has become extreme.

10 To get a fairer, and less panicky answer to the question, we must first make the distinction between a *lingua franca*° and a mother tongue.° Not all languages have the same value to their speakers. When a language spreads as a *lingua franca*, this is a matter of convenience, making direct communication possible where before it was difficult because of a language barrier. The result is a larger community mediated by the *lingua franca*, with no corresponding loss of any other links. But when a language spreads as a mother tongue, this means that someone grows up with a language which is different from the mother tongue of one or both parents: some other mother tongue has lost a potential learner in the new generation. So whereas the spread of a *lingua franca* can only increase an effective "global" community, the spread of a mother tongue may well decrease some local community. So only the latter contributes to language endangerment.

A confusion arises because a language like English has gained many speakers in both these ways. In North America and Australia, most immigrants and most of the indigenous° population have adopted English as a mother tongue, whereas, as a *lingua franca*, it is also widely used in countries which have never had a close political association with Britain. In many countries, though, such as India, Malaysia, South Africa, or Nigeria,° its status is more mixed and ambiguous.

But consider a language like Esperanto,° which only grows as a *lingua franca*: its spread is an asset to globalization, since it puts more people in touch with each other across the world, but it does not thereby replace any other linguistic competence. No one, and no language, need be afraid of Esperanto. This is one asset of a spreading *lingua franca*. Another one, potentially, is that it brings with it few, if any, cultural presumptions: it exists purely as a means of communication, not a badge of membership or a tradition. There seems to be an increasing impatience, in the world of Teaching English as a Foreign Language, with holding up the native speaker as an ideal, or accepting that any part of British or American culture is part of the subject.

This cultural emptiness of a *lingua franca* is a matter of degree. There is a literature, including poetry, even in Esperanto. And people who learn

lingua franca: a language systematically used to permit people who otherwise do not share a language to communicate. Increasingly, English is the lingua franca of business and tourism, for example; thus, a French tourist visiting Vietnam may use English with a Vietnamese waitress when ordering a meal, or an Arab businesswoman may use English when negotiating a contract with a counterpart in China.

mother tongue: the term speakers of British English use for native language.

indigenous: native to a place. Indigenous languages are those that were spoken in an area before later waves of settlers, often colonizers, arrived and became the dominant group; not surprisingly, indigenous languages that have managed to survive are disappearing quickly in the contemporary world. The heritage languages of Native Americans represent the indigenous languages of the United States.

India, Malaysia, South Africa, Nigeria: countries all colonized by Britain and, hence, part of the British Empire. Each of these countries has developed its own local variety of English.

any language in any way may derive from it some social benefits beyond the ability to communicate: indeed, those who know a *lingua franca* which is not their mother tongue may often be recognized as an elite, having greater prospects and potentially greater power. This is in fact the rule, with second-language learners of English, French, or Russian. But this does not supplant their mother tongue culture. They do not thereby have less access to their traditions.

Nevertheless, the net effect of globalization may be adverse° for minority languages, even if the spread of such *lingua francas* does them no direct harm. Increasing and denser international contacts are likely to raise the general climate of aspiration and ambition within a territory. The results have often been a stimulus to imperialism° in outsiders, nationalism° in the local elite and urban masses, and centralizing economic development° in both. All of these, by diminishing the role and independence of small traditional communities, usually damage minority languages. But this kind of damage is not by any means always brought about by the "usual suspects" among global languages, languages like English, French, Spanish, Portuguese, Arabic, Russian, Persian, or Chinese.

The Foundation for Endangered Languages' conference in 2006, held in 15
Mysore, southern India, focused on multilingualism as it affects endangered languages, and the relations revealed were very varied (Elangaiyan et al., 2006). In Nicaragua, the Tuahka language yields to its ancient neighbor Miskitu, unaffected by the recent overlays of English and Spanish. In Pakistan, urbanized Torwalis abandon their language for Pashto and Urdu, not English. The small Turung community in Assam° are finding that traditional pressures from Tai and Jinghpaw are morphing° into new relations with Assamese and English; but the process is still too complex to have a predictable outcome. Matthias Brenzinger, in a wide-ranging discussion of the language dynamics of southern and eastern Africa (Brenzinger, 2007), admits that there are languages now growing there at the expense of smaller languages, but these are Amharic, Swahili, Setswana, not English, and perhaps Kirundi and Kinyarwanda owe their present unchallenged status as national languages to previous spread.

Modern globalization can also bring about trends which are positive for minority languages. It can reveal the fact there are endangered languages all around the world, and so give their speakers a motive to contact one another, and build solidarity networks.° It can spread ideas of how languages can reverse a downward trend, as Welsh, Maori,° and Hawaiian appear to have done recently in their different corners of the world, or breathe new life into the apparent husk of a dead language, as Hebrew° did in the twentieth century.

Esperanto: an artificial language created in the late nineteenth century and based on European languages. Its founder, L. L. Zamenhoff, hoped to create an international language that was politically neutral, easy to learn, and fostered mutual understanding and peace between speakers of various languages.

adverse: negative, unfavorable, harmful.

imperialism: the expansion of a country's influence or power, most often by military force or direct colonization.

nationalism: allegiance to a country.

centralizing economic development: economic development focusing on and planned by a central government in contrast to more regionally focused methods of development.

Assam: a state in northeastern India just south of the Himalayas.

morphing: shifting or changing shape.

solidarity networks: social networks that can be used to effect social change.

Maori: the language of the indigenous people of New Zealand.

On the solidarity front, there has been since 1978 the American Indian Language Development Institute (AILDI), with its mission to document, revitalize, and promote indigenous languages, reinforcing the processes of intergenerational language transfer, and specifically organizing regular summer schools to train teachers. On the other side of the world, there are now winter schools to promote knowledge of the Latgalian language (de Graaf et al., 2008), closely related to Latvian, which has been transplanted to central Siberia, but which is now put back in contact with its erstwhile° linguistic neighbors in Latvia. This kind of parallel development is only possible in a globalized world.

The global trend of concern for endangered languages, wherever it may have started—if indeed it makes sense to look for a single source—has spread to influence governments and opinion-formers worldwide. We can instance activities, selected randomly in just four continents.

Here in Japan, there is now official concern for the Ainu,° where until 1997, and the Act for "Encouragement of Ainu Culture and the Diffusion and Enlightenment of Knowledge on Ainu Tradition," there was only resignation, if not negative discrimination (though in fact, only on 6 June 2008 did Japan formally recognize the Ainu as an indigenous group).

20 In Australia, since 1992 and the "Mabo" judgment which recognized Native Title and ended the doctrine of "Terra Nullius"—namely that no indigenous population had rights to territory before the advent of European claimants, official attitudes to indigenous people have turned around 180 degrees, with an Aboriginal Reconciliation Commission in the 1990s and networks of "Australian Language Centers" set up in the 2000s. Although there was something of retrenchment° under the Liberal administration, in 2008 the new Labor Government has issued a formal apology to them.

In Peru and other Andean countries, there is increasing acceptance that indigenous populations need special support. There is a national program in Peru of *Educación Intercultural Bilingüe*,° and this is not just for the benefit of the majority indigenous language Quechua. There is also AIDESEP (*Asociación Interétnica de Desarrollo de la Selva Peruana*°) which focuses on the education of speakers of Amazonian languages.

In Europe, the newly recognized duty to support minority languages has been cast into a treaty, which imposes specific obligations on national governments if they are prepared to accept it. This is the ECRML, the European Charter for Regional and Minority Languages, adopted in 1992 under the auspices of the Council of Europe, and so far ratified by twenty-one states. Effectively it mobilizes a supranational,° quasi-global organization in support of regional languages.

Hebrew: The reference here is to the revitalization of Hebrew. In late-nineteenth-century Europe, it was a liturgical language used only for religious purposes, but during the twentieth century, it became a spoken and written language used in all contexts in daily life in what is today Israel, where it serves as one of the two official languages.

erstwhile: former.

Ainu: the single surviving indigenous language of Japan, spoken on the northern island of Hokkaido.

retrenchment: a reversal or reduction.

Educación Intercultural Bilingüe: Spanish for "Intercultural Bilingual Education."

Asociación Interétnica de Desarrollo de la Selva Peruana: Spanish for "Interethnic Association for the Development of the Peruvian Rainforest."

supranational: having influence beyond the borders of a single nation; also used to describe an organization of nations such as the European Union or NATO (North Atlantic Treaty Organization).

Finally, one can mention the efforts of that quintessentially global organization, the United Nations. Since 1993 UNESCO's Intangible Heritage Section has had an Endangered Languages Program, and in 2003 adopted a Convention for the Safeguarding of Intangible Cultural Heritage which recognizes the essential role of language in its expression and transmission. Other symbolic initiatives include the recognition since 2000 of 21 February as International Mother Tongue Day (the date originally commemorating the re-institution of Bangla as official in East Pakistan), and indeed 2008 as the International Year of Languages.

It is over-simple, then, and misleading, to cast Globalization as a direct cause of language endangerment. If one is concerned for this crisis, it is important to try to "remember the enemy": not global languages themselves, for they are only an effect of globalization, and not necessarily in direct competition with languages that are endangered. What has led to the endangerment of languages is the imperialism, nationalism, and centralizing economic development, which are more about the concentration of power, and hence the disempowerment—and sometimes dissolution—of minority language communities.

We have seen that, in current conditions, globalization, by unleashing new forms of human solidarity, gives some—modest—grounds for hope that these enemies of endangered languages can be resisted.

Wade Davis has remarked that "Every language is an old-growth forest° of the mind, a watershed° of thought, an ecosystem° of spiritual possibilities." Globalization provides endless opportunities for cross-fertilization,° but to get its benefits as much as possible must survive of the different variant growths.° The best thing that we can do for endangered languages is to do our best to listen to the stories told in them, respect the people who tell those stories, and see them passed on to the next generation.

In one or other old-growth forest of the mind, we need to watch the trees grow.

old-growth forest: a largely undisturbed forest of considerable age that has developed a unique ecosystem.

watershed: area of land where water from several sources—rain, melting snow, melting ice—comes together and then enters another body of water such as a river or lake.

ecosystem: the system of living organisms in any place as they interact with the nonliving elements of the environment (e.g., soil, air, water).

cross-fertilization: pollination of one species by another.

variant growths: here, the various species in the old-growth forest.

References

Brenzinger, M. (Ed.). (2007). *Language diversity endangered*. Berlin, NY: Mouton de Gruyter.

de Graaf, T., Ostler, N., & Salverda, R. (Eds.). (2008). *Endangered languages and language learning*. Bath, England: Foundation for Endangered Languages.

Elangaiyan, R., Brown, R., Ostler, N., & Verma, M. (Eds.). (2006). *Vital voices: Endangered languages and multilingualism*. Bath, England: Foundation for Endangered Languages.

RESPOND

1. Briefly summarize Ostler's argument. In what way is it an example of a causal argument? (See Chapter 11 on causal arguments.)
2. How does Ostler structure his argument, and how does this structure help listeners follow his argument? To answer this question, start by dividing the text into sections, and then label the function of each based on the way it moves Ostler's argument forward. For example, in his opening sentence, Ostler defines what he means by globalization. The next several paragraphs provide historical information in chronological order. You can take it from here.
3. Ostler relies heavily on factual evidence to support his claims, offering many examples. In some cases, he offers a series of examples within a single paragraph; in others, he provides a series of paragraph-length examples. Study the text to find cases of each, and discuss with a classmate how these different ways of using examples are appropriate in context.
4. As noted, this selection was written as a conference paper to be read aloud, a fact that helps account for its short length and minimal use of references. Look for other features of the text that likely result from its being written to be read aloud. (A good way to think about this question would be to read the text aloud.) Here, consider matters related to sentence structure and length as well as the use of markers of structure like "finally." (Chapter 13 on style in arguments may help you here.) How has Ostler acknowledged the immediate context of the conference? How does this contribute to his ethos for the local audience? (See Chapter 3 about ethos.)
5. In the closing paragraphs of his talk, Ostler encourages his audience "to listen to the stories told in [an endangered language], respect the people who tell those stories, and see them passed on to the next generation." Do some research on an endangered language, choosing one to investigate in more detail. You may wish to investigate a Native American language spoken in your area or an endangered language elsewhere in the world. (The Wikipedia entry on "endangered languages" is a place to start, as are the Web sites mentioned in the next selection.) **Write a factual argument** in which you present information about the current vitality of the language—where it is spoken, how many speakers there are, whether the language is also written, etc.—and any efforts to document the language or to keep it alive. Perhaps, following Ostler's advice, you can find first-person accounts—stories—of efforts to preserve the language. (See Chapter 8 on arguments of fact.)

▶ *As her Web site roseveleth .com notes, Rose Eveleth is a Brooklyn-based "producer, designer, and writer" who has done freelance writing as well as audio and video production for a range of newspapers, magazines, and media outlets. She has a BS in ecology, behavior, and evolution and an MA in science, health, and environmental reporting. (She's got a video produced for* scienceline.org *called* "What the Heck Is Beer?" *that explains the science of beer.) This selection,* "Saving Languages through Korean Soap Operas," *appeared in the* Atlantic, *a magazine devoted to cultural and literary commentary, in September 2014. As you read this essay, think about how Eveleth manages to find unusual ways to draw readers into her subject.*

Saving Languages through Korean Soap Operas

ROSE EVELETH

About 350,000 people in the world speak Udmurt, a language native to eastern Russia. Nearly 50 percent of global languages are at risk of going extinct, and Udmurt is one of them — a so-called "endangered language." Preserving these languages is hard; as communities age and disperse, and as globalization pushes younger generations to study English, the incentives to learn an obscure, local language diminish.

But for Udmurt speakers, there's a new way to share the language: the movie *Apocalypto*. A team of translators has gone through the film and subtitled the whole thing in Udmurt. And it's not just *Apocalypto* either — the translation is part of a wider push to take popular television shows and movies and leverage them in the fight against language extinction.

Aleksey Shklyaev is the leader of the group that translated *Apocalypto*. His team has a number of projects going, all aimed at keeping Udmurt alive — everything from movie translations to inventing new words to keep the tongue up to date. Together they've created words for "PR" and "retail" and "crowd-sourcing," among others — and an online forum for promoting and sharing Udmurt.

So when Shklyaev stumbled upon a Web site called Viki — an online platform that licenses movies and television shows from around the world and opens them up

for crowd-sourced translation—he realized it would be a perfect place to bring his translation efforts. Shklyaev and his team are now translating into Udmurt everything from *Jungle Emperor Leo*, the 1997 Japanese movie that inspired *The Lion King*, to *The Heirs*, one of the most popular Korean dramas of the last decade.

Viki has teamed up with the Living Tongues Institute for Endangered 5
Languages to encourage those who speak endangered languages to contribute their own translations of the shows. They're currently adding projects for everything from Cherokee, a language spoken by about 18,000 people in the southeastern United States, to Maori, a language spoken in New Zealand by about 60,000. The most popular endangered language on the site is Basque, spoken by about 720,000 people in the Basque region on the border between Spain and France.

Viki wasn't designed as a safe haven for endangered languages. The company's goal when it launched in 2010 was to build translation communities, and have them share culture from other parts of the world. "We're opening up the world," Viki's CEO Razmig Hovaghimian told me.

"Not only the content travels, but the language, the nuance, the culture is suddenly crossing borders."

And in fact, the site has seen some interesting trends when it comes to who watches and translates what. A Korean series about an alien who falls in love with an actress is one of the most-watched shows in Hebrew and Arabic. Spanish speakers can't get enough of a Thai drama about a maid who winds up working for a mafioso in Hong Kong. Japanese shows are most commonly watched in Lithuanian. Viki's 33 million monthly visitors are just a slice of the world as a whole, but Hovaghimian says they offer clues about overlooked markets around the world that content producers may want to tap into.

When Shklyaev contacted Hovaghimian to find ways to work together, Hovaghimian said it was hard to say no. "I have a soft spot in my heart for this," he told me. "I'm struggling teaching my own kids Armenian."

David Harrison, a linguist at Swarthmore College and the director of research for 10
the Living Tongues Institute, thinks partnering with Viki is an effective way to bring languages like Udmurt to younger people. "Suddenly you have something that isn't a dry textbook or a grammar lesson," he says. "Seeing it on TV or on the Internet helps them see that it's not backwards or obsolete—it's suited for the

modern world. They can restore their pride in the language, which is really the X factor that causes language to be abandoned or to be saved by their speakers."

But there are still a number of challenges associated with this kind of preservation. Some communities in which endangered languages are spoken don't have access to reliable Internet, which makes it hard for them to participate. A full two-thirds of the world's languages don't have a written form, Harrison says, which makes subtitling difficult. And translation is hard work — it takes hours and hours to translate a single episode of a television show. Shklyaev has assembled a dedicated team of volunteers, but finding people who are willing or able to put the time in can be difficult.

Still, Harrison believes in the work groups like Viki are doing. "I think we're at a kind of threshold moment where we're going to pass through an extinction event in terms of languages, if we don't do anything about it," he says. And convincing people to care about that isn't easy. "Everybody knows that we benefit from biodiversity° and we'll suffer if we lose it. It's not clear to people why that's true for linguistic diversity." As Harrison sees it, losing traditional languages means losing a huge amount of knowledge about the world and history. But without concerted effort, languages like Udmurt and Cherokee and Maori may simply disappear. Or they could be saved — by Korean soap operas and Mel Gibson movies.

biodiversity: a measure of the number and variety of organisms in a particular environment or ecosystem; generally, higher levels of biodiversity are considered beneficial, though the biodiversity of different sorts of environments varies naturally.

RESPOND

1. In what ways does Eveleth provide evidence that technology and the accompanying phenomenon of crowd-sourcing offer endangered languages new resources for survival? What additional consequences might there be of a phenomenon like Viki? (To get a clearer idea of how Viki works, you may wish to visit its site: **viki.com/endangered languages**.) How does the quirkiness of these consequences contribute to the article?
2. In what ways does this selection support the claims made by Ostler in the previous selection, "Is It Globalization That Endangers Languages?" In what ways does it complicate his argument? (Some of David Harrison's comments may be especially helpful in this regard.) In what ways does this selection serve as an evaluative argument? (See Chapter 10 on evaluative arguments.)

3. Both the previous selection by Ostler, "Is It Globalization That Endangers Languages?," and this selection by Eveleth ultimately contain elements of a proposal argument. What is being proposed by Eveleth? By Ostler? To what extent do their proposals overlap? How do they differ? (Chapter 12 discusses proposal arguments.)
4. The last three paragraphs of this selection summarize comments by linguist David Harrison. Using his comments from either paragraph 10 or 12, **construct a Toulmin argument**. You will need to begin with Harrison's comments, map them onto the framework presented for a Toulmin argument, see whether there are any missing elements, and then try to fill them in. As you'll see, this exercise is a good way to test the strength of an argument. (See Chapter 7 for a discussion of Toulmin arguments.)
5. The selections in this chapter have all engaged the issue of language and globalization in some way. Choose some aspect of this topic and **develop an academic argument** that examines it in some detail. (Chapter 17 will help you think about the nature of academic arguments. The argument you construct may rely on fact, definition, or evaluation; it may analyze causes; or it may offer a proposal—the kinds of arguments treated in Chapters 8–12. Your argument will likely require research, and Chapters 18–22 will be most helpful there.)

25
Why Is Sustainability Important When It Comes to Food?

Left to right: Megan Haaga, for Open Gates, by permission; © Frank Fell/age fotostock; AP Photo/Kin Cheung

A major change in American culture over the past decade or so has been a growing interest in food; turn on the television at any hour of the day or night, and you can find someone demonstrating how to prepare food, generally on several different channels. At the same time, the notion of sustainability has become a hot topic and the topic of considerable debate. (There's a good chance that it, like diversity, has become or has been a buzzword on your campus in recent years.) What, then, would sustainable food look or taste like? And why does sustainability matter? The selections in this chapter will help you consider these issues and why they are far more complex than they might, at first glance, appear.

The chapter opens with an excerpt from Christian R. Weisser's 2014 book, *Sustainability: A Bedford Spotlight Reader*, which provides an extended definition of the term *sustainability* and explores why it matters. This selection will give you a framework for thinking about sustainability with regard to what we—and others—eat. The next three selections examine what qualifies as sustainable food. As you'll discover, there are sharp disagreements about this topic. In "Attention Whole Foods

Shoppers," political scientist Robert Paarlberg advocates the use of genetically modified seeds (and hence foods) as a way of helping to solve the food crisis in developing nations, an issue he contends has fallen off the radar of many Americans as they have become increasingly obsessed with what they eat. In an excerpt from *Animal, Vegetable, Miracle*, author Barbara Kingsolver and her husband, ornithologist Steven L. Hopp, argue with equal vigor that genetically modified seeds and plants are anathema: something to be loathed and even cursed. In the following selection, "Are Engineered Foods Evil?" from *Scientific American*, David H. Freedman promises to offer the truth about genetically engineered foods. You'll get to determine whether you believe what he delivers. You'll also immediately notice when comparing these three selections that different authors use different criteria for evaluation and thus, not surprisingly, they reach different conclusions, although they would contend they are arguing about the same topic.

This chapter's visual argument, "Apples to Oranges," by Claire Ironside, presents evidence that supports the "eat local" partisans while demonstrating what a carbon footprint is and how it figures into debates about sustainability and food. In the following selection, Eric Mortenson, a journalist who covers agricultural topics, writes about how the owners of a small farm outside Portland, Oregon, have gone organic and are diversifying their efforts to remain local and remain in business, another aspect of sustainability. In a similar vein, in an excerpt from her 2012 book, *Change Comes to Dinner: How Vertical Farmers, Urban Growers, and Other Innovators Are Revolutionizing How America Eats*, Katherine Gustafson examines some of the challenges found by those who eat locally and want to help others do the same. As this selection reminds us, eating sustainably at the local or international level, however defined, requires a great deal of effort on the parts of all kinds of folks.

▼ *We open this chapter, which is devoted to food, with a reading about sustainability by Christian R. Weisser, an associate professor of English at Penn State Berks. Two of Weisser's interests are environmental rhetoric and what we might term* public rhetoric, *moving rhetoric beyond classrooms into the world. He seeks to do just that in this selection, which is adapted from his introduction to* Sustainability: A Bedford Spotlight Reader *(2014). As Weisser notes, although the term was coined in Germany in 1804, discussions and debates about sustainability have grown exponentially in recent decades, representing one of the most significant discourses that define our era. And as you'll see in reading the selections in this chapter, discussions about food quickly turn to questions of sustainability, whether the issue is eating locally or food insecurity in developing nations. Thus, sustainability serves as an appropriate framework for thinking about the complexity of these issues. As you read this selection, pay special attention to the ways that Weisser defines sustainability and how he justifies its importance.*

Sustainability

CHRISTIAN R. WEISSER

What Is Sustainability?

You've probably heard the term "sustainability" in some context. It is likely that you've used some product or service that was labeled as sustainable, or perhaps you are aware of a campus or civic organization that focuses on sustainability. You may even recognize that sustainability has to do with preserving or maintaining resources; we often associate sustainability with things like recycling, using renewable energy sources like solar and wind power, and preserving natural spaces like rain forests and coral reefs. However, unless you have an inherent interest in sustainability, you probably haven't thought much about what the term actually means. In fact, many people do not have a clear sense of what sustainability is or why it is so important. The following description will provide a starting point for your investigations of sustainability.

Simply put, sustainability is the capacity to endure or continue. If a thing or an activity is sustainable, it can be reused, recycled, or repeated in some way because it has not exhausted all of the resources or energy required to create it. Sustainability can be broadly defined as the ability of something to maintain itself, and biological systems such as wetlands or forests are good examples of sustainability because they remain diverse and productive over long periods of time. Seen in this way, sustainability has to do with preserving resources and energy over the long term rather than exhausting them quickly to meet short-term needs or goals.

Many current discussions about sustainability focus on the ways in which human activity—and human life itself—can be maintained in the future without exhausting all of our current resources. Historically, there has been a close correlation between the growth of human society and environmental degradation—as communities grow, the environment often declines. Sustainability seeks new ways of addressing that relationship, which would allow human societies and economies to grow without destroying or overexploiting the environment or ecosystems in which those societies exist. The most widely quoted definition of sustainability comes from the Brundtland Report° by the World Commission on Environment and Development in 1987, which defined sustainability as meeting "the needs of the present without compromising the ability of future generations to meet their own needs."

Brundtland Report (1987): the name often used for the UN report entitled *Our Common Future: The World Commission on Environment and Development*, which is generally credited with igniting discussions at the international, national, and local levels about the nature of sustainable development. The commission was headed by Gro Harlem Brundtland. Brundtland is a Harvard-trained medical doctor, former prime minister of Norway, former director of the World Health Organization, former UN special envoy on climate change, currently a special envoy to the UN, and an internationally recognized leader in public health and sustainable development.

In other words, sustainability is based on the idea that human society should use industrial and biological processes that can be sustained indefinitely or at least for a very long time and that those processes should be cyclical rather than linear. The idea of "waste" is important here; a truly sustainable civilization would have little or no waste, and each turn of the industrial cycle would become the material for the next cycle. A basic premise of sustainability, then, is that many of our current practices are unsustainable and that human society will need to change to ensure that people in the future live in a world that is virtually no worse than the one we inherited.

5 As a quick example of sustainability, think about aluminum soda cans. In the past, many soda cans were used and thrown away without a whole lot of thought. Their creation, use, and disposal was a linear process, and lots of soda cans wound up in landfills and trash dumps. The practice of throwing them away was unsustainable because ready sources of aluminum are limited and landfills and trash dumps were filling with wasted cans. Consequently, governments and private corporations began to recycle aluminum soda cans, and today more than 100,000 soda cans are recycled each minute in the United States. In fact, today's typical used soda can returns as a new can in just sixty days. A billion-dollar recycling industry has emerged, creating jobs and profits for the workers and businesses employed in that enterprise, while at the same time using limited resources more thoughtfully and reducing the impact on the environment. The process has become cyclical, resulting in the continued use of materials, rather than linear, in which a soda can is used once and then becomes waste. Many questions remain

Gro Harlem Brundtland Jan-Philipp Strobel/picture-alliance/dpa/AP Images

about the actual benefits of recycling, but most people agree that recycling is a more-sustainable solution than pitching our used soda cans into the trash.

But sustainability is about more than just the economic benefits of recycling materials and resources. Although the economic factors are important, sustainability also accounts for the social and environmental consequences of human activity. This concept, referred to as the "three pillars of sustainability," asserts that true sustainability depends on three interlocking factors: social equity, environmental preservation, and economic viability. Some describe this three-part model as People, Planet, Profit. First, people and communities must be treated fairly and equally—particularly with regard to eradicating global poverty and ending the environmental exploitation of poor countries and communities. Second, sustainable human activities must protect the earth's environment. And, third, sustainability must be economically feasible—human development depends on the long-term production, use, and management of resources as part of a global economy. Only when all three of these pillars are incorporated can an activity or enterprise be described as sustainable. The following diagram illustrates the ways in which these three components intersect:

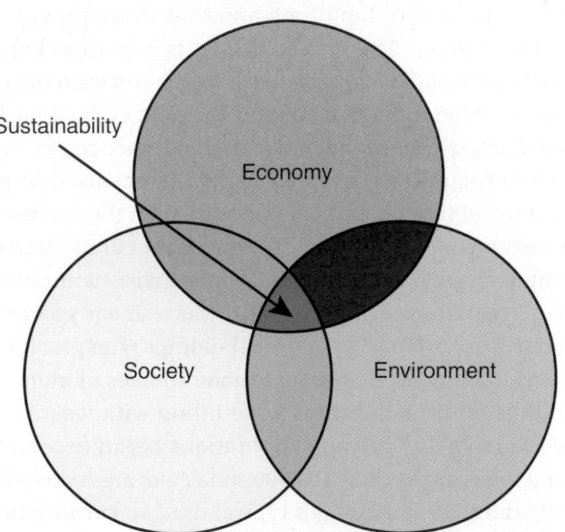

As this model should make clear, sustainability must consider the environment, society, and the economy to be successful. In fact, the earliest definitions of sustainability account for this relationship. The term *sustainability*

first appeared in forestry studies in Germany in the 1800s, when forest overseers began to manage timber harvesting for continued use as a resource. In 1804, German forestry researcher Georg Hartig described sustainability as "utilizing forests to the greatest possible extent, but still in a way that future generations will have as much benefit as the living generation" (Schmutzenhofer 1992).[1] Although our current definitions are quite different and much expanded from Hartig's, sustainability still accounts for the need to preserve natural spaces, to use resources wisely, and to maintain them in an equitable manner for all human beings, both now and in the future.

Our current definitions of sustainability—particularly in the United States—are deeply influenced by our historical and cultural relationship with nature. Many American thinkers, writers, and philosophers have focused on the value of natural spaces, and they have contributed to our collective understanding about the relationship between humans and the environment. Their ideas contributed to the environmentalist movement that emerged in the second half of the twentieth century. Environmentalism advocates for the protection and restoration of nature, and grassroots environmental organizations lobby for changes in public policy and individual behavior to preserve the natural world. The Sierra Club, for example, is one of the oldest, largest, and most influential environmental organizations in the United States.

Environmentalism and sustainability have a lot in common. In fact, some people think that our current conversations about sustainability are the next development or evolution of environmentalism. However, earlier environmental debates often pitted the environment against the economy—nature vs. jobs—and this dichotomy created a rift between those supporting one side of the debate against the other. The battle between the "tree huggers" and the "greedy industrialists" left a lot of people out of the conversation. Many current discussions involving sustainability hope to bridge that gap by looking for possibilities that balance a full range of perspectives and interests—a win-win solution rather than a win-lose scenario. Sustainability encourages and provides incentives for change rather than mandating change, and the three pillars of sustainability emphasize this incorporation. Many sustainability advocates imagine new technologies as mechanisms to protect the planet while also creating economic opportunities and growth; other sustainable approaches simply endorse new ways of thinking and

[1]Quoted in K. F. Wiersum, "200 Years of Sustainability in Forestry: Lessons from History," *Environmental Management* 19, no. 3 (1995): 321–29.

acting. In essence, sustainability looks for coordinated innovation to create a future that merges environmental, economic, and social interests rather than setting them in opposition.

Why Consider Sustainability?

Sustainability Is Important

In some ways, sustainability is the most important conversation taking place in 10
our society today. The earth is our home, and it provides all of the things we need for our survival and nourishment. However, that home has limited resources, and our collective future will depend on the successful management and use of those resources. We are living in a critical time, in which global supply of natural resources and ecosystem services is declining dramatically, while demand for these resources is escalating. From pollution, to resource depletion, to loss of biodiversity, to climate change, a growing human footprint is evident. This is not sustainable. We need to act differently if the world and its human and nonhuman inhabitants are to thrive in the future. Sustainability is about how we can preserve the earth and ensure the continued survival and nourishment of future generations. You and everyone you know will be affected in some way by the choices our society makes in the future regarding the earth and its resources. In fact, your very life may well depend on those choices.

Sustainability Is Relevant

Sustainability impacts nearly all human endeavors, and it is tied to nearly every social, academic, and professional arena. When you consider sustainability in relation to science, business, economics, political science, art, music, literature, history—or indeed any field of study—you will no doubt see that ideas and assumptions about sustainability are important both to the shape of those fields and to the work done within them. Indeed, debates and conversations about sustainability can be found all around us—in the news, on television, in film, and perhaps even among people in your own family or social circles. Therefore, understanding sustainability will help you understand an important facet of your future life and work.

Sustainability Is Complex

Sustainability is a complex subject that involves many different topics, conversations, and perspectives. Much of what we think and do concerning sustainability emerges from "expert" opinions on scientific, economic, and political issues, and it may seem daunting to try to form your own opinions based on your limited knowledge. Even the experts often disagree, and it can be confusing and difficult to sort through the complexity of the issues involved in the sustainability conversation. In fact, you may feel as if the subject is better left to those experts to address. However, you should recognize that it is that very complexity that makes the subject of sustainability worth addressing. Sustainability is a broad and diverse subject with no clear answer or set of answers.

Sustainability Is Interdisciplinary

Along with its complexity, sustainability is also an interdisciplinary subject. This means that it can be addressed or analyzed from many different academic perspectives and that various "disciplines" can be combined in its understanding. Interdisciplinary thinking is about crossing the boundaries of specific, traditional fields of study to look at a problem or subject in more holistic, comprehensive ways. In this respect, sustainability combines a variety of disciplines, including science, economics, politics, humanities, and others. In fact, it is hard to think of an academic discipline that could not contribute to the sustainability conversation.

Sustainability Is a "Discourse"

All intellectual endeavors involve participation in an ongoing conversation called a "discourse." This is not the same type of conversation you might have with a roommate or with a group of friends; it is the type of conversation that takes place among many people over many years in various methods of expression: books, essays, articles, speeches, and other kinds of articulations. All university students are expected to develop skills to absorb, assimilate, and synthesize information gathered from various sources within various discourses and to find their own voice within them. This is a basic pattern in the creation of knowledge. Sustainability is an emerging conversation or "discourse" in our society—its definition is still developing, and the reading, writing, thinking, and talking that you do can contribute to that definition.

Sustainability Is Political

Because sustainability is concerned with how we use limited resources on 15
the earth, it is essentially a political issue. All of the debates surrounding sustainability are political, since they seek to change the ways people think and act, often with the goal of influencing public policy and law.

Sustainability Is Rhetorical

Simply defined, rhetoric is about the ways in which speakers or writers attempt to persuade or motivate an audience. An effective writer will make careful choices in the language, delivery, timing, and other factors involved in a piece of writing because he or she wants those words to be understood, accepted, and acted on. Because sustainability is such an important, complex, and political issue, it is vital to analyze the words and images that are used to define it.

SUSTAINABILITY IS PERSONAL

Sustainability affects each of us on a personal level. The communities we live in, the foods we eat, our modes of transportation, the jobs we pursue—each of these aspects of our lives and countless others are shaped by sustainable (or unsustainable) choices. By learning more about sustainability, you will learn more about the world you live in and the influence it has on your own personal well-being. Furthermore, each of us has the ability to choose sustainable behaviors to improve our own lives and the lives of those around us. Your own perspective on sustainability will likely evolve, and that evolution will shape your values and decision-making, enabling you to create a healthier, happier, and more sustainable lifestyle.

RESPOND •

1. This selection represents an extended definitional argument. Make a list of the definitions, characterizations, and examples Weisser gives of the notion of sustainability, noting the paragraph in which each occurs. (The list may be quite long. Recall that explaining what something is not or how current ways of thinking about something differ from earlier ways of thinking about a related set of topics represents a kind of characterization.)
2. Take the list you created in response to question 1 and label each of the definitions, characterizations, or examples of sustainability in terms of the kind of definition it represents. (Chapter 9 on arguments of definition discusses kinds of definitions.)
3. In paragraph 4, Weisser writes that life-sustaining processes need to be or become "cyclical rather than linear." How, specifically, does he use the extended example of aluminum soda cans in paragraph 5 to illustrate and clarify the contrast between linear and cyclical processes?
4. Study the Venn diagram that Weisser uses to illustrate the meaning of sustainability (p. 604). (Slightly different versions of the diagram recur frequently in discussions of sustainability.) How does this diagram help clarify the notion of sustainability? Does it clarify or emphasize aspects of the notion that the written definition does not? How so? How does it help support the distinction Weisser draws between the

earlier environmentalist movement and current discussions of sustainability (paragraph 9)?

5. Using the information in this chapter and other research that you do, **write a definitional argument** in which you define the concept of sustainability. Obviously, you'll have to determine which aspects of this concept are most important for you. You'll also want to spend some time considering why you find these aspects to be the most important. What you learn may become part of your discussion. (If you quote or paraphrase this selection or other sources you consult, be sure to study Chapters 20–22, which give you practical advice about how to incorporate and document sources correctly.)

▼ *Robert Paarlberg teaches at Wellesley College, where he is the Betty Freyhof Johnson '44 Professor of Political Science; he is also an associate at Harvard's Weatherhead Center for International Affairs.*

The focus of Paarlberg's research is policy relating to food and agriculture, particularly in Africa and the developing world more broadly. His most recent book is Food Politics: What Everyone Needs to Know, *2nd ed. (2013). This selection, "Attention Whole Foods Shoppers," first appeared in April 2010 in* Foreign Policy, *an award-winning print magazine that publishes several international editions and a Web site focusing on domestic and international policy, global affairs, and contemporary events. Traditionally,* Foreign Policy *has sought to call into question commonly held opinions about the topics with which it is concerned. Its founders hoped that it would be "serious but not scholarly, lively but not glib." As you read this article, note carefully both the commonly held assumptions Paarlberg is questioning and the counterproposal he offers instead.*

Attention Whole Foods Shoppers

ROBERT PAARLBERG

From Whole Foods recyclable cloth bags to Michelle Obama's organic White House garden, modern eco-foodies are full of good intentions. We want to save the planet. Help local farmers. Fight climate change — and childhood obesity, too. But though it's certainly a good thing to be thinking about global welfare while chopping our certified organic onions, the hope that we can help others by changing our shopping and eating habits is being wildly oversold to Western consumers. Food has become an elite preoccupation in the West, ironically, just as the most effective ways to address hunger in poor countries have fallen out of fashion.

Helping the world's poor feed themselves is no longer the rallying cry it once was. Food may be today's *cause célèbre*,° but in the pampered West, that means trendy causes like making food "sustainable" — in other words, organic, local, and slow. Appealing as that might sound it is the wrong recipe for helping those who need it the most. Even our understanding of the global food problem is wrong these days, driven too much by the single issue of international prices. In

cause célèbre: a French expression used originally to refer to famous legal cases; speakers of English use it to refer to widespread controversies, often ones in which not all of the facts are well known.

Shoppers at Whole Foods. AP Photo/The Philadelphia Inquirer, Clem Murray

April 2008, when the cost of rice for export had tripled in just six months and wheat reached its highest price in twenty-eight years, a *New York Times* editorial branded this a "World Food Crisis." World Bank° President Robert Zoellick warned that high food prices would be particularly damaging in poor countries, where "there is no margin for survival." Now that international rice prices are down 40 percent from their peak and wheat prices have fallen by more than half, we too quickly conclude that the crisis is over. Yet 850 million people in poor countries were chronically undernourished before the 2008 price spike, and the number is even larger now, thanks in part to last year's global recession. This is the real food crisis we face.

It turns out that food prices on the world market tell us very little about global hunger. International markets for food, like most other international markets, are used most heavily by the well-to-do, who are far from hungry. The majority of truly undernourished people — 62 percent, according to the U.N. Food and Agriculture Organization — live in either

World Bank: a financial institution set up by the United Nations to reduce poverty in developing countries by lending them money for projects that will improve infrastructure there. Developing countries are those with a lower standard of living, found generally in Central and South America, Africa, and Asia. Infrastructure refers to things like roads, bridges, airports, railways, ports, and water systems that permit a country to function smoothly.

Africa or South Asia, and most are small farmers or rural landless laborers living in the countryside of Africa and South Asia. They are significantly shielded from global price fluctuations both by the trade policies of their own governments and by poor roads and infrastructure. In Africa, more than 70 percent of rural households are cut off from the closest urban markets because, for instance, they live more than a thirty-minute walk from the nearest all-weather road.

Poverty — caused by the low income productivity of farmers' labor — is the primary source of hunger in Africa, and the problem is only getting worse. The number of "food insecure"° people in Africa (those consuming less than 2,100 calories a day) will increase 30 percent over the next decade without significant reforms, to 645 million, the U.S. Agriculture Department projects.

5 What's so tragic about this is that we know from experience how to fix the problem. Wherever the rural poor have gained access to improved roads, modern seeds, less expensive fertilizer, electrical power, and better schools and clinics, their productivity and their income have increased. But recent efforts to deliver such essentials have been undercut by deeply misguided (if sometimes well-meaning) advocacy against agricultural modernization and foreign aid.

In Europe and the United States, a new line of thinking has emerged in elite circles that opposes bringing improved seeds and fertilizers to traditional farmers and opposes linking those farmers more closely to international markets. Influential food writers, advocates, and celebrity restaurant owners are repeating the mantra that "sustainable food" in the future must be organic, local, and slow. But guess what: Rural Africa already has such a system, and it doesn't work. Few smallholder° farmers in Africa use any synthetic chemicals, so their food is de facto° organic. High transportation costs force them to purchase and sell almost all of their food locally. And food preparation is painfully slow. The result is nothing to celebrate: average income levels of only $1 a day and a one-in-three chance of being malnourished.

If we are going to get serious about solving global hunger, we need to de-romanticize our view of preindustrial food and farming. And that means learning to appreciate the modern, science-intensive, and highly capitalized agricultural system we've developed in the West. Without it, our food would be more expensive and less safe. In other words, a lot like the hunger-plagued rest of the world.

Original Sins°

Thirty years ago, had someone asserted in a prominent journal or newspaper that the Green Revolution° was a failure, he or she would have been quickly dismissed. Today the charge is surprisingly common.

---

food insecure: not having regular access to affordable food.

smallholder: having less land than a farm.

de facto: a Latin phrase meaning "in fact"; it contrasts with *de jure*, "by law."

original sin: the Christian belief that when Adam ate the fruit of the tree of knowledge as recounted in the story of the Garden of Eden, humans, who had been without sin, became sinful, and that such sinfulness is passed on to future generations. Here, used figuratively, it refers to the sources of particular current problems.

Green Revolution: a series of advances in research, development, and technology that vastly improved worldwide agricultural production, especially in developing nations. While the Green Revolution began in the 1940s, it achieved its most spectacular results beginning in the late 1960s.

Celebrity author and eco-activist Vandana Shiva claims the Green Revolution has brought nothing to India except "indebted and discontented farmers." A 2002 meeting in Rome of five hundred prominent international NGOs,° including Friends of the Earth and Greenpeace, even blamed the Green Revolution for the rise in world hunger. Let's set the record straight.

The development and introduction of high-yielding wheat and rice seeds into poor countries, led by American scientist Norman Borlaug and others in the 1960s and 70s, paid huge dividends. In Asia these new seeds lifted tens of millions of small farmers out of desperate poverty and finally ended the threat of periodic famine. India, for instance, doubled its wheat production between 1964 and 1970 and was able to terminate all dependence on international food aid by 1975. As for indebted and discontented farmers, India's rural poverty rate fell from 60 percent to just 27 percent today. Dismissing these great achievements as a "myth" (the official view of Food First, a California-based organization that campaigns globally against agricultural modernization) is just silly.

10 It's true that the story of the Green Revolution is not everywhere a happy one. When powerful new farming technologies are introduced into deeply unjust rural social systems, the poor tend to lose out. In Latin America, where access to good agricultural land and credit has been narrowly controlled by traditional elites, the improved seeds made available by the Green Revolution increased income gaps. Absentee landlords° in Central America, who previously allowed peasants to plant subsistence crops° on underutilized land, pushed them off to sell or rent the land to commercial growers who could turn a profit using the new seeds. Many of the displaced rural poor became slum dwellers. Yet even in Latin America, the prevalence of hunger declined more than 50 percent between 1980 and 2005.

Aerial view of subsistence farmland. AP Photo/John McConnico

In Asia, the Green Revolution seeds performed just as well on small nonmechanized farms as on larger farms. Wherever small farmers had sufficient access to credit, they took up the new technology just as quickly as big farmers, which led to dramatic income gains and no increase in inequality or social friction. Even poor landless laborers gained, because

NGO: non-governmental organization, that is, an organization that is not part of a government or part of a for-profit company.

absentee landlord: a landowner who owns and rents land but lives elsewhere.

subsistence crops: crops that permit those growing them to survive but little or no more.

more abundant crops meant more work at harvest time, increasing rural wages. In Asia, the Green Revolution was good for both agriculture and social justice.

And Africa? Africa has a relatively equitable and secure distribution of land, making it more like Asia than Latin America and increasing the chances that improvements in farm technology will help the poor. If Africa were to put greater resources into farm technology, irrigation, and rural roads, small farmers would benefit.

Chapter 7 discusses the importance of understanding conditions of rebuttal. How well do you think Paarlberg anticipates rebuttals to his argument? Where should he anticipate additional rebuttals?

LINK TO P. 141

Organic Myths

There are other common objections to doing what is necessary to solve the real hunger crisis. Most revolve around caveats° that purist critics raise regarding food systems in the United States and Western Europe. Yet such concerns, though well-intentioned, are often misinformed and counterproductive — especially when applied to the developing world.

Take industrial food systems, the current bugaboo of American food writers. Yes, they have many unappealing aspects, but without them food would be not only less abundant but also less safe. Traditional food systems lacking in reliable refrigeration and sanitary packaging are dangerous vectors° for diseases. Surveys over the past several decades by the Centers for Disease Control and Prevention have found that the U.S. food supply became steadily safer over time, thanks in part to the introduction of industrial-scale technical improvements. Since 2000, the incidence of *E. coli*° contamination in beef has fallen 45 percent. Today in the United States, most hospitalizations and fatalities from unsafe food come not from sales of contaminated products at supermarkets, but from the mishandling or improper preparation of food inside the home. Illness outbreaks from contaminated foods sold in stores still occur, but the fatalities are typically quite limited. A nationwide scare over unsafe spinach in 2006 triggered the virtual suspension of all fresh and bagged spinach sales, but only three known deaths were recorded. Incidents such as these command attention in part because they are now so rare. Food Inc. should be criticized for filling our plates with too many foods that are unhealthy, but not foods that are unsafe.

15 Where industrial-scale food technologies have not yet reached into the developing world, contaminated food remains a major risk. In Africa, where many foods are still purchased in open-air markets (often uninspected, unpackaged, unlabeled, unrefrigerated, unpasteurized, and unwashed), an estimated 700,000 people die every year from food- and water-borne diseases, compared with an estimated 5,000 in the United States.

caveat: a warning with certain conditions or limitations. It was originally a Latin expression meaning "let a person beware."

vector: here, path along which or means by which diseases are easily transmitted.

E. coli: a bacteria, some forms of which can cause food poisoning.

Food grown organically—that is, without any synthetic nitrogen fertilizers or pesticides—is not an answer to the health and safety issues. The *American Journal of Clinical Nutrition* last year published a study of 162 scientific papers from the past fifty years on the health benefits of organically grown foods and found no nutritional advantage over conventionally grown foods. According to the Mayo Clinic,° "No conclusive evidence shows that organic food is more nutritious than is conventionally grown food."

Health professionals also reject the claim that organic food is safer to eat due to lower pesticide residues. Food and Drug Administration surveys have revealed that the highest dietary exposures to pesticide residues on foods in the United States are so trivial (less than one one-thousandth of a level that would cause toxicity°) that the safety gains from buying organic are insignificant. Pesticide exposures remain a serious problem in the developing world, where farm chemical use is not as well regulated, yet even there they are more an occupational risk for unprotected farmworkers than a residue risk for food consumers.

When it comes to protecting the environment, assessments of organic farming become more complex. Excess nitrogen fertilizer use on conventional farms in the United States has polluted rivers and created a "dead zone"° in the Gulf of Mexico, but halting synthetic nitrogen fertilizer use entirely (as farmers must do in the United States to get organic certification from the Agriculture Department) would cause environmental problems far worse.

Here's why: Less than 1 percent of American cropland is under certified organic production. If the other 99 percent were to switch to organic and had to fertilize crops without any synthetic nitrogen fertilizer, that would require a lot more composted animal manure. To supply enough organic fertilizer, the U.S. cattle population would have to increase roughly fivefold. And because those animals would have to be raised organically on forage crops, much of the land in the lower forty-eight states would need to be converted to pasture. Organic field crops also have lower yields per hectare.° If Europe tried to feed itself organically, it would need an additional 28 million hectares of cropland, equal to all of the remaining forest cover in France, Germany, Britain, and Denmark combined.

Mass deforestation probably isn't what organic 20
advocates intend. The smart way to protect against nitrogen runoff is to reduce synthetic fertilizer applications with taxes, regulations, and cuts in farm subsidies, but not try to go all the way to zero as required by the official organic standard. Scaling up registered organic farming would be on balance harmful, not helpful, to the natural environment.

Not only is organic farming less friendly to the environment than assumed, but modern conventional farming is becoming significantly more sustainable. High-tech farming in rich countries today is far safer for the environment, per bushel of production, than it was in the 1960s, when Rachel Carson criticized the indiscriminate farm use of DDT in her

---

Mayo Clinic: a not-for-profit Minnesota-based hospital and medical research facility, generally considered the best medical facility in the United States.

toxicity: the potential of a substance to harm an organism.

dead zone: area of the ocean where there is less oxygen than is necessary to sustain certain forms of life as a result of excessive pollution.

hectare: a metric measure, equivalent to 10,000 square meters or 2.47 acres.

environmental classic, *Silent Spring*.° Thanks in part to Carson's devastating critique, that era's most damaging insecticides were banned and replaced by chemicals that could be applied in lower volume and were less persistent in the environment. Chemical use in American agriculture peaked soon thereafter, in 1973. This was a major victory for environmental advocacy.

Read an excerpt of Rachel Carson's causal argument on the overuse of chemical pesticides.

LINK TO PP. 244–45

And it was just the beginning of what has continued as a significant greening of modern farming in the United States. Soil erosion on farms dropped sharply in the 1970s with the introduction of "no-till" seed planting, an innovation that also reduced dependence on diesel fuel because fields no longer had to be plowed every spring. Farmers then began conserving water by moving to drip irrigation and by leveling their fields with lasers to minimize wasteful runoff. In the 1990s, GPS equipment was added to tractors, autosteering the machines in straighter paths and telling farmers exactly where they were in the field to within one square meter, allowing precise adjustments in chemical use. Infrared sensors were brought in to detect the greenness of the crop, telling a farmer exactly how much more (or less) nitrogen might be needed as the growing season went forward. To reduce wasteful nitrogen use, equipment was developed that can insert fertilizers into the ground at exactly the depth needed and in perfect rows, only where it will be taken up by the plant roots.

These "precision farming" techniques have significantly reduced the environmental footprint of modern agriculture relative to the quantity of food being produced. In 2008, the Organization for Economic Cooperation and Development published a review of the "environmental performance of agriculture" in the world's thirty most advanced industrial countries — those with the most highly capitalized and science-intensive farming systems. The results showed that between 1990 and 2004, food production in these countries continued to increase (by 5 percent in volume), yet adverse environmental impacts were reduced in every category. The land area taken up by farming declined 4 percent, soil erosion from both wind and water fell, gross greenhouse gas emissions from farming declined 3 percent, and excessive

Silent Spring: Rachel Carson's 1962 book, often credited with bringing an awareness of environmental issues, particularly the consequences for birds of the overuse of pesticides, to the general American public.

Rachel Carson with her book Silent Spring. © The Everett Collection/age fotostock

nitrogen fertilizer use fell 17 percent. Biodiversity° also improved, as increased numbers of crop varieties and livestock breeds came into use.

Seeding the Future

Africa faces a food crisis, but it's not because the continent's population is growing faster than its potential to produce food, as vintage Malthusians° such as environmental advocate Lester Brown° and advocacy organizations such as Population Action International would have it. Food production in Africa is vastly less than the region's known potential, and that is why so many millions are going hungry there. African farmers still use almost no fertilizer; only 4 percent of cropland has been improved with irrigation; and most of the continent's cropped area is not planted with seeds improved through scientific plant breeding, so cereal° yields are only a fraction of what they could be. Africa is failing to keep up with population growth not because it has exhausted its potential, but instead because too little has been invested in reaching that potential.

25 One reason for this failure has been sharply diminished assistance from international donors. When agricultural modernization went out of fashion among elites in the developed world° beginning in the 1980s, development assistance° to farming in poor countries collapsed. Per capita food production in Africa was declining during the 1980s and 1990s and the number of hungry people on the continent was doubling, but the U.S. response was to withdraw development assistance and simply ship more food aid° to Africa. Food aid doesn't help farmers become more productive — and it can create long-term dependency.° But in recent years, the dollar value of U.S. food aid to Africa has reached twenty times the dollar value of agricultural development assistance.

---

biodiversity: the level of plant and animal life in a given environment; generally, a higher level of biodiversity is desirable.

Malthusian: subscribing to the thought of Robert Malthus, an eighteenth-century English thinker, that population grows exponentially while food supply grows, at best, arithmetically. In order to prevent a catastrophe, Malthus argued that ways had to be found to reduce natural population growth.

Lester Brown (1934–): an environmental analyst, founder of the Worldwatch Institute, and president of the Earth Policy Institute, both located in Washington, D.C. Brown has authored over forty books on environmental issues.

cereal: here, edible grains, e.g., corn, rice, wheat, barley.

developed world: countries with a higher standard of living, including the United States, Canada, Australia, and Europe.

development assistance: funds given by governments to support long-term development of various kinds in developing countries. It contrasts with humanitarian aid, funds given in response to a specific short-term problem. While the United States gave $31.55 billion of development assistance in 2013, first among the world's countries in amount donated, it ranked twentieth among nations in terms of percentage of the gross national income donated, 0.19 percent. The UN target for such donations is 0.7 percent, a goal met or exceeded that year by five countries: Norway, Sweden, Denmark, Luxembourg, and the United Kingdom.

food aid: food given with the explicit goal of preventing starvation.

long-term dependency: that is, the opposite of independence or self-sufficiency.

The alternative is right in front of us. Foreign assistance to support agricultural improvements has a strong record of success, when undertaken with purpose. In the 1960s, international assistance from the Rockefeller Foundation,° the Ford Foundation,° and donor governments led by the United States made Asia's original Green Revolution possible. U.S. assistance to India provided critical help in improving agricultural education, launching a successful agricultural extension service,° and funding advanced degrees for Indian agricultural specialists at universities in the United States. The U.S. Agency for International Development,° with the World Bank, helped finance fertilizer plants and infrastructure projects, including rural roads and irrigation. India could not have done this on its own — the country was on the brink of famine at the time and dangerously dependent on food aid. But instead of suffering a famine in 1975, as some naysayers had predicted, India that year celebrated a final and permanent end to its need for food aid.

Foreign assistance to farming has been a high-payoff investment everywhere, including Africa. The World Bank has documented average rates of return on investments° in agricultural research in Africa of 35 percent a year, accompanied by significant reductions in poverty. Some research investments in African agriculture have brought rates of return estimated at 68 percent. Blind to these realities, the United States cut its assistance to agricultural research in Africa 77 percent between 1980 and 2006.

When it comes to Africa's growing hunger, governments in rich countries face a stark choice: They can decide to support a steady new infusion of financial and technical assistance to help local governments and farmers become more productive, or they can take a "worry later" approach and be forced to address hunger problems with increasingly expensive shipments of food aid. Development skeptics and farm modernization critics keep pushing us toward this unappealing second path. It's time for leaders with vision and political courage to push back.

Rockefeller Foundation: New York–based private philanthropic organization whose primary mission is "to promote the well-being of humanity throughout the world." It began funding agriculture projects in the 1940s.

Ford Foundation: New York–based private philanthropic foundation whose mission is to advance human welfare.

agricultural extension service: in most cases, a government program that assists farmers at the local level by helping them use improved methods of growing, harvesting, marketing, and shipping.

U.S. Agency for International Development: U.S. federal agency that administers nonmilitary foreign aid; among its goals is helping eradicate extreme poverty at the international level.

return on investment (ROI): the benefit that results from some investment, with a high ROI indicating that, once the costs of the investment are deducted, the benefit or "profit" is high. ROI is a measure of the performance and efficiency of an investment.

RESPOND •

1. Summarize Paarlberg's proposal, being sure to include the problem it addresses, the claim it makes, the way(s) the proposal addresses the problem, and the feasibility of what is proposed. (See Chapter 12 on proposal arguments.)
2. Strong proposal arguments generally both acknowledge alternative proposals and demonstrate the superiority of the proposed solution to those alternatives. Summarize the alternative proposal(s) Paarlberg critiques as well as the evidence he offers to support the superiority of his proposal. (Chapter 12 on proposal arguments and Chapter 7 on structuring arguments may be useful to you in answering this question.)
3. Paarlberg relies heavily on hard evidence and reason as discussed in Chapter 4. Choose a paragraph where he uses hard evidence to support a point, and be prepared to explain to classmates why you find his use of evidence successful or less than successful.
4. How new was Paarlberg's argument for you? In what ways? How convincing do you find his proposal? Why? How might Christian R. Weisser, author of the previous selection from *Sustainability: A Bedford Spotlight Reader*, respond to it? Why?
5. To what extent does this essay from *Foreign Policy* live up to the publication's goals? (Rereading the headnote to this selection will give you the criteria you'll need to respond to this question, which, of course, asks for a brief evaluative argument of the sort discussed in Chapter 10.)
6. This selection confronts most American readers with facts that are new to them because most Americans tend to know little, or nothing, about issues related to food or agriculture in the developing world. Choose a country in the developing world and do research on issues related to food and agriculture there. Then **write an argument of fact** in which you identify the basic issues related to food and agricultural production in that country with the goal of explaining to your readers the challenges that particular country faces in this domain. If you and your classmates choose different countries around the globe and make short oral reports on your findings, you'll learn a great deal about international issues related to food and agriculture. (Chapter 8, which discusses arguments of fact, and Chapters 18–21 on research will likely prove useful here. If you are doing an oral report as well, consult Chapter 15.)

Barbara Kingsolver (1955–) is an American novelist, essayist, poet, and writer of nonfiction who has published over a dozen books. The best-known of these is The Poisonwood Bible *(1998), the story of a family of American missionaries living in the Congo. Kingsolver started college as a piano major but changed to biology and later received her master's degree in ecology and evolutionary biology. She often writes about issues relating to biodiversity and the environment. Steven L. Hopp, her husband and an ornithologist, is an adjunct faculty member at Emory and Henry College in Emory, Virginia. These selections come from* Animal, Vegetable, Miracle: A Year of Food Life *(2007), which Kingsolver wrote with the assistance of Hopp and her daughter, Camille Kingsolver. It details the family's efforts during 2005–2006 to eat locally by growing all their own food or obtaining it from nearby farms. (They did permit themselves to buy items they could not grow such as olive oil and coffee.) Barbara Kingsolver wrote nearly the entire book, but short pieces by Hopp and Camille Kingsolver appear throughout and complement the book's main argument. This selection includes an excerpt from the chapter entitled "Springing Forward," which includes Hopp's "The Strange Case of Percy Schmeiser." As you read these selections, think about how each text provides a context for the other. Also consider how Kingsolver and Hopp's perspective on genetically modified foods differs from the perspectives of Robert Paarlberg ("Attention Whole Foods Shoppers") and David H. Freedman ("Are Engineered Foods Evil?") and why that might be the case.*

"Springing Forward" and "The Strange Case of Percy Schmeiser," from *Animal, Vegetable, Miracle*

BARBARA KINGSOLVER AND STEVEN L. HOPP

Springing Forward (Barbara Kingsolver)

Bronze Arrowhead lettuces, Speckled Trout romaine, red kale—this is the rainbow of my April garden, and you'll find similar offerings then at a farmers' market or greengrocer. It's the reason I start our vegetables from seed, rather than planting out whatever the local nursery has to offer: variety, the splendor of vegetables. I have seen women looking at jewelry ads with a misty eye and one hand resting on the heart, and I only know what they're feeling because that's how I read the seed catalogs in January. In my mind the garden grows and grows, as I affix a sticky note to every page where there's something I need. I swoon over names like Moon and Stars watermelon, Cajun Jewel okra, Gold of Bacau pole bean, Sweet Chocolate pepper, Collective Farm Woman melon, Georgian Crystal garlic, mother-of-thyme. Steven walks by, eyes the toupee of yellow sticky notes bristling from the top of the catalog, and helpfully asks, "Why don't you just mark the one you *don't* want to order?"

Heirloom vegetables° are irresistible, not just for the poetry in their names but because these titles stand for real stories. Vegetables acquire histories when they are saved as seeds for many generations, carefully maintained and passed by hand from one gardener to another. Heirlooms are open-pollinated° — as opposed to hybrids, which are the onetime product of a forced cross between dissimilar varieties of a plant. These crosses do rely on the sex organs of the plant to get pollen into ovaries, so they're still limited to members of the same species: tall corn with early corn, for example, or prolific cucumbers with nonprickly ones, in blends that combine the ideal traits of both parents for one-time-only offspring. These whiz-kid hybrid seeds have slowly colonized° and then dominated our catalogs and our croplands. Because of their unnatural parentage they offer special vigor, but the next generation from these crosses will be of an unpredictable and mostly undesirable character. Thus, hybrid seeds have to be purchased again each year from the companies that create them.

Kingsolver defines the problem she sees with genetically modified crops, providing an important component to her proposal.

LINK TO P. 279

heirloom vegetable: a vegetable variety that has been maintained by farmers and gardeners because of its perceived strengths with regard to characteristics like taste, hardiness, or appearance. The notion obviously links these varieties to that of heirlooms generally, that is, something that is carefully selected, cared for, and handed down across generations.

Heirloom tomatoes AP Photo/ Journal Inquirer, Jared Ramsdell

open-pollinated: pollinated naturally by bees, birds, or the wind and, thus, a possible source of biodiversity. Open pollination contrasts with controlled pollination, which ensures that the seeds produced have only the traits of the parent plants.

colonized: here, reproduced across multiple generations.

Genetic modification (GM) takes the control even one step further from the farmer. Seed companies have made and sold hybrids since the 1920s (starting with the Hybrid Corn Company, now a subsidiary of DuPont), but GM is a newer process involving direct manipulation of genes in the laboratory. Freed from the limits of natural sex, the gene engineer may combine traits of creatures that aren't on speaking terms in the natural world: animal or bacterial genes spliced into the chromosomes of plants, for example, and vice versa. The ultimate unnatural product of genetic engineering is a "terminator gene" that causes a crop to commit genetic suicide after one generation, just in case some maverick° farmer might want to save seed from his expensive, patented crop, instead of purchasing it again from the company that makes it.

maverick: rebellious, nonconformist, often with the connotation of being reckless.

By contrast to both GM and hybridization, open-pollinated heirlooms are created the same way natural selection does it: by saving and reproducing specimens that show the best characteristics of their generation, thus gradually increasing those traits in the population. Once bred to a given quality, these varieties yield the same characteristics again when their seeds are saved and grown, year after year. Like sunshine, heirloom seeds are of little interest to capitalism if they can't be patented or owned. They have, however, earned a cult following among people who grow or buy and eat them. Gardeners collect them like family jewels, and Whole Foods Market can't refrain from poetry in its advertisement of heirlooms, claiming that the tomatoes in particular make a theatrical entrance in the summertime, "stealing the summer produce scene. Their charm is truly irresistible. Just the sound of the word 'heirloom' brings on a warm, snuggly, bespectacled grandmother knitting socks and baking pies kind of feeling."

They've hired some whiz-bang writers down at Whole Foods, for sure, but 5
the hyperbolic° claims are based on a genuine difference. Even a child who dislikes tomatoes could likely tell the difference between a watery mass-market tomato and a grandmotherly (if not pie-baking) heirloom. Vegetables achieve historical status only if they deserve it. Farmers are a class of people not noted for sentimentality or piddling around. Seeds get saved down the generations for a reason, or for many, and in the case of vegetables one reason is always flavor. Heirlooms are the tangiest or sweetest tomatoes, the most fragrant melons, the eggplants without a trace of bitterness.

hyperbolic: characterized by hyperbole, or extreme exaggeration.

Most standard vegetable varieties sold in stores have been bred for uniform appearance, mechanized harvest, convenience of packing (e.g. square tomatoes), and a tolerance for hard travel. None of these can be mistaken, in practice, for actual flavor. Homegrown tomatoes are famously superior to their supermarket counterparts, but the disparity° is just as great (in my experience) for melons, potatoes, asparagus, sweet corn, broccoli, carrots, certain onions, and the Japanese edible soybeans called edamame. I have

disparity: difference.

looked for something to cull from my must-grow list on the basis of its being reasonably similar to the supermarket version. I have yet to find that vegetable.

How did supermarket vegetables lose their palatability,° with so many people right there watching? The Case of the Murdered Flavor was a contract killing, as it turns out, and long-distance travel lies at the heart of the plot. The odd notion of transporting fragile produce dates back to the early twentieth century when a few entrepreneurs tried shipping lettuce and artichokes, iced down in boxcars, from California eastward over the mountains as a midwinter novelty. Some wealthy folks were charmed by the idea of serving out-of-season (and absurdly expensive) produce items to their dinner guests. It remained little more than an expensive party trick until mid-century, when most fruits and vegetables consumed in North America were still being produced on nearby farms.

palatability: pleasant flavor.

Then fashion and marketing got involved. The interstate highway system became a heavily subsidized national priority, long-haul trucks were equipped with refrigeration, and the cost of gasoline was nominal. The state of California aggressively marketed itself as an off-season food producer, and the American middle class opened its maw.° In just a few decades the out-of-season vegetable moved from novelty status to such an ordinary item, most North Americans now don't know what out-of season means.

maw: the mouth and jaws of an animal.

While marketers worked out the logistics of moving every known vegetable from every corner of the planet to somewhere else, agribusiness° learned to breed varieties that held up in a boxcar, truck, or ship's cargo hold. *Indestructible* vegetables, that is to say: creations that still looked decent after a road trip. Vegetable farmers had little choice but to grow what the market demanded. In the latter half of the twentieth century they gradually dropped from their repertoire thousands of flavorful varieties traditionally grown for the table, concentrating instead on the handful of new varieties purchased by transporters, restaurant chains, and processed-food manufacturers. Modern U.S. consumers now get to taste less than 1 percent of the vegetable varieties that were grown here a century ago. Those old-timers now lurk only in backyard gardens and on farms that specialize in direct sales—if they survive at all. Many heirlooms have been lost entirely.

agribusiness: (*agriculture + business*) relating to agriculture as a large-scale business, whether operating very large farms or providing goods or services for such farms and farmers.

10 The same trend holds in other countries, wherever the influence of industrial-scale agriculture holds sway. In Peru, the original home of potatoes, Andean farmers once grew some four thousand potato varieties, each with its own name, flavor, and use, ranging in size from tiny to gigantic and covering the color spectrum from indigo-purple to red, orange, yellow, and white. Now, even in the regions of Peru least affected by the modern market, only a few dozen potato varieties are widely grown. Other indigenous° crops

indigenous: native to the region.

elsewhere in the world have followed the same path, with the narrowing down of corn and amaranth° varieties in Central America, squashes in North America, apples in Europe, and grains in the Middle East. And it's not just plant varieties but whole species that are being lost. As recently as ten years ago farmers in India still grew countless indigenous oil crops,° including sesame, linseed, and mustards; in 1998 all the small mills that processed these oils were ordered closed, the same year a ban on imported soy oil was lifted. A million villages lost their mills, ten million farmers lost their living, and GM soy found a vast new market.

According to Indian crop ecologist Vandana Shiva,° humans have eaten some 80,000 plant species in our history. After recent precipitous changes, three-quarters of all human food now comes from just eight species, with the field quickly narrowing down to genetically modified corn, soy, and canola.° If woodpeckers and pandas enjoy celebrity status on the endangered-species list (dubious though such fame may be), food crops are the forgotten commoners. We're losing them as fast as we're losing rain forests. An enormous factor in this loss has been the new idea of plant varieties as patentable° properties, rather than God's gifts to humanity or whatever the arrangement was previously felt to be, for all of prior history. God lost that one in 1970, with the Plant Variety Protection Act.° Anything owned by humans, of course, can be taken away from others; the removal of crop control from farmers to agribusiness has been powerful and swift. Six companies—Monsanto, Syngenta, DuPont, Mitsui, Aventis, and Dow—now control 98 percent of the world's seed sales. These companies invest heavily in research whose purpose is to increase food production capacity only in ways that can be controlled strictly. Terminator technology is only one (extreme) example. The most common genetic modifications now contained in most U.S. corn, soy, cotton, and canola do one of two things: (1) put a bacterial gene into the plant that kills caterpillars, or (2) alter the crop's physiology

Amaranth AP Photo/Charlie Neilbergall

Vandana Shiva Christian Charisius/picture-alliance/dpa/AP Images

amaranth: grain that was widely consumed by the indigenous peoples of Mexico and Central and South America. It is a favorite of certain proponents of local, sustainable agriculture because it is easily grown and harvested, it contains a great deal of protein (far more than many competing grains), and it is easy to cook.

oil crops: crops that can be used as a source of cooking oil, e.g., coconut, corn, cottonseed, olives, palm, peanuts, safflower, sesame, and sunflower seeds as well as nuts of various kinds.

Vandana Shiva (1952–): award-winning Indian environmental activist known for her support of biodiversity and her opposition to globalization.

canola: rapeseed, a source commonly used for "healthy" cooking oil.

patentable: able to be patented; a patent grants the owner the exclusive rights to the use or sale of a product.

Plant Variety Protection Act (1970): U.S. intellectual property law that guarantees plant breeders up to twenty-five years of control over certain categories of the plants they create.

so it withstands the herbicide Roundup,° so that chemicals can be sprayed over the crop. (The crop stays alive, the weeds die.) If you guessed Monsanto controls sales of both the resistant seed and the Roundup, give yourself a star. If you think you'd never eat such stuff, you're probably wrong. GM plants are virtually everywhere in the U.S. food chain, but don't have to be labeled, and aren't. Industry lobbyists intend to keep it that way.

Roundup: the brand name of a highly debated glyphosate herbicide sold by Monsanto since the 1970s. It became especially popular with farmers when Monsanto later introduced crops that were resistant to Roundup, permitting the farmers to plant their crops, use Roundup, and destroy any weeds. A growing number of weeds have developed resistance to Roundup; in other words, it is not as effective as it once was. Debates about the product relate to its possible consequences for the environment and for humans.

Monsanto sells many package deals of codependent° seeds and chemicals, including so-called traitor technologies in which a crop's disease resistance relies on many engineered genes resting in its tissues—genes that can only be turned on, as each disease arises, by the right chemical purchased from Monsanto.

codependent: dependent on one another.

It's hardly possible to exaggerate the cynicism of this industry. In internal reports, Monsanto notes "growers who save seed from one year to the next" as significant competitors, and allocates a $10 million budget for investigating and prosecuting seed savers. Agribusinesses can patent plant varieties for the purpose of removing them from production (Seminis dropped 25 percent of its total product line in one recent year, as a "cost-cutting measure"), leaving farmers with fewer options each year. The same is true for home gardeners, who rarely suspect when placing seed orders from Johnny's, Territorial, Nichols, Stokes, and dozens of other catalogs that they're likely buying from Monsanto. In its 2005 annual report, Monsanto describes its creation of American Seeds Inc. as a licensing channel that "allows us to marry our technology with the high-touch, local face of regional seed companies." The marriage got a whopping dowry° that year when Monsanto acquired Seminis, a company that already controlled about 40 percent of the U.S. vegetable seed market. Garden seed inventories show that while about 5,000 nonhybrid vegetable varieties were available from catalogs in 1981, the number in 1998 was down to 600.

dowry: money or goods a woman's family gives to her future husband in some cultures.

Jack Harlan, a twentieth-century plant geneticist and author of the classic *Crops and Man*, wrote about the loss of genetic diversity in no uncertain terms: "These resources stand between us and catastrophic starvation on a scale we cannot imagine. . . . The line between abundance and disaster is becoming thinner and thinner."

The "resources" Harlan refers to are old varieties, heirlooms and land 15
races—the thousands of locally adapted varieties of every crop plant important to humans (mainly but not limited to wheat, rice, corn, and potatoes), which historically have been cultivated in the region where each crop was domesticated from its wild progenitor.° Peru had its multitude of potatoes, Mexico its countless kinds of corn, in the Middle East an infinity of wheats, each subtly different from the others, finely adapted to its region's various

progenitor: ancestor.

microclimates, pests and diseases, and the needs of the humans who grew it. These land races contain a broad genetic heritage that prepares them to coevolve with the challenges of their environments.

pathogen: virus or bacteria that causes disease.

Disease pathogens° and their crop hosts, like all other predators and prey, are in a constant evolutionary dance with each other, changing and improving without cease as one evolves a slight edge over its opponent, only to have the opponent respond to this challenge by developing its own edge. Evolutionary ecologists call this the Red Queen principle (named in 1973 by Leigh Van Valen), after the Red Queen in *Through the Looking Glass*, who observed to Alice: "In this place it takes all the running you can do to keep in the same place." Both predator and prey must continually change or go extinct. Thus the rabbit and fox both get faster over the generations, as their most successful offspring pass on more genes for speediness. Humans develop new and stronger medicines against our bacterial predators, while the bacteria continue to evolve antibiotic-resistant strains of themselves. (The people who don't believe in evolution, incidentally, are just as susceptible as the rest of us to this observable occurrence of evolution. Ignorance of the law is no excuse.)

broad-spectrum: wide-ranging.

mongrel: here, a dog resulting from the interbreeding of various kinds of dogs.

Plant diseases can attack their host plants in slightly new ways each season, encouraged by changes in prevailing conditions of climate. This is where genetic variability becomes important. Genetic engineering cannot predict or address such broad-spectrum° challenges. Under highly varied environmental conditions, the resilience of open-pollinated land races can be compared approximately with the robust health of a mixed-breed dog versus the finicky condition of a pooch with a highly inbred pedigree. The mongrel° may not perform as predictably under perfectly controlled conditions, but it has the combined smarts and longevity of all the sires that ever jumped over the fence. Some of its many different genes are likely to come in handy, in a pinch.

monoculture: in agriculture, growing a single crop for many years in the same large area, a common practice in contemporary industrial agriculture.

truncated: cut short.

The loss of that mongrel vigor puts food systems at risk. Crop failure is a possibility all farmers understand, and one reason why the traditional farmstead raised many products, both animal and vegetable, unlike the monocultures° now blanketing our continent's midsection. History has regularly proven it drastically unwise for a population to depend on just a few varieties for the majority of its sustenance. The Irish once depended on a single potato, until the potato famine rewrote history and truncated° many family trees. We now depend similarly on a few corn and soybean strains for the majority of calories (both animal and vegetable) eaten by U.S. citizens. Our addiction to just two crops has made us the fattest people who've ever lived, dining just a few pathogens away from famine.

The Strange Case of Percy Schmeiser (Steven L. Hopp)

In 1999, a quiet middle-aged farmer from Bruno, Saskatchewan, was sued by the largest biotech seed producer in the world. Monsanto Inc. claimed that Percy Schmeiser had damaged them, to the tune of $145,000, by having their patented gene in some of the canola plants on his 1,030 acres. The assertion was not that Percy had actually planted the seed, or even that he obtained the seed illegally. Rather, the argument was that the plants on Percy's land contained genes that belonged to Monsanto. The gene, patented in Canada in the early 1990s, gives genetically modified (GM) canola plants the fortitude to withstand spraying by glyphosate° herbicides such as Roundup, sold by Monsanto.

Canola, a cultivated variety of rapeseed, is one of over three thousand 20
species in the mustard family. Pollen from mustards is transferred either by insects, or by wind, up to one-third of a mile. Does the patented gene travel in the pollen? Yes. Are the seeds viable? Yes, and can remain dormant up to ten years. If seeds remain in the soil from previous years, it's illegal to harvest them. Further, if any of the seeds from a field contain the patented genes, it is illegal to save them for use. Percy had been saving his canola seeds for fifty years. Monsanto was suing for possession of intellectual property that had drifted onto his plants. The laws protect possession of the gene itself, irrespective of its conveyance.° Because of pollen drift° and seed contamination,° the Monsanto genes are ubiquitous in Canadian canola.

Percy lost his court battles: he was found guilty in the Federal Court of Canada, the conviction upheld in the court of appeals. The Canadian Supreme Court narrowly upheld the decision (5-4), but with no compensation to Monsanto. This stunning case has drawn substantial attention to the problems associated with letting GM genies out of their bottle. Organic canola farmers in Saskatchewan have now sued Monsanto and another company, Aventis, for making it impossible for Canadian farmers to grow organic canola. The National Farmers Union of Canada has called for a moratorium° on all GM foods. The issue has spilled over the borders as well. Fifteen countries have banned import of GM canola, and Australia has banned all Canadian canola due to the unavoidable contamination made obvious by Monsanto's lawsuit. Farmers are concerned about liability,° and consumers are concerned about choice. Twenty-four U.S. states have proposed or passed various legislation to block or limit particular GM products, attach responsibility for GM drift to seed producers, defend a farmer's right to save seeds, and require seed and food product labels to indicate GM ingredients (or allow "GM-free" labeling).

The U.S. federal government (corporate-friendly as ever) has stepped in to circumvent these proconsumer measures. In 2006 the House of

glyphosate: herbicide designed to kill particular weeds that compete with crops grown commercially.

conveyance: here, how the gene arrived where it did, that is, whether it was windborne, a part of pollen, or purposefully implanted in the seed.

pollen drift: cross-pollination among varieties of a plant that occurs naturally (e.g., by the wind or by insects).

seed contamination: here, the mixing of genetically altered seeds with those that are not, however it might occur (e.g., by tractors moving from one field to another).

moratorium: the suspension or delay of something.

liability: potential sources of harm or cost (e.g., being held legally and financially accountable for something that occurs).

Representatives passed the National Uniformity for Food Act,° which would eliminate more than two hundred state-initiated food safety and labeling laws that differ from federal ones. Thus, the weakest consumer protections would prevail (but they're *uniformly* weak!). Here's a clue about who really benefits from this bill: it's endorsed by the American Frozen Food Institute,° ConAgra,° Cargill,° Dean Foods,° Hormel,° and the National Cattlemen's Beef Association.° It's opposed by the Consumers Union,° the Sierra Club,° the Union of Concerned Scientists,° the Center for Food Safety,° and thirty-nine state attorneys general. Keeping GM's "intellectual" paws out of our bodies, and our fields, is up to consumers who demand full disclosure on what's in our food.

For more information, visit www.biotech-info.net or www.organicconsumers.org.

National Uniformity for Food Act (2006): a proposed law that would have limited the rights of state and local governments to enact laws relating to food safety, including in cases where the federal government had not acted. Thus, it would have nullified existing laws not identical to federal ones and prevented the passage of future laws.

American Frozen Food Institute: trade association and lobbying group for industries that manufacture or distribute frozen foods.

ConAgra: a U.S. manufacturer of packaged foods; its brands include Hunt's, Healthy Choice, Bertolli, Egg Beaters, and Orville Redenbacher's, among others.

Cargill: the largest privately held U.S. corporation; among its products are grains, vegetable oils and fats for use in processed food, livestock feed, and glucose syrup and starch for use in foods.

Dean Foods: a U.S. multinational food and beverage company that produces a number of national and regional brands. Its motto is "Healthy Food, Healthy Families."

Hormel: a U.S. food company that produces Spam as well as items marketed under the brand names Herdez, Dinty Moore, and Muscle Milk, among others.

National Cattlemen's Beef Association: lobbying group for beef producers in the United States.

Consumers Union: U.S. nonprofit advocacy organization concerned with a number of issues, including food safety and health care. Until 2012, it produced *Consumer Reports*; that year, the magazine and Web site became a separate company, leaving the Consumers Union to focus on advocacy.

Sierra Club: U.S. environmental organization that focuses on educating the public on environmental issues.

Union of Concerned Scientists: U.S. nonprofit advocacy organization focused on scientific matters; membership includes scientists as well as concerned citizens.

Center for Food Safety: a U.S. nonprofit advocacy organization focused on protecting human health as well as the environment. Genetically modified plants and food are among its major concerns.

RESPOND •

1. Obviously, both Kingsolver and Hopp oppose genetically modified plants and organisms. What arguments do they offer for their positions? How convincing do you find them?
2. How do these two selections work together? In other words, how does each provide a context for and comment on the other?
3. Kingsolver's use of language is especially noteworthy; in fact, it should come as no surprise that she is a successful writer of fiction and poetry. Choose several examples of interesting word choices or figurative language that she uses, and be prepared to discuss them and the ways that they contribute to her argument. (Chapter 13 on style in argument will help you here.) How does Kingsolver's use of language differ from Hopp's? Why might they differ in these ways?
4. Compare and contrast the arguments Kingsolver and Hopp offer against genetically modified food and organisms with the arguments offered in their favor by Robert Paarlberg in the previous selection, "Attention Whole Foods Shoppers," and by David H. Freedman in the next selection, "Are Engineered Foods Evil?" To what extent are they addressing the same sets of issues, and to what extent are they focusing on different aspects of those issues?
5. How might Kingsolver and Hopp respond to the opening selection in this chapter, Christian R. Weisser's "Sustainability"? What is sustainability for Kingsolver and Hopp?
6. As noted, Kingsolver's style is very much one that we associate with writers of fiction and poetry (despite her training as a scientist), and it contrasts markedly not only with the style used by Hopp but also with those used by Paarlberg and Freedman. In two to three healthy paragraphs, **summarize Kingsolver's arguments** about genetically modified foods, and present her arguments in the style of a research paper on this topic. In a very basic way, you will be constructing an argument of fact, as discussed in Chapter 8, where the facts you use come from Kingsolver's text. (Because you'll need to use paraphrases and direct quotations, Chapter 20 on using sources, Chapter 21 on plagiarism and academic integrity, and Chapter 22 on documenting sources will prove useful.)

▼ *David H. Freedman has written about science, business, and technology for a number of magazines, including* Inc. Magazine, *the* Harvard Business Review, *and* Wired, *as well as the* New York Times. *His latest book is* Wrong: Why Experts Keep Failing Us—And How to Know When Not to Trust Them *(2010). This selection, "Are Engineered Foods Evil?," appeared in an in-depth report in a September 2013 issue of* Scientific American *entitled "The Food Issue: The Science of Feast, Fuel, and Farm." (This same article has also been published with an alternate title, "The Truth about Genetically Modified Food.") As you read this selection, note the role that the visual elements—the illustration and the video that accompanied the original online article—play in the argument; likewise, consider the ethos Freedman is seeking to create as he offers what he sees as a solution to the dilemma over genetically modified foods.*

Genetically modified food?

Are Engineered Foods Evil?

DAVID H. FREEDMAN

Robert Goldberg sags into his desk chair and gestures at the air. "Frankenstein monsters, things crawling out of the lab," he says. "This the most depressing thing I've ever dealt with."

Goldberg, a plant molecular biologist at the University of California, Los Angeles, is not battling psychosis. He is expressing despair at the relentless need to confront what he sees as bogus fears over the health risks of genetically modified (GM) crops. Particularly frustrating to him, he says, is that this debate should have ended decades ago, when researchers produced a stream of exonerating° evidence: "Today we're facing the same objections we faced 40 years ago."

exonerating: clearing someone of guilt or responsibility.

Across campus, David Williams, a cellular biologist who specializes in vision, has the opposite complaint. "A lot of naïve science has been involved in pushing this technology," he says. "Thirty years ago we didn't know that when you throw any gene into a different genome,° the genome reacts to it. But now anyone in this field knows the genome is not a static environment. Inserted genes can be transformed by several different means, and it can happen generations later." The result, he insists, could very well be potentially toxic plants slipping through testing.

genome: an organism's genetic material; for humans, this would be the twenty-three pairs of chromosomes found in each cell.

Williams concedes that he is among a tiny minority of biologists raising sharp questions about the safety of GM crops. But he says this is only because the field of plant molecular biology is protecting its interests. Funding, much of it from the companies that sell GM seeds, heavily favors researchers who are exploring ways to further the use of genetic modification in agriculture. He says that biologists who point out health or other risks associated with GM crops—who merely report or defend experimental findings that imply there may be risks—find themselves the focus of vicious attacks on their credibility, which leads scientists who see problems with GM foods to keep quiet.

Whether Williams is right or wrong, one thing is undeniable: despite overwhelming 5
evidence that GM crops are safe to eat, the debate over their use continues to rage, and in some parts of the world, it is growing ever louder. Skeptics would argue that this contentiousness is a good thing—that we cannot be too cautious when tinkering with the genetic basis of the world's food supply. To researchers such as Goldberg, however, the persistence of fears about GM foods is nothing short of exasperating. "In spite of hundreds of millions of genetic experiments involving every type of organism on earth," he says, "and people eating billions of meals without a problem, we've gone back to being ignorant."

So who is right: advocates of GM or critics? When we look carefully at the evidence for both sides and weigh the risks and benefits, we find a surprisingly clear path out of this dilemma.

BENEFITS AND WORRIES

The bulk of the science on GM safety points in one direction. Take it from David Zilberman, a U.C. Berkeley agricultural and environmental economist and one of the few researchers considered credible by both agricultural chemical companies and their critics. He argues that the benefits of GM crops greatly outweigh the health risks, which so far remain theoretical. The use of GM crops "has lowered the price of food," Zilberman says. "It has increased farmer safety by allowing them to use less pesticide. It has raised the output of corn, cotton and soy by 20 to 30 percent, allowing some people to survive who would not have without it. If it were more widely adopted around the world, the price [of food] would go lower, and fewer people would die of hunger."

In the future, Zilberman says, those advantages will become all the more significant. The United Nations Food and Agriculture Organization° estimates

United Nations Food and Agriculture Organization: UN agency that seeks to end world hunger.

that the world will have to grow 70 percent more food by 2050 just to keep up with population growth. Climate change will make much of the world's arable° land more difficult to farm. GM crops, Zilberman says, could produce higher yields, grow in dry and salty land, withstand high and low temperatures, and tolerate insects, disease, and herbicides.

Despite such promise, much of the world has been busy banning, restricting, and otherwise shunning GM foods. Nearly all the corn and soybeans grown in the United States are genetically modified, but only two GM crops, Monsanto's MON810 maize° and BASF's Amflora potato, are accepted in the European Union. Eight E.U. nations have banned GM crops outright. Throughout Asia, including in India and China, governments have yet to approve most GM crops, including an insect-resistant rice that produces higher yields with less pesticide. In Africa, where millions go hungry, several nations have refused to import GM foods in spite of their lower costs (the result of higher yields and a reduced need for water and pesticides). Kenya has banned them altogether amid widespread malnutrition. No country has definite plans to grow Golden Rice, a crop engineered to deliver more vitamin A than spinach (rice normally has no vitamin A), even though vitamin A deficiency causes more than one million deaths annually and half a million cases of irreversible blindness in the developing world.

Globally, only a tenth of the world's cropland includes GM plants. Four 10
countries — the United States, Canada, Brazil, and Argentina — grow 90 percent of the planet's GM crops. Other Latin American countries are pushing away from the plants. And even in the United States, voices decrying genetically modified foods are becoming louder. At press time, at least twenty states are considering GM-labeling bills.

The fear fueling all this activity has a long history. The public has been worried about the safety of GM foods since scientists at the University of Washington developed the first genetically modified tobacco plants in the 1970s. In the mid-1990s, when the first GM crops reached the market, Greenpeace,° the Sierra Club,° Ralph Nader,° Prince Charles,° and a number of celebrity chefs took highly visible stands against them. Consumers in Europe became particularly alarmed: a survey conducted in 1997, for example, found that 69 percent of the Austrian public saw serious risks in GM foods, compared with only 14 percent of Americans.

In Europe, skepticism about GM foods has long been bundled with other concerns, such as a resentment of American agribusiness. Whatever it is based on,

arable: in technical discussions like this one, land that is actually being farmed; the term is sometimes used in the broader and earlier sense of land that could potentially be used to grow crops.

maize: corn.

Greenpeace: international non-governmental organization that works "to ensure the ability of the Earth to nurture life in all its diversity."

Sierra Club: U.S. environmental organization that focuses on educating the public on environmental issues.

Ralph Nader (1934–): Lebanese American political activist and former independent presidential candidate; environmentalism is among Nader's major concerns.

Ralph Nader AP Photo/Joe Magana

Prince Charles (1948–): Prince of Wales and the heir apparent to the British throne; he has been an advocate for environmental awareness since the early 1980s.

however, the European attitude reverberates across the world, influencing policy in countries where GM crops could have tremendous benefits. "In Africa, they don't care what us savages in America are doing," Zilberman says. "They look to Europe and see countries there rejecting GM, so they don't use it." Forces fighting genetic modification in Europe have rallied support for "the precautionary principle," which holds that given the kind of catastrophe that would emerge from loosing a toxic, invasive GM crop on the world, GM efforts should be shut down until the technology is proved absolutely safe.

But as medical researchers know, nothing can really be "proved safe." One can only fail to turn up significant risk after trying hard to find it—as is the case with GM crops.

A CLEAN RECORD

The human race has been selectively breeding crops, thus altering plants' genomes, for millennia. Ordinary wheat has long been strictly a human-engineered plant; it could not exist outside of farms, because its seeds do not scatter. For some sixty years scientists have been using "mutagenic"° techniques to scramble the DNA of plants with radiation and chemicals, creating strains of wheat, rice, peanuts, and pears that have become agricultural mainstays. The practice has inspired little objection from scientists or the public and has caused no known health problems.

mutagenic: relating to chemical or physical agents that trigger greater mutation in DNA than would normally be expected.

15 The difference is that selective breeding or mutagenic techniques tend to result in large swaths of genes being swapped or altered. GM technology, in contrast, enables scientists to insert into a plant's genome a single gene (or a few of them) from another species of plant or even from a bacterium, virus, or animal. Supporters argue that this precision makes the technology much less likely to produce surprises. Most plant molecular biologists also say that in the highly unlikely case that an unexpected health threat emerged from a new GM plant, scientists would quickly identify and eliminate it. "We know where the gene goes and can measure the activity of every single gene around it," Goldberg says. "We can show exactly which changes occur and which don't."

And although it might seem creepy to add virus DNA to a plant, doing so is, in fact, no big deal, proponents say. Viruses have been inserting their DNA into the genomes of crops, as well as humans and all other organisms, for millions of years. They often deliver the genes of other species while they are at it, which is why our own genome is loaded with genetic sequences that originated in viruses and nonhuman species. "When GM critics say that genes don't cross the species barrier in nature, that's just simple ignorance," says Alan McHughen, a plant molecular geneticist at U.C. Riverside. Pea aphids° contain fungi genes. Triticale is a century-plus-old hybrid of wheat and rye found in some flours and breakfast cereals. Wheat itself, for that matter, is a cross-species hybrid. "Mother Nature does it all the time, and so do conventional plant breeders," McHughen says.

pea aphid: a sap-sucking insect.

Could eating plants with altered genes allow new DNA to work its way into our own? It is theoretically possible but hugely improbable. Scientists have never found genetic material that could survive a trip through the human gut and make it into cells. Besides, we are routinely exposed to – we even consume – the viruses and bacteria whose genes end up in GM foods. The bacterium *B. thuringiensis*, for example, which produces proteins fatal to insects, is sometimes enlisted as a natural pesticide in organic farming. "We've been eating this stuff for thousands of years," Goldberg says.

In any case, proponents say, people have consumed as many as trillions of meals containing genetically modified ingredients over the past few decades. Not a single verified case of illness has ever been attributed to the genetic alterations. Mark Lynas, a prominent anti-GM activist who last year publicly switched to strongly supporting the technology, has pointed out that every single news-making food disaster on record has been attributed to non-GM crops, such as the *Escherichia coli*°-infected organic bean sprouts that killed fifty-three people in Europe in 2011.

Escherichia coli ***(more commonly*** **E. coli*):*** bacteria, some strains of which cause food poisoning.

Critics often disparage U.S. research on the safety of genetically modified foods, which is often funded or even conducted by GM companies, such as Monsanto.

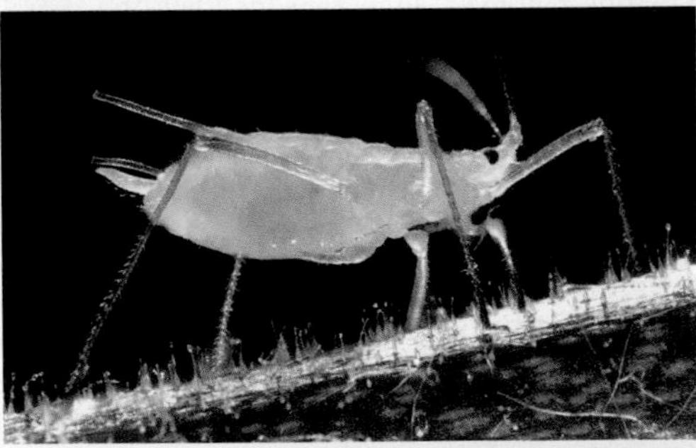

A pea aphid © Michael Weber/imageBROKER/age fotostock

But much research on the subject comes from the European Commission, the administrative body of the E.U., which cannot be so easily dismissed as an industry tool. The European Commission has funded 130 research projects, carried out by more than five hundred independent teams, on the safety of GM crops. None of those studies found any special risks from GM crops.

20 Plenty of other credible groups have arrived at the same conclusion. Gregory Jaffe, director of biotechnology at the Center for Science in the Public Interest, a science-based consumer-watchdog group in Washington, D.C., takes pains to note that the center has no official stance, pro or con, with regard to genetically modifying food plants. Yet Jaffe insists the scientific record is clear. "Current GM crops are safe to eat and can be grown safely in the environment," he says. The American Association for the Advancement of Science,° the American Medical Association,° and the National Academy of Sciences° have all unreservedly backed GM crops. The U.S. Food and Drug Administration,° along with its counterparts in several other countries, has repeatedly reviewed large bodies of research and concluded that GM crops pose no unique health threats. Dozens of review studies carried out by academic researchers have backed that view.

Opponents of genetically modified foods point to a handful of studies indicating possible safety problems. But reviewers have dismantled almost all of those reports. For example, a 1998 study by plant biochemist Árpád Pusztai, then at the Rowett Institute in Scotland, found that rats fed a GM potato suffered from stunted growth and immune system–related changes. But the potato was not intended for human consumption – it was, in fact, designed to be toxic for research purposes. The Rowett Institute later deemed the experiment so sloppy that it refuted the findings and charged Pusztai with misconduct.

Similar stories abound. Most recently, a team led by Gilles-Éric Séralini, a researcher at the University of Caen Lower Normandy in France, found that rats eating a common type of GM corn contracted cancer at an alarmingly high rate. But Séralini has long been an anti-GM campaigner, and critics charged that in his study, he relied on a strain of rat that too easily develops tumors, did not use enough rats, did not include proper control groups, and failed to report many details of the experiment, including how the analysis was performed. After a review, the European Food Safety Authority dismissed the study's findings. Several other European agencies came to the same conclusion. "If GM corn were that toxic, someone would have noticed by now," McHughen says. "Séralini has been refuted by everyone who has cared to comment."

American Association for the Advancement of Science: the world's largest scientific society; among its goals are increasing cooperation among scientists and supporting science education

American Medical Association: largest professional organization for doctors in the United States

National Academy of Science: U.S. honorary society for distinguished researchers in the sciences; its members serve as voluntary "advisers to the nation on science, engineering, and medicine."

Food and Drug Administration (FDA): U.S. agency tasked with protecting and promoting public health with regulatory authority over matters of food and drug safety.

Some scientists say the objections to GM food stem from politics rather than science—that they are motivated by an objection to large multinational corporations having enormous influence over the food supply; invoking risks from genetic modification just provides a convenient way of whipping up the masses against industrial agriculture. “This has nothing to do with science,” Goldberg says. “It’s about ideology.” Former anti-GM activist Lynas agrees. He recently went as far as labeling the anti-GM crowd “explicitly an antiscience movement.”

PERSISTENT DOUBTS

Not all objections to genetically modified foods are so easily dismissed, however. Long-term health effects can be subtle and nearly impossible to link to specific changes in the environment. Scientists have long believed that Alzheimer’s disease and many cancers have environmental components, but few would argue we have identified all of them.

And opponents say that it is not true that the GM process is less likely to cause 25
problems simply because fewer, more clearly identified genes are switched. David Schubert, an Alzheimer’s researcher who heads the Cellular Neurobiology Laboratory at the Salk Institute for Biological Studies° in La Jolla, CA, asserts that a single, well-characterized gene can still settle in the target plant’s genome in many different ways. “It can go in forward, backward, at different locations, in multiple copies, and they all do different things,” he says. And as U.C.L.A.’s Williams notes, a genome often continues to change in the successive generations after the insertion, leaving it with a different arrangement than the one intended and initially tested. There is also the phenomenon of “insertional mutagenesis,” Williams adds, in which the insertion of a gene ends up quieting the activity of nearby genes.

Salk Institute for Biological Studies: nonprofit, independent research institute in the life sciences; it is considered one of the most prestigious research institutions in the world.

True, the number of genes affected in a GM plant most likely will be far, far smaller than in conventional breeding techniques. Yet opponents maintain that because the wholesale swapping or alteration of entire packages of genes is a natural process that has been happening in plants for half a billion years, it tends to produce few scary surprises today. Changing a single gene, on the other hand, might turn out to be a more subversive action, with unexpected ripple effects, including the production of new proteins that might be toxins or allergens.

Opponents also point out that the kinds of alterations caused by the insertion of genes from other species might be more impactful, more complex, or more subtle than those caused by the intraspecies gene swapping of conventional breeding. And just because there is no evidence to date that genetic material from an altered crop can make it into the genome of people who eat it does not mean such a transfer will never happen — or that it has not already happened and we have yet to spot it. These changes might be difficult to catch; their impact on the production of proteins might not even turn up in testing. "You'd certainly find out if the result is that the plant doesn't grow very well," Williams says. "But will you find the change if it results in the production of proteins with long-term effects on the health of the people eating it?"

It is also true that many pro-GM scientists in the field are unduly harsh — even unscientific — in their treatment of critics. GM proponents sometimes lump every scientist who raises safety questions together with activists and discredited researchers. And even Séralini, the scientist behind the study that found high cancer rates for GM-fed rats, has his defenders. Most of them are nonscientists, or retired researchers from obscure institutions, or nonbiologist scientists, but the Salk Institute's Schubert also insists the study was unfairly dismissed. He says that as someone who runs drug-safety studies, he is well versed on what constitutes a good-quality animal toxicology study and that Séralini's makes the grade. He insists that the breed of rat in the study is commonly used in respected drug studies, typically in numbers no greater than in Séralini's study; that the methodology was standard; and that the details of the data analysis are irrelevant because the results were so striking.

Schubert joins Williams as one of a handful of biologists from respected institutions who are willing to sharply challenge the GM-foods-are-safe majority. Both charge that more scientists would speak up against genetic modification if doing so did not invariably lead to being excoriated° in journals and the media. These attacks, they argue, are motivated by the fear that airing doubts could lead to less funding for the field. Says Williams: "Whether it's conscious or not, it's in their interest to promote this field, and they're not objective."

excoriated: severely denounced and discredited.

Both scientists say that after publishing comments in respected journals 30
questioning the safety of GM foods, they became the victims of coordinated attacks on their reputations. Schubert even charges that researchers who turn up results that might raise safety questions avoid publishing their findings out of fear of repercussions. "If it doesn't come out the right way," he says, "you're going to get trashed."

There is evidence to support that charge. In 2009 *Nature* detailed the backlash to a reasonably solid study published in the *Proceedings of the National Academy of Sciences USA* by researchers from Loyola University Chicago and the University of Notre Dame. The paper showed that GM corn seemed to be finding its way from farms into nearby streams and that it might pose a risk to some insects there because, according to the researchers' lab studies, caddis flies° appeared to suffer on diets of pollen from GM corn. Many scientists immediately attacked the study, some of them suggesting the researchers were sloppy to the point of misconduct.

caddis fly: also known as sedge fly or rail fly; any of the 12,000 species of small insects similar to moths.

A WAY FORWARD

There is a middle ground in this debate. Many moderate voices call for continuing the distribution of GM foods while maintaining or even stepping up safety testing on new GM crops. They advocate keeping a close eye on the health and environmental impact of existing ones. But they do not single out GM crops for special scrutiny, the Center for Science in the Public Interest's Jaffe notes: all crops could use more testing. "We should be doing a better job with food oversight altogether," he says.

Even Schubert agrees. In spite of his concerns, he believes future GM crops can be introduced safely if testing is improved. "Ninety percent of the scientists I talk to assume that new GM plants are safety-tested the same way new drugs are by the FDA," he says. "They absolutely aren't, and they absolutely should be."

Stepped-up testing would pose a burden for GM researchers, and it could slow down the introduction of new crops. "Even under the current testing standards for GM crops, most conventionally bred crops wouldn't have made it to market," McHughen says. "What's going to happen if we become even more strict?"

That is a fair question. But with governments and consumers increasingly 35
coming down against GM crops altogether, additional testing may be the compromise that enables the human race to benefit from those crops' significant advantages.

RESPOND •

1. In this selection, David Freedman argues that there is a "surprisingly clear path out of [the] dilemma" of genetically modified foods, and he contends that he provides it for readers. What path does he offer? How does he go about offering it? In other words, how does he structure his argument? (Making an outline of the selection, listing the main points paragraph by paragraph, will likely help you here.)
2. Freedman is obviously making a proposal argument. What, specifically, does he propose as a solution to the dilemma referred to in question 1? Who is likely to be satisfied with his proposal? Who is likely to reject his proposal? Why? (You may wish to start thinking about this question by recalling the positions taken by the writers of the previous two selections, Paarlberg in "Attention Whole Foods Shoppers" and Kingsolver and Hopp in *Animal, Vegetable, Miracle*.)
3. Watch the video that originally accompanied this essay at **http://bit.ly/1uufK9Y**. How well does it help you to understand the notion of genetically modified food? How would you characterize this stance toward genetically modified food? In other words, what kind(s) of argument does the video make—an argument based on fact? On definition? On evaluation? A causal argument? A proposal? What kinds of argument would be most effective in this context? Why? Evaluate the success of each of these arguments. (Chapter 14 on visual rhetoric and Chapter 16 on multimedia arguments may be useful here.)
4. The writer, editor, and producer of the video mentioned in question 3, Eric Olson, draws an unproblematic parallel between what humans have done for millennia and what scientists are now capable of doing much more quickly and efficiently. How do you think Barbara Kingsolver, author of the previous selection, *Animal, Vegetable, Miracle*, would react to the parallel Olson has drawn? Why? You may also want to read the comments that have been posted about Olson's video. How do they respond to this parallel? How would Freedman, the author of this selection, likely respond to those comments?
5. You have now read four selections that deal with current debates about genetically modified food: Weisser's "Sustainability," Paarlberg's "Attention Whole Foods Shoppers," Kingsolver's *Animal, Vegetable, Miracle*, and David Freedman's "Are Engineered Foods Evil?" These

selections discuss many, but by no means all, of the issues relevant to this topic. **Write an academic argument** in which you analyze one or more of these issues in detail. Rather than providing the "right" answer, your goal should be to represent the complexity of the issue in as unbiased a way as possible. (See Chapter 17 for advice on writing academic arguments.)

▼ *Claire Ironside is an instructor of illustration at Sheridan College School of Animation, Art, and Design in Ontario, Canada, where she teaches in the applied illustration program. With training in environmental and communication design studies, she is especially interested in issues of social engagement and activism as well as sustainability. This selection, "Apples to Oranges," uses primarily visual means to make its argument. Its title plays on an everyday expression that is used when two things are compared unfairly because they are fundamentally different in one or more ways. We found this selection in* Food, *a 2008 book edited by John Knechtel. It appears in the Alphabet City series, copublished by Alphabet City Media and the MIT Press. Each volume focuses on a single theme and brings together artists and writers from diverse perspectives to encourage readers to question their basic assumptions about the topic. As you study this selection, think about what it would take to translate Ironside's argument into words alone and whether doing so is even possible. (By the way, to convert kilometers to miles, multiply the number of kilometers by .62 to get a rough equivalent.)*

Making a Visual Argument: Apples to Oranges

CLAIRE IRONSIDE

The Big Apple
Colborne, Ontario
photo: Claire Ironside

apples to oranges

claire ironside

The Orange Julep
Montreal, Quebec

photo: Simon Villeneuve

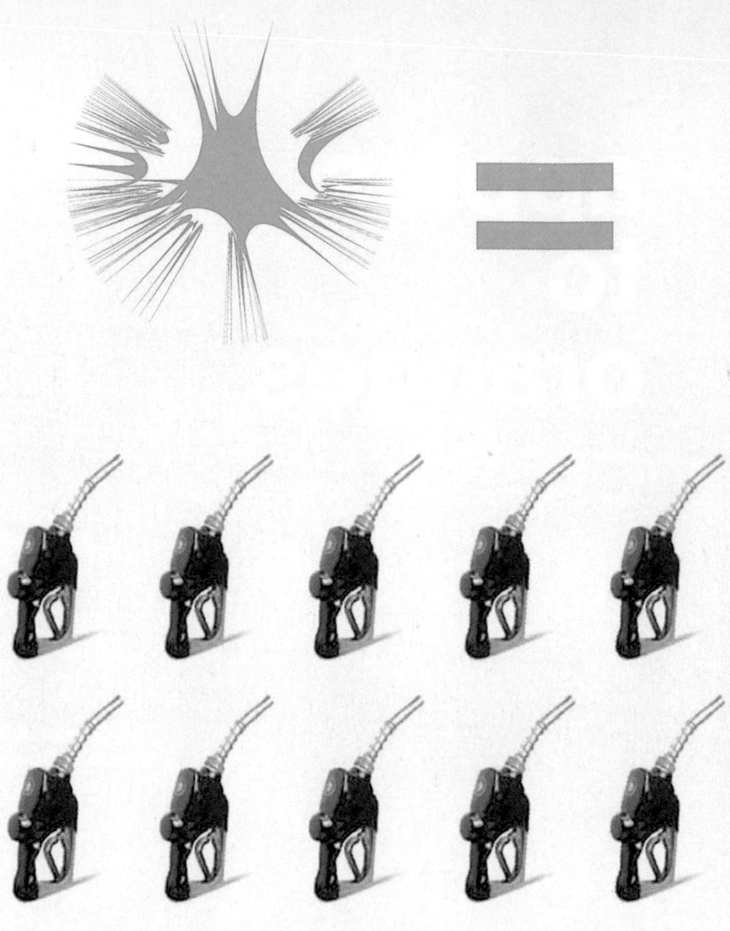

Your food travels an average distance of 2,414 kilometers to get to your plate, which is a large part of the reason every calorie you eat takes an average of 10 fossil fuel calories to produce.*

A look at the fossil fuel inputs of a locally grown, organic apple, and a California orange, both destined for the Toronto market, reveals the difference.

* Dr. Joseph Pimentel, Cornell University professor of ecology and agricultural science.

Colborne to Toronto
178 km

Orange County to Toronto
5,632 km

Fossil fuel inputs of a local, organic apple

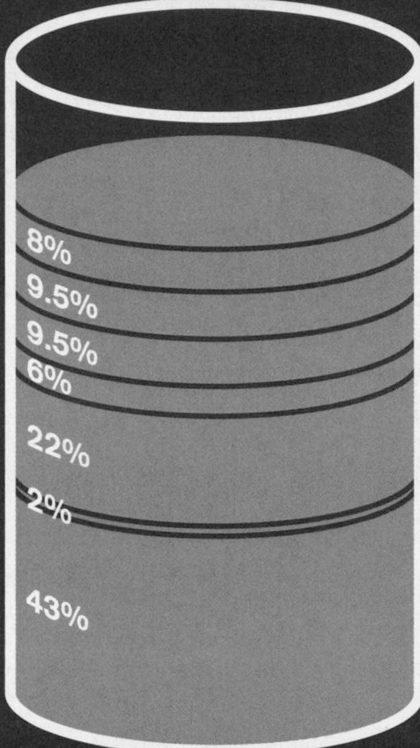

Fossil fuel inputs of a Californian orange

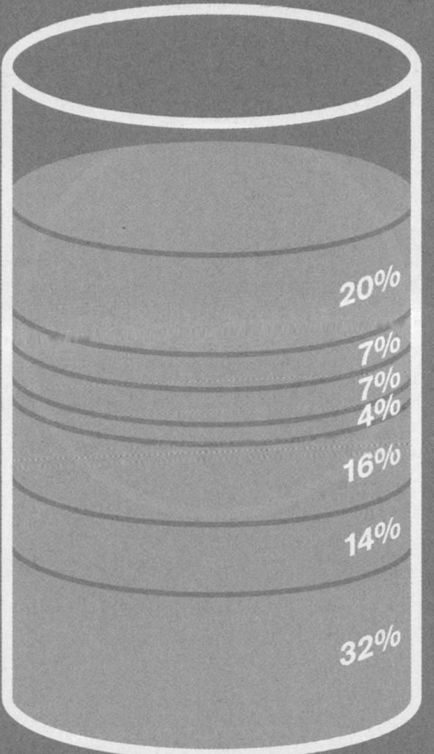

RESPOND

1. What is Ironside's explicit argument? What kind of argument is it (for example, of fact or definition)? Might she be making an implicit argument as well? If so, what would that implicit argument be, and what kind of argument is it?
2. Analyze each pair of pages in Ironside's argument. What does each juxtaposition contribute to her argument? How would you characterize the purpose of the comparison related to fossil-fuel inputs? What value might there be in the details given? What sorts of conclusions might we draw from this juxtaposition?
3. Evaluate the visual aspects of Ironside's argument, including her choice of colors.
4. Ironside's argument is part of a larger debate about carbon footprints. As this book goes to press, there are many Internet sites where you can calculate your own footprint. One is the Nature Conservancy's "What's My Carbon Footprint?" (**http://www.nature.org/greenliving/carboncalculator/**). After you've calculated your footprint at this site, visit others, and compare the calculations you get there. **Write an essay** in which you report your findings and discuss the factors that might account for any discrepancies. (For a discussion of arguments of fact and definition, see Chapters 8 and 9, respectively.)
5. Ironside takes a single fact (about the relationship between each calorie you consume and the fossil-fuel calories that are required to produce it) and illustrates this fact in a complex and sophisticated way. She compares two examples and demonstrates the nature of the average by showing an example that is above average and one that is below average. Choose a single fact about food and think of a visual argument that can illustrate it (as Ironside has here). You can either create the visual argument or describe it in words by discussing aspects of design (color, shape, images, and so on). (For a discussion of visual argument, see Chapter 14.)

▼ *Eric Mortenson has been a reporter in Oregon since 1980, working for both the* Eugene Register-Guard *and the* Oregonian, *the daily newspaper of the Portland metropolitan area, and currently* Capital Press *in Salem, Oregon, a weekly newspaper focusing on agricultural news related to the West Coast region. This selection first appeared in the* Oregonian *in September 2011. In an email to one of the authors of this textbook, Mortenson reports that he grew up in Hood River, Oregon, surrounded by orchards, and that his summer jobs involved picking fruit, operating combines, plowing, and driving wheat trucks. His older brother has spent his career working for a timber company. Mortenson hopes that these experiences give him a better understanding of the issues he writes about than someone who has not had these opportunities might have.*

As is often the case with newspapers that have print and online editions, this article appeared with two different titles. The online edition uses the title that we use below, while the print edition carried the title "Family Pulls In, Branches Out: Tom and Barbara Boyer Adapted Their 400 Acres to Fit a Changing Market, Lifestyle." As you read this article, consider which title you think is more appropriate; also pay attention to what this article teaches about the complexities of eating locally as well as the questions it raises about sustainability.

A Diversified Farm Prospers in Oregon's Willamette Valley by Going Organic and Staying Local

ERIC MORTENSON

MCMINNVILLE° — To hear Tom Boyer explain it, farming has a proper pace to it. He shakes his head at farmers who get too big too fast. The ones who get out ahead of themselves in terms of acreage, bank loans or expensive equipment. In their haste, those fellows are "right next to stumbling," he says.

Sometimes, of course, every farmer races from chore to chore, hustles to beat the weather and scrambles to solve the latest tractor breakdown. "It keeps you high-stepping to keep on top of it," Boyer says.

On their 400 acres° a mile south of McMinnville, Boyer and his wife, Barbara, face the challenge common to Oregon's 38,800 farmers: How do you keep your balance when markets change, costs increase and regulations crank?

How do you mesh what you love with the complications of water, fuel, fertilizer and financing? What about consumer expectations? What if traffic is so thick and fast you're scared to move bulky equipment to your next field down the highway? What if the neighbor sells out and plants condos instead of crops?

McMinnville: county seat of Yamhill County, Oregon, located about thirty-five miles southwest of Portland. It is the center of Oregon's wine industry and produces grains, timber, and tree-grown fruits as well as horticultural and dairy products.

acre: unit of surface measure commonly used in the United States, about 44,000 square feet, or about 90 percent of a standard American football field (not counting the end zones). It is about 40 percent of a hectare, the unit of surface measure used in the metric system.

How do you adapt, hold on and prosper?

This is one farm's walk. The Boyers found their pace by going organic and sticking local. By scaling back while reaching out, and by dialing in and diversifying.

Tom Boyer is 54, the fourth generation to farm in Oregon and the third on this ground, which hugs the curving contour of the South Yamhill River. He's a jacket and jeans guy, wears his cap to the dinner table and calls his wife Babs. He's bald, stocky, keeps a droopy 1970s mustache and is a central casting font° of laconic° country expressions.

Which can be misleading. He gets by on four hours sleep a night, and spends his time, when the house is quiet, reading and researching. "You're constantly fine-tuning," he says. "If you're not fine-tuning, you're out of business."

"I call him my Einstein," Barbara Boyer says.

She's 44, a Connecticut girl with a plant science degree who never imagined she'd end up an Oregon farmwife. She's dark-haired, gregarious and a natural organizer. She won election to the board of the Yamhill County Soil & Water Conservation District and in November will take a seat on the Oregon Board of Agriculture.

She co-founded and now manages the McMinnville Farmer's Market. She's leaning on the county's school districts to add local fruit and vegetables to lunch menus. A "no brainer" in such a fine agricultural county, she says.

The Boyer farm, under Tom's father and grandfather and in his first years, grew grain, multiple varieties of grass seed, and turnips, radish and mustard for seed. That changed after a seed marketing company folded and left him holding several million pounds of vegetable seed. Never again, he vowed, would he let a middleman control his destiny.

Diversify and Prosper

The Boyers set out to establish five "profit centers" at the farm — five ways to make money.

At the heart of it is their "Gourmet Hay."

The Boyers have always grown grass hay — some fields have produced 30 years running — but they began marketing to the many hobby farms and ranches in the area, people with a few horses, goats or cattle to feed. Although international demand has pushed the price of Oregon hay to $220 a ton or more, the Boyers sell for $130 to $160 a ton. Couldn't look customers in the eye if they gouged them, they say.

They produce 30,000 to 40,000 87-pound bales annually and deliver to about 450 regular customers. They restrict deliveries to a 50-mile radius. Haul beyond that, Tom Boyer says, and you're a trucker instead of a farmer.

They use organic techniques. Instead of chemical fertilizer, the Boyers buy 300 to 500 tons of pomace — grape skins and seeds left over from pressing at local wineries — and mix it with manure. They spread it on the hay fields in the fall. Tom Boyer calls it "trail mix" for earthworms, whose work makes for rich, healthy, well-drained soil. "Our worm count is way high," he says.

A second profit center emerged in 2004 from a conservation project along the South Yamhill River. Working with the federal Farm Service Agency, the Boyers and various community groups planted 10,000 trees over seven years. The Boyers estimate they gave up 24 acres of cropland by planting trees in a buffer zone stretching 180 feet from the riverbank, and the FSA pays them $6,000 annually as compensation. That's less than what they could earn if the land was kept in production, but the restored riparian° buffer cools the river and controls erosion.

"We want to have as nice a river to swim in as I did when I was a kid," Tom Boyer says.

Third is a Community Supported Agriculture° operation, in which

---

font: literally, a container, usually made of stone, for holding the water used in baptism in a Christian church; here, figuratively, a reservoir or source.

laconic: using few words; brief.

riparian: located on a riverbank.

Community Supported Agriculture (CSA): movement that began in Japan and Germany in the 1960s and came to the United States in the 1980s. The weekly boxes that subscribers receive contain whatever is ripe at the time and thus change seasonally.

subscribers pay for weekly boxes of fresh vegetables. The Boyers converted 1.5 acres of hay field into a garden, and grow tomatoes, carrots, beans, kale, cabbage, squash and other edibles.

They plan to expand the garden by another quarter acre and continue enriching it with the pomace treatment.

"If you caress a garden it will produce a third more," Tom Boyer says. "That's how you do it."

The fourth profit center is Barbara Boyer's job at McMinnville Farmer's Market, which pays $5,000 a year.

The fifth is a work in progress. They're fixing up the original farmhouse, a two-story, 1909 beauty, and plan to rent it to vacationers who want to experience a working farm. People ought to know, Tom Boyer says, there are "land rich, pocket poor" family farmers who are "out there busting their butts."

The restoration has a proper pace, as well. They pick one major project each year: replaced the roof in 2009, rebuilt the front porch last year and this fall will add stone steps, front and back.

Tom Boyer sees the house rental as a way to "keep the story alive."

His son, Ted, lives nearby and is beginning to show interest in returning to the farm. And Ted's young daughter, Josi, loves every aspect.

"If heritage were not important, why not just sell it and coast?" Tom asks.

His smile is his answer.

"I think it's worth punishing a few more generations," he says.

There's More

The Boyers have farmed up to 1,000 acres by leasing land, but found themselves "highway farmers" moving from field to field. They're scaling back to the home place, and believe they can maintain hay production with additional irrigation.

Even that comes with complications, however. The Boyers hold the oldest water rights on the South Yamhill. If they increase their take, some newcomer to the fast-growing county might get bumped off. They don't relish the prospect.

But farming is tough. There are testy times during harvest, when rain threatens the hay and the baler or stacker breaks down, when Tom Boyer says he has "a regular Jesus moment" and questions why he does it.

The answer lies deep. Farming, he says with a laugh, "gets in your blood and then you're screwed."

But good moments overcome bad. Delivering hay to somebody you like, he says, is like going to meet a friend.

Perspective and energy also arrive with the farm's idealistic "woofers," unpaid interns who come to the farm through a program called Worldwide Opportunities on Organic Farms.° In the past three years, the Boyers have hosted 79 woofers for two-week stays, putting them up in their basement. The current intern, Meghan Bender, was a waitress in Manhattan before ar-riving to pick beans and tomatoes and push a wheelbarrow for the first time.

"I spend most of the day in the garden," Bender says with a broad smile. "It feels really right."

That goes both ways.

"Maybe we are doing something right," Tom Boyer says. "These kids are coming from across the country to be here."

The Boyers have worked only two Sundays in 18 years; once when they had to catch up on the harvest after a friend's funeral on a Saturday, another time to help a friend whose equipment had broken down. Otherwise, Sundays are for spiritual recharge. Time to find that proper pace. Stay on the steady.

A reminder, Tom Boyer says, "That there's some sort of life other than on a tractor."

Worldwide Opportunities on Organic Farms (WWOOF): movement begun in England in the early 1970s to give individuals the opportunity to work on organic farms in rural areas or another country in exchange for room and board. There are about fifty national WWOOF organizations that form a loose network around the world.

RESPOND •

1. What arguments is Mortenson making in this article? In what ways does the information here help you understand the challenges of being an independent farmer in the United States at this historical moment? In what ways does it give you useful information about the relationship many Americans have with the food they consume?
2. What sorts of hard evidence does Mortenson use in this selection? How effectively does he use them? (You might imagine what the article would be like if he had not used these sources of evidence. For a discussion of hard evidence, see Chapter 4.)
3. As is often the case in such newspaper articles, Mortenson seeks to create the Boyers as three-dimensional characters by describing them in some detail. Watch the video posted with this article (**http://tinyurl.com/q40h0al**). In what ways has Mortenson captured aspects of each of the Boyers' personality? Are there other details he might have added? How do such details serve as arguments based on emotion, ethos, or fact? (See Chapters 2–4 on these arguments.)
4. Mortenson makes interesting stylistic choices in this article. How would you describe his style? To what extent and in what ways does his style seek to match the ways the Boyers—Tom, in particular—talk? Why might Mortenson have made these choices? How would the article have been different if Mortenson had used a more distant or academic style? Why? (Chapter 13 considers the role of style in arguments.)
5. **Write an essay** in which you explore some topic related to local independent farms in the area where you study or an area where you live. Using this article as a starting point, you might investigate the challenges independent farmers face generally; to tackle this topic, you'll want to do some research on the Internet or interview people knowledgeable about these issues, including farmers themselves. You could write an essay about Worldwide Opportunities on Organic Farms (WOOF) using information you get from its Web site or elsewhere on the Internet, from interviews with farmers in your area who participate in WWOOF, or from people who have been WWOOF volunteers. From a different perspective, you might check local news sources, especially newspapers, to discover issues currently relevant on topics related to independent farmers, farmers' markets, or the local food supply.

Katherine Gustafson is a self-employed writer and editor living in Seattle, Washington, whose articles have appeared in the Christian Science Monitor, Slate, *the* Huffington Post, *and the* Chronicle of Higher Education. *Her first book,* Change Comes to Dinner: How Vertical Farmers, Urban Growers, and Other Innovators Are Revolutionizing How America Eats *(2012), sought to find and share good news about the sustainable food movement, specifically some of the creative ways that Americans are finding to alter the status quo. Critics appreciate it for highlighting many positive aspects of the transformations occurring across the country. This selection, the first chapter of that book, focuses on the challenges one couple faced as they worked to change the way Americans relate to their food. As you read, think about why such changes are indeed challenging and how your understanding of these challenges has broadened from reading the selections in this chapter.*

School Bus Farmers' Market

AN UNUSUAL SMALL BUSINESS BRINGS FARM-FRESH TO THE CITY

KATHERINE GUSTAFSON

My hoperaking° journey began, like so many voyages of discovery do, on an old yellow school bus. This bus was not full of children, though, but food—tomatoes, potatoes, lettuce, apple cider, milk, ribs, chicken, barbeque sauce—all of it from farms within 150 miles of the Richmond street corner where I filled up my shopping basket in this unlikely vehicle.

Up by the steering wheel, Mark Lilly presided over the bus with a proprietary° air, greeting people as they came aboard to browse in the apple barrels, wooden shelves, and freezers he had installed, showing kids the baby chicks he was keeping in a cage out on the sidewalk. The products I picked out to purchase—a tub of frozen pit-cooked barbeque made by a Mennonite° family, a whole chicken from the famous Polyface Farm,° a glass bottle of yogurt topped with blackberry jam—were things that I had spent ten hours driving all over the Virginia countryside with Mark to pick up a few days before. I couldn't wait to see how they tasted.

A visit with a local-food entrepreneur like Mark was, I felt, the logical place to start my journey; the commitment to eating locally is the sacred cow° of the sustainable food movement. There seems to be a general—though sometimes only vaguely justified—consensus that sourcing as much of our food as possible from within a short driving distance of our houses is one of the most important things we can do to right the sinking ship of the U.S. food system.

hoperaking: a gathering (raking) of inspiration, a word Gustafson coins to contrast with *muckraking*, which is a term used for reform-focused journalism that seeks to expose social problems as well as corporate and government corruption.

proprietary: relating to ownership.

Mennonite: U.S. and Canadian Protestant group that frequently keeps apart from the rest of society, often wearing distinct clothing and having distinct hairstyles. Mennonites are pacifists.

Polyface Farm: a well-known organic farm in Virginia; it will be discussed in detail later in this selection.

sacred cow: a figure of speech, specifically a metaphor, referring to a topic that cannot be criticized or, in some cases, even questioned or discussed. The metaphor's origin is the esteem in which cows are held in Hindu society.

scapes: the immature flower stalks of a garlic plant; they are removed so that the garlic bulb will continue to grow.

A garlic scape Indigoiris/Shutterstock

AP Photo/The Herald-Palladium, John Madill

I wondered if this was true. Is relocalizing our food economy the answer to our woes? It seemed improbable to me that small farmers selling at urban markets—the image almost universally associated with the idea of "eating local"—could be the much sought-after solution to all the complicated problems of our industrially dominated food system. Aren't these local farms just too small and too few and too apt to be growing things like garlic scapes° and ramps,° which—let's be honest—sound more like pieces of equipment found in a skateboard park than food?

5 The most familiar argument for locavorism° arises from an objection to the massive distances that the vast majority of food eaten in the United States travels before it reaches dinner plates. The figure fifteen hundred miles is thrown around a lot, and while that number—calculated by the Leopold Center for Sustainable Agriculture°—is only kind of true and then only if you live in Chicago, the exact number doesn't really matter; the sticking point is that we eat many things that have flown on airplanes from other hemispheres or been trucked across continents (or back and forth between states in a pointless bureaucratic shuffle) to get to us.

The ghastly carbon footprint° of all that global food shipping is the more commonly reiterated reason to eat more locally. The environmental impact of getting an apple from five miles away, the logic goes, must surely be less than that of shipping your fruit in from New Zealand. Unfortunately for the locavores, the ecological argument for eating locally doesn't always stand up well to scrutiny. An apple in a load of millions shipped cross-country in an efficient

ramp: (also known as spring onion or wild garlic) a vegetable that grows in the early spring; it has a sharp onion flavor and a garlic-like smell.

locavorism: a preference for (or commitment to) eating locally grown and sourced food, often defined as food raised within one hundred miles.

Leopold Center for Sustainable Agriculture: a research and education center at the University of Iowa that works to improve farming while reducing its negative impact.

carbon footprint: the greenhouse gases created by a person, organization, product, or event.

© Frank Fell/age fotostock

eighteen-wheeler might well account for fewer carbon emissions than an apple in a single bushel driven thirty miles to a farmers' market in an old diesel farm truck. And that comparison doesn't account for the carbon dioxide expended by the shoppers getting to and from the place of purchase—a figure that might be lower for those who shop at grocery stores where only one trip is necessary than for those who take separate trips to farmers' markets, specialty shops, and other stores to put the week's menu together.

Making local and regional food distribution systems more robust and efficient would change the environmental calculus considerably. But as things stand now, other reasons for eating locally turn out to be far more compelling. What people want by and large, it seems to me, is to live in communities that are thriving, where they can find the means to be happy and healthy. What better way to make sure our communities thrive than by locating a chunk of the most important businesses of our lives—the work of feeding ourselves—close to our cities and in our own neighborhoods? Bolstering local food economies means creating and keeping local jobs, maintaining food producers' interest in and responsiveness to the needs and wants of the community (including the need for safe and healthy food), ensuring greater freshness, and providing local consumers with more instead of fewer options regarding where, when, and how to buy their food.

I still had my doubts about whether all those little guys farming their hearts out on their one-, five-, and twenty-acre parcels and dragging their wares to the farmers' market every week could feed our country effectively, but logic had it that they were doing vital work to keep our country from

inexorably: ruthlessly, relentlessly.

inexorably° being taken over part and parcel by corporate food concerns. Local-food entrepreneurs were on the front lines, bringing us all hope. And hope is what I was after. In trying to find some small answer to the question, "What would a better food system look like?" I clearly needed to see "local food" in action. If what I found didn't appear to be the final, glorious solution to our food dilemmas, perhaps I could gain some hints about what such a solution might be.

So one April evening I headed south from my home in Washington, DC, to Richmond, the capital of Virginia, where Mark is making a go of it with his school bus-cum-roving farmers' market, an unusual business venture he calls Farm to Family. His bus route follows a schedule, but he uses his BlackBerry to remind his thousands of Facebook and Twitter fans of his location and to update them about any change of plans, which happens occasionally due to parking problems, absence of shoppers, or previously unscheduled visits.

10 When I inquired whether I might see his operation, Mark had kindly invited me to stay at his house for the night so I could come on his purchasing rounds at local farms early the following day. That's how I found myself sitting at a dining room table in a cozy house somewhere in Richmond eating a bowl of yogurt criss-crossed with a drizzle of maple syrup, products Mark buys from local farmers and sells on his bus.

"This is the best stuff you've every tasted," Mark said, pointing at my bowl. Something about his friendly, low-key demeanor, shaved head, and sun-reddened cheeks reminded me obscurely of a firefighter. His wife Suzi, a warm woman in a teal° "eat local" T-shirt and reddish hair twisted up in a clip, chatted with me about her job in the alternative healing and body care section of Ellwood Thompson's, a unique Richmond grocery store focused on local food. Not long after my visit, she would begin working full-time with Mark on Farm to Family.

teal: a shade of blue-green.

Adisa/Shutterstock

"The Fs should be green, darker green. Don't you think?" Mark interrupted, leaning over and showing Suzi a picture on his BlackBerry—the drafts of a Farm to Family logo sent by his designer.

"It's a little busy," she said. "You have to picture it on everything."

He brooded on this for a few moments then stalked away from the table, leaving Suzi to install me in a sweet-smelling, crimson guest room with an antique bedstead, a shelf of Buddhist relics, and a tinkling wind chime made of slices of pink stone.

15 The next morning as we sped down the highway toward the Shenandoah Valley in his truck, dragging a trailer equipped with six giant plastic coolers, Mark told me how he got the idea for the bus venture after experiencing a political awakening about issues of industrial food during a master's program in disaster science and emergency management. A research project about California's San Joaquin Valley for a class called Hazards and Threats to

the Future led him into a sobering investigation of soil salination,° monocultures,° water shortages, labor issues, and petroleum's role in an area that grows almost 13 percent of the country's produce.

salination: the process of coming to contain salt, which, of course, means that the soil cannot be used for growing crops.

monoculture: growing a single crop over a large area for an extended period of time.

"It is really bad, what is going on out there," he said, propping his arm on the steering wheel. "If that system fails, that's going to have a major, major impact on the country." The idea for the bus venture started simmering in the back of his mind, but he would never have gone ahead if he hadn't lost his job working in food service at a university. By then he had already bought the old bus from Craigslist on a hunch.

All around us, spring had burst upon the countryside, the pink cotton candy fluff of redbud trees lacing the edges of the roadway. It was an unusually hot day for April; the temperature reading in the corner of the rearview mirror was climbing past eighty. The truck's AC was on the fritz.

"It all boils down to money," he went on. "What corporations do is they want to make as much money as they can and exploit anything in their path to get that done. These lobbyists and players in Washington—the government makes laws to benefit them, not to benefit the people." For a guy engaged in such a creative and optimistic business endeavor, he exuded a surprisingly intense sense of outrage.

We trundled off the highway onto a country road slicing through green hills and pulled into the parking lot of a McDonald's, of all places, where a white-bearded Mennonite farmer in a straw hat and his blue-skirted wife in a pale kerchief were waiting incongruously° for us next to their truck and trailer.

incongruously: being or seeming out of place, unusual. Here, the imagery refers to a Mennonite couple in a McDonald's parking lot.

20 This was Mike and Diana Puffenbarger, a thirty-years-married couple who run a farm, a barbeque business, and a hunting and fishing guide service. Mike's family has been producing maple syrup for five generations, and he himself has been at it for at least three decades. Their 4 × 4 sported a window sticker saying "TRUTH WILL SET YOU FREE, JOHN 8:32" alongside another emblazoned with a picture of a howling coyote in crosshairs surrounded by the motto "HUNT HARD, SHOOT STRAIGHT, KILL CLEAN, APOLOGIZE TO NO ONE."

As they helped load tubs of their pit-cooked barbeque and bottles of their syrup into Mark's truck, I asked Mike about their biggest challenge as small farmers.

"The government," he responded without a pause. "They're letting in all this junk from China. But *we* try to do something, they hammer us. We've been butchering meat for years from our farm and we've never had a recall. What's that tell you?" The Puffenbargers take their animals destined for sale as meat to a slaughterhouse as required by the USDA, the closest one being in Harrisonburg, eighty miles from their farm in Bolar, Virginia. They prefer to butcher at home the meat they eat themselves.

Mike's comment highlighted one of the many reasons local-food advocates cite for buying closer to home. The country's industrial food chain has been busy building itself an abysmal record on food safety. The USDA Web site posts hundreds of recalls of food products every year, the majority of them for posing a “possible health risk.” The word *salmonella*° makes a distressingly regular appearance on this list, as do *E. coli*° and *Listeria*,° a dangerous bacterium. One compelling reason to buy your food—especially your meat—from smaller-scale farmers who are involved in your community instead of from corporations whose operations are opaque, remote, and likely too massive to be handled safely is that smaller, closer-to-home producers are more likely to have both the ability and the motivation to make sure their products aren’t tainted.

salmonella: a bacterium that causes food poisoning and other diseases.

E. coli: a bacterium that causes food poisoning.

Listeria: a disease-causing bacterium.

Back on the road, the pungent odor of manure wafting in the window and the temperature in the truck climbing toward incendiary, Mark told me he had been totally unprepared for what he was getting into when he started the bus business. His original idea was to go into food deserts—urban areas where residents don’t have access to stores that carry fresh food—and sell his local meat and produce to these underserved communities. He got registered to accept food stamps and parked in poor neighborhoods, waiting for the rush of customers. But the people there looked at him like he was crazy and continued to spend their money in the corner store, where fresh vegetables are usually absent in favor of fried chicken, chips, and soda.

25 “I got blindsided. I was really naïve,” he said. “A for-profit business has no incentive to go into a food desert and set up shop. If you’re a for-profit business and you’re bringing in high-quality stuff, it costs. I would be out of business if I were to just go into low-income areas.” Mark was referencing one of the most prominent critiques of the locavore ethos: the cost of food from nearby small farms is almost always substantially higher than the products of industrial production you can buy in the average supermarket or at the corner store. Critics accuse the eat-local movement of promoting two separate food systems: one that’s supplied with healthy, “happy” food for all the people who can afford it, and another stocked with ecologically damaging, pesticide-laden, processed junk for everyone else.

But when you’re trying to start a business like Mark Lilly, you don’t have the time or money to fix the world’s problems. You find the customers who can help you succeed. So, while still doing some work in low-income communities, including occasionally giving away free food (efforts for which he has received high-profile publicity, including a three-page spread in *People* magazine), he has focused mostly on parts of town where people have a little extra money to spend and are attuned to the politics of local food. He runs his own version of a community-supported agriculture (CSA) program, which he calls a USA for “urban-supported agriculture,” that has people pay ahead of time for a season’s worth of biweekly boxes of fresh food. He also delivers milk to people's doors early in the morning, just like guys used to do back in my grandmother's time.

"I'm giving people a way to opt out of the current system," he proudly told me as we rattled up a long, dirt drive into the cluttered parking area of Mountain View Dairy Farm. Proprietor Christie Huger, dressed for the heat in a white T-shirt, athletic shorts, and sandals, greeted us as Mark backed the truck up to the loading area by a dilapidated trailer office. They consulted for a few moments by a set of glass-fronted refrigerators before starting to load jars of blackberry yogurt and glass bottles of milk into the coolers in Mark's trailer.

Christie's tousled hair and tired smile suggested that it had already been a long day despite it not yet being noon. She used to be an art teacher, she told me, but she quit teaching two years ago to attend full-time to the farm. I asked her if it's been a hard transition, and she answered unhesitatingly: "If I went back to teaching it'd be easier. When you get up at four-thirty and then force yourself to come inside at eight at night to feed your kids dinner, it's hard." I wondered aloud if she planned to go back to teaching, and her answer was again immediate: no way.

I followed Christie's daughter Isabelle, an energetic girl in a peach tank top and bowl haircut, toward a pen by the house where a tiny lamb was bleating manically. She grabbed a baby bottle full of water and kneeled down beside the animal.

"Do you want to be a farmer when you grow up?" I asked, thinking about 30
that statistic I had recently come across: the average age of farmers in the United States is fifty-five and rising. We badly need kids to take an interest in this kind of life.

"I already am," she said matter-of-factly, squinting up at me in the sunshine. "I'm a sheep farmer. Because we have this little baby sheep."

My heart melted, and I realized that this moment, as much as the fresh, delicious milk itself, was what the consumers on Mark's bus are buying. From Mennonite farmers to milk in glass bottles to the old yellow school bus, Mark's business plays on city dwellers' sense of nostalgia for what they see as a safe, picturesque, and pastoral yesteryear. A common theme in the movement to reinvigorate local food systems is the idea of a David-and-Goliath battle between corporate overlords and the small family farmer, with the corporation representing the evils of mechanized, overcrowded, stifling, isolating modern life and the little guy laying claim to a virtuous existence of nature, space, freedom, and community. Not to mention little baby sheep.

I mentioned this observation to Mark as we got back on the road heading to our next stop. On the bus, he told me, visitors often revel in memories of other types of roving food vendors that populated their long-ago childhoods.

Customers reminisce about the guys who used to come by their urban neighborhoods in trucks or with handcarts yelling "Fresh fish!" or "Watermelon!"

"Back in the day, there was the milkman and the meat delivery guy," Mark said. "You knew them. They came to your house. It was interactive. You chatted with them. That's what I try to do. I'm interactive. I chat with people."

Mark tries, in short, to give his customers "an experience." He brings baby 35
animals for children to hold. He talks to customers about what they can do with what he sells—how to cook a spaghetti squash, for instance, or which kind of barbeque sauce will go best on pulled pork. At the time of our journey, his bus was plastered with hand-lettered signs proclaiming a variety of riling slogans, such as "EAT AT HOME, COOK, HAVE FUN!" and "DON'T RELY ON A FAILING, HIGHLY PROCESSED UNSUSTAINABLE TOXIC FOOD SYSTEM! GROW AND PRESERVE YOUR OWN FOOD NOW!"

When he invites customers onto his bus, he's asking them not only to step inside the vehicle, but also to move into another way of looking at our world of food. The way he thinks of it, coming onto his bus is the next best thing to experiencing the bracing goodness of the farm itself. "I'm packaging a farm onto a school bus," he said, "and bringing it to them."

Supporters of local food and small farms will be the first to insist vociferously° that they are not in the business of rehashing some long-ago bucolic° utopia, but that they're building new networks of small enterprises that draw on some of the best lessons we've collectively learned in the past. But even so, the idea that we are suffering from modern ills because we have somehow gotten away from a good life of fresh air and honest manual work nonetheless animates a sizable amount of interest in local food. And people are willing to pay extra to have a vision of a return to that idealized time served up with their kale° and kohlrabi.° It's a powerful narrative. Regardless that I don't in any way believe that poverty equals virtue and toil under the hot sun cleanses the soul, I felt for a moment, as I thought about that lamb suckling enthusiastically at the bottle offered by the little girl, the tragedy of my concrete-bound city life that does not include this type of countrified charm.

But life is, of course, more complicated than all of these visions and dichotomies° can encompass. Even the man who spends his days driving from quaint farm to adorable homestead buying up yogurt in jars and field-raised poultry is as frenzied a denizen° of the modern-day rat race as I've ever seen. Mark's BlackBerry was never far from his hand, even while driving his truck and trailer, and he lamented that he had been up working until three the night before. He radiated a contained but manic energy, the kind that wouldn't allow for any slowdown for a lunchtime picnic of the local foods we had collected. Instead, we got Subway sandwiches from a gas station and ate them in the car.

vociferously: loudly.

bucolic: relating to a lifestyle associated with rural areas.

kale: a leafy vegetable that some consider to be "the world's healthiest food."

kohlrabi: a root vegetable, the root and leaves of which can be eaten. (Odds are that Gustafson chose *kohlrabi*, a vegetable that does show up at farmers' markets, at least partly because of the alliteration—"***k****ale and* ***k****ohlrabi*.")

dichotomies: contrasts between two items; opposition or contradiction.

denizen: inhabitant.

Usually, Mark insisted, he and Suzi eat almost exclusively the products they sell on the bus, which seems like it would be more challenging because of the time it takes to prepare fresh, whole foods than because of any lack of availability or variety, even in the winter. He listed off the things he might be carrying on a typical day in February: "Hydroponic° lettuce, tomatoes, eggs, bacon, sausage, barbeque, potatoes, apples, butternut squash, chestnuts, collard greens, kale, onions, sweet potatoes, milk, cheese, butter, yogurt, spaghetti squash. I have people who bake pies and breads and cookies for me. I've got maple syrup, apple butter, apple cider, peach cider . . ."

hydroponic: grown without soil in a solution of water supplemented by nutrients.

We pulled into a long straight drive labeled with a sign for the famous 40
Polyface Farm, owned by Joel Salatin, whose innovative farming practices have captured the imagination of sustainable food advocates. Salatin insists that growing food should replenish natural resources instead of depleting them, improving the health of the animals, the people, and the soil instead of degrading it. He's become an outspoken advocate for the development of laws that would enable the success of our country's small farmers and has been catapulted to niche stardom by his appearances in both Michael Pollan's seminal work *The Omnivore's Dilemma*° and in the Academy Award–nominated documentary *Food, Inc.*

Michael Pollan's . . .* The Omnivore's Dilemma: A Natural History of Four Meals *(2006): a highly acclaimed and much critiqued nonfiction account of Americans' relationship with food and eating; Pollan is a strong advocate of locavorism.

Food, Inc. ***(2008):*** American documentary criticizing agribusiness because of its effects on the environment, the animals it rears, and the people it employs. Michael Pollan was one of the film's narrators.

As Mark disappeared into a walk-in freezer to pick up his order of meat, a family from Wisconsin come to witness "that famous farm" for themselves was piling out of a minivan and ogling the chicken houses. The scene might not have lived up to their pastoral imaginings: the part of Polyface a casual visitor sees is chaotic and down-at-the-heels like any farm. Used-up equipment is stacked here and there, vehicles are parked every which way, and a worn, white farmhouse squats unpretentiously in the yard. The famous farmer was nowhere to be seen, but his son Daniel and some farmhands were lingering over by the barn, swatting at bees with shovels and laughing at one another's antics. "They bore into the wood," said Daniel, chuckling, his teeth blindingly white in the sunshine. "It's not good." With his handsome, tanned face and his straw cowboy hat, he could have been a Western movie star.

"We put our first batch of roasters° out on the field today," he told Mark. The Salatins have popularized the use of the chicken tractor, a wheeled coop with a mesh bottom moved from place to place, which allows the birds to fertilize the fields and get their nourishment from the grass, worms, and bugs. Raising poultry this way is more ecologically friendly and conducive to maintaining a thriving, diverse farm than the usual method of providing poultry feed and letting the birds' nitrogen-rich waste go to . . . well, waste.

roaster: here, a chicken; roasters are generally sold when they are less than eight months old and weigh between 3.5 and 5 pounds.

If only all people could have access to and afford the wonderful food produced by places like Polyface. But even this most prominent of small farms provides an instructive example of the difficulty of reaching that noble goal.

While Polyface does supply pork to two Chipotle Mexican Grill fast-food restaurants, the project took almost a year and a half of negotiations and logistical arrangements to succeed, and it required Salatin to double or even triple his production, a feat few small farms can manage. With more than 950 Chipotle locations across the country, Salatin's contribution is a drop in the bucket, and the majority of products from small producers remain the province of affluent individual buyers and high-end restaurants.

By two p.m., the temperature in the truck was up to eighty-six degrees, and we'd been on the road for seven hours. We still had several stops to go.

"These days are long and hard," Mark groaned as we pulled into Riverside 45
Plant, a Mennonite-owned plant business positioned in several spacious greenhouses across a gravel drive from a neat white house. Plain garments ordered by size flapped on a clothesline in the side yard. "I'm burning out right now," Mark continued. "I have nothing outside this business. I don't socialize. I don't sleep. It's brutal."

His laments, however, were mitigated by the pride of success. After just nine months, his business—launched with four thousand dollars of his savings—had started making a profit, and interest in his bus was growing. The business could easily expand if only he had the financing and infrastructure to make that happen. "I could have a fleet of these just in Richmond," he said. "I could create hundreds of jobs."

The idea of bolstering a local economy, of course, is another excellent argument advanced by boosters of local eating. Local-food production can be a key pillar of a community's economy: producing, distributing, and selling food in a local area requires a local workforce, and the fact that everyone needs food no matter the state of the nation's economy means that such jobs aren't likely to dry up with every downturn.

Chapter 10 notes that evaluation arguments always depend on evaluative criteria, such as the criteria of effectiveness that Gustafson discusses.

LINK TO P. 212

Farm to Family isn't creating any jobs yet, however. Mark's just one guy with a gas-guzzling truck and a trailer roaming the Virginia countryside, transporting the goods in and out of his central warehouse, an old flower shop on a run-down commercial strip outside Richmond, which, shortly after my visit, he turned into a nonroving local-foods shop.

And while the concept of a mobile supermarket is innovative and the nostalgia-inducing school bus is a good marketing hook, the idea of any city's main alternative to the Safeway being a fleet of old school buses kitted out with burlap and smelling of onions left me slightly deflated. Although a good example of a hopeful enterprise, Mark's venture seemed a somewhat cumbersome way to inject local food into the cityscape. I was interested in what a more sustainable food system might look like, and the project of driving all day in a hot truck to pick up a box of potatoes here, a cooler of yogurt there didn't strike me as all that sustainable, especially considering the guy behind the wheel was so tired he seemed fit to collapse at any moment.

A company like Mark's—especially one expanded and able to run effi- 50
ciently at a larger scale—can play an important role as part of a network of businesses and nonprofits offering a variety of alternatives, the presence of which alone makes for a more sustainable local community. But I could see that if I was going to showcase all that is hopeful in local food and discover its potential, I would need to find a more expansive example. What I needed to find next was a place where a proper network of locally oriented endeavors was starting to form a veritable alternative economy of local food.

RESPOND•

1. What questions sparked Gustafson's journey, both her literal journey and the larger, metaphorical journey? How do her doubts (paragraph 8) set the stage for what follows in this chapter?
2. At the end of this selection, we find that Gustafson is not satisfied with what she has thus far found. Why not? How do her experiences lead her to a deeper understanding of the challenges Americans face if they are to have a different relationship with the food they eat?
3. Make a list of the specific unsustainable aspects of the model of alternative food delivery that Gustafson describes in this selection, noting the paragraph where she discusses each. What benefits come from learning about these challenges in the way that Gustafson teaches us about them—through a narrative interspersed with her comments and analyses—rather than having them presented as, say, a factual argument such as the list you made, with comments on each challenge?
4. What sort of ethos does Gustafson create for herself in this chapter? How does her ethos influence your response to this selection? (Chapter 3 discusses arguments based on ethos.)
5. How might Christian R. Weisser, author of the first selection in this chapter, from *Sustainability: A Bedford Spotlight Reader*, respond to Gustafson's search for sustainable foodways? Why?
6. In this chapter, you've read selections that focus on various aspects of sustainability as they relate to food, in particular. **Write a proposal** in which you define a problem relating to food and sustainability and then offer a solution to it, based on the readings in the chapter and other research that you might do. For example, you may wish to take a stand on the issue of genetically modified foods in the United States (or elsewhere), or you may examine the strengths or weaknesses of the local food movement. These are just two possible ideas. (Chapter 12 offers advice on creating proposal arguments, while Chapters 18–22 will assist you with questions about research.)

26
What Should "Diversity on Campus" Mean and Why?

Left to right: Megan Haaga, for Open Gates, by permission; © Frank Fell/age fotostock; AP Photo/Kin Cheung

Visit your school's homepage, and look for information about diversity; if you don't find a link there, use the search function to see how long it takes to get information about diversity on your campus. We predict it won't take long. Once you find that information, see what's included—and what's not. Be sure to look at any images you find. If your school is like most, you might end up concluding that diversity has a meaning on campus that is narrower than the *Oxford English Dictionary*'s definition of the term: "the condition or quality of being diverse, different, or varied; difference, unlikeness." (For linguists, cases of semantic narrowing like this one often stand as evidence that social change of one sort or another is taking place in the community where the narrowing occurs.) The arguments in this chapter challenge you to think about the meaning of diversity on your own campus—what it might mean, what it should mean, and whether it's relevant at all.

The chapter opens with a portfolio of visual arguments about diversity in general or some specific facet of the topic. Each poster comes from a different campus, and each serves as a definitional argument of sorts. The second selection, "A Campus More Colorful Than Reality," is a transcript of a 2013 National Public Radio story that examines the common practice among colleges of overrepresenting the actual ethnic diversity found on campus in the images used in recruitment materials. The example examined involved Photoshopping the image of an African American student into a photo of an event he never attended.

Sarah Fraas, an undergraduate at Smith College, takes the discussion in a very different direction as she examines the situation of trans women at women's colleges, especially her own. Transgender students face challenges on all campuses, but they present a special challenge for single-sex institutions like women's colleges. The issue hinges on the definition of *woman*, which Fraas addresses in her editorial for her campus newspaper. Young M. Kim and James S. Cole, in an excerpt from their report *Student Veterans/Service Members' Engagement in College and University Life and Education*, consider another growing population on U.S. campuses: veterans and active service members. Recent U.S. military involvement in the Middle East, in particular, has resulted in a growing number of vets on campus. In an excerpt from her 2014 book, *Muslim American Women on Campus: Undergraduate Social Life and Identity*, Shabana Mir reports on her ethnographic study of the double bind in which Muslim women find themselves as they struggle to balance the expectations of the Muslim community and of peers against a background of strong cultural stereotypes of what it means to be a Muslim woman.

Georgetown Law professor Sheryll Cashin, in a selection from her 2014 book, *Place, Not Race*, offers what she terms a "new vision of fairness" for American campuses—and the society at large. Cashin wants us to shift our attention away from what she terms "optical diversity" to dealing with a broader set of issues than skin color alone. The chapter closes with a complementary excerpt from the introduction to Walter Benn Michaels's 2006 book, *The Trouble with Diversity: How We Learned to Love Identity and Ignore Inequality*. Michaels argues that our discussions of diversity, especially when focused on ethnic or racial diversity, are simply on the wrong track. Such discussions may keep us occupied, but they conveniently prevent us from dealing with deeper, more serious issues that we all work hard to avoid.

Making a Visual Argument: Diversity Posters

▶ *All these posters stand as evidence that the topic of diversity is a live one on college campuses today. Students, faculty, and administrators across the country are trying to figure out and to articulate what diversity is, why it matters, and how it should show up in college life, whether in dorms, in syllabi, or in images or photos of the campus. Some of these posters were clearly created as part of a campus competition; Western Washington University, for example, has a long history of such an annual contest. Others were created as part of a celebration commemorating the birthday of Dr. Martin Luther King Jr. or some other campus event or exhibition. As you study these images, consider each as a definitional argument: which aspect(s) of diversity does it consider, and which does it ignore?*

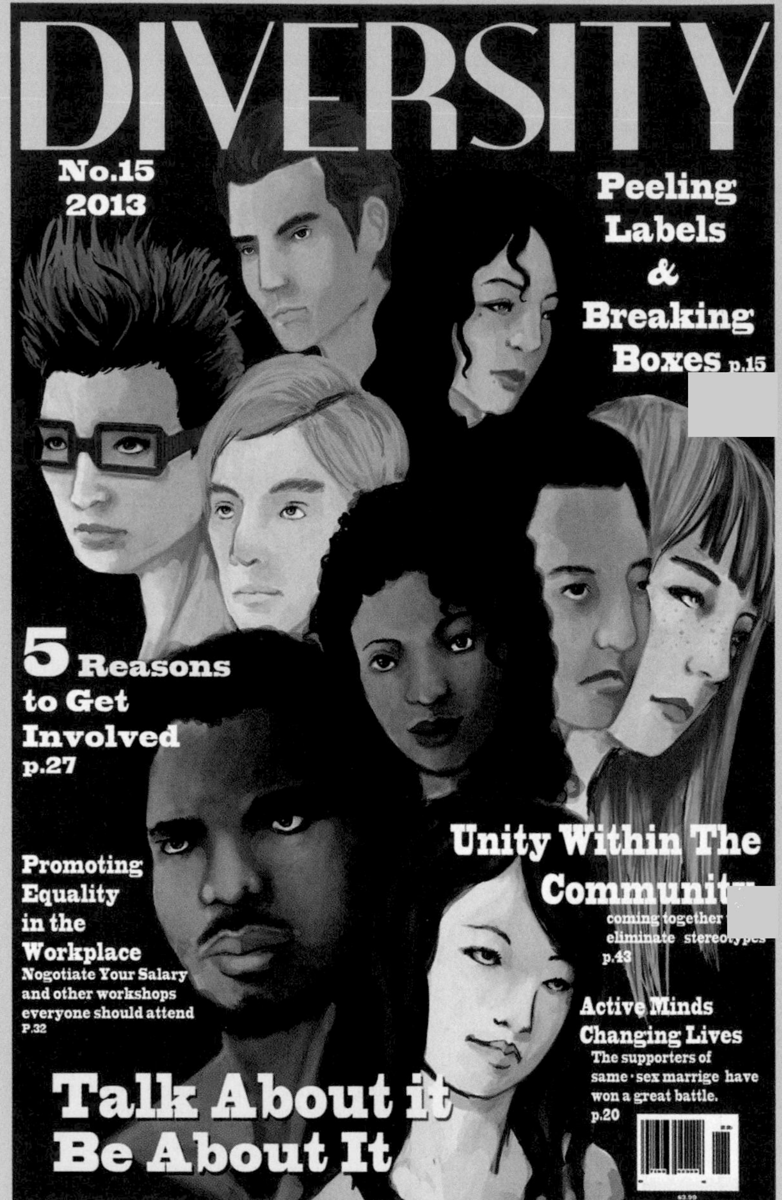

Wendy Aguilar, *Talk About It, Be About It,* Western Washington University, Bellingham, Washington © Wendy Aguilar, 2013 Diversity Poster Contest Winner, Western Washington University

Max Smith, *Unity within the Community,* Western Washington University, Bellingham, Washington © Max Smith, 2012 Diversity Poster Contest Winner, Western Washington University

Hayley Kuntz, *We All Come from Different Walks of Life*, University of North Dakota, Grand Forks, North Dakota Graphics: copyright Hayley Kuntz; photo: Yuri Arcurs/Getty Images

David Whittemore, *Diversity Is the Largest Picture*, Northeastern University, Boston, Massachusetts © David Whittemore Design

Dr. Lynda Kenney, *Diversity Makes Life Interesting*, University of North Dakota, Grand Forks, North Dakota

Jake Nicolella, *Reflect on Yesterday. Experience Today. Transform Tomorrow*. Penn State University, State College, Pennsylvania © Jake Nicolella, for Penn State University

Coleman Collins, *You Are Not Colorblind,* University of Notre Dame, South Bend, Indiana "You Are Not Colorblind." Original work © 2011 Coleman Collins.

RESPOND.

1. Which of these visual arguments do you find most appealing? Least appealing? Why? (Chapter 14 on visual rhetoric may prove useful here.)
2. Analyze the relationship between text (the words used) and the visual images and layout in each of the posters. What's the interaction between the text, on the one hand, and the visual images and layout, on the other, in each one? Which poster is most effective in this regard? Why?
3. If you take each of these posters to be a definitional argument, defining diversity in some way, what argument is each making? In other words, how does each poster define diversity? (For a discussion of definitional arguments, see Chapter 9.)
4. In defining and commenting on the notion of diversity, these posters range from approaching the topic in a didactic fashion (that is, seeking to teach a moral lesson) to approaching it much more vaguely. (Note the evaluative—and potentially negative—connotations the labels "didactic" and "vague" carry.) Choose the posters that you find most explicitly didactic and those that you find vaguer in their approach to the topic. Justify your choices. Which approach do you prefer? Why? Which do you believe is more effective in situations like this one? Why?
5. **Write an essay** in which you evaluate two of these posters, commenting on the definition of diversity presented or assumed (question 3); the relationship between text, on the one hand, and visual images and layout, on the other (question 2); and the artists' approach to the subject (question 4). (For a discussion of evaluative arguments, see Chapter 10.)
6. **Write a definitional essay** in which you define the notion of diversity as it might or should be understood on American college campuses today in general or on your campus specifically. (For a discussion of definitional arguments, see Chapter 9.)

Although the events this story refers to took place over a decade earlier, the questions they raise are still live wires on many campuses, something this feature, which aired on National Public Radio's Weekend Edition Sunday *on December 29, 2013, demonstrates. As sociologist Tim Pippert, who is interviewed in the feature, explains, colleges and universities want and need to market diversity, and the diversity represented in their promotional materials doesn't necessarily match campus demographics. This disparity leads to a number of questions, which this news feature and the accompanying information from the NPR Web site explore. (You can listen to the actual broadcast at n.pr/11PACBR.) Deena Prichep is a freelance journalist whose media include print and radio. Based in Portland, Oregon, she is a frequent contributor to various National Public Radio programs and to the Northwest News Network, and her radio features have appeared on Public Radio International's* The World *and* Marketplace *while her articles have appeared on* Salon.com, *in* Vegetarian Times, *and in* Portland Monthly. *She also blogs at* Mostly Foodstuffs. *As you listen to the news broadcast and read the information from the NPR Web site, consider how the two are similar, how they differ, and why that may be the case. Likewise, give some thought to the dilemma colleges and universities face and the possible alternatives they might have.*

A Campus More Colorful Than Reality: Beware That College Brochure

DEENA PRICHEP

NPR Transcript

JENNIFER LUDDEN, HOST: When it's time to apply to college, for many high school kids the process begins by leafing through a university brochure. But as Deena Prichep reports, when it comes to diversity, those glossy images may not paint an accurate picture.

DEENA PRICHEP, BYLINE: In 2000, Diallo Shabazz was a student at the University of Wisconsin. And he stopped by the admissions office.

DIALLO SHABAZZ: And one of the admissions counselors walked up to me and said, "Diallo, did you see yourself in the admissions booklet? Actually, you're on the cover this year."

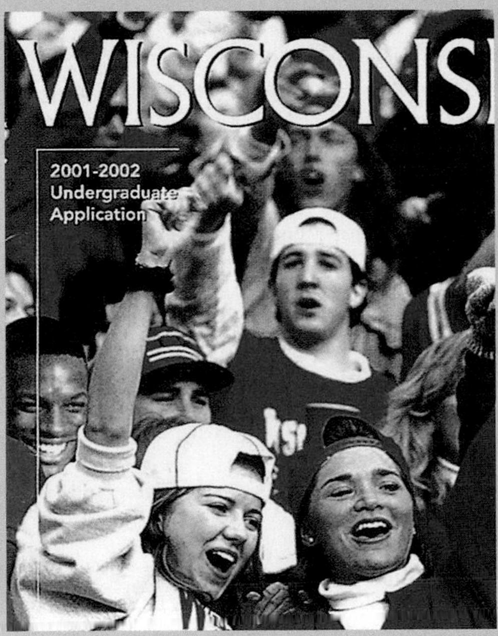

PRICHEP: Shabazz remembered seeing a cover shot of students at a football game. But he'd never been to a football game.

SHABAZZ: And so I flipped back and that's when I saw my head cut off, and kind of 5
pasted onto the front cover of the admissions booklet.

PRICHEP: This Photoshopped image became a classic example of how colleges miss the mark on diversity. Wisconsin stressed that it was just one person's bad choice. But Shabazz sees it as part of a bigger problem.

SHABAZZ: The admissions department that we've been talking about I believe was on the fourth floor, and the multicultural student center was on the second floor of that same building. So you didn't need to create false diversity in a picture. All you really needed to do was go downstairs.

TIM PIPPERT: Diversity is something that's being marketed.

PRICHEP: Tim Pippert is a sociologist at Augsberg College in Minnesota. He says that even without Photoshop colleges try to shape the picture.

PIPPERT: They're trying to sell a campus climate. They're trying to sell a future. 10
Campuses are trying to say: If you come here, you'll have a good time and you'll fit in.

PRICHEP: Pippert and his researchers looked at over ten thousand images from college brochures. They compared the racial breakdown of students in the pictures to the colleges' actual demographics. And they found that, overall, the whiter the school, the more the brochures skewed diversity—especially for certain groups.

PIPPERT: So, for example, when we looked at African-Americans in those schools that were predominantly white, the actual percentage in those campuses was only about 5 percent of the student body. They were photographed at 14.5 percent.

PRICHEP: While that may not sound like a lot, it's an overrepresentation of 188 percent. But where should colleges draw the line? Jim Rawlins directs admissions at the University of Oregon. He's also the past president of the National Association for College Admission Counseling.

JIM RAWLINS: If your campus is 20 percent racially and ethnically diverse, and I were to look at all your photos and you were 30 percent, is 30 unreasonable? Is 30 OK, but 35 would be too far? Is 20? I mean, where's that number?

PRICHEP: Rawlins says that showing inflated diversity can actually be a step toward 15
creating a more diverse campus. It helps students imagine themselves at those schools. But balancing representation and aspiration is difficult.

RAWLINS: I also wouldn't want to suggest it's something that we all feel we can easily quantify, and start counting faces in pictures and reach our answers to whether we're doing this right or not. I think very much any campus that wants to do this right has to talk with the students they have and see how they're doing.

PRICHEP: We checked in with a group of twelfth graders at Jefferson High School in Portland, Oregon, who are awash in college brochures. And none of them had any illusions, like Tobias Kelly.

TOBIAS KELLY: I see these as ads. So I think it's best if you are trying to go to a school to visit it for yourself, so you can really see, 'cause this can fool you sometimes.

PRICHEP: The students all stress that their highest priority is finding a school that will give them the best education. But many, like Brandon Williams, say that diversity is a part of that.

BRANDON WILLIAMS: When you go to college, it's not just about like the classrooms, 20
but it's also about like the stuff you learn from the people.

PRICHEP: And showing who those people are is something colleges continue to navigate. After his Photoshop experience, you'd think Diallo Shabazz would insist colleges stay absolutely true to the numbers. But Shabazz thinks that colleges can paint a picture with an eye toward the future — and they should.

SHABAZZ: I think that universities have a responsibility to portray diversity on campus, you know. And to portray the type of diversity that they would like to create — it shows what their value systems are. At the same time, I think they have a responsibility to be actively engaged in creating that diversity on campus that goes deeper than just what's in the picture.

PRICHEP: And Shabazz hopes that if schools take on that responsibility, the picture may change. For NPR News, I'm Deena Prichep.

(Soundbite of music)

LUDDEN: You're listening to NPR News.

RESPOND •

1. What evaluative argument is Prichep making in this radio feature and in the accompanying materials from the NPR Web site? What specific problems are discussed, and what possible solutions are proposed? (Note that, importantly, Prichep is not making an actual proposal although she is likely presuming that, after hearing the radio broadcast and/or reading the materials on the Web site, readers will want to take a stance on the issues discussed; that is, they will have proposals they wish to offer.) How are the various proposals for dealing with the problems Prichep discusses evaluated? (See Chapter 10 on criteria of evaluation in evaluative arguments; you may also want to review Chapter 12 so that you can understand clearly why Prichep is not, in fact, making a proposal argument.)
2. Does the information provided in this feature surprise you? Why or why not?
3. How sympathetic are you to the arguments made in this selection that promotional materials for a college must be aspirational, that is, they should represent what the university would like to be like? Can we distinguish such arguments from the argument that promotional materials represent the college as it wishes to be perceived at this time? What is the difference between the two arguments? Are there consequences to these differences?
4. How do the two versions of this feature — the transcript and audio link, on the one hand, and the printed information given on the NPR Web site, on the other — compare? What might account for the similarities? The differences?

5. Take Prichep's challenge. Examine carefully the promotional materials, whether print or electronic, for your college or university. How do they represent or fail to represent current reality? Do not consider issues of race or ethnicity alone; consider other kinds of diversity as well. (Also spend some time thinking about whether certain important kinds of diversity may not be visible.) You'll want to compare what you find with the latest available statistics about diversity on your campus. Once you've done this research, you have two options: **write a factual argument** about what you found or **write an evaluative argument** examining what you found. (Chapter 8 will help you with the first choice, while Chapter 10 will help you with the second.) This activity is also a great opportunity to work with a group. Each group should take a topic like race/ethnicity, sex/gender, or international students as its focus, and share what it finds.

▼ *As part of a successful campaign regarding admissions for transgender students who identify as female, this article appeared in April 2014 in the Sophian, the weekly independent, official, student-run newspaper of Smith College, in Northampton, Massachusetts. (Sophia is the Greek word for "wisdom," and Sophia was the goddess of wisdom in ancient Greece.) Smith is a private liberal arts college for women, and the largest of the Seven Sisters, an association of seven liberal arts colleges in New England that were traditionally women's colleges. Sarah Fraas was a sophomore when she wrote this piece, with, as she noted, the assistance of several friends; she is majoring in sociology and women's and gender studies. Ultimately, this selection focuses on an issue many campuses are studying: how best to include and meet the needs of their transgender students. It is, understandably, an especially complex issue for women's colleges. In May 2015, Smith announced that it would broaden its policy to begin admitting trans women in the fall. It would not admit trans men, that is, "those assigned female at birth but who now identify as male" or genderqueer or gender non-binary applicants because of its focus on women's education. As you read this selection, consider the definitional arguments it both makes and presupposes.*

Trans Women at Smith: The Complexities of Checking "Female"

SARAH FRAAS, CONTRIBUTING WRITER

April 24, 2014
(Written with the help of Raven Fowlkes-Witten, Maggie Peebles-Dorrin, and Jason McGourty)

Imagine a women's college that accepts all women. A feminist institution that supports women no matter what gender they were assigned at birth, or what legal documents they have, or whether or not their parent or high school supports them.

It might surprise some that this women's college does in fact exist — in Oakland, Calif. Mills College is open to "all women who claim a female gender identity." Yes, Mills accepts trans women without checking their papers and, no, the sky has not fallen. Smith and other women's colleges need to follow this example.

How is Smith's current policy different from this?

Every applicant has to have all female gender markers on four materials: the Common Application, their high school transcript, their midyear academic report, and three letters of recommendation.

Easy enough, right? Well, no. Not 5
for a lot of young women.

For starters, what if your teachers refuse to use "she" pronouns in your recommendation letters? What if you live in one of the countless school districts that don't allow gender changes on transcripts? What if you live in Washington, which has the official policy that schools are free to reject gender-marker changes as they

A student at Mount Holyoke, another of the Seven Sisters, makes a quick definitional argument. Megan Haaga, for Open Gates, by permission

Sarah Fraas proposes a series of hypothetical eventualities to build pathos, followed immediately by a fact from a recognizable authority. How does this contribute to the effectiveness of her argument? For more, see "Offering Evidence and Good Reasons" in Chapter 7.

LINK TO P. 131

please? What if changing your gender markers requires a $10,000+ surgery with months of painful and debilitating recovery time behind it, and what if that's a surgery you don't even want?

Essentially, the only trans women who can reasonably hope to apply have a supportive family, attend a supportive school, and have the luxury of free time to navigate bureaucratic processes.

A recent study by the National Gay and Lesbian Task Force found that less than half of trans high school students have been able to update their school documents. Eleven percent tried to do so and were flat-out denied.

Let's factor in school climate as well:

10 In another study of transgender K–12 students, 31 percent reported verbal harassment by teachers or staff for their gender. Another 5 percent reported physical assault by teachers and 3 percent reported sexual assault. The more harassment that students faced, the less likely they were to maintain higher GPAs, attend all their classes, and plan for college. But transmisogyny° doesn't just affect education — it's a life and death issue. In fact, 53 percent of those lost to anti-queer hate murders in 2012 were trans women.

In the words of Bet Power, Director of the Sexual Minorities Archives: "Trans girls dream big for their futures. There is no luxury in that. Education is the only chance at survival while living as trans."

Smith Q&A° is not asking that Smith suddenly adopt Mills's policy, although we hope to work toward that goal. We are simply demanding that Smith accept the proposal of a supplement to allow women with non-female gender markers on their documents to go here.

Smith Q&A drafted this proposal when the group was first formed. It suggests that if an application has "male" gender markers, Smith can request "letters of support or explanation from health providers, school administrators, teachers, guidance counselors, social workers, advisors, clergy, family, employers, etc." Smith admissions has always been concerned that someone might assert that they're a woman for the "wrong reasons" — this eliminates that risk as it would be hard to imagine two trusted adults getting in on such a "scheme."

Although we know that not every single trans woman will have two adults willing to affirm her identity, it's certainly a start.

15 That's why over one hundred students got up at 8:30 in the morning on Thursday, April 24, to rally in support of their trans sisters — to help make Smith an institution that empowers all women for the world.°

However, I have to address criticisms that are often hurled at student organizers: that we're too aggressive, that the administration is trying its best.

---

transmisogyny: *transphobia* "fear of transsexuals" + *misogyny* "hatred of women"; the intersection of transphobia and misogyny, or the particular kinds of discrimination faced by trans women.

Smith Q&A: a student organization at Smith with the goal of "abolishing Smith College's exclusionary admissions policies for trans women and making Smith a safe, inclusive space for trans women."

women for the world: the slogan of Smith College's recent $450 million fundraising campaign.

To that, I would say that of course this is not a personal attack on Smith administrators. We are all — myself included — a product of the ideologies we have been taught to believe are common sense. These often include inaccurate or harmful ideas about sex and gender that we have to unlearn. We know that many Smith administrators have good intentions and see themselves only as concerned with preserving Smith's status as a women's college.

However, the fact remains that Q&A has spent a year and a half trying to get this gender supplement proposal accepted. We met with higher education law experts who validated our sense that this was not actually a legal, or Title IX, issue — Smith College will not lose its status as a women's college by accepting our proposal. Heartened by this, Q&A conducted several negotiations with administrators, which did result in the change that gender markers no longer matter for Disability and Financial Aid application materials. This year, a trans woman applied to Smith, was accepted, and is now a student here. Once at Smith, she personally explained to administrators why Smith's policy is exclusionary. She urged them to accept the gender supplement proposal. Their reply was that they can't simply make a supplement for every specific situation in which a student cannot meet their requirements. The big difference here is that these requirements shouldn't even exist in the first place — womanhood does not reside in documentation.

In other words, a huge part of the problem is that Smith sees it as the applicant's responsibility to meet set-in-stone requirements, instead of Smith thinking about how to create a system that accommodates all women, particularly those who truly need it the most.

I hope you will stand with us. 20
If "women for the world" doesn't mean all women, it doesn't mean anything.

RESPOND

1. In what senses does this selection represent a definitional argument? What is being defined, and what are the competing definitions that are the source of the argument? (See Chapter 9 for a discussion of definitional arguments.)
2. What evidence does Fraas offer for why the current definition of who may apply to Smith is problematic? What kinds of appeals does this evidence represent? (See Chapter 1 for a discussion of kinds of appeals.)
3. In what senses is this selection a proposal argument? What is being proposed? How does the evidence discussed in response to question 2 support or fail to support the proposal that is made? (Chapter 12 will help you understand proposal arguments.)
4. The following information appears on the current Web site for Mount Holyoke College, another of the Seven Sisters, which has a different policy from Smith's policy with respect to this issue. (*Ze* is a gender-neutral pronoun; unlike *he* or *she*, *ze* does not indicate the biological

sex or gender identity of the person to whom it refers. It is one of several pronouns that transgender individuals sometimes use.)

Mount Holyoke College's policy on the admission of transgender students states that it welcomes applications for its undergraduate program from any qualified student who is female or identifies as a woman. Can you clarify "who is female or identifies as a woman"?

The following academically qualified students can apply for admission consideration:

- Biologically born female; identifies as a woman
- Biologically born female; identifies as a man
- Biologically born female; identifies as other/they/ze
- Biologically born female; does not identify as either woman or man
- Biologically born male; identifies as woman
- Biologically born male; identifies as other/they/ze and when "other/they" identity includes woman
- Biologically born with both male and female anatomy (Intersex); identifies as a woman

The following academically qualified students cannot apply for admission consideration:

- Biologically born male; identifies as man

Source: http://bit.ly/1rKYeDJ

In what ways does this list constitute a definitional argument? What kind of definition is it—a formal definition, an operational definition, or a definition by example? What criteria are involved? Why are they relevant in this case? Studying the information given in the headnote for this article (or consulting Smith's most recent FAQ on admissions), assess the extent to which Smith and Mount Holyoke define "female" in the same way.

5. The Web site quoted in question 4 also includes the following question and answer. (*Positionality* is a term from feminist theory; it focuses on how society positions [and values] individuals who are members of a socially constructed category. Thus, each of the following groups is differently positioned [and valued] in our society: women/men; bisexuals/asexuals/lesbians/gay men/heterosexuals; people of different ethnic or racial backgrounds; people from different social classes; the able-bodied and the differently able; etc.)

Is Mount Holyoke College changing the fundamental nature of its mission as a women's college by admitting transgender students?

Mount Holyoke remains committed to its historic mission as a women's college. Yet, concepts of what it means to be a woman are not static. Traditional binaries around who counts as a man or woman are

being challenged by those whose gender identity does not conform to their biology. Those bringing forth these challenges recognize that such categorization is not independent of political and social ideologies. Just as early feminists argued that the reduction of women to their biological functions was a foundation for women's oppression, we must acknowledge that gender identity is not reducible to the body. Instead, we must look at identity in terms of the external context in which the individual is situated. It is this positionality that biological and trans women share, and it is this positionality that is relevant when women's colleges open their gates for those aspiring to live, learn, and thrive within a community of women.

What arguments is Mount Holyoke making for the inclusion of trans women in its institution? How do these arguments link to the college's understanding of its historical mission? How do they help us appreciate the complexity of this issue?

6. Although the admission of transgender students represents a particular challenge to institutions that have traditionally accepted only women or only men, transgender students face challenges on all campuses. Investigate how your college or university is or is not attempting to assist transgender students as members of your community. This investigation may include consulting print or electronic resources, interviewing individuals in various campus organizations—transgender advocacy, queer student organizations, student services, health and counseling services on campus. You may wish to focus simply on information gathering (leading you to **write an argument of fact**), but likely far more interesting will be efforts to trace the ways that members of your school's community have been challenged to rethink their own ideas about gender and identity and about the ways this rethinking has or has not resulted in changed policies. In this latter case, you'll likely **write a causal argument** of some sort. (Chapter 8 considers arguments of fact, while Chapter 11 examines causal arguments.) As in some previous cases, your class may find it useful to divide into pairs or small groups, each of which focuses on a different aspect of campus life. Be aware that this issue is by and large a new one for most of us, so we all have a great deal to learn about it. Likewise, if there appear to be no transgender students on your campus, it does not mean that they are not there; they may simply not have disclosed the relevant information. If your campus has not dealt with this issue, imagine how it might.

▼ *This selection is an excerpt from a report by the American Council on Education (ACE), the major advocacy and leadership organization in higher education in the United States. The report itself comes out of the Center for Policy Research and Strategy, the research arm of ACE. Young M. Kim worked as a consultant to ACE on this project; James S. Cole, project manager for the Beginning College Survey of Student Engagement, is a research analyst at the Indiana University Center for Postsecondary Research.*

A decade ago, there was almost no discussion of veterans or service members on campus, although a small number of veterans and service members were present. The armed conflicts in the Middle East have changed that situation in very significant ways, and campuses across the country are struggling to catch up. They are aware that, thanks to the Post-9/11 Veterans Educational Assistance Act of 2008, veterans and service members represent a source of potential students and, hence, revenue; they are likewise aware that returning veterans and service members face a range of challenges that their nonveteran or civilian colleagues likely are not dealing with. This report examines how veterans and service members compare with their nonveteran or civilian classmates. The complete report compares veterans and service members with two populations: first all students, and then those who are twenty-five or older, or the age group to which the veterans and service members are more likely to belong. This excerpt focuses on comparisons with this latter group. It includes the executive summary (a summary of the goals and key findings of the entire project that appears at the beginning of a research report), an overview of the findings with respect to how student veterans and service members over twenty-five compare to their classmates in the same age cohort, the conclusion of the study, and the relevant references. (Not included are the sections on methodology and the section of the findings that compares the survey responses of veterans and service members with those of students of all ages.)

Student Veterans/Service Members' Engagement in College and University Life and Education

YOUNG M. KIM AND JAMES S. COLE

Executive Summary

Since the passage of the Post-9/11 Veterans Educational Assistance Act of 2008, also known as the Post-9/11 GI Bill,° the enrollment of active-duty service members and veterans in American colleges and universities has increased substantially. According to the Department of Veterans Affairs, more than three-quarters of a million veterans have used their earned benefit to enroll in postsecondary courses. In response to the influx of veteran student enrollment, a group of higher education associations and veterans'

GI Bill: (in popular usage, the term *GI* refers to a veteran, especially a veteran of World War II) legislation that provides specific benefits for veterans. Whereas the Post-9/11 Veterans Educational Assistance Act of 2008 provides educational benefits for veterans and, under certain circumstances, their spouse or children, the original GI Bill of 1944 provided subsidized mortgages and loans to start a business as well as payments for the cost of attending high school, vocational education, or college.

organizations collaborated in 2009 and 2012 on a study that asked college and university administrators whether their institutions had geared up campus programs and services specifically designed to support the unique needs of veterans.[1] The results indicated that administrators had indeed increased support levels, sometimes by quite significant margins.

But how do student veterans/service members[2] perceive their experiences at higher education institutions? To date, there is little or no information to assess whether the efforts by institutions to provide targeted programs and services are helpful to the veterans and service members enrolled in colleges and universities. Similarly, not much is known about the transition to postsecondary education from military service experienced by student veterans/service members, or whether these students are engaged in both academic programs and college and university life to their fullest potential. In this context, this issue brief explores student veteran/service member engagement in postsecondary education. The brief utilizes data from the 2012 National Survey of Student Engagement (NSSE), an annual survey of students enrolled in four-year universities, to assess how student veterans/service members perceive their integration on campus.

A key finding is that student veterans/service members are selective about the campus life and academic activities in which they invest their time. Student veterans/service members are more likely to be first-generation students—the first in their families to attend a college or university—and older than nonveteran/civilian students; they therefore tend to have responsibilities outside of higher education that put constraints on their time. Student veterans/service members report placing greater emphasis on academic areas that they find essential for academic progress than on college and

---

[1]The idea for this issue brief emerged as a result of *From Soldier to Student*, a research series on campus readiness to support the increasing number of post-9/11 veterans enrolling in higher education. The research was started by the American Council on Education (ACE), Servicemembers Opportunity Colleges, the American Association of State Colleges and Universities, NASPA: Student Affairs Administrators in Higher Education, and the National Association of Veteran's Programs Administrators, with the support of Lumina Foundation (Cook & Kim, 2009). *From Soldier to Student II* showed that campuses have increased programs and services specifically designed for post-9/11 veterans, in part propelled by the enactment of the Post-9/11 GI Bill in 2008 (McBain et al., 2012).

[2]This brief uses the term "student veterans/service members" to indicate college and university students who are either current or former members of the U.S. Armed Forces, Military Reserves, or National Guard. It uses the term "nonveteran/civilian students" to refer to students who have never served in the military.

university life and activities—academic or otherwise—that are not essential for success in the courses in which they are enrolled. Student veterans/service members are less likely to participate in co-curricular activities, and they dedicate less time to relaxing and socializing than nonveteran/civilian students. In particular:

- Student veterans/service members are less likely to participate in experiential learning opportunities, such as internships or practicums, learning communities, study abroad, or community service. Sixty-eight percent of student veterans/service members say they have plans to participate in or have already participated in community service or volunteer work, compared with 82 percent of nonveteran/civilian students.
- Student veterans/service members are more likely (70 percent) than nonveteran/civilian students (65 percent) to spend at least ten hours per week preparing for class.
- Student veterans/service members are also more likely (60 percent) than nonveteran/civilian students (58 percent) to discuss grades or assignments with their instructors.
- Forty-nine percent of student veterans/service members indicate that they collaborate with classmates outside of class to prepare class assignments, compared with 57 percent of nonveteran/civilian students.

In terms of student veterans/service members' relationships with others in their college or university communities, the results are mixed. For all students, forming good relationships with others is an important way to successfully engage in campus life and academics. While student veterans/service members are more likely than nonveteran and civilian students to state that they have a friendly and supportive relationship with faculty and staff, the reverse is true of their relationship with other students.

- While 61 percent of student veterans/service members say they have a positive relationship with faculty members, 54 percent of nonveteran and civilian students feel the same way.
- Similarly, 46 percent of student veterans/service members say they feel supported by and have a sense of belonging with administrative personnel, versus 36 percent of nonveteran/civilian students.
- But in terms of relationships with other students, 58 percent of student veterans/service members say they have friendly and supportive relationships, compared with 62 percent of nonveteran/civilian students.

The NSSE also explores students' personal experiences, achievements, and 5
skills acquisition. While there are a few areas of similarity, in general student veterans/service members are more likely than nonveteran/civilian students to report lower gains during their time as students in higher education.

- Seventy percent of student veterans/service members, compared with 78 percent of nonveteran/civilian students, indicate gains in working effectively with others.
- Sixty-eight percent of student veterans/service members indicate gains in learning effectively on their own, compared with 75 percent of other students.
- Fifty percent of nonveteran/civilian students report gains in contributing to the welfare of their community, compared with 40 percent of student veterans/service members.

The average age of student veterans/service members enrolled in four-year universities is 33, compared with nonveteran/civilian students, whose average age is 22. To capture differences and similarities in campus integration among student veterans/service members and nonveteran/civilian students of the same age, survey responses from student veterans age 25 and over—the age group to which veterans are more likely to belong—are compared with those of nonveteran/civilian students in the same age range. One aim of this study was to explore how students at a similar stage of life manage college and university life and education.

- Student veterans/service members age 25 and over are just as unlikely as nonveteran/civilian students to be engaged with faculty members on activities other than coursework, such as serving on committees, attending orientation, and participating in student life activities.
- Both student veterans/service members and nonveteran and civilian students age 25 and over invest their time in preparing for class. Approximately 72 percent of both groups report spending eleven or more hours per week studying.
- Student veterans/service members age 25 and over are less likely than nonveteran/civilian students to work with peers outside of class to prepare assignments.
- Student veterans and civilian students age 25 and over report lower gains in achievement as a result of their academic experiences than nonveteran/civilian students age 25 and over. Sixty-nine percent of

student veterans/service members report gains in working effectively with others, compared with 77 percent of nonveteran and civilian students. In addition, 57 percent of student veterans/service members report gains in solving complex real-world problems, compared with 65 percent of nonveteran and civilian students.

- Student veterans/service members age 25 and over show somewhat greater cultural sensitivity than nonveteran/civilian students age 25 and over.

demographic characteristics: easily quantifiable information about social categories like sex, age, race or ethnicity, and homeownership. Such information is then used as a way of interpreting other information about specific topics of interest gathered from a population.

In general, NSSE data are revealing as to student veterans/service members' preferences and their allocation of time, in addition to demographic characteristics° that can in part explain differences in their engagement in college and university life and education. Although their engagement is strong in some areas—especially in activities related to coursework—their engagement in co-curricular activities and other areas that form college and university life is not as strong as that of their nonveteran/civilian peers. Drawing attention to the unique experiences of student veterans/service members, which may not be well understood by faculty and staff, is important in institutions' efforts to create and adapt effective support systems for these students.

Who Are the Student Veterans/Service Members?

Student veterans/service members are racially and ethnically diverse, and compared with nonveteran/civilian students, they are older, more likely to be male than female, and more likely to represent the first generation in their families to attend a college or university (see Table 1). These characteristics reveal useful information about student preferences, explaining in part why student veterans/service members' views on their participation in classroom activities and their general integration on campus differ from those of other students. Take, for instance, the fact that 62 percent of student veterans/service members, versus 43 percent of nonveteran/civilian students, indicate they are first-generation students. A number of studies have shown the extent to which first-generation students' experiences differ from those of other students; for example, first-generation students are at greater risk of not persisting in higher education.[3]

[3]A report by the National Center for Education Statistics, *First-Generation Students in Postsecondary Education: A Look at Their College Transcripts*, found that first-generation students are less likely than other students to persist in postsecondary education. While 47 percent of first-generation students entering higher education between 1992 and 2000 obtained a postsecondary degree by 2000, 68 percent of students whose parents were college or university graduates did so during the same period (Chen & Carroll, 2005).

Table 1. General Survey-Respondent Demographic Information

	Student Veterans/Service Members	Nonveteran/Civilian Students
Age	%	%
18–24	21.1	86.5
25 and over	78.9	13.5
Total %	100.0	100.0
Gender	%	%
Male	73.3	34.1
Female	26.7	65.9
Total %	100.0	100.0
Race/ethnicity	%	%
White	68.2	71.4
African American	10.6	7.1
Hispanic	7.8	6.8
Asian American	3.1	4.1
American Indian	1.5	0.9
Multi-racial/ethnic	1.7	1.9
Other	7.1	7.7
Total %	100.0	100.0
First-generation student	%	%
Yes	61.8	42.8
No	38.2	57.2
Total %	100.0	100.0

Source: Indiana University Center for Postsecondary Research, National Survey of Student Engagement, 2012. Authors' calculation.

These students are less likely to have guidance to help them navigate through their postsecondary education, are more likely to come from families with fewer financial resources, and are more likely to be in need of academic support—in general, their experience may be wrought with more anxiety than that of a typical student (Engle, Bermeo, & O'Brien, 2006). Differences such as these have implications for how college and university administrators engage with student veterans/service members and provide them with effective support systems.

10 It is important to note that the majority of veterans starting higher education for the first time initially enroll in two-year institutions. According to the U.S. Department of Education, while 84 percent of veterans initially enroll in two-year institutions, 16 percent of veterans start in four-year institutions. While the focus of this issue brief is four-year institutions, readers should note that in the continuum of learning, student veterans/service members'

education can begin outside of four-year universities. It is also important to consider that some veterans started their higher education either before or during active duty.

Student Veterans/Service Members and Nonveteran/Civilian Students Over 25 Share Similar Experiences, with Some Exceptions

This issue brief has suggested that some of the differences in engagement among student veterans/service members and nonveteran/civilian students are, to a large extent, associated with responsibilities that older student veterans/service members have, and which nonveteran/civilian students do not. Nonveteran/civilian students, who are more likely to be younger than student veterans/service members, do not have as many interests competing for their time and thus may have more opportunities to integrate in campus and academic life. But how does the picture of engagement change when comparing students of similar age? By comparing individuals of similar age, it may be possible to observe nuances between student veterans/service members and their peers not visible when comparing students of all ages.

When comparing nonveteran/civilian students age 25 and over with student veterans/service members age 25 and over—the age group to which veterans and service members are more likely to belong—the results are mixed. Student veterans/service members age 25 and over are just as unlikely as nonveteran/civilian students age 25 and over to be engaged with faculty members on activities other than coursework (16 percent of student veterans/service members; 17 percent of nonveteran/civilian students). Given older students' likelihood of having family and job responsibilities, regardless of veteran status, the low percentage of participation in this area outside of essential classwork is not surprising.

On the other hand, older student veterans/service members are almost as likely as older nonveteran/civilian students to have worked with other students on projects during class (52 percent of student veterans/service members; 55 percent of nonveteran/civilian students). Older student veterans/service members and nonveteran/civilian students are equally likely to have talked about career plans with a faculty member or advisor. Both groups also indicate spending similar amounts of time preparing for class, with approximately 72 percent from each group indicating they spend eleven or more hours per week studying (see Table 2). These results, which indicate the seriousness with which both older student veterans/service members and nonveteran/civilian students approach their education, contrast with the comparison made earlier in the brief between student veterans/service

Table 2. Areas in Which Student Veterans/Service Members Age 25 and Over and Nonveteran/Civilian Students Age 25 and Over Are Similarly Engaged

Q: In your experience at your institution during the current school year, about how often have you done each of the following?

	Student Veterans/ Service Members Age 25 and Over	*Nonveteran/ Civilian Students Age 25 and Over*
Worked with other students on projects during class	%	%
Often/Very often	48.0	44.9
Sometimes/Never	52.0	55.1
Total %	100.0	100.0
Worked with faculty members on activities other than coursework	%	%
Often/Very often	15.6	16.7
Sometimes/Never	84.4	83.3
Total %	100.0	100.0
Talked about career plans with a faculty member or advisor	%	%
Often/Very often	[illegible]	38.6
Sometimes/Never	63.7	61.4
Total %	100.0	100.0
Preparing for class (studying, reading, writing, doing homework or lab work, analyzing data, rehearsing, and other academic activities)	%	%
11 hours or more	71.6	71.6
10 hours or less	28.4	28.4
Total %	100.0	100.0

Source: Indiana University Center for Postsecondary Research, National Survey of Student Engagement, 2012. Authors' calculation.

members and nonveteran/civilian students of all ages. In that instance, nonveteran/civilian students put less emphasis on essential areas of academic participation than did student veterans/service members of all ages.

While the engagement of student veterans/service members and nonveteran/civilian students is similar in some areas—namely in the areas of essential academic concerns and class preparation—it is not the same in all areas. For instance, older student veterans/service members are less likely to have worked with classmates outside of class to prepare class assignments than older nonveteran/civilian students (48 percent of student veterans/service members versus 54 percent of nonveteran/civilian students). Older student veterans/service members are also less likely to indicate that they spend as much time discussing ideas from readings or classes outside of class with others (65 percent of student veterans/service members versus 70 percent of nonveteran/civilian students). These student veterans/service members also report lower gains as a result of their academic experiences, compared with nonveteran/civilian students of similar age. For instance, student veterans/service members report lower gains in working effectively with others (69 percent compared with 77 percent); writing clearly and effectively (76 percent compared with 80 percent); and solving complex real-world problems (57 percent compared with 65 percent). When the older students answer the question, "To what extent does your institution emphasize helping you cope with your non-academic responsibilities?" student veterans/service members are less likely than nonveteran/civilian students to respond "quite a bit" or "very much" (25 percent of student veterans/service members versus 28 percent of nonveteran/civilian students) (see Table 3).

Kim and Cole offer both inartistic proofs, such as statistical evidence, and artistic proofs, those based on reason and common sense, to support their claims. For more on using logos in arguments, see Chapter 4.

LINK TO P. 51

In part, some of these differences may be a manifestation of veterans and 15
service members' unique backgrounds, which make the transition from the military to academia indeed challenging. But there certainly may be other possibilities, including the preference for independent work.

Conversely, student veterans/service members age 25 and over are more likely than nonveteran/civilian students age 25 and over to have had serious conversations with students of a different race or ethnicity than their own (58 percent of student veterans/service members; 54 percent of nonveteran/civilian students). Similarly, a greater share of student veterans/service members report having serious conversations with students who are very different from them in terms of their religious beliefs, political opinions, or personal values (58 percent of student veterans/service members; 55 percent of nonveteran/civilian students) (see Table 4). As mentioned earlier, student veterans/service members in general are more racially and ethnically diverse than nonveteran/civilian students. The greater cultural sensitivity of student veterans/service members is not surprising insofar as their own identity goes; being open to different views and individuals may be a reflection of the diverse nature of student veterans/service members in general. It is also true that, before entering academia, veterans and service members come from a U.S. military that is more racially and ethnically diverse than the U.S. population.[4] Student veterans/service members also reported higher-quality relationships with the administrative personnel and offices on their campus (50 percent) compared with nonveteran/civilian students (46 percent).

---

[4]Authors' calculation based on the Department of Defense's Armed Forces personnel data from the Defense Manpower Data Center and 2009 U.S. population data from the U.S. Census.

Table 3. Areas in Which Student Veterans/Service Members Age 25 and Over Fare Worse Than Nonveteran/Civilian Students Age 25 and Over

Q. In your experience at your institution during the current school year, about how often have you done the following?

Worked with classmates outside of class to prepare class assignments	***Student Veterans/ Service Members Age 25 and Over*** %	***Nonveteran/Civilian Students Age 25 and Over*** %
Often/Very often	48.0	54.0
Sometimes/Never	52.0	46.0
Total %	100.0	100.0
Discussed ideas from your readings or classes with others outside of class (students, family members, co-workers, etc.)	%	%
Often/Very often	64.8	69.8
Sometimes/Never	35.2	30.2
Total %	100.0	100.0

Q: To what extent has your experience at this institution contributed to your knowledge, skills, and personal development in the following areas?

Working effectively with others	%	%
Quite a bit/Very much	77.3	69.1
Some/Very little	22.7	30.9
Total %	100.0	100.0
Writing clearly and effectively	%	%
Quite a bit/Very much	75.8	80.3
Some/Very little	24.2	19.7
Total %	100.0	100.0
Solving complex real-world problems	%	%
Quite a bit/Very much	56.6	63.1
Some/Very little	43.4	36.9
Total %	100.0	100.0

Q: To what extent does your institution emphasize the following?

Helping you cope with your non-academic responsibilities (work, family, etc.)	%	%
Quite a bit/Very much	24.8	28.2
Some/Very little	75.2	71.8
Total %	100.0	100.0

Source: Indiana University Center for Postsecondary Research, National Survey of Student Engagement, 2012. Authors' calculation.

Table 4. Areas in Which Student Veterans/Service Members Age 25 and Over Fare Better Than Nonveteran/Civilian Students Age 25 and Over

Q: In your experience at your institution during the current school year, about how often have you done the following?

Had serious conversations with students of a different race or ethnicity than your own	***Student Veterans/ Service Members Age 25 and Over*** %	***Nonveteran/Civilian Students Age 25 and Over*** %
Often/Very often	57.9	53.5
Sometimes/Never	42.1	46.5
Total %	100.0	100.0
Had serious conversations with students who are very different from you in terms of their religious beliefs, political opinions, or personal values	%	%
Often/Very often	57.6	54.8
Sometimes/Never	42.4	45.2
Total %	100.0	100.0

Q: Select the circle that best represents the quality of your relationship with people at your institution.

Relationships with administrative personnel and offices	***Student Veterans/ Service Members Age 25 and Over*** %	***Nonveteran/Civilian Students Age 25 and Over*** %
Friendly, supportive, sense of belonging	49.5	46.6
Somewhat friendly	35.4	36.5
Unfriendly, unsupportive, sense of alienation	15.1	16.9
Total %	100.0	100.0

Source: Indiana University Center for Postsecondary Research, National Survey of Student Engagement, 2012. Authors' calculation.

While these results are not simple to interpret, they do show that the experiences of student veterans/service members, when compared with other students of a similar age, cannot be assumed to be the same. The results indicate that student veterans/service members tend to be older adults whose experiences of integrating into life at colleges and universities can be more challenging in some areas. Clearly, student veterans/service members of all ages engage in postsecondary education in ways that are different than nonveteran/civilian students of all ages. Many of the differences in engagement point to differences in maturity and the amount of responsibilities they may or may not have. But for a subset of the students (i.e., older students), the evidence shows that student veterans/service members and nonveteran and civilian students both are often equally engaged in ways that lead to academic progress and success. Student veterans/service members are more involved than older nonveteran/civilian students in certain areas, particularly in demonstrating greater cultural sensitivity to people not like them, while showing less investment in non-core, but still helpful, curricular activities in their academic pursuits.

Conclusion

Not surprisingly, this report provides additional evidence that many student veterans/service members attending baccalaureate-level institutions are older and more likely to be first-generation students and students of color than their nonveteran/civilian student peers. These differences provide an important backdrop for other results, which indicate that many veterans and service members are not feeling as supported by their institutions and are not as engaged in non-core academic areas as their peers. Student veterans/service members are more likely to report spending increased time on non-academic activities, such as dependent care and working for pay, which likely contributes to a more stressful academic experience. Though many student veterans/service members report good relationships with faculty, they are not as likely to report good relationships with other students and are less likely to engage with other students when completing class assignments. As a result, these student veterans/service members may not be benefiting from important interactions that lead to improved academic integration in their campus environment. Though many veterans and service members do report important gains in their experiences at institutions, they generally report lower gains as a group than their nonveteran/civilian peers in many academic-work-related skills.

The results also point to the seriousness with which student veterans/service members approach their academic programs. On activities they consider vital for successful progression, a greater percentage of veterans and service members than nonveteran/civilian students report investing time in those activities. Veterans and service members are more likely to prepare for class, discuss grades or assignments with an instructor, and discuss ideas from reading with faculty outside of class than nonveteran/civilian students.

One way that higher education administrators can approach the findings 20
of this brief is to seek to understand what is and is not important for student veterans/service members. Clearly, student veterans/service members want to do well academically, as demonstrated by their time investment. This

research also showed that overall, student veterans/service members, whether older than the average student or not, do not invest their energy on *traditional* "high-impact" areas, such as internships, community service, and study abroad. These high-impact, experiential programs and services may not fit the needs of veterans and service members because these students are more likely than nonveteran/civilian students to have responsibilities away from campus that compete for their time. Also, veterans and service members already bring with them valuable real-life experiences from the military that may make these high-impact programs less relevant. For veterans and service members, college and university administrators may want to develop new kinds of high-impact programs and services that bring more focus to learning opportunities. Veterans and service members seem more likely to engage in these activities than in those that are not essential to their academic progress.

References

Chen, X., & Carroll, C. D. (2005). *First-generation students in postsecondary education: A look at their college transcripts*. Washington, DC: U.S. Department of Education, National Center for Education Statistics.

Cook, B., & Kim, Y. (2009). *From soldier to student: Easing the transition of service members on campus*. Washington, DC: American Council on Education.

Engle, J., Bermeo, A., & O'Brien, C. (2006). *Straight from the source: What works for first-generation college students*. Washington, DC: Pell Institute for the Study of Opportunity in Higher Education.

McBain, L., Kim, Y., Cook, B. J., & Snead, K. M. (2012). *From soldier to student II: Assessing campus programs for veterans and service members*. Washington, DC: American Council on Education.

RESPOND •

1. Relying on the executive summary, explain how the experiences of veterans and service members compare with those of students generally. Relying on the entire selection, explain how their experiences differ from those of students twenty-five and older who have never served in the military.
2. Read footnote 2 carefully. What is its function? What sort of definition does it offer for the terms it discusses? Why is it necessary, especially in research studies like this one? (Chapter 9 on definitional arguments includes a discussion of kinds of definitions.)

3. What purposes do the tables in this selection serve? Pay special attention to the sorts of information that such visual displays of information contain that are not included in the text about them. Similarly, imagine what the selection would be like without any of the tables. How do the tables complement the discussions about them in the text?

4. Like many reports generated by research institutes, this selection is primarily an argument of fact. As is common, however, there are proposals (or at least recommendations) embedded within these factual arguments, with the facts serving as evidence for and justification of the proposed action. Find instances of such recommendations or proposals in this selection. Why might they be part of what is primarily a factual argument?

5. As is often the case, data from reports such as this one can be used to support multiple arguments. **Write a summary** of this selection that supports the claim that, by and large, the experiences of veterans and service members at college are not especially different from those of their age cohort, all students twenty-five and older. Then **write a second summary** of the selection that supports the claim that, in fact, the experiences of veterans and service members at college are quite distinct from those of their age cohort. In both cases, you will be constructing factual arguments, relying heavily on fact and statistics from surveys. (Chapter 4 on arguments based on fact and reason and Chapter 8 on arguments of fact will be helpful to you here.) You might imagine that these summaries are part of a larger research project on veterans and service personnel on college campuses; doing so will give you a context for this assignment.

Muslim American Women in Campus Culture

SHABANA MIR

▶ *Shabana Mir is currently an assistant professor at Millikin University in Decatur, Illinois, where she serves as Global Issues Coordinator.* Muslim American Women on Campus: Undergraduate Social Life and Identity *grew out of her dissertation research, which used ethnographic fieldwork to study female Muslim students at Georgetown University and George Washington University, both of which are private schools in Washington, D.C. A native of London and now a naturalized American, Mir spent most of her childhood and her early twenties in Pakistan.* Muslim American Women on Campus *received the Outstanding Book Award from the National Association for Ethnic Studies and the 2014 Critics Choice Book Award from the American Educational Studies Association. As you read this selection, consider how the situation of Muslim women on campus is like and not like that of other marginalized groups—a point Mir discusses in detail. Similarly, notice the concepts from social theory that Mir uses to help describe and account for those similarities and situations.*

A Perfect Identity Storm:° Muslims at College

For undergraduates, college is a life-change that can be exhilarating, terrifying, and confusing. For youth already in the throes of physical and social change, shuttling between their roles as dependents and adolescents, on the one hand, and financially independent adults and voting citizens, on the other. Add Muslim identity to the mix, fold in a post-9/11 nativist° racism, and we find that Muslim American college students have some painful growing up to do. Muslim, American, and youth—these identities effervesce and simmer in many Americans' minds like a chemistry experiment gone wrong. How can these different ingredients harmonize? How will the balance of identities shift, teeter, and settle? This book unpacks how dysfunction and confusion may result from not being free to *be*—to be American "like everyone else"; to be Muslim, Arab, or Pakistani; to be authentically American *as well as* a Somali (or white, Arab, or black) Muslim woman; to be Pakistani American and American simultaneously; to be a religious Muslim American, and/or to be an *irreligious* Muslim. *"I can't get anything right,"* my research participants seemed to say; "I'm damned no matter what I do."

In the United States, Muslim identity is typically a source of "stigma" (Goffman, 1963). Conversely, behaving like a "normal" American youth can be a source of stigma in Muslim communities. In terms of American identity politics, young Muslim American women are beset by a perfect identity storm. The experiences of Muslim American women serve as a distinctive lens whence to examine the social spaces of American campus culture. Let us start with Latifa, an effusively cheerful Arab American freshman trying to find her way at Georgetown.

Limited Liberty: Marginal Identities on Campus

> LATIFA: Yeah, I came with some baggage, but my whole approach to college is, I'm starting on a new slate, so whatever I was taught in that home is definitely not being reinforced here.

College is popularly visualized as a world of freedom, mobility, and personal maturity. This is where girls become women and boys become men.

Syahrir Anuar/Shutterstock

Moreover, in the liberal narrative of college, there is an inherent claim—a promise, a "university imaginary," an individualistic, universal dream of full humanity that is accessible to all regardless of their particular characteristics (Abelmann, 2009, pp. 1–2). Yet this supposedly egalitarian community where diverse individuals may come together, share, and celebrate is not equally hospitable to all student identities; rather, it is a ranked array of decidedly unequal cliques° and coteries.° Latifa swiftly recognized that her home identities and cultural capital° were identity possibilities blocked off in campus spaces and repackaged as "baggage." Latifa's religious, civic, youthful, and gendered identities stretched the conceptions of majority Americans and traditional Muslims; the "freedom" within self-consciously pluralistic° campus cultures was not a very meaningful commodity° to her.

Through Muslim women's narratives, I call attention to the noiselessly marginalizing processes in campus social spaces that constrain Muslim American women's identities and turn home cultures into baggage. I investigate how Muslim American undergraduates engage with the college environment and how these girls become women, negotiating multiple norms under the twin towers of surveillance by Muslim communities and the American majority. In this chapter I discuss the Orientalist° discursive construction° of Muslims and contextualize my research findings relative to the scholarly literature on campus culture and Muslim Americans.

perfect storm: a rare violent storm resulting from an unusual combination of factors; used here metaphorically.

nativist: anti-immigrant.

clique: a small group of people who share interests; cliques are generally closed to outsiders.

coteries: a synonym for *cliques*.

cultural capital: the assets one has, apart from money, that encourage or permit social mobility, including one's manner of speech, level of education, appearance, and manner of dress.

pluralistic: characterized by difference.

commodity: something of value.

Orientalist: a general patronizing Western attitude toward Middle Eastern, Asian, and North African societies. For literary scholar Edward Said, who wrote extensively about the topic, the West essentializes these societies, seeing them as backward and unchanging. In representing these cultures in this way, Western societies construct themselves as being the opposite: modern, flexible, rational, and, of course, superior.

discursive construction: created through discourse, that is, culturally preferred ways of conceptualizing and talking about a topic.

Sociability and Hedonism° in College Peer Culture

Peer culture is one of the most powerful factors in shaping the behavior of college students (Renn & Arnold, 2003, p. 263; Renn, 2000, p. 400; Astin, 1997, p. 53), whether majority American or minority youth. Beyond university policies, regulations, official documents, and course syllabi, it is the people on campus who co-construct and consume campus culture. Since the late 1960s, when universities relinquished the *in loco parentis*° role, sociability and hedonism have grown ubiquitous° in higher education, so that "many campuses have come to be seen as increasingly chaotic and dangerous to a number of students and parents . . . places where men and women share dorm rooms and where drugs and alcohol are easily available" (Miller, 2006, p. 6). Sociability and hedonism, which play central roles in the marketing of college brands, are manufactured and indulged in by college undergraduates. 5

hedonism: the pursuit of pleasure, often at all costs.

in loco parentis: Latin for "in place of parents"; prior to the 1960s, colleges and universities generally saw themselves as playing the role of parents; thus, daily life on campuses was restricted in ways that are currently unimaginable on nearly all campuses.

ubiquitous: found everywhere.

imprudence: lack of consideration for the possible consequences of one's actions.

to do "being drunk": researchers who focus on human interaction often use the phrase *to do X* to emphasize the fact that in much of daily life we are, in some profound sense, acting. Thus, *to do "being drunk"* means to behave as if one were drunk though one is, in fact, not.

In American popular culture, college—at the corner of adolescence and adulthood—represents a selective mimicry of "adult" hedonistic behaviors combined with youthful imprudence.° Undergraduates are customarily described as being frivolous, "'drowning' in a campus sea of secularism, hedonism, and materialism" (Magolda & Gross, 2009, p.315), and immersed in an "anti-intellectual student ethos" (Renn & Arnold, 2003, p. 263). Getting trashed, flirting with abandon, (aspiring to) wild promiscuity, cutting classes—these are all familiar tropes that popularly represent the college years in the popular imagination (CoEd Staff, 2008).

Peer culture constitutes marginality for many who are ugly, uncool, frumpy, unpopular, nonwhite, foreign, or poor. With important regional and rural-urban variations, "cool" students are (or seem) mellow or blasé in relation to, well, everything: academic work, sex, religion, morality, politics, and regulations—everything except having a good time. Nothing is supposed to faze normal youth, and certainly not a judicious measure of debauchery. If you were significantly disengaged from such "normal" youth behaviors, you would be marked as "different." And if you simply performed being drunk at parties the way my research participant Heather did during her high school days, well, "everyone else is being ridiculously drunk, so the fact that you're screaming, really no one knows whether you're drunk or not." You would *want* to do "being drunk"° when "everyone" is doing the same.

© Jim West/Photoshot

When sober, youth could only *pretend* to be part of the real fun. As for non-participants in hedonistic campus culture—and Latifa did not even attend parties, let alone feign inebriation—they were particularly marginal. To use a heuristic° spatial metaphor, the social world of undergraduate culture comprised a core, a periphery,° and a semi-periphery.° Members of campus culture who possessed the requisite cultural capital could locate themselves in the core, and others would be relegated to a lower status. Latifa was *peripheral* to campus culture. Even Heather—white, attractive, non-immigrant, and upper class—was in the cultural periphery. Within the secularity of campus culture, religiosity—particularly Islamic religiosity with its distinctive racial, political, and historical connotations—is commonly represented as "weird," incongruous, outdated, and marginal (Magolda & Gross, 2009). This cultural placement of individuals was a shifting affair, as the same person could be core, peripheral, or semi-peripheral depending on her actions and contextual factors.

heuristic: useful for thinking with.

periphery: the outside edges, as opposed to the core or center.

semi-periphery: the area near the outside edges.

College Peer Culture and Unauthorized or Informal Policy

The undergraduate social world is the site of crucial identity work° and the source of what Levinson, Sutton, and Winstead (2009) describe as "unauthorized or informal policy" (p. 768). Whatever "authorized policy" in the form of university policy statements may claim about diversity, student life, and alcohol, "normal" students drink: the designation of university spaces as "dry" and of underage students as non-drinking is often meaningless because "everyone" drinks in dorms and in bars with fake IDs.

identity work: the conscious and less-than-conscious energy individuals devote to creating a coherent identity for themselves as individuals and as members of social groups.

10 Many persons of admirable intent (myself included) are drawn to policy studies by the emancipatory° promise of virtuous power, believing that, when delivered top-down (by authorities within government, the policy community, higher education, etc.), policy promises to rid the world of injustice and create triumphant spaces of liberty and equality for marginal individuals and groups. Policy is a creature far more unpredictable and slippery and far less tractable° and pliant° than it is usually imagined. Rather than this top-down (unrealistic and incomplete) conception of policy, Levinson, Sutton, and Winstead (2009) conceive of policy broadly, unpacking° it "as a kind of social practice, specifically, a practice of power" or a "complex set of interdependent sociocultural practices" (pp. 767–68). In shaping undergraduate identities, the street-level practice of student leisure culture is far more compelling than university regulations. As peers are "the single most potent source of influence" (Astin, 1997, p. 398), the student community's unspoken consent forms much of the "unauthorized policy" world of undergraduates (Levinson, Sutton, & Winstead, 2009, p. 770). Systemic and powerful, unauthorized policy defeats Band-Aid solutions that are incompatible with cultural ideology and neutralizes the theater of much "diversity work."

emancipatory: liberating.

tractable: easily influenced or controlled.

pliant: bendable or flexible.

unpack: in academic contexts, to explain further.

The Discursive Construction of Muslim Americans

It does not take much scholarly research, ethnographic or otherwise, to know what most Americans tend to think when they meet a Muslim man, or a Muslim woman. In social encounters, the Muslim and the non-Muslim are both aware of a set of notions about Muslim traditionalism, fanaticism, anti-modernity, xenophobia,° violence, and gender oppression. In that shared psychological space, battles are won and lost; but the accusation hangs in the air, and the power differential remains. When an Arab or an African American is *essentialized* and assumed to have an essential, unchanging, fundamental, core identity—for example, being prone to fanaticism or violence—the awareness of this stereotype can inflict symbolic violence° and inwardly reduce the stereotyped individual (Bourdieu, 1977). The stereotyping gaze, manifested through a fearful glance, a racial slur, a snide joke, or a thoughtless remark, exercises power over stereotyped persons. People *construct* what we know about Others through *discourses*, or sets of ideas, expressed in words, attitudes, beliefs, and practices (Foucault, 1980, 1979; Fanon, [1952] 2008). People who circulate racial stereotypes in everyday speech, books, newspapers, television shows, movies, and music can be said to possess the discursive power to construct the truth about people of color and their supposedly *essential* identities.

xenophobia: fear of strangers or those who are different.

symbolic violence: social and cultural domination that those who are dominated may not even be aware of.

Among these essentializing stereotypes, *Orientalist* stereotypes project Muslims and Muslim societies as racially and religiously homogeneous and predictable and the opposite of the "West" (Said, 1978; Haddad, Smith, & Moore, 2006, pp. 21–40). Muslim men are exoticized and assumed to be homogeneously primitive, religious, threatening, misogynistic, oversexed, xenophobic, and violent, while Muslim females are perceived to be oppressed, fragile, immobile, shy, and hyperfeminine. As "the Western episteme,° supported by administrative, corporate and academic institutions, has enabled the West to simultaneously represent and dominate the Orient" (Kapoor, 2003, p. 562), Orientalism operates freely in diverse cultural and educational spaces in the multicultural metropolis (Mir, 2009, p. 250), remaining unnamed by virtue of its pervasiveness, exerting "intellectual authority over the Orient within Western culture" (Said, 1978, p. 19). So, whether a woman is jailed for adultery in Nigeria or a suicide bomber blows up a bus in Israel, the surveillance of Muslim Americans is ratcheted up, because they are symbolically representative of a worldwide Muslim community.

episteme: knowledge (in contrast to opinion or common belief).

A racist Orientalist image of the Muslim Other is the necessary corollary° to an idealized self-conception of "the West" (Said, 1978). Orientalist notions posit "us" as egalitarian, free, secular, and progressive, because "they" are authoritarian, backward, religious, and traditional. "We" are, in part,

corollary: a proposition that follows logically from something that has already been proved.

constructed by the Other's representations of us, and by our construction of the Other.

My Muslim American female participants continually encountered in the gaze of the Other this conviction about Muslim women's inferior status and underdeveloped personhood. Muslim women's religious identities were hypervisible in their social encounters on campus, and they were assumed to be "Muslim"—purely religious beings—*rather than* "American," in that exclusive binary.° For Muslim women, continued *double consciousness* (Du Bois, [1903] 1995) meant awareness that Americans believed Muslim women to be oppressed, immobile, weak, and hyperfeminine (as Muslim women) on the one hand and threatening, primitive, xenophobic, and fanatical (as Muslims) on the other. It meant that Muslim women were constantly aware of being considered irrevocably *different* and alien.

exclusive binary: either/or situation.

double consciousness: a term first used by W. E. B. Du Bois in *The Souls of Black Folk* (1903) to discuss the challenges of "always looking at one's self through the eyes of others" with reference to the situation of African Americans because they could not (and cannot) help but see themselves through their own eyes and the eyes of the dominant society. The metaphor is often applied to the situations of other marginalized groups.

15 Besides being a source of psychological strain for the minority individual, double consciousness° and the internalization of stereotypes can be a useful tool for comprehensive control by the modern nation-state of population groups that are subversive, suspect, or just plain eyesores. Since overt oversight and inordinate enforcement can be costly and violent, a system of internalized psychological self-surveillance can cause marginal groups to feel as though they are always being watched, with a minimum of state effort. In Foucault's° words: "There is no need for arms, physical violence, material constraints. Just a gaze. An inspecting gaze, a gaze which each individual under its weight will end by interiorisation to the point that he is his own overseer, each individual thus exercising this surveillance over, and against, himself. A superb formula: power exercised continuously and for what turns out to be minimal cost" (1980, p. 155).

Michel Foucault (1926–1984): French philosopher who died of AIDS, his work was much concerned with the relationship between knowledge and power and the nature of social control.

Covering to Be Normal

While Muslims, blacks, Latinos, Jews, and gays are stereotyped and imagined as having fixed core identities, identities are socially *constructed* rather than inherent, essential, and unchanging. Anthropological analysis indicates that our behaviors are not a pure manifestation of some inner unchanging core and that social interactions result in complex combinations of identities that, moreover, change in composition in different environments. Socially, we engage with people's opinions of us and with others' views on acceptable behavior. No one is entirely "free" to be who she is or wants to be. We are wrapped within a matrix°—of social connections, roles, personae, rituals, and expectations—that blocks entire worlds of possibility, in the manner of the Keanu Reaves° blockbuster. The roles and personae we adopt do not stay frozen forever; situationally, we don and remove roles like shoes, but—unlike

matrix: the political, cultural, and social environment within which something develops or occurs.

Keanu Reaves (1964–): Canadian actor, director, and musician who starred in the *Matrix* trilogy.

a pair of shoes—multiple identities may be worn at the same time in particular circumstances.

Certain types of identities are more stigmatized, more radioactive than others. In the United States, Muslim youth, like women and gays, learn to "play down" their "outsider identities to blend into the mainstream." The American dream holds out a promise: "Just conform, the dream whispers, and you will be respected, protected, accepted" (Yoshino, 2007, pp. 20–21). This (usually) unspoken *demand* to conform—the reason why "outsiders" play down racial, religious, sexual, and gendered identities—is wrapped into a promise for better things. Blacks, Latinos, Muslims, Asians, and professional women learn to disguise, or *cover* (Goffman, 1963), stigmatized identities in order to survive and succeed. Today, discrimination targets not entire racial or religious groups, but subgroups that fail to tone down awkward identities, to "*act* white, male, straight, Protestant, and able-bodied" (Yoshino, 2007, pp. 17–18), and to blend into the majority, conforming, harmonizing, and becoming all but indistinguishable. In this book, I explore Muslim American female students' responses to identity *constriction*, or to the demand to cover and mute their identities in campus culture.

Muslim American women regularly experience such identity silencing demands on campus. This is not to say that all Muslim American women who are indistinguishable from their peers are always responding to the demand to cover. It is to say that the *choice* to be openly, publicly Muslim is not an easy one because the stigma against Muslim identities breeds ambivalence, contradiction, and disavowal vis-à-vis° their identity backgrounds (Bhabha, 1994; Khan, 2002). Under the oppressive awareness of the stigma they bear, Muslim women often try to be "ordinary" (Sacks, 1984) by projecting "normal American" (mainstream Anglo, Judeo-Christian) identities. In table 1, I show the dominant constructions imposed on Muslim American women (left column), and their corresponding attempts at being normal in response to stereotypes (right column). This performance entails downplaying or "covering" their Muslim backgrounds, and sometimes even concealing Muslim identity to "pass" as "normal" (Goffman, 1963).

vis-à-vis: French for "face-to-face"; with respect to.

White Christian Americans are typically unaware of the existence of racism or of "covering demands" on racial and religious minorities. Minority persons, on the other hand, are acutely aware of the content of "normal American" identities, of what norms they must obey and what behaviors they must choose and reject to adopt or approximate such American normalcy. These choices form the generally hidden assumptions of a culture. Most people work to be "normal" in various ways, but through a fine-grained ethnographic analysis of marginal individuals' identity strategies I examine the process of becoming so. Ethnographically investigating how religious Muslim students *work* to "pass" as normal drinking and dating college students reveals "the strategies of the stigmatized" and how marginal individuals are unobtrusively silenced within college cultures. Such ethnographic analysis also shows how we all conform within "the routines that we all use unconsciously each day"—a clue to "every life's inevitable existential compromise" (Rymes & Pash, 2001, p. 280). Minority students frequently *perform* conformity, resistance, and accommodation to the hidden curriculum° of campus culture. By so doing, minority students explicate the hidden curriculum and the implicit assumptions and norms buried in everyday campus interactions. Ethnographic analysis of these performances reveals the cultural checkpoints that obstruct certain persons, behaviors, and ideas from crossing over into normalcy.

hidden curriculum: the lessons one learns at school that are not explicitly taught; those related to the beliefs, norms, and values that schools reward. Such lessons often replicate social inequality in complex ways by reinforcing assumptions about what society values.

Table 1. Stereotypes of Muslim Women and Their Performative Responses to Them

Stereotypes	***"Normal" Attributes***
Marginal	Core
Restricted, oppressed	Free, independent, exercising choice
Uptight, boring, a "stickler"	Uninhibited, easygoing, fun, broad-minded
Shy, timid	Confident, adventurous, extroverted
Naïve, provincial	Sophisticated, worldly, cosmopolitan
Terrorist, pugnacious	Peaceful, friendly, "mainstream" activist
"Extreme"	"Moderate"
Weird	Normal, ordinary

References

Abelmann, N. (2009). *The intimate university: Korean American students and the problems of segregation*. Durham, NC: Duke University Press.

Astin, A. W. (1997). *What matters in college? Four critical years revisited*. San Francisco, CA: Jossey-Bass.

Bhabha, H. (1994). *The location of culture*. London, England: Routledge.

Bourdieu, P. (1997). *Outline of a theory of practice*. (R. Nice, Trans.). Cambridge, England: Cambridge University Press.

CoEd Staff. (2008, August 6). The real campuses behind the top nineteen college movies of all time. *CoEd Magazine*. Retrieved from http://coedmagazine.com/

Du Bois, W. E. B. (1995). *The souls of black folk*. New York, NY: Signet/Penguin Books. (Original work published 1903)

Fanon, F. (2008). *Black skin, white masks*. (R. Philcox, Trans.). New York, NY: Grove Press.

Foucault, M. (1979). *Discipline and punish: The birth of the prison*. (A. Sheridan, Trans.). New York, NY: Vintage.

Foucault, M. (1980). *Power/knowledge: Selected interviews and other writings, 1972–1977*. (C. Gordon, Ed. and Trans.). Brighton, England: Harvester Press.

Goffman, E. (1963). *Stigma: Notes on the management of spoiled identity.* Englewood Cliffs, N.J.: Prentice Hall.

Haddad, Y. Y., Smith, J. I., & Moore, K. M. (2006). *Muslim women in America: The challenge of Islamic identity today.* Oxford, England: Oxford University Press.

Kapoor, I. (2003). Acting in a tight spot: Homi Bhabha's postcolonial politics. *New Political Science, 25*(4), 561–577.

Khan, S. (2002). *Aversion and desire: Negotiating Muslim female identity in the diaspora.* Toronto, Canada: Women's Press.

Levinson, B. A., Sutton, M., & Winstead, T. (2009). Education policy as a practice of power: Theoretical tools, ethnographic methods, democratic options. *Educational Policy, 23*(6), 767–795.

Magolda, P, & Gross, K. E. (2009). *It's all about Jesus! Faith as an oppositional collegiate subculture.* Sterling, VA: Stylus Publishing.

Miller, M. A. (2006, March–April). Religion on campus. *Change*, 6–7.

Mir, (2009). 'Not too college-like, not too normal': American Muslim undergraduate women's gendered discourses. *Anthropology and Education Quarterly* 40(3), 237–256.

Renn, K. A. (2000). Patterns of situational identity among biracial and multiracial college students. *Review of Higher Education, 23*(4), 399–420.

Renn, K. A., & Arnold, K. D. (2003). Reconceptualizing research on college student peer culture. *Journal of Higher Education, 74*(3), 261–291.

Rymnes, B., & Pash, D. (2001). Questioning identity: The case of one second-language learner. *Anthropology and Education Quarterly, 32*(3), 276–300.

Sacks, H. (1984). On doing 'being ordinary.' In J. M. Atkinson & J. Heritage (Eds.), *Structures of social action: Studies in conversation analysis* (pp. 413–429). Cambridge, England: Cambridge University Press.

Said, E. (1978). *Orientalism: Western conceptions of the Orient.* New York, NY: Vintage.

Yoshino, K. (2007). *Covering: The hidden assault on our civil rights.* New York, NY: Random House.

RESPOND •

1. What particular confluence of historical events has created the context (the "perfect storm") Mir discusses with respect to the challenges Muslim women face on college campuses?
2. In what ways is the situation of Muslim women on campus like that of all groups that might be labeled "marginalized"?
3. Do you agree with Mir's claim that much of college life—or at least campus life—focuses on sociability and hedonism? Why or why not?
4. During an interview about her book (which can be read at **http://bit.ly/1o2PpgF**), Mir was asked whether the women she studied had a

difficult time reconciling their identities as Muslims and Americans. Here is her reply:

> My participants knew that observers and others thought that their "Muslim" and "American" identities were in perpetual conflict. None of them said that they experienced this conflict. Where they saw conflict was in the way others saw what it means to be "American" and "Muslim." In other words, if you think an "American" young person is a White, Christian person who drinks at college then, yes, there is conflict between being "American" and an observant Muslim. There are certainly plenty of Muslims, Jews, Hindus, and Christians who do not participate in hedonistic youth culture, and plenty who do. When we assume that an "American" and/or a "Muslim" has an "essence" that is religious or irreligious, liberal or conservative, etc., that is when we engage with the problem of conflict between these incommensurable identities. Intisar (a Somali American student), for instance, is personally comfortable with praying in the prayer-room as well as attending a dance show; Teresa, a White convert, is comfortable with being an observant Muslim as well as smoking; but neither of them is comfortable being seen doing these "conflicting" things. The problem is not in being this complicated person. The problem is that the observer just can't take it all in. These real, complicated, mixed people simply do not compute.

What does Mir's comment teach us about the nature of identity, especially when one belongs to a group that is placed on the periphery? What does it teach us about the challenge of diversity on college campuses and in society generally?

5. Mir uses a large number of constructs from social theory to discuss the situation of the women she studied, including stigma, cultural capital, informal policy, Orientalist discourse, essentialism, double consciousness, and covering. Use one or more of these constructs to discuss the situation of other minority groups on campus.

6. Like most theorists in any discipline who currently write about issues of identity, Mir argues that it is socially constructed, that is, it is not simply something that is given or assigned but something that is achieved through a complex process—a dialogue, and often a painful one—with one's family, friends, and the communities of which one is a part. Not surprisingly, it often involves the feeling that one must cover aspects of one's identity, at least in certain contexts. **Write a causal essay** in which you examine some aspect of your understanding of your identity, including, perhaps, some prejudice that you possess that has changed over time. In the essay be sure to help readers understand the series of events that led you to change. (Chapter 11 discusses causal arguments. Chapters 2 and 3 on arguments based on emotion and character, respectively, will likely prove useful resources as well.)

median wage: the wage in the middle, when wages are arranged from lowest to highest. In cases where data are not evenly distributed, the median is the best measure of central tendency. Wages and housing prices are instances in which there are many data points at the low end but disproportionately far fewer ones at the high end. In such cases, tracking the median will give us more information than tracking the mean, or average.

knowledge economy: an economy based not on what one produces (e.g., in a factory or on a farm) but on what one knows or can do with information and knowledge.

structural barrier: a barrier in the social system that prevents someone from achieving a goal. For example, someone who is not comfortable using the Internet or does not have access to a computer with Wi-Fi will face challenges getting basic information about health care because much of that information is to be found online.

opportunity hoarding: a method whereby the elite maintain their advantages by limiting the access of other groups to the resources (e.g., attending schools that offer good educations) that originally afforded the elite their advantage.

▼ *Sheryll Cashin obtained her undergraduate engineering degree at Vanderbilt, but today she is a professor of law at Georgetown University, where she teaches courses on constitutional law as well as courses that deal with race as it relates to American law. Along the way, as she explains, she was a Marshall Scholar at Oxford and completed her law degree at Harvard. After law school, she clerked for Justice Thurgood Marshall. Cashin is a native of Huntsville, Alabama; both her parents were political activists during the civil rights era. She and her husband are the parents of two sons, a fact that influences how she thinks about issues of race and ethnicity in America, as you'll also see. This selection is the introduction to her latest book,* Place, Not Race: A New Vision of Opportunity in America *(2014), a book that is highly critical of affirmative action programs but one that likely offends many readers on the right as much as it offends many readers on the left. It is a densely argued book, drawing widely on legal precedent and theory, on the one hand, and social science research, on the other. It is also very much a book directly out of the prophetic tradition of the African American church, a book that challenges readers to imagine and work to realize a better society. As you read this selection, pay particular attention to how Cashin creates an ethos of trustworthiness and fairness.*

Introduction from *Place, Not Race: A New Vision of Opportunity in America*

SHERYLL CASHIN

This book is about fairness. The U.S. economy has become a pyramid in which nearly three-quarters of the jobs that will become available in this decade are predicted to pay a median wage° of less than $35,000 a year and require only a high school diploma or less.[1] The so-called knowledge economy° belongs to the few able to enter it, and the traditional gateway is selective higher education. I focus in this book on the structural barriers° to accessing high-opportunity colleges for this reason. Fairness requires that their doors be open to all exceptional achievers, not just those who are already advantaged. The stratifications of K-12 education are mirrored in higher education, and in both systems the phenomenon of "opportunity hoarding"° described by sociologist Charles Tilly seems to be at work.[2]

Those blessed to occupy golden neighborhoods and schools are most likely to enter equally golden colleges. Intentionally or not, they can block access by those outside their advantaged networks through in-group sanctioned practices like legacy preferences,° "merit" aid,° and the overuse of standardized test scores that track income status. Ironically, race-based affirmative action may also contribute to the hoarding phenomenon because advantaged racial minorities are most likely to benefit from the policy, and, as I argue, the optical diversity° this creates undermines the possibility that elite colleges will rethink exclusionary practices.

legacy preferences: preferences granted in college admissions to the children (or grandchildren) of an institution's graduates.

"merit" aid: financial aid awarded on the basis of achievement.

optical diversity: what appears to be diversity at first glance but is not, in fact, diversity in a broader, more representative sense.

In this book, I challenge universities to reform both affirmative action and the entire admissions process. But hoarding of selective education is only one strain of the unfairness that pervades America. My aim is to begin a larger conversation about how to create a politics of fairness that will help the vast majority of Americans who will not attend Harvard, Yale, or the University of Illinois.

A professional black woman describes to me her sister's fury when black children from low-income neighborhoods were given preferences to improve their access to sought-after magnet programs in Chicago public schools. The sister was angry when her middle class black kids who did not live in the 'hood did not gain entrance, although they had better academic records. Is this what America has come to—a country where advantaged people of all colors look at growing inequality and are reduced to invoking numerical standards that block out others, and complaining when those others do gain access? Is this the country you want to live in, dear reader?

Fairness in College Admissions

Abigail Fisher had a complaint that resonated with most Americans. The 5
cherub-faced strawberry blond wanted her dream school, the University of Texas, to evaluate her and her competitors without any consideration of race. She did not want to be seen as a white girl from a suburb named Sugar Land, presumably the wrong race and place in a withering competition that has gone global. Nor did she think it fair that other applicants might benefit from having more melanin.° "There were people in my class with lower grades who weren't in all the activities I was in, who were being accepted into UT, and the only difference between us was the color of our skin," she said in a YouTube video posted by her lawyers.[3]

melanin: the pigment that is primarily responsible for human skin color; greater concentrations of melanin result in darker skin color.

Her argument is one we've heard before. Blacks and Latinos with lower test scores and grades than hers got in and that, she concluded, violated her right to equal protection under the Constitution. It didn't matter to Fisher or her lawyers that forty-two white applicants with lower numbers than hers were also admitted. They focused on the theoretical possibility that the five applicants of color with lower scores who gained entrance may have succeeded where Fisher failed, solely because of their race.[4]

Who knows for certain why Fisher did not emerge from ambiguity? Had she graduated in the top 10 percent of her high school class, she would have gained automatic entrance to the flagship university° that both her father and sister attended. Instead she and other less stellar applicants had to compete head to head for the remaining 19 percent of slots in the UT Class of 2012. Her application probably landed in the "maybe" pile, its occupants neither obvious admits nor rejects. These are the applications conscientious admissions officers agonize over. A strong, authentic voice crying out from an absorbing personal essay or a soaring letter of recommendation that rings as true can make the difference.

flagship university: generally, the best-known, most selective, and best-funded university in a state system.

In addition to high school rank and standardized test scores, UT considered personal achievement based upon two essays and factors like leadership, socioeconomic status, and — the eternal bugaboo — race. Fisher's argument that race played a definitive role certainly resonates with how most white people feel about affirmative action in higher education. They think it is unfair to them and their children, and this explains why many institutions have been retreating from considering race in admissions.

The Supreme Court's 2013 compromise decision in *Fisher v. Texas* extended the life of race-based affirmative action. But there will always be another Abigail Fisher. When a disgruntled applicant sues, defenders of an affirmative action policy must convince the court that there are "no workable race-neutral alternatives" to achieve the educational benefits of diversity. Conservatives will continue to attack the policy in courts and through politics. With one exception, every time the issue of affirmative action has been placed on a state ballot, voters have banned the policy. As this book went to print, the Supreme Court had heard argument but not issued a decision in the case of *Schuette v. Coalition to Defend Affirmative Action,*° in which the ability of Michigan voters to ban affirmative action is challenged. At oral argument, conservative justices seemed inclined to uphold the ban. However the court rules, political opposition to use of race in college admissions will continue.

Schuette v. Coalition to Defend Affirmative Action: 2014 Supreme Court ruling that upheld Michigan's voter-sanctioned prohibition on the use of race in university admissions and other public institutions, with a limited number of exceptions.

This is particularly easy politics for Republicans. On the day Barack Obama 10
was re-elected president, voters in Oklahoma approved an amendment to their state constitution to prohibit affirmative action based upon race, gender, ethnicity, or national origin in public employment, education, and contracting.[5] At the time this was the third ban successfully sponsored by

Republican state legislators in three years. They no longer needed a black man, Ward Connerly,° for cover. Political mobilization against affirmative action accords with the mood of a browning country in which white guys increasingly feel victimized. White anxiety about changing demographics° shows up in online comments like one by "Andrew," who identified himself as living in the South. Opining° on a *New York Times* story about California universities that had responded to a state ban on racial preferences by spending as much as $85 million on outreach and mentoring to expand the pipeline of college-ready applicants of color, Andrew wrote:

> *Diversity* = fewer white people, even in places where white people are already a minority, both in terms of their representation in the general population and their presence on campuses. If judges ban affirmative action, the ideologues who run our institutions of higher education will simply ignore the law and proclaim "holistic admission practices" in order to decrease the number of white students admitted, much as they have done in California, Michigan, and elsewhere in recent years.

His was among the most recommended comments on the story, presumably because it resonated with many white readers. White anxiety will continue to rise as more whites become minorities in their states or communities. Institutions necessarily are changing to accommodate domestic demographic change and globalization. The future is Rice University: today, at this preeminent school founded on a "whites-only" charter, less than half of the undergraduates are white Americans.[6] At Rice, native students of color and international students are taking places that literally were once reserved for white people, and some whites are not dealing well with such transitions.

The Perception Gap

A student of mine testifies to the angst° whites share with him because he is a member of that club—honest tribal talk that I will only hear if a race traitor° like my student shares it with me. My student—I will call him Ted—tells me about a former Dalton School classmate who was livid when his four-year-old did not get into their alma mater's pre-K class, half of which was now populated by the rainbow. Dalton is an elite prep school on New York's Upper East Side with a reputation for progressivism° that decided in 2007 to make diversity "an integral part of school life," according to its mission statement. By 2011, the numbers of non-white kindergarteners went from 6 percent to 47 percent of the entering class, with predictable commentary from disappointed parents on UrbanBaby.com.[7] "*They* took my kid's spot!" Ted's

Ward Connerly (1939–): African American businessman, political activist, and former regent in the University of California system who worked tirelessly to oppose and dismantle any form of affirmative action.

Ward Connerly AP Photo/Bill Wolf

changing demographics: here, the shifting racial and ethnic makeup of the country.

opine: to offer an opinion; a verb used frequently in legal discourse.

angst: deep fear, dread, or anxiety.

race traitor: someone who acts (or is perceived to act) against the interest of his/her own racial or ethnic group; the term is almost always used pejoratively, that is, in a negative way.

progressivism: a movement that supports social justice and a number of social causes deemed liberal in the United States.

ostensibly liberal, shut-out former classmate exclaimed. Even one-percenters are forced to adapt. As Ted relates the story to me, he titters with nervous laughter and recognition. When friends or strangers raise this complaint, should he question their underlying assumptions of entitlement and superiority, or just let them vent?

Such gripes, and worse, are easy to find online. Just read the comments to any news story about affirmative action. Jonica Witherspoon, a graduate of Northwestern, confessed to a reporter in the *Chicago Sun-Times* that given her scores on standardized tests, she "probably wouldn't have made the cut to attend Northwestern" if she were not African American. She did not begrudge affluent Jamaicans and Nigerians, "who may have taken a spot that would have gone to somebody from, say, Chicago's West Side." "It's good for you," she said. "You see these successful, smart people out there who are black and you think, 'Maybe I can be one of them. Maybe I can do better.'"[8] An online commenter identified as Razz Barry felt differently: "I resent her taking the place of some white man, with higher test scores, who may have discovered a cure for cancer, invented a fuel to end our dependency on Arab oil . . ." He trailed off.

Barry's suggestion that affirmative action squelches opportunity for would-be white heroes overlooks the fact that Superman leaps over obstacles. Were he rejected by Northwestern, most likely Clark Kent would be accepted and thrive elsewhere. Abigail Fisher declined an offer to attend a different Texas institution, with a possibility of later transferring to UT. Instead she sued, leaving her case to activist lawyers and heading off to Louisiana State University, where she graduated with a degree in finance in 2012. Through her own resilience and determination, her life did not grind to a halt. That said, many people feel her pain.

In a 2012 Rasmussen poll, 55 percent of respondents opposed affirmative action in college admissions.[9] In a 2009 Quinnipiac University poll of registered voters, 55 percent said affirmative action should be abolished.[10] Although proponents of affirmative action argue that such programs advance only qualified minorities and don't disadvantage others, as the Quinnipiac pollsters put it, "voters see a zero-sum game° in which someone—generally white males—loses when someone else gains."[11] For the white parent who fills Adderall prescriptions for a teenager for whom "above average" is not good enough, observing Cosby kids° advance is a provocation.

Although legions of non-blacks and women have benefited from affirma- 15
tive action, inconveniently for its proponents, the policy has a black face and remains a dog whistle° for political mobilization. It is hard for non-blacks to see blacks as disadvantaged and needing affirmative action when examples

zero-sum game: a situation in which one person's or group's gain necessarily represents a loss for someone else or another party. An example would be sharing a pie: the larger my piece, the smaller yours will necessarily be.

Cosby kids: reference to the animated television program that ran from 1972 to 1985; it was created and hosted by Bill Cosby and was based on his recollections of childhood friends.

dog whistle: an ultrasonic whistle that dogs can hear but humans can't; used here metaphorically.

of black success are ubiquitous,° from Obama to Oprah to Jay Z, not to mention black bosses non-blacks may report to, fictional black surgeons and lawyers they encounter on TV, and well-dressed black people driving expensive cars they occasionally notice on their daily commute. Americans are also now regularly offered steamy examples of interracial romance on small and large screens. Even a dark-skinned brother is now allowed to seduce a pale woman, the ultimate suggestion of black equality.

ubiquitous: found everywhere.

While non-blacks see real and virtual examples of black success every day, they don't see black poverty, because they are removed from the deprivations of ghetto neighborhoods. Not surprisingly, only 49 percent of participants in a 2009 Pew survey believed that African Americans were subject to "a lot of discrimination." A majority of survey participants did perceive *other* groups as enduring serious discrimination: Latinos (52 percent), Muslims (58 percent), and gays and lesbians (64 percent).[12]

African Americans have arrived, in the minds of many non-blacks. In a 2007 Pew survey of racial attitudes, 84 percent of participants had a favorable view of African Americans, while only 10 percent expressed an unfavorable view of them.[13] Since Barack Obama was elected president, however, more people express explicitly anti-black views.[14] And a large body of research by social psychologists demonstrates that most people harbor subconscious biases about black people.[15] Americans remain complicated about race. We are at war with ourselves inside our heads. Despite biases against "the other," the vast majority of all Americans view racial discrimination as wrong, even un-American, and self-identify as anti-racist. Their anti-racist identity coupled with ubiquitous examples of black success likely inform their judgment that affirmative action is unfair and no longer necessary.

Trayvon-esque: in the manner of Trayvon Martin (1995–2012), an African American youth who was shot and killed by George Zimmerman, who was a member of a neighborhood watch group.

Trayvon Martin AP Photo/The Miami Herald/Marsha Halper

In opinion polls, African Americans register the strongest support for affirmative action. This is not hard to understand. Those on the receiving end of real or perceived racial discrimination—from taxis that pass them by to security guards who trail them in clothing stores to bad schools or incarcerated family members—also harbor a sense of grievance. The civil rights revolution is not over yet. Watching Obama on TV and the race pride that engenders does not make up for twice the unemployment, nearly three times the poverty, and six times the incarceration that white people endure.[16] In the consciously black mind, history and present-day inequalities are frontal. Black folks live with a constant awareness of the myriad ways in which race can obstruct, interfere, or in nightmarish, Trayvon-esque° scenarios, ruin one's life. For many African Americans, affirmative action is a modest palliative,° but a fair one, given the systemic forces black people endured historically and continue to face.

palliative: a treatment that eases pain but does not deal with the underlying causes of the pain.

As I describe in this book, these gaps of perception about race undermine possibilities for opponents and proponents of affirmative action to join forces to make systems of education and opportunity better and more responsive to everyone. To borrow an apt phrase from a self-described "gun guy" who seeks common ground between his gun-toting brothers and gun-control advocates who may be clueless or dismissive about the culture of huntsmen, "there is no tree for these folks to gather under."[17] On the issue of affirmative action, there are no forums for addressing common concerns, or even building a sense of the common good. The civil rights tent is not viewed as a place where the concerns of struggling whites will be heard. Movement conservatives° allied against affirmative action are viewed with suspicion by many people of color. This perception gap puts universities that are serious about diversity in a quandary. Going forward, should they still try to use race and risk lawsuits from disappointed white applicants? Or risk the ire of Republican state legislators who have picked up the movement Ward Connerly began?

movement conservatives: a term used by U.S. political conservatives to describe those whose conservative ideology focuses on the evils of big government.

I prefer place, rather than race, as the focus of affirmative action for the 20
pragmatic reason that it will foster more social cohesion and a better politics. More importantly, it will help those *actually* disadvantaged by segregation. Those who suffer the deprivations of high-poverty neighborhoods and schools are deserving of special consideration. Those blessed to come of age in poverty-free havens are not. Race still matters in American society, particularly in the criminal justice system. But race is under-inclusive. As Walter Benn Michaels, professor at the University of Illinois, bluntly put it to the *Journal of Blacks in Higher Education*: "When students and faculty activists struggle for cultural diversity, they are in large part battling over what skin color the rich kids have."[18]

As I will show in subsequent chapters, race does not, by definition, capture those who suffer the structural disadvantages of segregated schools and neighborhoods. Race is also over-inclusive in that it can capture people with dark skin who are exceedingly advantaged. African immigrants, on average, are better educated than *every* American subgroup, including Asians and whites. The mantra° of diversity might be applied to a school that admits African elites or their American cousins, like Sasha, Malia,° Blue Ivy,° or my kids. But diversity by phenotype° puts no pressure on institutions to dismantle underlying systems of exclusion that propagate inequality.

mantra: a frequently repeated slogan or motto.

Sasha, Malia: the Obama daughters.

Blue Ivy: the daughter of Beyoncé Knowles and Shawn "Jay Z" Carter.

phenotype: appearance in terms of a society's racial or ethnic categories.

When President Lyndon Johnson framed the argument for affirmative action at a commencement address at Howard University in 1965, the Civil Rights Act of 1964 was an infant. The antidiscrimination principle the act embodied, so widely embraced today, was also new and meeting resistance. About half of blacks, still "Negroes" at the time, lived below the poverty line. The black middle class was beginning to emerge. A two-parent black professional family, for example a teacher and an equal employment opportunity officer at IBM, would likely have been trained at historically black institutions and needed a lift to gain entry into predominately white ones. Centuries of exclusionary habits didn't die easily; affirmative efforts were needed, Johnson argued. "This is the next and more profound stage of the battle for civil rights," he intoned. "We seek not just freedom . . . but equality as a fact and as a result."[19]

Back then, race and gender were appropriate markers for the type of exclusion practiced by most predominately white universities. Today, place is a more appropriate indicator of who gets excluded from consideration by admissions officers at selective institutions. Every high school in America has a cadre° of strivers. Diversity by skin color enables universities to bypass achievers from inner-city, rural, and struggling suburban environs—kids who weren't handed perfection but did their very best with what they had. Phenotypic diversity also assuages what is left of white guilt and helps mask exclusion. Affluent people of all colors who call an SAT score merit are complicit in this.

cadre: a committed group.

The Promise of *Brown v. Board of Education*°

Brown v. Board of Education *(1954):* landmark Supreme Court ruling that struck down segregated schooling; for many, this court decision signals a major shift in American society's understanding of racial issues.

In 1954, the Supreme Court determined that segregated public education deprived "children of the minority group" of equal educational opportunity. Six decades later, public education remains largely segregated. As we celebrate or distance ourselves from the latest decennial anniversary of the Supreme Court's decision in *Brown v. Board of Education*, we must contend with the reality that high-quality K-12 education is not widely distributed. The discourse in America about segregation is dishonest. On the surface, we pretend that the values of *Brown v. Board of Education* have been met, although most of us know in our hearts that public education usually betrays those values.

25 This result was not inevitable. As a post–civil rights baby, I attended integrated public schools in Alabama during the era when the state and nation were making good on the promise of *Brown v. Board of Education*. I graduated from S. R. Butler High School in Huntsville in 1980. At the time it was one of the largest schools in the state. Our mascot was the Butler Rebel, a confederate colonel who appeared more avuncular° than defiant. Butler was an integrated but majority-white powerhouse in sports and a place where a nerd like me could take Advanced Placement classes and gain entrance to great colleges. Kids from housing projects and sturdy, middle-class neighborhoods attended the same school, albeit with a degree of sorting into racially identifiable academic tracks. We played on sports fields together, attended the same "fifth quarter" dances, and generally got along.

avuncular: like an uncle.

At our thirtieth reunion, my classmates and I bemoaned Butler's demise. Enrollment at the school we had thrived at and loved had dwindled to 35 percent of capacity, depleted by demographic change. It had become an impoverished, predominately black, low-opportunity school and the object of derision, despite its string of state basketball championships in the 2000s. Barely half of its seniors graduated, and its students *were* being "left behind" as families with options moved on and standardized test scores declined. Middle-class people exited the neighborhoods surrounding the school, opting for greener, higher-opportunity acres in rapidly growing suburban Madison County. The state accelerated the school's isolation when it built an interstate highway connector that mowed down scores of homes in Butler's attendance zone. As in most other cities where links to the interstate were laid decades before, this created a concrete firewall between the majority-white, affluent and majority-black, declining sides of town, with predictable results for our alma mater. A similar story of race and class segregation could be told in most American cities with a critical mass of people of color.

I feel blessed to have come of age in the 1970s, when there was still much opportunity to live a middle-class life. Despite being the child of broke activists who paid dearly for challenging Alabama-style apartheid,° my high-quality, free public education set me on an extraordinary path. As a co-valedictorian from Butler, I was able to enter Vanderbilt University on an honors scholarship and found that, despite an SAT score that was solid but not stratospheric, Butler had prepared me to compete. I chose to study engineering because Wernher von Braun° had made rocket science a common occupation in Huntsville and it was an easy route to scholarships and financial security for a black girl who got As in physics and trigonometry.

apartheid: a policy of racial segregation, usually associated with South Africa.

Wernher von Braun (1912–1977): the father of the modern rocket. Born in Germany, he immigrated to the United States in 1945.

Vanderbilt became my financial parent, as did the British government when I parlayed a summa degree in electrical engineering into a Marshall Scholarship to study law at Oxford University. I recall writing a letter from Oxford to my AP English teacher at Butler, Mrs. Calloway, thanking her for teaching me how to compose a coherent essay. As I endured the trauma of the British approach to finals—eight closed-book exams in eight days covering two years of material—I was steadied by the fundamentals of good writing that I learned from this gifted, passionate public school teacher. I went on to graduate from Harvard Law School and to work as a law clerk for Justice Thurgood Marshall, the chief oral advocate for *Brown* who had done so much to make my trajectory possible.

As my generation of post–civil rights era babies was integrating schools and preparing for life, politicians started culture wars, a war on drugs, and a cynical politics of racial resentment. And our nation retreated from the promise of *Brown*. Ten years ago, in marking the fiftieth anniversary of the decision, I wrote a book with the happy title *The Failures of Integration* arguing that the only route to true equality was the hardest one, integration. Since then racial segregation in neighborhoods has continued to decline modestly, even as the affluent have become more separated from everyone else. As a result, place—where one lives—powerfully structures opportunity. Exclusion from the good life, good schools and jobs, and middle-class stability is no longer based primarily on race, as was the case in the Jim Crow° era. While race certainly plays a role in the geographic sorting that goes on in residential housing markets, it is no longer a definitive marker for who is disadvantaged, because a person of color who has the means can escape admittedly racialized segregation. Meanwhile, for those of any color relegated to low-opportunity environs, geography is largely destiny.

Jim Crow: the term used for the laws in the southern United States that institutionalized legal racial segregation; put in place during Reconstruction, these laws were in force until 1965, although they continue to have consequences of various sorts with regard to matters like housing patterns.

Sign over a segregated restroom.
AP/Wide World Photos

In this book I reflect on how twenty-first-century segregation contributes 30
to the achievement gap that has made race-based affirmative action necessary. Less than one-third of black and Latino children live in middle-class neighborhoods; exposure to extensive poverty is the norm for most of them, while the opposite is true for most white and Asian children. That said, not all white and Asian children are privileged, and not all black and Latino children are poor.

Moral Clarity

The rub for proponents of affirmative action is that as long as they hold on to race as the *sine qua non*° of diversity, they stymie possibilities for transformative change. The civil rights community, for example, expends energy on a policy that primarily benefits the most advantaged children of color, while contributing to a divisive politics that makes it difficult to create quality K-12 education for all children. I argue that the next generation of diversity strategies should encourage rather than discourage cross-racial alliances and social mobility. I contend that meaningful diversity can be achieved if institutions rethink exclusionary practices, cultivate strivers from overlooked places, and give special consideration to highly qualified applicants of all races that have had to overcome structural disadvantages like segregation. I call it "diversity practice" because we need to jettison° the label affirmative action, with its loaded meanings, and create new, fairer structures of opportunity through daily effort. The goal, over time, is to create a society where getting ahead is not a function of circumstances of birth.

sine qua non: Latin for "without which (there is) nothing"; essential condition or element, prerequisite.

jettison: to discard, generally by throwing overboard.

That august° task will require a more cohesive politics, and any winning majority necessarily will be multiracial. Our present collective goal must be the same one Dr. Martin Luther King Jr. articulated at the dawn of the civil rights movement. In championing nonviolence as the means to dismantling

august: noble, dignified, stately.

Jim Crow, King always reminded his audience of his ultimate vision for America. "[T]he end is reconciliation; the end is redemption," he said, and "the creation of the beloved community." To "make it possible for men to live together as brothers in a community, and not continually live with bitterness and friction"—that was King's end, and the unfinished work to which each generation of Americans must be dedicated.[20]

The moral authority that flowed from John Lewis° and others volunteering to get their heads beat in on the Edmund Pettus Bridge° did much to render the movement "everybody's fight"—the words Viola Liuzzo° used to justify leaving her five children in Michigan to join with civil rights activists in Alabama. King saw in the Freedom Riders and his increasingly multiracial band of civil rights soldiers an early example of the beloved community he espoused. The movement itself could be an approximation of the spirit of agape° love and community that he envisioned for the whole of America. One expression of this love for community was seeing the mutuality in all types of human suffering. As King famously said, "Injustice anywhere is a threat to justice everywhere."[21] In the end, he did not turn away from the hardest part of community building. In his last book, King wrote, "Our loyalties must transcend our race, our tribe, our class, and our nation."[22]

There are obvious lessons here for proponents of diversity. Race-based affirmative action buys some diversity for a relative few, but not serious inclusion. It doesn't help to build a movement to attack underlying systems of inequality that are eating away at the soul of our nation. Among other transformations, we need corporations that share more profits with workers and pay them equitably. We need a financial system that doesn't exploit average people. We need governments that invest wisely in pre–K-12 education and the nonselective higher education that at least half of high school graduates attend. We also need government that does not over-incarcerate high school dropouts of all colors.[23]

35 The means of race pushes away potential allies in a way that makes it mathematically impossible to build multiracial alliances for sanity and common sense. Throughout this book, I draw on social science research to explain how race can and cannot be used effectively to build cross-racial alliances. In the context of promoting diversity on college campuses, place is a better mechanism that will also encourage alliances among those mutually excluded by current systems. Ultimately, I argue that, given our nation's failure to live up to *Brown*, we have an obligation to acknowledge and ameliorate° the injustices of segregation—a moral imperative more important than diversity itself. The idea of America will only become true when those who suffer mutual oppressions unite to create real opportunity for everyone.

John Lewis (1940–): civil rights activist and member of the House of Representatives from Georgia (1987–). He is the only living member of the "Big Six," the men who led the civil rights movement.

Edmund Pettus Bridge: Selma, Alabama, bridge named for a Confederate army officer and site of one of the bloodiest events of the civil rights era when, on March 7, 1965, armed officers attacked nonviolent demonstrators as they sought to cross the bridge.

Viola Liuzzo (1925–1965): a martyr of the civil rights era. Liuzzo, a Unitarian Universalist civil rights activist, traveled from her Michigan home to participate in the marches in Selma, Alabama. While there, she was shot by members of the Ku Klux Klan.

agape: selfless or unconditional love, a term from Greek, where *agape* contrasts with the love of intimate partners (*eros*), love between siblings or friends (*philia*), and the love of parents for their children or vice versa (*storge*).

ameliorate: improve.

Notes

1. C. Brett Lockhard and Michael Wolf, "Employment Outlook 2010–2020: Occupational Employment Projections to 2020," *Monthly Labor Review* 84 (January 2012): 106, table 6, which identifies "[j]ob openings due to growth and replacement needs, 2010–2020."
2. Charles Tilly, "How to Hoard Opportunities," in *Durable Inequality* (Berkeley: University of California Press, 1998), 147–69.
3. "Abigail Fisher v. University of Texas at Austin," YouTube video, posted by "FairRepresentation," September 4, 2012, http://www.youtube.com/watch?v=sXSpx9PZZj4.
4. Brief for Respondents University of Texas at Austin at 16, Fisher v. University of Texas at Austin, 132 S. Ct. 1536 (2012), no. 11–345.
5. Okla. Const. art. 2, § 36.
6. Rice University Office of Institutional Research, *Students and Scholars: Race and Ethnicity*, http://oir.rice.edu/Factbook/Students/Enrollment/Race_and_Ethnicity.
7. Sophia Hollander, "At Dalton, a Push for Change," *Wall Street Journal*, August 11, 2011, online.wsj.com/article/SB10001424053111903918104576500653887399330.html.
8. Tom McNamee, "Who Really Benefits from Colleges' Affirmative Action?" *Chicago Sun-Times*, July 19, 2004.
9. Rasmussen Reports, "55% Oppose Affirmative Action Policies for College Admissions," February 16, 2012, http://www.rasmussenreports.com/public_content/politics/general_politics/february_2012/55_oppose_affirmative_action_policies_for_college_admissions.
10. Quinnipiac University Polling Institute, "US Voters Disagree 3–1 with Sotomayor on Key Case, Quinnipiac University National Poll Finds; Most Say Abolish Affirmative Action," June 3, 2009, http://www.quinnipiac.edu/institutes-and-centers/polling-institute/national/release-detail?ReleaseID=1307.
11. Ibid.
12. Pew Research Center Religion and Public Life Project, "Muslims Widely Seen as Facing Discrimination," September 9, 2009, http://www.pewforum.org/2009/09/09/muslims-widely-seen-as-facing-discrimination.
13. Paul Taylor, "Race, Ethnicity and Campaign '08," Pew Research Center, January 17, 2008, http://www.pewresearch.org/2008/01/17/race-ethnicity-and-campaign-08.
14. In 2012, "51 percent of Americans express[ed] explicit anti-black attitudes, compared with 48 percent in a similar 2008 survey. When measured by an implicit racial attitudes test, the number of Americans with anti-black sentiments jumped to 56 percent, up from 49 percent during the last presidential election." Sonya Ross and Jennifer Agiesta, "AP Poll: Majority Harbor Prejudice against Blacks," Associated Press, October 27, 2012, http://bigstory.ap.org/article/ap-poll-majority-harbor-prejudice-against-blacks.
15. See Jerry Kang, "Trojan Horses of Race," *Harvard Law Review* 118 (2005): 1489–1593, which presents an overview of social psychology literature on implicit bias.
16. Pew Research Center Social and Demographic Trends Project, "King's Dream Remains an Elusive Goal; Many Americans See Racial Disparities," August 22, 2013, http://www.pewsocialtrends.org/files/2013/08/final_full_report_racial_disparities.pdf.
17. Joe Nocera, "What Gun Lovers Think," *New York Times*, April 6, 2013, www.nytimes.com/2013/04/07/opinion/sunday/nocera-what-gun-lovers-think.html?pagewanted=all&_r=o.
18. "Most Black Students at Harvard Are from High-Income Families," *Journal of Blacks in Higher Education* 52 (Summer 2006): 13.

19. Lyndon B. Johnson, "To Fulfilll These Rights" (speech, Washington, DC, June 4, 1965), LBJ Presidential Library, http://www.lbjlib.utexas.edu/johnson/archives.hom/speeches.hom/650604.asp.
20. Martin Luther King Jr., "Justice without Violence" (speech, Waltham, MA, April 4, 1957), King Center, http://www.thekingcenter.org/archive/document/mlk-justice-without-violence.
21. Martin Luther King Jr., "Letter from Birmingham Jail," in *Why We Can't Wait* (New York: Harper & Row, 1964), 77–100.
22. Martin Luther King Jr., *A Testament of Hope: The Essential Writings and Speeches of Martin Luther King, Jr.* (New York: HarperCollins, 1990), 253.
23. Sam Dillon, "Study Finds High Rate of Imprisonment among Dropouts," *New York Times*, October 9, 2009, www.nytimes.com/2009/10/09/education/09dropout.html?_r=o.

RESPOND •

1. For Cashin, what's wrong with affirmative action? What does she propose instead?
2. As noted in the introductory material on page 712, Cashin's position and the claims she makes sooner or later offend nearly everyone. Think of the various aspects of Cashin's arguments that various groups—liberals, conservatives, African Americans, white Americans, graduates of elite schools, etc.—will probably not find pleasing about her position.
3. What sort of ethos does Cashin create? How does she demonstrate her educational background? Her membership in the African Ameri can community and her loyalty to it? (Here, be sure to consider the language she uses as well as the cultural allusions she employs.) The values to which she is committed? (See Chapter 3 for information about arguments based on character.)
4. In what ways is Cashin's book an American book? Putting aside the historical and social contexts, what "American" values does Cashin seek to appeal to in her readers, regardless of their own personal background or political affiliation? (See Chapter 2 on arguments based on pathos, or appeals to the audience's emotions and values.)
5. Pay careful attention to how Cashin structures her argument and how she acknowledges the perspectives held by others. How specifically is her argument structured? Try to summarize her argument, putting it in the form of a Toulmin argument. (See Chapter 7 for a discussion of Toulmin argumentation.)
6. **Write an evaluative argument** in which you seek to evaluate Cashin's proposal that place, rather than race or ethnicity, should be the primary concern of those committed to fairness in American society. Obviously, you'll need to restate her position fairly (something question 5 should help you do) and to give the criteria you use in evaluating her position. (Chapter 10 on evaluative arguments will help you here.)

▼ *Walter Benn Michaels is currently a professor of English at the University of Illinois at Chicago, where he teaches literary theory and American literature. His influential essay "Against Theory," coauthored with Steven Knapp, was published in 1982, and his books include* The Shape of the Signifier: 1967 to the End of History *(2004). This selection is an excerpt from the introduction to his book* The Trouble with Diversity: How We Learned to Love Identity and Ignore Inequality *(2006). Michaels begins this selection with an extended discussion of a literary text, F. Scott Fitzgerald's* The Great Gatsby, *one of the most famous American novels, which was published in 1925. Its central character, Jay Gatsby, seeks to win back Daisy Buchanan, a beautiful woman whom he had courted years earlier when he was a poor soldier but who had married a man from an "old money" background like her own. After meeting her, Gatsby changed his name to cover up his German immigrant roots at a time when people of most immigrant backgrounds were not fully accepted in elite society. He had also become wealthy, but his money was "new money"; though readers never learn exactly where it comes from, its sources are clearly disreputable and likely illegal. Many scholars now see* The Great Gatsby *as one of the best literary depictions and critiques of American life and values. While you read this selection, consider how his arguments mesh and do not mesh with those of Sheryll Cashin in the introduction to her book* Place, Not Race.

The Trouble with Diversity: How We Learned to Love Identity and Ignore Inequality

WALTER BENN MICHAELS

"The rich are different from you and me" is a famous remark supposedly made by F. Scott Fitzgerald to Ernest Hemingway,° although what made it famous—or at least made Hemingway famously repeat it—was not the remark itself but Hemingway's reply: "Yes, they have more money." In other words, the point of the story, as Hemingway told it, was that the rich really aren't very different from you and me. Fitzgerald's mistake, he thought, was that he mythologized or sentimentalized the rich, treating them as if they were a different kind of person instead of the same kind of person with more money. It was as if,

Ernest Hemingway (1899–1961): an American writer and Nobel Prize winner. His first novel was *The Sun Also Rises* (1926).

A. S. Alexander Collection of Ernest Hemingway. Department of Rare Books and Special Collections, Princeton University Library.

according to Fitzgerald, what made rich people different was not what they *had*—their money—but what they *were*, "a special glamorous race."

To Hemingway, this difference—between what people owned and what they were—seemed obvious, and it was also obvious that the important thing was what they were. No one cares much about Robert Cohn's° money in *The Sun Also Rises*, but everybody feels the force of the fact that he's a "race-conscious" "little kike."° And whether or not it's true that Fitzgerald sentimentalized the rich and made them more glamorous than they really were, it's certainly true that he, like Hemingway, believed that the fundamental differences—the ones that really mattered—ran deeper than the question of how much money you had. That's why in *The Great Gatsby*, the fact that Gatsby has made a great deal of money isn't quite enough to win Daisy Buchanan back. Rich as he has become, he's still "Mr. Nobody from Nowhere," not Jay Gatsby but Jimmy Gatz. The change of name is what matters. One way to look at *The Great Gatsby* is as a story about a poor boy who makes good, which is to say, a poor boy who becomes rich—the so-called American dream. But *Gatsby* is not really about someone who makes a lot of money; it is instead about someone who tries and fails to change who he is. Or, more precisely, it's about someone who pretends to be something he's not; it's about Jimmy Gatz pretending to be Jay Gatsby. If, in the end, Daisy Buchanan is very different from Jimmy Gatz, it's not because she's rich and he isn't (by the end, he is) but because Fitzgerald treats them as if they really do belong

Robert Cohn: a Jewish character in *The Sun Also Rises* who develops an inferiority complex as a result of his outsider status.

kike: an ethnic slur referring to Jews that was widely used in the early twentieth century.

Leonardo DiCaprio played the lead in the 2013 film The Great Gatsby.
Kobal Collection at Art Resource, NY

to different races, as if poor boys who made a lot of money were only "passing" as rich. "We're all white here," someone says, interrupting one of Tom Buchanan's racist outbursts. Jimmy Gatz isn't quite white enough.

What's important about *The Great Gatsby*, then, is that it takes one kind of difference (the difference between the rich and the poor) and redescribes it as another kind of difference (the difference between the white and the not-so-white). To put the point more generally, books like *The Great Gatsby* (and there have been a great many of them) give us a vision of our society divided into races rather than into economic classes. And this vision has proven to be extraordinarily attractive. Indeed, it's been so attractive that the vision has survived even though what we used to think were the races have not. In the 1920s, racial science° was in its heyday; now very few scientists believe that there are any such things as races. But many of those who are quick to remind us that there are no biological entities called races are even quicker to remind us that races have not disappeared; they should just be understood as social entities instead. And these social entities have turned out to be remarkably tenacious, both in ways we know are bad and in ways we have come to think of as good. The bad ways involve racism, the inability or refusal to accept people who are different from us. The good ways involve just the opposite: embracing difference, celebrating what we have come to call diversity.

Indeed, in the United States, the commitment to appreciating diversity emerged out of the struggle against racism, and the word *diversity* itself began to have the importance it does for us today in 1978 when, in *Bakke v. Board of Regents*,° the Supreme Court ruled that taking into consideration the race of an applicant to the University of California (in this case, it was the medical school at UC Davis) was an acceptable practice if it served "the interest of diversity." The point the Court was making here was significant. It was not asserting that preference in admissions could be given, say, to black people because they had previously been discriminated against. It was saying instead that universities had a legitimate interest in taking race into account in exactly the same way they had a legitimate interest in taking into account what part of the country an applicant came from or what his or her nonacademic interests were. They had, in other words, a legitimate interest in having a "diverse student body," and racial diversity, like geographic diversity, could thus be an acceptable goal for an admissions policy.

5 Two things happened here. First, even though the concept of diversity was not originally connected with race (universities had long sought diverse student bodies without worrying about race at all), the two now came to be firmly associated. When universities publish their diversity statistics today, they're not talking about how many kids come from Oregon. My

racial science: the scientific investigation of and debate about matters related to race. The field often attracts those who are seeking to find evidence for the existence of distinct races and for ranking them in a hierarchy, though many scientists studying these issues disavow both aims.

Bakke v. Board of Regents: *Regents of the University of California v. Bakke*, a 1978 U.S. Supreme Court decision. Bakke, a white man, claimed that he had been discriminated against in violation of federal and state laws when he was not admitted to the UC-Davis medical school in 1973 and 1974 even though nonwhite candidates with significantly lower test scores were. In a 5–4 decision, the court ruled that quota systems for admissions are illegal but that schools can consider race as one of many factors in admissions decisions. (Subsequent Supreme Court decisions have largely maintained this position.) Bakke was later admitted to and graduated from the UC-Davis medical school; his name and this case continue to be associated with the notion of reverse discrimination.

university—the University of Illinois at Chicago—is ranked as one of the most diverse in the country, but well over half the students in it come from Chicago. What the rankings measure is the number of African Americans and Asian Americans and Latinos we have, not the number of Chicagoans.

end run: a football play in which the person carrying the ball tries to run around the end of the opposing team's line. As a figure of speech, it is any action that tries to get around opponents or difficulties without confronting them directly, often through the use of trickery.

And, second, even though the concept of diversity was introduced as a kind of end run° around the historical problem of racism (the whole point was that you could argue for the desirability of a diverse student body without appealing to the history of discrimination against blacks and so without getting accused by people like Alan Bakke of reverse discrimination against whites), the commitment to diversity became deeply associated with the struggle against racism. Indeed, the goal of overcoming racism, which had sometimes been identified as the goal of creating a "color-blind" society, was now reconceived as the goal of creating a diverse, that is, a color-conscious, society.[1] Instead of trying to treat people as if their race didn't matter, we would not only recognize but celebrate racial identity. Indeed, race has turned out to be a gateway drug for all kinds of identities, cultural, religious, sexual, even medical. To take what may seem like an extreme case, advocates for the disabled now urge us to stop thinking of disability as a condition to be "cured" or "eliminated" and to start thinking of it instead on the model of race: we don't think black people should want to stop being black; why do we assume the deaf want to hear?[2]

The general principle here is that our commitment to diversity has redefined the opposition to discrimination as the appreciation (rather than the elimination) of difference. So with respect to race, the idea is not just that racism is a bad thing (which of course it is) but that race itself is a good thing. Indeed, we have become so committed to the attractions of race that (as I've already suggested above [. . .]) our enthusiasm for racial identity has been utterly undiminished by scientific skepticism about whether there is any such thing. Once the students in my American literature classes have taken a course in human genetics, they just stop talking about black and white and Asian races and start talking about black and European and Asian cultures instead. We love race, and we love the identities to which it has given birth.

Michaels offers several different arguments, but perhaps the richest and most complex is his causal argument that traces the effects of our traditional thinking about diversity. For more on how causal arguments work, see Chapter 11.

LINK TO P. 240

The fundamental point of this book is to explain why this is true. The argument, in its simplest form, will be that we love race—we love identity—because we don't love class.[3] We love thinking that the differences that divide us are not the differences between those of us who have money and those who don't but are instead the differences between those of us who are black and those who are white or Asian or Latino or whatever. A world where some of us don't have enough money is a world where the differences between us present a problem: the need to get rid of inequality or to justify it. A world where some of us are black and some of us are white—or biracial or Native American or transgendered—is a world where the differences between us present a solution: appreciating our diversity. So we like to talk about the differences we can appreciate, and we don't like to talk about the ones we can't. Indeed, we don't even like to acknowledge that they exist. As survey after survey has shown, Americans are very reluctant to identify themselves as belonging to the lower class and even more reluctant to identify themselves as belonging to the upper class. The class we like is the middle class.

But the fact that we all like to think of ourselves as belonging to the same class doesn't, of course, mean that we actually do belong to the same class. In reality, we obviously and increasingly don't. "The last few decades," as *The Economist*° puts it, "have seen a huge increase in inequality in America."[4] The rich *are* different from you and me, and one of the ways they're different is that they're getting richer and we're not. And while it's not surprising that most of the rich and their apologists on the intellectual right are unperturbed by this development, it is at least a little surprising that the intellectual left has managed to remain almost equally unperturbed. Giving priority to issues like affirmative action and committing itself to the celebration of difference, the intellectual left has responded to the increase in economic inequality by insisting on the importance of cultural identity. So for thirty years, while the gap between the rich and the poor has grown larger, we've been urged to respect people's identities—as if the problem of poverty would be solved if we just appreciated the poor. From the economic standpoint, however, what poor people want is not to contribute to diversity but to minimize their contribution to it—they want to stop being poor. Celebrating the diversity of American life has become the American left's way of accepting their poverty, of accepting inequality.

The Economist: a weekly newsmagazine based in London and focusing on international affairs. Its target audience is affluent and highly educated.

10 I have three goals in writing this book. The first is to show how our current notion of cultural diversity—trumpeted as the repudiation of racism and biological essentialism°—in fact grew out of and perpetuates the very concepts it congratulates itself on having escaped. The second is to show how and why the American love affair with race—especially when you can dress race up as culture—has continued and even intensified. Almost everything we say about culture (that the significant differences between us are cultural, that such differences should be respected, that our cultural heritages should be perpetuated, that there's a value in making sure that different cultures survive) seems to me mistaken, and this book will try to show why. And the

essentialism: the assumption that all members of a category are alike or share similar, if not identical, characteristics. Essentialist arguments take the form of "All X's are Y" and often appear in arguments about social difference. Examples include claims that gay men aren't athletic, straight men aren't empathetic, and people from a specific ethnic group are (or are not) intelligent.

third goal is—by shifting our focus from cultural diversity to economic equality—to help alter the political terrain of contemporary American intellectual life.

Notes

1. Consciousness of color was, it goes without saying, always central to American society insofar as that society was a committedly racist one. The relevant change here—marked rather than produced by *Bakke*—involved (in the wake of both the successes and failures of the civil rights movement) the emergence of color consciousness as an antiracist position. The renewed black nationalism in the 1960s is one standard example of this transition, but the phenomenon is more general. You can get a striking sense of it by reading John Okada's *No-No Boy*, a novel about the Japanese Americans who answered no to the two loyalty questions on the questionnaire administered to them at the relocation centers they were sent to during World War II. The novel itself, published in 1957, is a pure product of the civil rights movement, determined to overcome race (and ignore class) in the imagination of a world in which people are utterly individualized—"only people." It began to become important, however, as an expression of what Frank Chin, in an article written in 1976 and included as an appendix to the current edition, calls "yellow soul," and when it's taught today in Asian American literature classes, reading it counts toward the fulfillment of diversity requirements that Okada himself would not have understood.
2. Simi Linton, *Claiming Disability* (New York: New York University Press, 1998), 96.
3. The relations between race and class have been an important topic in American writing at least since the 1930s, and in recent years they have, in the more general form of the relations between identity and inequality, been the subject of an ongoing academic discussion. Some of the more notable contributions include *Culture and Equality* (2000) by Brian Barry, *Redistribution or Recognition* (2003), an exchange between Nancy Fraser and Axel Honneth, and *The Debate on Classes* (1990), featuring an important essay by Erik Olin Wright and a series of exchanges about that essay. And in my particular field of specialization, American literature, Gavin Jones is about to publish an important and relevant book called *American Hunger*. I cite these texts in particular because, in quite different ways, they share at least some of my skepticism about the value of identity. And I have myself written in an academic context about these issues, most recently in *The Shape of the Signifier* (2004). *The Trouble with Diversity* is in part an effort to make some of the terms of the discussion more vivid to a more general audience. More important, however, it is meant to advance a particular position in that discussion, an argument that the concept of identity is incoherent and that its continuing success is a function of its utility to neoliberalism.
4. *The Economist*, December 29, 2004.

RESPOND

1. What, for Walter Benn Michaels, is the real issue that American society needs to confront? How, for him, does defining *diversity* in terms of a celebration of difference, especially ethnic difference, prevent Americans from both seeing the real issue and doing anything about it? In what ways does our society's focus on ethnic and cultural diversity necessarily perpetuate racism and biological essentialism (paragraph 10)?
2. Why and how are these issues relevant to discussions of diversity on campus in general? On the campus you attend?
3. Later in this introduction, Michaels, a liberal, points out ways in which both conservatives and liberals in American public life, first, focus on racial or ethnic differences rather than issues of social inequality and, second, benefit from doing so. In a 2004 essay, "Diversity's False Solace," he notes:

   > [W]e like policies like affirmative action not so much because they solve the problem of racism but because they tell us that racism is the problem we need to solve. . . . It's not surprising that universities of the upper middle class should want their students to feel comfortable [as affirmative action programs enable and encourage them to do]. What is surprising is that diversity should have become the hallmark of liberalism.

   Analyze the argument made in this paragraph as a Toulmin argument. (For a discussion of Toulmin argumentation, see Chapter 7.)
4. How would you characterize Michaels's argument? In what ways is it an argument of fact? A definitional argument? An evaluative argument? A causal argument? A proposal? (For a discussion of these kinds of arguments, see Chapters 8–12.)
5. Imagine a dialogue between Walter Benn Michaels and Sheryll Cashin, author of the previous selection. What would they agree on with respect to diversity on campuses? And where might there be disagreements? Why?
6. This chapter has provided many perspectives on an issue that is hotly debated on American campuses and in American society at large—diversity. Should diversity be something that schools strive for? If so, what kinds of diversity? What should a diverse campus look like, and why? **Write a proposal essay** in which you define and justify the sort(s) of diversity, if any, that your school should aim for. Seek to draw widely on the perspectives that you've read in this chapter—in terms of topics discussed and also approaches to those or other topics that you might consider. If you completed the assignment in question 6 for the first selection in this chapter (p. 677), you will surely want to reread your essay, giving some thought to how and why your understanding of diversity has or has not changed as you have read the selections in this chapter. (For a discussion of proposals, see Chapter 12.)

27

How Has the Internet Changed the Meaning of Privacy?

Left to right: Megan Haaga, for Open Gates, by permission; © Frank Fell/age fotostock; AP Photo/Kin Cheung

The last time you downloaded a software update, did you stop to read the agreement listing the rights and information you were giving away when you clicked ACCEPT? Likely not. Even if you had, odds are you would've realized that given our reliance on (and addiction to) technology, we have little choice but to "share" all sorts of information about who we are and what we do online—and to do so freely. But there is also the issue of the information we don't give away, information that someone—governments and big corporations, for example—manages to obtain about our online and offline selves, whether they do so legally, illegally, or in that gray space in between. The selections in this chapter give you a chance to investigate these issues and the impact they have on you as someone who depends on technology.

The chapter opens with a selection from Daniel J. Solove's 2011 book, *Nothing to Hide: The False Tradeoff between Privacy and Security*. Solove, a law professor, does his best to demolish the argument that most of us needn't worry about issues of privacy online because we're law-abiding citizens with nothing to hide. The second selection, Rebecca Greenfield's

"What Your Email Metadata Told the NSA about You," explains and illustrates the important concept of metadata and how it can be used by organizations like the U.S. National Security Agency (NSA). As you'll see when you geolocate yourself, every time you use a computer, someone somewhere could be learning all sorts of things about you. The third selection, the chapter's visual argument, asks you to analyze three cartoons dealing with privacy and government surveillance.

The next two selections consider privacy and surveillance with respect to technology companies in particular. In an excerpt from their conference paper *Six Provocations for Big Data*, researchers danah boyd (who spells her name all lowercase) and Kate Crawford explain what constitutes "Big Data," how such data can be used, and why all of us should be paying attention to who gets access to it. "It's Not OK Cupid," an interview from *The Takeaway*, a Public Radio International program, gives Christian Rudder, co-founder of OkCupid, a popular dating site, a chance to defend experiments his site conducted on its unsuspecting users, manipulating the messages they received about good and bad matches. (After listening to the program and reading the transcript, you may want to say that program host Todd Zwillich takes Rudder to task for what his company did, demonstrating the very different conclusions individuals with different assumptions about privacy come to about what Rudder would label "business as usual.")

The final two selections in the chapter return to the question of privacy and the government, but the focus is a 2014 Supreme Court ruling in *Riley v. California*, which made it illegal for law enforcement officials to search the contents of someone's cell phone without first obtaining a warrant. This narrowing of the rights of law enforcement with regard to searches of cell phones represents a major victory for privacy advocates—at least in certain situations. The final selection in the chapter, Amy Davidson's "Four Ways the *Riley* Ruling Matters for the NSA," argues that the *Riley* ruling will have major consequences for continuing debates and court cases about the behavior of the NSA, although she also admits that not everyone agrees.

So who's watching over your shoulder as you type away, and what do they see that you likely don't realize is visible? The selections in this chapter will give you new perspectives on what it means to be wired and on the tradeoffs you're making, whether or not you realize it.

When the topic of government surveillance comes up, some folks are quick to respond, "It's OK. I have nothing to hide." In this selection, Daniel J. Solove, the John Marshall Harlan Research Professor of Law at the George Washington University Law School and a leading expert on privacy law, seeks to demonstrate the fallacy of such a claim. The selection, which comes from Solove's 2011 book Nothing to Hide: The False Tradeoff between Privacy and Security, *has been praised by John W. Dean, who served as White House counsel for President Nixon, as "the best brief analysis of this issue." As noted in the subtitle of Solove's book, tradeoffs are quite relevant to this topic and to legal questions generally because courts, including the U.S. Supreme Court, find themselves balancing the competing interests of various parties. In this case, the relevant parties are individuals, on the one hand, and corporations or governments, on the other. As you read, notice the ways in which Solove is ultimately constructing a definitional argument about the complex nature of privacy, particularly in our contemporary society. You may also want to give some thought to things about your life you might not want made public; doing so will help you appreciate why Solove's argument matters.*

The Nothing-to-Hide Argument

DANIEL J. SOLOVE

When the government gathers or analyzes personal information, many people say they're not worried. "I've got nothing to hide," they declare. "Only if you're doing something wrong should you worry, and then you don't deserve to keep it private."

The nothing-to-hide argument pervades discussions about privacy. The data security expert Bruce Schneier calls it the "most common retort° against privacy advocates."[1] The legal scholar Geoffrey Stone refers to it as an "all-too-common refrain."[2] In its most compelling form, it is an argument that the privacy interest is generally minimal, thus making the balance against security concerns a foreordained° victory for security. In this chapter, I'll demonstrate how the argument stems from certain faulty assumptions about privacy and its value.

retort: a sharp and often angry reply.

foreordained: decided in advance.

"I've Got Nothing to Hide"

The nothing-to-hide argument is everywhere. In Britain, for example, the government has installed millions of public surveillance cameras in cities and towns, which are watched by officials via closed-circuit television. In a campaign slogan for the program, the government declares: "If you've got nothing to hide, you've got nothing to fear."[3] In the United States, one anonymous individual comments: "If [government officials] need to read my e-mails . . . so be it. I have nothing to hide. Do you?"[4] Variations of nothing-to-hide arguments frequently appear in blogs, letters to the editor, television news interviews, and other forums. One blogger, in reference to profiling people for national security purposes, declares: "Go ahead and profile me, I have nothing to hide."[5] Another blogger proclaims: "So I don't mind people wanting to find out things about me, I've got nothing to hide! Which is why I support [the government's] efforts to find terrorists by monitoring our phone calls!"[6] Some other examples include:

- I don't have anything to hide from the government. I don't think I had that much hidden from the government in the first place. I don't think they care if I talk about my ornery neighbor.[7]
- Do I care if the FBI monitors my phone calls? I have nothing to hide. Neither does 99.99 percent of the population. If the wire-tapping stops one of these Sept. 11 incidents, thousands of lives are saved.[8]
- Like I said, I have nothing to hide. The majority of the American people have nothing to hide. And those that have something to hide should be found out, and get what they have coming to them.[9]

The nothing-to-hide argument is not of recent vintage. One of the characters in Henry James's° 1888 novel *The Reverberator* muses: "If these people had done bad things they ought to be ashamed of themselves and he couldn't pity them, and if they hadn't done them there was no need of making such a rumpus° about other people knowing."[10]

I encountered the nothing-to-hide argument so frequently in news interviews, discussions, and the like that I decided to probe° the issue. I asked the readers of my blog, *Concurring Opinions*, whether there are good responses to the nothing-to-hide argument.[11] I received a torrent° of comments:

- My response is "So do you have curtains?" or "Can I see your credit card bills for the last year?"
- So my response to the "If you have nothing to hide . . ." argument is simply, "I don't need to justify my position. You need to justify yours. Come back with a warrant."°

Henry James (1843–1916): American novelist and critic who spent much of his adult life in Britain and ultimately became a British subject. He is a major figure among late-nineteenth-century literary realists, known for his exploration of human consciousness and perception through the characters of his novels.

rumpus: commotion, uproar.

probe: to examine something or someone with great care.

torrent: literally, a powerful stream of fast-moving liquid, often water; here, used figuratively.

warrant: in legal contexts, a document that authorizes its holder to carry out actions such as making an arrest, searching and perhaps seizing property, or ensuring that a judgment is carried out. In Toulmin argument (as discussed in Chapter 7), a warrant is the connection, often an unstated principle or assumed chain of reasoning, between a particular claim and the reason(s) that supports it—the glue that holds the claim and reason together.

- I don't have anything to hide. But I don't have anything I feel like showing you, either.
- If you have nothing to hide, then you don't have a life.
- Show me yours and I'll show you mine.
- It's not about having anything to hide, it's about things not being anyone else's business.
- Bottom line, Joe Stalin° would [have] loved it. Why should anyone have to say more?[12]

On the surface it seems easy to dismiss the nothing-to-hide argument. 5
Everybody probably has something to hide from somebody. As the author Aleksandr Solzhenitsyn° declared, "Everyone is guilty of something or has something to conceal. All one has to do is look hard enough to find what it is."[13] Likewise, in Friedrich Dürrenmatt's° novella *Traps*, which involves a seemingly innocent man put on trial by a group of retired lawyers for a mock trial° game, the man inquires what his crime shall be. "'An altogether minor matter,' the prosecutor replied. . . . 'A crime can always be found.'"[14]

One can usually think of something that even the most open person would want to hide. As a commenter to my blog post noted, "If you have nothing to hide, then that quite literally means you are willing to let me photograph you naked? And I get full rights to that photograph—so I can show it to your neighbors?"[15] The Canadian privacy expert David Flaherty expresses

Joseph Stalin (1878–1953): dictator of the Soviet Union from 1924 until his death. Although his policies, which emphasized a state-controlled economy and collectivism, transformed the USSR from a rural society into an industrial power, he is also known for his brutality: millions of Soviets labeled "enemies of the state" were exiled, imprisoned, or executed at various periods during this era.

Aleksandr Solzhenitsyn (1918–2008): Nobel Prize–winning novelist and historian known for his outspoken criticism of Soviet efforts to control the public and private lives of its citizens. His novel *The Gulag Archipelago* (published in the West in 1973 and in Russia in 1989) is based on his research into the history of the Soviet system of labor camps and the eight years he spent in a correctional labor camp after making a disparaging remark about Stalin in a letter to a friend.

Friedrich Dürrenmatt (1921–1990): Swiss author and playwright who created works for the stage and radio (before television was widespread, radio plays were quite popular). His work, often controversial, explored philosophical themes popular in Europe after World War II.

mock trial: a trial that is for practice or fun rather than one that has legal consequences.

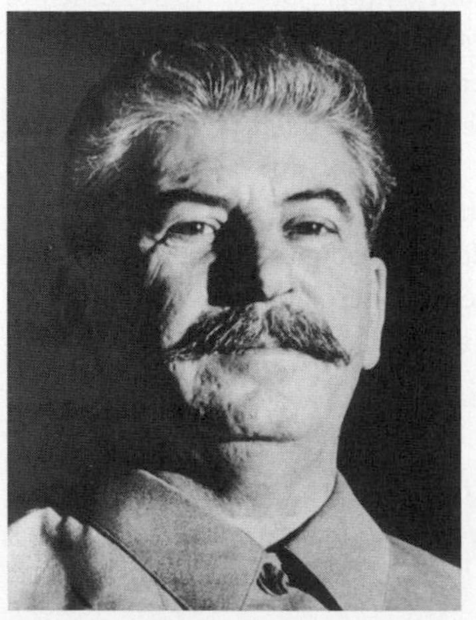

Joseph Stalin AP Photo, 1943

Aleksandr Solzhenitsyn © Bettmann/Corbis

a similar idea when he argues: "There is no sentient° human being in the Western world who has little or no regard for his or her personal privacy; those who would attempt such claims cannot withstand even a few minutes' questioning about intimate aspects of their lives without capitulating to the intrusiveness of certain subject matters."[16]

sentient: conscious, capable of feeling and perceiving.

Such responses attack the nothing-to-hide argument only in its most extreme form, which isn't particularly strong. In a less extreme form, the nothing-to-hide argument refers not to all personal information but only to the type of data the government is likely to collect. Retorts to the nothing-to-hide argument about exposing people's naked bodies or their deepest secrets are relevant only if the government is likely to gather this kind of information. In many instances, hardly anyone will see the information, and it won't be disclosed to the public. Thus, some might argue, the privacy interest is minimal, and the security interest in preventing terrorism is much more important. In this less extreme form, the nothing-to-hide argument is a formidable one.

Understanding Privacy

To evaluate the nothing-to-hide argument, we should begin by looking at how its adherents understand privacy. Nearly every law or policy involving privacy depends upon a particular understanding of what privacy is. The way problems are conceived has a tremendous impact on the legal and policy solutions used to solve them. As the philosopher John Dewey° observed, "A problem well put is half-solved."[17]

John Dewey (1859–1952): American philosopher, educational theorist and reformer, and psychologist.

What is "privacy"? Most attempts to understand privacy do so by attempting to locate the essence of privacy—its core characteristics or the common denominator that links together the various things we classify under the rubric of "privacy." Privacy, however, is too complex a concept to be reduced to a singular essence. It is a plurality° of different things that do not share one element in common but that nevertheless bear a resemblance to each other.[18] For example, privacy can be invaded by the disclosure of your deepest secrets. It might also be invaded if you're watched by a Peeping Tom, even if no secrets are ever revealed to anyone. With the disclosure of secrets, the harm is that your concealed information is spread to others. With the Peeping Tom, the harm is that you're being watched. You'd probably find it creepy regardless of whether the peeper finds out anything sensitive or discloses any information to others.

plurality: here, multitude.

There are many other forms of invasion of privacy, such as blackmail or 10
the improper use of your personal data. Your privacy can also be invaded if the government compiles an extensive dossier° about you. Privacy thus

dossier: collection of documents or information, a file.

involves so many different things that it is impossible to reduce them all to one simple idea. We need not do so.

In many cases, privacy issues never get balanced against conflicting interests because courts, legislators, and others fail to recognize that privacy is implicated. People don't acknowledge certain problems because they don't fit into their particular one-size-fits-all conception of privacy. Regardless of whether we call something a "privacy" problem, it still remains a problem, and problems shouldn't be ignored. We should pay attention to all the different problems that spark our desire to protect privacy.

To describe the problems created by the collection and use of personal data, many commentators use a metaphor based on George Orwell's° *Nineteen Eighty-Four*.[19] Orwell depicted a harrowing totalitarian society ruled by a government called Big Brother that watched its citizens obsessively and demanded strict discipline. The Orwell metaphor, which focuses on the harms of surveillance (such as inhibition and social control), might be apt to describe government monitoring of citizens. But much of the data gathered in computer databases isn't particularly sensitive, such as one's race, birth date, gender, address, or marital status. Many people don't care about concealing the hotels they stay at, the cars they own, or the kind of beverages they drink. Frequently, though not always, people wouldn't be inhibited or embarrassed if others knew this information.

A different metaphor better captures the problems: Franz Kafka's° *The Trial*. Kafka's novel centers around a man who is arrested but not informed

George Orwell (1903–1950): pen name of Eric Arthur Blair, an English writer known for his prose style, his allegiance to democratic socialism, and his efforts to fight what he perceived as social injustice. Orwell wrote novels, essays, and criticism and is also known for his journalistic writings. He coined several terms that are now part of the English language, including *cold war*, *thought crime*, *thought police*, *Big Brother*, and *doublethink*—all things he railed against. His name has also become part of the language: *Orwellian* refers, always pejoratively, to authoritarian or totalitarian states or practices.

Franz Kafka (1883–1924): writer born in Prague whose works were especially influential after his death. In fact, the word *Kafkaesque* now refers to situations like those described in Kafka's writings, which are characterized by alienation, brutality, and inescapable bureaucracies. Though he claimed German, the language in which he wrote, as his native language, he also spoke Czech fluently. As nationalism increased among Czech- and German-speakers in Prague, the city of his birth, he, like the Jews of the city generally, was left to question where, and if, he belonged.

George Orwell Keystone/Getty Images

Franz Kafka AP Photo

why. He desperately tries to find out what triggered his arrest and what's in store for him. He finds out that a mysterious court system has a dossier on him and is investigating him, but he's unable to learn much more. *The Trial* depicts a bureaucracy with inscrutable purposes that uses people's information to make important decisions about them, yet denies the people the ability to participate in how their information is used.[20] The problems portrayed by the Kafkaesque metaphor are of a different sort from the problems caused by surveillance. They often do not result in inhibition. Instead, they are problems of information processing—the storage, use, or analysis of data—rather than of information collection. They affect the power relationships between people and the institutions of the modern state. They not only frustrate the individual by creating a sense of helplessness and powerlessness, they also affect social structure by altering the kind of relationships people have with the institutions that make important decisions about their lives.

Legal and policy solutions focus too much on the problems under the Orwellian metaphor—those of surveillance—and aren't adequately addressing the Kafkaesque problems—those of information processing.[21] The difficulty is that commentators are trying to conceive of the problems caused by databases in terms of surveillance when, in fact, these problems are different.

The Problem with the Nothing-to-Hide Argument

Commentators often attempt to refute the nothing-to-hide argument by 15
pointing to things people want to hide. But the problem with the nothing-to-hide argument is the underlying assumption that privacy is about hiding bad things. By accepting this assumption we concede far too much ground and invite an unproductive discussion of information people would likely want to hide. As Bruce Schneier aptly notes, the nothing-to-hide argument stems from a faulty "premise that privacy is about hiding a wrong."[22] Surveillance, for example, can inhibit such lawful activities as free speech, free association, and other First Amendment rights essential for democracy.

The deeper problem with the nothing-to-hide argument is that it myopically° views privacy as a form of secrecy. In contrast, understanding privacy as a plurality of related issues demonstrates that the disclosure of bad things is just one among many difficulties caused by government security measures. To return to my discussion of literary metaphors, the problems are not just Orwellian but Kafkaesque. Government information-gathering programs are problematic even if no information people want to hide is uncovered. In

myopically: literally and metaphorically, in a shortsighted manner.

The Trial, the problem is not inhibited behavior but rather a suffocating powerlessness and vulnerability created by the court system's use of personal data and its denial to the protagonist of any knowledge of or participation in the process. The harms are bureaucratic ones—indifference, error, abuse, frustration, and lack of transparency and accountability.

One such harm, for example, which I call *aggregation*, emerges from the fusion of small bits of seemingly innocuous° data. When combined, the information becomes much more telling. By joining pieces of information we might not take pains to guard, the government can glean information about us that we might indeed wish to conceal. For example, suppose you bought a book about cancer. This purchase isn't very revealing on its own, for it just indicates an interest in the disease. Suppose you bought a wig. The purchase of a wig, by itself, could be for a number of reasons. But combine these two pieces of information, and now the inference can be made that you have cancer and are undergoing chemotherapy.

innocuous: unimportant or not harmful.

Another potential problem with the government's harvest of personal data is one I call *exclusion*. Exclusion occurs when people are prevented from having knowledge about how information about them is being used, and when they are barred from accessing and correcting errors in that data. Many government national security measures involve maintaining a massive database of information that individuals cannot access. Indeed, because they involve national security, the very existence of these programs is often kept secret. This kind of information processing, which blocks subjects' knowledge and involvement, resembles in some ways a kind of due-process problem. It is a structural° problem involving the way people are treated by government institutions and creating a power imbalance between individuals and the government. To what extent should government officials have such a significant power over citizens? This issue isn't about what information people want to hide but about the power and the structure of government.

structural: here, part of the structure of the social system, including government.

A related problem involves *secondary use*. Secondary use is the exploitation of data obtained for one purpose for an unrelated purpose without the subject's consent. How long will personal data be stored? How will it be used? What could it be used for in the future? The potential future uses of any piece of personal information are vast, and without limits on or accountability for how that information is used, it is hard for people to assess the dangers of the data's being in the government's control.

Yet another problem with government gathering and use of personal data 20
is *distortion*. Although personal information can reveal quite a lot about people's personalities and activities, it often fails to reflect the whole person.

It can paint a distorted picture, especially since records are reductive°—they often capture information in a standardized format with many details omitted.

reductive: here, overly simplistic.

For example, suppose government officials learn that a person has bought a number of books on how to manufacture methamphetamine. That information makes them suspect that he's building a meth lab. What is missing from the records is the full story: The person is writing a novel about a character who makes meth. When he bought the books, he didn't consider how suspicious the purchase might appear to government officials, and his records didn't reveal the reason for the purchases. Should he have to worry about government scrutiny of all his purchases and actions? Should he have to be concerned that he'll wind up on a suspicious-persons list? Even if he isn't doing anything wrong, he may want to keep his records away from government officials who might make faulty inferences from them. He might not want to have to worry about how everything he does will be perceived by officials nervously monitoring for criminal activity. He might not want to have a computer flag him as suspicious because he has an unusual pattern of behavior.

The problem with the nothing-to-hide argument is that it focuses on just one or two particular kinds of privacy problems—the disclosure of personal information or surveillance—while ignoring others. It assumes a particular view about what privacy entails to the exclusion of other perspectives.

It is important to distinguish here between two ways of justifying a national security program that demands access to personal information. The first way is not to recognize a problem. This is how the nothing-to-hide argument works—it denies even the existence of a problem. The second manner of justifying such a program is to acknowledge the problems but contend that the benefits of the program outweigh the privacy sacrifice. The first justification influences the second, because the low value given to privacy is based upon a narrow view of the problem. The key misunderstanding is that the nothing-to-hide argument views privacy in a particular way—as a form of secrecy, as the right to hide things. But there are many other types of harm involved beyond exposing one's secrets to the government.

Blood, Death, and Privacy

One of the difficulties with the nothing-to-hide argument is that it looks for a singular and visceral° kind of injury. Ironically, this underlying conception of injury is sometimes shared by those advocating for greater privacy protections. For example, the law professor Ann Bartow argues that in order to have

visceral: relating to feelings rather than reason.

resonance: here, effect on people's emotions.

a real resonance,° privacy problems must "negatively impact the lives of living, breathing human beings beyond simply provoking feelings of unease." She urges that privacy needs more "dead bodies" and that privacy's "lack of blood and death, or at least of broken bones and buckets of money, distances privacy harms from other [types of harm]."[23]

25 Bartow's objection is actually consistent with the nothing-to-hide argument. Those advancing the nothing-to-hide argument have in mind a particular kind of appalling privacy harm, one where privacy is violated only when something deeply embarrassing or discrediting is revealed. Like Bartow, proponents of the nothing-to-hide argument demand a dead-bodies type of harm.

Bartow is certainly right that people respond much more strongly to blood and death than to more abstract concerns. But if this is the standard to recognize a problem, then few privacy problems will be recognized. Privacy is not a horror movie, most privacy problems don't result in dead bodies, and demanding more palpable harms will be difficult in many cases.

egregious: horrible, shocking.
accretion: a gradual accumulation or increase.

In many instances, privacy is threatened not by a single egregious° act but by the accretion° of a slow series of relatively minor acts. In this respect, privacy problems resemble certain environmental harms which occur over time through a series of small acts by different actors. Although society is more likely to respond to a major oil spill, gradual pollution by a multitude of different actors often creates worse problems.

Privacy is rarely lost in one fell swoop. It is often eroded over time, little bits dissolving almost imperceptibly until we finally begin to notice how much is gone. When the government starts monitoring the phone numbers people call, many may shrug their shoulders and say, "Ah, it's just numbers, that's all." Then the government might start monitoring some phone calls. "It's just a few phone calls, nothing more," people might declare. The government might install more video cameras in public places, to which some would respond, "So what? Some more cameras watching in a few more places. No big deal." The increase in cameras might ultimately expand to a more elaborate network of video surveillance. Satellite surveillance might be added, as well as the tracking of people's movements. The government might start analyzing people's bank records. "It's just my deposits and some of the bills I pay—no problem." The government may then start combing through credit card records, then expand to Internet service provider (ISP) records, health records, employment records, and more. Each step may seem incremental, but after a while, the government will be watching and knowing everything about us.

"My life's an open book," people might say. "I've got nothing to hide." But now the government has a massive dossier of everyone's activities, interests, reading habits, finances, and health. What if the government leaks the information to the public? What if the government mistakenly determines that based on your pattern of activities, you're likely to engage in a criminal act? What if it denies you the right to fly? What if the government thinks your financial transactions look odd—even if you've done nothing wrong—and freezes your accounts? What if the government doesn't protect your information with adequate security, and an identity thief obtains it and uses it to defraud you? Even if you have nothing to hide, the government can cause you a lot of harm.

"But the government doesn't want to hurt me," some might argue. In 30
many cases, this is true, but the government can also harm people inadvertently, due to errors or carelessness.

Silencing the Nothing-to-Hide Argument

When the nothing-to-hide argument is unpacked,° and its underlying assumptions examined and challenged, we can see how it shifts the debate to its terms, then draws power from its unfair advantage. The nothing-to-hide argument speaks to some problems, but not to others. It represents a singular and narrow way of conceiving of privacy, and it wins by excluding consideration of the other problems often raised with government security measures. When engaged directly, the nothing-to-hide argument can ensnare°, for it forces the debate to focus on its narrow understanding of privacy. But when confronted with the plurality of privacy problems implicated by government data collection and use beyond surveillance and disclosure, the nothing-to-hide argument, in the end, has nothing to say.

unpacked: here, analyzed with care.

ensnare: catch in a trap.

Notes

1. Bruce Schneier, "The Eternal Value of Privacy," *Wired*, May 18, 2006. http://www.wired.com/news/columns/1,70886-0.html.
2. Geoffrey R. Stone, "Freedom and Public Responsibility," *Chicago Tribune*, May 21, 2006.
3. Jeffrey Rosen, *The Naked Crowd: Reclaiming Security and Freedom in an Anxious Age* (New York: Random House, 2004), 36.
4. NonCryBaby to Security Focus, February 12, 2003, http://www.securityfocus.com/comments/articles/2296/18105#18105.
5. Yoven, comment on DanielPipes.org, June 14, 2006, http://www.danielpipes.org/comments/47675.
6. "Look All You Want, I've Got Nothing to Hide!" *Reach for the Stars!* (blog), May 14, 2006, http://greatcarrieoakey.blogspot.com/2006/05/look-all-you-want-ive-got-nothing-to.html.

7. Annegb, comment on *Concurring Opinions*, (blog) May 23, 2006, http://www.concurringopinions.com/archives/2006/05/is_there_a_good.html.
8. Joe Schneider, letter to the editor, *St. Paul Pioneer Press*, August 24, 2006, 11B.
9. Alix Spiegel, "Polls Suggest Americans Approve NSA Monitoring," *Day to Day*, NPR, radio broadcast, May 19, 2006, http://www.npr.org/templates/story/story.php?storyId=5418066/.
10. Henry James, *The Reverberator* (1888; repr. New York: Library of America, 1989), 687.
11. Daniel J. Solove, "Is There a Good Response to the 'Nothing-to-Hide' Argument?" *Concurring Opinions* (blog), May 23, 2006, http://www.concurringopinions.com/archives/2006/05/is_there_a_good.html
12. Comments on Daniel J. Solove, "Is There a Good Response to the 'Nothing-to-Hide' Argument?" *Concurring Opinions* (blog), May 23, 2006, http://www.concurringopinions.com/archives/2006/05/is_there_a_good.html.
13. Aleksandr Solzhenitsyn, *Cancer Ward*, trans. Nicholas Bethell and David Burg (New York: Farrar, Straus and Giroux, 1991), 192.
14. Friedrich Dürrenmatt, *Traps*, trans. Richard and Clara Winston (New York: Ballantine, 1960), 23.
15. Andrew, comment on Daniel J. Solove, "Is There a Good Response to the 'Nothing-to-Hide' Argument?" *Concurring Opinions* (blog), October 16, 2006, http://www.concurringopinions.com/archives/2006/05/is_there_a_good.html.
16. David H. Flaherty, "Visions of Privacy: Past, Present, and Future," in *Visions of Privacy: Policy Choices for the Digital Age*, ed. Colin J. Bennett and Rebecca Grant (Toronto: University of Toronto, 1999), 31.
17. John Dewey, *Logic: The Theory of Inquiry* (1938; repr. vol. 12 of *The Later Works of John Dewey*, Carbondale, IL: Southern Illinois University Press, 1991), 112.
18. I discuss the various privacy problems in more depth in my book *Understanding Privacy*, where I set forth a taxonomy to help identify the many different kinds of distinct yet related privacy problems. See Daniel J. Solove, *Understanding Privacy* (2008).
19. See George Orwell, *Nineteen Eighty-Four* (1949).
20. Franz Kafka, *The Trial* (1937; trans. Willa and Edwin Muir, New York: Schocken, 1956), 50–58.
21. Daniel J. Solove, *The Digital Person: Technology and Privacy in the Information Age* (New York: New York University Press, 2004), 27–75.
22. Schneier, *Eternal Value*.
23. Ann Bartow, "A Feeling of Unease about Privacy Law," *University of Pennsylvania Law Review* 155, (2006), http://www.pennumbra.com/responses/11-2006/Bartow.pdf.

RESPOND •

1. How does Solove characterize (that is, define) the nothing-to-hide argument? What, for Solove, are its limitations?
2. Solove contends that privacy is a large and complex concept composed of a number of related elements that, nevertheless, do not exactly overlap. Review this selection, and write down the various definitions of *privacy* Solove explores along with the limitations that

he offers of each; for each, note the paragraph(s) where it occurs. (This list will help you understand the structure and arrangement of Solove's argument.)

3. Solove quotes John Dewey as having noted, "A problem well put is half-solved" (paragraph 8). As you'll see throughout the selections in this chapter, writers are struggling to define privacy in ways that match the complexity of the reality of everyday life. What does Dewey's aphorism demonstrate about the value and importance of arguments of definition? (Chapter 9 on definitional argument will help you here.)
4. In paragraphs 12–14, Solove discusses two common metaphors for analyzing privacy and does so using the example of two well-known literary works, George Orwell's *1984* and Franz Kafka's *The Trial*. How does Solove use these metaphors to illustrate the difference between information collection and information processing? Why is this distinction key in understanding privacy? From a different perspective, how has Solove written about these two literary works so that, even if you have not read them, you understand his point? What do these examples demonstrate about the potential value of figurative language in explaining concepts? (See Chapter 13 for a discussion of figurative language and metaphor in particular.)
5. **Write a rhetorical analysis** of this selection. (Chapter 6 will be especially helpful here.) As you begin to examine Solove's argument in detail, you may decide that you wish to limit your discussion to one particular aspect of it, for example, its arguments based on emotion, character, or facts and reasoning or perhaps the arrangement of the argument (that is, the steps moving from the beginning to the end of the argument).

National Security Agency (NSA): intelligence agency of the U.S. government; as stated on its Web site, its role is "[to] collect (including through clandestine means), process, analyze, produce, and disseminate signals intelligence information and data for foreign intelligence and counterintelligence purposes . . . and [to] act as the National Manager for National Security Systems as established in law and policy. . . ." Signals intelligence refers to "communications systems, radars, and weapons systems" and thus includes electronic data.

metadata: literally, data about data; here, the concern is descriptive metadata, or information about the creation of an electronic message like a particular email, text, or posting.

Edward Snowden (1983–): computer professional who leaked classified information from the NSA, where he had been a contract employee; as this textbook goes to press, he is currently living in temporary exile in Russia. Snowden is the subject of the 2014 documentary *Citizenfour*. He is depicted in the image to the right.

▼ *Rebecca Greenfield is currently a staff writer at* Fast Company, *an award-winning magazine and Web site about technology, business, and design. Formerly, she was a staff writer at the* Atlantic Wire, *where her focus was technology and where this selection first appeared in June 2013. (The* Atlantic Wire, *now the* Wire, *is still associated with the* Atlantic *magazine and includes original reporting as well as news and opinion pieces aggregated from a number of media outlets.) As you read this selection, consider how Daniel J. Solove, author of the previous selection, "The Nothing-to-Hide Argument," might respond to it; you might also consider a comment posted on the* Wire *Web site in response to this article: "the point is that if they can get their hands on the headers, they certainly can read the message content too."*

What Your Email Metadata Told the NSA about You

REBECCA GREENFIELD

President Obama said "nobody is listening to your telephone calls," even though the National Security Agency° could actually track you from cellphone metadata.° Well, the latest from the Edward Snowden° leaks shows that Obama eventually told the NSA to stop collecting your email communications in 2011, apparently

Edward Snowden AP Photo/Kin Cheung

because the so-called StellarWind program "was not yielding much value," even when collected in bulk. But how much could the NSA learn from all that email metadata, really? And was it more invasive than phone data collection? The agency is well beyond its one trillionth° metadata record, after all, so they must have gotten pretty good at this.

trillion: a million millions or 1,000,000,000,000.

To offer a basic sense of how StellarWind collection worked—and how much user names and IP addresses can tell a spy about a person, even if he's not reading the contents of your email—we took a look at the raw source code of an everyday email header. It's not the exact kind of information the NSA was pulling, of course, but it shows the type of information attached to every single one of your emails.

Below is what the metadata looks like as it travels around with an email—we've annotated the relevant parts, based on what the *Guardian*° reported today as the legally allowed (and apparently expanded) powers of the NSA to read without your permission. After all, it's right there behind your words:

***the* Guardian:** a center-left British newspaper. (Unlike in the United States, British newspapers are clearly identified with a political orientation and even a party.)

```
Delivered-To: rgreenfield@theatlantic.com 1.
Received: by 10.52.27.45 with SMTP id q13csp154992vdg; 2.
        Thu, 27 Jun 2013 08:49:25 -0700 (PDT)
X-Received: by 10.236.83.210 with SMTP id q58mr4956210yhe.25.1372348165480;
        Thu, 27 Jun 2013 08:49:25 -0700 (PDT)
Return-Path: <LittleMonsterscom-tldkulkljdtiiimulj@cmail5.com>
Received: from mx104.d.outbound.createsend.com (mx104.d.outbound.createsend.com. [27.126.148.104]) 3.
        by mx.google.com with ESMTP id e68si475804yha.377.2013.06.27.08.49.25
        for <rgreenfield@theatlantic.com>;
        Thu, 27 Jun 2013 08:49:25 -0700 (PDT)
Received-SPF: pass (google.com: domain of LittleMonsterscom-tldkulkljdtiiimulj@cmail5.com designates 27.126.148.10
Authentication-Results: mx.google.com;
       spf=pass (google.com: domain of LittleMonsterscom-tldkulkljdtiiimulj@cmail5.com designates 27.126.148.104 a
tldkulkljdtiiimulj@cmail5.com;
       dkim=pass header.i=info=3Dthebackplane.com@cmail5.com
DKIM-Signature: v=1; a=rsa-sha1; c=relaxed/relaxed; s=cs2013; d=cmail5.com;
 h=From:To:Reply-To:Date:Subject:MIME-Version:Content-Type:List-Unsubscribe:Sender:Message-ID; i=info=3Dthebackpla
 bh=NQKeEz8ocSLYEAYpwTWTTM/Q4Zk=;
 b=QP/8qBkgDEAqXsu0X60EXxhqsNnklUtBxsVA0QNGZnx+vMn2y9gt2JRd3aufxP5UkkoU9/jwqyc9
   MzUszRVYokDvdE6Blq5SvrFAZEjPBbdpO4Byq6h7v3roL5TahDeB/Tc//juMk4soz3apCMAcujGR
   YvJCoOMmbw4QMkuNu6M=
DomainKey-Signature: a=rsa-sha1; c=nofws; q=dns; s=cs2013; d=cmail5.com;
 b=umyQJrmiu6kGR1NjnV7l1OQmr+Vtc2G3FKgqIJRrBZPA3DUB5YXhkPoxHueVfCNn2hqTxO5Ri+I4
   OKUCmi4kl++tsYWqpzCY4xnBrj7tirzIvUIoEmN8xhQ0zFQ+4K7UmoNWbjCh4Dvj+quRzhmMEZJi
   zKfqIOhmgkv8PfJtpr0=;
Received: by mx104.d.outbound.createsend.com id hphfgalhsps5 for <rgreenfield@theatlantic.com>; Fri, 28 Jun 2013 0
tldkulkljdtiiimulj@cmail5.com>)
From: "LittleMonsters.com" <info@thebackplane.com>4.
To: "R" <rgreenfield@theatlantic.com>
Reply-To: info@thebackplane.com
Date: Fri, 28 Jun 2013 01:40:47 +1000 5.
Subject: Incredible News!
MIME-Version: 1.0
Content-Type: multipart/alternative;
       boundary="_=aspNetEmail=_8d5bc72b464041778a98a365f54ad49a"
X-Mailer: Create Send
X-Complaints-To: abuse@cmail5.com
List-Unsubscribe: <http://unsub.cmail5.com/t/i-u-tldkulk-idtiiimu/>
```

1. Recipient Email
2. Recipient IP Address (location)
3. Sender IP Address (location)
4. Recipient Email
5. Date and Time

As you can see, at the bare minimum, your average email metadata offers location (through the IPs), plus names (or at least email addresses), and dates (down to the second). The *Guardian*'s Glenn Greenwald and Spencer Ackerman report that Attorney General Michael Mukasey and Defense Secretary Bob Gates signed a document that OK'd the collection and mining of "the information appearing on the 'to,' 'from,' or 'bcc' lines of a standard email or other electronic communication" from, well, you and your friends and maybe some terrorists.

But email metadata is more revealing than that — even more revealing than what 5
the NSA could do with just the time of your last phone call and the nearest cell tower. For operation StellarWind, it must have been all about that IP, or Internet protocol, address. Hell, it'd be easy enough for your grandma to geolocate° both parties from a couple of IPs: there are countless free services on Google that turn those numbers you give to the IT guy into your exact location. For example, using the two IP addresses in the email sent to me above, we can easily determine that it was sent from Victoria, Australia:

geolocate: to locate the street address (in contrast to the geographic coordinates) of an object such as a mobile phone or computer; try it at mapbox.com.

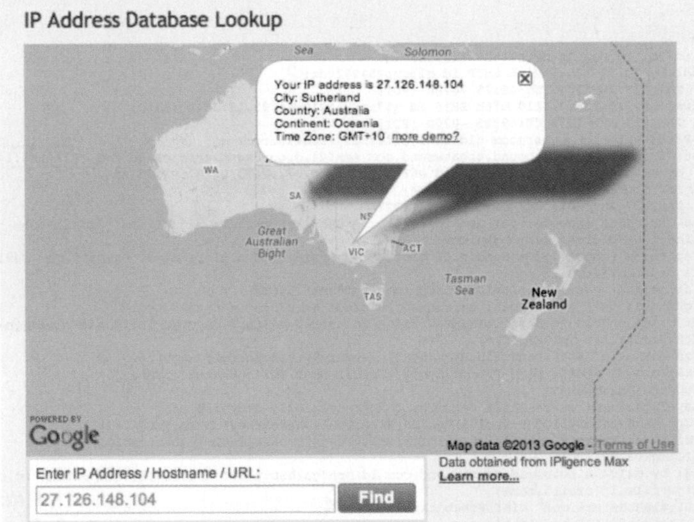

homing pigeon: also called *carrier pigeon*; a variety of pigeon that is able to fly back to its home even though it was released over a thousand miles away. Homing pigeons have been used to transport messages, including across enemy lines, during wartime.

The IP address is like a homing pigeon,° and that's why the revelations of email metadata being authorized under the Bush and Obama administrations amount to a seriously revealing breach of personal security in the name of terror-hunting.

"Seeing your IP logs — and especially feeding them through sophisticated analytic tools — is a way of getting inside your head that's in many ways on par with reading your diary," Julian Sanchez of the Cato Institute° told the *Guardian*. Of course, the administration has another party line, telling the *Los Angeles Times* that operation StellarWind was discontinued because it wasn't adding up to enough good intelligence of "value." But with one of the many "sophisticated analytic tool" sets developed by the NSA over the last decade or so and leaked during the last month — like, say, EvilOlive, "a near-real-time metadata analyzer" described in yet another *Guardian* scoop today — America's intelligence operation certainly can zero in on exactly where Americans are. Even if you're just emailing your hip grandma.

Cato Institute: a Washington-based think tank whose mission is "to originate, disseminate, and increase understanding of public policies based on the principles of individual liberty, limited government, free markets, and peace."

RESPOND •

1. Was the information presented in this selection new to you? Why or why not? How would you expect privacy advocates to respond to this selection? And what about those who argue that, in the name of national defense, the U.S. government needs to collect such data? How do you anticipate that Daniel J. Solove, author of the previous selection, "The Nothing-to-Hide Argument," would respond? Why?
2. How would you characterize this selection: is it an argument of fact, of definition, or of evaluation; a causal argument; or a proposal argument? (The discussion of kinds of arguments in Chapter 1 will help you decide.) How would you characterize its function or purpose? (Chapter 6 on rhetorical analysis may help you here.)
3. Greenfield, like many people who write professionally for various Internet sites, uses a complex mix of styles: some parts of the article are quite informal while other parts could be part of an academic research paper. Choose several instances of particularly informal writing that would not be appropriate in an academic research paper, and explain why. How does Greenfield use comments about "grandma" to help structure the selection's argument? (Chapter 13 discusses style in argument.)
4. Visual arguments play an important role in this selection. Evaluate the role that each of the visual arguments plays by discussing how the selection would have been different without it. (Chapter 14 on visual rhetoric will help you respond to this question.)

5. When Edward Snowden released confidential data from the NSA in 2013, he was immediately labeled a traitor by some and a hero by others. Collect and examine examples of discussions of Snowden — the comments posted in the *Wire* about this selection would be an easy place to begin — and **write an evaluative argument** in which you describe and evaluate the criteria used in making such an assessment by one side or the other. (In other words, your task is not to evaluate Snowden or his actions but to examine and evaluate the criteria his supporters or detractors used in reaching that conclusion.) An interesting challenge would be first to assess your own response to Snowden's actions and second to evaluate the criteria used by those who share your opinion of his actions to come to such a conclusion. Doing so will require you to examine the tradeoffs you're willing to make in balancing competing interests when the debate is about privacy. (Chapter 10 on evaluative arguments will help you consider and evaluate the criteria used in these discussions.)

Nick Anderson, whose Pulitzer Prize–winning work is syndicated in over one hundred newspapers, currently draws cartoons for the *Houston Chronicle*, where this cartoon appeared in June 2014, shortly after the Supreme Court decision that limited cell phones from being searched without a warrant. You'll be reading an excerpt from this decision later in this chapter. Why might the cap worn by the speaker holding the cell phone be relevant? (Recall that Anderson lives in Texas.) How is it used to characterize the speaker?

Making a Visual Argument: The Issue of Privacy

▲ *You may never have stopped to consider it, but producing an effective cartoon requires an interesting and complex set of skills. Cartoonists have a limited amount of space to convey their argument; the ones represented here use no more than two frames. The message has to be pithy—much like a tweet—but it has to combine words with one or more images. The words, of course, may take the form of a caption, or they may be part of the image. The images have multiple functions: they have to capture the reader's attention, but they must also thrust the reader into a story, one that unfolds almost instantaneously.*

Cartoons likewise have to rely on the two-edged sword of humor—always risky—to make their point. In this regard, even simple cartoons represent sophisticated visual rhetoric that merits careful examination. As you consider the three cartoons in this selection, all of which examine the themes of privacy and surveillance in the electronic age, use your rhetorical skills to analyze how each of the cartoonists manages to pack what is often an implied but powerful argument into such a small package.

Internationally known cartoonist Alfredo Martirena lives and works in Cuba, the country of his birth. This cartoon gives us some insight into how discussions of the NSA play outside the United States, particularly in Cuba, a country with which our nation has a troubled relationship. In studying this 2013 cartoon, consider, first, how you'd feel if you turned on your cell phone to find such an electronic notice and, second, how you respond to the fact that people outside the United States may be mocking it, however gently, for its behavior. www.CartoonStock.com

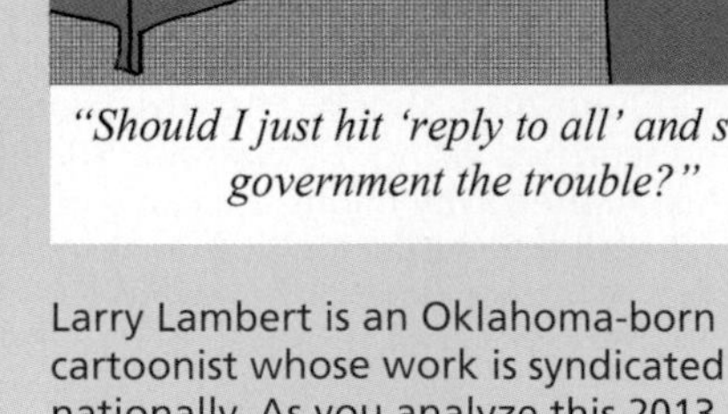

"Should I just hit 'reply to all' and save the government the trouble?"

Larry Lambert is an Oklahoma-born cartoonist whose work is syndicated nationally. As you analyze this 2013 cartoon, focus on how the setting—an office—makes its concerns about privacy different, at least slightly, from the concerns of the two previous cartoons. www.CartoonStock.com

RESPOND.

1. Which of these three cartoons do you find most effective at communicating its message? How does it encourage readers to think about issues of privacy in an electronic environment? Why? (The discussion of evaluative criteria in Chapter 10 may be useful here.)
2. Analyze how each of these cartoons works as a visual argument, as discussed in Chapter 14. Consider the visual design, including the images and colors used, the style of drawing, and the relationship between the images and text of each.
3. Choose one of the cartoons, and analyze it in terms of its appeals to emotions, to the character of its creator, and to the facts or reasoning the cartoon represents. (These appeals are discussed in Chapter 1 and again in Chapters 2–4, respectively.)
4. Someone searching databases for cartoons generally uses a keyword search, as discussed in Chapter 18. The keywords listed for the cartoon by Alfredo Martirena are *National Security Agency*, *NSA*, *domestic espionage*, *domestic spying*, *Prism*, *Tempora*, *Edward Snowden*, *spying scandal*, *spying scandals*, *intelligence agency*, *intelligence agencies*, *privacy*, and *surveillance society*, while those for the cartoon by Larry Lambert are *domestic spying*, *espionage*, *surveillance*, *spy*, *spies*, *spying*, *email*, *emails*, *CIA*, *FBI*, *NSA*, *political scandal*, *political scandals*, *reply*, *replies*, *intrusions*, *government*, *governments*, *emailing*, *private*, *privacy*, and *personal freedoms*. Why would these be appropriate keywords to use in searching for each of these cartoons? (By the way, you may need to check out the meanings of *Prism* and *Tempora*; we did. Do so by Googling *Prism, spying* and *Tempora, spying*; adding *spying* limits the search, of course.) What might account for overlap and differences in the lists, given the content of each cartoon? Can you think of other terms that someone might have used to search for these cartoons? Can you imagine why they weren't included in the list of keywords?
5. Many writers struggle with incorporating a visual of any kind—a cartoon, a figure, a table—into a text they are writing in a way that helps readers understand the meaning and significance of the visual argument with regard to the ongoing argument. Imagine that you are writing an essay about the nature of privacy in electronic environments and that you decide to use one of these cartoons to illustrate a point you wish to make. Specify the point you wish to make, and then **write a healthy paragraph** that could be used to incorporate the cartoon into the text. You will need both to describe the cartoon to some degree and to explain its message or significance. Using a phrase like "the cartoon shows . . ." or "in the cartoon, the reader sees . . ." will help you as you describe the cartoon. (This will be a **factual argument** of the sort discussed in Chapter 8; the discussion of using visuals in your own arguments in Chapter 14 should help you with this task.)

In this excerpt from Six Provocations for Big Data, *a conference presentation at Oxford University in September 2011 as part of "A Decade in Internet Time: Symposium on the Dynamics of the Internet and Society," danah boyd and Kate Crawford provoke debate by making six potentially controversial claims. These claims are that (1) automating research changes the definition of knowledge, (2) claims to objectivity and accuracy are misleading, (3) bigger data are not always better data, (4) not all data are equivalent, (5) just because it's accessible doesn't make it ethical, and (6) limited access to Big Data creates new digital divides. Given the focus of this chapter, this excerpt includes the paper's introduction, part of the section devoted to the first claim, and all of the section devoted to the fifth claim. danah boyd wears many hats. A principal researcher at Microsoft Research and founder of Data & Society Research Institute, she has academic affiliations with the Department of Media, Culture, and Communication at New York University (NYU), the University of New South Wales (UNSW) in Australia, and the Berkman Center for Internet & Society at Harvard University. Her work has focused on the intersection of technology and society, particularly how young people use social media in their daily lives. More recently, her research has shifted toward the topic of this selection, Big Data and privacy. Like boyd, Kate Crawford, her coauthor, is also a principal researcher at Microsoft Research as well as a visiting professor at the MIT Center for Civic Media, a senior fellow at NYU's Information Law Institute, and an associate professor in the Journalism and Media Research Center at UNSW. Crawford is also a composer who has released three albums of electronic music. Her research focuses on power and ethics with respect to social media. As you read, be alert to how boyd and Crawford define the term* Big Data *and why they think all of us should be concerned about it and its uses.*

Six Provocations for Big Data

danah boyd AND KATE CRAWFORD

> Technology is neither good nor bad; nor is it neutral . . . technology's interaction with the social ecology is such that technical developments frequently have environmental, social, and human consequences that go far beyond the immediate purposes of the technical devices and practices themselves.
>
> —Melvin Kranzberg (1986, p. 545)

> We need to open a discourse—where there is no effective discourse now—about the varying temporalities, spatialities, and materialities that we might represent in our databases, with a view to designing for maximum flexibility and allowing as possible for an emergent polyphony° and polychrony.° Raw data is both an oxymoron° and a bad idea; to the contrary, data should be cooked with care.
>
> —Geoffrey Bowker (2005, pp. 183–184)

The era of Big Data has begun. Computer scientists, physicists, economists, mathematicians, political scientists, bio-informaticists, sociologists, and many others are clamoring for access to the massive quantities of information produced by and about people, things, and their interactions. Diverse groups argue about the potential benefits and costs of analyzing information from Twitter, Google, Verizon, 23andMe,° Facebook, Wikipedia, and every space where large groups of people leave digital traces and deposit data. Significant questions emerge. Will large-scale analysis of DNA help cure diseases? Or will it usher in a new wave of medical inequality? Will data analytics help make people's access to information more efficient and effective? Or will it be used to track protesters in the streets of major cities? Will it transform how we study human communication and culture, or narrow the palette° of research options and alter what "research" means? Some or all of the above?

---

polyphony: music having more than one part in harmony.

polychrony: in computing, polychronous systems are those with "multiple clocks" that can accommodate the different rates of sampling images or sounds that movies and the television systems of the United States and Europe use as they sample the continuous image that is being recorded.

oxymoron: a contradictory term, e.g., *living dead*, *open secret*, *organized mess*.

23andMe: a California-based biotechnology and personal genomics company that uses a test based on a person's saliva sample to determine ancestry. From 2006 until 2013, it also used this test to provide customers with health-related results, but the U.S. Food and Drug Administration forced it to stop providing that information. In 2014, it began marketing both products in Canada.

palette: the board on which a painter mixes the colors she/he uses, or, by extension, the range of colors a painter uses. In computing, it's the number of colors a given system can manage; here, used figuratively to mean the issues researchers might think worth investigating.

This piece begins by making a definitional argument about Big Data. That definition informs all the other arguments that boyd and Crawford make. For more on arguments of definition, see Chapter 9.

LINK TO P. 185

relationality: how something relates to other things.

mine (data): to analyze data from multiple perspectives.

aggregate (data): to combine (presumably anonymous) data from individual records to form a larger data set that can be used for research purposes.

salience: the quality of being noticeable, of standing out from other similar things.

actuary: someone who specializes in calculating the potential financial impact of risks and various kinds of uncertainties for purposes relating to insurance of all kinds, financial resource management, and the likely costs of social programs in the short and long terms.

algorithm: a set of procedures to be followed in performing a calculation, solving a problem, or manipulating data, especially by a computer.

Big Data is, in many ways, a poor term. As Lev Manovich (2011) observes, it has been used in the sciences to refer to data sets large enough to require supercomputers, although now vast sets of data can be analyzed on desktop computers with standard software. There is little doubt that the quantities of data now available are indeed large, but that's not the most relevant characteristic of this new data ecosystem. Big Data is notable not because of its size, but because of its relationality° to other data. Due to efforts to mine° and aggregate° data, Big Data is fundamentally networked. Its value comes from the patterns that can be derived by making connections between pieces of data, about an individual, about individuals in relation to others, about groups of people, or simply about the structure of information itself.

Furthermore, Big Data is important because it refers to an analytic phenomenon playing out in academia and industry. Rather than suggesting a new term, we are using Big Data here because of its popular salience° and because it is the phenomenon around Big Data that we want to address. Big Data tempts some researchers to believe that they can see everything at a 30,000-foot view. It is the kind of data that encourages the practice of apophenia: seeing patterns where none actually exist, simply because massive quantities of data can offer connections that radiate in all directions. Due to this, it is crucial to begin asking questions about the analytic assumptions, methodological frameworks, and underlying biases embedded in the Big Data phenomenon.

While databases have been aggregating data for over a century, Big Data is no longer just the domain of actuaries° and scientists. New technologies have made it possible for a wide range of people—including humanities and social science academics, marketers, governmental organizations, educational institutions, and motivated individuals—to produce, share, interact with, and organize data. Massive data sets that were once obscure and distinct are being aggregated and made easily accessible. Data is increasingly digital air: the oxygen we breathe and the carbon dioxide that we exhale. It can be a source of both sustenance and pollution.

How we handle the emergence of an era of Big Data is critical: while it is 5
taking place in an environment of uncertainty and rapid change, current decisions will have considerable impact in the future. With the increased automation of data collection and analysis—as well as algorithms° that can extract and inform us of massive patterns in human behavior—it is necessary to ask which systems are driving these practices, and which are regulating them. In *Code*, Lawrence Lessig (1999) argued that systems are regulated

by four forces: the market, the law, social norms, and architecture°—or, in the case of technology, code. When it comes to Big Data, these four forces are at work and, frequently, at odds. The market sees Big Data as pure opportunity: marketers use it to target advertising, insurance providers want to optimize their offerings, and Wall Street bankers use it to read better readings on market temperament. Legislation has already been proposed to curb the collection and retention of data, usually over concerns about privacy (for example, the Do Not Track Online Act of 2011 in the United States). Features like personalization allow rapid access to more relevant information, but they present difficult ethical questions and fragment the public in problematic ways (Pariser, 2011).

architecture: with respect to computing, the structure of the system, both the hardware and the software.

There are some significant and insightful studies currently being done that draw on Big Data methodologies, particularly studies of practices in social network sites like Facebook and Twitter. Yet, it is imperative that we begin asking critical questions about what all this data means, who gets access to it, how it is deployed, and to what ends. With Big Data come big responsibilities. In this essay, we are offering six provocations that we hope can spark conversations about the issues of Big Data. Social and cultural researchers have a stake in the computational culture of Big Data precisely because many of its central questions are fundamental to our disciplines. Thus, we believe that it is time to start critically interrogating this phenomenon, its assumptions, and its biases.

1. Automating Research Changes the Definition of Knowledge

In the early decades of the twentieth century, Henry Ford devised a manufacturing system of mass production, using specialized machinery and standardized products. Simultaneously, it became the dominant vision of technological progress. Fordism meant automation and assembly lines, and for decades onward, this became the orthodoxy° of manufacturing: out with skilled craftspeople and slow work, in with a new machine-made era (Baca, 2004). But it was more than just a new set of tools. The twentieth century was marked by Fordism at a cellular° level: it produced a new understanding of labor, the human relationship to work, and society at large.

orthodoxy: Greek for "correct belief"; a generally accepted belief or set of beliefs.

cellular: here, at the level of the small unit, the individual.

Big Data not only refers to very large data sets and the tools and procedures used to manipulate and analyze them, but also to a computational turn in thought and research (Burkholder, 1992). Just as Ford changed the way we made cars—and then transformed work itself—Big Data has emerged as a system of knowledge that is already changing the objects of knowledge, while also having the power to inform how we understand human networks and community. "Change the instruments, and you will change the entire social theory that goes with them," Latour° reminds us (2009, p. 9).

[. . .]

5. Just Because It Is Accessible Doesn't Make It Ethical

In 2006, a Harvard-based research project started gathering the profiles of 1,700 college-based Facebook users to study how their interests and friendships changed over time (Lewis et al., 2008). This supposedly anonymous data was released to the world, allowing other researchers to explore and analyze it. What other researchers quickly discovered was that it was possible to de-anonymize parts of the data set: compromising the privacy of students, none of whom were aware their data was being collected (Zimmer, 2008).

The case made headlines, and raised a difficult issue for scholars: what is 10
the status of so-called "public" data on social media sites? Can it simply be used, without requesting permission? What constitutes best ethical practice for researchers? Privacy campaigners already see this as a key battleground where better privacy protections are needed. The difficulty is that privacy breaches are hard to make specific—is there damage done at the time? What about twenty years hence? "Any data on human subjects inevitably raise privacy issues, and the real risks of abuse of such data are difficult to quantify" (*Nature*, cited in Berry, 2011).

Even when researchers try to be cautious about their procedures, they are not always aware of the harm they might be causing in their research. For example, a group of researchers noticed that there was a correlation between self-injury ("cutting"°) and suicide. They prepared an educational intervention seeking to discourage people from engaging in acts of self-injury, only to learn that their intervention prompted an increase in suicide attempts. For some, self-injury was a safety valve that kept the desire to attempt suicide at bay. They immediately ceased their intervention (Emmens & Phippen, 2010).

Institutional Review Boards° (IRBs)—and other research ethics committees—emerged in the 1970s to oversee research on human subjects. While unquestionably problematic in implementation (Schrag, 2010), the goal of IRBs is to provide a framework for evaluating the ethics of a particular line of research inquiry and to make certain that checks and balances are put into place to protect subjects. Practices like "informed consent"° and protecting the privacy of informants are intended to empower participants in light of earlier abuses in the medical and social sciences (Blass, 2004; Reverby,

Bruno Latour (1947–): French philosopher and sociologist of science whose work often focuses on careful analysis of how scientists in fact do their work.

cutting: form of self-harm often involving razor blades. It is generally not done with the intention to commit suicide, but it represents the cutter's attempt to deal with extreme anger, frustration, or emotional pain.

Institutional Review Boards: federally mandated committees at colleges, universities, and research institutes that approve and oversee all research involving human subjects. While their primary function is to protect the rights of those who participate as research subjects, these boards also work to protect the institution and the researchers involved from risk.

informed consent: here, the process for getting someone's permission before he/she participates in a research study; with rare exception, informed consent requires that individuals understand the nature of the research they are participating in even if there may be sound reasons for not revealing all the details of the research. The point here is that, minimally, individuals must be aware that they are agreeing to be part of a research study and that data collected from them is being analyzed.

2009). Although IRBs cannot always predict the harm of a particular study—and, all too often, prevent researchers from doing research on grounds other than ethics—their value is in prompting scholars to think critically about the ethics of their research.

With Big Data emerging as a research field, little is understood about the ethical implications of the research being done. Should someone be included as a part of a large aggregate of data? What if someone's "public" blog post is taken out of context and analyzed in a way that the author never imagined? What does it mean for someone to be spotlighted or to be analyzed without knowing it? Who is responsible for making certain that individuals and communities are not hurt by the research process? What does consent look like?

It may be unreasonable to ask researchers to obtain consent from every person who posts a tweet, but it is unethical for researchers to justify their actions as ethical simply because the data is accessible. Just because content is publicly accessible doesn't mean that it was meant to be consumed by just anyone (boyd & Marwick, 2011). There are serious issues involved in the ethics of online data collection and analysis (Ess, 2002). The process of evaluating the research ethics cannot be ignored simply because the data is seemingly accessible. Researchers must keep asking themselves—and their colleagues—about the ethics of their data collection, analysis, and publication.

15 In order to act in an ethical manner, it is important that scholars reflect on the importance of accountability. In the case of Big Data, this means both accountability to the field of research and accountability to the research subjects. Academic researchers are held to specific professional standards when working with human participants in order to protect their rights and well-being. However, many ethics boards do not understand the processes of mining and anonymizing Big Data, let alone the errors that can cause data to become personally identifiable. Accountability to the field and to human subjects requires rigorous thinking about the ramifications of Big Data, rather than assuming that ethics boards will necessarily do the work of ensuring people are protected. Accountability here is used as a broader concept than privacy, as Troshynski et al. (2008) have outlined, where the concept of accountability can apply even when conventional expectations of privacy aren't in question. Instead, accountability is a multi-directional relationship: there may be accountability to superiors, to colleagues, to participants, and to the public (Dourish & Bell, 2011).

There are significant questions of truth, control, and power in Big Data studies: researchers have the tools and the access, while social media users as a whole do not. Their data was created in highly context-sensitive spaces, and it is entirely possible that some social media users would not give permission for their data to be used elsewhere. Many are not aware of the multiplicity of agents and algorithms currently gathering and storing their data for future use. Researchers are rarely in a user's imagined audience; neither are users necessarily aware of all the multiple uses, profits, and other gains that come from information they have posted. Data may be public (or semipublic) but this does not simplistically equate with full permission being given for all uses. There is a considerable difference between being in public and being public, which is rarely acknowledged by Big Data researchers.

Acknowledgements

We wish to thank Heather Casteel for her help in preparing this article. We are also deeply grateful to Eytan Adar, Tarleton Gillespie, and Christian Sandvig for inspiring conversations, suggestions, and feedback.

References

Baca, G. (2004). Legends of Fordism: Between myth, history, and foregone conclusions. *Social Analysis* 48(3), 169–178.

Berry, D. (2011). The computational turn: Thinking about the digital humanities. *Culture Machine* 12. Retrieved from http://www.culturemachine.net/index.php/cm/article/view/440/470

Blass, T. (2004). *The man who shocked the world: The life and legacy of Stanley Milgram.* New York, NY: Basic Books.

Bowker, G. C. (2005). *Memory practices in the sciences.* Cambridge, MA: MIT Press.

boyd, d., & Marwick, A. (2011). *Social privacy in networked publics: Teens' attitudes, practices, and strategies.* Paper presented at Oxford Internet Institute Decade in Time Conference, Oxford, England.

Burkholder, L. (Ed.). (1992). *Philosophy and the computer.* Boulder, CO: Westview Press.

Dourish, P., & Bell, G. (2011). *Divining a digital future: Mess and mythology in ubiquitous computing.* Cambridge, MA: MIT Press.

Emmens, T., & Phippen, A. (2010). Evaluating online safety programs. Harvard Berkman Center for Internet and Society. Retrieved from http://cyber.law.harvard.edu/sites/cyber.law.harvard.edu/files/Emmens_Phippen_Evaluating-Online-Safety-Programs_2010.pdf

Ess, C. (2002). Ethical decision-making and Internet research: Recommendations from the AOIR ethics working committee. Association of Internet Researchers. Retrieved from http://aoir.org/reports/ethics.pdf

Kranzberg, M. (1986). Technology and history: Kranzberg's laws. *Technology and Culture* 27(3), 544–560.

Latour, B. (2009). Tarde's idea of quantification. In M. Candea (Ed.), *The social after Gabriel Tarde: Debates and assessments* (pp. 145–162). London, England: Routledge.

Lessig, L. (1999). *Code: And other laws of cyberspace*. New York, NY: Basic Books.

Lewis, K., Kaufman, J., Gonzalez, M., Wimmer, A., & Christakis, N. (2008). Tastes, ties, and time: A new social network dataset using Facebook.com. *Social Networks* 30, 330–342.

Manovich, L. (2011). Trending: The promises and the challenges of big social data. In M. K. Gold (Ed.), *Debates in the digital humanities*. Minneapolis: University of Minnesota.

Pariser, E. (2011). *The filter bubble: What the Internet is hiding from you*. New York, NY: Penguin.

Reverby, S. M. (2009). *Examining Tuskegee: The infamous syphilis study and its legacy*. Chapel Hill: University of North Carolina.

Schrag, Z. M. (2010). *Ethical imperialism: Institutional review boards and the social sciences, 1965–2009*. Baltimore, MD: Johns Hopkins University.

Troshynski, E., Lee, C., & Dourish, P. (2008). Accountabilities of presence: Reframing location-based systems. *CHI '08 Proceedings of the SIGCHI Conference on Human Factors in Computing Systems*, 487–496. doi:10.1145/1357054.1357133

Zimmer, M. (2008). More on the "anonymity" of the Facebook dataset—It's Harvard College [Blog post]. Retrieved from http://www.michaelzimmer.org/2008/01/03/more-on-the-anonymity-of-the-facebook-dataset-its-harvard-college/

RESPOND •

1. How, for boyd and Crawford, do automating research and using Big Data change the definition of knowledge? And what specific ethical issues does Big Data raise for these authors? Why?
2. boyd and Crawford quote Bruno Latour, who notes, "Change the instruments, and you will change the entire social theory that goes with them" (paragraph 8). What does Latour mean? How does it relate to boyd and Crawford's stance at this point in the selection and throughout their argument? What sort of causal argument is this? (Chapter 11 discusses the forms of causal argument that we usually encounter.)
3. As in much academic writing, definitional arguments play an important role in boyd and Crawford's discussion. Examine how the authors define the following terms and how they use them to further their own argument: *Big Data* (paragraphs 1–3), *apophenia* (paragraph 3), *Fordism* (paragraphs 7–8), *self-injury* (paragraph 11), and *accountability*

(paragraph 15). How do boyd and Crawford both offer a definition or characterization of the concept and then employ that notion to support or explain a point they wish to make? By the way, note that in none of these situations do the authors quote *Webster's* or some other dictionary; instead, they construct their definitions in other ways. (Chapter 9 on arguments of definition may prove useful in helping you answer this question.)

4. Another interesting (and common) feature of boyd and Crawford's academic writing style is the use of figurative language. What sort of figurative language is being used in these examples?
   a. Will it transform how we study human communication and culture, or narrow the palette of research options and alter what "research" means? (paragraph 1)
   b. Data is increasingly digital air: the oxygen we breathe and the carbon dioxide that we exhale. (paragraph 4)
   c. The twentieth century was marked by Fordism at a cellular level: it produced a new understanding of labor, the human relationship to work, and society at large. (paragraph 7)

   How does the use of this figurative language help advance the arguments being made? (Chapter 13 on style in arguments discusses figurative language.)

5. Begin where boyd and Crawford end their essay. What is the difference between being in public and being public with respect to the sorts of Big Data that these authors discuss? Investigate two forms of social media that you are familiar with (or, better yet, that you use) to see what sorts of access those who frequent each site give the developers with respect to the use of data about their behavior on that site or others that are tracked. (In other words, when someone clicks "Agree" on one of these sites, what information is now "public" to the developers of the site?) **Write an argument of fact** in which you present your findings, linking them to the contrast between "being in public" online and "being public" online. (Chapter 8 will be useful here.) You may also wish to use this information **to evaluate** the situation (Chapter 10) or **make a proposal** about it (Chapter 12).

▼ *In this interview from July 30, 2014, with Christian Rudder, one of the co-founders of the dating site OkCupid and author of* Dataclysm: Who We Are (When We Think No One Is Looking) *(2014), Todd Zwillich, Washington correspondent for* The Takeaway, *a Public Radio International program of news and commentary, asks probing questions about experiments OkCupid ran on users without their foreknowledge or permission. Zwillich has been a journalist in Washington for fifteen years, working first in print; he has been in public radio since 2006. In contrast to the first three selections in this chapter, this piece focuses on industry, not government, and it concerns exactly the sorts of issues raised by boyd and Crawford in the previous selection,* Six Provocations for Big Data.

If you listen to this interview (at http://bit.ly/1HK3VHb), you'll be reminded that speakers have resources to communicate that differ in important ways from those writers have and that spoken and written language—at least in academic contexts—can be quite distinct. For example, you'll notice that Rudder frequently uses intonation in interesting ways: his pitch will often go up when he is emphasizing new or important information. A writer would have to find other ways to show this emphasis. Similarly, you'll hear Rudder using hedges like "kind of" or "sort of." Linguists have demonstrated that speakers often use such expressions to minimize the force of what follows, that is, to try to lessen its impact. Pay attention to where they occur; as you'll see, it's no surprise that the title of this interview in the original URL (rather than the shortened one given above) is "are-okcupids-experiments-users-ethical." You'll get to be the judge of whether they are or aren't as we continue exploring issues of privacy and surveillance.

It's Not OK Cupid: Co-Founder Defends User Experiments

TODD ZWILLICH AND CHRISTIAN RUDDER

Note on the transcript: We've tried to stick as close as possible to the interview in transcribing this interaction. In other words, we haven't cleaned up the *um*'s, the repeated words, or the occasions when a speaker corrects himself to encourage you to think about the complex relationship between spoken and written language. In the transcript, *overlap* refers to two people talking at once; as you'll hear, neither speaker seems to treat the overlap that occurs as interruption.

Danil Nevsky/Shutterstock

TODD ZWILLICH: Dating online can feel like a shot in the dark when you're looking for love, but for those in the business of selling matchmaking services online, there's not a whole lot of mystery to it. It's not about magic; it's all about data and algorithmic° calculations. But this week, online dating giant OkCupid came under a little bit of fire for taking the scientific approach to matchmaking to the next level when it revealed it had conducted experiments on its own users. Ricardo Sanchez sent us this tweet: "Not cool," he writes. "The participants were drafted without their permission."

algorithmic: relating to algorithms, sets of procedures to be followed in performing a calculation, solving a problem, or manipulating data, especially by a computer.

And it's not the first time OkCupid has done research like this on the behavior of its members. In the past, the site's team has used its trove of data to identify things like whether you should use a smiley or a flirty face in your profile to get more response, how much skin to show in a photo, even what kind of camera takes the best headshot. But what makes the online-dating company's latest research a little different is that it actually involved manipulating the information that users received about potential matches. Did they learn anything by doing this? Christian Rudder, co-founder of OkCupid, joins me now. He's also author of the forthcoming book *Dataclysm*. Christian, welcome.

CHRISTIAN RUDDER: Thank you, glad to be here.

TZ: Everybody heard about Facebook and . . .

CR: Right. (CR *overlaps* TZ *in a low voice.*)

TZ: Everybody heard about the experiment that Facebook was conducting° on its users. Explain how your manipulations of your users are different.

CR: You know, we're a dating site, so we took groups of people who, uh, we thought were bad matches and told them they were good—for each other, and we took a group of people who were people we thought would be good for each other, and told them that we were bad, that they were bad—uh, for each other. And the goal was kind of to test our estimation of how compatible they were against like the kind of like, uh, null hypothesis,° you know, from the scientific method, essentially. We had our method, and then we had essentially nonsense—a random° recommendation—and we wanted to see how we did against that.

TZ: And that's all you did? What else did you do?

CR: Um, the other stuff is fairly straightforward Web design stuff. Like, we showed some profiles, um, with the picture and the text that the user entered, and then sometimes just with the picture, and kind of tracked the difference in how people judged that particular person. It came out about 90 percent the same, so your picture is 90 percent of the, uh, of that first impression.

TZ: I think that surprises nobody.

CR: No, of course not! Yeah. (*laughs*) Um, and then, one was kind of an implied experiment: There was a day in 2013 when we turned off all the photos on the site, for, uh, about seven hours and kind of, uh, let users use OkCupid without being able to see who they were talking to. And then so if you compare that against a normal day, uh, you see that the site is actually a lot healthier in terms of how people reply to messages, and kind of like length and sort of velocity of conversations is actually a lot better when there's no photos, except that people just don't want to use a dating site with no photos, so we would be a better and infinitely smaller site.

TZ: Getting back to the first thing that you mentioned . . .

CR: Uh-hm.

TZ: The power of suggestion: telling people that they weren't good matches when maybe your algorithm thought that they were, or vice versa.

CR: Exactly.

TZ: This is the part that a lot of people had a problem with, primarily, I think, because somebody might have thought, "Somebody who might have been a

experiment that Facebook was conducting: this experiment and the questions it raised were discussed by boyd and Crawford (paragraphs 9–10).

null hypothesis: the assumption that there is no statistically significant relationship between A and B; in other words, any apparent relationship is, in fact, due to chance and not real. Researchers in the social and natural sciences who analyze quantitative data always begin with the assumption of the null hypothesis and then attempt to disprove it by demonstrating that the relationship between A and B likely does exist because it is statistically significant, that is, it can be demonstrated that the findings did not occur by chance.

random: it is not clear here whether Rudder is using this term in its everyday or its technical sense. In its everyday sense, *random* would mean something like "having no rhyme or reason" while in its technical sense, it would mean "governed by the laws of chance or probability so that any possible match would have an equal chance of being offered."

good match for me, I might have missed them because I was told they weren't, and I'm not, uh, you know, I might have missed my, 'the one,'" I guess.

CR: Sure, yeah, I definitely understand people's misgiving. But first of all, like every user who sent a message under this kind of test "match-percentage" was notified after the fact of the experiment. You know, say, if we were matched together: "Hey, Christian, you know, your match percentage with Todd was misstated because of a test. Uh, the correct percentage is 30" or whatever. Also, it's—we see it as just a part of the continuum of experiments that we are always doing on the site. I mean, just for match-percentage alone, we might change or reweight a variable, and inevitably, people are going to see two different numbers. It's a continuum. It's kind of at the end of it, but it's still part of . . . normal business.

TZ: Um, I'm not quite sure I understand how this manipulation of users, which I'm sure was allowed under your user agreement . . .

CR: Right.

TZ: I'm not quite sure I understand—what that tells you about your own algorithm. It certainly tells you the power of suggestion, which is, if you tell somebody that somebody's no good for them, they're likely to believe it. That I get. But what did you learn about your own business? Because it's, uh, not obvious to me.

Christian Rudder Jayne Orenstein/The Washington Post/Getty Images

CR: Well, I think the reason it's not obvious is that we found that the algorithm actually kind of worked. But imagine it in the other way around; like, what if we had tested our best guess about compatibility against kind of a nonsense measure, which is what we did, and the nonsense one was better, that our best guess was actually worse than random, you know. Then obviously, we got to go back to the drawing board, and our whole reason for existence is called into question at that point. 'Cause I mean, the other option, if we just did nothing, you know, we obviously misled a small number of users as part of this experiment. If we don't test it, the possibility that we're misleading the four million people who come to the site every month, every day, uh, that's the other kind of thing that hangs in the balance.

TZ: So we should be clear: When people write stories about what OkCupid did, or even what Facebook did, social scientists are commenting on how these types of experiments are important. You didn't do this for any redeeming social value whatsoever; you did this for your own purposes and to test your own algorithms and your own model.

CR: Yeah, for sure. This, these particular experiments were kind of part of the normal course of our business. Unlike Facebook's, which, I mean, um, I'm a Facebook user like anyone else—I don't own shares or anything like this—and the one thing that has kind of gone under the radar is that they have put together like a world-class scholarship academic team to do, basically, public research for the public good.

TZ: Right. But yours was different.

CR: No, no, ours was definitely different. (*Overlaps with* TZ)

TZ: This, this was not for the public good.

CR: No, no. (*Continued overlap with* TZ)

TZ: This was for your good.

CR: That's right.

TZ: And people need to understand that.

CR: Of course, yeah, yeah. And, and, look, if there's kind of a public-facing part of what we did, it's to point out to every person that uses the Internet, that every site does these experiments. It's not just OkCupid. Google, you know, their search algorithm gets better because they test version A against version B, and, you know, it sounds a little bit trivial or boring, but that means that for the people in the various groups, they kind of like, truth in the world is reordered by those search results, you know. And so, all of these things are always happening all the time.

TZ: Let's talk about the trust factor a little bit.

CR: Sure.

TZ: Um, it's probably clear, again, that in your user agreement that somebody clicked, buried in there somewhere, it says, you can do this, . . .

CR: Sure.

TZ: So it's not like . . .

CR: You bet.

TZ: There. Right. It's not like there wasn't disclosure. Not that anybody reads those things.

CR: Yeah. Uh.

TZ: That's their own problem. But what about the trust factor? It is the case that, uh, when people are on a site like yours, they are trying to meet someone, whether it's just for a casual date or to find the one for them.

CR: Absolutely.

TZ: If they feel that not everything is necessarily straightforward, and that the people they are seeing or meeting or talking to has something else behind it besides love (maybe), um, how do you answer them?

CR: Well, I would say that people come to us expecting us to do a good job finding them sex, a date, a marriage, whatever: uh, it's totally right. And, uh, they trust us to do that, and part of us delivering on that trust is actually making sure that what we do, works. Like, so, we try to prove it. And of course, that involves — an experiment. Um, and we take a small group of users and test any idea — you know, this is one particular test, but we test it. And then so those small groups of users bear a sort of cost for keeping the site good for everyone else and for themselves. As soon as we end the experiment, we make the site better. So, it's part of delivering on the promise rather than betraying it.

TZ: Well, Christian Rudder, uh, let's sum it up a bit. After all this, what did you learn?

banal: obvious or not very interesting.

CR: Well, um, you know, the company learned a few banal° things: you know, pictures matter and, and the power of suggestion works, like you said. But I guess for us institutionally, um, or for me personally, I learned there's a long way to go until the public sort of understands the way Web sites work, and I think, obviously, we, we sensationalized it a little bit, but I think it's a discussion that needs to continue.

TZ: And that maybe everybody, every time they go on a Web site, should have it in their mind that they are being watched.

CR: Absolutely. Not only being watched, but, you know, there's someone that's looking at that exact same Web page that's seeing something different.

TZ: Christian Rudder is the co-founder and president of OkCupid. He's the author of the forthcoming book *Dataclysm*.

RESPOND

1. What issues does this interview raise about Big Data, social media sites, research, and ethics?
2. Characterize the stance that Christian Rudder takes with regard to the issues raised in question 1 above. Based on his questions and comments, what do you imagine the stance of Todd Zwillich to be? If you cannot characterize his stance or are not sure about it, do you see that situation as a good or bad thing, given Zwillich's role as interviewer and radio host? Why?
3. At one point, Rudder comments:

   > There was a day in 2013 when we turned off all the photos on the site, for, uh, about seven hours and kind of, uh, let users use OkCupid without being able to see who they were talking to. And then so if you compare that against a normal day, uh, you see that the site is actually a lot healthier in terms of how people reply to messages, and kind of like length and sort of velocity of conversations is actually a lot better when there's no photos.

   Why might it be the case that the site was "healthier" when there were no photos? And why don't people want to use a dating site without photos, even one that might be healthier?
4. Characterize the ethos that Zwillich and Rudder create for themselves in this interview. How would you describe Zwillich's performance as an interviewer and radio host? How would you describe Rudder's ability to respond to Zwillich's questions and to support the claims he makes? (Information from Chapter 3 on arguments based on ethos, or character, will likely be useful in answering this question.)

5. Examine the contexts in which Rudder uses "sort of" or "kind of." (The best way to do this is to underline or highlight each occurrence of it along with whatever occurs after it, e.g., "And the goal was *kind of to test our estimation* of how compatible they were.") When does Rudder tend to use either of these expressions? (Certainly, his use of them is not conscious or intentional.) If we treat them as hedges, which seek to soften the impact of whatever follows, what might Rudder be weakening the force of? How does such a pattern of use influence the ethos he creates for himself? Why?

6. As noted, unplanned spoken talk of the sort that occurs during interviews is quite different in many ways from highly planned and edited written academic discourse even when the topic is the same. **Write a one-page summary** of this interview as if you were planning to use the summary, or part of it, in an academic research paper. If you wish to use direct quotations, you'll likely want to choose them carefully or edit them carefully to avoid passages that contain fillers like "um" or repeated words; you'll also need to incorporate any quotations, whether phrases or sentences, into your text correctly. Paraphrases may prove especially useful precisely because of the spoken nature of this selection. (The section on synthesizing information in Chapter 20 will help you with this task. You'll need to use the information in Chapter 22 on documenting sources to help you determine the correct format for citing the interview.)

▼ *In June 2014, the U.S. Supreme Court issued a landmark ruling regarding cell phones and privacy, addressing the question of whether law enforcement officials could search the cell phone of someone who has been arrested without first obtaining a warrant*° *to do so. With its decision that such warrantless searches are unconstitutional, the court redefined the criteria for balancing the competing interests of law enforcement officials, on the one hand, and individuals who own cell phones and who are concerned about their privacy, on the other. The excerpt of the ruling included here gives you an opportunity to see the arguments made by the court about privacy as it relates to cell phones while examining how legal argumentation works generally.*

As will become immediately clear when you begin reading, legal discourse seems to be a world of its own. In the next few paragraphs, we try to give you a road map to help you understand this legal ruling and legal discourse generally, particularly its system of documentation. We hope this information will help you see the ways that legal opinions represent stasis theory in action. Their structure is completely predictable. After stating the legal question at issue, they move to an argument of fact in which the relevant facts of the case are presented, then an argument of definition in which the relevant laws and prior legal rulings are reviewed, followed by an evaluative argument in which the facts of the case are evaluated in light of the law, and, finally, a holding, or judgment, along with the reasoning behind that judgment.

With regard to this specific ruling, the court examined two cases that pose the same question: whether the police can legally search an individual's cell phone without having a warrant to do so. The first case, from which the ruling takes its name, Riley v. California, *involves events that occurred in 2009. The relevant details of this case are included in the excerpt below. In court cases, the plaintiff, or complaining party who has filed the lawsuit, also called the petitioner, is named first while the defendant, or party being sued, is named second. In the original case, David Riley sued the State of California. (Often, in writing and conversation, the case is simply referred to as* Riley *if there is no chance of confusion.)*

The second case the court considered in this ruling is U.S. v. Brima Wurie. *The details of this are relevant to understanding this excerpt. In this case, the police stopped Brima Wurie in 2007 for making what appeared to be a drug sale while he was in his car. They also confiscated two cell phones, one of which was an older flip phone. Using information found on this older phone, the police were able to locate Wurie's home address, obtain a search warrant, and seize "215 grams of crack cocaine, marijuana, drug*

warrant: in legal contexts, a document that authorizes its holder to carry out actions such as making an arrest, searching and perhaps seizing property, or ensuring that a judgment is carried out. In Toulmin argument (as discussed in Chapter 7), a warrant is the connection, often an unstated principle or assumed chain of reasoning, between a particular claim and the reason(s) supporting it—in short, the glue that holds the claim and reason together.

paraphernalia, a firearm, and ammunition." Wurie was later sentenced to nearly twenty-two years in prison for crimes relating to the drug sale and the seized drugs and firearms. During Wurie's trial, his attorneys argued that information obtained from the search of their client's apartment should not be admissible° because the seizure of his cell phones was illegal under the Fourth Amendment,° which prevents unreasonable seizures. The district court rejected this argument and permitted information obtained from the search to be heard at trial. Wurie appealed his case on the grounds that the district court's ruling on this issue was faulty.

admissible: able to be heard in court, thus becoming part of the facts of the trial.

Fourth Amendment: the Fourth Amendment of the U.S. Constitution protects anyone in the country from "unreasonable searches and seizures."

The appeals court overturned the decision of the district court, agreeing with Wurie that the information obtained from the search of his apartment should not have been heard in court. Thus, Wurie's sentence was dropped. In its ruling, the appeals court argued that cell phones cannot be searched without a warrant because unlike the other sorts of possessions a person might have on his/her body—a wallet, a note, or a piece of mail—all of which can be searched without a warrant, cell phones can contain far more personal data than these other items.

After Wurie won the appeal, the case was appealed to the Supreme Court, whose decision is binding and becomes the law of the land. The U.S. Department of Justice considered the question of whether cell phones could be searched without a warrant to be an important legal issue and, therefore, became part of the case. When the United States appealed this case to the Supreme Court, the court ultimately accepted the appeals court's argument and built upon it, as you will see in the excerpt.

As you read this excerpt from Riley v. California, *consider how this redefinition of the nature of privacy with regard to cell phones has consequences for you and your legal rights as well as how it illustrates the power of stasis theory and argument to change the nature of what we experience as reality.*

A Word about Legal Documentation

The legal profession uses a system of documenting sources that is all its own. Although you do not need to understand the details, the following observations may help you appreciate how the system works as well as how legal professionals provide support for their claims.

First, there are many references to laws, earlier court decisions, or to other relevant sources. These will often be introduced by "See" or "Compare" as in the example "See Cal. Penal Code Ann. §§12025(a)(1), 12031(a)(1) (West 2009)" *(paragraph 3), which refers the reader to specific sections of the California Penal Code as annotated by Thomson West. You'll also find abbreviations you may not be familiar with:* App. *(appendix),* supra *(cited above), and* Id. *(the previous cited reference). While you can ignore the specifics of such citations, pay attention to the frequency with which they occur. In some legal writing, every sentence will be followed by a citation to various laws, previous court rulings, or other reliable sources of information.*

Finally, the version of the ruling excerpted here is a slip opinion. Slip opinions represent an early stage in a ruling becoming official; in other words, they are semi-official drafts, issued shortly after a ruling, allowing for its broad dissemination. They are, however, subject to correction, which includes the addition of official case reference and page numbers. The court later compiles the corrected version of the ruling along with other rulings from the same period into a bound volume, at which point the ruling becomes fully official. Because slip opinions have no case numbers or page numbers, you'll see earlier slip opinions cited in this ruling in the following way: "See United States v. Jones, 565 U.S. ___, ___ (2012) (SOTOMAYOR, J., concurring) (slip op., at 3)." *Interestingly, legal professionals use* "at" *to mean* "on page."

The Supreme Court AP Photo/Pablo Martinez Monsivais

Opinion of the Court

SUPREME COURT OF THE UNITED STATES

Nos. 13–132 and 13–212

DAVID LEON RILEY, PETITIONER
13–132 *v.*
CALIFORNIA

ON WRIT OF CERTIORARI° TO THE COURT OF APPEAL OF CALIFORNIA, FOURTH APPELLATE DISTRICT, DIVISION ONE

UNITED STATES, PETITIONER
13–212 *v.*
BRIMA WURIE

ON WRIT OF CERTIORARI TO THE UNITED STATES COURT OF APPEALS FOR THE FIRST CIRCUIT

[June 25, 2014]

CHIEF JUSTICE ROBERTS delivered the opinion of the Court.

These two cases raise a common question: whether the police may, without a warrant, search digital information on a cell phone seized from an individual who has been arrested.

writ of certiorari: decision of the Supreme Court to hear an appeal about a case decided by a lower appeals court.

I

A

In the first case, petitioner David Riley was stopped by a police officer for driving with expired registration tags. In the course of the stop, the officer also learned that Riley's license had been suspended. The officer impounded Riley's car, pursuant to department policy, and another officer conducted an inventory search of the car. Riley was arrested for possession of concealed and loaded firearms when that search turned up two handguns under the car's hood. See Cal. Penal Code Ann. §§12025(a)(1), 12031(a)(1) (West 2009).

An officer searched Riley incident to the arrest and found items associated with the "Bloods"° street gang. He also seized a cell phone from Riley's pants pocket. According to Riley's uncontradicted assertion, the phone was a "smart phone," a cell phone with a broad range of other functions based on advanced computing capability, large storage capacity, and Internet

Bloods and Crips: two rival gangs that often engage in violent criminal action, including exterminating one another's members.

Opinion of the Court

connectivity. The officer accessed information on the phone and noticed that some words (presumably in text messages or a contacts list) were preceded by the letters "CK" — a label that, he believed, stood for "Crip Killers," a slang term for members of the Bloods gang.

At the police station about two hours after the arrest, a detective specializing in gangs further examined the contents of the phone. The detective testified that he "went through" Riley's phone "looking for evidence, because . . . gang members will often video themselves with guns or take pictures of themselves with the guns." App. in No. 13–132, p. 20. Although there was "a lot of stuff" on the phone, particular files that "caught [the detective's] eye" included videos of young men sparring while someone yelled encouragement using the moniker° "Blood." *Id.*, at 11–13. The police also found photographs of Riley standing in front of a car they suspected had been involved in a shooting a few weeks earlier. 5

Riley was ultimately charged, in connection with that earlier shooting, with firing at an occupied vehicle, assault with a semiautomatic firearm, and attempted murder. The State alleged that Riley had committed those crimes for the benefit of a criminal street gang, an aggravating factor° that carries an enhanced sentence.° Compare Cal. Penal Code Ann. §246 (2008) with §186.22(b)(4)(B) (2014). Prior to trial, Riley moved to suppress all evidence° that the police had obtained from his cell phone. He contended that the searches of his phone violated the Fourth Amendment, because they had been performed without a warrant and were not otherwise justified by exigent circumstances.° The trial court rejected that argument. App. in No. 13–132, at 24, 26. At Riley's trial, police officers testified about the photographs and videos found on the phone, and some of the photographs were admitted into evidence. Riley was convicted on all three counts and received an enhanced sentence of fifteen years to life in prison.

[. . .]

II

The Fourth Amendment provides:

> "The right of the people to be secure in their persons, houses, papers, and effects, against unreasonable searches and seizures, shall not be violated, and no Warrants shall issue, but upon probable cause,° supported by Oath or affirmation, and particularly describing the place to be searched, and the persons or things to be seized."

moniker: nickname.

aggravating factor: something that could increase the seriousness of a criminal act; here, the fact that the crime was claimed to be gang-related.

enhanced sentence: a longer sentence or a more onerous sentence (e.g., a higher fine) resulting from the presence of one or more aggravating factors.

suppress all evidence: prevent evidence from being introduced in court and becoming part of the facts of the case.

exigent circumstances: urgent situations that permit a law officer legally to search a building or part of a building without a warrant.

probable cause: reasonable legal grounds.

Opinion of the Court

As the text makes clear, "the ultimate touchstone° of the Fourth Amendment is 'reasonableness.'" *Brigham City* v. *Stuart*, 547 U. S. 398, 403 (2006). Our cases have determined that "[w]here a search is undertaken by law enforcement officials to discover evidence of criminal wrongdoing, . . . reasonableness generally requires the obtaining of a judicial warrant." *Vernonia School Dist. 47J* v. *Acton*, 515 U. S. 646, 653 (1995). Such a warrant ensures that the inferences to support a search are "drawn by a neutral and detached magistrate instead of being judged by the officer engaged in the often competitive enterprise of ferreting out° crime." *Johnson* v. *United States*, 333 U. S. 10, 14 (1948). In the absence of a warrant, a search is reasonable only if it falls within a specific exception to the warrant requirement. See *Kentucky* v. *King*, 563 U. S. ___, ___ (2011) (slip op., at 5–6).

The two cases before us concern the reasonableness of a warrantless search incident to a lawful arrest. In 1914, this Court first acknowledged in dictum° "the right on the part of the Government, always recognized under English and American law,° to search the person of the accused when legally arrested to discover and seize the fruits or evidences of crime." *Weeks* v. *United States*, 232 U. S. 383, 392. Since that time, it has been well accepted that such a search constitutes an exception to the warrant requirement. Indeed, the label "exception" is something of a misnomer° in this context, as warrantless searches incident to arrest° occur with far greater frequency than searches conducted pursuant to a warrant.° See 3 W. LaFave, Search and Seizure §5.2(b), p. 132, and n. 15 (5th ed. 2012).

Although the existence of the exception for such searches has been rec- 10
ognized for a century, its scope° has been debated for nearly as long. See *Arizona* v. *Gant*, 556 U. S. 332, 350 (2009) (noting the exception's "checkered° history"). That debate has focused on the extent to which officers may search property found on or near the arrestee. Three related precedents set forth the rules governing such searches:

The first, *Chimel* v. *California*, 395 U. S. 752 (1969), laid the groundwork for most of the existing search incident to arrest doctrine. Police officers in that case arrested Chimel inside his home and proceeded to search his entire three-bedroom house, including the attic and garage. In particular rooms, they also looked through the contents of drawers. *Id.*, at 753–754.

The Court crafted the following rule for assessing the reasonableness of a search incident to arrest:

touchstone: figuratively, the standard or most commonly used criterion by which something is evaluated.

ferret out: to discover though a process of thorough or crafty research much as a trained ferret hunts.

dictum (plural* dicta*): expression of judicial opinion in a court case that is not considered part of the ruling (that is, the holding) so it does not have the legal status that the ruling does.

English and American law: much of American law is based on English common law; the U.S. and English legal systems differ in fundamental ways from the legal systems of Continental Europe.

misnomer: an inaccurate name or characterization.

incident to arrest: occurring at the same time as the arrest.

pursuant to a warrant: based on a warrant or once a warrant has been obtained.

scope: range of applicability.

checkered: figuratively, characterized by both failures and successes, as a checkerboard has squares of two colors.

Opinion of the Court

> "When an arrest is made, it is reasonable for the arresting officer to search the person arrested in order to remove any weapons that the latter might seek to use in order to resist arrest or effect his escape. Otherwise, the officer's safety might well be endangered, and the arrest itself frustrated. In addition, it is entirely reasonable for the arresting officer to search for and seize any evidence on the arrestee's person in order to prevent its concealment or destruction. . . . There is ample justification, therefore, for a search of the arrestee's person and the area 'within his immediate control'—construing that phrase to mean the area from within which he might gain possession of a weapon or destructible evidence." *Id.*, at 762–763.

The extensive warrantless search of Chimel's home did not fit within this exception, because it was not needed to protect officer safety or to preserve evidence. *Id.*, at 763, 768.

Four years later, in *United States* v. *Robinson*, 414 U. S. 218 (1973), the Court applied the Chimel analysis in the context of a search of the arrestee's person. A police officer had arrested Robinson for driving with a revoked license. The officer conducted a patdown search and felt an object that he could not identify in Robinson's coat pocket. He removed the object, which turned out to be a crumpled cigarette package, and opened it. Inside were 14 capsules of heroin. *Id.*, at 220, 223.

[. . .]

The Court thus concluded that the search of Robinson was reasonable even though there was no concern about the loss of evidence, and the arresting officer had no specific concern that Robinson might be armed. *Id.*, at 236. In doing so, the Court did not draw a line between a search of Robinson's person and a further examination of the cigarette pack found during that search. It merely noted that, "[h]aving in the course of a lawful search come upon the crumpled package of cigarettes, [the officer] was entitled to inspect it." *Ibid.* A few years later, the Court clarified that this exception was limited to "personal property . . . immediately associated with the person of the arrestee." *United States* v. *Chadwick*, 433 U. S. 1, 15 (1977) (200-pound, locked footlocker could not be searched incident to arrest), abrogated° on other grounds by *California* v. *Acevedo*, 500 U. S. 565 (1991).

abrogate: overturn or repeal.

[. . .]

III

These cases require us to decide how the search incident to arrest doc- 15
trine applies to modern cell phones, which are now such a pervasive and insistent part of daily life that the proverbial° visitor from Mars might conclude they were an important feature of human anatomy. A smartphone of the sort taken from Riley was unheard of ten years ago; a significant majority of American adults now own such phones. See A. Smith, Pew Research Center, Smartphone Ownership — 2013 Update (June 5, 2013). Even less sophisticated phones like Wurie's, which have already faded in popularity since Wurie was arrested in 2007, have been around for less than fifteen years. Both phones are based on technology nearly inconceivable just a few decades ago, when *Chimel* and *Robinson* were decided.

proverbial: here, a frequently used example of.

Absent° more precise guidance from the founding era, we generally determine whether to exempt a given type of search from the warrant requirement "by assessing, on the one hand, the degree to which it intrudes upon an individual's privacy and, on the other, the degree to which it is needed for the promotion of legitimate governmental interests." *Wyoming* v. *Houghton*, 526 U. S. 295, 300 (1999). Such a balancing of interests supported the search incident to arrest exception in *Robinson*, and a mechanical application of *Robinson* might well support the warrantless searches at issue here.

absent: without.

But while *Robinson*'s categorical rule strikes the appropriate balance in the context of physical objects, neither of its rationales has much force with respect to digital content on cell phones. On the government interest side, *Robinson* concluded that the two risks identified in *Chimel* — harm to officers and destruction of evidence — are present in all custodial arrests.° There are no comparable risks when the search is of digital data. In addition, *Robinson* regarded any privacy interests retained by an individual after arrest as significantly diminished by the fact of the arrest itself. Cell phones, however, place vast quantities of personal information literally in the hands of individuals. A search of the information on a cell phone bears little resemblance to the type of brief physical search considered in *Robinson*.

custodial arrest: one in which the defendant is immediately arrested (in contrast to, e.g., being given a citation and told to appear in court at some later date).

We therefore decline to extend *Robinson* to searches of data on cell phones, and hold° instead that officers must generally secure a warrant before conducting such a search.

hold: issue a legal decision, that is, the court decides that given these facts in light of existing laws, here is the result. Holdings, which have the status of law, contrast with *dicta*, defined above.

[. . .]

Digital data stored on a cell phone cannot itself be used as a weapon to harm an arresting officer or to effectuate° the arrestee's escape. Law enforcement officers remain free to examine the physical aspects of a phone to ensure that it will not be used as a weapon — say, to determine whether

effectuate: cause to happen.

there is a razor blade hidden between the phone and its case. Once an officer has secured a phone and eliminated any potential physical threats, however, data on the phone can endanger no one.

20 Perhaps the same might have been said of the cigarette pack seized from Robinson's pocket. Once an officer gained control of the pack, it was unlikely that Robinson could have accessed the pack's contents. But unknown physical objects may always pose risks, no matter how slight, during the tense atmosphere of a custodial arrest. The officer in *Robinson* testified that he could not identify the objects in the cigarette pack but knew they were not cigarettes. See 414 U. S., at 223, 236, n. 7. Given that, a further search was a reasonable protective measure. No such unknowns exist with respect to digital data. As the First Circuit explained, the officers who searched Wurie's cell phone "knew exactly what they would find therein: data. They also knew that the data could not harm them." 728 F. 3d, at 10.

[. . .]

The United States [as petitioner in *U.S.* v. *Wurie*] asserts that a search of all data stored on a cell phone is "materially indistinguishable"° from searches of these sorts of physical items. Brief for United States in No. 13–212, p. 26. That is like saying a ride on horseback is materially indistinguishable from a flight to the moon. Both are ways of getting from point A to point B, but little else justifies lumping them together. Modern cell phones, as a category, implicate privacy concerns far beyond those implicated by the search of a cigarette pack, a wallet, or a purse. A conclusion that inspecting the contents of an arrestee's pockets works no substantial additional intrusion on privacy beyond the arrest itself may make sense as applied to physical items, but any extension of that reasoning to digital data has to rest on its own bottom.°

materially indistinguishable: the same for the purposes at hand.

rest on its own bottom: that is, stand on its own without assistance.

[. . .]

Cell phones differ in both a quantitative and a qualitative sense from other objects that might be kept on an arrestee's person. The term "cell phone" is itself misleading shorthand; many of these devices are in fact minicomputers that also happen to have the capacity to be used as a telephone. They could just as easily be called cameras, video players, rolodexes, calendars, tape recorders, libraries, diaries, albums, televisions, maps, or newspapers. One of the most notable distinguishing features of modern cell phones is their immense storage capacity. Before cell phones, a search of a person was limited by physical realities and tended as a general matter to constitute only a narrow intrusion on privacy. See Kerr, Foreword: Accounting for Technological Change, 36 Harv. J. L. & Pub. Pol'y 403, 404–405 (2013). Most people cannot lug around every piece of mail they have received for the past several months, every picture they have taken, or every book or article they have read — nor would they have any reason to attempt to do so. And if they did, they would have to drag behind them a trunk of the sort held to require a search warrant in *Chadwick*, *supra*,° rather than a container the size of the cigarette package in *Robinson*.

supra: cited above.

But the possible intrusion on privacy is not physically limited in the same way when it comes to cell phones. The current top-selling smartphone has a standard capacity of 16 gigabytes (and is available with up to 64 gigabytes). Sixteen gigabytes translates to millions of pages of text, thousands of pictures, or hundreds of videos. See Kerr, *supra*, at 404; Brief for Center for Democracy & Technology et al. as *Amici Curiae*° 7–8. Cell phones couple that capacity with the ability to store many different types of information: Even the most basic phones that sell for less than twenty dollars might hold photographs, picture messages, text messages, Internet browsing history, a calendar, a thousand-entry phone book, and so on. See *Id.*, at 30; *United States* v. *Flores-Lopez*, 670 F. 3d 803, 806 (CA7 2012). We expect that the gulf between physical practicability and digital capacity will only continue to widen in the future.

Amici Curiae ***(plural of*** **Amicus Curiae*)*:** Latin for "friend of the court"; here, documents and testimony provided by parties not involved in the legal case at hand that examine the possible legal effects of a ruling that would go beyond the case being considered. Courts have the discretion to consider or ignore such documents and testimony.

The storage capacity of cell phones has several interrelated consequences for privacy. First, a cell phone collects in one place many distinct types of information — an address, a note, a prescription, a bank statement, a video — that reveal much more in combination than any isolated record. Second, a cell phone's capacity allows even just one type of information to convey far more than previously possible. The sum of an individual's private life can be reconstructed through a thousand photographs labeled with dates, locations, and descriptions; the same cannot be said of a photograph or two of loved ones tucked into a wallet. Third, the data on a phone can date back to the purchase of the phone, or even earlier. A person might carry in his pocket a slip of paper reminding him to call Mr. Jones; he would not carry a record of all his communications with Mr. Jones for the past several months, as would routinely be kept on a phone.[1]

Finally, there is an element of pervasiveness that characterizes cell phones 25
but not physical records. Prior to the digital age, people did not typically carry a cache° of sensitive personal information with them as they went about their day. Now it is the person who is not carrying a cell phone, with

cache: here, collection.

[1] Because the United States and California agree that these cases involve *searches* incident to arrest, these cases do not implicate the question whether the collection or inspection of aggregated digital information amounts to a search under other circumstances.

all that it contains, who is the exception. According to one poll, nearly three-quarters of smartphone users report being within five feet of their phones most of the time, with 12% admitting that they even use their phones in the shower. See Harris Interactive, 2013 Mobile Consumer Habits Study (June 2013). A decade ago police officers searching an arrestee might have occasionally stumbled across a highly personal item such as a diary. See, e.g., *United States* v. *Frankenberry*, 387 F. 2d 337 (CA2 1967) (*per curiam*°). But those discoveries were likely to be few and far between. Today, by contrast, it is no exaggeration to say that many of the more than 90% of American adults who own a cell phone keep on their person a digital record of nearly every aspect of their lives — from the mundane° to the intimate. See *Ontario* v. *Quon*, 560 U. S. 746, 760 (2010). Allowing the police to scrutinize such records on a routine basis is quite different from allowing them to search a personal item or two in the occasional case.

per curiam: Latin for "by a court"; the unsigned decision of a single judge or the unanimous decision of a court consisting of several judges hearing a case on appeal (in contrast to an opinion whose author is identified).

mundane: boring or dull.

Although the data stored on a cell phone is distinguished from physical records by quantity alone, certain types of data are also qualitatively different. An Internet search and browsing history, for example, can be found on an Internet-enabled phone and could reveal an individual's private interests or concerns — perhaps a search for certain symptoms of disease, coupled with frequent visits to WebMD. Data on a cell phone can also reveal where a person has been. Historic location information is a standard feature on many smartphones and can reconstruct someone's specific movements down to the minute, not only around town but also within a particular building. See *United States* v. *Jones*, 565 U. S. ___, ___ (2012) (SOTOMAYOR, J., concurring) (slip op., at 3) ("GPS monitoring generates a precise, comprehensive record of a person's public movements that reflects a wealth of detail about her familial, political, professional, religious, and sexual associations.").

Mobile application software on a cell phone, or "apps," offer a range of tools for managing detailed information about all aspects of a person's life. There are apps for Democratic Party news and Republican Party news; apps for alcohol, drug, and gambling addictions; apps for sharing prayer requests; apps for tracking pregnancy symptoms; apps for planning your budget; apps for every conceivable hobby or pastime; apps for improving your romantic life. There are popular apps for buying or selling just about anything, and the records of such transactions may be accessible on the phone indefinitely. There are over a million apps available in each of the two major app stores; the phrase "there's an app for that" is now part of the popular lexicon.° The average smartphone user has installed thirty-three apps, which together can form a revealing montage of the user's life. See Brief for Electronic Privacy Information Center as *Amicus Curiae* in No. 13–132, p. 9.

lexicon: here, vocabulary.

Billings Learned Hand (1872–1961): U.S. judge and philosopher of law; his writings have been quoted more often in Supreme Court rulings than have the writings of all other judges serving in lower courts.

In 1926, Learned Hand° observed (in an opinion later quoted in *Chimel*) that it is "a totally different thing to search a man's pockets and use against him what they contain, from ransacking his house for everything which may incriminate him." *United States* v. *Kirschenblatt*, 16 F. 2d 202, 203 (CA2). If his pockets contain a cell phone, however, that is no longer true. Indeed, a cell phone search would typically expose to the government far more than the most exhaustive search of a house: A phone not only contains in digital form many sensitive records previously found in the home; it also contains a broad array of private information never found in a home in any form — unless the phone is.

[. . .]

IV

We cannot deny that our decision today will have an impact on the ability of law enforcement to combat crime. Cell phones have become important tools in facilitating coordination and communication among members of criminal enterprises, and can provide valuable incriminating information about dangerous criminals. Privacy comes at a cost. Our holding, of course, is not that the information on a cell phone is immune from search; it is instead that a warrant is generally required before such a search, even when a cell phone is seized incident to arrest. Our cases have historically recognized that the warrant requirement is "an important working part of our machinery of government," not merely "an inconvenience to be somehow 'weighed' against the claims of police efficiency." *Coolidge* v. *New Hampshire*, 403 U. S. 443, 481 (1971). Recent technological advances similar to those discussed here have, in addition, made the process of obtaining a warrant itself more efficient. See *McNeely*, 569 U. S., at ___ (slip op., at 11–12); *id.*, at ___ (ROBERTS, C. J., concurring in part and dissenting in part) (slip op., at 8) (describing jurisdiction where "police officers can e-mail warrant requests to judges' iPads [and] judges have signed such warrants and e-mailed them back to officers in less than fifteen minutes").

[. . .]

* * *

30 Our cases have recognized that the Fourth Amendment was the founding generation's response to the reviled "general warrants"° and "writs of assistance"° of the colonial era, which allowed British officers to rummage through homes in an unrestrained search for evidence of criminal activity. Opposition to such searches was in fact one of the driving forces behind the Revolution itself. In 1761, the patriot James Otis° delivered a speech in

general warrant: a type of warrant issued by the British government during the American colonial period that permitted an officer of the law to search unspecified people or places in hope of finding some unspecified object — in other words, an open-ended search warrant. The Fourth Amendment of the U.S. Constitution rendered such warrants illegal.

writ of assistance: a court-issued document instructing an officer of the law to carry out some task.

James Otis (1725–1783): colonial patriot who coined the motto "Taxation without representation is tyranny." A lawyer, legislator, pamphleteer, and political activist who originally saw himself as a loyal subject of the British government, Otis nevertheless argued against the use of writs of assistance, a move that helped give rise to the American Revolution.

Boston denouncing the use of writs of assistance. A young John Adams° was there, and he would later write that "[e]very man of a crowded audience appeared to me to go away, as I did, ready to take arms against writs of assistance." 10 Works of John Adams 247–248 (C. Adams ed. 1856). According to Adams, Otis's speech was "the first scene of the first act of opposition to the arbitrary claims of Great Britain. Then and there the child Independence was born." *Id.*, at 248 (quoted in *Boyd* v. *United States*, 116 U. S. 616, 625 (1886)).

John Adams (1735–1826): first vice president of the United States and second president of the country; one of the founding fathers. He helped draft the Declaration of Independence and negotiate the treaty with Britain that ended the American Revolution.

Modern cell phones are not just another technological convenience. With all they contain and all they may reveal, they hold for many Americans "the privacies of life," *Boyd*, *supra*, at 630. The fact that technology now allows an individual to carry such information in his hand does not make the information any less worthy of the protection for which the Founders fought. Our answer to the question of what police must do before searching a cell phone seized incident to an arrest is accordingly simple — get a warrant.

We reverse the judgment of the California Court of Appeal in No. 13–132 and remand° the case for further proceedings not inconsistent with this opinion. We affirm the judgment of the First Circuit in No. 13–212.

remand: return a case to a lower court requiring that its decision be reconsidered in light of the current ruling.

It is so ordered.

Opinion of ALITO, J.

JUSTICE ALITO, concurring in part and concurring in the judgment.

35 I agree with the Court that law enforcement officers, in conducting a lawful search incident to arrest, must generally obtain a warrant before searching information stored or accessible on a cell phone. I write separately to address two points [only one of which is included here].

[. . .]

B

Despite my view on the point discussed above, I agree that we should not mechanically apply the rule used in the predigital era to the search of a cell phone. Many cell phones now in use are capable of storing and accessing a quantity of information, some highly personal, that no person would ever have had on his person in hard-copy form. This calls for a new balancing of law enforcement and privacy interests. The Court strikes this balance in favor of privacy interests with respect to all cell phones and all information found in them, and this approach leads to anomalies.° For example, the Court's broad holding favors information in digital form over information in hard-copy form. Suppose that two suspects are arrested. Suspect number

anomalies: irregularities, inconsistencies.

one has in his pocket a monthly bill for his land-line phone, and the bill lists an incriminating call to a long-distance number. He also has in his wallet a few snapshots, and one of these is incriminating. Suspect number two has in his pocket a cell phone, the call log of which shows a call to the same incriminating number. In addition, a number of photos are stored in the memory of the cell phone, and one of these is incriminating. Under established law, the police may seize and examine the phone bill and the snapshots in the wallet without obtaining a warrant, but under the Court's holding today, the information stored in the cell phone is out.

While the Court's approach leads to anomalies, I do not see a workable alternative. Law enforcement officers need clear rules regarding searches incident to arrest, and it would take many cases and many years for the courts to develop more nuanced° rules. And during that time, the nature of the electronic devices that ordinary Americans carry on their persons would continue to change.

nuanced: subtle, making finer or more careful distinctions.

[. . .]

RESPOND.

1. As mentioned in the headnote, U.S. legal opinions represent stasis theory in action: they contain an argument of fact in which the relevant facts of the case are presented, an argument of definition in which the relevant laws and prior legal rulings are reviewed, an evaluative argument in which the facts of the case are evaluated in light of the law, and, finally, a holding, or judgment, along with the reasoning behind that judgment. Divide the selection into these component parts. (Be careful! It's easy to make a mistake here.)
2. Reduce the Supreme Court's reasoning in this decision to a Toulmin argument, as discussed in Chapter 7. In other words, map the legal issues and arguments being made onto the outline used to illustrate Toulmin argumentation (p. 143). You'll likely learn the most about this case, legal reasoning, and Toulmin arguments if you work with a classmate. Then, compare and contrast your analysis of the arguments with the analyses done by your other classmates.
3. Not surprisingly, Justice Roberts acknowledges the "impact [of the *Riley* ruling] on the ability of law enforcement to combat crime" (paragraph 29). How does Roberts make explicit the limits of the court's holding, or ruling? Why might we expect such qualifications of a claim in opinions from the Supreme Court? (Chapter 7 on structuring arguments discusses the use of qualifiers in its treatment of Toulmin argumentation.)

4. How do the comments in Justice Alito's opinion contextualize the court's decision by highlighting and problematizing the need to balance the needs of law enforcement and the rights of individuals to privacy?
5. Examine with great care footnote 1. Why might the word *searches* have been italicized? What bearing might this explicit statement in the court's decision have on future legal debates and decisions about the issues of data aggregation and mining in the name of national security discussed in other selections in this chapter, specifically, Solove's "The Nothing-to-Hide Argument," Greenfield's "What Your Email Metadata Told the NSA about You," and the visual arguments relating to domestic spying?
6. Roberts argues that "cell phones differ in both a quantitative and qualitative sense from other objects" that someone who is arrested might have on her/his person (paragraph 22). **Summarize his arguments** in a few healthy paragraphs so that you could use them in a research paper on the topic of cell phones and privacy. Be sure to distinguish between the quantitative and qualitative criteria Roberts uses and to link the arguments he makes explicitly to the issue of an individual's privacy. Likely the simplest way to complete this assignment is to begin by making a list of arguments in each category and then to turn the lists into paragraphs. (Chapter 10 on evaluative arguments discusses the use of quantitative and qualitative criteria, and Chapters 20–22 provide information on using and documenting sources.)

The executive editor of newyorker.com, Amy Davidson focuses on topics related to national security, politics, and international issues. In this selection from June 29, 2014, Davidson reflects on the Supreme Court's decision in Riley v. California, *part of which appears as the previous selection in this chapter. She puts that ruling in context by linking it to the debates you have been examining throughout this chapter, especially those that relate to the government's right to collect and monitor the sorts of personal information contained on an individual's cell phone. In paragraph 3 of this selection, she refers to a podcast she made the same week with Jeffrey Toobin, an attorney and legal analyst for the* New Yorker *and CNN. (The podcast is available at http://nyr.kr/1AY3xTr.) During her conversation with Toobin, Davidson contends that the case is in many ways about language, specifically, whether the thing we call a* mobile telephone *should be treated as comparable to what earlier court rulings had in mind when they ruled on* telephones. *As noted in paragraph 3, Toobin and she interpret the significance of the* Riley *decision quite differently: he distinguishes sharply between the criminal justice system and the system of laws governing matters of national security (an issue touched on in question 5 of the previous selection), and between data on a specific individual's phone and anonymous data of the sort aggregated by the NSA. In reading this selection, reflect again on the ways in which stasis theory and arguments of fact, definition—when does X count as Y?—and evaluation form the basis of legal discourse. Likewise, give some thought to the power of the law to shape our lives and to the changing nature of privacy and our understanding of it as a result of changes in technology.*

Four Ways the *Riley* Ruling Matters for the NSA

AMY DAVIDSON

On March 16, 1976, police officers in Baltimore, Maryland, spotted a man driving a Chevrolet Monte Carlo; the car matched one a witness to a crime had seen drive slowly by her house. By noting the license plates, they were able to get the home phone number of the driver, Michael Smith. On August 22, 2009, in a separate case a continent away, police officers stopped a Lexus making its way through the Lincoln Park neighborhood of San Diego, California, with expired tags; the license of the driver, David Riley, wasn't valid, either, and there were two guns under the hood of the car. The police also took his Samsung Instinct M800 smartphone which, they said, had been in his pocket.

There is a single trajectory that joins the car ride in Baltimore and the one in San Diego, thirty-three years apart, by way of two major Supreme Court cases: *Smith v. Maryland*° (https://supreme.justia.com/cases/federal/us/442/735/case.html), decided in 1979, which said that the police were within their rights to trace Smith's phone calls without a warrant (and is often cited in defense of the National Security Agency's° bulk collection of data on Americans); and *Riley v. California* (http://www2.bloomberglaw.com/public/desktop/document/Riley_v_California_No_13132_and_13212_US_June_25_2014_Cc) decided last week, in which the Court said that the police were not right to trawl° through the data on Riley's cell phone—texts, contact lists, pictures, videos of street-boxing bouts—without a warrant. The decision in *Riley* was unanimous and essential. The opinion, written by Chief Justice John Roberts, did not mention the NSA, but it reflects the debate about the agency that has taken place in the past year, thanks to documents leaked by Edward Snowden,° an NSA contractor.

A trawler bikeriderlondon/Shutterstock

trawl: to fish in a boat equipped with a wide-mouth net that makes catching large numbers of fish easy and quick; used here figuratively.

So how might *Riley v. California* affect the cases that are surely headed to the Supreme Court, post Snowden? Jeffrey Toobin and I talked about this question, along with others related to the Court's recent decisions, in this week's Political Scene podcast (http://www.newyorker.com/online/blogs/newsdesk/2014/06/political-scene-big-decisions-from-the-supreme-court.html). (I should say that

---

Smith v. Maryland: the legal case *Smith v. Maryland*. In court cases, the plaintiff, or complaining party who has filed the lawsuit, is named first while the defendant, or party being sued, is named second. Here, Smith was suing the State of Maryland. Often, in writing and conversation, the case will be referred to simply as *Smith*.

NSA (National Security Agency): intelligence agency of the U.S. government; as stated on its Web site, its role is "[to] collect (including through clandestine means), process, analyze, produce, and disseminate signals intelligence information and data for foreign intelligence and counterintelligence purposes . . . and [to] act as the National Manager for National Security Systems as established in law and policy. . . ." Signals intelligence refers to "communications systems, radars, and weapons systems" and thus includes electronic data.

Edward Snowden (1983–): computer professional who leaked classified information from the NSA, where he had been a contract employee; as this textbook goes to press, he is currently living in temporary exile in Russia. Snowden is the subject of the 2014 documentary *Citizenfour*.

jurisprudence: theory of law and methods of legal reasoning.

Toobin and I have a somewhat different view on the subject, in part because of the gulf he sees between national-security and criminal-justice jurisprudence.°) These cases, together, will help define the future of the Fourth Amendment, which affirms "the right of the people to be secure in their persons, houses, papers, and effects, against unreasonable searches and seizures" in the absence of a warrant. They also touch on questions of language and technology, and the way one shapes the other.

Each of Davidson's four points is a causal argument, exploring the impact of the *Riley* ruling (pp. 774–84) on the law. For more on causal arguments, see Chapter 11.

LINK TO P. 240

Here are four ways *Riley* matters when thinking about the NSA:

morph: to change shape or nature.

sleight of hand: a technique used by magicians to manipulate cards, coins, or other objects in such a way as to fool viewers.

stage help: in live theater, the people who assist backstage and whose important work is invisible to the audience; here, used figuratively.

Foreign Intelligence Surveillance Court: U.S. federal court that authorizes requests from various federal law enforcement agencies for surveillance warrants to track suspected foreign intelligence agents inside the country.

1. **A phone is not a phone.** Or rather, it is only accidentally called one. 5
"The term 'cell phone' is itself misleading shorthand," Roberts wrote in his opinion. "Many of these devices are in fact minicomputers that also happen to have the capacity to be used as a telephone. They could just as easily be called cameras, video players, rolodexes, calendars, tape recorders, libraries, diaries, albums, televisions, maps, or newspapers." Roberts's language here is very much like that of Judge Richard Leon, of the D.C. District Court, who noted, in an opinion last year, "Cell phones have also morphed° into multi-purpose devices. They are now maps and music players. . . . They are cameras. . . . They are even lighters that people hold up at rock concerts." One of the NSA's sleights of hand,° for which it had the stage help° of the Foreign Intelligence Surveillance Court,° was acting as though a police man standing next to a telephone technician in 1976 to find out what number a single, identifiable suspect was dialing on a single rotary phone was legally indistinguishable from the mass collection of records of the cell-phone calls of virtually all Americans – phones, records, nothing else to see. For Leon, the non-phoneness of modern phones rendered this absurd. Roberts's opinion suggests that this shelving of *Smith v. Maryland* might find some sympathy on the Court.
2. **A phone is also not a cigarette pack filled with heroin.** In *United States v. Robinson*, a 1973 decision that also involved the police pulling over a car – a 1965 Cadillac, in this case – the court found that a police officer could search a soft cigarette pack he came across patting down a man named Willie Robinson Jr. The pack, which the officer opened because it felt strange, turned out to contain fourteen hard capsules of heroin. That falls in the category of searches that are reasonable, Justice William Rehnquist wrote in the majority opinion, to see what a person is carrying when he's arrested, in case there's, say, a weapon or something hazardous – and whatever was in that pack "he knew it was not cigarettes." But when it comes to a suspect's

phone, Roberts wrote, the police know what it is and what they will find: data. Roberts explicitly rejects the idea that there are simple analogies between the search of physical objects (tangible things) and the data to which a phone is a portal. "Modern cell phones, as a category, implicate privacy concerns far beyond those implicated by the search of a cigarette pack, a wallet, or a purse."

Similarly, Roberts points out that earlier rulings that let police search pockets were based on the assumption that a pocket couldn't possibly hold very much. But, he writes,

> If his pockets contain a cell phone, however, that is no longer true. Indeed, a cell phone search would typically expose to the government far more than the most exhaustive search of a house: A phone not only contains in digital form many sensitive records previously found in the home; it also contains a broad array of private information never found in a home in any form – unless the phone is.

New technology doesn't mean that law enforcement gets a bonanza;° it means that precedents need to be re-examined before they are uncritically applied – and that the NSA's advocates will have some real work to do. As Roberts puts it, "Any extension of that reasoning to digital data has to rest on its own bottom."°

3. **If it's "My House," it is not "just" metadata.°** Since the Snowden revelations, we have been constantly reassured that much (though not all) of what the government collects without a warrant is "just" metadata – and what could be the harm in that? Metadata is supposedly distinguishable from content – it is information about a communication, the labels affixed to it, the addresses and the contacts, the times and the dates, and perhaps the locations. The reply is that an enormous amount can be learned from putting pieces of metadata together, and an awareness of that is present in *Riley v. California* and its companion case, *United States v. Wurie.* After the police took Brima Wurie's phone, they saw calls from a number that came up as "My House"; that was used to connect him to evidence found at the address associated with the number. Police looking at Riley's phone saw that some names on his contact list were designated "CK," which they took to be shorthand for "Crip killer," and part of their evidence for his affiliation with the Bloods gang.° (Another piece of evidence was a photo on his cell phone of Riley with yet another car, a red Oldsmobile – the Bloods' color – that had been at the scene of a gang shooting.) "We also reject the United States' final suggestion that officers should always be able to search a phone's call log, as

bonanza: a large amount of something desired; a source of unanticipated profit, good luck, etc.

to rest on its own bottom: that is, to stand on its own without assistance.

metadata: literally, data about data. Here, the concern is descriptive metadata, or information about the creation of an electronic message like a particular email, text, or posting.

Crips and Bloods: two rival gangs that often engage in violent criminal action, including exterminating one another's members.

they did in Wurie's case," Roberts wrote, noting that "the Government relies on *Smith v. Maryland*":

> The Court in that case, however, concluded that the use of a pen register° was not a "search" at all under the Fourth Amendment. See *id.*,° at 745–746. There is no dispute here that the officers engaged in a search of Wurie's cell phone. Moreover, call logs typically contain more than just phone numbers; they include any identifying information that an individual might add, such as the label "my house" in Wurie's case.

4. **Judges *really* need to know the technology when evaluating the government's claims.** But, the government said, we can't wait to get a warrant; criminals will have their data remotely erased by their confederates;° they will spring geofencing° traps that will wipe the phones clean; there might be only moments before the phone locks; the evidence will be out of our reach forever before we can reach a judge. This all sounds very alarming—geofencing!—but, luckily, someone told the Justices that you can deal with a lot of the issues with simple measures, like removing batteries, using the window before a phone is locked to change the locking settings, or just putting the thing in what are called Faraday bags:° "They are essentially sandwich bags made of aluminum foil: cheap, lightweight, and easy to use." Technical awareness and skepticism of government claims about ticking time bombs: these are two easy-to-use items that will be helpful to the Court in the coming NSA cases. 10

We are not on a different planet than we were four decades ago, but we move through it differently, with pockets bigger than our houses. In his decision, Roberts wrote that pretending that delving into cell-phone data is "materially indistinguishable"° from the old way of searching the things a person carried is "like saying a ride on horseback is materially indistinguishable from a flight to the moon. Both are ways of getting from point A to point B, but little else justifies lumping them together." A horse is not a moon rocket. A 1975 Monte Carlo isn't even a Lexus in Lincoln Park.

pen register: a mechanical device that records all the telephone numbers dialed from a particular landline.

id.: Latin for "the same"; in legal documentation and certain other documentation systems, *idem* is used to refer back to the immediately prior source, for which complete publication information has been given.

confederate: accomplice.

geofencing traps: in this case, software settings that would wipe the phone clean if it were taken into a specific area or to a specific locale.

Faraday bag: a container that blocks all external electrical fields, hence, protecting contents that are electronic from being altered or damaged from exposure to any sort of electromagnetic waves.

materially indistinguishable: the same for the purposes at hand.

RESPOND •

1. Davidson's argument is obviously an evaluative one. What, specifically, is she evaluating, what criteria does she use, and what evidence does she present? How does the layout of her text help the reader navigate it easily? (Chapter 10 discusses these aspects of evaluative arguments.)

2. Having read an excerpt from the *Riley* ruling as the previous selection, you are in a position to evaluate how well Davidson provided the necessary background about the case for readers who have little or no information about it so that they can understand the issues she is discussing. The criterion here would be the Goldilocks Test: not too much and not too little but just the right amount. What grade would you give her for this aspect of the selection? Why? If, in your opinion, she gives too little information, what should be added? If she gives too much, what could be omitted?
3. Davidson argues, "Technical awareness and skepticism of government claims about ticking time bombs . . . will be helpful to the Court in the coming NSA cases." What is she referring to with this claim? How does her stance on "technical awareness" relate to Justice Alito's observations in his concurring opinion, excerpted in the previous selection? Has Davidson provided evidence for the second item—the "ticking time bombs"? Do you agree with her contention? Why or why not?
4. Reread footnote 1 in the previous selection, an excerpt from the *Riley* case (p. 780). How do the qualifications of the *Riley* ruling made in the paragraph complicate Davidson's claim that the *Riley* case has clear implications for upcoming court cases about the NSA?
5. As the headnote makes clear, Davidson pays attention to matters of language, a fact that shows up in her own writing. It is quite clear that Davidson is no admirer of the NSA and its practices and is likely critical of the liberties taken by police more broadly. How do her word choices and particularly her figurative use of words with concrete meanings help demonstrate her stance? Choose several specific examples, noting where they occur and what function they serve. (Chapter 13's discussion of style in language will help you with this question.)
6. The readings in this chapter have challenged and equipped you to consider in some detail issues related to privacy and surveillance by governments and entities like social media. How has your thinking about these issues changed from reading these selections? **Construct a causal argument** in which you define and evaluate these changes, thinking about them in terms of cause and effect. In short, what effect have these readings had on your thinking and why? You'll likely want to begin by brainstorming about how your thinking has changed and then try to link those changes to specific selections or passages in selections, to class discussions, to homework exercises, or to things you're exposed to outside class. (Chapter 11 will help you design your causal argument.)

GLOSSARY

academic argument writing that is addressed to an audience well informed about the topic, that aims to convey a clear and compelling point in a somewhat formal style, and that follows agreed-upon conventions of usage, punctuation, and formats.

accidental condition in a definition, an element that helps to explain what's being defined but isn't essential to it. An accidental condition in defining a bird might be "ability to fly" because most, but not all, birds can fly. (See also *essential condition* and *sufficient condition*.)

***ad hominem* argument** a fallacy of argument in which a writer's claim is answered by irrelevant attacks on his/her character.

allusion an indirect reference. Saying "watch out or you'll create the next Edsel" contains an allusion to the Ford Edsel, a disastrously unpopular and unsuccessful product of the late 1950s.

analogy an extended comparison between something unfamiliar and something more familiar for the purpose of illuminating or dramatizing the unfamiliar. An analogy might, say, compare nuclear fission (less familiar) to a pool player's opening break (more familiar).

anaphora a figure of speech involving repetition, particularly of the same word at the beginning of several clauses.

antithesis the use of parallel structures to call attention to contrasts or opposites, as in *Some like it hot; some like it cold.*

antonomasia use of a title, epithet, or description in place of a name, as in *Your Honor* for *Judge*.

argument (1) a spoken, written, or visual text that expresses a point of view; (2) the use of evidence and reason to discover some version of the truth, as distinct from *persuasion*, the attempt to change someone else's point of view.

artistic appeal support for an argument that a writer creates based on principles of reason and shared knowledge rather than on facts and evidence. (See also *inartistic appeal*.)

assumption a belief regarded as true, upon which other claims are based.

assumption, cultural a belief regarded as true or commonsensical within a particular culture, such as the belief in individual freedom in American culture.

audience the person or persons to whom an argument is directed.

authority the quality conveyed by a writer who is knowledgeable about his/her subject and confident in that knowledge.

background the information a writer provides to create the context for an argument.

backing in Toulmin argument, the evidence provided to support a warrant.

bandwagon appeal a fallacy of argument in which a course of action is recommended on the grounds that everyone else is following it.

begging the question a fallacy of argument in which a claim is based on the very grounds that are in doubt or dispute: *Rita can't be the bicycle thief; she's never stolen anything.*

causal argument an argument that seeks to explain the effect(s) of a cause, the cause(s) of an effect, or a causal chain in which A causes B, B causes C, C causes D, and so on.

ceremonial argument an argument that deals with current values and addresses questions of praise and blame. Also called *epideictic*, ceremonial arguments include eulogies and graduation speeches.

character, appeal based on a strategy in which a writer presents an authoritative, credible self-image in order to gain the trust of an audience.

circumstantial evidence in legal cases, evidence from which conclusions cannot be drawn directly but have to be inferred.

claim a statement that asserts a belief or truth. In arguments, most claims require supporting evidence. The claim is a key component in Toulmin argument.

classical oration a highly structured form of an argument developed in ancient Greece and Rome to defend or refute a thesis. The oration evolved to include six parts—*exordium*, *narratio*, *partitio*, *confirmatio*, *refutatio*, and *peroratio*.

confirmatio the fourth part of a classical oration, in which a speaker or writer offers evidence for the claim.

connotation the suggestions or associations that surround most words and extend beyond their literal meaning, creating associational effects. *Slender* and *skinny* have similar meanings, for example, but carry different connotations, the former more positive than the latter.

context the entire situation in which a piece of writing takes place, including the writer's purpose(s) for writing; the intended audience; the time and place of writing; the institutional, social, personal, and other influences on the piece of writing; the material conditions of writing (whether it's, for instance, online or on paper, in handwriting or in print); and the writer's attitude toward the subject and the audience.

conviction the belief that a claim or course of action is true or reasonable. In a proposal argument, a writer must move an audience beyond conviction to action.

credibility an impression of integrity, honesty, and trustworthiness conveyed by a writer in an argument.

criterion (*plural* criteria) in evaluative arguments, a standard by which something is measured to determine its quality or value.

deductive reasoning a process of thought in which general principles are applied to particular cases.

definition, argument of an argument in which the claim specifies that something does or doesn't meet the conditions or features set forth in a definition: *Pluto is not a major planet.*

deliberative argument an argument that deals with action to be taken in the future, focusing on matters of policy. Deliberative arguments include parliamentary debates and campaign platforms.

delivery the presentation of an argument.

dogmatism a fallacy of argument in which a claim is supported on the grounds that it's the only conclusion acceptable within a given community.

either/or choice a fallacy of argument in which a complicated issue is misrepresented as offering only two possible alternatives, one of which is often made to seem vastly preferable to the other.

emotional appeal a strategy in which a writer tries to generate specific emotions (such as fear, envy, anger, or pity) in an audience to dispose it to accept a claim.

enthymeme in Toulmin argument, a statement that links a claim to a supporting reason: *The bank will fail* (claim) *because it has lost the support of its largest investors* (reason). In classical rhetoric, an enthymeme is a syllogism with one term understood but not stated: *Socrates is mortal because he is a human being.* (The understood term is *All human beings are mortal.*) (See also *syllogism.*)

epideictic argument See *ceremonial argument.*

equivocation a fallacy of argument in which a lie is given the appearance of truth, or in which the truth is misrepresented in deceptive language.

essential condition in a definition, an element that must be part of the definition but, by itself, isn't enough to define the term. An essential condition in defining a bird might be "winged": all birds have wings, yet wings alone don't define a bird since some insects and mammals also have wings. (See also *accidental condition* and *sufficient condition.*)

ethical appeal See *character, appeal based on*, and *ethos.*

ethnographic observation a form of field research involving close and extended observation of a group, event, or phenomenon; careful and detailed note-taking during the observation; analysis of the notes; and interpretation of that analysis.

ethos the self-image a writer creates to define a relationship with readers. In arguments, most writers try to establish an ethos that suggests authority, fairness, and credibility.

evaluation, argument of an argument in which the claim specifies that something does or doesn't meet established criteria: *The Nikon D4s is the most sophisticated digital SLR camera currently available.*

evidence material offered to support an argument. (See *artistic appeal* and *inartistic appeal.*)

example, definition by a definition that operates by identifying individual examples of what's being defined: *sports car—Corvette, Viper, Miata, Cayman.*

exordium the first part of a classical oration, in which a speaker or writer tries to win the attention and goodwill of an audience while introducing a subject.

experimental evidence evidence gathered through experimentation; often evidence that can be quantified (for example, a survey of students before and after an election might yield statistical evidence about changes in their attitudes toward the candidates). Experimental evidence is frequently crucial to scientific arguments.

fact, argument of an argument in which the claim can be proved or disproved with specific evidence or testimony: *The winter of 2012 was the warmest on record for the United States.*

fallacy of argument a flaw in the structure of an argument that renders its conclusion invalid or suspect. (See ad hominem *argument, bandwagon appeal, begging the question, dogmatism, either/or choice, equivocation, false authority, faulty analogy, faulty causality, hasty generalization, non sequitur, scare tactic, sentimental appeal, slippery slope*, and *straw man.*)

false authority a fallacy of argument in which a claim is based on the expertise of someone who lacks appropriate credentials.

faulty analogy a fallacy of argument in which a comparison between two objects or concepts is inaccurate or inconsequential.

faulty causality a fallacy of argument making the unwarranted assumption that because one event follows another, the first event causes the second. Also called *post hoc, ergo propter hoc*, faulty causality forms the basis of many superstitions.

firsthand evidence data—including surveys, observations, personal interviews, etc.—collected and personally examined by the writer. (See also *secondhand evidence*.)

forensic argument an argument that deals with actions that have occurred in the past. Sometimes called *judicial arguments*, forensic arguments include legal cases involving judgments of guilt or innocence.

formal definition a definition that identifies something first by the general class to which it belongs (see *genus*) and then by the characteristics that distinguish it from other members of that class (see *species*): *Baseball is a game* (genus) *played on a diamond by opposing teams of nine players who score runs by circling bases after striking a ball with a bat* (species).

genus in a definition, the general class to which an object or a concept belongs: *baseball is a* sport; *green is a* color.

grounds in Toulmin argument, the evidence provided to support a claim and reason—that is, an *enthymeme*.

hard evidence support for an argument using facts, statistics, testimony, or other evidence the writer finds.

hasty generalization a fallacy of argument in which an inference is drawn from insufficient data.

hyperbole use of overstatement for special effect.

hypothesis a well-informed guess at what the conclusion of one's research will reveal. Hypotheses must be tested against evidence, opposing arguments, and so on.

immediate reason the cause that leads directly to an effect, such as an automobile accident that results in an injury to the driver. (See also *necessary reason* and *sufficient reason*.)

inartistic appeal support for an argument using facts, statistics, eyewitness testimony, or other evidence the writer finds rather than creates. (See also *artistic appeal*.)

inductive reasoning a process of thought in which particular cases lead to general principles.

infotention a term coined by Howard Rheingold to describe the digital literacy skills of managing the technology we use and synthesizing the information we find online.

intended readers the actual, real-life people whom a writer consciously wants to address in a piece of writing.

invention the process of finding and creating arguments to support a claim.

inverted word order moving grammatical elements of a sentence out of their usual order (subject-verb-object/complement) for special effect, as in *Tired I was; sleepy I was not*.

invitational argument a term used by Sonja Foss and Cindy Griffin to describe arguments that are aimed not at vanquishing an opponent but at inviting others to collaborate in exploring mutually satisfying ways to solve problems.

invoked readers the readers implied in a text, which may include some whom the writer didn't consciously intend to reach. An argument that refers to *those who have experienced a major trauma*, for example, invokes all readers who have undergone this experience.

irony use of language that suggests a meaning in contrast to the literal meaning of the words.

kairos the opportune moment; in arguments, the timeliness of an argument and the most opportune ways to make it.

line of argument a strategy or an approach used in an argument. Argumentative strategies include appeals to the heart (emotional appeals), to character (ethical appeals), and to facts and reason (logical appeals).

logical appeal a strategy in which a writer uses facts, evidence, and reason to convince audience members to accept a claim.

logos See *logical appeal*.

metaphor a figure of speech that makes a comparison, as in *The ship was a beacon of hope*.

metonymy a rhetorical trope in which a writer uses a particular object to stand for a general concept, as in referring to businesspeople as "suits" or to the English monarchy as "the crown."

narratio the second part of a classical oration, in which a speaker or writer presents the facts of a case.

necessary reason a cause that must be present for an effect to occur; for example, infection with a particular virus is a necessary reason for the development of mumps. (See also *immediate reason* and *sufficient reason*.)

non sequitur a fallacy of argument in which claims, reasons, or warrants fail to connect logically; one point doesn't follow from another: *If you're really my friend, you'll lend me five hundred dollars*.

operational definition a definition that identifies an object by what it does or by the conditions that create it: *A line is the shortest distance between two points*.

oxymoron a rhetorical trope that states a paradox or contradiction, as in "jumbo shrimp."

parallelism use of similar grammatical structures or forms for clarity, emphasis, and/or artfulness: *in the classroom, on the playground, and at the mall*.

paraphrase a restatement of the meaning of a piece of writing using different words from the original.

partitio the third part of a classical oration, in which a speaker or writer divides up the subject and explains what the claim will be.

patchwriting a misuse of sources in which a writer's phrase, clause, or sentence stays too close to the original language or syntax of the source.

pathos, appeal to See *emotional appeal*.

peroratio the sixth and final part of a classical oration, in which a speaker or writer summarizes the case and moves the audience to action.

persuasion the act of seeking to change someone else's point of view.

plagiarism the act of using the words, phrases, and expressions of others without proper citation or acknowledgment.

precedents actions or judgments in the past that have established a pattern or model for subsequent decisions. Precedents are particularly important in legal cases.

premise a statement or position regarded as true and upon which other claims are based.

propaganda an argument advancing a point of view without regard to reason, fairness, or truth.

proposal argument an argument in which a claim is made in favor of or opposing a specific course of action: *Sport-utility vehicles should have to meet the same fuel economy standards as passenger cars.*

purpose the goal of an argument. Purposes include entertaining, informing, convincing, exploring, and deciding, among others.

qualifiers words or phrases that limit the scope of a claim: *usually; in a few cases; under these circumstances.*

qualitative argument an argument of evaluation that relies on non-numerical criteria supported by reason, tradition, precedent, or logic.

quantitative argument an argument of evaluation that relies on criteria that can be measured, counted, or demonstrated objectively.

quantitative data the sort of data that can be observed and counted.

reason in writing, a statement that expands a claim by offering evidence to support it. The reason may be a statement of fact or another claim. In Toulmin argument, a reason is attached to a claim by a warrant, a statement that establishes the logical connection between claim and supporting reason. (See also *Toulmin argument.*)

rebuttal an answer that challenges or refutes a specific claim or charge. Rebuttals may also be offered by writers who anticipate objections to the claims or evidence they offer.

rebuttal, conditions of in Toulmin argument, potential objections to an argument. Writers need to anticipate such conditions in shaping their arguments.

red herring a fallacy of argument in which a writer abruptly changes the topic in order to distract readers from potentially objectionable claims.

refutatio the fifth part of a classical oration, in which a speaker or writer acknowledges and refutes opposing claims or evidence.

reversed structures a figure of speech that involves the inversion of clauses: *What is good in your writing is not original; what is original is not good.*

rhetoric the art of persuasion. Western rhetoric originated in ancient Greece as a discipline to prepare citizens for arguing cases in court.

rhetorical analysis an examination of how well the components of an argument work together to persuade or move an audience.

rhetorical questions questions posed to raise an issue or create an effect rather than to get a response: *You may well wonder, "What's in a name?"*

rhetorical situation the relationship between topic, author, audience, and other contexts (social, cultural, political) that determine or evoke an appropriate spoken or written response.

Rogerian argument an approach to argumentation based on the principle, articulated by psychotherapist Carl Rogers, that audiences respond best when they don't feel threatened. Rogerian argument stresses trust and urges those who disagree to find common ground.

scare tactic a fallacy of argument presenting an issue in terms of exaggerated threats or dangers.

scheme a figure of speech that involves a special arrangement of words, such as inversion.

secondhand evidence any information taken from outside sources, including library research and online sources. (See also *firsthand evidence.*)

sentimental appeal a fallacy of argument in which an appeal is based on excessive emotion.

signifying a distinctive trope found extensively in African American English in which a speaker or writer cleverly and often humorously needles another person.

simile a comparison that uses *like* or *as*: *My love is like a red, red rose* or *I wandered lonely as a cloud.*

slippery slope a fallacy of argument exaggerating the possibility that a relatively inconsequential action or choice today will have serious adverse consequences in the future.

species in a definition, the particular features that distinguish one member of a genus from another: *Baseball is a sport* (genus) *played on a diamond by teams of nine players* (species).

stacking the deck a fallacy of argument in which the writer shows only one side of an argument.

stance the writer's attitude toward the topic and the audience.

stasis theory in classical rhetoric, a method for coming up with appropriate arguments by determining the nature of a given situation: a question of fact; of definition; of quality; or of policy.

straw man a fallacy of argument in which an opponent's position is misrepresented as being more extreme than it actually is, so that it's easier to refute.

sufficient condition in a definition, an element or set of elements adequate to define a term. A sufficient condition in defining God, for example, might be "supreme being" or "first cause." No other conditions are necessary, though many might be made. (See also *accidental condition* and *essential condition.*)

sufficient reason a cause that alone is enough to produce a particular effect; for example, a particular level of smoke in the air will set off a smoke alarm. (See also *immediate reason* and *necessary reason.*)

summary a presentation of the substance and main points of a piece of writing in very condensed form.

syllogism in formal logic, a structure of deductive logic in which correctly formed major and minor premises lead to a necessary conclusion:

Major premise	All human beings are mortal.
Minor premise	Socrates is a human being.
Conclusion	Socrates is mortal.

testimony a personal experience or observation used to support an argument.

thesis a sentence that succinctly states a writer's main point.

Toulmin argument a method of informal logic first described by Stephen Toulmin in *The Uses of Argument* (1958). Toulmin argument describes the key components of an argument as the claim, reason, warrant, backing, and grounds.

trope a figure of speech that involves a change in the usual meaning or signification of words, such as *metaphor*, *simile*, and *analogy*.

understatement a figure of speech that makes a weaker statement than a situation seems to call for. It can lead to powerful or to humorous effects.

values, appeal to a strategy in which a writer invokes shared principles and traditions of a society as a reason for accepting a claim.

warrant in Toulmin argument, the statement (expressed or implied) that establishes the logical connection between a claim and its supporting reason.

Claim	Don't eat that mushroom.
Reason	It's poisonous.
Warrant	What is poisonous should not be eaten.

ACKNOWLEDGMENTS

Doug Bandow. "A New Military Draft Would Revive a Very Bad Old Idea" from *Forbes*, July 16, 2012, copyright © 2012 by Forbes, LLC. All rights reserved. Used by permission and protected by the Copyright Laws of the United States. The printing, copying, redistribution, or retransmission of this Content without express written permission is prohibited.

Sara Barbour. From "Kindle vs. Books: The Dead Trees Society," first published in the *Los Angeles Times*, June 17, 2011. Reprinted by permission of the author.

danah boyd and Kate Crawford. *Six Provocations for Big Data*. Paper presented at Oxford Internet Institute's "A Decade in Internet Time: Symposium on the Dynamics of the Internet and Society," September 21, 2011. Used by permission of the authors.

David Brooks. "It's Not about You" from the *New York Times*, May 31, 2011. Copyright © 2011 by The New York Times. All rights reserved. Used by permission and protected by the Copyright Laws of the United States. The printing, copying, redistribution, or retransmission of this Content without express written permission is prohibited.

Melinda C. R. Burgess et al. "Playing with Prejudice: The Prevalence and Consequences of Racial Stereotypes in Video Games" by Melinda C. R. Burgess, Karen E. Dill, S. Paul Stermer, Stephen R. Burgess, and Brian P. Brown. Copyright © 2011 from Media Psychology. Reproduced by permission of Taylor & Francis Group, LLC (http://www.tandfonline.com).

Sheryll Cashin. Introduction from *Place, Not Race: A New Vision of Opportunity in America*. Copyright © 2014 by Sheryll Cashin. Reprinted by permission of Beacon Press, Boston.

Amy Davidson. "Four Ways the *Riley* Ruling Matters for the NSA" from the *New Yorker*, June 29, 2014, is reprinted by permission of Condé Nast. Copyright © 2014 Condé Nast Publications.

Edye Deloch-Hughes. From "So God Made a Black Farmer Too," reprinted by permission of the author. http://eldhughes.com/2013/02/05/so-god-made-a-farmer-dodge-ram/

Digital First Media. "Coca-Cola's Multilingual 'America' Ad Didn't Hit Any Wrong Notes," first published in the *Lebanon Daily News*, February 3, 2014, is reprinted by permission of the Lebanon Daily News and Digital First Media.

Jon Dolan. "Drake, 'Draft Day'" by Jon Dolan, from *Rolling Stone*, Issue 1207, April 24, 2014. Copyright © 2014 by Rolling Stone, LLC. All rights reserved. Used by permission.

Roger Ebert. From a review of *Toy Story* (1995). Used by permission of Ebert Digital, LLC.

Rose Eveleth. "Saving Languages through Korean Soap Operas" from the *Atlantic*, September 23, 2014, is reprinted by permission. Copyright © 2014 The Atlantic Media Co. All rights reserved. Distributed by Tribune Content Agency, LLC.

Sarah Fraas. "Trans Women at Smith: The Complexities of Checking 'Female'" by Sarah Fraas, written with the help of Raven Fowlkes-Witten, Maggie Peebles-Dorrin, and Jason McGourty, from the *Smith Sophian*, April 14, 2014. Copyright © 2014 by Sarah Fraas. Published by Smith College, Northampton, MA. Used by permission of the publisher. All rights reserved.

David H. Freedman. "The Truth about Genetically Modified Food" from *Scientific American*, September 1, 2013. Copyright © 2013 by Scientific American, a Division of Nature America, Inc. All rights reserved. Reproduced with permission.

Rebecca Greenfield. "What Your Email Metadata Told the NSA about You," first published in the *Atlantic*, June 27, 2013, is reprinted by permission. Copyright © 2013 The Atlantic Media Co. All rights reserved. Distributed by Tribune Content Agency, LLC.

Katherine Gustafson. From "School Bus Farm Market" [editor's title "School Bus Farmers' Market"], from *Change Comes to Dinner: How Vertical Farmers, Urban Growers, and Other Innovators Are Revolutionizing How America Eats*. Copyright © 2012 by Katherine Gustafson. Reprinted by permission of St. Martin's Press. All rights reserved.

Stephanie Hanes. "Little Girls or Little Women? The Disney Princess Effect" from the *Christian Science Monitor*, posted September 24, 2011. Reprinted by permission of the author.

Neil Irwin. "What the Numbers Show about N.F.L. Player Arrests" from the *New York Times*, September 13, 2014. Copyright © 2014 by The New York Times. All rights reserved. Used by permission and protected by the Copyright Laws of the United States. The printing, copying, redistribution, or retransmission of this Content without express written permission is prohibited.

Raven Jiang. "Dota 2: The Face of Professional Gaming" from the *Stanford Daily*, August 5, 2011, is reprinted by permission of the *Stanford Daily* and Raven Jiang.

Young M. Kim and James S. Cole. From *Student Veterans/Service Members' Engagement in College and University Life and Education* is republished with permission of the American Council on Education via the Copyright Clearance Center, Inc. Copyright © 2013.

Barbara Kingsolver. Excerpt from *Animal, Vegetable, Miracle* by Barbara Kingsolver, Steven Hopp, and Camille Kingsolver. Copyright © 2007 by Barbara Kingsolver, Steven L. Hopp, and Camille Kingsolver. Reprinted by permission of HarperCollins Publishers.

Joyce Xinran Liu. "Friending: The Changing Definition of Friendship in the Social Media Era" by Joyce Xinran Liu, from *Vitamin IMC*, March 6, 2014. Reprinted by permission of the author.

Walter Russell Mead. From "It All Begins with Football," first published in the *American Interest*, December 4, 2011. Reprinted by permission of the author.

Walter Benn Michaels. Excerpt from the introduction to *The Trouble with Diversity: How We Learned to Love Identity and Ignore Inequality*. Copyright © 2006 by Walter Benn Michaels. Used by permission of Henry Holt and Company, LLC. All rights reserved.

Shabana Mir. From *Muslim American Women on Campus: Undergraduate Social Life and Identity*. Copyright © 2014 by the University of North Carolina Press. Used by permission of the publisher. http://www.uncpress.unc.edu

Scott L. Montgomery. From *Does Science Need a Global Language? English and the Future of Research*. Copyright © 2013 by Scott L. Montgomery. Reprinted by permission of the publisher, the University of Chicago Press.

Eric Mortenson. "A Diversified Farm Prospers in Oregon's Willamette Valley by Going Organic and Staying Local" from OregonLive.com, September 30, 2011. Copyright © 2011 by Oregonian Publishing Company. Reprinted by permission of the publisher via Copyright Clearance Center.

Nicholas Ostler. "Is It Globalization That Endangers Languages?" from UNESCO/UNU Conference, August 27–28, 2008. Reprinted by permission of the author.

Robert Paarlberg. "Attention Whole Foods Shoppers" is reprinted by permission of Foreign Policy from *Foreign Policy*, No. 179 (May/June 2010), pp. 80–85. Copyright © 2010 Washingtonpost.Newsweek Interactive, LLC. Permission conveyed through Copyright Clearance Center, Inc.

Virginia Postrel. "Let's Charge Politicians for Wasting Our Time" from *Bloomberg View*, June 3, 2014. Reprinted by permission of Bloomberg L.P. Copyright © 2014. All rights reserved.

Deena Prichep. "A Campus More Colorful Than Reality: Beware That College Brochure" from *Weekend Edition*, National Public Radio, Dec. 29, 2013, is reprinted by permission of the author and National Public Radio International.

Charles A. Riley II. *Disability and the Media: Prescriptions for Change* is reprinted by permission of the publisher. Copyright © University Press of New England, Lebanon, N.H.

Kirk Semple. "Immigrants Who Speak Indigenous Languages Encounter Isolation" from the *New York Times*, July 11, 2014. Copyright © 2014 by The New York Times. All rights reserved. Used by permission and protected by the Copyright Laws of the United States. The printing, copying, redistribution, or retransmission of this Content without express written permission is prohibited.

Daniel J. Solove. "The Nothing-to-Hide Argument" from *Nothing to Hide: The False Tradeoff between Privacy and Security*. Copyright © 2013 by Yale University Press. Reprinted by permission of the publisher.

Claude M. Steele. From *Whistling Vivaldi and Other Clues to How Stereotypes Affect Us*, copyright © 2010 by Claude M. Steele. Used by permission of W. W. Norton & Company, Inc.

Amy Stretten. "Appropriating Native American Imagery Honors No One but the Prejudice" from Fusion.net, September 18, 2013, is reprinted with permission. Copyright © 2014 by Fusion Media Network, LLC. All rights reserved.

The Takeaway. "It's Not OK Cupid: Co-Founder Defends User Experiments," interview with Christian Rudder, originally aired on *The Takeaway* episode July 30, 2014. Used with permission of New York Public Radio.

Deborah Tannen. "Why Is 'Compromise' Now a Dirty Word?," first published in *Politico*, June 15, 2011. Copyright © Deborah Tannen. Used by permission of the author.

John Tierney. "Can a Playground Be Too Safe?" by John Tierney from the *New York Times*, July 18, 2011. Copyright © 2011 by The New York Times. All rights reserved. Used by permission and protected by the Copyright Laws of the United States. The printing, copying, redistribution, or retransmission of this Content without express written permission is prohibited.

Hayley Tsukayama. "My Awkward Week with Google Glass" from the *Washington Post*, April 29, 2014. Copyright © 2014 by The Washington Post Company. All rights reserved. Used by permission and protected by the Copyright Laws of the United States. The printing, copying, redistribution, or retransmission of this Content without express written permission is prohibited.

Christian R. Weisser. Excerpt from *Sustainability: A Bedford Spotlight Reader*, copyright © 2015 by Bedford/St. Martin's. Used by permission of the publisher.

Sean Wilsey. From "The Things They Buried" from the *New York Times Book Review* section, June 18, 2006. Copyright © 2006 by The New York Times. All rights reserved. Used by permission and protected by the Copyright Laws of the United States. The printing, copying, redistribution, or retransmission of this Content without express written permission is prohibited.

Lan Xue. "China: The Prizes and Pitfalls of Progress" from *Nature* magazine, vol. 454, July 2008. Reprinted by permission from Macmillan Publishers, Ltd. via the Copyright Clearance Center. Copyright © 2008 by Nature Publishing Group.

Amy Zimmerman. "It Ain't Easy Being Bisexual on TV" from the *Daily Beast*, August 14, 2014, copyright © 2014 The Daily Beast Company, LLC. All rights reserved. Used by permission and protected by the Copyright Laws of the United States. The printing, copying, redistribution, or retransmission of this Content without express written permission is prohibited.

INDEX

Missing something? Instructors may assign the online materials that accompany this text. For access to them, visit **macmillanhighered.com /everythingsanargument7e**.

Inside LaunchPad for *Everything's an Argument with Readings*

LaunchPad for *Everything's an Argument with Readings* includes tutorials on

Critical Reading

- Active Reading Strategies
- Reading Visuals: Audience
- Reading Visuals: Purpose

Documentation and Working with Sources

- Do I Need to Cite That?
- How to Cite in MLA Style
- How to Cite in APA Style

Digital Writing

- Photo Editing Basics with GIMP
- Audio Editing with Audacity
- Presentations
- Word Processing
- Online Research Tools
- Job Search/Personal Branding

LearningCurve adaptive quizzing, including new LearningCurve Argument activities